CHILTON'S
REPAIR MANUAL

FORD RANGER/BRONCO II EXPLORER
1983-91
Covers all U.S and Canadian Models

Sr. Vice President	Ronald A. Hoxter
Publisher and Editor-In-Chief	Kerry A. Freeman, S.A.E.
Managing Editors	Peter M. Conti, Jr. □ W. Calvin Settle, Jr., S.A.E.
Assistant Managing Editor	Nick D'Andrea
Senior Editors	Richard J. Rivele, S.A.E. □ Ron Webb
Director of Manufacturing	Mike D'Imperio
Manager of Manufacturing	John F. Butler

CHILTON BOOK COMPANY

ONE OF THE DIVERSIFIED PUBLISHING COMPANIES,
A PART OF CAPITAL CITIES/ABC, INC.

CONTENTS

1 GENERAL INFORMATION and MAINTENANCE

2 ENGINE PERFORMANCE and TUNE-UP

3 ENGINE and ENGINE OVERHAUL

4 EMISSION CONTROLS

5 FUEL SYSTEM

6 CHASSIS ELECTRICAL

DRIVE TRAIN

SUSPENSION and STEERING

BRAKES

BODY

MECHANIC'S DATA

SAFETY NOTICE

Proper service and repair procedures are vital to the safe, reliable operation of all motor vehicles, as well as the safety of those performing repairs. This book outlines procedures for servicing and repairing vehicles using safe effective methods. The procedures contain many NOTES, CAUTIONS and WARNINGS which should be followed along with standard safety procedures to eliminate the possibility of personal injury or improper service which could damage the vehicle or compromise its safety.

It is important to note that repair procedures and techniques, tools and parts for servicing motor vehicles, as well as the skill and experience of the individual performing the work vary widely. It is not possible to anticipate all of the conceivable ways or conditions under which vehicles may be serviced, or to provide cautions as to all of the possible hazards that may result. Standard and accepted safety precautions and equipment should be used during cutting, grinding, chiseling, prying, or any other process that can cause material removal or projectiles.

Some procedures require the use of tools specially designed for a specific purpose. Before substituting another tool or procedure, you must be completely satisfied that neither your personal safety, nor the performance of the vehicle will be endangered.

Although the information in this guide is based on industry sources and is as complete as possible at the time of publication, the possibility exists that the manufacturer made later changes which could not be included here. While striving for total accuracy, Chilton Book Company cannot assume responsibilty for any errors, changes, or omissions that may occur in the compilation of this data.

PART NUMBERS

Part numbers listed in the reference are not recommendations by Chilton for any product by brand name. They are references that can be used with interchange manuals and aftermarket supplier catalogs to locate each brand supplier's discrete part number.

SPECIAL TOOLS

Special tools are recommended by the vehicle manufacturer to perform their specific job. Use has been kept to a minimum, but where absolutely necessary, they are referred to in the text by the part number of the tool manufacturer. These tools can be purchased, under the appropiate part number, from the Owatonna Tool Company, Owatonna, MN 55060 or an equivalent tool can be purchased locally from a tool supplier or parts outlet. Before substituting any tool for the one recommended, read the SAFETY NOTICE at the top of this page.

ACKNOWLEDGEMENTS

Chilton Book Company expresses appreciation to Ford Motor Company; Ford Parts and Service Division, Service Technical Communications Department, Dearborn, Michigan for their generous assistance

Chilton's Repair Manual: Ford Ranger/Bronco II/Explorer 1983–91
ISBN 0–8019–8160–3 pbk.
Library of Congress Catalog Card No. 90–055480

General Information and Maintenance

1

HOW TO USE THIS BOOK

Chilton's Repair Manual for Ford Ranger/Bronco II/Explorer models from 1983 through 1991 is intended to teach you about the inner workings of your vehicle and save you money on its upkeep.

The first two Chapters will be the most used, since they contain maintenance and tune-up information and procedures. Studies have shown that a properly tuned and maintained engine can get at least 10% better gas mileage (which translates into lower operating costs) and periodic maintenance will catch minor problems before they turn into major repair bills. The other Chapters deal with the more complex systems of your vehicle. Operating systems from engine through brakes are covered. This book will give you detailed instructions to help you change your own brake pads and shoes, tune-up the engine, replace spark plugs and filters, and do many more jobs that will save you money, give you personal satisfaction and help you avoid expensive problems.

A secondary purpose of this book is a reference guide for owners who want to understand their vehicle and/or their mechanics better. In this case, no tools at all are required. Knowing just what a particular repair job requires in parts and labor time will allow you to evaluate whether or not you're getting a fair price quote and help decipher itemized bills from a repair shop.

Before attempting any repairs or service on your vehicle, read through the entire procedure outlined in the appropriate Chapter. This will give you the overall view of what tools and supplies will be required. There is nothing more frustrating than having to walk to the bus stop on Monday morning because you were short one gasket on Sunday afternoon. So read ahead and plan ahead. Each operation should be approached logically and all procedures thoroughly understood before attempting any work. Some special tools that may be required can often be rented from local automotive jobbers or places specializing in renting tools and equipment. Check the yellow pages of your phone book.

All Chapters contain adjustments, maintenance, removal and installation procedures, and overhaul procedures. When overhaul is not considered practical, we tell you how to remove the failed part and then how to install the new or rebuilt replacement. In this way, you at least save the labor costs. Backyard overhaul of some components (such as the alternator or water pump) is just not practical, but the removal and installation procedure is often simple and well within the capabilities of the average owner.

Two basic mechanic's rules should be mentioned here. First, whenever the LEFT side of the vehicle or engine is referred to, it is meant to specify the DRIVER'S side of the vehicle. Conversely, the RIGHT side of the vehicle means the PASSENGER'S side. Second, all screws and bolts are removed by turning counterclockwise, and tightened by turning clockwise (left loosen, right tighten).

Safety is always the MOST important rule. Constantly be aware of the dangers involved in working on or around any vehicle and take proper precautions to avoid the risk of personal injury or damage to the vehicle. See the section in this Chapter, Servicing Your Vehicle Safely, and the SAFETY NOTICE on the acknowledgment page before attempting any service procedures and pay attention to the instructions provided. There are 3 common mistakes in mechanical work:

1. Incorrect order of assembly, disassembly or adjustment. When taking something apart or putting it together, doing things in the wrong order usually just costs you extra time;

however it CAN break something. Read the entire procedure before beginning disassembly. Do everything in the order in which the instructions say you should do it, even if you can't immediately see a reason for it. When you're taking apart something that is very intricate (for example a carburetor), you might want to draw a picture of how it looks when assembled at one point in order to make sure you get everything back in its proper position. We will supply exploded views whenever possible, but sometimes the job requires more attention to detail than an illustration provides. When making adjustments (especially tune-up adjustments), do them in order. One adjustment often affects another and you cannot expect satisfactory results unless each adjustment is made only when it cannot be changed by any other.

2. Overtorquing (or undertorquing) nuts and bolts. While it is more common for overtorquing to cause damage, undertorquing can cause a fastener to vibrate loose and cause serious damage, especially when dealing with aluminum parts. Pay attention to torque specifications and utilize a torque wrench in assembly. If a torque figure is not available remember that, if you are using the right tool to do the job, you will probably not have to strain yourself to get a fastener tight enough. The pitch of most threads is so slight that the tension you put on the wrench will be multiplied many times in actual force on what you are tightening. A good example of how critical torque is can be seen in the case of spark plug installation, especially where you are putting the plug into an aluminum cylinder head. Too little torque can fail to crush the gasket, causing leakage of combustion gases and consequent overheating of the plug and engine parts. Too much torque can damage the threads or distort the plug, which changes the spark gap at the electrode. Since more and more manufacturers are using aluminum in their engine and chassis parts to save weight, a torque wrench should be in any serious do-it-yourselfer's tool box.

There are many commercial chemical products available for ensuring that fasteners won't come loose, even if they are not torqued just right (a very common brand is Loctite®). If you're worried about getting something together tight enough to hold, but loose enough to avoid mechanical damage during assembly, one of these products might offer substantial insurance. Read the label on the package and make sure the product is compatible with the materials, fluids, etc. involved before choosing one.

3. Crossthreading. This occurs when a part such as a bolt is screwed into a nut or casting at the wrong angle and forced, causing the threads to become damaged. Crossthreading is more likely to occur if access is difficult. It helps to clean and lubricate fasteners, and to start threading with the part to be installed going straight in, using your fingers. If you encounter resistance, unscrew the part and start over again at a different angle until it can be inserted and turned several times without much effort. Keep in mind that many parts, especially spark plugs, use tapered threads so that gentle turning will automatically bring the part you're threading to the proper angle if you don't force it or resist a change in angle. Don't put a wrench on the part until it's been turned in a couple of times by hand. If you suddenly encounter resistance and the part has not seated fully, don't force it. Pull it back out and make sure it's clean and threading properly.

Always take your time and be patient; once you have some experience, working on your vehicle will become an enjoyable hobby.

TOOLS AND EQUIPMENT

Naturally, without the proper tools and equipment it is impossible to properly service your vehicle. It would be impossible to catalog each tool that you would need to perform each or every operation in this book. It would also be unwise for the amateur to rush out and buy an expensive set of tools an the theory that he may need one or more of them at sometime.

The best approach is to proceed slowly, gathering together a good quality set of those tools that are used most frequently. Don't be misled by the low cost of bargain tools. It is far better to spend a little more for better quality. Forged wrenches, 6- or 12-point sockets and fine tooth ratchets are by far preferable to their less expensive counterparts. As any good mechanic can tell you, there are few worse experiences than trying to work on any vehicle with bad tools. Your monetary savings will be far outweighed by frustration and mangled knuckles.

Certain tools, plus a basic ability to handle them, are required to get started. A basic mechanics tool set, a torque wrench and a Torx® bits set. Torx® bits are hexlobular drivers which fit both inside and outside on special Torx® head fasteners used in various places on modern vehicles. Begin accumulating those tools that are used most frequently; those associated with routine maintenance and tune-up.

In addition to the normal assortment of screwdrivers and pliers you should have the following tools for routine maintenance jobs (your

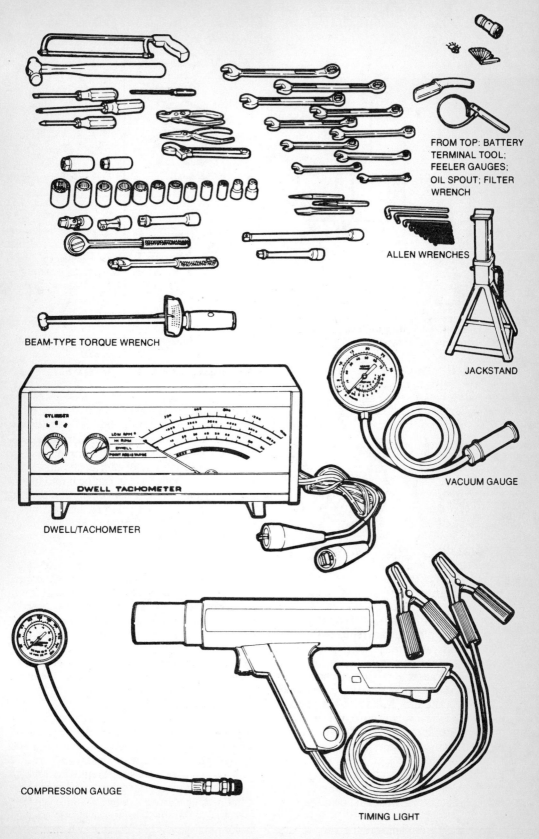

FROM TOP: BATTERY TERMINAL TOOL; FEELER GAUGES; OIL SPOUT; FILTER WRENCH

ALLEN WRENCHES

BEAM-TYPE TORQUE WRENCH

JACKSTAND

DWELL TACHOMETER

DWELL/TACHOMETER

VACUUM GAUGE

COMPRESSION GAUGE

TIMING LIGHT

This basic collection of tools and test instruments is all you need for most maintenance on your truck.

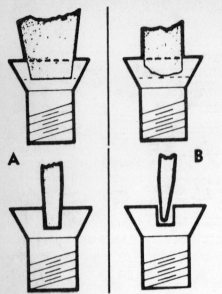

Keep screwdrivers in good shape. They should fit the slot as shown 'A'. If they look like those in 'B', they need grinding or replacing.

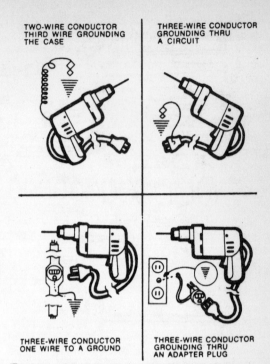

TWO-WIRE CONDUCTOR THIRD WIRE GROUNDING THE CASE

THREE-WIRE CONDUCTOR GROUNDING THRU A CIRCUIT

THREE-WIRE CONDUCTOR ONE WIRE TO A GROUND

THREE-WIRE CONDUCTOR GROUNDING THRU AN ADAPTER PLUG

When using electric tools, make sure they are properly grounded.

When using an open-end wrench, use the exact size needed and position it squarely on the flats of the bolt or nut.

Ranger/Bronco II and Explorer uses both SAE and metric fasteners):

1. SAE/Metric wrenches, sockets and combination open end/box end wrenches in sizes from $1/8$ in. (3mm) to $3/4$ in. (19mm) and a spark plug socket ($13/16$ in. or $5/8$ in.). If possible, buy various length socket drive extensions. One break in this department is that the metric sockets available in the U.S. will all fit the ratchet handles and extensions you may already have ($1/4$ in., $3/8$ in., and $1/2$ in. drive).

2. Jackstands for support.
3. Oil filter wrench.
4. Oil filter spout for pouring oil.
5. Grease gun for chassis lubrication.
6. Hydrometer for checking the battery.
7. A container for draining oil.
8. Many rags (paper or cloth) for wiping up the inevitable mess.

In addition to the above items there are several others that are not absolutely necessary, but handy to have around. These include a hydraulic floor jack, oil-dry, a transmission funnel and the usual supply of lubricants, antifreeze and fluids, although these can be purchased as needed. This is a basic list for routine maintenance, but only your personal needs and desires can accurately determine your list of necessary tools.

The second list of tools is for tune-ups. While the tools involved here are slightly more sophisticated, they need not be outrageously expensive. There are several inexpensive tach/dwell meters on the market that are every bit as good for the average mechanic as an expensive professional model. Just be sure that it goes to at least 1,200–1,500 rpm on the tach scale and that it works on 4, 6 and 8 cylinder engines. A basic list of tune-up equipment could include:

1. Tach/dwell meter.
2. Spark plug wrench.
3. Timing light (a DC light that works from the vehicle's battery is best, although an AC light that plugs into 110V house current will suffice at some sacrifice in brightness).
4. Wire spark plug gauge/adjusting tools.

Here again, be guided by your own needs. While not absolutely necessary, an ohmmeter can be useful in determining whether or not a spark plug wire is any good by measuring its resistance. In addition to these basic tools, there are several other tools and gauges you may find useful. These include:

1. A compression gauge. The screw-in type is slower to use, but eliminates the possibility of a faulty reading due to escaping pressure.

2. A manifold vacuum gauge.

3. A test light.

4. An induction meter. This is used for determining whether or not there is current in a wire. These are handy for use if a wire is broken somewhere in a wiring harness.

As a final note, you will probably find a torque wrench necessary for all but the most basic work. The beam type models are perfectly adequate, although the newer click (breakaway) type are more precise, and you don't have to crane your neck to see a torque reading in awkward situations. The breakaway torque wrenches are more expensive and should be recalibrated periodically.

Torque specification for each fastener will be given in the procedure in any case that a specific torque value is required. If no torque specifications are given, use the following values as a guide, based upon fastener size:

Bolts marked 6T

6mm bolt/nut — 5–7 ft. lbs.

8mm bolt/nut — 12–17 ft. lbs.

10mm bolt/nut — 23–34 ft. lbs.

12mm bolt/nut — 41–59 ft. lbs.

14mm bolt/nut — 56–76 ft. lbs.

Bolts marked 8T

6mm bolt/nut — 6–9 ft. lbs.

8mm bolt/nut — 13–20 ft. lbs.

10mm bolt/nut — 27–40 ft. lbs.

12mm bolt/nut — 46–69 ft. lbs.

14mm bolt/nut — 75–101 ft. lbs.

Special Tools

Normally, the use of special factory tools is avoided for repair procedures, since these are not readily available for the do-it-yourself mechanic. When it is possible to perform the job with more commonly available tools, it will be pointed out, but occasionally a special tool was designed to perform a specific function and should be used. Before substituting another tool, you should be convinced that neither your safety nor the performance of the vehicle will be compromised. Where possible, an illustration of the special tool will be provided so that an equivalent tool may be used.

Some special tools are available commercially from Owatonna Tool Co., Owatonna, MN 55060. Others can be purchased through your Ford dealer or local parts supplier.

SERVICING YOUR VEHICLE SAFELY

It is virtually impossible to anticipate all of the hazards involved with maintenance and service work, but care and common sense will prevent most accidents.

The rules of safety for mechanics range from "don't smoke around gasoline," to "use the proper tool for the job." The trick to avoiding injuries is to develop safe work habits and take every possible precaution.

Dos

• Do keep a fire extinguisher and first aid kit within easy reach.

• Do wear safety glasses or goggles when cutting, drilling or prying, even if you have 20–20 vision. If you wear glasses for the sake of vision, they should be made of hardened glass that can also serve as safety glasses, or wear safety goggles over your regular glasses.

• Do shield your eyes whenever you work around the battery. Batteries contain sulphuric acid. In case of contact with the eyes or skin, flush the area with water or a mixture of water and baking soda and get medical attention immediately.

• Do use safety stands for any under vehicle service. Jacks are for raising vehicles; safety stands are for making sure the vehicle stays raised until you want it to come down. Whenever the vehicle is raised, block the wheels remaining on the ground and set the parking brake.

• Do use adequate ventilation when working with any chemicals. Like carbon monoxide, the asbestos dust resulting from brake lining wear can be poisonous in sufficient quantities.

• Do disconnect the negative battery cable when working on the electrical system. The primary ignition system can contain up to 40,000 volts.

• Do follow manufacturer's directions whenever working with potentially hazardous materials. Both brake fluid and antifreeze are poisonous if taken internally.

• Do properly maintain your tools. Loose hammerheads, mushroomed punches and chisels, frayed or poorly grounded electrical cords, excessively worn screwdrivers, spread wrenches (open end), cracked sockets, slipping ratchets, or faulty droplight sockets can cause accidents.

• Do use the proper size and type of tool for the job being done.

• Do when possible, pull on a wrench handle rather than push on it, and adjust your stance to prevent a fall.

• Do be sure that adjustable wrenches are tightly adjusted on the nut or bolt and pulled so that the face is on the side of the fixed jaw.

• Do select a wrench or socket that fits the nut or bolt. The wrench or socket should sit straight, not cocked.

• Do strike squarely with a hammer—avoid glancing blows.

• Do set the parking brake and block the drive wheels if the work requires that the engine be running.

Don'ts

• Don't run an engine in a garage or anywhere else without proper ventilation—EVER! Carbon monoxide is poisonous. It takes a long time to leave the human body and you can build up a deadly supply of it in your blood stream by simply breathing in a little every day. You may not realize you are slowly poisoning yourself. Always use power vents, windows, fans or open the garage doors.

• Don't work around moving parts while wearing a necktie or other loose clothing. Short sleeves are much safer than long, loose sleeves and hard-toed shoes with neoprene soles protect your toes and give a better grip on slippery surfaces. Jewelry such as watches, fancy belt buckles, beads or body adornment of any kind is not safe working around any vehicle. Long hair should be hidden under a hat or cap.

• Don't use pockets for toolboxes. A fall or bump can drive a screwdriver deep into your body. Even a wiping cloth hanging from the back pocket can wrap around a spinning shaft or fan.

• Don't smoke when working around gasoline, cleaning solvent or other flammable material.

• Don't smoke when working around the battery. When the battery is being charged, it gives off explosive hydrogen gas.

• Don't use gasoline to wash your hands; there are excellent soaps available. Gasoline may contain lead, and lead can enter the body through a cut, accumulating in your blood stream until you are very ill. Gasoline also removes all the natural oils from the skin so that bone dry hands will suck up oil and grease.

• Don't service the air conditioning system unless you are equipped with the necessary tools and training. The refrigerant, R-12, is extremely cold and when exposed to the air, will instantly freeze any surface it comes in contact with, including your eyes. Although the refrigerant is normally non-toxic, R-12 becomes a deadly poisonous gas (phosgene) in the presence of an open flame. One good whiff of the vapors from burning refrigerant can be fatal.

SERIAL NUMBER IDENTIFICATION

Vehicle Identification (VIN) Number

A 17 digit combination of numbers and letters forms the vehicle identification number (VIN). The VIN is stamped on a metal tab that is riveted to the instrument panel close to the windshield. The VIN plate is visible by looking through the windshield on the driver's side. The VIN number is also found on the Safety Compliance Certification Label which is described below.

By looking at the 17 digit VIN number, a variety of information about the vehicle can be determined.

• The 1st digit identifies the country of origin. 1 = USA; 2 = Canada.

• The 2nd digit identifies the manufacturer. F = Ford.

• The 3rd digit identifies the type of vehicle.

    C = Basic (stripped) chassis
    D = Incomplete vehicle
    M = Multi-purpose vehicle
    T = Truck (complete vehicle)

• The 4th digit identifies the gross vehicle weight rating (GVWR Class) and brake system. For incomplete vehicles, the 4th digit determines the brake system only. All brake systems are hydraulic.

    A = up to 3,000 lbs.
    B = 3,001–4,000 lbs.
    C = 4,001–5,000 lbs.
    D = 5,001–6,000 lbs.
    E = 6,001–7,000 lbs.
    F = 7,001–8,000 lbs.
    G = 8,001–8,500 lbs.
    H = 8,500–9,000 lbs.
    J = 9,001–10,000 lbs.

• The 5th digits identifies the model or line. R = Ranger U = Bronco II and Explorer.

• The 6th and 7th digits identify chassis and body type.

    10 = 4x2 pickup regular cab
    11 = 4x4 pickup regular cab
    14 = 4x2 pickup super cab
    15 = 4x4 pickup super cab
    12 = 4x2 standard Bronco II
    14 = 4x4 standard Bronco II
    22 = 4x2 standard Explorer 2 dr.
    24 = 4x4 standard Explorer 2 dr.
    32 = 4x2 standard Explorer 4 dr.
    34 = 4x4 standard Explorer 4 dr.

• The 8th digit identifies the engine.

    C = 2.0L 4-cylinder
    P = 2.2L 4-cylinder
    A = 2.3L 4-cylinder

(UNITED STATES)

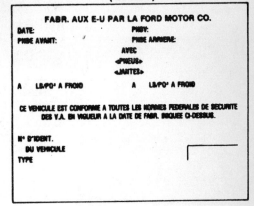

MFD. BY FORD MOTOR CO. IN U.S.A.

DATE: 2/83   GVWR: 3740 LBS/1696 KG

FRONT GAWR: 1910 LBS   REAR GAWR: 2012 LBS

866 KG   WITH   866 KG   WITH
P195/75R14SL   TIRES   P195/75R14SL   TIRES
14x5.0JJ   RIMS   14x5.0JJ   RIMS
AT 35 PSI COLD   AT 35 PSI COLD

THIS VEHICLE CONFORMS TO ALL APPLICABLE FEDERAL MOTOR VEHICLE SAFETY STANDARDS IN EFFECT ON THE DATE OF MANUFACTURE SHOWN ABOVE

VEHICLE IDENTIFICATION NO. 1FTCR10Z 5DUA00001

TYPE   TRUCK

EXTERIOR PAINT COLORS   DSO

WB	TYPE GVW	BODY	TRANS	AXLE

(QUEBEC)

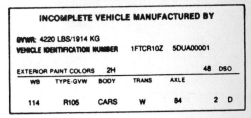

FABR. AUX E-U PAR LA FORD MOTOR CO.

DATE: PNBV:

PNBE AVANT: PNBE ARRIERE:

AVEC
‹PNEUS›
‹JANTES›

A   LB/PO² A FROID   A   LB/PO² A FROID

CE VEHICULE EST CONFORME A TOUTES LES NORMES FEDERALES DE SECURITE DES V.A. EN VIGUEUR A LA DATE DE FABR. INDIQUEE CI-DESSUS.

N° D'IDENT.
DU VEHICULE

TYPE

FOR VEHICLES MFD IN U.S.A. FOR QUEBEC, CANADA.

INCOMPLETE VEHICLES

THE INCOMPLETE VEHICLE RATING DECAL IS INSTALLED ON THE DRIVER'S DOOR LOCK PILLAR IN PLACE OF THE SAFETY STANDARD CERTIFICATION LABEL.

VEHICLE RATING DECAL

INCOMPLETE VEHICLE MANUFACTURED BY

GVWR: 4220 LBS/1914 KG

VEHICLE IDENTIFICATION NUMBER   1FTCR10Z 5DUA00001

EXTERIOR PAINT COLORS   2H   48   DSO

WB	TYPE-GVW	BODY	TRANS	AXLE		
114	R105	CARS	W	84	2	D

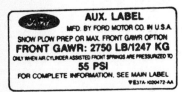

AUX. LABEL

MFD. BY FORD MOTOR CO. IN U.S.A.

SNOW PLOW PREP OR MAX. FRONT GAWR OPTION

FRONT GAWR: 2750 LB/1247 KG

ONLY WHEN AIR CYLINDER ASSISTED FRONT SPRINGS ARE PRESSURIZED TO

55 PSI

FOR COMPLETE INFORMATION, SEE MAIN LABEL

E37A-1020472-AA

977

DECAL APPLIED TO ALL CANADIAN BUILT UNITS AND ALL U.S.A. BUILT UNITS SOLD IN CANADA

Vehicle certification labels

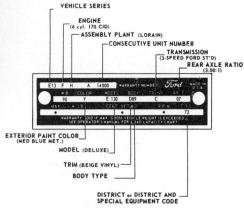

VEHICLE SERIES
ENGINE (6 cyl. 170 CID)
ASSEMBLY PLANT (LORAIN)
CONSECUTIVE UNIT NUMBER
TRANSMISSION (3-SPEED FORD ST'D)
REAR AXLE RATIO (3.00:1)

| E13 | F | H | A | 14000 | WARRANTY NUMBER | Ford | MADE IN U.S.A. |

| WB | COLOR | MODEL | BODY | TRANS | AX R |
| 90 | Y | E 130 | D89 | C | 07 |

MAX G.V.W.P. | CERT NET H.P. | R.P.M. | MAX R
| | | | 72 |

WARRANTY VOID IF MAX. GROSS VEHICLE WEIGHT IS EXCEEDED SEE OPERATOR'S MANUAL FOR LOAD CAPACITY CHART.

EXTERIOR PAINT COLOR (MED BLUE MET.)
MODEL (DELUXE)
TRIM (BEIGE VINYL)
BODY TYPE
DISTRICT or DISTRICT AND SPECIAL EQUIPMENT CODE

Vehicle Identification Plate

E = 2.3L 4-cylinder
S = 2.8L 4-cylinder
T = 2.9L 6-cylinder
U = 3.0L 6-cylinder
X = 4.0L 6-cylinder

- The 9th digit is a check digit.
- The 10th digit identifies the model year.
  D = 1983
  E = 1984

F = 1985
G = 1986
H = 1987
J = 1988
K = 1989
L = 1990
M = 1991

- The 11th digit identifies the assembly plant.

C = Ontario, Canada
H = Lorain, OH
K = Claycomo, MO
L = Wayne, MI
N = Norfolk, VA
P = St. Paul, MN
U = Louisville, KY
Z = Hazlewood, MO

- Digits twelve through seventeen make up the sequential serial and warranty number. Digit twelve uses the letter A until the production or sequence of 99,999 units (digits thirteen through seventeen) is reached. Letter A then becomes B for the next production sequence of vehicles.

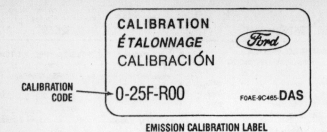

EMISSION CALIBRATION LABEL

CALIBRATION CODE

Use the following to interpret the calibration code from the Emission Calibration Label:

(1) MODEL YEAR—This number represents the model year in which the Calibration was first introduced. As shown below, the model year is 1990. (Represented by the Number 0)

(2) CALIBRATION DESIGN LEVEL—Represents the design level assigned to the engine (25F).

(3) CALIBRATION REVISION LEVEL—Represents the revision level of the calibration (R00). These numbers will advance as revisions occur.

CALIBRATION CODE

Emission calibration label

A. Position 1, 2, and 3—Manufacturer, Make and Type (World Manufacturer Identifier)
B. Position 4—Brake System/GVWR
C. Position 5, 6, and 7—Model or Line, Series, Chassis, Cab Type
D. Position 8—Engine Type
E. Position 9—Check Digit
F. Position 10—Model Year
G. Position 11—Assembly Plant
H. Position 12—Constant "A" until sequence number of 99,999 is reached, then changes to a constant "B" and so on
I. Position 13 through 17—Sequence number—begins at 00001

Sample VIN number

Build Date Stamp Location

The vehicle build date is stamped on the front surface of the radiator support on the passenger side of the vehicle. Yellow ink is used for the date stamp. When the marking surface is painted the body color, the date stamp will be marked in red ink. Units from the Ontario truck plant (code C) will be marked with silver ink.

Vehicle Data

The vehicle data appears on the Safety Compliance Certification Label on the second and third lines following the identification number. The code set (two numbers or a number and letter) above COLOR identify the exterior paint color, with two sets of codes designating two tone paint. The three digits under W.N. designate the wheelbase in inches. The letter and three digits under TYPE/G.V.W. designate the truck model within a series and the gross vehicle weight rating. The letters and/or numbers under BODY designate the interior trim, seat and body type. The transmission installed in the vehicle is identified under TRANS by an alphabetical code.

A letter and a number or two numbers under AXLE identify the rear axle ratio and, when required, a letter or number is also stamped after the rear axle code to identify the front axle. The letters and/or numerals under TAPE designate

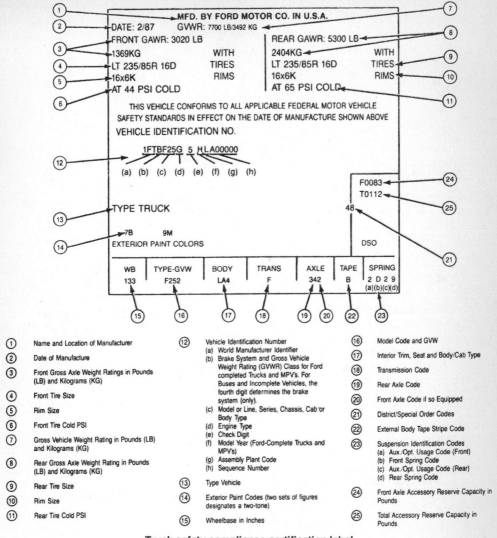

① MFD. BY FORD MOTOR CO. IN U.S.A.
② DATE: 2/87   GVWR: 7700 LB/3492 KG
③ FRONT GAWR: 3020 LB   REAR GAWR: 5300 LB
   1369KG   WITH   2404KG   WITH
④ LT 235/85R 16D   TIRES   LT 235/85R 16D   TIRES
⑤ 16x6K   RIMS   16x6K   RIMS
⑥ AT 44 PSI COLD   AT 65 PSI COLD

THIS VEHICLE CONFORMS TO ALL APPLICABLE FEDERAL MOTOR VEHICLE
SAFETY STANDARDS IN EFFECT ON THE DATE OF MANUFACTURE SHOWN ABOVE
VEHICLE IDENTIFICATION NO.

⑫   1FTBF25G 5 HLA00000
     (a) (b) (c) (d) (e) (f) (g) (h)

F0083 ㉔
T0112 ㉕

⑬ TYPE TRUCK   48

⑭ 7B   9M   DSO
   EXTERIOR PAINT COLORS

WB	TYPE-GVW	BODY	TRANS	AXLE	TAPE	SPRING
133	F252	LA4	F	342	B	2 D 2 9 (a)(b)(c)(d)

① Name and Location of Manufacturer	⑫ Vehicle Identification Number	⑯ Model Code and GVW
② Date of Manufacture	(a) World Manufacturer Identifier	⑰ Interior Trim, Seat and Body/Cab Type
③ Front Gross Axle Weight Ratings in Pounds (LB) and Kilograms (KG)	(b) Brake System and Gross Vehicle Weight Rating (GVWR) Class for Ford completed Trucks and MPV's. For Buses and Incomplete Vehicles, the fourth digit determines the brake system (only).	⑱ Transmission Code
④ Front Tire Size		⑲ Rear Axle Code
⑤ Rim Size	(c) Model or Line, Series, Chassis, Cab or Body Type	⑳ Front Axle Code if so Equipped
⑥ Front Tire Cold PSI	(d) Engine Type	㉑ District/Special Order Codes
⑦ Gross Vehicle Weight Rating in Pounds (LB) and Kilograms (KG)	(e) Check Digit (f) Model Year (Ford-Complete Trucks and MPV's)	㉒ External Body Tape Stripe Code
⑧ Rear Gross Axle Weight Rating in Pounds (LB) and Kilograms (KG)	(g) Assembly Plant Code (h) Sequence Number	㉓ Suspension Identification Codes (a) Aux./Opt. Usage Code (Front) (b) Front Spring Code (c) Aux./Opt. Usage Code (Rear) (d) Rear Spring Code
⑨ Rear Tire Size	⑬ Type Vehicle	
⑩ Rim Size	⑭ Exterior Paint Codes (two sets of figures designates a two-tone)	㉔ Front Axle Accessory Reserve Capacity in Pounds
⑪ Rear Tire Cold PSI	⑮ Wheelbase in Inches	㉕ Total Accessory Reserve Capacity in Pounds

Truck safety compliance certification label

the external body side tape stripe code. The spring usage codes for the vehicle are identified under SPRING.

A two digit number is stamped above D.S.O. to identify the district which originally ordered the vehicle. If the vehicle is built to special order (Domestic Special Order, Foreign Special Order, Limited Production Option or other special order), the complete order number will also appear above D.S.O.

Safety Compliance Certification Label

The English Safety Compliance Certification Label is affixed to the door latch edge on the driver's side door. The French Safety Compliance Certification Label is affixed to the door latch edge on the passenger's side door. The label contains the following information: name of manufacturer, the month and year of manufacture, the certification statement, and the Vehicle Identification number. The label also contains information on Gross Vehicle weight ratings, Wheel and tire data, and additional vehicle data information codes.

Emission Calibration Label

The emission calibration number label is attached to the left side door or the left door post pillar. This label plate identifies the engine calibration number, engine code number and the revision level. These numbers are used to determine if parts are unique to specific engines. The engine codes and calibration are necessary for ordering parts and asking questions related to the engine.

ENGINE IDENTIFICATION CHART

VIN Code	Engine Displacement Liter/CID	No. of Cylinders	Fuel System	Manufacturer
C	2.0/122	4	Gas	Ford
P	2.2/134	4	Diesel	Ford
A	2.3/140	4	Gas	Ford
E	2.3/140	4	Diesel	Mitsubishi
S	2.8/173	6	Gas	Ford
T	2.9/177	6	Gas	Ford
U	3.0/183	6	Gas	Ford
X	4.0/241	6	Gas	Ford

TRANSMISSION IDENTIFICATION CHART

Code	Transmission Type
V	Automatic—C3
W	Automatic—C5
T	Automatic—4 speed OD (A4LD)
X	Manual—4 Speed
5	Manual—5 Speed Overdrive
M/D	Manual—5 Speed Overdrive

Engine

The engine identification code is a letter located in the eighth digit of the Vehicle Identification Number stamped on a metal tab that is riveted to the instrument panel close to the windshield. Specific engine data is located on a label attached to the timing cover.

Transmission

The transmission code may be found in two places on the vehicle. One is on the Safety Standard Certification label attached to the left driver's side door lock post. The code appears as a letter in the "Trans" column of the label.

M = 5-speed manual transmission; T = 4-speed automatic transmission.

The other location is on the transmission body itself. On manual transmissions, the identification number is located on a plate attached to the main transmission case. On the plate you find Ford's assigned part number, the serial number and a bar code used for inventory purposes. On automatic transmissions, the identification number is stamped on plate that hangs from the lower left extension housing bolt. The plate identifies when the transmission was built, it's code letter and model number.

Transfer Case

All vehicles can be equipped with a mechanical or electronic shift transfer case. The identification number is stamped on a plate on the side of the case.

Front Drive Axle

The identification number is stamped on a plate on the differential housing.

REAR AXLE IDENTIFICATION CHART

Model	Code	Description	# Capacity	Ratio
Bronco II	42	Regular	2640	3.45
	44	Regular	2640	3.73
	47	Regular	2500	4.10
	D2	Limited Slip	2500	3.45
	D4	Limited Slip	2640	3.73
	D7	Limited Slip	2500	4.10
Ranger	72	Regular	2200	3.08
	74	Regular	2200	3.45
	82	Regular	2700	3.08
	84	Regular	2700	3.45
	85	Regular	2750	3.55
	86	Regular	2700	3.73
	87	Regular	2700	4.10
	96	Regular	3200	3.73
	F4	Limited Slip	2700	3.45
	F5	Limited Slip	2750	3.55
	F6	Limited Slip	2700	3.73
	F7	Limited Slip	2700	4.10
	K6	Limited Slip	3200	4.10
Explorer	43	Regular	3200	3.08
	41	Regular	3200	3.27
	45	Regular	3200	3.55
	04	Limited Slip	3200	3.73

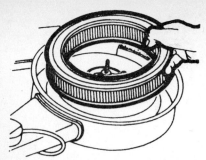

Removing the carburetor air cleaner element

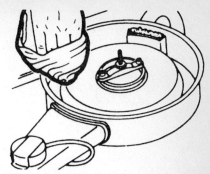

Clean out the air cleaner body before installing the new filter

Rear Axle

The rear axle code may be found in two places on the vehicle. One is on the Safety Standard Certification label attached to the left driver's side door lock post. The code appears as a number or letter/number combination in the "Axle" column of the label. The rear axle identification code is also stamped on a metal tag hanging from the axle cover-to-carrier bolt at the 2 o'clock position in the cover bolt circle.

ROUTINE MAINTENANCE

Air Cleaner

The air cleaner is a paper element type. The paper cartridge should be replaced according to the Preventive Maintenance Schedule at the end of this Chapter.

NOTE: *Check the air filter more often if the vehicle is operated under severe dusty conditions and replace or clean it as necessary.*

REPLACEMENT

Carbureted Engines

1. Open the engine compartment hood.
2. Remove the wing nut holding the air cleaner assembly to the top of the carburetor.
3. Disconnect the crankcase ventilation hose at the air cleaner and remove the entire air cleaner assembly from the carburetor.
4. Remove and discard the old filter element, and inspect the condition of the air cleaner mounting gasket. Replace the gasket as necessary.

NOTE: *A crankcase ventilation filter is located in the side of the air cleaner body. The filter should be replaced rather than cleaned. Simply pull the old filter out of the body every 20,000 miles (or more frequently if the vehi-*

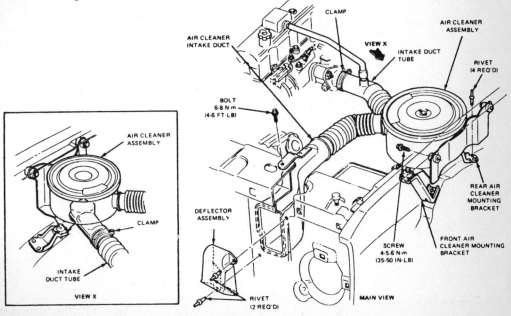

Air cleaner assembly — 2.2L diesel engine

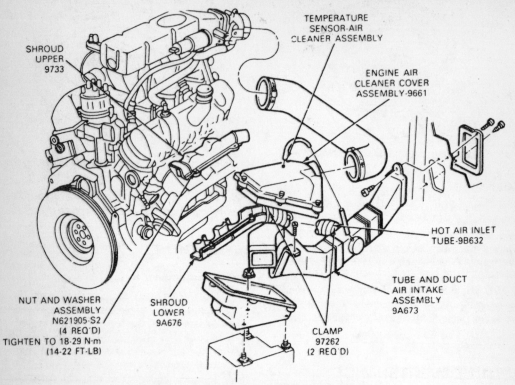

SHROUD
UPPER
9733

TEMPERATURE
SENSOR-AIR
CLEANER ASSEMBLY

ENGINE AIR
CLEANER COVER
ASSEMBLY-9661

HOT AIR INLET
TUBE-9B632

TUBE AND DUCT
AIR INTAKE
ASSEMBLY
9A673

NUT AND WASHER
ASSEMBLY
N621905-S2
(4 REQ'D)
TIGHTEN TO 18-29 N·m
(14-22 FT-LB)

SHROUD
LOWER
9A676

CLAMP
97262
(2 REQ'D)

Air cleaner assembly — 2.9L fuel injected engine

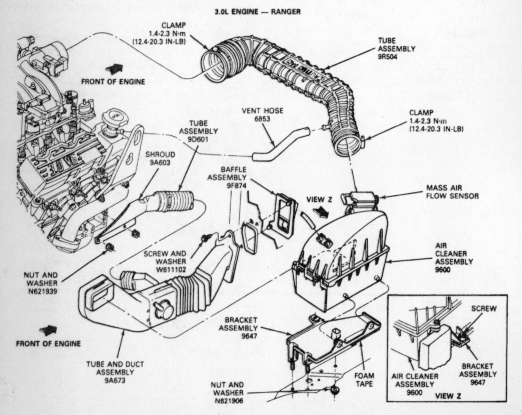

3.0L ENGINE — RANGER

CLAMP
1.4-2.3 N·m
(12.4-20.3 IN-LB)

TUBE
ASSEMBLY
9R504

FRONT OF ENGINE

TUBE
ASSEMBLY
9D601

VENT HOSE
6853

CLAMP
1.4-2.3 N·m
(12.4-20.3 IN-LB)

SHROUD
9A603

BAFFLE
ASSEMBLY
9F874

VIEW Z

MASS AIR
FLOW SENSOR

AIR
CLEANER
ASSEMBLY
9600

SCREW AND
WASHER
W611102

NUT AND
WASHER
N621939

FRONT OF ENGINE

TUBE AND DUCT
ASSEMBLY
9A673

BRACKET
ASSEMBLY
9647

NUT AND
WASHER
N621906

FOAM
TAPE

SCREW

AIR CLEANER
ASSEMBLY
9600

BRACKET
ASSEMBLY
9647

VIEW Z

Air cleaner assembly — 3.0L fuel injected engine

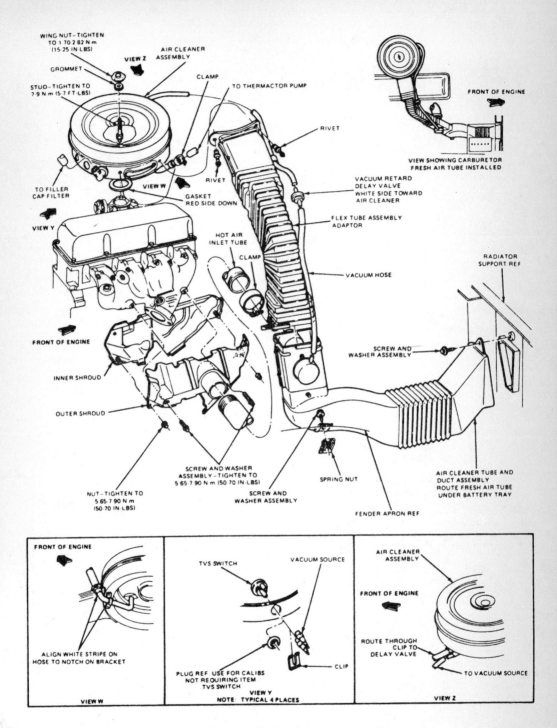

WING NUT – TIGHTEN TO 1 70-2 B2 N m (15-25 IN-LBS)

AIR CLEANER ASSEMBLY

VIEW Z

GROMMET

STUD – TIGHTEN TO 7-9 N m (5 7 FT-LBS)

CLAMP

TO THERMACTOR PUMP

RIVET

VIEW SHOWING CARBURETOR FRESH AIR TUBE INSTALLED

FRONT OF ENGINE

TO FILLER CAP FILTER

VIEW W

RIVET

GASKET RED SIDE DOWN

VIEW Y

VACUUM RETARD DELAY VALVE WHITE SIDE TOWARD AIR CLEANER

FLEX TUBE ASSEMBLY ADAPTOR

HOT AIR INLET TUBE

CLAMP

VACUUM HOSE

RADIATOR SUPPORT REF

FRONT OF ENGINE

SCREW AND WASHER ASSEMBLY

INNER SHROUD

OUTER SHROUD

SCREW AND WASHER ASSEMBLY – TIGHTEN TO 5 65-7 90 N m (50-70 IN-LBS)

SPRING NUT

SCREW AND WASHER ASSEMBLY

AIR CLEANER TUBE AND DUCT ASSEMBLY ROUTE FRESH AIR TUBE UNDER BATTERY TRAY

NUT – TIGHTEN TO 5 65-7 90 N m (50-70 IN-LBS)

FENDER APRON REF

FRONT OF ENGINE

ALIGN WHITE STRIPE ON HOSE TO NOTCH ON BRACKET

VIEW W

TVS SWITCH

VACUUM SOURCE

CLIP

PLUG REF. USE FOR CALIBS NOT REQUIRING ITEM TVS SWITCH

VIEW Y
NOTE: TYPICAL 4 PLACES

AIR CLEANER ASSEMBLY

FRONT OF ENGINE

ROUTE THROUGH CLIP TO DELAY VALVE

TO VACUUM SOURCE

VIEW Z

Air cleaner assembly — 2.0L and 2.3L fuel carbureted engines

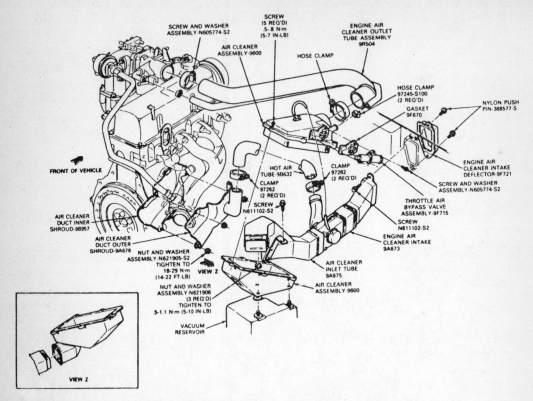

SCREW AND WASHER ASSEMBLY-N605774-S2

AIR CLEANER ASSEMBLY-9600

SCREW (5 REQ'D) 5-8 N·m (5-7 IN·LB)

HOSE CLAMP

ENGINE AIR CLEANER OUTLET TUBE ASSEMBLY 9R504

HOSE CLAMP 97245-S100 (2 REQ'D)

GASKET 9F670

NYLON PUSH PIN-388577-S

FRONT OF VEHICLE

HOT AIR TUBE 9B632

CLAMP 97262 (2 REQ'D)

SCREW N611102-S2

CLAMP 97262 (2 REQ'D)

ENGINE AIR CLEANER INTAKE DEFLECTOR-9F721

SCREW AND WASHER ASSEMBLY-N605774-S2

THROTTLE AIR BYPASS VALVE ASSEMBLY-9F715

SCREW N611102-S2

ENGINE AIR CLEANER INTAKE 9A673

AIR CLEANER DUCT INNER SHROUD-9B957

AIR CLEANER DUCT OUTER SHROUD-9A676

NUT AND WASHER ASSEMBLY-N621905-S2 TIGHTEN TO 18-29 N·m (14-22 FT·LB)

VIEW Z

NUT AND WASHER ASSEMBLY-N621906 (3 REQ'D) TIGHTEN TO .5-1.1 N·m (5-10 IN·LB)

AIR CLEANER INLET TUBE 9A675

AIR CLEANER ASSEMBLY-9600

VACUUM RESERVOIR

VIEW Z

Air cleaner assembly — 2.3L fuel injected engine

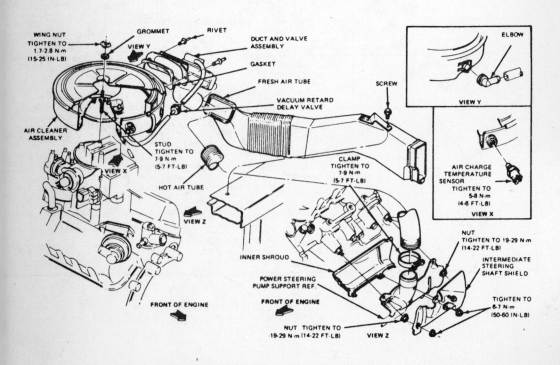

WING NUT TIGHTEN TO 1.7-2.8 N·m (15-25 IN·LB)

GROMMET

RIVET

VIEW Y

DUCT AND VALVE ASSEMBLY

GASKET

FRESH AIR TUBE

SCREW

ELBOW

VIEW Y

AIR CLEANER ASSEMBLY

VACUUM RETARD DELAY VALVE

AIR CHARGE TEMPERATURE SENSOR TIGHTEN TO 5-8 N·m (4-6 FT·LB)

VIEW X

STUD TIGHTEN TO 7-9 N·m (5-7 FT·LB)

VIEW X

HOT AIR TUBE

VIEW Z

CLAMP TIGHTEN TO 7-9 N·m (5-7 FT·LB)

NUT TIGHTEN TO 19-29 N·m (14-22 FT·LB)

INTERMEDIATE STEERING SHAFT SHIELD

INNER SHROUD

POWER STEERING PUMP SUPPORT REF.

FRONT OF ENGINE

FRONT OF ENGINE

NUT TIGHTEN TO 19-29 N·m (14-22 FT·LB)

VIEW Z

TIGHTEN TO 6-7 N·m (50-60 IN·LB)

Air cleaner assembly — 2.8L carbureted engine

cle has been used in extremely dusty conditions) and push a new filter into place.

5. Install the air cleaner body on the carburetor so that the word **FRONT** faces toward the front of the vehicle.

6. Place the new filter element in the air cleaner body and install the cover and tighten the wing nut. If the word **TOP** appears on the element, make sure that the side that the word appears on is facing up when the element is in place.

7. Connect the crankcase ventilation hose to the air cleaner.

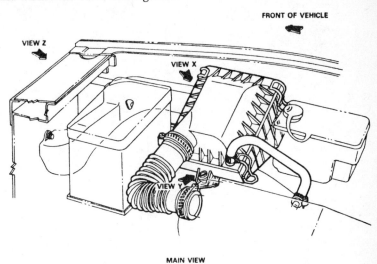

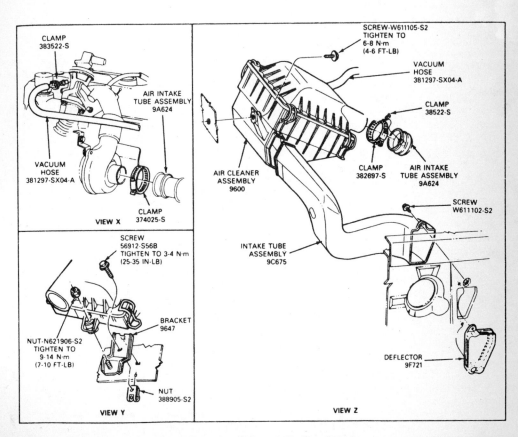

Air cleaner assembly — 2.3L diesel engine

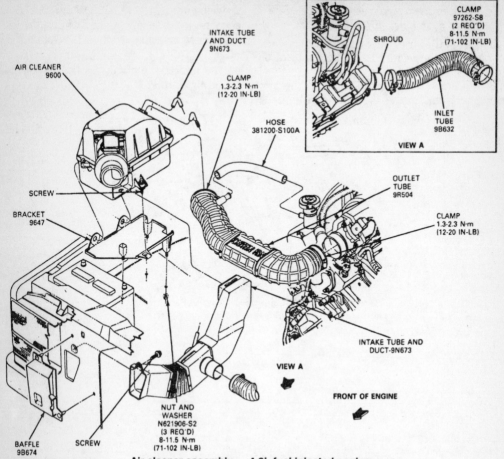

Air cleaner assembly — 4.0L fuel injected engine

Fuel Injected Engines

1. Loosen the clamps that secure the hose assembly to the air cleaner.
2. Remove the screws that attach the air cleaner to the bracket.
3. Disconnect the hose and inlet tube from the air cleaner.
4. Remove the screws attaching the air cleaner cover.
5. Remove the air filter and tubes.
6. Installation is the reverse of removal. Don't overtighten the hose clamps! A torque of 12–15 inch lbs. is sufficient.

Diesel Engines

2.2L ENGINE

1. Open the engine compartment hood.
2. Remove the wing nut holding the air cleaner assembly.
3. Remove and discard the old filter element, and inspect the condition of the air cleaner mounting gasket. Replace the gasket as necessary.

4. Place the new filter element in the air cleaner body and install the cover and tighten the wing nut.

2.3L ENGINE

1. Open the engine compartment hood.
2. Remove the clips holding the air cleaner assembly.
3. Remove and discard the old filter element, and inspect the condition of the air cleaner mounting gasket. Replace the gasket as necessary.
4. Place the new filter element in the air cleaner body and install the cover and tighten the wing nut.

Fuel Filter

REPLACEMENT

It is recommended that the fuel filter be replaced periodically. The filter is of one piece construction and cannot be cleaned, it must be replaced.

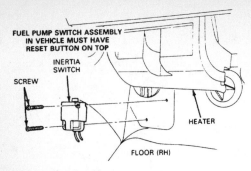

Inertia switch location

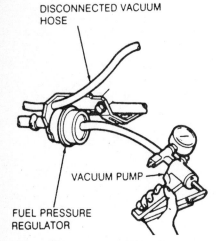

Relieving fuel pressure on EFI engines

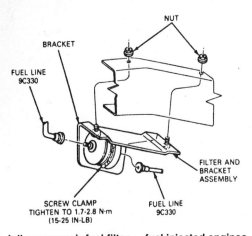

Inline reservoir fuel filter — fuel injected engines

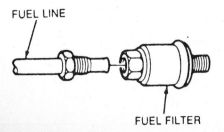

Carbureted engine fuel filter

Gasoline Engines

CARBURETED ENGINES

1. Remove the air cleaner.
2. Loosen and remove the fuel tube from the filter.
3. Unscrew the filter from the carburetor.
4. Apply Loctite® or equivalent to the external threads of the new filter and screw the filter into the carburetor.
5. Hand start the tube nut into the fuel filter. While holding the filter with a wrench to prevent it from turning, tighten the fuel line tube nut.
6. Start the engine and check for fuel leaks.
7. Replace the air cleaner.

FUEL INJECTED ENGINES

NOTE: *The inline reservoir type fuel filter should last the left of the vehicle under normal driving conditions. If the filter does need to be replaced, proceed as follows:*

CAUTION: *If the fuel filter is being serviced with the rear of the vehicle higher than the front, or if the tank is pressurized, fuel leakage or siphoning from the tank fuel lines could occur. to prevent this condition, maintain the vehicle front end at or above the level of the rear of vehicle. also, relieve tank pressure by loosening the fuel fill cap. cap should be tightened after pressure is relieved.*

1. Shut the engine off. Depressurize the fuel system as follows:

On the 2.3L EFI engine, a valve is located on the throttle body for this purpose. The valve can be located by removing the air cleaner.

On the 2.9L EFI engine use the following steps:

- Remove the gas cap.
- Disconnect the vacuum hose from the pressure regulator located on the engine fuel rail.
- Using a hand vacuum pump, apply approximately 25 in.Hg pressure to the pressure regulator.

Fuel pressure will be released into the fuel tank through the fuel return hose.

On most EFI engines the fuel pressure can be relieved as follows. Use special tool T80L-9974-B or equivalent attached to the pressure measuring port on the engine fuel rail. Direct the drain hose to a suitable container and depress the pressure relief button.

An alternate method of relieving the fuel system pressure is to disconnect the electrical connector from the inertia switch and crank the engine for about 15–30 seconds until it runs out of fuel and dies.

2. Raise and support the vehicle safely.

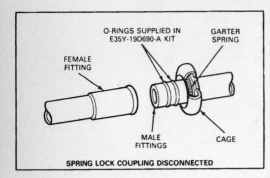

O-RINGS SUPPLIED IN
E35Y-19D690-A KIT

GARTER
SPRING

FEMALE
FITTING

MALE
FITTINGS

CAGE

SPRING LOCK COUPLING DISCONNECTED

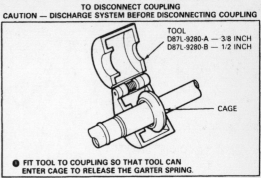

TO DISCONNECT COUPLING
CAUTION — DISCHARGE SYSTEM BEFORE DISCONNECTING COUPLING

TOOL
D87L-9280-A — 3/8 INCH
D87L-9280-B — 1/2 INCH

CAGE

❶ FIT TOOL TO COUPLING SO THAT TOOL CAN
ENTER CAGE TO RELEASE THE GARTER SPRING.

TO CONNECT COUPLING

GARTER
SPRING

REPLACEMENT GARTER SPRINGS
3/8 INCH — E1ZZ-19E576-A
1/2 INCH — E1ZZ-19E576-B
ALSO AVAILABLE IN
E35Y-19D690-A KIT

❶ CHECK FOR MISSING OR DAMAGED GARTER
SPRING — REMOVE DAMAGED SPRING WITH
SMALL HOOKED WIRE — INSTALL NEW
SPRING IF DAMAGED OR MISSING.

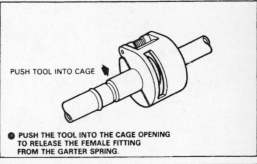

PUSH TOOL INTO CAGE

❷ PUSH THE TOOL INTO THE CAGE OPENING
TO RELEASE THE FEMALE FITTING
FROM THE GARTER SPRING.

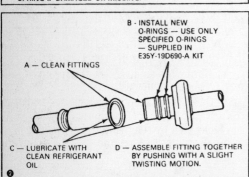

B - INSTALL NEW
O-RINGS — USE ONLY
SPECIFIED O-RINGS
— SUPPLIED IN
E35Y-19D690-A KIT

A — CLEAN FITTINGS

C — LUBRICATE WITH
CLEAN REFRIGERANT
OIL

D — ASSEMBLE FITTING TOGETHER
BY PUSHING WITH A SLIGHT
TWISTING MOTION.

❷

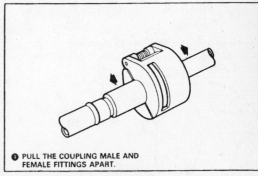

❸ PULL THE COUPLING MALE AND
FEMALE FITTINGS APART.

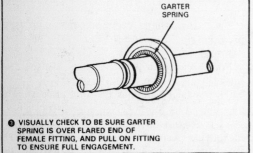

GARTER
SPRING

❸ VISUALLY CHECK TO BE SURE GARTER
SPRING IS OVER FLARED END OF
FEMALE FITTING, AND PULL ON FITTING
TO ENSURE FULL ENGAGEMENT.

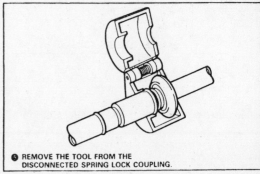

❺ REMOVE THE TOOL FROM THE
DISCONNECTED SPRING LOCK COUPLING.

Installing fuel lines

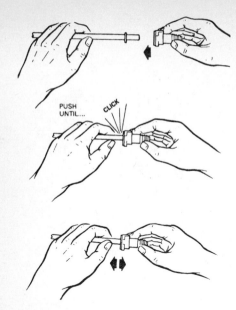

PUSH
UNTIL....   CLICK

Installing fuel lines

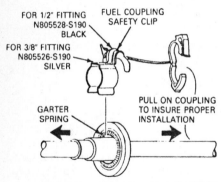

FOR 1/2" FITTING
N805528-S190
BLACK

FUEL COUPLING
SAFETY CLIP

FOR 3/8" FITTING
N805526-S190
SILVER

GARTER
SPRING

PULL ON COUPLING
TO INSURE PROPER
INSTALLATION

**SPRING LOCK COUPLING – FOR FUEL LINE TO
ENGINE FUEL RAIL CONNECTIONS**

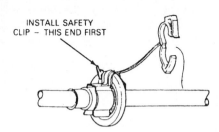

INSTALL SAFETY
CLIP – THIS END FIRST

THEN POSITION
CLAMP END
AND SNAP SHUT

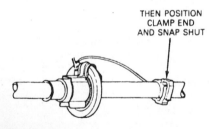

Installing fuel lines

3. Remove the push connect fittings at both ends of fuel filter. Install new retainer clips in each push connect fitting.

4. Remove the filter from the bracket by loosening the filter retaining clamp enough to allow the filter to pass through.

NOTE: *The **flow** arrow direction should be positioned as installed in the bracket to ensure proper flow of fuel through the replacement filter.*

5. Install the filter in the bracket, ensuring proper direction of flow as noted by arrow. Tighten clamp to 15–25 inch lbs.

6. Install the push connect fittings at both ends of the filter.

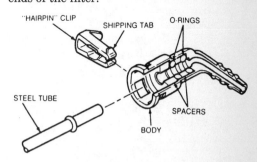

"HAIRPIN" CLIP   SHIPPING TAB   O-RINGS

STEEL TUBE

BODY   SPACERS

$\frac{5}{16}$ in. quick connect fuel fitting

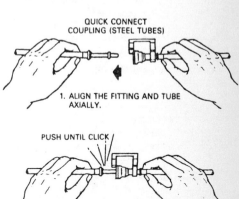

QUICK CONNECT
COUPLING (STEEL TUBES)

1. ALIGN THE FITTING AND TUBE
AXIALLY.

PUSH UNTIL CLICK

2. PUSH THE TUBE INTO THE FITTING.
WHEN PROPERLY ENGAGED, A DEFINITE
"CLICK" WILL BE HEARD.

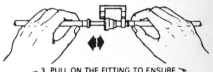

3. PULL ON THE FITTING TO ENSURE
IT IS FULLY ENGAGED.

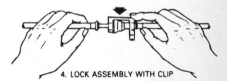

4. LOCK ASSEMBLY WITH CLIP

Installing fuel lines

7. Lower the vehicle.

8. Start the engine and check for leaks.

Clean all dirt and/or grease from the fuel filter fittings. "Quick Connect" fittings are used on models equipped with a pressurized fuel system. These fittings must be disconnected using the proper procedure or the fittings may be damaged. The fuel filter uses a "hairpin" clip retainer. Spread the two hairpin clip legs about $\frac{1}{8}$ in. (3mm) each to disengage it from the fitting, then pull the clip outward. Use finger pressure only; do not use any tools. Push the quick connect fittings onto the filter ends. Ford recommends that the retaining clips be replaced whenever removed. The fuel tubes used on these fuel systems are manufactured in $\frac{5}{16}$ in. and $\frac{3}{8}$ in. diameters. Each fuel tube takes a different size harpin clip, so keep this in mind when purchasing new clips. A click will be heard when the hairpin clip snaps into its

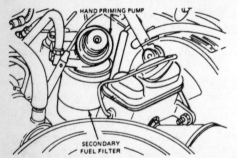

Priming the pump and fuel filter assembly — 2.2L diesel engine

proper position. Pull on the lines with moderate pressure to ensure proper connection. Start the engine and check for fuel leaks. If the inertia switch (reset switch) was disconnected to relieve the fuel system pressure, cycle the ignition switch from the **OFF** to **ON** position several times to re-charge the fuel system before attempting to start the engine.

Diesel Engines

2.2L DIESEL ENGINE

1. Remove the spin on filter by turning counterclockwise with hands or suitable tool, and discard filter.

2. Clean the filter mounting surfaces.

3. Coat the gasket of the new filter with clean diesel fuel.

4. Tighten the filter until the gasket touches the filter header, then tighten an additional $\frac{1}{2}$ turn.

5. Air Bleed the fuel system using the following procedure:

    a. Loosen the fuel filter air vent plug.

    b. Pump the priming pump on the top of

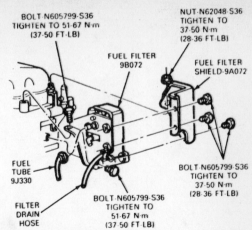

Fuel conditioner filter replacement — 2.3L diesel engine

the filter adapter.

    c. Continue pumping until clear fuel, free from air bubbles, flows from the air vent plug.

    d. Depress the priming pump and hold down while closing the air vent plug.

6. Start the engine and check for fuel leaks.
NOTE: *To avoid fuel contamination do not add fuel directly to the new filter.*

2.3L DIESEL ENGINE

The 2.3L diesel engine fuel filter is the paper element cartridge type and the conditioner housing includes an air vent screw to bleed air from the fuel lines.

1. Remove the rear bracket shield, attaching bolts, and unplug the electrical connectors attached to the shield. These connectors pull apart by pulling on the wire bundle on each side. Be resting the shield on the engine valve cover, the electrical connector halves leading to the fuel conditioner can be left attached to the shield.

2. Remove the rectangular filter element cartridge by unlatching holddown clamps by hand or with suitable tool, and pull element cartridge rear ward until it clears the base.

3. Clean the filter mounting pad.

4. Install the new element by pushing straight on after lining up filter element grommet holes with corresponding inlet/outlet tubes on the base.

5. Snap on the clamps.

6. Install the rear bracket shield, tighten the bolts to specification and plug the electrical connections back together. If the connectors were pulled away from the shield, push the locators back in the holes provided in the shield to secure the electrical connectors.
NOTE: *To avoid fuel contamination do not add fuel directly to the new filter.*

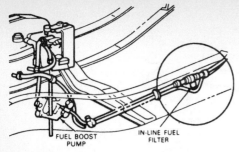

Inline filter replacement — 2.3L diesel engine

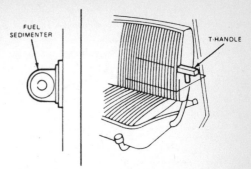

Diesel fuel sedimenter draining — 2.2L diesel engine

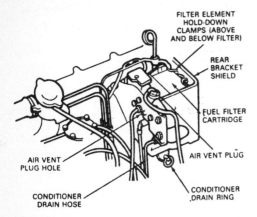

Purging and priming the fuel filter — 2.3L diesel engine

2.3L DIESEL ENGINE w/FRAME MOUNTED INLINE FUEL FILTER

The inline fuel filter is a molded plastic mesh type designed to protect the electrical fuel boost pump from contamination. It is located on the LH side frame rail about tow feet rear of the fuel boost pump.

1. Pinch off the fuel hose to the rear of the inline filter using a rubber coated clamp or other suitable device to prevent fuel from siphoning from the tank. Care must be taken not to damage the fuel hose.

2. Remove the two hose clamps closest to the inline filter and remove filter.

3. Install replacement filter and two new clamps. Remove the hose pinch-off clamp.

2.3L DIESEL ENGINE — PURGING AIR AND PRIMING FUEL FILTER

1. Turn the ignition switch **ON** to activate the electric fuel boost pump.

2. Loosen the air vent plug on the conditioner housing until fuel flows from the air vent plug hole free of bubbles.

3. Tighten the air vent plug securely.

4. Start the engine and check for leaks.

WARNING: *DO NOT OPEN AIR VENT PLUG WITH THE ENGINE RUNNING!*

Diesel Fuel Sedimenter 2.2L Engine

SERVICE

2.2L Diesel Engine

Water should be changed from the diesel fuel sedimenter whenever the light on the instrument panel comes on or every 5,000 miles. More frequent drain intervals may be required depending on the quality of the fuel used.

CAUTION: *The vehicle must be stopped with the engine off when draining the sedimenter. Fuel may ignite if sedimenter is drained while the engine is running or the vehicle is moving.*

The instrument panel warning light **(WATER IN FUEL)** will glow when approximately 1/2 liter of water has accumulated in the sedimenter. When the warning light glows, shut off the engine as soon as safely possible. A suitable drain pan or container should be placed under the sedimenter, which is mounted inside the frame rail, underneath the driver's side of the cab. To drain the fuel sedimenter, pull up on the T-handle (located on the cab floor behind the driver's seat) until resistance is felt. Turn the ignition switch to the **ON** position so the warning light glows and hold T-handle up for approximately 45 seconds after light goes out.

To stop draining fuel, release T-handle and inspect sedimenter to verify that draining has stopped. Discard drained fluid suitably.

PCV Valve

REMOVAL AND INSTALLATION

Check the PCV valve according to the Preventive Maintenance Schedule at the end of this Chapter to see if it is free and not gummed up, stuck or blocked. To check the valve, remove it from the engine and work the valve by sticking a screwdriver in the crankcase side of the valve. It should move. It is possible to

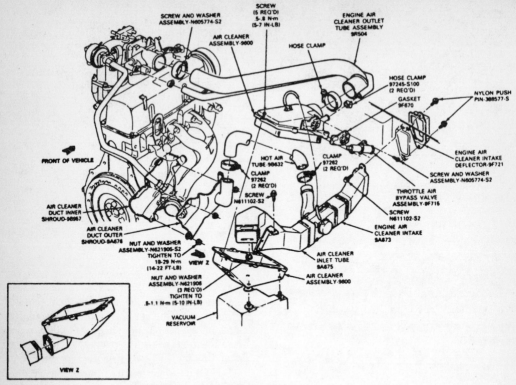

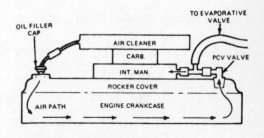

PCV system

clean the PCV valve by soaking it in a solvent and blowing it out with compressed air. This can restore the valve to some level of operating order.

This should be used only in emergency situations. Otherwise, the valve should be replaced. Always check PCV valve hose for wear or cracks during service procedure.

Evaporative Canister

The fuel evaporative emission control canister should be inspected for damage or leaks at

PCV system

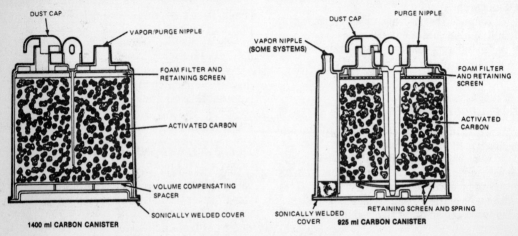

Carbon canister cross-sections

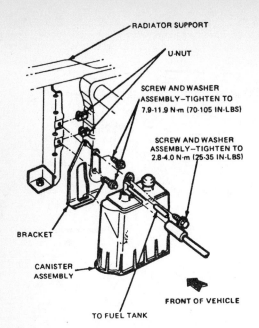

RADIATOR SUPPORT

U-NUT

SCREW AND WASHER
ASSEMBLY—TIGHTEN TO
7.9-11.9 N·m (70-105 IN-LBS)

SCREW AND WASHER
ASSEMBLY—TIGHTEN TO
2.8-4.0 N·m (25-35 IN-LBS)

BRACKET

CANISTER
ASSEMBLY

FRONT OF VEHICLE

TO FUEL TANK

Evaporative canister

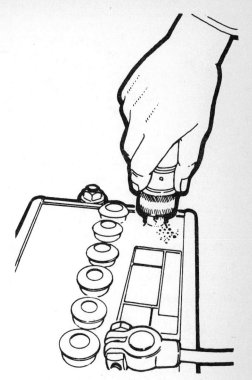

Clean the battery posts with a wire terminal cleaner

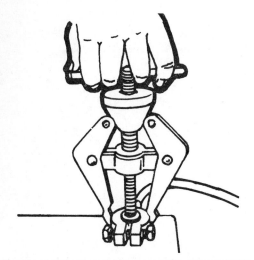

Top terminal battery cables are easily removed with this inexpensive puller

the hose fittings. Repair or replace any old or cracked hoses. Replace the canister if it is damaged in any way. The canister is located on the left side radiator support, under the hood.

Battery

Loose, dirty, or corroded battery terminals are a major cause of "no-start." Every 3 months or so, remove the battery terminals and clean them, giving them a light coating of petroleum jelly when you are finished. This will help to retard corrosion.

Check the battery cables for signs of wear or

Clean the cable ends with a stiff cable cleaning tool (male end)

chafing and replace any cable or terminal that looks marginal. Battery terminals can be easily cleaned and inexpensive terminal cleaning tools are an excellent investment that will pay for themselves many times over. They can usually be purchased from any well equipped auto store or parts department. Side terminal batteries require a different tool to clean the threads in the battery case. The accumulated white powder and corrosion can be cleaned from the top of the battery with an old toothbrush and a solution of baking soda and water.

Unless you have a maintenance free battery, check the electrolyte level (see Battery under Fluid Level Checks in this Chapter) and check the specific gravity of each cell. Be sure that the vent holes in each cell cap are not blocked by grease or dirt. The vent holes allow hydrogen gas, formed by the chemical reaction in the battery, to escape safely.

REPLACEMENT BATTERIES

The cold power rating of a battery measures battery starting performance and provides an approximate relationship between battery size and engine size. The cold power rating of a replacement battery should match or exceed your engine size in cubic inches.

FLUID LEVEL (EXCEPT MAINTENANCE FREE BATTERIES)

Check the battery electrolyte level at least

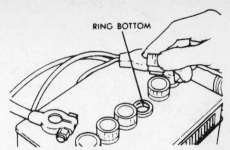

Fill each battery cell to the bottom of the split ring with distilled water

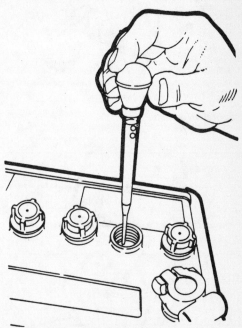

The specific gravity of the battery can be checked with a simple float-type hydrometer

once a month, or more often in hot weather or during periods of extended vehicle operation. The level can be checked through the case on translucent polypropylene batteries; the cell caps must be removed on other models. The electrolyte level in each cell should be kept filled to the split ring inside, or the line marked on the outside of the case.

If the level is low, add only distilled water, or colorless, odorless drinking water, through the opening until the level is correct. Each cell is completely separate from the others, so each must be checked and filled individually.

If water is added in freezing weather, the vehicle should be driven several miles to allow the water to mix with the electrolyte. Otherwise, the battery could freeze.

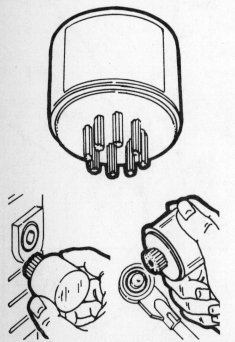

Side terminal batteries require a special wire brush for cleaning

SPECIFIC GRAVITY (@ 80°F.) AND CHARGE	
Specific Gravity Reading (use the minimum figure for testing)	
Minimum	Battery Charge
1.260	100% Charged
1.230	75% Charged
1.200	50% Charged
1.170	25% Charged
1.140	Very Little Power Left
1.110	Completely Discharged

Battery specific gravity. Some testers have colored balls which correspond to the numerical values in the left column

SPECIFIC GRAVITY (EXCEPT MAINTENANCE FREE BATTERIES)

At least once a year, check the specific gravity of the battery. It should be between 1.20 in.Hg and 1.26 in.Hg at room temperature.

The specific gravity can be check with the use of an hydrometer, an inexpensive instrument available from many sources, including auto parts stores. The hydrometer has a squeeze bulb at one end and a nozzle at the other. Battery electrolyte is sucked into the hydrometer until the float is lifted from its seat. The specific gravity is then read by noting the position of the float. Generally, if after charging, the specific gravity between any two cells varies more than 50 points (0.50), the battery is bad and should be replaced.

It is not possible to check the specific gravity in this manner on sealed (maintenance free) batteries. Instead, the indicator built into the top of the case must be relied on to display any signs of battery deterioration. If the indicator is dark, the battery can be assumed to be OK. If the indicator is light, the specific gravity is low, and the battery should be charged or replaced.

CABLES AND CLAMPS

Once a year, the battery terminals and the cable clamps should be cleaned. Loosen the clamps and remove the cables, negative cable first. On batteries with posts on top, the use of a puller specially made for the purpose is recommended. These are inexpensive, and available in auto parts stores. Side terminal battery cables are secured with a bolt.

Clean the cable lamps and the battery terminal with a wire brush, until all corrosion, grease, etc., is removed and the metal is shiny. It is especially important to clean the inside of the clamp thoroughly, since a small deposit of foreign material or oxidation there will prevent a sound electrical connection and inhibit either starting or charging. Special tools are available for cleaning these parts, one type for conventional batteries and another type for side terminal batteries.

Before installing the cables, loosen the battery holddown clamp or strap, remove the battery and check the battery tray. Clear it of any debris, and check it for soundness. Rust should be wire brushed away, and the metal given a coat of anti-rust paint. Replace the battery and tighten the holddown clamp or strap securely, but be careful not to overtighten, which will crack the battery case.

After the clamps and terminals are clean, reinstall the cables, negative cable last; do not hammer on the clamps to install. Tighten the clamps securely, but do not distort them. Give the clamps and terminals a thin external coat of grease after installation, to retard corrosion.

Check the cables at the same time that the terminals are cleaned. If the cable insulation is cracked or broken, or if the ends are frayed, the cable should be replaced with a new cable of the same length and gauge.

CAUTION: *Keep flame or sparks away from the battery; it gives off explosive hydrogen gas. Battery electrolyte contains sulphuric acid. If you should splash any on your skin or in your eyes, flush the affected area with plenty of clear water. If it lands in your eyes, get medical help immediately.*

Belts

INSPECTION

The V-ribbed belt design, belts do not show wear readily. It is a good idea, therefore, to visually inspect the belts regularly and replace them, routinely, in accordance with the intervals specified in the Maintenance Interval chart at the end of this Chapter. The drive belts must always be properly adjusted. Loose drive belts will allow the belt to slip on the pulley causing noise or will not allow proper operation of the accessory (many a battery has died due to a

HOW TO SPOT WORN V-BELTS

V-Belts are vital to efficient engine operation—they drive the fan, water pump and other accessories. They require little maintenance (occasional tightening) but they will not last forever. Slipping or failure of the V-belt will lead to overheating. If your V-belt looks like any of these, it should be replaced.

Cracking or weathering

This belt has deep cracks, which cause it to flex. Too much flexing leads to heat build-up and premature failure. These cracks can be caused by using the belt on a pulley that is too small. Notched belts are available for small diameter pulleys.

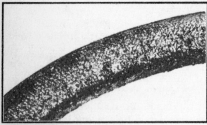

Softening (grease and oil)

Oil and grease on a belt can cause the belt's rubber compounds to soften and separate from the reinforcing cords that hold the belt together. The belt will first slip, then finally fail altogether.

Glazing

Glazing is caused by a belt that is slipping. A slipping belt can cause a run-down battery, erratic power steering, overheating or poor accessory performance. The more the belt slips, the more glazing will be built up on the surface of the belt. The more the belt is glazed, the more it will slip. If the glazing is light, tighten the belt.

Worn cover

The cover of this belt is worn off and is peeling away. The reinforcing cords will begin to wear and the belt will shortly break. When the belt cover wears in spots or has a rough jagged appearance, check the pulley grooves for roughness.

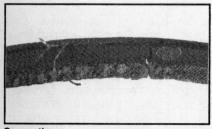

Separation

This belt is on the verge of breaking and leaving you stranded. The layers of the belt are separating and the reinforcing cords are exposed. It's just a matter of time before it breaks completely.

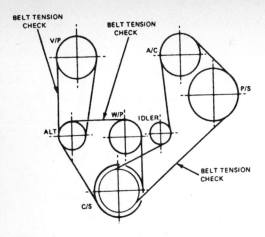

Belt tension adjustments — 2.3L diesel engine

loose alternator belt). On the other hand, overly tight belts will place strain on accessory bearings causing them to fail prematurely.

ADJUSTMENT

Belt tension can be checked by pressing on the belt at the center point of its longest straight run. The belt should give about $1/4$–$1/2$ in.. If the belt is loose, it will slip. If the belt is too tight it will damage bearings in the driven unit. Those units being driven, such as the alternator, power steering pump or compressor, have a bolt which when loosened allows the unit to move for belt adjustment. Sometimes it is necessary to loosen the pivot bolt also, to make the adjustment.

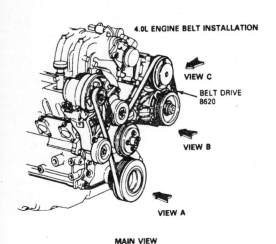

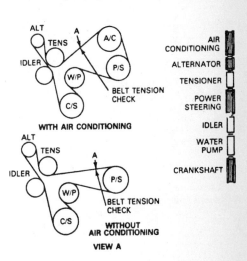

Belt tension adjustments — 4.0L engine

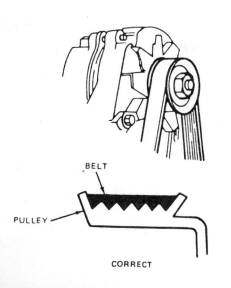

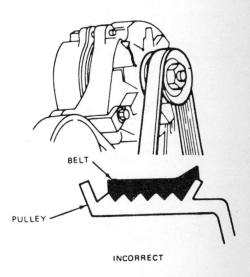

Serpentine belt installation

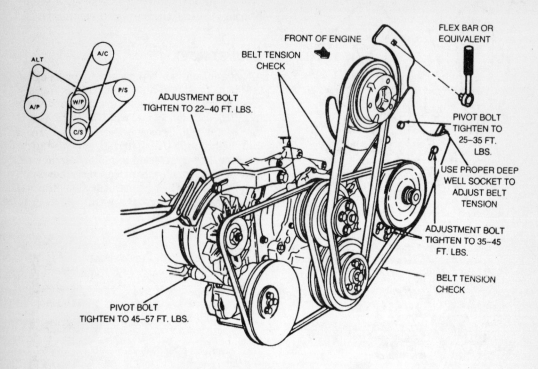

Belt tension adjustments — 2.8L engine

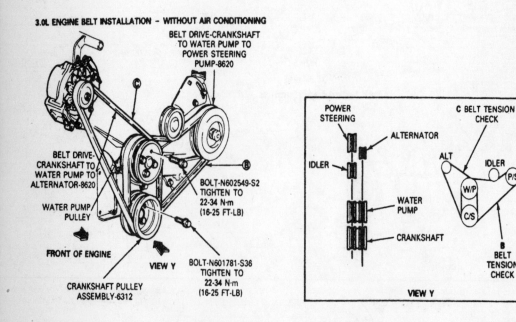

Belt tension adjustments — 3.0L engine without A/C

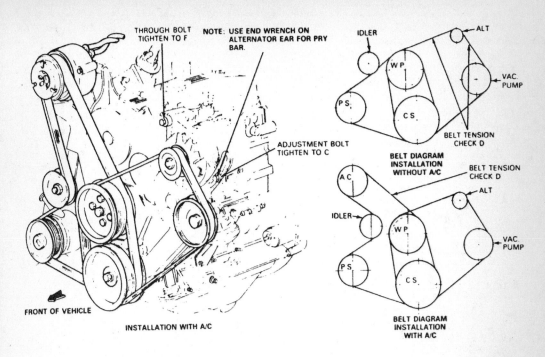

Belt tension adjustments — 2.3L diesel engine

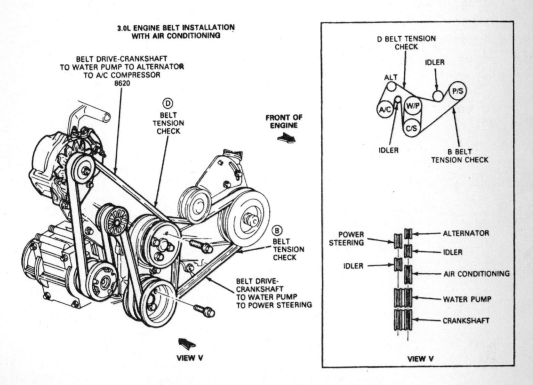

Belt tension adjustments — 3.0L engine with A/C

REMOVAL AND INSTALLATION

To remove a drive belt, simply loosen the accessory being driven and move it on its pivot point to free the belt. Then, remove the belt. If an idler pulley is used, it is often necessary, only, to loosen the idler pulley to provide enough slack to slip the belt from the pulley.

It is important to note, however, that on engines with many driven accessories, several or all of the belts may have to be removed to get at the one to be replaced.

Hoses

REPLACEMENT

1. Drain the existing antifreeze and coolant. Open the radiator and engine drain petcocks, or disconnect the bottom radiator hose, at the radiator outlet.

CAUTION: *When draining the coolant, keep in mind that cats and dogs are attracted by the ethylene glycol antifreeze, and are quite likely to drink any that is left in an uncov-*

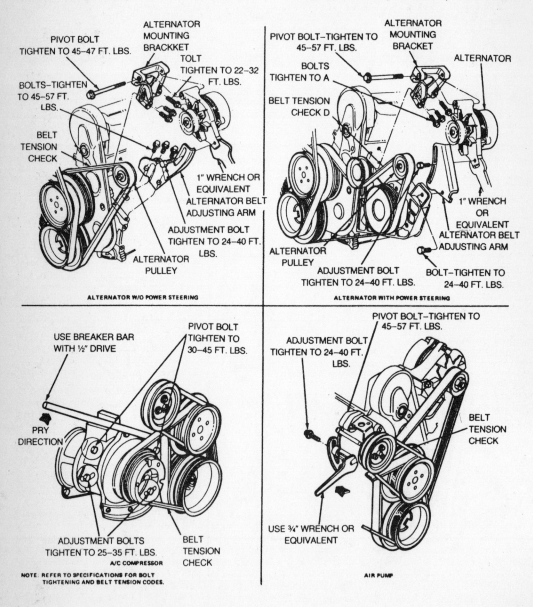

Belt tension adjustments — 2.0L, 2.3L engines

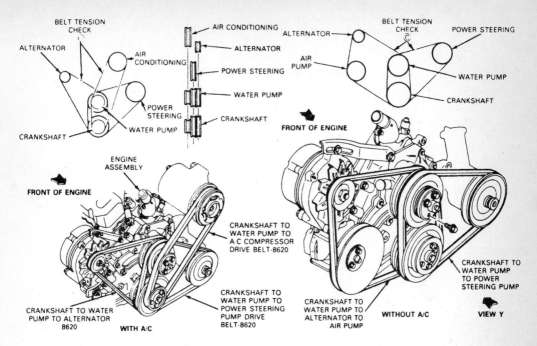

Belt tension adjustments — 2.9L engine

ered container or in puddles on the ground. This will prove fatal in sufficient quantity. Always drain the coolant into a sealable container. Coolant should be reused unless it is contaminated or several years old.

NOTE: *Before opening the radiator petcock, spray it with some penetrating lubricant.*

2. Loosen the clamp on each end of the hose to be removed.

3. Slide the hose off the connections.

4. Position the clamps on each end of the new hose.

5. Slide the hose onto the connections, then tighten the clamps. If the connections have a bead around the edges, make sure the clamps are located beyond the beads.

6. Refill the cooling system with coolant. Run the engine for several minutes, then check the hose connections for leaks.

Cooling System

CAUTION: *Never remove the radiator cap under any conditions while the engine is running! Failure to follow these instructions could result in damage to the cooling system or engine and/or personal injury. To avoid having scalding hot coolant or steam blow out of the radiator, use extreme care when removing the radiator cap from a hot radiator. Wait until the engine has cooled, then wrap a thick cloth around the radiator cap and turn it slowly to the first stop. Step back*

while the pressure is released from the cooling system. When you are sure the pressure has been released, press down on the radiator cap (still have the cloth in position) turn and remove the radiator cap.

At least once every 2 years, the engine cooling system should be inspected, flushed, and refilled with fresh coolant. If the coolant is left in the system too long, it loses its ability to prevent rust and corrosion. If the coolant has too much water, it won't protect against freezing.

The pressure cap should be looked at for signs of age or deterioration. Fan belt and other drive belts should be inspected and adjusted to the proper tension. (See checking belt tension).

Hose clamps should be tightened, and soft or cracked hoses replaced. Damp spots, or accumulations of rust or dye near hoses, water pump or other areas, indicate possible leakage, which must be corrected before filling the system with fresh coolant.

CHECK THE RADIATOR CAP

While you are checking the coolant level, check the radiator cap for a worn or cracked gasket. It the cap doesn't seal properly, fluid will be lost and the engine will overheat.

Worn caps should be replaced with a new one.

CLEAN RADIATOR OF DEBRIS

Periodically clean any debris — leaves, paper, insects, etc. — from the radiator fins. Pick the

HOW TO SPOT BAD HOSES

Both the upper and lower radiator hoses are called upon to perform difficult jobs in an inhospitable enviorment. They are subject to nearly 18 psi at under hood temperature often over 280F., and must circulate an hour-3 good reasons to have good hoses.

Swollen hose

A good test for any hose is to feel it for soft or spongy spots. Frequently these will appear as swollen areas of the hose. The most likely cause is oil soaking. This hose could burst at any time, when hot or under pressure.

Cracked hose

Cracked hoses can usually be seen but feel the hoses to be sure they have not hardened; a prime cause of cracking. This hose has cracked down to the reinforcing cords and could split at any of the cracks.

Frayed hose end (due to weak clamp)

Weakened clamps frequently are the cause of hose and cooling system failure. The connection between the pipe and hose has deteriorated enough to allow coolant to escape when the engine is hot.

Debris in cooling system

Debris, rust and scale in the cooling system can cause the inside of a hose to weaken. This can usually be felt on the outside of the hose as soft or thinner areas.

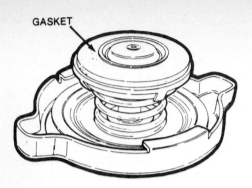

Check the radiator cap gasket for cracks or wear

Open the radiator petcock to drain the cooling system

Keep the radiator fins clear of debris for maximum cooling

large pieces off by hand. The smaller pieces can be washed away with water pressure from a hose.

Carefully straighten any bent radiator fins with a pair of needle nose pliers. Be careful — the fins are very soft. Don't wiggle the fins back and forth too much. Straighten them once and try not to move them again.

DRAIN AND REFILL THE COOLING SYSTEM

Completely draining and refilling the cooling system every two years at least will remove accumulated rust, scale and other deposits. Coolant in late model vehicles is a 50/50 mixture of ethylene glycol and water for year round use. Use a good quality antifreeze with water pump lubricants, rust inhibitors and other corrosion inhibitors along with acid neutralizers.

1. Drain the existing antifreeze and coolant. Open the radiator and engine drain petcocks, or disconnect the bottom radiator hose, at the radiator outlet.

CAUTION: *When draining the coolant, keep in mind that cats and dogs are attracted by the ethylene glycol antifreeze, and are quite likely to drink any that is left in an uncovered container or in puddles on the ground. This will prove fatal in sufficient quantity. Always drain the coolant into a sealable con-*

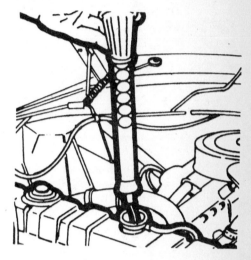

Check antifreeze protection with an inexpensive tester

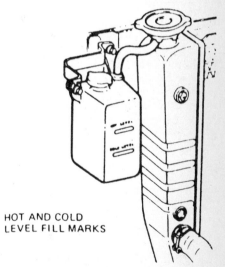

HOT AND COLD
LEVEL FILL MARKS

The system should be pressure tested once a year

tainer. Coolant should be reused unless it is contaminated or several years old.
NOTE: *Before opening the radiator petcock, spray it with some penetrating lubricant.*

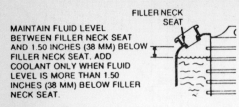

MAINTAIN FLUID LEVEL BETWEEN FILLER NECK SEAT AND 1.50 INCHES (38 MM) BELOW FILLER NECK SEAT. ADD COOLANT ONLY WHEN FLUID LEVEL IS MORE THAN 1.50 INCHES (38 MM) BELOW FILLER NECK SEAT.

FILLER NECK SEAT

Coolant level check

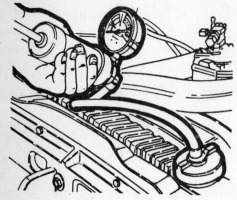

The system should be pressure tested once a year

2. Close the petcock or reconnect the lower hose and fill the system with water.

3. Add a can of quality radiator flush.

4. Idle the engine until the upper radiator hose gets hot.

5. Drain the system again.

6. Repeat this process until the drained water is clear and free of scale.

7. Close all petcocks and connect all the hoses.

8. If equipped with a coolant recovery system, flush the reservoir with water and leave empty.

9. Determine the capacity of your coolant system (see capacities specifications). Add a 50/50 mix of quality antifreeze (ethylene glycol) and water to provide the desired protection.

10. Run the engine to operating temperature.

11. Stop the engine and check the coolant level.

12. Check the level of protection with an antifreeze tester, replace the cap and check for leaks.

Air Conditioning

PREVENTIVE MAINTENANCE CHECKS

Antifreeze

In order to prevent heater core freeze-up during A/C operation, it is necessary to maintain permanent type antifreeze protection of +15°F (–9°C) or lower. A reading of –15°F (–

26°C) is ideal since this protection also supplies sufficient corrosion inhibitors for the protection of the engine cooling system.

WARNING: *Do not use antifreeze longer than specified by the manufacturer.*

Radiator Cap

For efficient operation of an air conditioned cooling system, the radiator cap should have a holding pressure which meets manufacturer's specifications. A cap which fails to hold these pressure should be replaced.

Condenser

Any obstruction of or damage to the condenser configuration will restrict the air flow which is essential to its efficient operation. It is therefore, a good rule to keep this unit clean and in proper physical shape.

NOTE: *Bug screens are regarded as obstructions.*

Condensation Drain Tube

This single molded drain tube expels the condensation, which accumulates on the bottom of the evaporator housing, into the engine compartment.

If this tube is obstructed, the air conditioning performance can be restricted and condensation buildup can spill over onto the vehicle's floor.

SAFETY PRECAUTIONS

Because of the importance of the necessary safety precautions that must be exercised when working with air conditioning systems and R-12 refrigerant, a recap of the safety precautions are outlined.

1. Avoid contact with a charged refrigeration system, even when working on another part of the air conditioning system or vehicle. If a heavy tool comes into contact with a section of copper tubing or a heat exchanger, it can easily cause the relatively soft material to rupture.

2. When it is necessary to apply force to a fitting which contains refrigerant, as when checking that all system couplings are securely tightened, use a wrench on both parts of the fitting involved, if possible. This will avoid putting torque on the refrigerant tubing. (It is advisable, when possible, to use tube or line wrenches when tightening these flare nut fittings.)

3. Avoid applying heat to any refrigerant line or storage vessel. Charging may be aided by using water heated to less than 125°F (52°C) to warm the refrigerant container. Never allow a refrigerant storage container to sit out in the

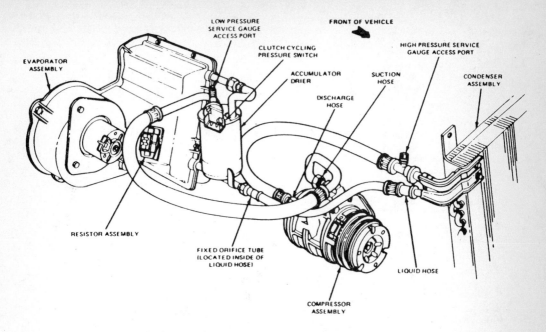

A/C system, showing all components

sun, or near any other source of heat, such as a radiator.

4. Always wear goggles when working on a system to protect the eyes. If refrigerant contacts the eye, it is advisable in all cases to see a physician as soon as possible.

5. Frostbite from liquid refrigerant should be treated by first gradually warming the area with cool water, and then gently applying petroleum jelly. A physician should be consulted.

6. Always keep refrigerant can fittings capped when not in use. Avoid sudden shock to the can which might occur from dropping it, or from banging a heavy tool against it. Never carry a refrigerant can in the passenger compartment of a vehicle.

7. Always completely discharge the system before painting the vehicle (if the paint is to be baked on), or before welding anywhere near the refrigerant lines.

TEST GAUGES

Most of the service work performed in air conditioning requires the use of a set of two gauges, one for the high (head) pressure side of the system, the other for the low (suction) side.

The low side gauge records both pressure and vacuum. Vacuum readings are calibrated from 0 to 30 inches Hg and the pressure graduations read from 0 to no less than 60 psi.

The high side gauge measures pressure from 0 to at last 600 psi.

Both gauges are threaded into a manifold that contains two hand shut-off valves. Proper manipulation of these valves and the use of the

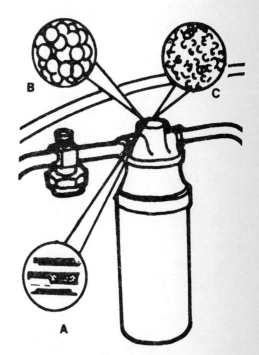

Sight glass check w/accumulator

attached test hoses allow the user to perform the following services:

1. Test high and low side pressures.
2. Charge the system (with refrigerant).

The manifold valves are designed so that they have no direct effect on gauge readings, but serve only to provide for, or cut off, flow of refrigerant through the manifold. During all

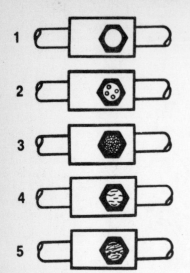

1 Clear sight glass — system correctly charged or overcharged

2 Occasional bubbles — refrigerant charge slightly low

3 Oil streaks on sight glass — total lack of refrigerant

4 Heavy stream of bubbles — serious shortage of refrigerant

5 Dark or clouded sight glass — contaminent present

Sight glass inspection

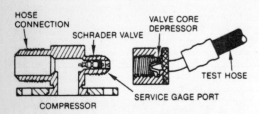

Schrader valve

testing and hook-up operations, the valves are kept in a close position to avoid disturbing the refrigeration system. The valves are opened only to purge the system or refrigerant or to charge it.

INSPECTION

CAUTION: *The compressed refrigerant used in the air conditioning system expands into the atmosphere at a temperature of −21.7°F (−30°C) or lower. This will freeze any surface, including your eyes, that it contacts. In addition, the refrigerant decomposes into a poisonous gas in the presence of a flame. Do not open or disconnect any part of the air conditioning system.*

Sight Glass Check

You can safely make a few simple checks to determine if your air conditioning system needs service. The tests work best if the temperature is warm (about 70°F [21.1°C]).

NOTE: *If your vehicle is equipped with an aftermarket air conditioner, the following system check may not apply. You should contact the manufacturer of the unit for instructions on systems checks.*

1. Place the automatic transmission in Park or the manual transmission in Neutral. Set the parking brake.

2. Run the engine at a fast idle (about 1,500 rpm) either with the help of a friend or by temporarily readjusting the idle speed screw.

3. Set the controls for maximum cold with the blower on High.

4. Locate the sight glass in one of the system lines. Usually it is on the left alongside the top of the radiator.

5. If you see bubbles, the system must be recharged. Very likely there is a leak at some point.

6. If there are no bubbles, there is either no refrigerant at all or the system is fully charged. Feel the two hoses going to the belt driven compressor. If they are both at the same temperature, the system is empty and must be recharged.

7. If one hose (high pressure) is warm and the other (low pressure) is cold, the system may be all right. However, you are probably making these tests because you think there is something wrong, so proceed to the next step.

Some sight glasses are in the A/C lines

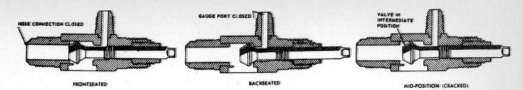

Manual service valve positions

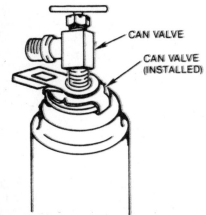

One pound R-12 can with opener valve connected

8. Have an assistant in the vehicle turn the fan control on and off to operate the compressor clutch. Watch the sight glass.

9. If bubbles appear when the clutch is disengaged and disappear when it is engaged, the system is properly charged.

10. If the refrigerant takes more than 45 seconds to bubble when the clutch is disengaged, the system is overcharged. This usually causes poor cooling at low speeds.

WARNING: *If it is determined that the system has a leak, it should be corrected as soon as possible. Leaks may allow moisture to enter and cause a very expensive rust problem. Exercise the air conditioner for a few minutes, every two weeks or so, during the cold months. This avoids the possibility of the compressor seals drying out from lack of lubrication.*

TESTING THE SYSTEM

1. Connect a gauge set.
2. Close (clockwise) both gauge set valves.
4. Park the vehicle in the shade, at least 5 feet from any walls. Start the engine, set the parking brake, place the transmission in NEUTRAL and establish an idle of 1,100–1,300 rpm.
5. Run the air conditioning system for full cooling, in the MAX or COLD mode.
6. The low pressure gauge should read 5–20 psi; the high pressure gauge should indicate 120–180 psi.

WARNING: *These pressures are the norm for an ambient temperature of 70–80°F (21–27°C). Higher air temperatures along with high humidity will cause higher system pressures. At idle speed and an ambient temperature of 110°F (43°C), the high pressure reading can exceed 300 psi. Under these extreme conditions, you can keep the pressures down by directing a large electric floor fan through the condenser.*

LEAK TESTING

Some leak tests can be performed with a soapy water solution. There must be at least a $1/2$ lb. charge in the system for a leak to be detected. The most extensive leak tests are performed with either a Halide flame type leak tester or the more preferable electronic leak tester.

In either case, the equipment is expensive, and, the use of a Halide detector can be **extremely** hazardous!

CHARGING THE SYSTEM

CAUTION: *NEVER OPEN THE HIGH PRESSURE SIDE WITH A CAN OF REFRIGERANT CONNECTED TO THE SYSTEM! OPENING THE HIGH PRESSURE SIDE WILL OVER PRESSURIZE THE CAN, CAUSING IT TO EXPLODE!*

1. Connect the gauge set.
2. Close (clockwise) both gauge set valves.
3. Connect the center hose to the refrigerant can opener valve.
4. Make sure the can opener valve is closed, that is, the needle is raised, and connect the valve to the can. Open the valve, puncturing the can with the needle.
5. Loosen the center hose fitting at the pressure gauge, allowing refrigerant to purge the hose of air. When the air is bled, tighten the fitting.

CAUTION: *IF THE LOW PRESSURE GAUGE SET HOSE IS NOT CONNECTED TO THE ACCUMULATOR/DRIER, KEEP THE CAN IN AN UPRIGHT POSITION!*

6. Disconnect the wire harness snap-lock connector from the clutch cycling pressure switch and install a jumper wire across the two terminals of the connector.
7. Open the low side gauge set valve and the

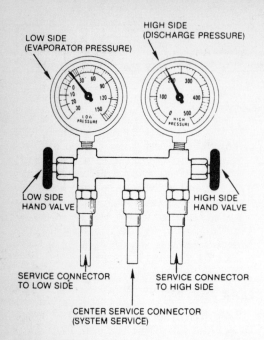

LOW SIDE
(EVAPORATOR PRESSURE)

HIGH SIDE
(DISCHARGE PRESSURE)

LOW SIDE
HAND VALVE

HIGH SIDE
HAND VALVE

SERVICE CONNECTOR
TO LOW SIDE

SERVICE CONNECTOR
TO HIGH SIDE

CENTER SERVICE CONNECTOR
(SYSTEM SERVICE)

Typical manifold gauge set

can valve.

8. Allow refrigerant to be drawn into the system.

9. When no more refrigerant is drawn into the system, start the engine and run it at about 1,500 rpm. Turn on the system and operate it at the full high position. The compressor will operate and pull refrigerant gas into the system.

NOTE: *To help speed the process, the can may be placed, upright, in a pan of warm water, not exceeding 125°F (52°C).*

10. If more than one can of refrigerant is needed, close the can valve and gauge set low side valve when the can is empty and connect a new can to the opener. Repeat the charging process until the sight glass indicates a full charge. The frost line on the outside of the can will indicate what portion of the can has been used.

CAUTION: *NEVER ALLOW THE HIGH PRESSURE SIDE READING TO EXCEED 240 psi!*

11. When the charging process has been completed, close the gauge set valve and can valve. Remove the jumper wire and reconnect the cycling clutch wire. Run the system for at least five minutes to allow it to normalize. Low pressure side reading should be 4–25 psi; high pressure reading should be 120–210 psi at an ambient temperature of 70–90°F (21–32°C).

12. Loosen both service hoses at the gauges to allow any refrigerant to escape. Remove the gauge set and install the dust caps on the service valves.

NOTE: *Multi-can dispensers are available which allow a simultaneous hook-up of up to four 1 lb. cans of R-12.*

CAUTION: *Never exceed the recommended maximum charge for the system! The maximum charge for systems is 3 lb.*

Windshield Wipers

Intense heat from the sun, snow and ice, road oils and the chemicals used in windshield washer solvents combine to deteriorate the rubber wiper refills. The refills should be replaced about twice a year or whenever the blades begin to streak or chatter.

WIPER REFILL REPLACEMENT

Normally, if the wipers are not cleaning the windshield properly, only the refill has to be replaced. The blade and arm usually require replacement only in the event of damage. It is not necessary (except on new Tridon refills) to remove the arm or the blade to replace the refill (rubber part), though you may have to position the arm higher on the glass. You can do this turning the ignition switch **ON** and operating the wipers. When they are positioned where they are accessible, turn the ignition switch **OFF**.

There are several types of refills and your vehicle could have any kind, since aftermarket blades and arms may not use exactly the same refill as the original equipment.

Most Anco styles use a release button that is pushed down to allow the refill to slide out of the yoke jaws. The new refills slide in and locks in place. Some Anco refills are removed by locating where the metal backing strip or the refill is wider. Insert a small screwdriver blade between the frame and metal backing strip. Press down to release the refill from the retaining tab.

The Trico style is unlocked at one end by squeezing 2 metal tabs, and the refill is slid out of the frame jaws. When the new refill is installed, the tabs will click into place, locking the refill.

The polycarbonate type is held in place by a locking lever that is pushed downward out of the groove in the arm to free the refill. When the new refill is installed, it will lock in place automatically.

The Tridon refill has a plastic backing strip with a notch about 1 in. from the end. Hold the blade (frame) on a hard surface so that the frame is tightly bowed. Grip the tip of the backing strip and pull up while twisting counterclockwise. The backing strip will snap out of the retaining tab. Do this for the remaining tabs until the refill is free of the arm. The length of

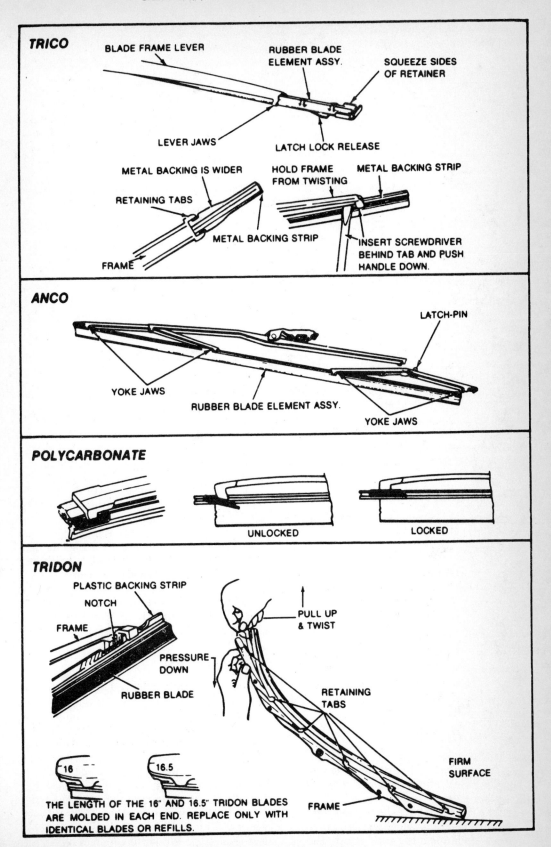

Popular styles of wiper refills

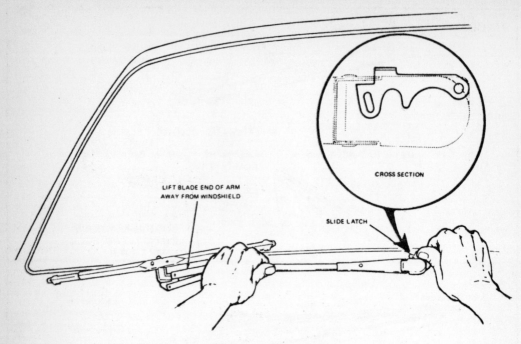

LIFT BLADE END OF ARM
AWAY FROM WINDSHIELD

CROSS SECTION

SLIDE LATCH

Wiper arm replacement

these refills is molded into the end and they should be replaced with identical types.

No matter which type of refill you use, be sure that all of the frame claws engage the refill. Before operating the wipers, be sure that no part of the metal frame is contacting the windshield.

WIPER ARM REPLACEMENT

To remove the arm and blade assembly, raise the blade end of the arm off of the windshield and move the slide latch away from the pivot shaft. The wiper arm can now be removed from the shaft without the use of any tools.

To install, push the main head over the pivot shaft. Be sure the wipers are in the pared position, and the blade assembly is in its correct position. Hold the main arm head onto the pivot shaft while raising the blade end of the wiper arm and push the slide latch into the lock under the pivot shaft head. Then, lower the blade to the windshield. If the blade does not lower to the windshield, the slide latch is not completely in place.

Tires and Wheels

The tires should be rotated as specified in the Maintenance Intervals Chart. Refer to the accompanying illustrations for the recommended rotation patterns.

The tires on your vehicle should have built-in tread wear indicators, which appear as $1/2$ in. (12.7mm) bands when the tread depth gets as low as $1/16$ in. (1.5mm). When the indicators appear in 2 or more adjacent grooves, it's time for new tires.

For optimum tire life, you should keep the tires properly inflated, rotate them often and have the wheel alignment checked periodically.

Some late models have the maximum load pressures listed in the V.I.N. plate on the left door frame. In general, pressure of 28–32 psi would be suitable for highway use with moderate loads and passenger truck type tires (load range B, non-flotation) of original equipment size. Pressures should be checked before driving, since pressure can increase as much as 6 psi due to heat. It is a good idea to have an accurate gauge and to check pressures weekly. Not all gauges on service station air pumps are to be trusted. In general, truck type tires require higher pressures and flotation type tires, lower pressures.

TIRE ROTATION

It is recommended that you have the tires rotated every 6,000 miles. There is no way to give a tire rotation diagram for every combination of tires and vehicles, but the accompanying diagrams are a general rule to follow. Radial tires should not be cross-switched; they last longer if their direction of rotation is not changed. Truck tires sometimes have directional tread, indicated by arrows on the sidewalls; the arrow shows the direction of rotation. They will wear very rapidly if reversed. Studded snow tires will lose their studs if their direction of rotation is reversed.

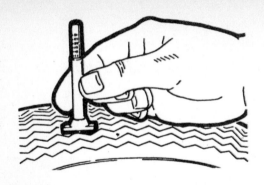

Checking tread depth with an inexpensive depth gauge

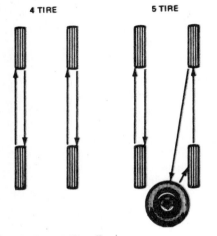

Radial-ply tire rotation diagram

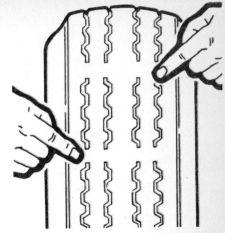

Tread wear indicators are built into all new tires. When they appear, it's time to trash that old rubber for some new skins

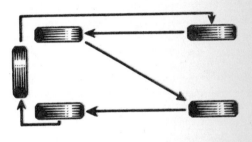

Bias-ply tire rotation diagram

Tread depth can be checked with a penny; when the top of Lincoln's head is visible, it's time for new tires

NOTE: *Mark the wheel position or direction of rotation on radial tires or studded snow tires before removing them.*

If your vehicle is equipped with tires having different load ratings on the front and the rear, the tires should not be rotated front to rear. Rotating these tires could affect tire life (the tires with the lower rating will wear faster, and could become overloaded), and upset the handling of the vehicle.

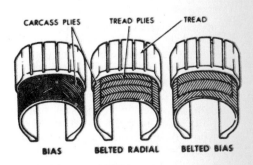

Types of tire construction

TIRE USAGE

The tires on your vehicle were selected to provide the best all around performance for normal operation when inflated as specified. Oversize tires (Load Range D) will not increase the maximum carrying capacity of the vehicle, although they will provide an extra margin of tread life. Be sure to check overall height before using larger size tires which may cause interference with suspension components or wheel wells. When replacing conventional tire sizes with other tire size designations, be sure to check the manufacturer's recommendations. Interchangeability is not always possible because of differences in load ratings, tire dimensions, wheel well clearances, and rim size. Also due to differences in handling characteristics, 70 Series and 60 Series tires should be used only in pairs on the same axle; radial tires should be used only in sets of four.

The wheels must be the correct width for the tire. Tire dealers have charts of tire and rim compatibility. A mismatch can cause sloppy handling and rapid tread wear. The old rule of thumb is that the tread width should match the rim width (inside bead to inside bead) within 1 in.. For radial tires, the rim width should be 80% or less of the tire (not tread) width.

The height (mounted diameter) of the new tires can greatly change speedometer accuracy, engine speed at a given road speed, fuel mileage, acceleration, and ground clearance. Tire manufacturers furnish full measurement specifications. Speedometer drive gears are available for correction.

NOTE: *Dimensions of tires marked the same size may vary significantly, even among tires from the same manufacturer.*

The spare tire should be usable, at least for low speed operation, with the new tires.

TIRE DESIGN

For maximum satisfaction, tires should be used in sets of five. Mixing or different types (radial, bias-belted, fiberglass belted) should be avoided. Conventional bias tires are constructed so that the cords run bead-to-bead at an angle. Alternate plies run at an opposite angle. This type of construction gives rigidity to both tread and sidewall. Bias-belted tires are similar in construction to conventional bias ply tires. Belts run at an angle and also at a 90° angle to the bead, as in the radial tire. Tread life is improved considerably over the conventional bias tire. The radial tire differs in construction, but instead of the carcass plies running at an angle of 90° to each other, they run at an angle of 90° to the bead. This gives the tread a great deal of rigidity and the sidewall a great deal of flexibility and accounts for the characteristic bulge associated with radial tires.

Radial tire are recommended for use on all Ford trucks. If they are used, tire sizes and wheel diameters should be selected to maintain ground clearance and tire load capacity equivalent to the minimum specified tire. Radial tires should always be used in sets of five, but in an emergency radial tires can be used with caution on the rear axle only. If this is done, both tires on the rear should be of radial design.

NOTE: *Radial tires should never be used on only the front axle.*

FLUIDS AND LUBRICANTS

Oil and Fuel Recommendations

Gasoline Engines

All Ford Ranger/Bronco II/Explorer must use lead-free gasoline.

The recommended oil viscosities for sustained temperatures ranging from below 0°F (−18°C) to above 32°F (0°C) are listed in this Section. They are broken down into multi-viscosities and single viscosities. Multi-viscosity oils are recommended because of their wider range of acceptable temperatures and driving conditions.

When adding oil to the crankcase or changing the oil or filter, it is important that oil of an equal quality to original equipment be used in your vehicle. The use of inferior oils may void the warranty, damage your engine, or both.

The SAE (Society of Automotive Engineers) grade number of oil indicates the viscosity of the oil (its ability to lubricate at a given temperature). The lower the SAE number, the lighter the oil; the lower the viscosity, the easier it is to crank the engine in cold weather but the less the oil will lubricate and protect the engine in high temperatures. This number is marked on every oil container.

Oil viscosities should be chosen from those oils recommended for the lowest anticipated temperatures during the oil change interval. Due to the need for an oil that embodies both good lubrication at high temperatures and easy cranking in cold weather, multi-grade oils have been developed. Basically, a multi-grade oil is thinner at low temperatures and thicker at high temperatures. For example, a 10W–40 oil (the W stands for winter) exhibits the characteristics of a 10 weight (SAE 10) oil when the vehicle is first started and the oil is cold. Its lighter weight allows it to travel to the lubricating surfaces quicker and offer less resistance to starter motor cranking than, say, a straight 30 weight (SAE 30) oil. But after the engine reaches operating temperature, the 10W–40 oil begins acting like straight 40 weight (SAE 40) oil, its heavier weight providing greater lubrication with less chance of foaming than a straight 30 weight oil.

The API (American Petroleum Institute) designations, also found on the oil container, indicates the classification of engine oil used under certain given operating conditions. Only oils des-

This is the oil's SAE viscosity grade. The numbers followed by a 'W' indicate an oil with low temperature performance characteristics and the 'non-W' numbers describe an oil with high temperature character-istics. If there is one number, it is a single grade. Two or more numbers indicate a 'multi-viscosity' oil which has both low and high temperature characteristics.

This means that the oil will protect expensive engine components. Even if your car is no longer under warranty, it indicates that the oil is of good quality.

This is the manufacturer's brand name.

These letters generally mean that the oil meets or exceeds established standards for use in gasoline (indicated by 'S' and a following letter) and diesel and commercial engines (indicated by 'C' and a following letter). These designations replace the older classifications which may be called for in some owners' manuals. The SF rating is the highest standard for gasoline automobiles.

The top of the oil can will tell you all you need to know about the oil

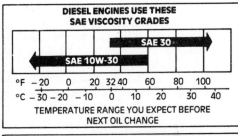

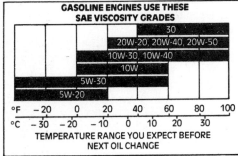

Engine oil viscosities

ignated for use Service SG heavy duty deter-gent should be used in your vehicle. Oils of the SG type perform may functions inside the engine besides their basic lubrication. Through a balanced system of metallic detergents and pol-ymeric dispersants, the oil prevents high and low temperature deposits and also keeps sludge and dirt particles in suspension. Acids, particu-larly sulphuric acid, as well as other by-prod-ucts of engine combustion are neutralized by the oil. If these acids are allowed to concen-trate, they can cause corrosion and rapid wear of the internal engine parts.

CAUTION: *Non-detergent motor oils or straight mineral oils should not be used in your Ford gasoline engine.*

Diesel Engines

Diesel engines require different engine oil from those used in gasoline engines. Besides doing the things gasoline engine oil does, diesel oil must also deal with increased engine heat and the diesel blow-by gases, which create sulphuric acid, a high corrosive.

Under the American Petroleum Institute (API) classifications, gasoline engine oil codes begin with an **S**, and diesel engine oil codes begin with a **C**. This first letter designation is followed by a second letter code which explains what type of service (heavy, moderate, light) the oil is meant for. For example, the top of a typical oil can will include: API SERVICES SG, CD. This means the oil in the can is a superior, heavy duty engine oil when used in a diesel engine.

Many diesel manufacturers recommend an oil with both gasoline and diesel engine API clas-sifications.

NOTE: *Ford specifies the use of an engine oil conforming to API service categories of both SG and CD. DO NOT use oils labeled as only SG or only CD as they could cause engine damage.*

FUEL

Fuel makers produce two grades of diesel fuel, No. 1 and No. 2, for use in automotive diesel engines. Generally speaking, No. 2 fuel is recommended over No. 1 for driving in temper-atures above 20°F (–7°C). In fact, in many areas, No. 2 diesel is the only fuel available. By comparison, No. 2 diesel fuel is less volatile than No. 1 fuel, and gives better fuel economy. No. 2 fuel is also a better injection pump lubri-cant.

Two important characteristics of diesel fuel are its cetane number and its viscosity.

The cetane number of a diesel fuel refers to

ENGINE OIL DIPSTICK   MAINTAIN LEVEL HERE

Checking engine oil level

the ease with which a diesel fuel ignites. High cetane numbers mean that the fuel will ignite with relative ease or that it ignites well at low temperatures. Naturally, the lower the cetane number, the higher the temperature must be to ignite the fuel. Most commercial fuels have cetane numbers that range from 35 to 65. No. 1 diesel fuel generally has a higher cetane rating than No. 2 fuel.

Viscosity is the ability of a liquid, in this case diesel fuel, to flow. Using straight No. 2 diesel fuel below 20°F (–7°C) can cause problems, because this fuel tends to become cloudy, meaning wax crystals begin forming in the fuel. 20°F (–7°C) is often call the cloud point for No. 2 fuel. In extremely cold weather, No. 2 fuel can stop flowing altogether. In either case, fuel flow is restricted, which can result in no start condition or poor engine performance. Fuel manufacturers often winterize No. 2 diesel fuel by using various fuel additives and blends (no. 1 diesel fuel, kerosene, etc.) to lower its winter time viscosity. Generally speaking, though, No. 1 diesel fuel is more satisfactory in extremely cold weather.

NOTE: *No. 1 and No. 2 diesel fuels will mix and burn with no ill effects, although the engine manufacturer recommends one or the other. Consult the owner's manual for information.*

Depending on local climate, most fuel manufacturers make winterized No. 2 fuel available seasonally.

Many automobile manufacturers publish pamphlets giving the locations of diesel fuel stations nationwide. Contact the local dealer for information.

Do not substitute home heating oil for automotive diesel fuel. While in some cases, home heating oil refinement levels equal those of diesel fuel, many times they are far below diesel engine requirements. The result of using dirty home heating oil will be a clogged fuel system, in which case the entire system may have to be dismantled and cleaned.

One more word on diesel fuels. Don't thin diesel fuel with gasoline in cold weather. The

lighter gasoline, which is more explosive, will cause rough running at the very least, and may cause extensive damage to the fuel system if enough is used.

OIL LEVEL CHECK

Check the engine oil level every time you fill the gas tank. The oil level should be above the ADD mark and not above the FULL mark on the dipstick. Make sure that the dipstick is inserted into the crankcase as far as possible and that the vehicle is resting on level ground. Also, allow a few minutes after turning off the engine for the oil to drain into the pan or an inaccurate reading will result.

1. Open the hood and remove the engine oil dipstick.

2. Wipe the dipstick with a clean, lint-free rag and reinsert it. Be sure to insert it all the way.

3. Pull out the dipstick and note the oil level. It should be between the **SAFE** (MAX) mark and the **ADD** (MIN) mark.

4. If the level is below the lower mark, replace the dipstick and add fresh oil to bring the level within the proper range. Do not overfill.

5. Recheck the oil level and close the hood.

NOTE: *Use a multi-grade oil with API classification SG.*

OIL AND FILTER CHANGE

NOTE: *The engine oil and oil filter should be changed at the same time, at the recommended intervals on the maintenance schedule chart.*

The oil should be changed more frequently if the vehicle is being operated in very dusty areas. Before draining the oil, make sure that the engine is at operating temperature. Hot oil will hold more impurities in suspension and will flow better, allowing the removal of more oil and dirt.

Loosen the drain plug with a wrench, then, unscrew the plug with your fingers, using a rag to shield your fingers from the heat. Push in on the plug as you unscrew it so you can feel when all of the screw threads are out of the hole. You

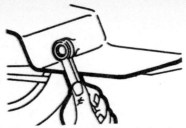

Loosen, but do not remove, the drain plug on the bottom of the oil pan. Get your drain pan ready

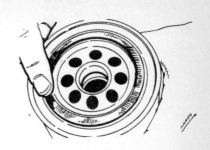

Wipe clean engine oil around the rubber gasket on the new filter. This helps ensure a good seal

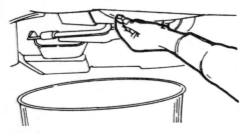

Unscrew the plug by hand. Keep an inward pressure on the plug as you unscrew it, so the oil won't escape until you pull the plug away.

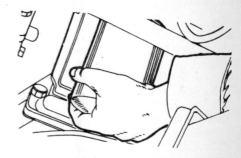

Install the new filter by hand only; DO NOT use a strap wrench to install

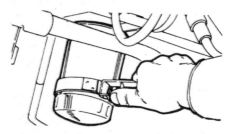

Move the drain pan underneath the oil filter. Use a strap wrench to remove the filter — remember it is still filled with about a quart of hot, dirty oil

Don't forget to install the drain plug before refilling the engine with fresh oil

can then remove the plug quickly with the minimum amount of oil running down your arm and you will also have the plug in your hand and not in the bottom of a pan of hot oil. Drain the oil into a suitable receptacle. Be careful of the oil. If it is at operating temperatures it is hot enough to burn you.

CAUTION: *The EPA warns that prolonged contact with used engine oil may cause a number of skin disorders, including cancer! You should make every effort to minimize your exposure to used engine oil. Protective gloves should be worn when changing the oil. Wash your hands and any other exposed skin areas as soon as possible after exposure to used engine oil. Soap and water, or waterless hand cleaner should be used.*

The oil filter SHOULD BE changed every time the oil is changed. To remove the filter, you may need an oil filter wrench since the

filter may have been fitted too tightly and the heat from the engine may have made it even tighter. A filter wrench can be obtained at an auto parts store and is well worth the investment, since it will save you a lot of grief. Loosen the filter with the filter wrench. With a rag wrapped around the filter, unscrew the filter from the boss on the side of the engine. Be careful of hot oil that will run down the side of the filter. Make sure that you have a pan under the filter before you start to remove it from the engine; should some of the hot oil happen to get on you, you will have a place to dump the filter in a hurry. Wipe the base of the mounting boss with a clean, dry cloth. When you install the new filter, smear a small amount of oil on the gasket with your finger, just enough to coat the entire surface, where it comes in contact with the mounting plate. When you tighten the filter, rotate if only a half turn after it comes in contact with the mounting boss.

Manual Transmission

FLUID RECOMMENDATION

The lubricant in the transmission should be checked and changed periodically, except when the vehicle has been operated in deep water and water has entered the transmission. When this happens, change the lubricant in the transmission as soon as possible. Use Standard Transmission Lube SAE 80 in the manual transmission.

LEVEL CHECK

Before checking the lubricant level in the transmission, make sure that the vehicle is on level ground. Remove the fill plug from the transmission. Remove the plug slowly when it starts to reach the end of the threads on the plug. Hold the plug up against the hole and move it away slowly. This is to minimize the loss of lubricant through the fill hole. The level of the lubricant should be up to the bottom of the fill hole. If lubricant is not present at the bottom of the fill hole, add Standard Transmission Lube SAE 80 until it reaches the proper level. A squeeze bottle or siphon gun is used to fill a manual transmission with lubricant.

DRAIN AND REFILL

Drain and refill the transmission daily if the vehicle has been operating in water. All you have to do is remove the drain plug which is located at the bottom of the transmission. Allow all the lubricant to run out before replacing the plug. Replace the oil with the correct fluid. If you are experiencing hard shifting and the weather is very cold, use a lighter weight fluid in the transmission. If you don't have a pressure gun to install the oil, use a suction gun.

Automatic Transmission

FLUID RECOMMENDATION

Refer to the dipstick to confirm automatic transmission fluid specifications. With a C5 automatic transmission, add only Type H automatic transmission fluid. With the C3 and A4LD automatic transmissions, use only Dexron® II automatic transmission fluid.

LEVEL CHECK

The fluid level in an automatic transmission is checked when the transmission is at operating temperatures. If the vehicle has been sitting and is cold, drive it at highway speeds for at least 20 minutes to warm up the transmis-

AUTOMATIC TRANSMISSION DIPSTICK

Automatic transmission dipstick is located towards the rear of the engine

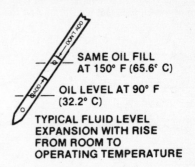

SAME OIL FILL AT 150° F (65.6° C)

OIL LEVEL AT 90° F (32.2° C)

TYPICAL FLUID LEVEL EXPANSION WITH RISE FROM ROOM TO OPERATING TEMPERATURE

Checking automatic transmission fluid level. Check transmission when it is warmed to operating temperature

sion. The transmission dipstick is located under the hood, against the firewall, on the right side.

1. With the transmission in Park, the engine running at idle speed, the foot brakes applied and the vehicle resting on level ground, move the transmission gear selector through each of the gear positions, including Reverse, allowing time for the transmission to engage. Return the shift selector to the Park position and apply the parking brake. Do not turn the engine off, but leave it running at idle speed.

2. Clean all dirt from around the transmission dipstick cap and the end of the filler tube.

3. Pull the dipstick out of the tube, wipe it off with a clean cloth, and push it back into the tube all the way, making sure that it seats completely.

4. Pull the dipstick out of the tube again and read the level of the fluid on the stick. The level should be between the ADD and FULL marks. If fluid must be added, add enough fluid through the tube to raise the level up to between the ADD and FULL marks. Do not overfill the transmission because this will cause foaming and loss of fluid through the vent and malfunctioning of the transmission.

DRAIN AND REFILL

The transmission is filled at the factory with a high quality fluid that both transmits power and lubricates and will last a long time. In most cases, the need to change the fluid in the automatic transmission will never arise under

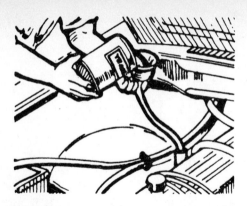

Fill the transmission with the required amount of fluid. Do not overfill. Start the engine and run the selector through all shift points. Check the fluid and add as necessary.

normal use. But since this is a truck and most likely will be subjected to more severe operating conditions than a conventional vehicle, the fluid may have to be replaced. An internal leak in the radiator could develop and contaminate the fluid, necessitating fluid replacement.

The extra load of operating the vehicle in deep sand, towing a heavy trailer, etc., causes the transmission to create more heat due to increased friction. This extra heat is transferred to the transmission fluid and, if the oil is al-

lowed to become too hot, it will change its chemical composition or become scorched. When this occurs, valve bodies become clogged and the transmission doesn't operate as efficiently as it should. Serious damage to the transmission can result.

You can tell if the transmission fluid is scorched by noting a distinctive **burned** smell and discoloration. Scorched transmission fluid is dark brown or black as opposed to its normal bright, clear red color. Since transmission fluid **cooks** in stages, it may develop forms of sludge or varnish. Pull the dipstick out and place the end on a tissue or paper towel. Particles of sludge can be seen more easily this way. If any of the above conditions do exist, the transmission fluid should be completely drained, the filtering screens cleaned, the transmission inspected for possible damage and new fluid installed. Refer to Chapter 7 under Automatic Transmission for Pan Removal and Filter Service Procedures.

CAUTION: *Use of a fluid other than those specified could result in transmission malfunction and/or failure.*

NOTE: *If it is necessary to completely drain and refill the transmission, it will be necessary to remove the residual fluid from the torque converter and the cooler lines.*

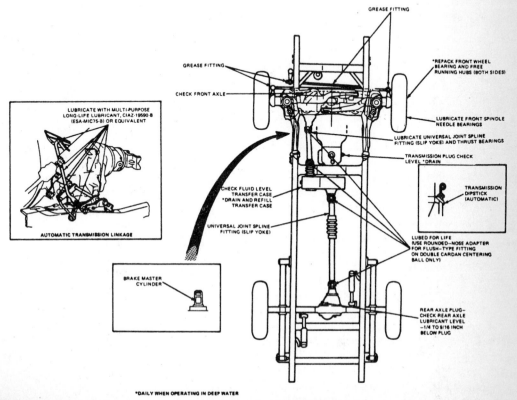

Lubrication chart — 4WD models

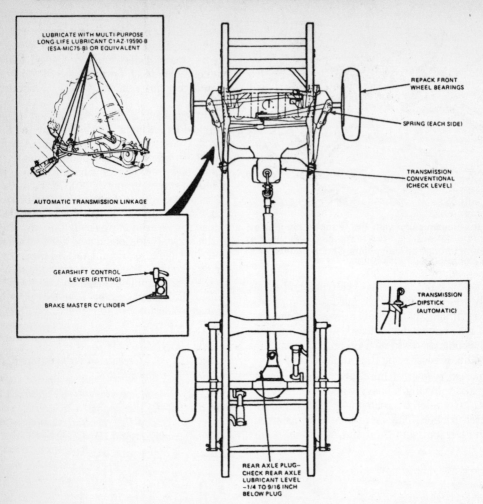

LUBRICATE WITH MULTI-PURPOSE
LONG LIFE LUBRICANT C1AZ-19590-B
(ESA-MIC75-B) OR EQUIVALENT

AUTOMATIC TRANSMISSION LINKAGE

GEARSHIFT CONTROL
LEVER (FITTING)

BRAKE MASTER CYLINDER

REPACK FRONT
WHEEL BEARINGS

SPRING (EACH SIDE)

TRANSMISSION
CONVENTIONAL
(CHECK LEVEL)

TRANSMISSION
DIPSTICK
(AUTOMATIC)

REAR AXLE PLUG—
CHECK REAR AXLE
LUBRICANT LEVEL
–1/4 TO 9/16 INCH
BELOW PLUG

Lubrication chart — 2WD models

The procedure for partial drain and refill, for a vehicle that is in service, is as follows:

1. Place a drain pan under the transmission. Loosen the pan bolts and pull one corner down to start the fluid draining. Remove and empty the pan.

2. When all the fluid has drained from the transmission, remove and clean the pan and screen. Make sure not to leave any solvent residue or lint from the rags in the pan.

3. Install the pan with a new gasket and tighten the bolts in a crisscross pattern.

4. Add three quarts of fluid through the dipstick tube.   With a C5 automatic transmission, add only fluid meeting Ford Specification ESP-MZC166-H, Type H automatic transmission fluid. With a C3 and A4LD automatic transmission, use only DEXRON®II automatic transmission fluid. The level should be at or below the ADD mark.

5. Check the fluid level as soon as the transmission reaches operating temperature for the first time. Make sure that the level is between ADD and FULL.

To drain the torque converter:

1. Remove the converter housing lower cover.

2. Rotate the torque converter until the drain plug comes into view.

3. Remove the drain plug and allow the transmission fluid to drain.

4. Flush the cooler lines completely.

Front and Rear Axle

FLUID RECOMMENDATION

Use hypoid gear lubricant SAE 80 or 90.

NOTE: *On models with the front locking differential, add 2 oz. of friction modifier Ford part No. EST-M2C118-A. On models with the rear locking differential, use only locking differential fluid Ford part No. ESP-M2C154-A or its equivalent, and add 4 oz. of friction modifier Ford part No. EST-M2C118-A.*

LEVEL CHECK

Clean the area around the fill plug, which is located in the housing cover, before removing the plug. The lubricant level should be maintained to the bottom of the fill hole with the axle in its normal running position. If lubricant does not appear at the hole when the plug is removed additional lubricant should be added.

DRAIN AND REFILL

Drain and refill the front and rear axle housings according to the Preventive Maintenance Schedule at the end of this Chapter. Remove the oil with a suction gun. Refill the axle housings with the proper oil. Be sure and clean the area around the drain plug before removing the plug.

Transfer Case

FLUID RECOMMENDATION

Use Dexron®II automatic transmission fluid when refilling or adding fluid to the transfer case.

LEVEL CHECK

Position the vehicle on level ground. Remove the transfer case fill plug (the upper plug) located on the rear of the transfer case. The fluid level should be up to the fill hole. If lubricant doesn't run out when the plug is removed, add lubricant until it does run out and then replace the fill plug.

DRAIN AND REFILL

The transfer case is serviced at the same time and in the same manner as the transmission. Clean the area around the filler and drain plugs and remove the filler plug on the side of the transfer case. Remove the drain plug on the bottom of the transfer case and allow the lubricant to drain completely. Clean and install the drain plug. Add the proper lubricant.

Brake Master Cylinder

The master cylinder reservoir is located under the hood, on the left side firewall.

FLUID RECOMMENDATION

Fill the master cylinder with a good quality Heavy-Duty Dot 3 Brake Fluid.

LEVEL CHECK

Before removing the master cylinder reservoir cap, make sure the vehicle is resting on level ground and clean all dirt away from the top of the master cylinder. Pry off the retaining clip and remove the cap. The brake fluid level should be within 1/4 in. of the top of the reservoir.

If the level of the brake fluid is less than half the volume of the reservoir, it is advised that you check the brake system for leaks. Leaks in a hydraulic brake system most commonly occur at the wheel cylinder.

There is a rubber diaphragm in the top of the master cylinder cap. As the fluid level lowers in the reservoir due to normal brake shoe wear or leakage, the diaphragm takes up the space. This is to prevent the loss of brake fluid out the vented cap and contamination by dirt. After filling the master cylinder to the proper level with brake fluid, but before replacing the cap, fold the rubber diaphragm up into the cap, then replace the cap on the reservoir and tighten the retaining bolt or snap the retaining clip into place.

Clutch Master Cylinder

The clutch master cylinder reservoir is located under the hood, on the left side firewall.

FLUID RECOMMENDATION

Fill the clutch master cylinder reservoir with a good quality Heavy-Duty Brake Fluid.

LEVEL CHECK

The fluid level in the clutch reservoir should be visible at or above the step in the translu-

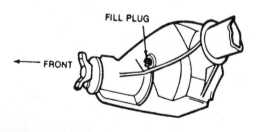

Differential fill plug location, 2WD shown. The 4WD front axle is similar

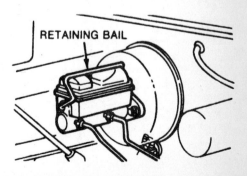

Brake master cylinder assembly

cent reservoir body, filling above this point is not necessary.

NOTE: *The fluid level in the clutch reservoir will slowly increase as the clutch wears.*

Before removing the clutch master cylinder reservoir cap, make sure the vehicle is resting on level ground and clean all dirt away from the top of the reservoir.

Power Steering Reservoir

FLUID RECOMMENDATION

Fill the power steering reservoir with a good quality power steering fluid or Auto. Trans. Fluid-Type **F**.

LEVEL CHECK

Position the vehicle on level ground. Run the engine until the fluid is at normal operating temperature. Turn the steering wheel all the way to the left and right several times. Position the wheels in the straight ahead position, then shut off the engine. Check the fluid level on the dipstick which is attached to the reservoir cap. The level should be between the ADD and FULL marks on the dipstick. Add fluid accordingly. Do not overfill.

Steering Gear

The steering gear is factory-filled with steering gear grease. Changing of this lubricant should not be performed and the housing should not be drained, lubricant is not required for the life of the steering gear.

Chassis Greasing

The preceding charts indicate where the grease fittings are located on the vehicle, and other level checks that should be made at the time of the chassis grease job. The vehicle should be greased according to the Preventive Maintenance Schedule at the end of this Chapter, and more often if the vehicle is operating in

dust areas or under heavy-duty conditions. If the vehicle is operated in deep water, lubricate the chassis every day.

Body Lubrication

Lubricate the door and tailgate hinges, door locks, door latches, and the hood latch when they become noisy or difficult to operate. A high quality Polyethylene Grease should be used as a lubricant.

Front Hub Assembly

For 4WD vehicles, see Chapter 7.

Wheel Bearings

It is recommended that the front wheel bearings be cleaned, inspected and repacked periodically and as soon as possible after the front hubs have been submerged in water.

NOTE: *Sodium based grease is not compatible with lithium based grease. Be careful not to mix the two types. The best way to prevent this is to completely clean all of the old grease from the hub assembly before installing any new grease.*

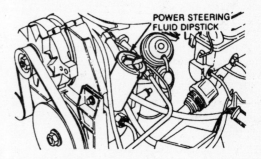

Power steering pump reservoir

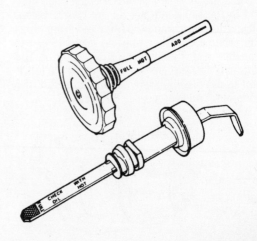

Power steering pump reservoir dipsticks

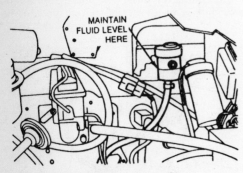

Clutch master cylinder reservoir

Before handling the bearings there are a few things that you should remember to do and try to avoid. DO the following:

1. Remove all outside dirt from the housing before exposing the bearing.

2. Treat a used bearing as gently as you would a new one.

3. Work with clean tools in clean surroundings.

4. Use clean, dry canvas gloves, or at least clean, dry hands.

5. Clean solvents and flushing fluids are a must.

6. Use clean paper when laying out the bearings to dry.

7. Protect disassembled bearings from rust and dirt. Cover them up.

8. Use clean rags to wipe bearings.

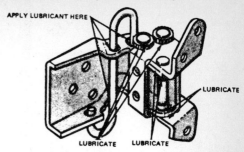

Door hinge lubrication points

9. Keep the bearings in oil-proof paper when they are to be stored or are not in use.

10. Clean the inside of the housing before replacing the bearing.

Do NOT do the following:

1. Don't work in dirty surroundings.

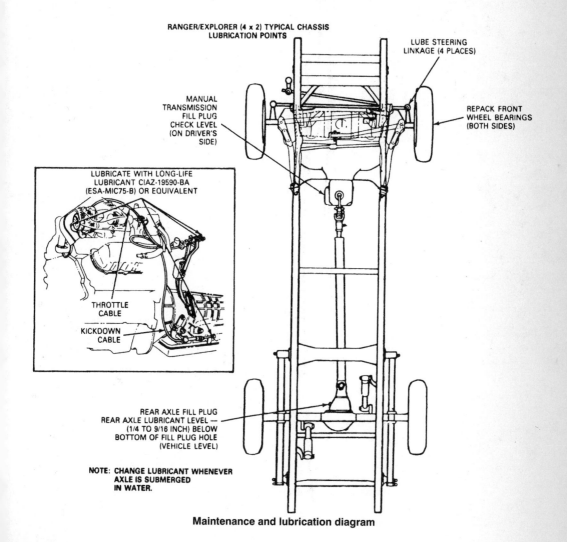

Maintenance and lubrication diagram

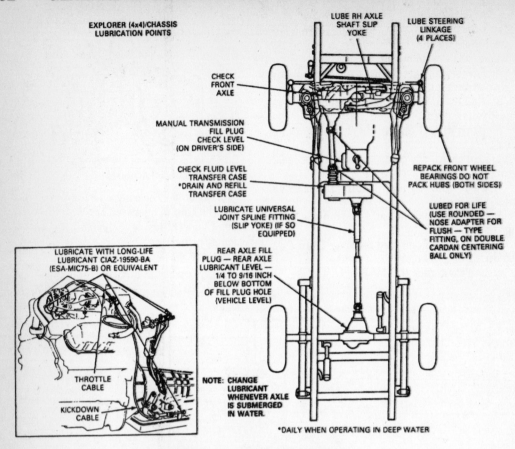

EXPLORER (4x4)/CHASSIS
LUBRICATION POINTS

LUBE RH AXLE
SHAFT SLIP
YOKE

LUBE STEERING
LINKAGE
(4 PLACES)

CHECK
FRONT
AXLE

MANUAL TRANSMISSION
FILL PLUG
CHECK LEVEL
(ON DRIVER'S SIDE)

REPACK FRONT WHEEL
BEARINGS DO NOT
PACK HUBS (BOTH SIDES)

CHECK FLUID LEVEL
TRANSFER CASE
*DRAIN AND REFILL
TRANSFER CASE

LUBED FOR LIFE
(USE ROUNDED —
NOSE ADAPTER FOR
FLUSH — TYPE
FITTING, ON DOUBLE
CARDAN CENTERING
BALL ONLY)

LUBRICATE UNIVERSAL
JOINT SPLINE FITTING
(SLIP YOKE) (IF SO
EQUIPPED)

LUBRICATE WITH LONG-LIFE
LUBRICANT C1AZ-19590-BA
(ESA-MIC75-B) OR EQUIVALENT

REAR AXLE FILL
PLUG — REAR AXLE
LUBRICANT LEVEL —
1/4 TO 9/16 INCH
BELOW BOTTOM
OF FILL PLUG HOLE
(VEHICLE LEVEL)

THROTTLE
CABLE

KICKDOWN
CABLE

NOTE: CHANGE
LUBRICANT
WHENEVER AXLE
IS SUBMERGED
IN WATER.

*DAILY WHEN OPERATING IN DEEP WATER

Maintenance and lubrication diagram

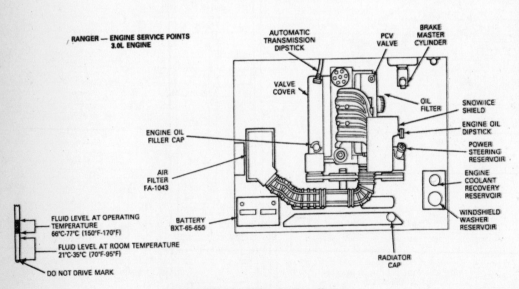

RANGER — ENGINE SERVICE POINTS
3.0L ENGINE

AUTOMATIC
TRANSMISSION
DIPSTICK

PCV
VALVE

BRAKE
MASTER
CYLINDER

VALVE
COVER

OIL
FILTER

SNOW/ICE
SHIELD

ENGINE OIL
FILLER CAP

ENGINE OIL
DIPSTICK

POWER
STEERING
RESERVOIR

AIR
FILTER
FA-1043

ENGINE
COOLANT
RECOVERY
RESERVOIR

FLUID LEVEL AT OPERATING
TEMPERATURE
66°C-77°C (150°F-170°F)

BATTERY
BXT-65-650

WINDSHIELD
WASHER
RESERVOIR

FLUID LEVEL AT ROOM TEMPERATURE
21°C-35°C (70°F-95°F)

RADIATOR
CAP

DO NOT DRIVE MARK

Maintenance and lubrication diagram

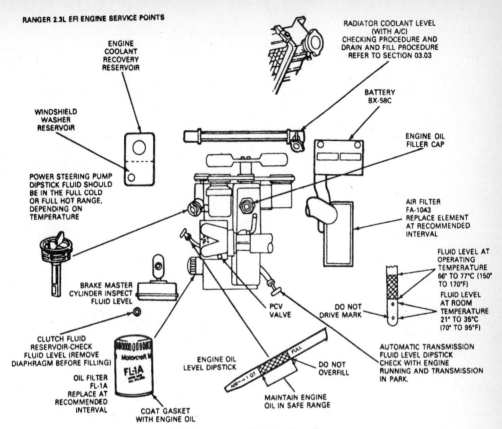

RANGER 2.3L EFI ENGINE SERVICE POINTS

Maintenance and lubrication diagram

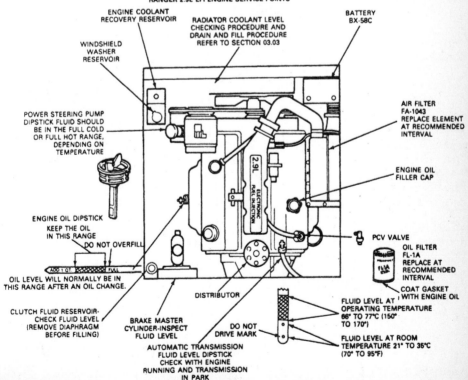

RANGER 2.9L EFI ENGINE SERVICE POINTS

Maintenance and lubrication diagram

RANGER-EXPLORER — ENGINE SERVICE POINTS
4.0L ENGINE

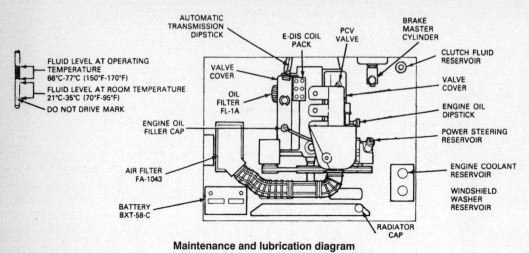

Maintenance and lubrication diagram

RANGER (4 x 4) CHASSIS LUBRICATION POINTS

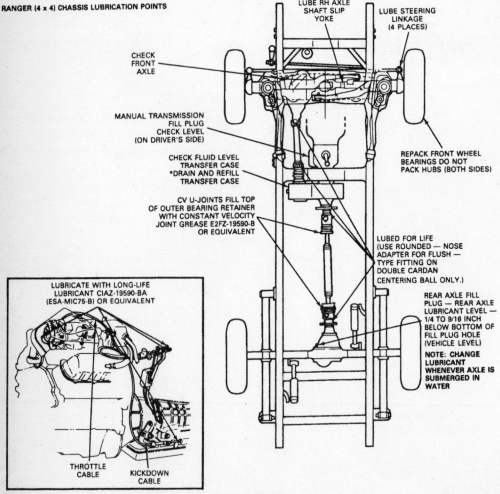

*DAILY WHEN OPERATING IN DEEP WATER

Maintenance and lubrication diagram

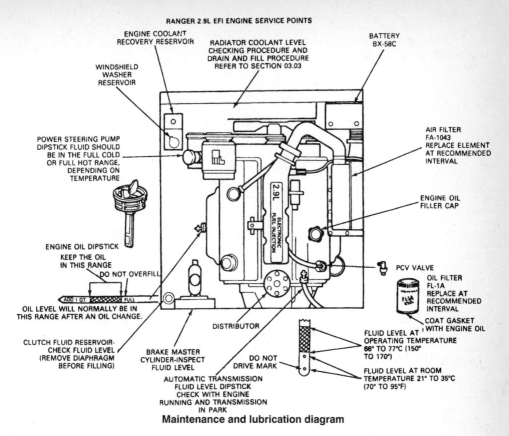

RANGER 2.9L EFI ENGINE SERVICE POINTS

ENGINE COOLANT
RECOVERY RESERVOIR

RADIATOR COOLANT LEVEL
CHECKING PROCEDURE AND
DRAIN AND FILL PROCEDURE
REFER TO SECTION 03.03

BATTERY
BX-58C

WINDSHIELD
WASHER
RESERVOIR

POWER STEERING PUMP
DIPSTICK FLUID SHOULD
BE IN THE FULL COLD
OR FULL HOT RANGE,
DEPENDING ON
TEMPERATURE

AIR FILTER
FA-1043
REPLACE ELEMENT
AT RECOMMENDED
INTERVAL

ENGINE OIL
FILLER CAP

2.9L
ELECTRONIC
FUEL INJECTION

ENGINE OIL DIPSTICK
KEEP THE OIL
IN THIS RANGE
DO NOT OVERFILL

PCV VALVE

OIL FILTER
FL-1A
REPLACE AT
RECOMMENDED
INTERVAL

ADD 1 QT.   FULL

OIL LEVEL WILL NORMALLY BE IN
THIS RANGE AFTER AN OIL CHANGE.

COAT GASKET
WITH ENGINE OIL

DISTRIBUTOR

FLUID LEVEL AT
OPERATING TEMPERATURE
66° TO 77°C (150°
TO 170°)

CLUTCH FLUID RESERVOIR-
CHECK FLUID LEVEL
(REMOVE DIAPHRAGM
BEFORE FILLING)

BRAKE MASTER
CYLINDER-INSPECT
FLUID LEVEL

DO NOT
DRIVE MARK

FLUID LEVEL AT ROOM
TEMPERATURE 21° TO 35°C
(70° TO 95°F)

AUTOMATIC TRANSMISSION
FLUID LEVEL DIPSTICK
CHECK WITH ENGINE
RUNNING AND TRANSMISSION
IN PARK

Maintenance and lubrication diagram

2. Don't use dirty, chipped, or damaged tools.

3. Try not to work on wooden work benches, or use wooden mallets.

4. Don't handle bearings with dirty or moist hands.

5. Do not use gasoline for cleaning; use a safe solvent.

6. Do not spin-dry bearings with compressed air. They will be damaged.

7. Do not spin unclean bearings.

8. Avoid using cotton waste or dirty clothes to wipe bearings.

9. Try not to scratch or nick bearing surfaces.

10. Do not allow the bearing to come in contact with dirt or rust at any time.

REMOVAL AND INSTALLATION

NOTE: *For 4WD vehicles, see Chapter 7.*

1. Raise the vehicle and support with jackstands. Remove the wheel from the rotor.

2. Remove the caliper and support it from the underbody with a piece of wire.

3. Remove the grease cap from the hub and the cotter pin, nut lock, adjusting nut, and the flat washer from the spindle. Remove the outer bearing assembly from the hub.

4. Carefully pull the hub and rotor assembly off the spindle.

5. Carefully drive out the inner bearing cone and grease seal from the hub.

6. Clean the inner and outer bearing cups with solvent. Inspect the cups for scratches, pits, excessive wear, and other damage. The cups are removed from the hub by driving them out with a drift pin. They are installed in the same manner.

7. If it is determined that the cups are in satisfactory condition and are to remain in the hub, clean and inspect the cones (bearings). Replace the bearings if necessary. When replacing either the cone or the cup, both parts should be replaced as a unit.

8. Thoroughly clean all components in a suitable solvent and blow them dry with com-

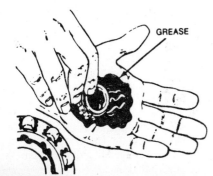

GREASE

Packing the wheel bearing with grease

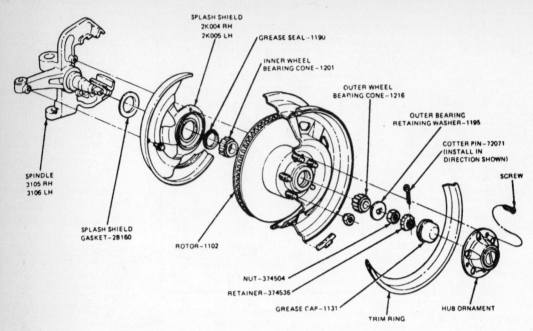

SPLASH SHIELD
2K004 RH
2K005 LH

GREASE SEAL - 1190

INNER WHEEL
BEARING CONE - 1201

OUTER WHEEL
BEARING CONE - 1216

OUTER BEARING
RETAINING WASHER - 1195

COTTER PIN - 72071
(INSTALL IN
DIRECTION SHOWN)

SCREW

SPINDLE
3105 RH
3106 LH

SPLASH SHIELD
GASKET - 2B160

ROTOR - 1102

NUT - 374504

RETAINER - 374536

GREASE CAP - 1131

TRIM RING

HUB ORNAMENT

Exploded view of the wheel bearings, grease seal and front hub

pressed air or allow them to dry while resting on clean paper.

NOTE: *Do not spin the bearings with compressed air while drying them.*

9. Cover the spindle with a clean cloth, and brush all loose dirt from the dust shield. Carefully remove the cloth to prevent dirt from falling from it.

10. Install the inner or outer bearing cups if they were removed. Thoroughly clean the old grease from the surrounding surfaces.

11. Pack the inside of the hub with wheel bearing grease. Add grease to the hub until the grease is flush with the inside diameter of the bearing cup.

12. Pack the bearing cone and roller assembly with wheel bearing grease. A bearing packer is desirable for this operation. If a packer is not available, place a large portion of grease into the palm of your hand and sliding the edge of the roller cage through the grease with your other hand, work as much grease in between the rollers as possible.

13. Position the inner bearing cone and roller assembly in the inner cup. Apply a light film of grease to the lips of a new grease seal and install the seal into the hub.

14. Carefully position the hub and rotor assembly onto the spindle. Be careful not to damage the grease seal.

15. Place the outer bearing into position on the spindle and into the bearing cup. Install the adjusting nut finger tight.

16. Adjust the wheel bearings as shown in

the illustration. Install the grease cap.

17. Install the caliper to the spindle and the wheel to the hub.

18. Remove the jackstands and lower the vehicle. Torque the lug nuts to 85–115 ft. lbs.

TRAILER TOWING

Factory trailer towing packages are available on most trucks. However, if you are installing a trailer hitch and wiring on your truck, there are a few thing that you ought to know.

Trailer Weight

Trailer weight is the first, and most important, factor in determining whether or not your vehicle is suitable for towing the trailer you have in mind. The horsepower-to-weight ratio should be calculated. The basic standard is a ratio of 35:1. That is, 35 pounds of GVW for every horsepower.

To calculate this ratio, multiply you engine's rated horsepower by 35, then subtract the weight of the vehicle, including passengers and luggage. The resulting figure is the ideal maximum trailer weight that you can tow. One point to consider: a numerically higher axle ratio can offset what appears to be a low trailer weight. If the weight of the trailer that you have in mind is somewhat higher than the weight you just calculated, you might consider changing your rear axle ratio to compensate.

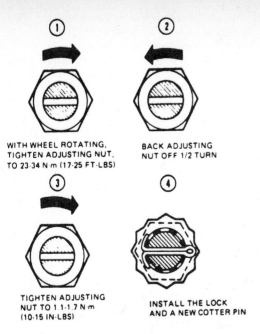

① WITH WHEEL ROTATING, TIGHTEN ADJUSTING NUT, TO 23-34 N·m (17-25 FT-LBS)

② BACK ADJUSTING NUT OFF 1/2 TURN

③ TIGHTEN ADJUSTING NUT TO 1.1-1.7 N·m (10-15 IN-LBS)

④ INSTALL THE LOCK AND A NEW COTTER PIN

Front wheel bearing adjustment procedures

Hitch Weight

There are three kinds of hitches: bumper mounted, frame mounted, and load equalizing.

Bumper mounted hitches are those which attach solely to the vehicle's bumper. Many states prohibit towing with this type of hitch, when it attaches to the vehicle's stock bumper, since it subjects the bumper to stresses for which it was not designed. Aftermarket rear step bumpers, designed for trailer towing, are acceptable for use with bumper mounted hitches.

Frame mounted hitches can be of the type which bolts to two or more points on the frame, plus the bumper, or just to several points on the frame. Frame mounted hitches can also be of the tongue type, for Class I towing, or, of the receiver type, for Classes II and III.

Load equalizing hitches are usually used for large trailers. Most equalizing hitches are welded in place and use equalizing bars and chains to level the vehicle after the trailer is hooked up.

The bolt-on hitches are the most common,

Recommended Equipment Checklist

Equipment	Class I Trailers Under 2,000 pounds	Class II Trailers 2,000-3,500 pounds	Class III Trailers 3,500-6,000 pounds	Class IV Trailers 6,000 pounds and up
Hitch	Frame or Equalizing	Equalizing	Equalizing	Fifth wheel Pick-up truck only
Tongue Load Limit**	Up to 200 pounds	200-350 pounds	350-600 pounds	600 pounds and up
Trailer Brakes	Not Required	Required	Required	Required
Safety Chain	3/16" diameter links	1/4" diameter links	5/16" diameter links	–
Fender Mounted Mirrors	Useful, but not necessary	Recommended	Recommended	Recommended
Turn Signal Flasher	Standard	Constant Rate or heavy duty	Constant Rate or heavy duty	Constant Rate or heavy duty
Coolant Recovery System	Recommended	Required	Required	Required
Transmission Oil Cooler	Recommended	Recommended	Recommended	Recommended
Engine Oil Cooler	Recommended	Recommended	Recommended	Recommended
Air Adjustable Shock Absorbers	Recommended	Recommended	Recommended	Recommended
Flex or Clutch Fan	Recommended	Recommended	Recommended	Recommended
Tires	•••	•••	•••	•••

NOTE The information in this chart is a guide. Check the manufacturer's recommendations for your car if in doubt.

*Local laws may require specific equipment such as trailer brakes or fender mounted mirrors. Check your local laws
Hitch weight is usually 10-15% of trailer gross weight and should be measured with trailer loaded

**Most manufacturer's do not recommend towing trailers of over 1,000 pounds with compacts. Some intermediates cannot tow Class III trailers

***Check manufacturer's recommendations for your specific car trailer combination
–Does not apply

since they are relatively easy to install.

Check the gross weight rating of your trailer. Tongue weight is usually figured as 10% of gross trailer weight. Therefore, a trailer with a maximum gross weight of 2,000 lb. will have a maximum tongue weight of 200 lb. Class I trailers fall into this category. Class II trailers are those with a gross weight rating of 2,000–3,500 lb., while Class III trailers fall into the 3,500–6,000 lb. category. Class IV trailers are those over 6,000 lb. and are for use with fifth wheel trucks, only.

When you've determined the hitch that you'll need, follow the manufacturer's installation instructions, exactly, especially when it comes to fastener torques. The hitch will subjected to a lot of stress and good hitches come with hardened bolts. Never substitute an inferior bolt for a hardened bolt.

Wiring

Wiring the vehicle for towing is fairly easy. There are a number of good wiring kits available and these should be used, rather than trying to design your own. All trailers will need brake lights and turn signals as well as tail lights and side marker lights. Most states require extra marker lights for overly wide trailers. Also, most states have recently required back-up lights for trailers, and most trailer manufacturers have been building trailers with back-up lights for several years.

Additionally, some Class I, most Class II and just about all Class III trailers will have electric brakes.

Add to this number an accessories wire, to operate trailer internal equipment or to charge the trailer's battery, and you can have as many as seven wires in the harness.

Determine the equipment on your trailer and buy the wiring kit necessary. The kit will contain all the wires needed, plus a plug adapter set which included the female plug, mounted on the bumper or hitch, and the male plug, wired into, or plugged into the trailer harness.

When installing the kit, follow the manufacturer's instructions. The color coding of the wires is standard throughout the industry.

One point to note, some domestic vehicles, and most imported vehicles, have separate turn signals. On most domestic vehicles, the brake lights and rear turn signals operate with the same bulb. For those vehicles with separate turn signals, you can purchase an isolation unit so that the brake lights won't blink whenever the turn signals are operated, or, you can go to your local electronics supply house and buy four diodes to wire in series with the brake and turn signal bulbs. Diodes will isolate the brake

and turn signals. The choice is yours. The isolation units are simple and quick to install, but far more expensive than the diodes. The diodes, however, require more work to install properly, since they require the cutting of each bulb's wire and soldering in place of the diode.

One final point, the best kits are those with a spring loaded cover on the vehicle mounted socket. This cover prevents dirt and moisture from corroding the terminals. Never let the vehicle socket hang loosely. Always mount it securely to the bumper or hitch.

Cooling

ENGINE

One of the most common, if not THE most common, problem associated with trailer towing is engine overheating.

With factory installed trailer towing packages, a heavy duty cooling system is usually included. Heavy duty cooling systems are available as optional equipment on most trucks, with or without a trailer package. If you have one of these extra-capacity systems, you shouldn't have any overheating problems.

If you have a standard cooling system, without an expansion tank, you'll definitely need to get an aftermarket expansion tank kit, preferably one with at least a 2 quart capacity. These kits are easily installed on the radiator's overflow hose, and come with a pressure cap designed for expansion tanks.

Another helpful accessory is a Flex Fan. These fan are large diameter units are designed to provide more airflow at low speeds, with blades that have deeply cupped surfaces. The blades then flex, or flatten out, at high speed, when less cooling air is needed. These fans are far lighter in weight than stock fans, requiring less horsepower to drive them. Also, they are far quieter than stock fans.

If you do decide to replace your stock fan with a flex fan, note that if your truck has a fan clutch, a spacer between the flex fan and water pump hub will be needed.

Aftermarket engine oil coolers are helpful for prolonging engine oil life and reducing overall engine temperatures. Both of these factors increase engine life.

While not absolutely necessary in towing Class I and some Class II trailers, they are recommended for heavier Class II and all Class III towing.

Engine oil cooler systems consist of an adapter, screwed on in place of the oil filter, a remote filter mounting and a multi-tube, finned heat exchanger, which is mounted in front of the radiator or air conditioning condenser.

TRANSMISSION

An automatic transmission is usually recommended for trailer towing. Modern automatics have proven reliable and, of course, easy to operate, in trailer towing.

The increased load of a trailer, however, causes an increase in the temperature of the automatic transmission fluid. Heat is the worst enemy of an automatic transmission. As the temperature of the fluid increases, the life of the fluid decreases.

It is essential, therefore, that you install an automatic transmission cooler.

The cooler, which consists of a multi-tube, finned heat exchanger, is usually installed in front of the radiator or air conditioning compressor, and hooked inline with the transmission cooler tank inlet line. Follow the cooler manufacturer's installation instructions.

Select a cooler of at least adequate capacity, based upon the combined gross weights of the truck and trailer.

Cooler manufacturers recommend that you use an aftermarket cooler in addition to, and not instead of, the present cooling tank in your truck's radiator. If you do want to use it in place of the radiator cooling tank, get a cooler at least two sizes larger than normally necessary.

NOTE: *A transmission cooler can, sometimes, cause slow or harsh shifting in the transmission during cold weather, until the fluid has a chance to come up to normal operating temperature. Some coolers can be purchased with or retrofitted with a temperature bypass valve which will allow fluid flow through the cooler only when the fluid has reached operating temperature, or above.*

PUSHING AND TOWING

To push-start your vehicle, (manual transmissions only) follow the procedures below. Check to make sure that the bumpers of both vehicles are aligned so neither will be damaged. Be sure that all electrical system components are turned off (headlights, heater, blower, etc.). Turn on the ignition switch. Place the shift lever in Third or Fourth and push in the clutch pedal. At about 15 mph, signal the driver of the pushing vehicle to fall back, depress the accelerator pedal, and release the clutch pedal slowly. The engine should start.

When you are doing the pushing or pulling, make sure that the two bumpers match so you won't damage the vehicle you are to push. Another good idea is to put an old tire between the two vehicles. If the bumpers don't match, perhaps you should tow the other vehicle. If the other vehicle is just stuck, use First gear to slowly push it out. Tell the driver of the other vehicle to go slowly too. try to keep your truck right up against the other vehicle while you are pushing. If the two vehicles do separate, stop and start over again instead of trying to catch up and ramming the other vehicle. Also try, as much as possible, to avoid riding or slipping the clutch. When the other vehicle gains enough traction, it should pull away from your vehicle.

If you have to tow the other vehicle, make sure that the two chain or rope is sufficiently long and strong, and that it is attached securely to both vehicles at a strong place. Attach the chain at a point on the frame or as close to it as possible. Once again, go slowly and tell the other driver to do the same. Warn the other driver not to allow too much slack in the line when he gains traction and can move under his own power. Otherwise he may run over the tow line and damage both vehicles. If your truck

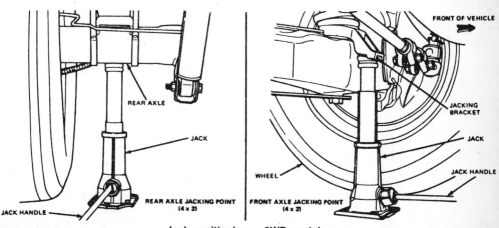

REAR AXLE

JACK

REAR AXLE JACKING POINT
(4 x 2)

JACK HANDLE

FRONT OF VEHICLE

JACKING BRACKET

JACK

JACK HANDLE

WHEEL

FRONT AXLE JACKING POINT
(4 x 2)

Jack positioning — 2WD models

has to be towed by a tow truck, it can be towed forward for any distance with the driveshaft connected as long as it is dine fairly slowly. If your truck has to be towed backward and is a 4WD model, unlock the front axle driving hubs, to prevent the front differential from rotating and place the transfer case in neutral. Also clamp the steering wheel on all models, in the straight ahead position with a clamping device designed for towing service.

JACKING AND HOSTING

It is very important to be careful about running the engine, on vehicles equipped with limited slip differentials, while the vehicle is up on a jack. This is because if the drive train is engaged, power is transmitted to the wheel with the best traction and the vehicle will drive off the jack, resulting in possible damage or injury.

Jack the truck from under the axles, radius arms, or spring hangers and the frame. Be sure and block the diagonally opposite wheel to prevent the vehicle from moving. Place jackstands under the vehicle at the points mentioned above when you are going to work under the vehicle.

CAUTION: *On models equipped with an under chassis mounted spare tire, remove the tire, wheel or tire carrier from the vehicle before it is placed in a high lift position in order to avoid sudden weight release from the chassis.*

When raising the vehicle on a hoist, position the front end adapters under the center of the lower suspension arm or the spring supports as near to the wheels as practical. The rear hoist adapters should be placed under the spring mounting pads or the rear axle housing. Be careful not to touch the rear shock absorber mounting brackets.

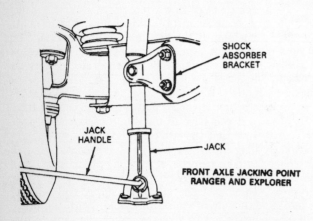

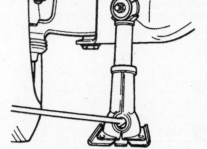

Jack positioning

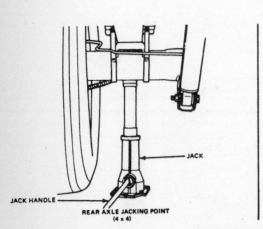

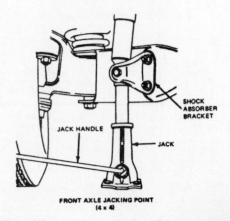

Jack positioning — 4WD models

JUMP STARTING A DEAD BATTERY

The chemical reaction in a battery produces explosive hydrogen gas. This is the safe way to jump start a dead battery, reducing the chances of an accidental spark that could cause an explosion.

Jump Starting Precautions

1. Be sure both batteries are of the same voltage.
2. Be sure both batteries are of the same polarity (have the same grounded terminal).
3. Be sure the vehicles are not touching.
4. Be sure the vent cap holes are not obstructed.
5. Do not smoke or allow sparks around the battery.
6. In cold weather, check for frozen electrolyte in the battery. Do not jump start a frozen battery.
7. Do not allow electrolyte on your skin or clothing.
8. Be sure the electrolyte is not frozen.
CAUTION: *Make certain that the ignition key, in the vehicle with the dead battery, is in the OFF position. Connecting cables to vehicles with on-board computers will result in computer destruction if the key is not in the OFF position.*

Jump Starting Procedure

1. Determine voltages of the two batteries; they must be the same.
2. Bring the starting vehicle close (they must not touch) so that the batteries can be reached easily.
3. Turn off all accessories and both engines. Put both cars in Neutral or Park and set the handbrake.
4. Cover the cell caps with a rag—do not cover terminals.
5. If the terminals on the run-down battery are heavily corroded, clean them.
6. Identify the positive and negative posts on both batteries and connect the cables in the order shown.
7. Start the engine of the starting vehicle and run it at fast idle. Try to start the car with the dead battery. Crank it for no more than 10 seconds at a time and let it cool off for 20 seconds in between tries.
8. If it doesn't start in 3 tries, there is something else wrong.
9. Disconnect the cables in the reverse order.
10. Replace the cell covers and dispose of the rags.

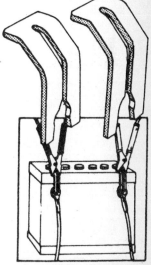

Side terminal batteries occasionally pose a problem when connecting jumper cables. There frequently isn't enough room to clamp the cables without touching sheet metal .Side terminal adaptors are available to alleviate this problem and should be removed after use.

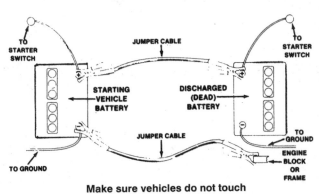

Make sure vehicles do not touch

This hook–up for negative ground cars only

1991 MAINTENANCE SCHEDULE B — NORMAL DRIVING CONDITIONS
Ranger/Explorer 2.3L 4-Cylinder, 2.9L, 3.0L and 4.0L 6-Cylinder Engines

B — Required for all vehicles.

b — Required for 49 States vehicles (all States except California); recommended, but not required, for California and Canada vehicles.

(b) — This item not required to be performed. However, Ford recommends that you also perform maintenance on items designated by a "(b)" in order to achieve best vehicle operation. Failure to perform this recommended maintenance will not invalidate the vehicle emissions warranty or manufacturer recall liability.

MAINTENANCE OPERATION — MILES (Thousands)	7.5	15	22.5	30	37.5	45	52.5	60	67.5	75	82.5	90	97.5	105	112.5	120
KILOMETERS (Thousands)	12	24	36	48	60	72	84	96	108	120	132	144	156	168	181	193
EMISSION CONTROL SYSTEMS																
Change Engine Oil and Oil Filter — every 6 months OR	B	B	B	B	B	B	B	B	B	B	B	B	B	B	B	b
Replace Spark Plugs: Standard				B				B				B				b
Platinum Type 3.0L/4.0L								B								b
Replace Coolant — every 36 months OR				B				B				B				b
*Check Cooling System, Hoses and Clamps	ANNUALLY															
Replace Air Cleaner Filter				B				b				b				b
*Check/Clean Idle Speed Control Air Bypass Valve (2.3L)								(b)								(b)
*Check/Clean Throttle Body								(b)								(b)
Replace PCV Valve (1)								b/1								b
Replace Ignition Wires								b								b
Inspect Drive Belt Condition and Tension — 2.3L								b								b
OTHER SYSTEMS																
Check Wheel Lug Nut Torque§	B	B	B	B	B	B	B	B								
Rotate Tires	B		B		B		B									
Check Clutch Reservoir Fluid Level	B	B	B	B	B	B	B	B								
Inspect and Lubricate Automatic Transmission Shift Linkage (Cable System)	B	B	B	B	B	B	B	B								
Inspect and Lubricate Front Wheel Bearings				B				B								
Inspect Disc Brake System and Lubricate Caliper Slide Rails		B		B		B		B								
Inspect Drum Brake Linings, Lines and Hoses		B		B		B		B								
Inspect Exhaust System for Leaks, Damage or Loose Parts				B				B								
Inspect and Remove any Foreign Material Trapped by Exhaust System Shielding	B	B	B	B	B	B	B	B								
Lubricate Driveshaft U-Joints if Equipped with Grease Fitting	B	B	B	B	B	B	B	B								
Inspect Parking Brake System for Damage and Operation		B		B		B		B								
Lubricate Throttle/Kick Down Cable Ball Stud				B				B								
Lubricate Rear Driveshaft Double Cardan Joint Centering Ball (Ranger SWB 4x4)	B	B	B	B	B	B	B	B								
Lubricate Front Drive Axle R.H. Axle — Shaft Slip Yoke (4x4)				B				B								
Inspect Spindle Needle Bearing Spindle Thrust Bearing Lubrication (4x4)				B				B								
Inspect Hub Lock Lubrication (4x4)				B				B								
Change Transfer Case Oil (4x4)								B								
Lubricate Steering Linkage Joints if equipped with Grease Fittings	B	B	B	B	B	B	B	B								

Beyond 60,000 miles/96 000 km, continue recommended maintenance operations at intervals indicated for 0-60,000 miles/96 000 km.

*   Check means a function measurement of system's operation (performance, leaks or conditions of parts). Correct as required.

§   Wheel lug nuts must be retightened to proper torque specifications at 500 miles/800 km of new vehicle operation (100 miles/160 km and 500 miles/800 km for vehicles equipped for snowplowing). See your Owner Guide for proper torque specifications. Also retighten to proper torque specification at 500 miles/800 km after (1) any wheel change or (2) any other time the wheel lug nuts have been loosened.

/1   At 60,000 miles/96 000 km, your dealer will replace the PCV Valve at no cost on 2.3L, 2.9L, 3.0L and 4.0L engines except California and Canada vehicles. NOTE: Refer to page 2 of the Maintenance Schedule Record Book for "NO COST PCV VALVE REPLACEMENT."

NOTE: Change rear axle lubrication at 100,000 miles.

NOTES:

Unique Driving Conditions

If your driving habits FREQUENTLY include one or more of the following conditions:
- Operating when outside temperatures remain below freezing and most trips are less than 16 km (10 miles).
- Operating during HOT WEATHER in stop-and-go "rush hour" traffic.
- Towing a trailer, using a camper or roof-top carrier, or carrying maximum loads.
- Operating in severe dust conditions.
- Extensive idling, such as police, taxi or door-to-door delivery service.
- High speed operation with a fully loaded vehicle (MAX. GVW).
- Snow plowing on low speed operation.

Change ENGINE OIL and OIL FILTER every 3 months or 4 800 km (3,000 miles) whichever occurs first.

Check/Regap SPARK PLUGS every 15,000 miles (24,000 km).

AIR CLEANER AND CRANKCASE VENTILATION FILTERS –

If operating in severe dust conditions, ask your dealer for proper replacement intervals.

AUTOMATIC TRANSMISSION FLUID — Change each 30,000 miles (48 000 km) — If your driving habits FREQUENTLY include one or more of the following conditions:
- Operating during hot weather (above 90°F, 32°C) and carrying heavy loads and driving in hilly terrain.
- Towing a trailer or slide-in camper.
- Door-to-door delivery, police or taxi.

Extreme Service Items

If vehicle is operated off-highway, perform the following items every 1,000 miles (1 600 km).

If vehicle is operated in mud and/or water perform the following items daily:
- Inspect disc brake system, lube caliper slide rails.
- Inspect drum brake system, hoses, and lines.
- Lubricate automatic transmission external controls (Cable system).
- Inspect front wheel bearings and lubrication.
- Inspect exhaust system for leaks, damage or loose parts and remove any foreign material trapped by shielding.
- Lubricate front axle, steering and clutch linkages, axle and driveshaft U-joints and slip yoke if equipped with fittings.

CAPACITIES

Year	Model	Engine Displacement Liter/CID	Engine Crankcase with Filter (qts)	Transmission Manual (pts)	Automatic (qts)	Transfer Case (pts)	Drive Axle Front (pts)	Rear (pts)	Fuel Tank (gal)	Cooling System wo/AC (qts)	w/AC (qts)
1983	Ranger	2.0/122	5	3①	8②	2	1	5	15	6.5	—
		2.2/134 Diesel	7	3①	8②	2	1	5	15	10.0	10.7
		2.3/140	6	3①	8②	2	1	5	15	6.5	7.2
1984	Bronco II	2.8/173	5	3①	8②	2	1	5.5	23	7.2	7.8
	Ranger	2.0/122	5	3①	8②	2	1	5	15	6.5	—
		2.2/134 Diesel	7	3①	8②	2	1	5	15	10.0	10.7
		2.3/140	6	3①	8②	2	1	5	15	6.5	7.2
		2.8/173	5	3①	8②	2	1	5	15	7.2	7.8
1985	Bronco II	2.8/173	5	3①	8②	2	1	5.5	23	7.2	7.8
	Ranger	2.0/122	5	3①	8②	2	1	5	15	6.5	—
		2.3/140	6	3①	8②	2	1	5	15	6.5	7.2
		2.3/144 Diesel	7	3①	8②	2	1	5	15	13	13
		2.8/173	5	3①	8②	2	1	5.5	15	7.2	7.8
1986	Bronco II	2.9/177	5	3①	8②	2	1	5.5	23	7.2	7.8
	Ranger	2.0/122	5	3①	8②	2	1	5	15	6.5	—
		2.3/140	6	3①	8②	2	1	5	15	6.5	7.2
		2.3/144 Diesel	7	3①	8②	2	1	5	15	13	13
		2.9/177	5	3①	8②	2	1	5.5	15	7.2	7.8
1987	Bronco II	2.9/177	5	3①	8②	2	1	5.5	23	7.2	7.8
	Ranger	2.0/122	5	3①	8②	2	1	5	15	6.5	—
		2.3/130	6	3①	8②	2	1	5	15	6.5	7.2
		2.3/144 Diesel	7	3①	8②	2	1	5	15	13	13
		2.9/177	5	3①	8②	2	1	5.5	15	7.2	7.8
1988	Bronco II	2.9/177	5	3①	8②	2	1	5.5	23	7.2	7.8
	Ranger	2.0/122	5	3①	8②	2	1	5	15	6.5	—
		2.3/140	6	3①	8②	2	1	5	15	6.5	7.2
		2.9/177	5	3①	8②	2	1	5.5	15	7.2	7.8
1989	Bronco II	2.9/177	5	3①	8②	2	3	5.5	15	7.2	7.8
	Ranger	2.3/140	5	3①	8②	2	3	5	15	6.5	7.2
		2.9/177	5	3①	8②	2	3	5.5	15	7.2	7.8
1990	Bronco II	2.9/177	5	3①	8②	2	3	5.5	15	7.2	7.8
	Ranger	2.3/140	5	3①	8②	2	3	5	15	6.5	7.2
		2.9/177	5	3①	8②	2	3	5.5	15	7.2	7.8
		4.0/241	5	5	10	2	3	5	16.3③	7.8	8.6
1991	Explorer	4.0/241	5	5	10	2	3	5	19.3	7.8	8.6
	Ranger	2.3/140	5	5	10	2	3	5	16.3③	6.5	7.2
		2.9/177	5	5	10	2	3	5	16.3③	7.2	7.8
		3.0/183	5	5	10	2	3	5	16.3③	9.5	10.2
		4.0/241	5	5	10	2	3	5	16.3③	7.8	8.6

wo–A/C: without Air Conditioning
w–A/C: with Air Conditioning
① 5-speed overdrive transmission: 3.6 pints
② C-5 transmission (2WD): 7.5 quarts
③ 19.6 optional

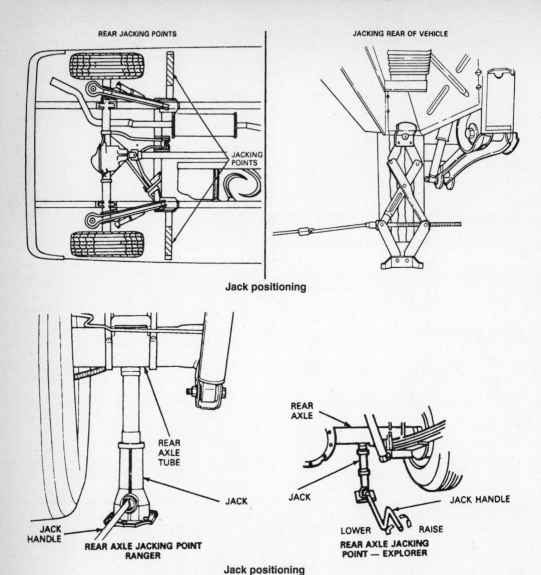

REAR JACKING POINTS

JACKING REAR OF VEHICLE

JACKING POINTS

Jack positioning

REAR AXLE TUBE

JACK

JACK HANDLE

REAR AXLE JACKING POINT RANGER

REAR AXLE

JACK

JACK HANDLE

LOWER   RAISE

REAR AXLE JACKING POINT — EXPLORER

Jack positioning

Engine Performance and Tune-Up

2

GASOLINE ENGINE TUNE-UP PROCEDURES

Spark Plugs

A typical spark plug consists of a metal shell surrounding a ceramic insulator. A metal electrode extends downward through the center of the insulator and protrudes a small distance. Located at the end of the plug and attached to the side of the outer metal shell is the side electrode. The side electrode bends in at a 90° angle so that its tip is even with, and parallel to, the tip of the center electrode. The distance between these two electrodes (measured in thousandths of an inch) is called the spark plug gap. The spark plug in no way produces a spark but merely provides a gap across which the current can arc. The coil produces anywhere from 20,000 to 40,000 volts which travels to the distributor where it is distributed through the spark plug wires to the spark plugs. The current passes along the center electrode and jumps the gap to the side electrode, and, in do doing, ignites the air/fuel mixture in the combustion chamber.

Spark plugs ignite the air and fuel mixture in the cylinder as the piston reaches the top of the compression stroke. The controlled explosion that results forces the piston down, turning the crankshaft and the rest of the drive train.

The average life of a spark plug is dependent on a number of factors: the mechanical condition of the engine; the type of engine; the type of fuel; driving conditions; and the driver.

When you remove the spark plugs, check their condition. They are a good indicator of the condition of the engine. It it a good idea to remove the spark plugs at regular intervals, such as every 2,000 or 3,000 miles, just so you can keep an eye on the mechanical state of your engine.

A small deposit of light tan or gray material on a spark plug that has been used for any period of time is to be considered normal.

The gap between the center electrode and the side or ground electrode can be expected to increase not more than 0.001 in. every 1,000 miles under normal conditions.

When a spark plug is functioning normally or, more accurately, when the plug is installed in an engine that is functioning properly, the plugs can be taken out, cleaned, regapped, and reinstalled in the engine without doing the engine any harm.

When, and if, a plug fouls and beings to misfire, you will have to investigate, correct the cause of the fouling, and either clean or replace the plug.

There are several reasons why a spark plug will foul and you can learn which is at fault by just looking at the plug. A few of the most common reasons for plug fouling, and a description of the fouled plug's appearance, are listed in the Color Section, which also offers solutions to the problems.

SPARK PLUG HEAT RANGE

Spark plug heat range is the ability of the plug to dissipate heat. The longer the insulator (or the farther it extends into the engine), the hotter the plug will operate; the shorter the insulator the cooler it will operate. A plug that absorbs little heat and remains too cool will quickly accumulate deposits of oil and carbon since it is not hot enough to burn them off. This leads to plug fouling and consequently to misfiring. A plug that absorbs too much heat will have no deposits, but, due to the excessive heat, the electrodes will burn away quickly and in some instances, preignition may result. Preignition takes place when plug tips get so hot that they glow sufficiently to ignite the fuel/air mixture before the actual spark occurs. This

GASOLINE ENGINE TUNE-UP SPECIFICATIONS

Year	Model	Engine Displacement Liter/CID	Spark Plugs Type*	Gap (in.)	Ignition Timing (deg.) MT	AT	Fuel Pump Pressure (psi)	Compression Pressure (psi)	Idle Speed (rpm) MT	AT	Valve Clearance Intake	Exhaust
1983	Ranger	2.0/122	①	①	①	①	5–7	②	①	①	Hyd.	Hyd.
		2.3/140	①	①	①	①	5–7	②	①	①	Hyd.	Hyd.
1984	Bronco II	2.8/173	AWSF-42	0.044	10B	10B	4.5–6.5	②	①	①	0.014	0.016
	Ranger	2.0/122	AWSF-42	0.044	8B	8B	5–7	②	800	800	Hyd.	Hyd.
		2.3/140	AWSF-44	0.044	①	①	5–7	②	800	800	Hyd.	Hyd.
		2.8/173	AWSF-42	0.044	10B	10B	4.5–6.5	②	①	①	0.014	0.016
1985	Bronco II	2.8/173	AWSF-42C	0.044	10B	10B	4.5–6.5	②	①	①	0.014	0.016
	Ranger	2.0/122	AWSF-52C	0.044	6B	6B	5–7	②	800	800	Hyd.	Hyd.
		2.3/140	AWSF-44C	0.044	10B	10B	30–40	②	①	①	Hyd.	Hyd.
		2.8/173	AWSF-42C	0.044	10B	10B	4.5–6.5	②	①	①	0.014	0.016
1986	Bronco II	2.9/177	AWSF-42C	0.044	10B	10B	30–40	②	①	①	Hyd.	Hyd.
	Ranger	2.0/122	AWSF-52C	0.044	6B	6B	5–7	②	800	800	Hyd.	Hyd.
		2.3/140	AWSF-44C	0.044	10B	10B	30–40	②	①	①	Hyd.	Hyd.
		2.9/177	AWSF-42C	0.044	10B	10B	30–40	②	①	①	Hyd.	Hyd.
1987	Bronco II	2.9/177	AWSF-42C	0.044	10B	10B	30–40	②	①	①	Hyd.	Hyd.
	Ranger	2.0/122	AWSF-52C	0.044	6B	6B	5–7	②	800	800	Hyd.	Hyd.
		2.3/140	AWSF-44C	0.044	10B	10B	30–40	②	①	①	Hyd.	Hyd.
		2.9/177	AWSF-42C	0.044	10B	10B	30–40	②	①	①	Hyd.	Hyd.
1988	Bronco II	2.9/177	AWSF-42C	0.044	10B	10B	30–40	②	①	①	Hyd.	Hyd.
	Ranger	2.0/122	AWSF-52C	0.044	6B	6B	5–7	②	800	800	Hyd.	Hyd.
		2.3/140	AWSF-44C	0.044	10B	10B	30–40	②	①	①	Hyd.	Hyd.
		2.9/177	AWSF-42C	0.044	10B	10B	30–40	②	①	①	Hyd.	Hyd.
1989	Bronco II	2.9/177	AWSF-42C	0.044	10B	10B	30–40	②	①	①	Hyd.	Hyd.
	Ranger	2.3/140	AWSF-44C	0.044	10B	10B	30–40	②	①	①	Hyd.	Hyd.
		2,8/177	AWSF-42C	0.044	10B	10B	30–40	②	①	①	Hyd.	Hyd.
1990	Bronco II	2.9/177	AWSF-42C	0.044	10B	10B	30–40	②	①	①	Hyd.	Hyd.
	Ranger	2.3/140	AWSF-44C	0.044	10B	10B	30–40	②	①	①	Hyd.	Hyd.
		2.9/177	AWSF-42C	0.044	10B	10B	30–40	②	①	①	Hyd.	Hyd.
		4.0/241	AWSF-42C	①	10B	10B	30–40	②	①	①	Hyd.	Hyd.
1991	Ranger	2.3	①	①	10B	10B	30–40	②	①	①	Hyd.	Hyd.
		2.9	AWSF-42C	0.044	10B	10B	30–40	②	①	①	Hyd.	Hyd.
		3.0	AWSF-32P	0.044	10B	10B	30–40	②	①	①	Hyd.	Hyd.
		4.0	AWSF-42C	①	10B	10B	30–40	②	①	①	Hyd.	Hyd.
	Explorer	4.0	AWSF-42C	①	10B	10B	30–40	②	①	①	Hyd.	Hyd.

NOTE: The underhood specification sticker often reflects tune-up specification changes made in production. Sticker figures must be used if they conflict with those in this chart.

*Spark plugs shown are original equipment. Part numbers in this reference are not recommendations by Chilton for any product by brand name.

① See underhood specification sticker.

② The lowest compression reading should be within 75 percent of the highest reading.

ALWAYS REFER TO VEHICLE EMISSION CONTROL INFORMATION DECAL FOR SPECIFICATIONS AND TIMING PROCEDURES.

early ignition will usually cause a pinging during low speeds and heavy loads.

The general rule of thumb for choosing the correct heat range when picking a spark plug is: if most of your driving is long distance, high speed travel, use a colder plug; if most of your driving is stop and to, use a hotter plug. Original equipment plugs are compromise plugs, but most people never have occasion to change their plugs from the factory-recommended heat range.

REPLACING SPARK PLUGS

Ford recommends that spark plugs be changed every 30,000 miles with electronic ignition systems. Under severe driving conditions, those intervals should be halved. Severe driving conditions are:

1. Extended periods of idling or low speed operation, such as off-road or door-to-door delivery.

2. Driving short distances (less than 10

DIESEL TUNE-UP SPECIFICATIONS

Year	Model	Engine Displacement Liter/CID	Valve Clearance (warm) Intake (in.)	Exhaust (in.)	Injection Timing (ATDC)	Injection Nozzle Pressure (psi)	Idle Speed (rpm)	Cranking Compression Pressure (psi)
1983	Ranger	2.2/134 Diesel	0.012	0.012	2	1957	700	427 ②
1984	Ranger	2.2/134 Diesel	0.012	0.012	2	1957	700	427 ②
1985	Ranger	2.2/140 Diesel	0.010	0.010	①	1707	①	384 ③
1986	Ranger	2.2/140 Diesel	0.010	0.010	①	1707	①	384 ③
1987	Ranger	2.2/140 Diesel	0.010	0.010	①	1707	①	384 ③

① See underhood specification sticker
② At 200 rpm
③ At 250 rpm

miles) when the average temperature is below 10° for 60 days or more.

3. Excessive dust or blowing dirt conditions.

When you're removing spark plugs, you should work on one at a time. Don't start by removing the plug wires all at once, because unless you number them, they may become mixed up. Take a minute before you begin and number the wires with tape. The best location for numbering is near where the wires come out of the cap.

1. Twist the spark plug boot and remove the boot and wire form the plug. Do not pull on the wire itself as this will ruin the wire.

2. If possible, use a brush or rag to clean the area around the spark plug. Make sure that all the dirt is removed so that none will enter the cylinder after the plug is removed.

3. Remove the spark plug using the proper size socket. Turn the socket counterclockwise to remove the plug. Be sure to hold the socket straight on the plug to avoid breaking the plug, or rounding off the hex on the plug.

4. Once the plug is out, check it against the plugs shown in this Chapter to determine engine condition. This is crucial since plug readings are vital signs of engine condition.

5. Use a round wire feeler gauge to check the plug gap. The correct size gauge should pass through the electrode gap with a slight drag. If you're in doubt, try one size smaller and one size larger. The smaller gauge should go through easily while the larger one shouldn't go through at all. If the gap is incorrect, use the electrode bending tool on the end of the gauge to adjust the gap. When adjusting the gap, always bend the side electrode. The center electrode is non-adjustable.

6. Squirt a drop of penetrating oil on the threads of the new plug and install it. Don't oil the treads too heavily. Turn the plug in clockwise by hand until it is snug.

7. When the plug is finger tight, tighten it with a wrench.

NOTE: *Whenever a high tension wire is removed for any reason from a spark plug, coil or distributor terminal housing, silicone grease must be applied to the boot before it is reconnected. Using a small clean tool, coat the entire interior surface of the boot with Ford silicone grease D7AZ-19A331-A or equivalent.*

8. Install the plug boot firmly over the plug. Proceed to the next plug.

Spark Plug Wires

INSPECTION

Visually inspect the spark plug cables for burns, cuts, or breaks in the insulation. Check the spark plug boots and the nipples on the distributor cap and coil. Replace any damaged wiring. If no physical damage is obvious, the wire can be checked with an ohmmeter for excessive resistance.

When installing a new set of spark plug cables, replace the cables one at a time so there will be no mixup. Start by replacing the longest

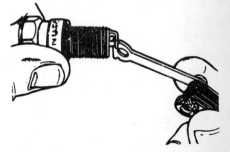

Adjust the electrode gap by bending the electrode

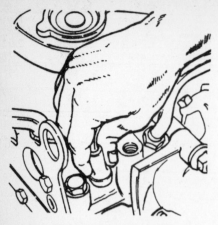

Twist and pull on the rubber boot to remove the spark wires; never pull on the wire itself

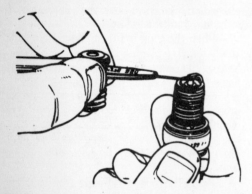

Always use a wire gauge to check the electrode gap; a flat feeler gauge may not give the proper reading.

cables first. Install the boot firmly over the spark plug. Route the wire exactly the same as the original. Insert the nipple firmly into the tower on the distributor cap. Repeat the process for each cable.

REMOVAL

When removing spark plug wires, use great care. Grasp and twist the insulator back and forth on the spark plug to free the insulator. Do not pull on the wire directly as it may become separated from the connector inside the insulator.

INSTALLATION

NOTE: *Whenever a high tension wire is removed for any reason form a spark plug, coil or distributor terminal housing, silicone grease must be applied to the boot before it is reconnected. Using a small clean tool, coat the entire interior surface of the boot with Ford silicone grease D7AZ-19A331-A or equivalent.*

1. Install each wire in or on the proper terminal of the distributor cap. Be sure the terminal connector inside the insulator is fully seated. The No. 1 terminal is identified on the cap.

2. Remove wire separators from old wire set and install them on new set in approximately same position.

3. Connect wires to proper spark plugs. Install ignition coil wire. Be certain all wires are fully seated on terminals.

TESTING

1. Remove the distributor cap from the distributor assembly.

2. Visually inspect the spark plug wires for burns, cuts or breaks in the insulation. Check the spark plug boots and the nipples on the distributor cap and coil. Replace any damaged wiring.

3. Inspect the spark plug wires to insure that they are firmly seated on the distributor cap.

4. Disconnect the spark plug wire(s) thought to be defective at the spark plug.

5. Using an ohmmeter, measure the resistance between the distributor cap terminal and the spark plug terminal.

NOTE: *Make certain that a good connection exists between the distributor cap and the spark terminal. Never, under any circumstances, measure resistance by puncturing the spark plug wire.*

6. If the measured resistance is less than 7000Ω per foot of wire, the wire is good. If the

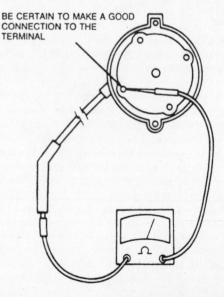

BE CERTAIN TO MAKE A GOOD CONNECTION TO THE TERMINAL

Testing spark plug wire resistance with an ohmmeter

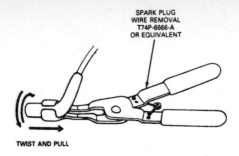

SPARK PLUG
WIRE REMOVAL
T74P-6666-A
OR EQUIVALENT

TWIST AND PULL

Spark plug boot removal tool

measured resistance is greater than 7000Ω per foot, the wire is defective and should be replaced.

FIRING ORDERS

NOTE: *To avoid confusion, replace spark plugs and wires one at a time.*

Electronic Ignition

The 2.0L and the 2.3L (1983-84) engines are equipped with Dura Spark II ignition system. However, depending on engine calibration, the Dura Spark II system may use a standard module or a **Universal Ignition Module.** The Universal Ignition Module (UIM) is capable of providing spark timing retard in response to barometric or engine sensors, or MCU signal.

The Ranger/Bronco II equipped with the 2.3L (1985-88), 2.8L, 2.9L or 3.0L engines uses a universal distributor design which incorporates an integrally mounted TFI-IV module.

NOTE: *On some models, 2.3L (twin plug) and 4.0L engine applications use a distributorless ignition system. This system consists of the following components: Crankshaft timing sensor, EDIS or DIS ignition module, one or two Ignition coil packs, EEC-IV module and related wiring. Initial timing is*

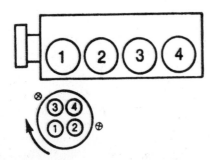

2.0L, 2.3L engines
Firing order: 1-3-4-2
Distributor rotation: clockwise

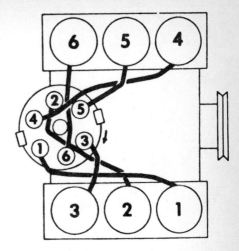

2.8L, 2.9L, 3.0L engines
Firing order: 1-4-2-5-3-6
Distributor rotation: clockwise

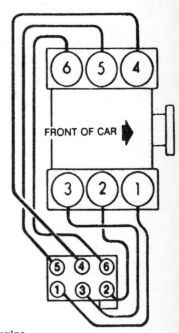

FRONT OF CAR ➡

4.0L engine
Firing order: 1-4-2-5-3-6
Distributor rotation: no distributor

PRESET at 10°BTDC and is NOT ADJUSTABLE.

The distributor uses a **Hall Effect** vane switch stator assembly and has provision for fixed octane adjustment. A new cap, adapter and rotor are designed for use on the Universal Distributor. The Thick Film Integrated (TFI) module is contained in molded thermo-plastic and is mounted on the distributor base. The TFI-IV features a **push start** mode which allows push starting of the vehicle, if necessary.

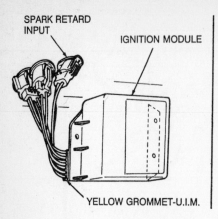

SPARK RETARD INPUT
IGNITION MODULE
YELLOW GROMMET-U.I.M.

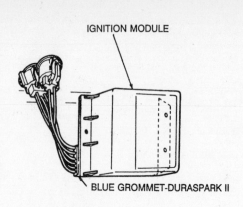

IGNITION MODULE
BLUE GROMMET-DURASPARK II

Two types of Dura Spark II ignition modules

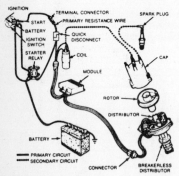

Dura Spark II Ignition system

The TFI-IV system uses an **E-Core** ignition coil, which replaces the oil-filled coil found on other systems.

DUAL MODE TIMING IGNITION MODULE

On some applications, a special Dura Spark II ignition module is used with altitude compensation. This special module plus the barometric pressure switch, allows the base engine timing to be modified to suit altitude conditions. All other elements and performance characteristics of this module are identical in both modes of operation to the basic Dura Spark II system. All Dura Spark II modules equipped with altitude features, have three connectors instead of the normal two. A barometric switch provides an automatic retard signal to the module at different altitudes, giving appropriate advanced timing at higher altitude and retard mode for spark knock control at lower altitudes.

DISTRIBUTOR

The distributors are equipped with both vacuum and centrifugal spark advances which operate the same regardless of the type of ignition system used. A dual vacuum advance is used on certain engines to provide ignition retard during engine closed throttle operation, to help control engine exhaust emissions.

CIRCUIT OPERATION

All systems consist of a primary (low voltage) and secondary (high voltage) circuit.
The Primary Circuit:
The components involved in the primary circuit are:
1. Battery
2. Ignition switch
3. Integral primary circuit resistance wire
4. Primary windings of the ignition coil
5. Magnetic pickup coil assembly in the distributor
6. Ignition module
The Secondary Circuit:
The components of the secondary circuit are:
1. Secondary windings of the ignition coil
2. Distributor rotor
3. Distributor cap and adapter
4. Secondary spark plug wires
5. Spark plugs

Operation

With the ignition switch in the **ON** position, the primary circuit is energized and the magnetic field is built up by the current flowing through the primary windings of the ignition coil. When the armature spokes align with the center of the magnetic pickup coil, the module turns off the coil primary current and the high voltage is produced in the secondary circuit by the collapsing magnetic field. High voltage is produced each time the magnetic field is caused to collapse due to a timing circuit in the module, which starts and stops the primary circuit through the coil. The high voltage flows through the coil secondary lead to the distributor cap, where the rotor distributes the spark to the proper spark plug terminal in the distrib-

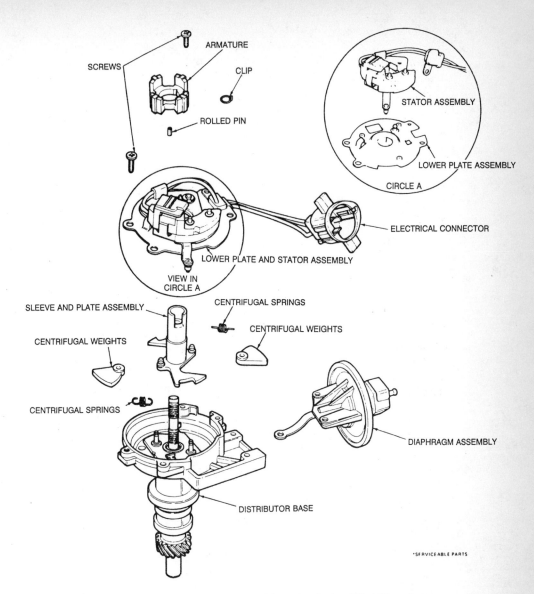

Dura Spark II distributor assembly — 4 cylinder 122, 140 engines

utor cap. The secondary current then flows through the secondary wire to the spark plug.

System Adjustments

No adjustments are made to the Dura Spark II ignition system except the initial timing and spark plug gap.

SECONDARY WIRE USAGE

Spark plug wires that are used with the Dura Spark II system are 8mm in size, to contain the higher output voltage. Two types of wires are used in this system and some engines will have both types. It is important to identify the type of wire to a cylinder before a replacement is obtained and installed. Both types are blue in color and have silicone jacketing. The insula-

tion material underneath the jacketing can be a EPDM or have another silicone layer, separated by glass braid. EPDM wires are used where the engine temperatures are cooler and are identified by the letters **SE**. The silicone jacket type are used where the engine temperatures are high and are identified by the letters **SS**.

NOTE: *Whenever a Dura Spark II high tension wire is removed for any purpose from a spark plug, coil or distributor cap, silicone grease must be applied to the boot before it is reconnected.*

The spark plug wires are marked with the cylinder number, model year and date of cable manufacture (quarter and year). Service replacement wires do not have this information.

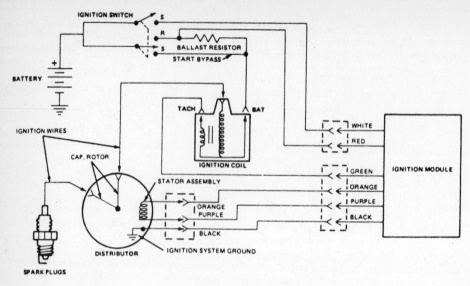

Dura Spark II circuit operation

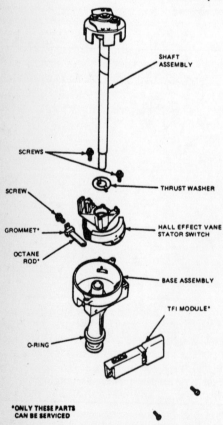

Exploded view of the EEC-IV distributor

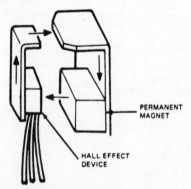

Magnetic Flux Field

EEC-IV Electronic Engine Control

The EEC-IV system utilizes microprocessor technology for instantaneous detection and response to the engine operation conditions. A significant advantage of the EEC-IV system over the earlier electronic-control systems is the capacity to process almost a million control commands a second through two microcircuits which are integrated into one semiconductor chip about 1/4 in. square.

NOTE: *Except for the cap, adapter, rotor, TFI module, O-ring and the octane rod, no other distributor parts are replaceable. There is no calibration required with the universal distributor.*

TFI-IV Electronic Ignition System

This system has a universal distributor design which is gear driven and has a die cast metal base that incorporates an integrally mounted TFI-IV ignition module.

The distributor uses a "Hall Effect" stator assembly and eliminates the conventional centrifugal and vacuum advance mechanisms. No distributor calibration is required and it is not normally necessary to adjust initial timing. The cap, adapter and rotor are designed for use with the universal distributor and the ignition

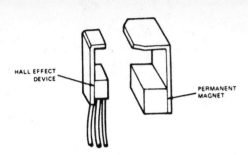

Hall effect Device

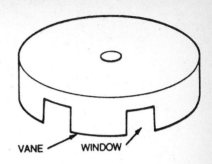

Rotary Vane cap

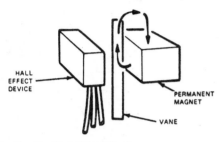

Activating the Hall Effect Device

module is a Thick Film Integrated (TFI) design. The module is contained in molded thermoplastic and is mounted on the distributor base retained by two screws. The distributor assembly can be identified by the part number in-

formation printed on a decal attached to the side of the distributor base.

In addition to the Hall Effect switch, the ignition module contains the Profile Ignition Pick-up (PIP) sensor, which sends an electronically oriented crankshaft position signal to the ECA and the TFI module circuitry. The ECA, after taking all the sensors information, produces a new signal called the Spout. This Spout signal is then sent back to the TFI module for comparison with the PIP signal. The TFI-IV module then uses both of these signals to fire the ignition coil at the proper timing interval. A modification to the circuitry allows for a Push-Start mode for manual transmission equipped vehicles.

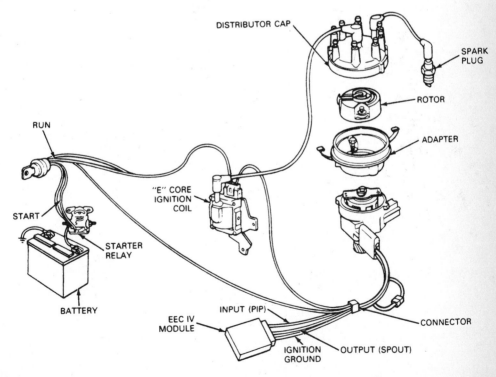

TFI components

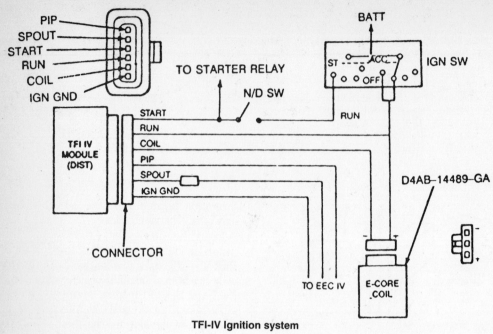

TFI-IV Ignition system

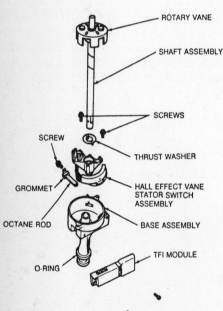

Exploded view of Hall Effect distributor

EEC-IV EDIS Electronic Ignition System

In the distributorless ignition system (DIS) used on the 4.0L V6, all engine timing and spark distribution is handled electronically with no moving parts. This system has fewer parts that require replacement and provides a more accurately timed spark. During basic operation, the EEC-IV determines the ignition timing required by the engine and a DIS module determines which ignition coil to fire.

IGNITION TIMING

Ignition timing is the measurement, in degrees of crankshaft rotation, of the point at which the spark plugs fire in each of the cylinders. It is measured in degrees before or after Top Dead Center (TDC) of the compression stroke.

Ideally, the air/fuel mixture in the cylinder will be ignited by the spark plug just as the piston passes TDC of the compression stroke. If this happens, the piston will be beginning the power stroke just as the compressed and ignited air/fuel mixture starts to expand. The expansion of the air/fuel mixture then forces the piston down on the power stroke and turns the crankshaft.

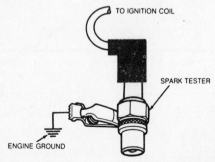

Checking ignition coil secondary voltage with spark tester

Because it takes a fraction of a second for the spark plug to ignite the mixture in the cylinder, the spark plug must fire a little before the piston reaches TDC. Otherwise, the mixture will not be completely ignited as the piston passes TDC and the full power of the explosion will not be used by the engine.

The timing measurement is given in degrees of crankshaft rotation before the piston reaches TDC (BTDC, or Before Top Dead Center). If the setting for the ignition timing is 5° BTDC, each spark plug must fire 5° before each piston reaches TDC. This only holds true, however, when the engine is at idle speed.

As the engine speed increases, the piston go faster. The spark plugs have to ignite the fuel even sooner if it is to be completely ignited when the piston reaches TDC.

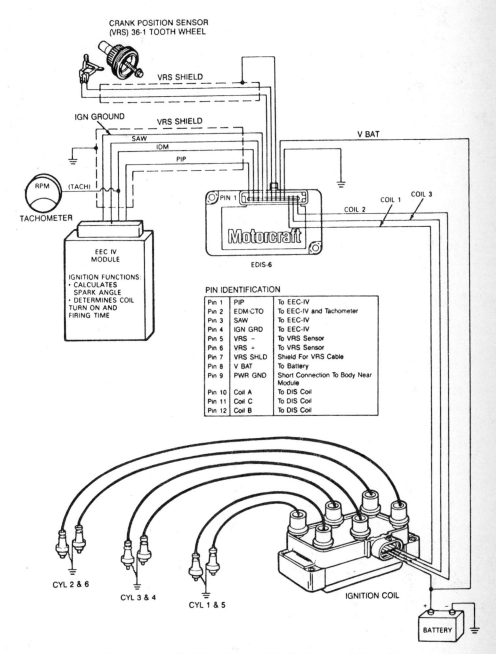

EDIS (Electronic Distributorless Ignition System) — 4.0L engine

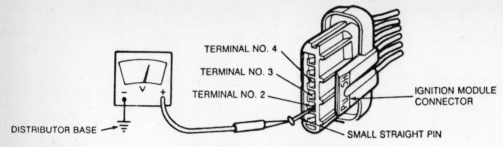

Wiring harness connector test

With the Dura Spark II system, the distributor has a means to advance the timing of the spark as the engine speed increases. This is accomplished by centrifugal weights within the distributor and a vacuum diaphragm mounted on the side of the distributor. It is necessary to disconnect the vacuum lines from the diaphragm when the ignition timing is being set.

With the TFI-IV and EEC-IV EDIS systems, ignition timing is calculated at all phases of vehicle operation.

If the ignition is set too far advanced (BTDC), the ignition and expansion of the fuel in the cylinder will occur too soon and tend to force the piston down while it is still traveling up. This causes engine ping. If the ignition spark is set too far retarded after TDC (ATDC), the piston will have already passed TDC and started on its way down when the fuel is ignited. This will cause the piston to be forced down for only a portion of its travel. This will result in poor engine performance and lack of power.

The timing is best checked with a timing light. This device is connected in series with the No. 1 spark plug. The current that fires the spark plug also causes the timing light to flash.

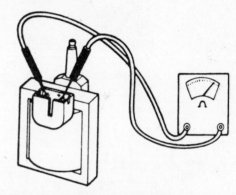

Ignition coil primary resistance test

IGNITION TIMING ADJUSTMENT

With the Dura Spark II system, only an initial timing adjustment is possible. Ignition timing is not considered to be a part of tune-up or routine maintenance.

With the TFI-IV and EEC-IV EDIS systems no ignition timing adjustment is possible (preset at the factory-computer controlled) and none should be attempted.

IGNITION TIMING CHECK

Dura Spark II Systems

NOTE: *Check the underhood Vehicle Emission Control Information decal for specifica-*

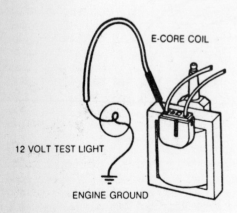

Ignition coil primary circuit switching test

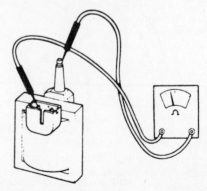

Ignition coil secondary test

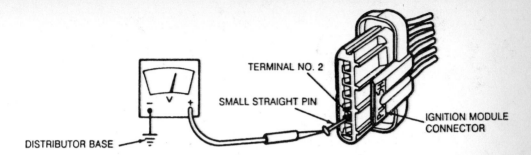

Primary circuit continuity test

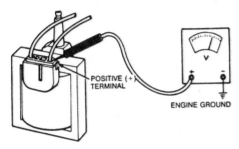

Ignition coil supply voltage test

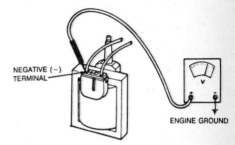

Ignition coil primary voltage test

tions and any special instructions.

1. Locate the timing marks on the crankshaft pulley and the front of the engine.

2. Clean off the timing marks so that you can see them.

3. Mark the timing marks with a piece of chalk or with paint. Color the mark on the scale that will indicate the correct timing when it is aligned with the mark on the pulley or the pointer. It is also helpful to mark the notch in the pulley or the tip of the pointer with a small dab of color.

4. Attach a tachometer to the engine.

5. Attach a timing light according to the manufacturer's instructions.

6. Check to make sure that all of the wires clear the fan and then start the engine.

7. Adjust the idle to the correct setting.

8. Aim the timing light at the timing marks. If the marks that you put on the pulley and the engine are aligned when the light flashes, the timing is correct. Turn off the engine and remove the tachometer and the timing light. If the marks are not in alignment, proceed with the following stops.

9. Loosen the distributor lockbolt just a security-type holddown bolt. Use Distributor Holddown Wrench, Tool T82L-12270-A, or equivalent, to loosen the holddown bolt.

10. With the timing light aimed at the pulley and the marks on the engine, turn the distributor in the direction of rotor rotation to retard the spark, and in the opposite direction of rotor rotation to advance the spark. Align the marks

on the pulley and the engine with the flashes of the timing light.

11. When the marks are aligned, tighten the distributor lockbolt and recheck the timing with the timing light to make sure that the distributor did not move when you tightened the lockbolt.

12. Turn off the engine and remove the timing light.

VALVE LASH

Valve adjustment determines how far the valves enter the cylinder and how long they stay open and closed.

If the valve clearance is too large, part of the life of the camshaft will be used to removing the excessive clearance. Consequently, the valve will not be opening as far as it should. This condition has two effects: the valve train components will emit a tapping sound as they take up the excessive clearance and the engine will perform poorly because the valves don't open fully and allow the proper amount of gases to flow into and out of the engine.

If the valve clearance is too small, the intake valve and the exhaust valves will open too far and they will not fully seat on the cylinder head when they close. When a seat on the cylinder head when they close. When a valve seats itself on the cylinder head, it does two things: it seals the combustion chamber so that none of the

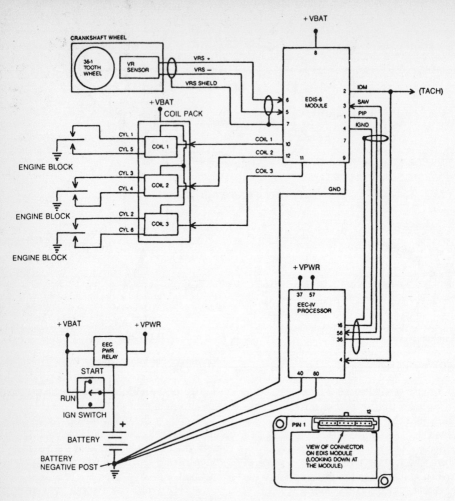

EDIS wiring schematic

gases in the cylinder escape and it cools itself by transferring some of the heat it absorbs from the combustion in the cylinder to the cylinder head and to the engine's cooling system. If the valve clearance is too small, the engine will run poorly because of the gases escaping from the combustion chamber. The valves will also become overheated and will warp, since they cannot transfer heat unless they are touching the valve seat in the cylinder head.

NOTE: *While all valve adjustments must be made as accurately as possible, it is better to have the valve adjustment slightly loose than slightly tight as a burned valve may result from overly tight adjustments.*

ADJUSTMENT

2.0L, 2.3L Engines

NOTE: *The 4-cylinder gasoline engines in this vehicle are equipped with hydraulic valve lash adjusters. Adjustment is not necessary as a tune up procedure. To check the*

valve lash use the following procedure. THE ALLOWABLE COLLAPSED TAPPET GAP IS 0.035–0.055 in. AT THE CAMSHAFT. THE DESIRED COLLAPSED TAPPET GAP IS 0.040–0.050 in. AT THE CAMSHAFT.

1. Disconnect the battery ground cable.
2. Remove the rocker arm cover following the procedure in Chapter 3.
3. Position the camshaft so that the base circle of the lobe is facing the cam follower of the valve to be checked.
4. Using tool T74P-6565-A, slowly apply pressure to the cam follower until the lash adjuster is completely collapsed. Hold the follower in this position and insert the proper size feeler gauge between the base circle of the cam and the follower.
5. If the clearance is excessive, remove the cam follower and inspect for damage.
6. If the cam follower appears to be intact, and not excessively worn, measure the valve

spring damper assembly assembled height to be sure the valve is not sticking.

7. If the valve spring damper spring assembled height is correct, check the dimensions of the camshaft following the procedure in Chapter 3.

8. If the camshaft dimensions are to specifications, remove, clean and test the lash adjuster.

9. Reinstall the lash adjuster and check the clearance. Replace damaged or worn parts as necessary.

2.8L Engine

NOTE: *The following procedure should be performed on a cold engine.*

1. Disconnect the battery ground cable.
2. Remove the rocker arm cover following the procedure in Chapter 3.
3. Place your finger on the adjusting screw of the intake valve rocker arm for the number 5 cylinder. You should be able to feel any movement in the rocker arm.
4. Using a remote starter switch, **bump** the engine over until the intake valve for the number 5 cylinder just begins to open. The valves on the number 1 cylinder may now be adjusted.
5. Adjust the number 1 intake valve so that a 0.35mm feeler gauge has a light drag and a 0.38mm feeler gauge is very tight. Turn the adjusting screw clockwise to decrease the gap and counterclockwise to increase the gap. The adjusting screws are self-locking and will stay in position once they are set.

NOTE: *When checking the valve lash, be sure to insert the feeler gauge between the rocker arm and the valve tip at the front or (rear) edge of the valve and move it toward the opposite edge with a rearward or (forward) motion. DO NOT insert the feeler gauge at the outer edge and move toward the inner edge (inward toward the carburetor), this will produce an incorrect reading which will result in overly tight valves.*

6. Using the same method, adjust the number 1 exhaust valve lash so that a 0.40mm feeler gauge has a light drag and a 0.43mm feeler gauge is very tight.
7. Adjust the remaining valves in the same manner, in the firing order (1-4-2-5-3-6) by positioning the camshaft according to the chart below.
8. Install the rocker arm covers following the procedure in Chapter 3 under **Engine Mechanical**.
9. Reconnect the battery ground cable.
10. Start the engine and check for oil and vacuum leaks.

2.9L Engine

NOTE: *The following procedure should be performed on a cold engine.*

1. On the cylinder to be adjusted, position the cams so that the tappets are in the base circle area.
2. Loosen the adjusting screws until a distinct lash between the roller arm pad and the valve tip can be noticed.

NOTE: *The plunger of the hydraulic tappet should now be fully extended under the load of the internal spring.*

3. Carefully screw in the adjustment screws until the roller arms slightly touch the valves.

To adjust both valves for cylinder number	1	4	2	5	3	6
The intake valve must be opening for cylinder number	5	3	6	1	4	2

Valve adjusting arrangement — 2.8L engine

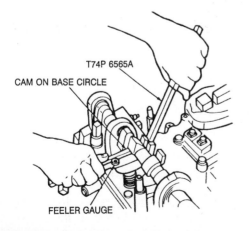

Checking valve lash — 2.0L, 2.3L engines

Valve adjustment — 2.8L engine

4. To achieve the normal working position of the plunger, screw in the adjusting screw $1^1/_2$ turns, equivalent to 2mm.

FUEL SYSTEM

This Chapter contains only tune-up adjustment procedures for the carburetor. Descriptions, adjustments and overhaul procedures for the carburetor can be found in Chapter 5.

When the engine in your vehicle is running, the air/fuel mixture from the carburetor is being drown into the engine by a partial vacuum created by the downward movement of the pistons on the intake stroke. The amount of air/fuel mixture that enters the engine is controlled by the throttle plate(s) in the bottom of the carburetor. When the engine is not running, the throttle plates are closed, completely blocking off the air/fuel passage(s) at the bottom of the carburetor. The throttle plates are connected by the throttle linkage to the accelerator pedal in the passenger compartment of the truck. When you depress the pedal, you open the throttle plates in the carburetor to admit more air/fuel mixture to the engine.

When the engine is idling, it is necessary to have the throttle plates open slightly. To prevent having to hold your foot on the pedal, an idle speed adjusting screw is located on the carburetor linkage.

The idle adjusting screw contacts a lever (throttle lever) on the outside of the carburetor. When the screw is turned, it opens or closes the throttle plates of the carburetor, raising or lowering the idle speed of the engine. This screw is called the curb idle adjusting screw. There are three different types of carburetors used on the Ford Ranger/Bronco II. The 4-2.0L, 2.3L engines use the Carter model YFA 1-bbl. carburetor except on the California and High Altitude models which are equipped with the Carter model YFA 1-bbl. Feedback carburetor. The 6-2.8L engine is equipped with a Motorcraft model 2150 2-bbl. carburetor.

IDLE SPEED ADJUSTMENTS

2.0L, 2.3L Engines with Carter YFA-1V & YFA-1V Feedback Carburetor

1. Block the wheels and apply the parking brake.

2. Place the transmission in Neutral or Park.

3. Bring engine to normal operating temperature.

4. Place the air conditioning selector in the Off position.

5. Place transmission in specified position as referred to on the emission decal.

6. Check/adjust curb idle RPM. If adjustment is required, turn the hex head adjustment at the rear of the TSP (throttle solenoid positioner) housing.

7. Place the transmission in Neutral or Park. Rev the engine momentarily. Place transmission in specified position and recheck curb idle RPM. Readjust if required.

8. Turn the ignition key to the Off position.

9. If a curb idle RPM adjustment was required and the carburetor is equipped with a dashpot, adjust the dashpot clearance to specification as follows:

a. Turn key to On position. Open throttle to allow TSP solenoid plunger to extend to the curb idle position.

b. Collapse dashpot plunger to maximum extent. Measure clearance between tip of plunger and extension pad on throttle vent lever. If required, adjust to specification. Tighten dashpot locknut. Recheck clearance. Turn key to Off position.

10. If curb idle adjustment was required:

a. Turn ignition key to the On position to activate the TSP (engine not running). Open throttle to allow the TSP solenoid plunger to extend to the curb idle position.

b. Secure the choke plate in the wide open position.

c. Open throttle so that the throttle vent lever does not touch the bowl vent rod. Close the throttle to the idle set position and measure the travel of the fuel bowl vent rod from the open throttle position.

d. Travel of the bowl vent rod should be 2.5-3.5mm.

e. If out of specification, bend the throttle vent lever at notch to obtain required travel.

11. Remove all test equipment and reinstall air cleaner assembly. Tighten the holddown bolt.

2.8L Engine with Motorcraft 2150A-2V Carburetor

NOTE: *On models equipped with air conditioning, the air conditioner-On RPM speed must be set prior to setting the Curb Idle Speed adjustment. This adjustment is made with the vacuum operated throttle modulator (VOTM) on.*

AIR CONDITIONER-ON RPM ADJUSTMENT

1. Remove the air cleaner and disconnect and plug the vacuum lines.

2. Block the wheels, apply the parking brake, turn off all accessories, start the engine and run it to normalize underhood temperatures.

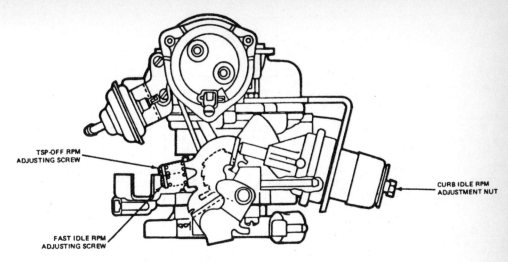

TSP-OFF RPM
ADJUSTING SCREW

CURB IDLE RPM
ADJUSTMENT NUT

FAST IDLE RPM
ADJUSTING SCREW

Carter YFA-1V & YFA-1V Feedback carburetor — idle speed adjustment

3. Check that the chile plate is fully open and connect a tachometer according to the manufacturer's instructions.

4. Disconnect the air conditioner clutch wire at the compressor.

5. Place the heater control selector to maximum cooling and set the blower switch in the high position.

6. Place the manual transmission in neutral; the automatic transmission in drive.

7. Using the saddle bracket adjusting screw, adjust the air conditioner-ON RPM to the specifications shown on the under hood emission sticker.

8. Reconnect the air conditioner compressor clutch wire.

9. Proceed to step 4 below and set the Curb Idle Speed adjustment.

CURB IDLE SPEED ADJUSTMENT

1. Remove the air cleaner and disconnect and plug the vacuum lines.

2. Block the wheels, apply the parking brake, turn off all accessories, start the engine and run it to normalize underhood temperatures.

3. Check that the choke plate is fully open and connect a tachometer according to the manufacturer's instructions.

4. Place the manual transmission in neutral; the automatic transmission in drive and make certain the (TSP) throttle stop positioner plunger is extended.

5. Turn the saddle bracket adjustment screw (non-air conditioned), or the hex head protruding from the rear of the TSP diaphragm assembly (air conditioned models) until the specified idle speed is obtained.

6. Check the TSP-off speed as follows:

a. disconnect the TSP wire.

b. place the transmission in neutral and check the RPM. If necessary, adjust to the specified TSP-off speed with the throttle adjusting screw. Check the underhood sticker for specifications.

7. Install the air cleaner and connect the vacuum lines. Recheck the idle speed. Adjust, if necessary, with the air cleaner on.

IDLE MIXTURE ADJUSTMENT

NOTE: *For this procedure, Ford recommends a propane enrichment procedure. This requires special equipment not available to the general public. In lieu of this equipment the following procedure may be followed to obtain a satisfactory idle mixture.*

Removing Limiter Plugs

2.0L, 2.3L ENGINES WITH CARTER YFA-1V FEEDBACK CARBURETORS

1. Remove the carburetor from the engine as described in Chapter 5.

2. Drain the fuel from the carburetor into a suitable container.

3. Invert the carburetor and cover all vacuum and fuel connection openings with tape. With a hack saw, carefully saw a slot lengthwise through the metal thickness of the cup. Use care to prevent contact between the saw blade and throttle body. Insert a screwdriver in the slot just cut, and twist, spreading the outer cup sufficiently to allow removal of the inner cap. After removing cap, count the number of turns required to seat the mixture screw needle lightly. This information will be used in assembly. Remove the screw and cap.

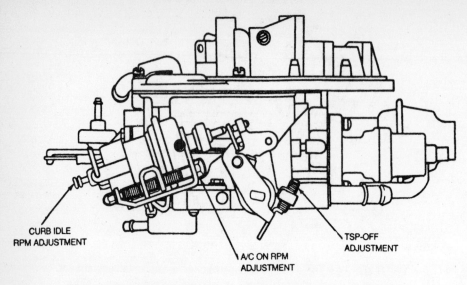

CURB IDLE
RPM ADJUSTMENT

A/C ON RPM
ADJUSTMENT

TSP-OFF
ADJUSTMENT

Motorcraft 2150A-2V carburetor — idle speed adjustment with A/C

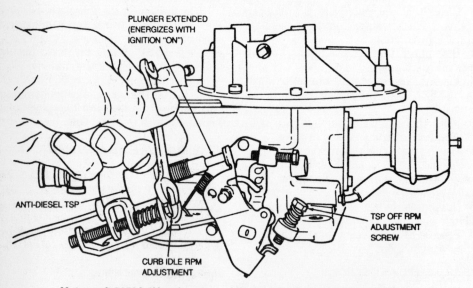

PLUNGER EXTENDED
(ENERGIZES WITH
IGNITION "ON")

ANTI-DIESEL TSP

CURB IDLE RPM
ADJUSTMENT

TSP OFF RPM
ADJUSTMENT
SCREW

Motorcraft 2150A-2V carburetor — idle speed adjustment without A/C

After cleaning the metal shavings from the carburetor, remove the tape from the openings.

4. Install the idle mixture screw and spring, and a new adjustment limiting cup. Set the screw to the same number of turns out from the lightly seated position as noted during disassembly.

5. Install the carburetor on the vehicle and perform the idle mixture setting procedure.

6. After making the mixture adjustment, install the mixture limiting cap.

2.8L ENGINE WITH MOTORCRAFT 2150A-2V CARBURETOR

The idle mixture adjusting screws are covered with a two-piece tamper-resistant limiter plugs. To adjust the idle mixture the plugs must be removed using the following procedure:

1. Remove and drain the carburetor using the procedure in Chapter 5 under **Fuel System**.

2. Turn the carburetor over and locate the locking tab on each locking cap.

3. Using a blunt punch and a light hammer, tap the locking cap until the locking tab has cleared the detent in the locking plug.

NOTE: *Support the area under the limiter plug when removing it to prevent the adjusting screw from bending.*

4. Remove the locking cap from the locking plug and remove the support form under the

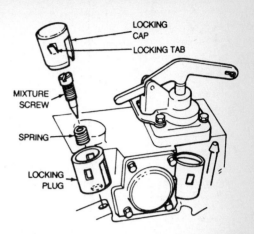

Mixture screw locking caps — Motorcraft 2150-2V

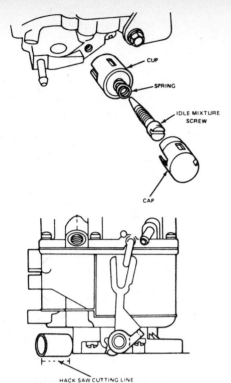

Mixture screw locking caps — Carter YFA-1V & YFA-1V Feedback carburetor

locking cap.

5. Repeat steps 3 and 4 for the other locking cap.

6. Install the carburetor on the engine and perform the idle mixture adjustment.

7. To install the cap, align with the detent in the plug and press the cap into the plug.

Mixture Adjustment

1. Block the wheels, set the parking brake and run the engine to bring it to normal operating temperature.

2. Disconnect the hose between the emission canister and the air cleaner.

3. On engines equipped with the Thermactor air injection system, the routing of the vacuum lines connected to the dump valve will have to be temporarily changed. Mark them for reconnection before switching them.

4. For valves with one or two vacuum lines at the side, disconnect and plug the lines.

5. For valves with one vacuum line at the top, check the line to see if it is connected to the intake manifold or an intake manifold source such as the carburetor or distributor vacuum line. If not, remove and plug the line at the dump valve and connect a temporary length of vacuum hose from the dump valve fitting to a source of intake manifold vacuum.

6. Remove the limiter caps form the mix-

ture screws by CAREFULLY cutting them with a sharp knife.

7. Place the transmission in neutral and run the engine at 2500 rpm for 15 seconds.

8. Place the automatic transmission in Drive; the manual in neutral.

9. Adjust the idle speed to the higher of the two figures given on the underhood sticker.

10. Turn the idle mixture screws to obtain the highest possible rpm, leaving the screws in the leanest position that will maintain this rpm.

11. Repeat steps 7 through 10 until further adjustment of the mixture screws does not increase the rpm.

12. Turn the screws in until the lower of the two idle speed figures is reached. Turn the screws in $1/4$ turn increments each to insure a balance.

13. Turn the engine off and remove the tachometer. Reinstall all equipment.

Fuel Injected Engines

These engines have idle speed controlled by the TFI-IV/EEC-IV system and no adjustment is possible.

DIESEL ENGINE TUNE-UP PROCEDURES

Due to the relative simplicity of the diesel engine as compared to the gasoline engine, tune-up procedures consist of adjusting the valves and adjusting the engine idle speed.

Valve Lash

ADJUSTMENT

1. Warm the engine until normal operating temperature is reached.

2. Remove the valve cover. Check the head bolt torque in sequence. Refer to Chapter 3 under **Cylinder Head** for this procedure.

3. Turn the engine to bring the No. 1 piston to TDC (top dead center) of the compression stroke.

4. Adjust the following valves:
- No. 1 Intake
- No. 1 Exhaust
- No. 2 Intake
- No. 3 Exhaust

5. Rotate the crankshaft 360° and bring No. 4 piston to TDC of the compression stroke.

6. Adjust the following valves:
- No. 2 Exhaust
- No. 3 Intake
- No. 4 Intake
- No. 4 Exhaust

7. To adjust the valves, loosen the locknut on the rocker arm. Rotate the adjusting screw clockwise to reduce clearance, counterclockwise to increase clearance. Clearance is checked with a flat feeler gauge (0.012 inch gauge intake and 0.012 gauge exhaust-engine must be hot on the 2.2L diesel engine) (0.010 inch gauge intake and 0.010 gauge exhaust-engine must be hot on the 2.3L Turbo diesel engine) that is passed between the rocker arm and valve stem.

8. After adjustments are made, be sure the locknuts are tight. Be sure mounting surfaces are clean. Install the valve cover and new valve cover gasket.

Setting the Idle Speed

NOTE: *A special tachometer is required to check engine RPM on a diesel engine.*

1. Block the wheels and apply the parking brake.

2. Start and run engine until the normal operating temperature is reached. Shut off engine.

3. Connect diesel engine tachometer.

4. Start engine and check RPM. Refer to emissions decal for latest specifications. RPM is usually adjusted in Neutral for manual transmissions and Drive for automatic models.

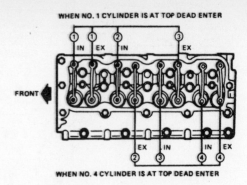

Diesel engine valve adjusting sequence

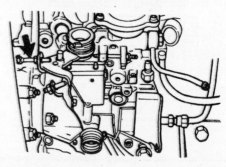

Diesel engine idle speed adjustment location — 2.2L shown 2.3L similar

5. The adjustment bolt is located on the bell crank at the top of the injector pump. The upper bolt is for curb idle, the lower for maximum speed.

6. Loosen the locknut. Turn the adjustment screw clockwise to increase RPM, counterclockwise to lower the RPM.

7. Tighten the locknut, Increase engine speed several times and recheck idle. Readjust if necessary

Injection Timing

NOTE: *For injection pump timing please refer to Chapter 5 under Diesel Fuel Systems.*

ENGINE ELECTRICAL

Ignition Coil

REMOVAL AND INSTALLATION

1. Disconnect the battery ground.
2. Disconnect the two small and one large wires from the coil.
3. Disconnect the condenser connector from the coil, if equipped.
4. Unbolt and remove the coil.
5. Installation is the reverse of service removal procedure.

Ignition Module

REMOVAL AND INSTALLATION

Removing the module, on all models, is a matter of simply removing the fasteners that attach it to the fender firewall and pulling apart the connectors. When unplugging the connectors, pull them apart with a firm, straight pull. NEVER PRY THEM APART! To pry them will cause damage. When reconnecting them, coat the mating ends with silicone dielectric grease to waterproof the connection. Press the connectors together firmly to overcome any vacuum lock caused by the grease.

NOTE: *If the locking tabs weaken or break, don't replace the unit. Just secure the connection with electrical tape or tie straps.*

Distributor Cap, Adapter and Rotor

REMOVAL AND INSTALLATION

1. Tag all spark plug wires with a piece of tape according to cylinder number for reference when installing the wires, then remove them from the distributor cap. Note the position of No. 1 spark plug tower.

2. Unclip the distributor cap and lift it straight up and off the distributor.
3. Using a screwdriver, loosen the adapter attaching screws and remove the adapter.
4. Loosen the screws attaching the rotor to the distributor and remove the rotor.
5. Wipe the distributor cap and rotor with a clean, damp cloth. Inspect the cap for cracks, broken carbon button, carbon tracks, dirt or corrosion on the terminals and replace the cap if questionable. Replace the rotor if cracks, carbon tracks, burns, damaged blade or a damaged spring is noted.
6. Position the distributor rotor with the square and round locator pins matched to the rotor mounting plate. Tighten the screws to 24–36 inch lbs. (2–4 Nm).
7. Install the adapter and tighten the attaching screws to 18–23 inch lbs. (2–3 Nm).
8. Install the cap, noting the square alignment locator, then tighten the holddown screws to 18–23 inch lbs. (2–3 Nm).
9. Install the spark plug wires in firing order, starting from No. 1 tower and working in sequence around the cap. Refer to the firing order illustrations in Chapter 2, if necessary. Make sure the ignition wires are installed correctly and are firmly seated in the distributor cap towers.

TFI Ignition Module

REMOVAL AND INSTALLATION

1. Remove the distributor cap with the ignition wires attached and position it out of the way. Remove the adapter.
2. Disconnect the TFI harness connector.
3. Remove the distributor from the engine as previously described.
4. Place the distributor on a clean workbench and remove the two TFI module attaching screws.
5. Pull the right side of the module down

toward the distributor mounting flange and then back up to disengage the module terminals from the connector in the distributor base. The module may then be pulled toward the flange and away from the distributor.

CAUTION: *Do not attempt to lift the module from its mounting surface prior to moving the entire TFI module toward the distributor flange or you will break the pins at the distributor/module connector.*

6. Coat the metal base of the new TFI module with a $\frac{1}{32}$ in. (0.8mm) thick film of Silicone Dielectric Compound D7AZ–19A331–A or equivalent. This is extremely important to help dissipate the heat when the module is operating.

7. Place the TFI module on the distributor base mounting flange.

8. Carefully position the TFI module assembly toward the distributor bowl and engage the three distributor connector pins securely. Be careful when performing this step. It is very easy to bend one of the connector pins when installing.

9. Install the two TFI mounting screws and tighten them to 15–35 inch lbs. (1–4 Nm).

10. Install the distributor on the engine as previously described.

11. Install the distributor cap and tighten the mounting screws to 18–23 inch lbs. (2–3 Nm).

12. Reconnect the TFI wiring harness connector.

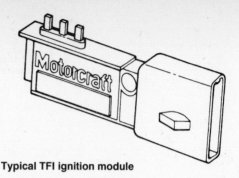

Typical TFI ignition module

13. Attach a timing light according to the manufacturer's instructions and set the initial timing.

Octane Rod

REMOVAL AND INSTALLATION

1. Remove the distributor cap, adapter and rotor as previously described.

2. Remove the octane rod 4mm retaining screw carefully. Don't drop it.

3. Slide the octane rod grommet out to a point where the rod can be disengaged from the stator retaining post and remove the octane rod. Retain the grommet for use with the new octane rod.

4. Install the grommet on the new octane rod.

5. Install the octane rod into the distributor, making sure it engages the stator retaining post.

6. Install the retaining screw and tighten it to 15–35 inch lbs. (2–4 Nm).

7. Install the rotor, adapter and cap as described above.

NOTE: *The 4.0L engine is equipped with the EDIS distributorless ignition system. The 2.3L (twin plug) and 4.0L engine have ignition systems which do not use a distributor assembly. The 2.3L (twin plug) engine uses a distributorless ignition system. This system consists of the following components: Crankshaft timing sensor, DIS ignition module, two ignition coil packs, EEC-IV module and related wiring. Initial timing is PRESET at 10°BTDC and is NOT ADJUSTABLE. Refer to service procedures below.*

Crankshaft Timing Sensor Assembly

REMOVAL AND INSTALLATION

1. Disconnect the negative battery cable. Disconnect the crankshaft timing sensor electrical connectors from the engine harness.

2. Remove the large electrical connector (mark location of wires for correct installation)

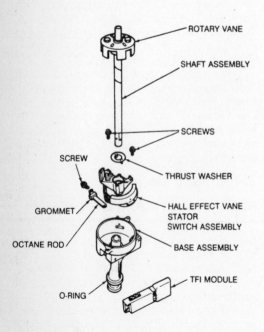

ROTARY VANE

SHAFT ASSEMBLY

SCREWS

SCREW

THRUST WASHER

GROMMET

HALL EFFECT VANE STATOR SWITCH ASSEMBLY

OCTANE ROD

BASE ASSEMBLY

TFI MODULE

O-RING

Exploded view of the universal distributor assembly

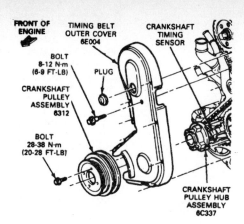

Engine ignition — 2.3L Twin Plug Engine

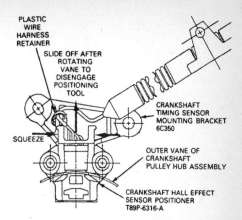

Installation of Crankshaft Hall Effect Sensor Positioner

from the crankshaft timing sensor assembly by prying out the red retaining clip and removing the four wires.

3. Remove the crankshaft pulley assembly by removing the accessory drive belts and then the four bolts that retain it the crankshaft pulley hub assembly.

4. Remove the timing belt cover outer cover.

5. Rotate the crankshaft so that the keyway is at 10 O'CLOCK position. This will place the vane window of both inner and outer vane cups over the crankshaft timing sensor assembly. The vane cups are attached to the crankshaft pulley hub assembly.

6. Remove the 2 crankshaft timing sensor assembly retaining bolts, wire harness retainer which secures the crankshaft timing sensor harness to its mounting bracket. Remove the crank-

shaft timing sensor assembly by sliding the electrical wires out from behind the inner timing belt cover.

To install:

7. Remove the large electrical connector from the new crankshaft timing sensor assembly. Position the crankshaft timing sensor assembly. First, slide the electrical wires behind the inner timing belt cover. Then, hold the sensor assembly loosely in place with the retaining bolts, but do not tighten at this time.

8. Install the large electrical connector (electrical connector must be installed in the proper

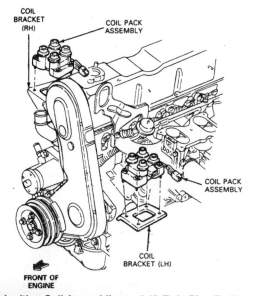

Ignition Coil Assemblies — 2.3L Twin Plug Engine

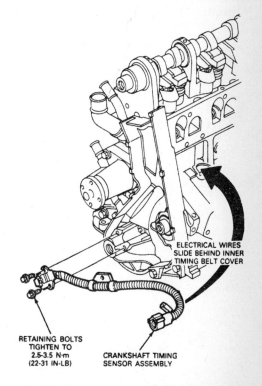

Crankshaft timing sensor assembly — 2.3L Twin Plug Engine

location) to the crankshaft timing sensor assembly.

9. Reconnect both of the crankshaft timing sensor electrical connectors to the engine harness.

10. Rotate the crankshaft such that the outer vane on the crankshaft pulley hub assembly engages both sides of the Crankshaft Hall Sensor Positioner Tool 89P–6316–A or equivalent and tighten sensor bolts to 22–31 inch lbs.

11. Rotate the crankshaft, then remove the Special Tool. Install new wire harness retainer and secure the crankshaft timing sensor harness to its mounting bracket. Trim off the excess as necessary.

12. Install the timing belt outer cover. Install the crankshaft pulley assembly and tighten retaining bolts to 20–28 ft. lbs. Install drive belts. Reconnect battery, start engine and check for proper operation.

DIS Module Assembly

REMOVAL AND INSTALLATION

1. Disconnect the negative battery cable.

2. Disconnect each electrical connector of the DIS ignition module assembly by pushing down the connector locking tabs where it is stamped **PUSH** and then pull it away from the module.

3. Remove the 3 retaining screws, remove the ignition module assembly from the lower intake manifold.

To install:

4. Apply an even coat (approximately $\frac{1}{32}$ in.) of a suitable silicone dielectric compound to the mounting surface of the DIS module.

5. Mount the DIS module assembly onto the intake assembly and install the retaining screws. Torque the screws to 22–31 inch lbs.

6. Install the electrical connectors to the DIS ignition module assembly. Reconnect the negative battery cable.

Ignition Coil Pack

REMOVAL AND INSTALLATION

1. Disconnect the negative battery cable.

2. Disconnect the electrical harness connector from the ignition coil pack.

3. Remove the spark plug wires by squeezing the locking tabs to release the coil boot retainers.

4. Remove the coil pack mounting screws and remove the coil pack.

NOTE: *On vehicle equipped with power steering it may be necessary to remove the intake (left hand) coil and bracket as an assembly.*

To install:

5. Install the coil pack and the retaining

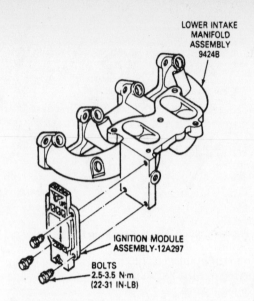

DIS ignition module — 2.3L Twin Plug Engine

screws. Torque the retaining screws to 40–62 inch lbs.

6. Connect the spark plug wires and connect the electrical connector to the coil pack.

7. Reconnect the negative battery cable.

NOTE: *Be sure to place some dielectric compound into each spark plug boot prior to installation of the spark plug wire.*

Distributor

REMOVAL AND INSTALLATION

2.0L & 1983–84 2.3L Engines
Dura Spark II Ignition System

1. Remove one alternator mounting bolt and drive belt. Swing the alternator to one side.

2. Remove the distributor cap. Position it and ignition wires to one side.

3. Disconnect and plug the vacuum advance hose.

4. Separate the distributor connector from the wiring harness.

5. Rotate the engine to align the stator assembly pole and any armature pole.

6. Scribe a mark on the distributor body and engine block to indicate the position of distributor in the engine, and the position of the rotor.

7. Remove the distributor holddown bolt and clamp.

8. Remove the distributor from the engine. Do not rotate the engine while the distributor is removed.

9. If the engine was rotated while the distributor was removed:

a. Rotate the engine until number 1 piston is on the compression stroke.

b. Align the timing marks for correct initial timing.

c. Install the distributor with rotor pointing at number one terminal position in the cap, and the armature and the stator assembly poles aligned.

d. Make sure the oil pump intermediate shaft properly engages the distributor shaft. It may be necessary to crank the engine after the distributor gear is partially engaged in order to engage the oil pump intermediate shaft and fully seat the distributor in the block.

e. If it was necessary to crank the engine, again rotate the engine until the number 1 piston is on compression stroke and align the timing marks for the correct initial timing.

f. Rotate the distributor in the block to align the armature and the stator assembly poles, and verify the rotor is pointing at the number one cap terminal.

g. Install the distributor holddown bolt and clamp; do not tighten.

10. If the engine was not rotated while the distributor was removed and the original distributor is being replaced:

a. Position the distributor in the engine with the rotor and distributor aligning with the previously scribed mark. The armature and stator assembly poles should also align, if the distributor is fully seat the distributor in block.

b. Install the distributor holddown bolt and clamp; do not tighten.

11. If the engine was not rotated while distributor was removed and the new distributor is being installed:

a. Position the distributor in the engine with the rotor aligned with the previously scribed mark. If necessary, crank the engine to fully seat the distributor.

b. Rotate the engine until the timing marks for the correct initial timing align and the rotor is pointing at the number one cap terminal.

c. Rotate the distributor in the block to align the armature and stator assembly poles.

d. Install the distributor holddown bolt and clamp; do not tighten.

12. If in steps 9–11 above, the armature and stator assembly poles cannot be aligned by rotating the distributor in the block, pull the distributor out of the block enough to disengage the distributor gear and rotate the distributor shaft to engage a different distributor gear tooth and re-install the distributor. Repeat steps 9–11 as necessary.

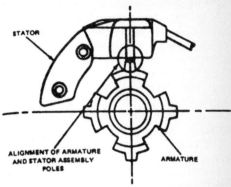

TOOTH MUST BE PERFECTLY ALIGNED WITH TIMING MARKS

STATOR

ALIGNMENT OF ARMATURE AND STATOR ASSEMBLY POLES

ARMATURE

Dura Spark II armature-stator assembly alignment

13. Connect the distributor wiring harness.

14. Install the distributor cap and ignition wires. Check that the ignition wires are securely connected to the distributor cap and spark plugs.

15. Reinstall the alternator mounting bolt and drive belt. Adjust to specification. Refer to Belt Tension Adjustment, described later in this Chapter.

16. Set the initial timing per specification on the Vehicle Emission Control Information Decal.

17. Tighten the distributor holddown bolt to 17–25 ft.lbs.

18. Recheck the initial timing. Readjust if necessary.

19. Connect the vacuum advance hose.

2.3L 1985–88, 2.8L, 2.9L and 3.0L Engines TFI-IV Ignition

1. Remove the air cleaner assembly, taking note of the hose locations.

2. Disconnect the primary wiring connector from the distributor.

NOTE: *Before removing the distributor cap, mark the position of the No. 1 wire tower on the distributor base for future reference.*

3. Using a screwdriver, remove the distributor cap and adapter and position it and the attached wires out of the way.

4. Remove the rotor and place it out of the way to avoid damage.

5. Remove the Thick Film Integrated module connector.

6. Remove the distributor holddown bolt and clamp and remove the distributor.

NOTE: *Some engines may be equipped with a security-type holddown bolt. Use Distributor Holddown Wrench, Tool T82L–12270–A, or equivalent, to remove the holddown bolt.*

7. Rotate the engine until the No. 1 piston is on the compression stroke.

8. Align the timing marks for the correct initial timing.

9. Rotate the distributor shaft so that the rotor tip is pointing toward the mark previously made on the distributor base.

10. Continue rotating slightly so that the leading edge of the vane is centered in the vane switch stator assembly.

11. Rotate the distributor in the engine block to align the leading edge of the vane and the vane switch and verify that the rotor is pointing at No. 1 cap terminal.

NOTE: *If the vane and vane switch stator cannot be aligned by rotating the distributor out of the block, pull the distributor out of the block enough to disengage the distributor and rotate the distributor to engage a different distributor gear tooth. Repeat Steps 8, 9 and 10 as necessary.*

12. Install the distributor holddown bolt and clamp. Do not tighten at this time.

13. Connect the distributor Thick Film Integrated (TFI) and the primary wiring harnesses.

14. Install the distributor rotor and tighten the attaching screws.

15. Install the distributor cap adapter and tighten the attaching screws.

16. Install the distributor cap and wires. Check that the ignition wires are securely attached to the cap and spark plugs.

NOTE: *Before installing the plug wires, coat the inside of each boot with silicone lubricant.*

17. Set the initial timing, with a timing light, to specification. Refer to the underhood Vehicle Emission Control Information Decal.

18. Tighten the distributor hold-down bolt to 17–25 ft. lbs.

19. Recheck and adjust the timing, if necessary.

Alternator

ALTERNATOR PRECAUTIONS

To prevent damage to the alternator and regulator, the following precautionary measures must be taken when working with the electrical system.

1. Never reverse battery connections. Always check the battery polarity visually. This should be done before any connections are made to be sure that all of the connections correspond to the battery ground polarity of the truck.

2. Booster batteries for starting must be connected properly. Make sure that the positive cable of the booster battery is connected to the positive terminal of the battery that is getting the boost. The same applies to the negative cables.

3. Disconnect the battery cables before using a fast charger; the charger has a tendency to force current through the diodes in the opposite direction for which they were designed. This burns out the diodes.

4. Never use a fast charger as a booster for starting the vehicle.

5. Never disconnect the voltage regulator while the engine is running.

6. Do not ground the alternator output terminal.

7. Do not operate the alternator on an open circuit with the field energized.

8. Do not attempt to polarize an alternator.

REMOVAL AND INSTALLATION

1. Open the hood and disconnect the battery ground cable.

2. Remove the adjusting arm bolt and loosen the pivot bolt.

3. Remove the drive belt from the alternator pulley.

4. Label all the leads to the alternator so that they can be reinstalled correctly and remove the leads from the alternator.

5. Remove the alternator pivot bolt and

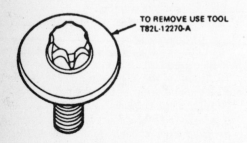

Security type hold-down bolt

TO REMOVE USE TOOL
T82L-12270-A

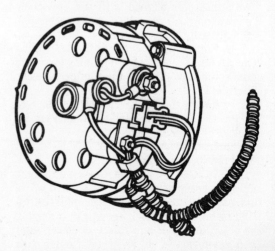

Side terminal alternator

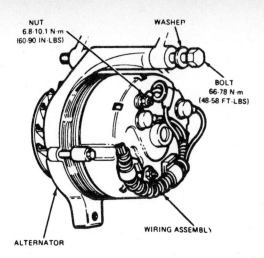

Rear terminal alternator contact locations

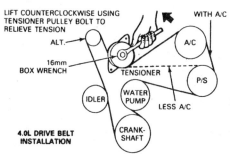

Drive belt installation and adjustment — 4.0L engine

remove the alternator from the truck.

6. To install, reverse the above service procedure.

BELT TENSION ADJUSTMENT

The fan belt drives the alternator and water pump. If the belt is too loose, it will slip and the alternator will not be able to produce its rated current.

Also, the water pump will not operate efficiently and the engine could overheat. Check the tension of the fan belt by pushing your thumb down on the longest span of the belt, midway between the pulleys. Belt deflection should be approximately $1/2$ in.

1. Loosen the alternator mounting bolt and the adjusting arm bolts.

2. Apply pressure on the alternator front housing only, moving the alternator away from the engine to tighten the belt. Do not apply pressure to the rear of the cast aluminum housing of an alternator; damage to the housing could result.

3. Tighten the alternator mounting bolt and the adjusting arm bolts when the correct tension is reached.

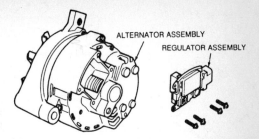

Removing the voltage regulator from the alternator

Regulator

The alternator regulator has been designed to control the charging system's rate of charge and to compensate for seasonal temperature changes. This regulator is 100 percent solid state, consisting of transistors, diodes, and resistors. The operating functions are achieved in basically four circuits: The output stage, the voltage control stage, the solid state relay, and the field circuit overload protection stage. There are two different regulators used on your Ford vehicle. The units both look alike, but are not interchangeable due to the different wiring connector plugs. One unit is used on trucks equipped with an ammeter and the other is used on alternator warning light equipped trucks. The regulators are calibrated by the manufacturer and no adjustment is required or possible on these units.

REMOVAL AND INSTALLATION

1. Disconnect the positive terminal of the battery.

2. Disconnect all of the electrical leads at the regulator. Label them as removed, so you can replace them in the correct order on the replacement unit.

3. Remove all of the hold-down screws, then remove the unit from the vehicle.

4. Install the new voltage regulator using the hold-down screws from the old one, or new ones if they are provided with the replacement regulator. Tighten the hold-down screws.

5. Connect all the leads to the new regulator.

Battery

REMOVAL AND INSTALLATION

1. Disconnect the negative cable then positive cable. (ALWAYS DISCONNECT THE NEGATIVE BATTERY CABLE FIRST) To do this, loosen the cable end-clamp bolts and twist the end-clamps until they are free. You can also buy an inexpensive clamp puller which makes the job easier.

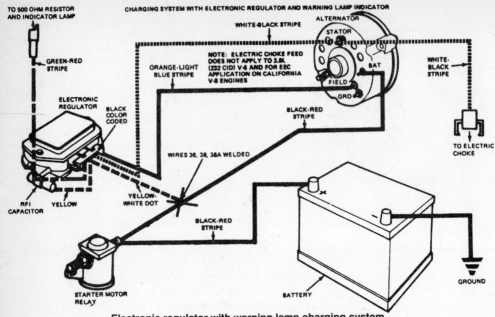

Electronic regulator with warning lamp charging system

ALTERNATOR SPECIFICATION CHART

| Supplier | Rating | | Slip-Ring Turning | | | | Brush Length | | | | Pulley Nut |
| | Amperes @ 15V | Watts @ 15V | Min. Diameter | | Max. Runout | | New | | Wear Limit | | Lb-Ft |
			MM	Inches	MM	Inches	MM	Inches	MM	Inches	
Ford	40A	600W	31	1.22	.013	0.0005	12.19	.480	6.35	.25	60–100
Ford	40A HE	600W	31	1.22	.013	0.0005	12.19	.480	6.35	.25	60–100
Ford	60A	900W	31	1.22	.013	0.0005	12.19	.480	6.35	.25	60–100
Ford	65A	975W	31	1.22	.013	0.0005	12.19	.480	6.35	.25	60–100
Ford	75A	1125W	31	1.22	.013	0.0005	12.19	.480	6.35	.25	60–100
Ford	80A	1200W	31	1.22	.013	0.0005	12.19	.480	6.35	.25	60–100

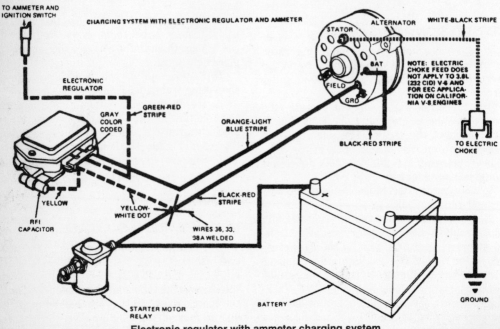

Electronic regulator with ammeter charging system

2. Remove the battery hold-down clamps.

3. Using a battery lifting strap, lift the battery from the vehicle.

4. Installation is the reverse of service removal procedure.

NOTE: *Keeping the battery top clean and dry reduces the need for service and extends battery life. Baking soda and water is excellent for this procedure also it neutralize corrosion. Always lubricate each battery post to help prevent corrosion with long-life lubricant or equivalent.*

Before installing the battery in the vehicle, make sure that the battery terminals are clean and free from corrosion. Use a battery terminal cleaner on the terminals and on the inside of the battery cable ends. If a cleaner is not available, use coarse grade sandpaper to remove the corrosion. A mixture of baking soda and water poured over the terminals and cable ends will help remove and neutralize any acid build up. Before installing the cables onto the terminals, cut a piece of felt cloth or something similar into a circle about the size of the battery terminals at their base. Push the cloth pieces over the terminals so they lie flat on the top of the battery. Soak the pieces of cloth with oil or equivalent. This will keep the formation of oxidized acid to a minimum. Place the battery in the vehicle. Install the cables onto the terminals. Tighten the nuts on the cable ends. Smear a light coating of grease on the cable ends and tops of the terminals. This will further prevent the build up of oxidized acid on the terminals and the cable ends. Install and tighten the nuts of the battery hold bracket.

Starter Motor

REMOVAL AND INSTALLATION

All Gasoline Engines
Except 4.0L Engine

1. Disconnect the negative battery cable.

2. Raise the vehicle and support it safely on jackstands.

3. Disconnect the relay-to-starter cable at the starter terminal.

4. Remove the starter mounting bolts and lower the starter from the engine.

To install:

5. Position the new starter assembly to the flywheel housing and start the mounting bolts in by hand.

6. Snug all bolts while holding the starter squarely against its mounting surface and fully inserted into the pilot hole. Tighten the mounting bolts to 15–20 ft. lbs.

7. Reconnect the relay-to-starter cable as-

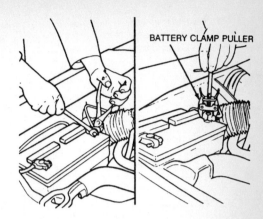

BATTERY CLAMP PULLER

Disconnecting the battery

sembly to the starter motor. Tighten the screw and washer assemblies to 70–130 inch lbs..

8. Lower the vehicle, then connect the negative battery cable.

4.0L Engine

1. Disconnect the negative battery cable.

2. Raise the vehicle and support it safely on jackstands.

3. Matchmark and disconnect the wires at the starter terminals.

4. Remove the starter mounting bolts and lower the starter from the engine.

To install:

5. Position the new starter assembly to the flywheel housing and start the mounting bolts in by hand.

6. Snug all bolts while holding the starter squarely against its mounting surface. Starting with the topmost bolt, tighten the mounting bolts to 15–20 ft. lbs. (21–27 Nm).

7. Reconnect the wires.

8. Lower the vehicle, then connect the negative battery cable.

Diesel Engines

1. Disconnect the battery ground cables from both batteries.

2. Remove the air intake hose between the air cleaner and the intake manifold.

3. Remove the No. 1 glow plug relay from the starter and position it out of the way.

4. Disconnect the starter solenoid wiring.

5. Remove the three starter mounting bolts, and remove the starter.

To install:

6. Position the starter on the engine and install the mounting bolts. Tighten bolts to 48–65 ft. lbs.

7. Connect the starter solenoid wiring.

8. Install the No. 1 glow plug relay on the starter.

9. Connect the air intake hose to the intake

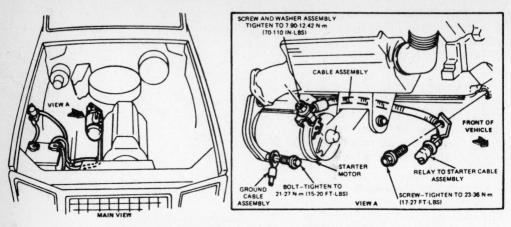

Starter installation exploded view — gasoline engines

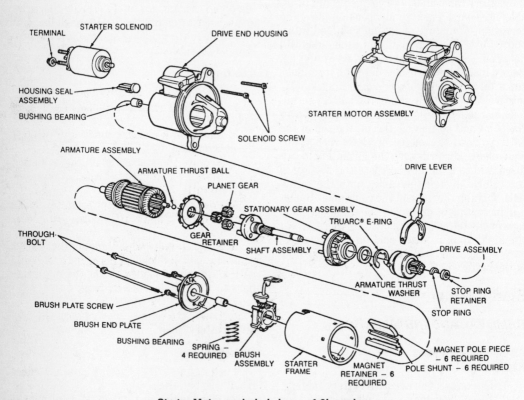

Starter Motor exploded view — 4.0L engine

manifold and air cleaner.

10. Connect the battery ground cables to both batteries.

11. Check the starter operation.

STARTER RELAY REPLACEMENT

Gasoline Engine

The starter relay is mounted on the inside of the right wheel well. To replace it, disconnect the positive battery cable from the battery, disconnect all of the electrical leads from the relay

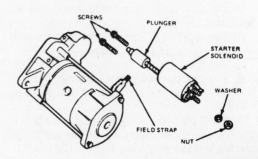

Removing the starter solenoid

and remove the relay from the fender well. Replace in the reverse order of removal procedure.

STARTER SOLENOID REPLACEMENT

Diesel Engine

1. Remove the starter as described in this Chapter.

2. Remove the nut and washer from the M terminal of the starter solenoid and position the field strap out of the way.

3. Position the solenoid on the starter and install the attaching screws. Tighten to 5–7 ft. lbs.

4. Position the strap to the M terminal on the solenoid and install the nut and washer. Tighten to 80–120 inch lbs.

5. Install the starter as described in this Chapter.

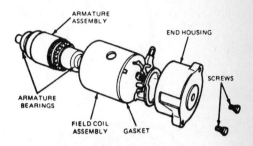

Removing the armature from the starter

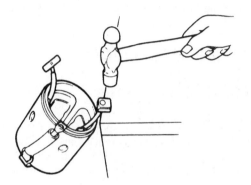

Removing brush from the lead wire — diesel engine starter

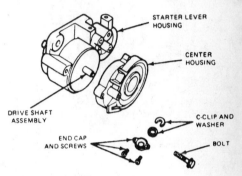

Removing the center housing

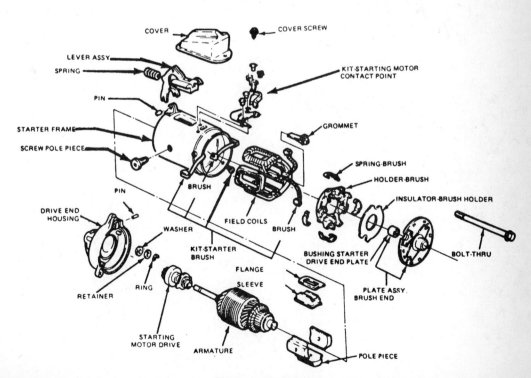

Starter, exploded view

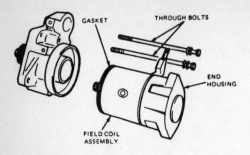

Removing the starter through bolts

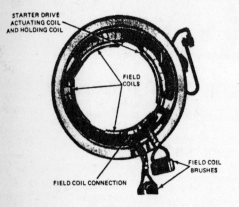

Starter motor field coil assembly with brushes

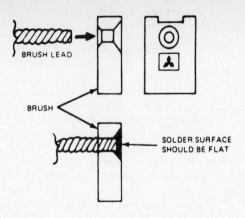

Installing brush to the lead wire — diesel engine starter

ENGINE MECHANICAL

Engine Overhaul Tips

Most engine overhaul procedures are fairly standard. In addition to specific parts replacement procedures and complete specifications for your individual engine, this section also is a guide to accept rebuilding procedures. Exam-

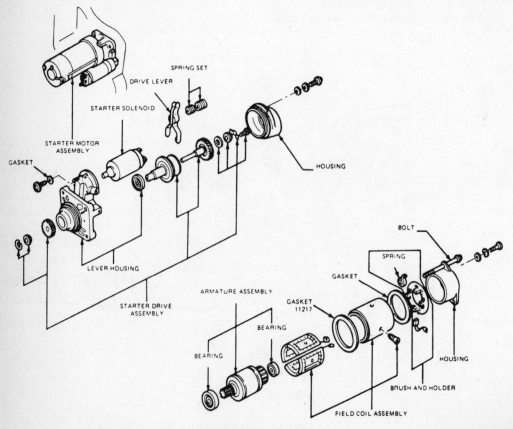

Starter exploded view — diesel engine

BATTERY AND STARTER SPECIFICATIONS

| | | Battery | | | Starter | | | | | Brush |
| | | | | | Lock Test | | No Load Test | | | |
Year	Engine	Ampere/ Hour Capacity	Volts	Ground	Amps	Volts	Amps	Volts	Cranking Speed RPM	Spring Tension (oz)
1983–88	Gas	45	12	Neg.	200	12	70	12	180–250	40
	Gas	63	12	Neg.	180	12	80	12	150–290	80
	Diesel	54	12	Neg.	500	12	180	12	150–220	
1989–91	Gas ①	—	12	Neg.	150–200	12	80	12	180–250	80
	Gas ②	—	12	Neg.	140–200	12	70	12	170–220	64

NOTE: Maximum starting circuit voltage drop between battery positive terminal to starter assembly terminal at normal engine temperature is 0.5 volt.
① 4 inch diameter starter motor
② 3 inch diameter starter motor

ples of standard rebuilding practice are shown and should be used along with specific details concerning your particular engine.

Competent and accurate machine shop services will ensure maximum performance, reliability and engine life.

In most instances it is more profitable for the do-it-yourself mechanic to remove, clean and inspect the component, buy the necessary parts and deliver these to a shop for actual machine work.

On the other hand, much of the rebuilding work (crankshaft, block, bearings, piston rods, and other components) is well within the scope of the do-it-yourself mechanic.

TOOLS

The tools required for an engine overhaul or parts replacement will depend on the depth of your involvement. With a few exceptions, they will be the tools found in a mechanic's tool kit. More in-depth work will require any or all of the following:
• a dial indicator (reading in thousandths) mounted on a universal base
• micrometers and telescope gauges
• jaw and screw-type pullers
• scraper
• valve spring compressor
• ring groove cleaner
• piston ring expander and compressor
• ridge reamer
• cylinder hone or glaze breaker
• Plastigage®
• engine stand

The use of most of these tools is illustrated in this Chapter. Many can be rented for a one-time use from a local parts jobber or tool supply house specializing in automotive work.

Occasionally, the use of special tools is called for. See the information on Special Tools and Safety Notice in the front of this book before substituting another tool.

INSPECTION TECHNIQUES

Procedures and specifications are given in this Chapter for inspecting, cleaning and assessing the wear limits of most major components. Other procedures such as Magnaflux® and Zyglo® can be used to locate material flaws and stress cracks. Magnaflux® is a magnetic process applicable only to ferrous materials. The Zyglo® process coats the material with a fluorescent dye penetrant and can be used on any material Check for suspected surface cracks can be more readily made using spot check dye. The dye is sprayed onto the suspected area, wiped off and the area sprayed with a developer. Cracks will show up brightly.

OVERHAUL TIPS

Aluminum has become extremely popular for use in engines, due to its low weight. Observe the following precautions when handling aluminum parts:
• Never hot tank aluminum parts (the caustic hot tank solution will eat the aluminum.
• Remove all aluminum parts (identification tag, etc.) from engine parts prior to the tanking.
• Always coat threads lightly with engine oil or anti-seize compounds before installation, to prevent seizure.
• Never over torque bolts or spark plugs especially in aluminum threads.

Stripped threads in any component can be repaired using any of several commercial repair kits (Heli-Coil®, Microdot®, Keenserts®, etc.).

When assembling the engine, any parts that will be frictional contact must be prelubed to provide lubrication at initial start-up. Any product specifically formulated for this purpose can

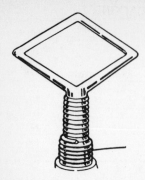

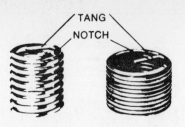

Screw the inert onto the installation tool until the tang engages the slot. Screw the insert into the tapped hole until it is 1/4 to 1/2 turn below the top surface. After installation, break off the tang with a hammer and punch

be used, but engine oil is not recommended as a prelube.

When semi-permanent (locked, but removable) installation of bolts or nuts is desired, threads should be cleaned and coated with Loctite® or other similar, commercial non-hardening sealant.

REPAIRING DAMAGED THREADS

Several methods of repairing damaged threads are available. Heli-Coil® (shown here), Keenserts® and Microdot® are among the most widely used. All involve basically the same principle—drilling out stripped threads, tapping the hole and installing a prewound insert—making welding, plugging and oversize fasteners unnecessary.

Two types of thread repair inserts are usually supplied: a standard type for most Inch Coarse, Inch Fine, Metric Course and Metric Fine thread sizes and a spark lug type to fit most spark plug port sizes. Consult the individual manufacturer's catalog to determine exact applications. Typical thread repair kits will contain a selection of prewound threaded inserts, a tap (corresponding to the outside diameter threads of the insert) and an installation tool. Spark plug inserts usually differ because they require a tap equipped with pilot threads and a combined reamer/tap section. Most manufacturers also supply blister-packed thread repair inserts separately in addition to a master kit containing a variety of taps and inserts plus installation tools.

Before effecting a repair to a threaded hole, remove any snapped, broken or damaged bolts or studs. Penetrating oil can be used to free frozen threads. The offending item can be removed with locking pliers or with a screw or stud extractor. After the hole is clear, the thread can be repaired, as shown in the series of accompanying illustrations.

Damaged bolt holes can be repaired with Standard thread repair insert (left) and spark plug thread insert (right)

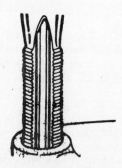

Drill out the damaged threads with the specified drill bit. Drill completely through the hole or to the bottom of the blind hole

With the tap supplied, tap the hole to receive the insert. Keep the tap well oiled and back it out frequently to avoid clogging he threads

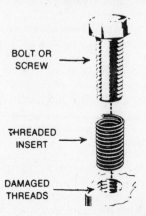

Thread repair insert kits can restore damaged threads

VALVE SPECIFICATIONS

Year	Model	Engine Displacement Liter/CID	Seat Angle (deg)	Face Angle (deg)	Spring Test Pressure (lbs @ in.)	Spring Installed Height (in.)	Stem-to-Guide Clearance (in.)		Stem Diameter (in.)	
							Intake	Exhaust	Intake	Exhaust
1983	Ranger	2.0/122	45	44	149 @ 1.12	1.49–1.55	0.0010–0.0027	0.0015–0.0032	0.3416–0.3423	0.3411–0.3418
		2.2/134 Diesel	①	①	②	③	0.0015–0.0046	0.0020–0.0051	0.3150	0.3150
		2.3/140	45	44	149 @ 1.12	1.53–1.59	0.0010–0.0027	0.0015–0.0032	0.3416–0.3423	0.3411–0.3418
1984	Bronco II	2.8/173	45	44	143 @ 1.22	1.58–1.61	0.0008–0.0025	0.0018–0.0035	0.3159–0.3167	0.3149–0.3156
	Ranger	2.0/122	45	44	149 @ 1.12	1.49–1.55	0.0010–0.0027	0.0015–0.0032	0.3416–0.3423	0.3411–0.3418
		2.2/134 Diesel	①	①	②	③	0.0015–0.0046	0.0020–0.0051	0.3150	0.3150
		2.3/140	45	44	149 @ 1.12	1.53–1.59	0.0010–0.0027	0.0015–0.0032	0.3416–0.3423	0.3411–0.3418
		2.8/173	45	44	143 @ 1.22	1.58–1.61	0.0008–0.0025	0.0018–0.0035	0.3159–0.3167	0.3149–0.3156
1985	Bronco II	2.8/173	45	44	143 @ 1.22	1.58–1.61	0.0008–0.0025	0.0018–0.0035	0.3159–0.3167	0.3149–0.3156
	Ranger	2.0/122	45	44	149 @ 1.12	1.49–1.55	0.0010–0.0027	0.0015–0.0032	0.3416–0.3423	0.3411–0.3418
		2.3/140	45	44	149 @ 1.12	1.53–1.59	0.0010–0.0027	0.0015–0.0032	0.3416–0.3423	0.3411–0.3418
		2.3/140 Diesel	45	44	61 @ 1.591	1.591	0.0012–0.0024	0.0020–0.0035	0.3150	0.3150
		2.8/173	45	44	143 @ 1.22	1.58–1.61	0.0008–0.0025	0.0018–0.0035	0.3159–0.3167	0.3149–0.3156
1986	Bronco II	2.9/177	45	44	143 @ 1.22	1.58–1.61	0.0008–0.0025	0.0018–0.0035	0.3159–0.3167	0.3149–0.3156
	Ranger	2.0/122	45	44	149 @ 1.12	1.49–1.55	0.0010–0.0027	0.0015–0.0032	0.3416–0.3423	0.3411–0.3418
		2.3/140	45	44	149 @ 1.12	1.53–1.59	0.0010–0.0027	0.0015–0.0032	0.3416–0.3423	0.3411–0.3418
		2.3/140 Diesel	45	44	61 @ 1.591	1.591	0.0012–0.0024	0.0020–0.0035	0.3150	0.3150
		2.9/177	45	44	143 @ 1.22	1.58–1.61	0.0008–0.0025	0.0018–0.0035	0.3159–0.3167	0.3149–0.3156
1987	Bronco II	2.9/177	45	44	143 @ 1.22	1.58–1.61	0.0008–0.0025	0.0018–0.0035	0.3159–0.3167	0.3149–0.3156
	Ranger	2.0/122	45	44	149 @ 1.12	1.49–1.55	0.0010–0.0027	0.0015–0.0032	0.3416–0.3423	0.3411–0.3418
		2.3/140	45	44	149 @ 1.12	1.53–1.59	0.0010–0.0027	0.0015–0.0032	0.3416–0.3423	0.3411–0.3418
		2.3/140 Diesel	45	44	61 @ 1.591	1.591	0.0012–0.0024	0.0020–0.0035	0.3150	0.3150
		2.9/177	45	44	143 @ 1.22	1.58–1.61	0.0008–0.0025	0.0018–0.0035	0.3159–0.3167	0.3149–0.3156

VALVE SPECIFICATIONS

Year	Model	Engine Displacement Liter/CID	Seat Angle (deg)	Face Angle (deg)	Spring Test Pressure (lbs @ in.)	Spring Installed Height (in.)	Stem-to-Guide Clearance (in.) Intake	Exhaust	Stem Diameter (in.) Intake	Exhaust
1988	Bronco II	2.9/177	45	44	143 @ 1.22	1.58–1.61	0.0008–0.0025	0.0018–0.0035	0.3159–0.3167	0.3149–0.3156
	Ranger	2.0/122	45	44	149 @ 1.12	1.49–1.55	0.0010–0.0027	0.0015–0.0032	0.3416–0.3423	0.3411–0.3418
		2.3/140	45	44	149 @ 1.12	1.53–1.59	0.0010–0.0027	0.0015–0.0032	0.3416–0.3423	0.3411–0.3418
		2.9/177	45	44	143 @ 1.22	1.58–1.61	0.0008–0.0025	0.0018–0.0035	0.3159–0.3167	0.3149–0.3156
1989	Bronco II	2.9/177	45	44	143 @ 1.22	1.58–1.61	0.0008–0.0025	0.0018–0.0035	0.3159–0.3167	0.3149–0.3156
	Ranger	2.3/140	45	44	149 @ 1.12	1.49–1.55	0.0010–0.0027	0.0015–0.0032	0.3416–0.3423	0.3411–0.3418
		2.9/177	45	44	143 @ 1.22	1.58–1.61	0.0008–0.0025	0.0018–0.0035	0.3159–0.3167	0.3149–0.3156
1990	Bronco II	2.9/177	45	44	143 @ 1.22	1.58–1.61	0.0008–0.0025	0.0018–0.0035	0.3159–0.3167	0.3149–0.3156
	Ranger	2.3/140	45	44	149 @ 1.12	1.49–1.55	0.0010–0.0027	0.0015–0.0032	0.3416–0.3423	0.3411–0.3418
		2.9/177	45	44	143 @ 1.22	1.58–1.61	0.0008–0.0025	0.0018–0.0035	0.3159–0.3167	0.3149–0.3156
		4.0/241	45	44	138 @ 1.22	1.58–1.61	0.0008–0.0025	0.0018–0.0035	0.3159–0.3167	0.3149–0.3156
1991	Ranger	2.3/140	45	44	149 @ 1.12	1.49–1.55	0.0010–0.0027	0.0015–0.0032	0.3416–0.3423	0.3411–0.3418
		2.9/177	45	44	143 @ 1.22	1.58–1.61	0.0008–0.0025	0.0018–0.0035	0.3159–0.3167	0.3149–0.3156
		3.0/183	45	44	180 @ 1.16	1.85	0.0010–0.0027	0.0015–0.0032	0.3134–0.3126	0.3129–0.3121
		4.0/241	45	44	138 @ 1.22	1.58–1.61	0.0008–0.0025	0.0018–0.0035	0.3159–0.3167	0.3149–0.3156
	Explorer	4.0/241	45	44	138 @ 1.22	1.58–1.61	0.0008–0.0025	0.0018–0.0035	0.3159–0.3167	0.3149–0.3156

① Intake: 45 degrees Exhaust: 30 degrees
② Outer: 40 @ 1.59 in.
   Inner: 28 @ 1.49 in.
③ Outer: 1.587 in.
   Inner: 1.488 in.

Checking Engine Compression

A noticeable lack of engine power, excessive oil consumption and/or poor fuel mileage measured over an extended period are all indicators of internal engine war. Worn piston rings, scored or worn cylinder bores, blown head gaskets, sticking or burnt valves and worn valve seats are all possible culprits here. A check of each cylinder's compression will help you locate the problems.

As mentioned earlier, a screw-in type compression gauge is more accurate that the type you simply hold against the spark plug hole, although it takes slightly longer to use. It's worth it to obtain a more accurate reading. Follow the procedures below.

Gasoline Engines

1. Warm up the engine to normal operating temperature.

2. Remove all the spark plugs.

3. Disconnect the high tension lead from the ignition coil.

4. On fully open the throttle either by operating the carburetor throttle linkage by hand or by having an assistant floor the accelerator pedal.

5. Screw the compression gauge into the no.1 spark plug hole until the fitting is snug.

WARNING: *Be careful not to crossthread the plug hole. On aluminum cylinder heads use extra care, as the threads in these heads are easily ruined.*

6. Ask an assistant to depress the accelerator pedal fully on both carbureted and fuel injected vehicles. Then, while you read the compression gauge, ask the assistant to crank the engine two or three times in short bursts using the ignition switch.

7. Read the compression gauge at the end of each series of cranks, and record the highest

CRANKSHAFT AND CONNECTING ROD SPECIFICATIONS

All measurements are given in inches.

Year	Model	Engine Displacement Liter/CID	Crankshaft				Connecting Rod		
			Main Brg Journal Dia.	Main Brg Oil Clearance	Shaft End-play	Thrust on No.	Journal Diameter	Oil Clearance	Side Clearance
1983	Ranger	2.0/122	2.3982–2.3990	0.0008–0.0015	0.004–0.008	3	2.0462–2.0472	0.0008–0.0015	0.0035–0.0105
		2.2/134 Diesel	2.5591	0.0016–0.0036	0.0055–0.0154	3	2.0866	0.0014–0.0030	0.0094–0.0134
		2.3/140	2.3982–2.3990	0.0008–0.0015	0.004–0.008	3	2.0462–2.0472	0.0008–0.0015	0.0035–0.0105
1984	Bronco II	2.8/173	2.2433–2.2441	0.0008–0.0015	0.004–0.008	3	2.1252–2.1260	0.0006–0.0016	0.004–0.011
	Ranger	2.0/122	2.3982–2.3990	0.0008–0.0015	0.004–0.008	3	2.0462–2.0472	0.0008–0.0015	0.0035–0.0105
		2.2/134 Diesel	2.5591	0.0016–0.0036	0.0055–0.0154	3	2.0866	0.0014–0.0030	0.0094–0.0134
		2.3/140	2.3982–2.3990	0.0008–0.0015	0.004–0.008	3	2.0462–2.0472	0.0008–0.0015	0.0035–0.0105
		2.8/173	2.2433–2.2441	0.0008–0.0015	0.004–0.008	3	2.1252–2.1260	0.0006–0.0016	0.004–0.011
1985	Bronco II	2.8/173	2.2433–2.2441	0.0008–0.0015	0.004–0.008	3	2.1252–2.1260	0.0006–0.0016	0.004–0.011
	Ranger	2.0/122	2.3982–2.3990	0.0008–0.0015	0.004–0.008	3	2.0462–2.0472	0.0008–0.0015	0.0035–0.0105
		2.2/134 Diesel	2.5591	0.0016–0.0036	0.0055–0.0154	3	2.0866	0.0014–0.0030	0.0094–0.0134
		2.3/140	2.3982–2.3990	0.0008–0.0015	0.004–0.008	3	2.0462–2.0472	0.0008–0.0015	0.0035–0.0105
		2.8/173	2.2433–2.2441	0.0008–0.0015	0.004–0.008	3	2.1252–2.1260	0.0006–0.0016	0.004–0.011
1986	Bronco II	2.9/177	2.2433–2.2441	0.0008–0.0015	0.004–0.008	3	2.1252–2.1260	0.0006–0.0016	0.004 0.011
	Ranger	2.0/122	2.3982–2.3990	0.0008–0.0015	0.004–0.008	3	2.0462–2.0472	0.0008–0.0015	0.0035–0.0105
		2.3/140	2.3982–2.3990	0.0008–0.0015	0.004–0.008	3	2.0462–2.0472	0.0008–0.0015	0.0035–0.0105
		2.3/140 Diesel	2.5980	0.0008–0.0015	0.0008–0.0020	3	2.087	0.0008–0.0024	0.004–0.010
		2.9/177	2.2433–2.2441	0.0008–0.0015	0.004–0.008	3	2.1252–2.1260	0.0006–0.0016	0.004–0.011
1987	Bronco II	2.9/177	2.2433–2.2441	0.0008–0.0015	0.004–0.008	3	2.1252–2.1260	0.0006–0.0016	0.004–0.011
	Ranger	2.0/122	2.3982–2.3990	0.0008–0.0015	0.004–0.008	3	2.0462–2.0472	0.0008–0.0015	0.0035–0.0105
		2.3/140	2.3982–2.3990	0.0008–0.0015	0.004–0.008	3	2.0462–2.0472	0.0008–0.0015	0.0035–0.0105
		2.3/140 Diesel	2.5980	0.0008–0.0015	0.0008–0.0020	3	2.087	0.0008–0.0024	0.004–0.010
		2.9/177	2.2433–2.2441	0.0008–0.0015	0.004–0.008	3	2.1252–2.1260	0.0006–0.0016	0.004–0.011
1988	Bronco II	2.9/177	2.2433–2.2441	0.0008–0.0015	0.004–0.008	3	2.1252–2.1260	0.0006–0.0016	0.004–0.011
	Ranger	2.0/122	2.3982–2.3990	0.0008–0.0015	0.004–0.008	3	2.0462–2.0472	0.0008–0.0015	0.0035–0.0105
		2.3/140	2.3982–2.3990	0.0008–0.0015	0.004–0.008	3	2.0462–2.0472	0.0008–0.0015	0.0035–0.0105
		2.9/177	2.2433–2.2441	0.0008–0.0015	0.004–0.008	3	2.1252–2.1260	0.0006–0.0016	0.004–0.011

CRANKSHAFT AND CONNECTING ROD SPECIFICATIONS

All measurements are given in inches.

Year	Model	Engine Displacement Liter/CID	Crankshaft				Connecting Rod		
			Main Brg Journal Dia.	Main Brg Oil Clearance	Shaft End-play	Thrust on No.	Journal Diameter	Oil Clearance	Side Clearance
1989	Bronco II	2.9/177	2.2433–2.2441	0.0008–0.0015	0.004–0.008	3	2.1252–2.1260	0.0006–0.0016	0.004–0.011
	Ranger	2.3/140	2.3982–2.3990	0.0008–0.0015	0.004–0.008	3	2.0462–2.0472	0.0008–0.0015	0.0035–0.0105
		2.9/177	2.2433–2.2441	0.0008–0.0015	0.004–0.008	3	2.1252–8.1260	0.0006–0.0016	0.004–0.011
1990	Bronco II	2.9/177	2.2433–2.2441	0.0008–0.0015	0.004–0.008	3	2.1252–2.1260	0.0006–0.0016	0.004–0.011
	Ranger	2.3/140	2.3982–2.3990	0.0008–0.0015	0.004–0.008	3	2.0462–2.0472	0.0008–0.0015	0.0035–0.0105
		2.9/177	2.2433–2.2441	0.0008–0.0015	0.004–0.008	3	2.1252–2.1260	0.0006–0.0016	0.004–0.011
		4.0/241	2.2433–2.2441	0.0008–0.0015	0.0160–0.0126	—	2.1252–2.1260	0.0003–0.0024	0.0002–0.0025
1991	Ranger	2.3/140	2.3982–2.3990	0.0008–0.0015	0.004–0.008	3	2.0462–2.0472	0.0008–0.0015	0.0035–0.0105
		2.9/177	2.2433–2.2441	0.0008–0.0015	0.004–0.008	3	2.1252–2.1260	0.0006–0.0016	0.004–0.011
		3.0/183	2.5190–2.5198	0.0010–0.0014	0.004–0.008	3	2.1253–2.1261	0.0010–0.0014	0.0060–0.0140
		4.0/241	2.2433–2.2441	0.0008–0.0015	0.0160–0.0126	—	2.1252–2.1260	0.0003–0.0024	0.0002–0.0025
	Explorer	4.0/241	2.2433–2.2441	0.0008–0.0015	0.0160–0.0126	—	2.1252–2.1260	0.0003–0.0024	0.0002–0.0025

of these readings. Repeat this procedure for each of the engine's cylinders. Compare the highest reading of each cylinder to the compression pressure specification in the Tune-Up Specifications chart. The specs in this chart are maximum values.

A cylinder's compression pressure is usually acceptable if it is not less than 80% of maximum. The difference between any two cylinders should be no more than 12–14 pounds.

8. If a cylinder is unusually low, pour a tablespoon of clean engine oil into the cylinder through the spark plug hole and repeat the compression test. If engine compression comes up after adding the oil, it appears that the cylinder's piston rings or bore are damaged or worn.

If the pressure remains low, the valves may not be seating properly (a valve job is needed), or the head gasket may be blown near that cylinder. If compression in any two adjacent cylinders is low, and if the addition of oil doesn't help the compression, there is leakage past the head gasket. Oil and coolant water in the combustion chamber can result from this problem. There may be evidence of water droplets on the engine dipstick when a head gasket has blown.

Diesel Engines

Checking cylinder compression on diesel engines is basically the same procedure as on gasoline engines except for the following:

1. A special compression gauge adaptor suit-

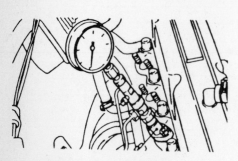

Diesel engines require a special compression gauge adaptor

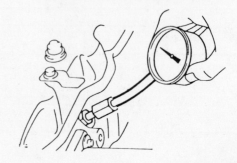

The screw-in type compression gauge is more accurate

GENERAL ENGINE SPECIFICATIONS

Year	Model	Engine Displacement Liter/CID	Net Horsepower (@ rpm)	Net Torque (@ rpm)	Bore × Stroke (in.)	Compression Ratio	Oil Pressure (@ 2000 rpm)
1983	Ranger	2.0/122	73 @ 4000	107 @ 2400	3.52 × 3.13	9.0:1	40–60
		2.2/134 Diesel	59 @ 4000	90 @ 2500	3.50 × 3.50	22:1	51③
		2.3/140	79 @ 3800①	124 @ 2200②	3.78 × 3.13	9.0:1	40–60
1984	Bronco II	2.8/173	115 @ 4600	150 @ 2600	3.66 × 2.70	8.7:1	40–60
	Ranger	2.0/122	73 @ 4000	107 @ 2400	3.52 × 3.13	9.0:1	40–60
		2.2/134 Diesel	59 @ 4000	90 @ 2500	3.50 × 3.50	22:1	51③
		2.3/140	79 @ 3800①	124 @ 2200②	3.78 × 3.13	9.0:1	40–60
		2.8/173	115 @ 4600	150 @ 2600	3.66 × 2.70	8.7:1	40–60
1985	Bronco II	2.8/173	115 @ 4600	150 @ 2600	3.66 × 2.70	8.7:1	40–60
	Ranger	2.0/122	73 @ 4000	107 @ 2400	3.52 × 3.13	9.0:1	40–60
		2.3/140	79 @ 3800①	124 @ 2200②	3.78 × 3.13	9.0:1	40–60
		2.3/140 Diesel	86 @ 4200	134 @ 2000	3.59 × 3.54	21:1	11.4④
		2.8/173	115 @ 4600	150 @ 2600	3.66 × 2.70	8.7:1	40–60
1986	Bronco II	2.9/177	140 @ 4600	170 @ 2600	3.66 × 2.83	9.0:1	40–60
	Ranger	2.0/122	73 @ 4000	107 @ 2400	3.52 × 3.13	9.0:1	40–60
		2.3/140	90 @ 4000	130 @ 1800	3.78 × 3.13	9.0:1	40–60
		2.3/140 Diesel	86 @ 4200	134 @ 2000	3.59 × 3.54	21:1	11.4④
		2.9/177	140 @ 4600	170 @ 2600	3.66 × 2.83	9.0:1	40–60
1987	Bronco II	2.9/177	140 @ 4600	170 @ 2600	3.66 × 2.83	9.0:1	40–60
	Ranger	2.0/122	80 @ 4200	106 @ 2600	3.52 × 3.13	9.0:1	40–60
		2.3/140	90 @ 4000	134 @ 2000	3.78 × 3.13	9.0:1	40–60
		2.3/140 Diesel	86 @ 4200	134 @ 2000	3.59 × 3.54	21:1	11.4④
		2.9/177	140 @ 4600	170 @ 2600	3.66 × 2.83	9.0:1	40–60
1988	Bronco II	2.9/177	140 @ 4600	170 @ 2600	3.66 × 2.83	9.0:1	40–60
	Ranger	2.0/122	80 @ 4200	106 @ 2600	3.52 × 3.13	9.0:1	40–60
		2.3/140	90 @ 4000	134 @ 2000	3.78 × 3.13	9.0:1	40–60
		2.9/177	140 @ 4600	170 @ 2600	3.66 × 2.83	9.0:1	40–60
1989	Bronco II	2.9/177	140 @ 4800	170 @ 2600	3.66 × 2.83	9.0:1	40–60
	Ranger	2.3/140	100 @ 4600	133 @ 2600	3.78 × 3.13	9.2:1	40–60
		2.9/177	140 @ 4600	170 @ 2600	3.66 × 2.83	9.0:1	40–60
1990	Bronco II	2.9/177	140 @ 4600	170 @ 2600	3.66 × 2.83	9.0:1	40–60
	Ranger	2.3/140	100 @ 4600	133 @ 2600	3.78 × 3.13	9.2:1	40–60
		2.9/177	140 @ 4600	170 @ 2600	3.66 × 2.83	9.0:1	40–60
		4.0/241	155 @ 4200	220 @ 2400	3.94 × 3.31		40–60
1991	Ranger	2.3/140	100 @ 4600	133 @ 2600	3.78 × 3.13	9.2:1	40–60
		2.9/177	140 @ 4600	170 @ 2600	3.66 × 2.83	9.0:1	40–60
		3.0/183	145 @ 4800	165 @ 3600	3.50 × 3.14	9.3:1	40–60
		4.0/241	155 @ 4200	220 @ 2400	3.94 × 3.31	9.0:1	40–60
	Explorer	4.0/241	155 @ 4200	220 @ 2400	3.94 × 3.31	9.0:1	40–60

① Auto. trans.: 82 @ 4200
② Auto. trans.: 126 @ 2200
③ @ 3600 rpm
④ @ Idle

PISTON AND RING SPECIFICATIONS

All measurements are given in inches.

Year	Model	Engine Displacement Liter/CID	Piston to Bore Clearance	Ring Side Clearance			Ring Gap		
				Top Compression	Bottom Compression	Oil Control	Top Compression	Bottom Compression	Oil Control
1983	Ranger	2.0/122	0.0014–0.0022	0.0020–0.0040	0.0020–0.0040	Snug	0.010–0.020	0.010–0.020	0.015–0.055
		2.2/134 Diesel	0.0021–0.0031	0.0020–0.0035	0.0016–0.0031	.0012–.0028	0.0157–0.0217	0.0118–0.0157	0.0138–0.0217
		2.3/140	0.0014–0.0022	0.0020–0.0040	0.0020–0.0040	Snug	0.010–0.020	0.010–0.020	0.015–0.055
1984	Bronco II	2.8/173	0.0011–0.0019	0.0020–0.0033	0.0020–0.0033	Snug	0.015–0.023	0.015–0.023	0.015–0.023
	Ranger	2.0/122	0.0014–0.0022	0.0020–0.0040	0.0020–0.0040	Snug	0.010–0.020	0.010–0.020	0.015–0.055
		2.2/134 Diesel	0.0021–0.0031	0.0020–0.0035	0.0016–0.0031	.0012–.0028	0.0157–0.0217	0.0118–0.0157	0.0138–0.0217
		2.3/140	0.0014–0.0022	0.0020–0.0040	0.0020–0.0040	Snug	0.010–0.020	0.010–0.020	0.015–0.055
		2.8/173	0.0011–0.0019	0.0020–0.0033	0.0020–0.0033	Snug	0.015–0.023	0.015–0.023	0.015–0.023
1985	Bronco II	2.8/173	0.0011–0.0019	0.0020–0.0033	0.0020–0.0033	Snug	0.015–0.023	0.015–0.023	0.015–0.023
	Ranger	2.0/122	0.0014–0.0022	0.0020–0.0040	0.0020–0.0040	Snug	0.010–0.020	0.010–0.020	0.015–0.055
		2.3/140	0.0014–0.0022	0.0020–0.0040	0.0020–0.0040	Snug	0.010–0.020	0.010–0.020	0.015–0.055
		2.3/140 Diesel	0.0021–0.0031	0.0020–0.0035	0.0016–0.0031	.0012–.0028	0.0157–0.0217	0.0118–0.0157	0.0138–0.0217
		2.8/173	0.0011–0.0019	0.0020–0.0033	0.0020–0.0033	Snug	0.015–0.023	0.015–0.023	0.015–0.023
1986	Bronco II	2.9/177	0.0011–0.0019	0.0020–0.0033	0.0020–0.0033	Snug	0.015–0.023	0.015–0.023	0.015–0.023
	Ranger	2.0/122	0.0014–0.0022	0.0020–0.0040	0.0020–0.0040	Snug	0.010–0.020	0.010–0.020	0.015–0.055
		2.2/134 Diesel	0.0021–0.0031	0.0020–0.0035	0.0016–0.0031	.0012–.0028	0.0157–0.0217	0.0118–0.0157	0.0138–0.0217
		2.3/140	0.0014–0.0022	0.0020–0.0040	0.0020–0.0040	Snug	0.010–0.020	0.010–0.020	0.015–0.055
		2.9/177	0.0011–0.0019	0.0020–0.0033	0.0020–0.0033	Snug	0.015–0.023	0.015–0.023	0.015–0.023
1987	Bronco II	2.9/177	0.0011–0.0019	0.0020–0.0033	0.0020–0.0033	Snug	0.015–0.023	0.015–0.023	0.015–0.023
	Ranger	2.0/122	0.0014–0.0022	0.0020–0.0040	0.0020–0.0040	Snug	0.010–0.020	0.010–0.020	0.015–0.055
		2.3/140	0.0014–0.0022	0.0020–0.0040	0.0002–0.0040	Snug	0.010–0.020	0.010–0.020	0.015–0.055
		2.3/140 Diesel	0.0021–0.0031	0.0020–0.0035	0.0016–0.0031	.0012–.0028	0.0157–0.0217	0.0118–0.0157	0.0138–0.0217
		2.9/177	0.0011–0.0019	0.0020–0.0033	0.0020–0.0033	Snug	0.015–0.023	0.015–0.023	0.015–0.023

PISTON AND RING SPECIFICATIONS

All measurements are given in inches.

Year	Model	Engine Displacement Liter/CID	Piston to Bore Clearance	Ring Side Clearance			Ring Gap		
				Top Compression	Bottom Compression	Oil Control	Top Compression	Bottom Compression	Oil Control
1988	Bronco II	2.9/177	0.0011–0.0019	0.0020–0.0033	0.0020–0.0033	Snug	0.015–0.023	0.015–0.023	0.015–0.023
	Ranger	2.0/122	0.0014–0.0022	0.0020–0.0040	0.0020–0.0040	Snug	0.010–0.020	0.010–0.020	0.015–0.055
		2.3/140	0.0014–0.0022	0.0020–0.0040	0.0020–0.0040	Snug	0.010–0.020	0.010–0.020	0.015–0.055
		2.9/177	0.0011–0.0019	0.0020–0.0033	0.0020–0.0033	Snug	0.015–0.023	0.015–0.023	0.015–0.023
1989	Bronco II	2.9/177	0.0011–0.0019	0.0020–0.0033	0.0020–0.0033	Snug	0.015–0.023	0.015–0.023	0.015–0.055
	Ranger	2.3/140	0.0014–0.0022	0.0020–0.0040	0.0020–0.0040	Snug	0.010–0.020	0.010–0.020	0.010–0.049
		2.9/177	0.0011–0.0019	0.0020–0.0033	0.0020–0.0033	Snug	0.015–0.023	0.015–0.023	0.015–0.055
1990	Bronco II	2.9/177	0.0011–0.0019	0.0020–0.0033	0.0020–0.0033	Snug	0.015–0.023	0.015–0.023	0.015–0.055
	Ranger	2.3/140	0.0014–0.0022	0.0020–0.0040	0.0020–0.0040	Snug	0.010–0.020	0.010–0.020	0.010–0.049
		2.9/177	0.0011–0.0019	0.0020–0.0033	0.0020–0.0033	Snug	0.015–0.023	0.015–0.023	0.015–0.055
		4.0/241	0.0008–0.0019	0.0020–0.0033	0.0020–0.0033	Snug	0.015–0.023	0.015–0.023	0.015–0.055
1991	Ranger	2.3/140	0.0014–0.0022	0.0020–0.0040	0.0020–0.0040	Snug	0.010–0.020	0.010–0.020	0.010–0.049
		2.9/177	0.0011–0.0019	0.0020–0.0033	0.0020–0.0033	Snug	0.015–0.023	0.015–0.023	0.015–0.055
		3.0/183	0.0012–0.0023	0.0016–0.0037	0.0016–0.0037	Snug	0.010–0.020	0.010–0.020	0.010–0.049
	Explorer	4.0/241	0.0008–0.0019	0.0020–0.0033	0.0020–0.0033	Snug	0.015–0.023	0.015–0.023	0.015–0.055

able for diesel engines (because these engines have much greater compression pressures) must be used.

2. Remove the injector tubes and remove the injectors from each cylinder.

WARNING: *Do not forget to remove the washer underneath each injector. Otherwise, it may get lost when the engine is cranked.*

3. When fitting the compression gauge adaptor to the cylinder head, make sure the bleeder of the gauge (if equipped) is closed.

4. When reinstalling the injector assemblies, install new washers underneath each injector.

Engine

REMOVAL AND INSTALLATION

2.0L, 2.3L Engines

1. Raise the hood and install protective fender covers. Drain the coolant from the radiator. On the carbureted engines remove the air cleaner and duct assembly. On the 2.3L EFI engine, disconnect the air cleaner outlet tube at the throttle body, idle speed control hose and the heat riser tube.

CAUTION: *When draining the coolant, keep in mind that cats and dogs are attracted by the ethylene glycol antifreeze, and are quite likely to drink any that is left in an uncovered container or in puddles on the ground. This will prove fatal in sufficient quantity. Always drain the coolant into a sealable container. Coolant should be reused unless it is contaminated or several years old.*

2. Disconnect the battery ground cable at the engine and disconnect the battery positive cable at the battery and set aside.

3. Mark the location of the hood hinges and remove the hood.

4. Disconnect the upper and lower radiator hoses from the engine. Remove the radiator shroud screws. Remove the radiator upper supports.

5. Remove engine fan and shroud assembly. Then remove the radiator. Remove the oil fill cap.

6. Disconnect the coil primary wire at the coil. Disconnect the oil pressure and the water

TORQUE SPECIFICATIONS
All readings in ft. lbs.

Year	Model	Engine Displacement Liter/CID	Cylinder Head Bolts	Main Bearing Bolts	Rod Bearing Bolts	Crankshaft Pulley Bolts	Flywheel to Crankshaft Bolts	Manifold	
								Intake	Exhaust
1983	Ranger	2.0/122	80–90[1]	80–90[1]	30–36[2]	100–120	56–64	14–21[3]	16–23[4]
		2.2/134 Diesel	80–85	80–85	50–54	253–289	95–137	12–17	17–20[7]
		2.3/140	80–90[1]	80–90[1]	30–36[2]	100–120	56–64	14–21[3]	16–23[4]
1984	Bronco II	2.8/173	70–85[5]	65–75	19–24	85–96	47–52	15–18[6]	20–30
	Ranger	2.0/122	80–90[1]	80–90[1]	30–36[2]	100–120	56–64	14–21[3]	16–23[4]
		2.2/134 Diesel	80–85	80–85	50–54	253–289	95–137	12–17	17–20[7]
		2.3/140	80–90[1]	80–90[1]	30–36[2]	100–120	56–64	14–21[3]	16–23[4]
		2.8/173	70–85[5]	65–75	19–24	85–96	47–52	15–18[6]	20–30
1985	Bronco II	2.8/173	70–85[5]	65–75	19–24	85–96	47–52	15–18[6]	20–30
	Ranger	2.0/122	80–90[1]	80–90[1]	30–36[2]	100–120	56–64	14–21[3]	16–23[4]
		2.3/140	80–90[1]	80–90[1]	30–36[2]	100–120	56–64	14–21[3]	16–23[4]
		2.3/140 Diesel	76–83[8]	55–61	33–34	123–137	94–101	11–14	11–14
		2.8/173	70–85[5]	65–75	19–24	85–96	47–52	15–18[6]	20–30
1986	Bronco II	2.9/177	[9]	65–75	19–24	85–96	47–52	15–18[6]	20–30
	Ranger	2.0/122	80–90[1]	80–90[1]	30–36[2]	100–120	56–64	14–21[3]	16–23[4]
		2.3/140	80–90[1]	80–90[1]	30–36[2]	100–120	56–64	14–21[3]	16–23[4]
		2.3/140 Diesel	76–83[8]	55–61	33–34	123–137	94–101	11–14	11–14
		2.9/177	[9]	65–75	19–24	85–96	47–52	15–18[6]	20–30
1987	Bronco II	2.9/177	[9]	65–75	19–24	85–96	47–52	15–18[6]	20–30
	Ranger	2.0/122	80–90[1]	80–90[1]	30–36[2]	100–120	56–64	14–21[3]	16–23[4]
		2.3/140	80–90[1]	80–90[1]	30–36[2]	100–120	56–64	14–21[3]	16–23[4]
		2.3/140 Diesel	76–83[8]	55–61	33–34	123–137	94–101	11–14	11–14
		2.9/177	[9]	65–75	19–24	85–96	47–52	15–18[6]	20–30
1988	Bronco II	2.9/177	[9]	65–75	19–24	85–96	47–52	15–18[6]	20–30
	Ranger	2.0/122	80–90[1]	80–90[1]	30–36[2]	100–120	56–64	14–21[3]	16–23[4]
		2.3/140	80–90[1]	80–90[1]	30–36[2]	100–120	56–64	14–21[3]	16–23[4]
		2.9/177	[9]	65–75	19–24	85–96	47–52	15–18[6]	20–30
1989	Bronco II	2.9/177	[9]	65–75	19–24	85–96	47–52	15–18[6]	20–30
	Ranger	2.3/140	80–90[1]	75–85[10]	30–36[2]	103–133	56–64	14–21[3]	16–23[4]
		2.9/177	[9]	65–75	19–24	85–96	47–52	15–18[6]	20–30
1990	Bronco II	2.9/177	[9]	65–75	19–24	85–96	47–52	15–18[6]	20–30
	Ranger	2.3/140	80–90[1]	75–85[10]	30–36[2]	103–133	56–64	14–21[3]	20–30
		2.9/177	[9]	65–75	19–24	85–96	47–52	15–18[6]	20–30
		4.0/241	[11]	66–77	18–24	N/A	N/A	[11]	20

temperature sending unit wires from the sending units.

7. Disconnect the alternator wire from the alternator, the starter cable from the starter and the accelerator cable from the carburetor. If so equipped, disconnect the transmission kickdown rod.

8. If so equipped, remove the A/C compressor from the mounting bracket and position it out of the way, leaving the refrigerant lines attached.

9. Disconnect the power brake vacuum hose. Disconnect the heater hoses from the engine.

10. On the carbureted engines, disconnect the fuel line from the fuel pump. On the 2.3L EFI engine depressurize the fuel system, then disconnect the 2 push connect fittings at the engine fuel rail.

11. Remove the engine mount nuts. Raise the vehicle and safely support on jackstands.

TORQUE SPECIFICATIONS

All readings in ft. lbs.

Year	Model	Engine Displacement Liter/CID	Cylinder Head Bolts	Main Bearing Bolts	Rod Bearing Bolts	Crankshaft Pulley Bolts	Flywheel to Crankshaft Bolts	Manifold Intake	Manifold Exhaust
1991	Ranger	2.3/140	80–90 ①	75–85 ⑩	30–36 ②	103–133	56–64	14–21 ③	20–30
		2.9/177	⑨	65–75	19–24	85–96	47–52	15–18 ⑥	20–30
		3.0/183	68 ⑫	60	26	107	59	18 ⑫	19
		4.0/241	⑪	66–77	18–24	N/A	N/A	⑪	20
	Explorer	4.0/241	⑪	66–77	18–24	N/A	N/A	⑪	20

① Torque in two steps: 1st 50–60 ft. lbs.,
2nd 80–90 ft. lbs.
② Torque in two steps: 1st 25–30 ft. lbs.,
2nd 30–36 ft. lbs.
③ Torque in two steps: 1st 5–7 ft. lbs.,
2nd 14–21 ft. lbs.
④ Torque in two steps: 1st 5–7 ft. lbs.,
2nd 16–23 ft. lbs.
⑤ Torque in three steps: 1st 29–40 ft. lbs.,
2nd 40–51 ft. lbs., 3rd 70–85 ft. lbs.
⑥ Torque in five steps: 1st Hand start and snug
nuts, 2nd 3–6 ft. lbs., 3rd 6–11 ft. lbs.,
4th 11–15 ft. lbs., 5th 15–18 ft. lbs.,
Repeat Step 5 after warm up.

⑦ Retorque after warm up.
⑧ Cold, 84–90 ft. lbs. Hot
⑨ Torque in three steps: 1st 22 ft. lbs.,
2nd 51–55 ft. lbs., 3rd Turn 90 degrees
⑩ Torque in 2 steps:
Step 1: 50–60 ft. lbs.
Step 2: 75–85 ft. lbs.
⑪ Refer to text for procedure
⑫ Torque in 2 steps
N/A—Not available at time of publication
NOTE: Always refer to text for sequence before starting torque procedure.

Drain the engine oil from the crankcase. Remove the starter motor.

> CAUTION: *The EPA warns that prolonged contact with used engine oil may cause a number of skin disorders, including cancer! You should make every effort to minimize your exposure to used engine oil. Protective gloves should be worn when changing the oil. Wash your hands and any other exposed skin areas as soon as possible after exposure to used engine oil. Soap and water, or waterless hand cleaner should be used.*

12. Disconnect the muffler exhaust inlet pipe at the exhaust manifold.

13. Remove the dust cover (manual transmission) or converter inspection plate (automatic transmission).

14. On vehicles with a manual transmission, remove the flywheel housing cover lower attaching bolts. On vehicles with automatic transmissions, remove the converter-to-flywheel bolts, then remove the converter housing lower attaching bolts.

15. Remove clutch slave cylinder (manual transmission). Lower the vehicle.

16. Support the transmission and flywheel or converter housing with a jack.

17. Remove the flywheel housing or converter housing upper attaching bolts.

18. Attach the engine lifting hooks to the existing lifting brackets. Carefully, so as not to damage any components, lift the engine out of the vehicle.

To install the engine:

19. If clutch was removed, reinstall. Carefully lower the engine into the engine compartment. On a vehicle with automatic transmission, start the converter pilot into the crankshaft. On a vehicle with a manual transmission, start the transmission main drive gear into the clutch disc. It may be necessary to adjust the position of the transmission in relation to the engine if the input shaft will not enter the clutch disc. If the engine hangs up after the shaft enters, turn the crankshaft in the clockwise direction slowly (transmission in gear), until the shaft splines mesh with the clutch disc splines.

20. Install the flywheel or converter housing upper attaching bolts. Remove the engine lifting hooks from the lifting brackets.

21. Remove the jack from under the transmission. Raise the vehicle and safely support on jackstands.

22. On a vehicle with a manual transmission, install the flywheel lower housing bolts and tighten to specifications. On a vehicle with an automatic transmission, attach the converter to the flywheel bolts and tighten to specifications. Install the converter housing-to-engine bolts and tighten to specifications.

23. Install clutch slave cylinder.

24. Install the dust cover (manual transmission). Correct the exhaust inlet pipe to the exhaust manifold.

25. Install the starter motor and connect the starter cables.

26. Lower the vehicle. Install the engine mounting nuts and tighten to 65–85 ft. lbs.

27. Connect the heater hoses to the engine. On the carbureted engines, connect the fuel line to the fuel pump. On the 2.3L EFI engine connect the 2 push connect fittings at the

engine fuel rail. Connect the power brake vacuum hose.

28. Connect the alternator wire to the alternator, connect the accelerator cable to the carburetor. If so equipped, connect the transmission kickdown rod. If so equipped, install the A/C compressor to the mounting bracket.

29. Connect the coil primary wire at the coil.

Connect the oil pressure and water temperature sending unit wires. Install oil fill cap.

30. Install the radiator and secure with upper support brackets. Install the fan and shroud assembly. Connect upper and lower radiator hoses.

31. Install the hood and align.

32. On the carbureted engines install the air

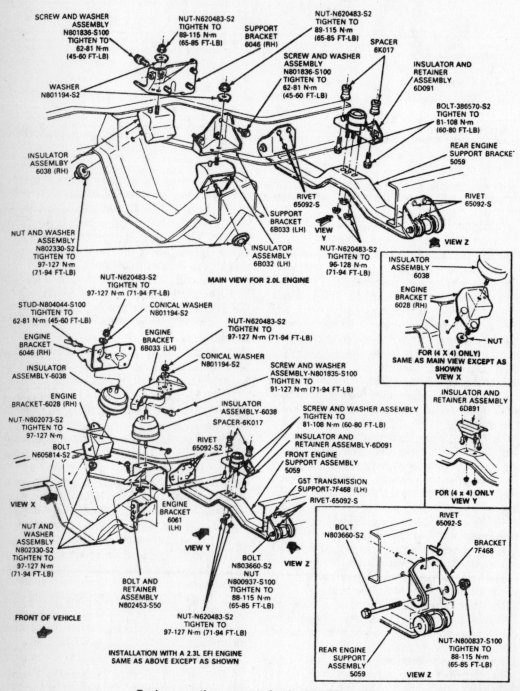

Engine mounting supports for the 2.3L EFI engine

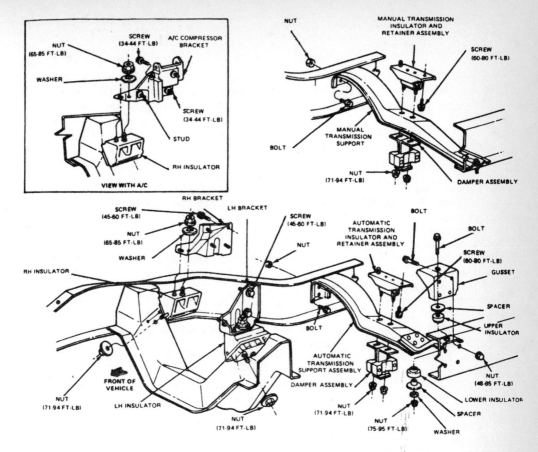

Engine mounting supports for the 2.0L & 2.3L engines 1985–1988

cleaner and duct assembly. On the 2.3L EFI engine, connect the air cleaner outlet tube, the idle speed control hose, and the heat riser tube at the throttle body. Fill and bleed the cooling system.

33. Fill the crankcase with specified oil. Connect battery ground cable to engine and battery positive cable to battery.

34. Start the engine and check for leaks.

2.8L Engine

Remove or disconnect the Thermactor system parts that will interfere with the removal or installation of the engine.

1. Disconnect the battery ground cable and drain the cooling system.

CAUTION: *When draining the coolant, keep in mind that cats and dogs are attracted by the ethylene glycol antifreeze, and are quite likely to drink any that is left in an uncovered container or in puddles on the ground. This will prove fatal in sufficient quantity. Always drain the coolant into a sealable container. Coolant should be reused unless it is contaminated or several years old.*

2. Remove the hood.

3. Remove the air cleaner and intake duct assembly.

4. Disconnect the radiator upper and lower hoses at the radiator.

5. Remove the fan shroud attaching bolts and position the shroud over the fan. Remove the radiator and shroud.

6. Remove the alternator and bracket. Position the alternator out of the way. Disconnect the alternator ground wire from the cylinder block.

7. Remove A/C compressor and power steering and position them out of the way, if so equipped. DO NOT disconnect the A/C refrigerant lines.

8. Disconnect the heater hoses at the block and water pump.

9. Remove the ground wires from the cylinder block.

10. Disconnect the fuel tank to fuel pump fuel line at the fuel pump. Plug the fuel tank line.

11. Disconnect the throttle cable linkage at the carburetor and intake manifold.

12. Label and disconnect the primary wires from the ignition coil. Disconnect the brake booster vacuum hose. Label and disconnect the

wiring from the oil pressure and engine coolant temperature senders.

13. Raise the vehicle and secure with jackstands.

14. Disconnect the muffler inlet pipes at the exhaust manifolds.

15. Disconnect the starter cable and remove the starter.

16. Remove the engine front support to crossmember attaching nuts or through bolts.

17. If equipped with automatic transmission:

a. Remove the converter inspection cover and disconnect the flywheel from the converter.

b. Remove the kickdown rod.

c. Remove the converter housing-to-cylinder block bolts and the adapter plate-to-converter housing bolt.

18. On vehicles equipped with a manual transmission, remove the clutch linkage.

19. Lower the vehicle.

20. Attach an engine lifting sling and hoist to the lifting brackets at the exhaust manifolds.

21. Position a jack under the transmission.

22. Raise the engine slightly and carefully pull it from the transmission. Carefully lift the engine out of the engine compartment. Install the engine on a work stand.

To install:

If clutch pressure plate and disc have been removed, install by following procedures in Chapter 7.

23. Attach an engine lifting sling and hoist to the lifting brackets at the exhaust manifolds.

24. Lower the engine carefully into the engine compartment. Make sure the exhaust manifolds are properly aligned with the muffler inlet pipes.

25. On a vehicle with a manual transmission, start the transmission in relation to the engine if the input shaft will not enter the clutch disc. If the engine hangs up after the shaft enters, turn the crankshaft slowly (transmission in gear) until the shaft splines mesh with the clutch disc splines.

26. On a vehicle with an automatic transmission, start the converter pilot into the crankshaft.

27. Install the clutch housing or converter housing upper bolts, making sure that the dowels in the cylinder block engage the flywheel housing. Remove the jack from under the transmission.

28. Remove the lifting sling from the engine.

29. On a vehicle with an automatic transmission, position the kickdown rod on the transmission and engine.

30. Raise the vehicle and secure with jackstands.

31. On a vehicle with an automatic transmission, position the transmission linkage bracket and install the remaining converter housing bolts. Install the adapter plate-to-converter housing bolt. Install the converter-to-flywheel nuts and install the inspection cover. Connect the kickdown rod on the transmission.

32. Install the starter and connect the cable.

33. Connect the muffler inlet pipes at the exhaust manifolds.

34. Install the engine front support nuts and washer attaching it to the crossmember or through bolts.

35. Lower the vehicle.

36. Install the battery ground cable.

37. Connect the ignition coil primary wires, then connect the coolant temperature sending unit and oil pressure sending unit. Connect the brake booster vacuum hose.

38. Install the throttle linkage.

39. Connect the fuel tank line at the fuel pump.

40. Connect the ground cable at the cylinder block.

41. Connect the heater hoses to the water pump and cylinder block.

42. Install the alternator and bracket. Connect the alternator ground wire to the cylinder block. Install the drive belt and adjust the belt tension, refer to Chapter 1 Belt Tension Adjustment.

43. Install A/C compressor and power steering pump, if so equipped.

44. Position the fan shroud over the fan. Install the radiator and connect the radiator upper and lower hoses. Install the fan shroud attaching bolts.

45. Fill and bleed the cooling system. Fill the crankcase with the proper grade and quantity of oil.

46. Reconnect the battery ground cable.

47. Operate the engine at fast idle until it reaches normal operating temperature and check all gaskets and hose connections for leaks. Adjust the ignition timing and the idle speed.

48. Install the air cleaner and intake duct. Install and align the hood.

2.9L Engine

Remove or disconnect the Thermactor system parts that will interfere with the removal or installation of the engine.

1. Disconnect the battery ground cable and drain the cooling system.

CAUTION: *When draining the coolant, keep in mind that cats and dogs are attracted by the ethylene glycol antifreeze, and are quite likely to drink any that is left in an uncovered container or in puddles on the ground.*

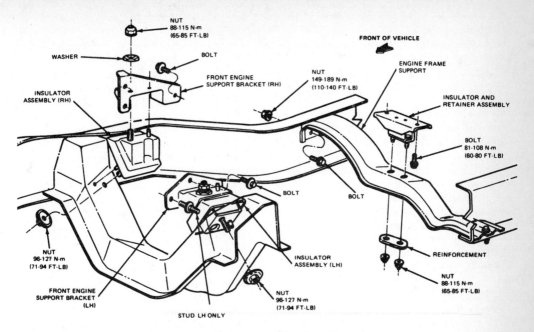

Engine mounting supports for the 2.8L engine

This will prove fatal in sufficient quantity. Always drain the coolant into a sealable container. Coolant should be reused unless it is contaminated or several years old.

2. Remove the hood.

3. Remove the air cleaner and intake hose.

4. Disconnect the radiator upper and lower hoses at the radiator.

5. Remove the fan shroud attaching bolts and position the shroud over the fan. Remove the radiator and shroud.

6. Remove the alternator and bracket. Position the alternator out of the way. Disconnect the alternator ground wire from the cylinder block.

7. Remove A/C compressor and power steering and position them out of the way, if so equipped. DO NOT disconnect the A/C refrigerant lines.

8. Disconnect the heater hoses at the block and water pump.

9. Remove the ground wires from the cylinder block.

10. Disconnect the fuel tank to fuel pump fuel line at the fuel pump. Plug the fuel tank line.

11. Disconnect the throttle cable shield and linkage at the throttle body and intake manifold. Disconnect the vacuum hoses from the EGR valve, the front fitting in the upper intake manifold and position them out of the way. Also, disconnect all vacuum connectors from the rear vacuum fitting in the upper intake manifold.

12. Label and disconnect the primary wires

from the ignition coil. Disconnect the brake booster vacuum hose. Label and disconnect the wiring from the oil pressure and engine coolant temperature senders. Also the injector harness, air charge temperature sensor, throttle position sensor and the EGR pressure sensor.

13. Raise the vehicle and secure with jackstands.

14. Disconnect the muffler inlet pipes at the exhaust manifolds. Disconnect the starter cable and remove the starter.

15. If equipped with manual transmission, remove the clutch housing attaching bolts. Remove the hydraulic clutch hose.

16. Remove the engine front support to crossmember attaching nuts or through bolts.

17a. If equipped with automatic transmission:

  a. Remove the converter inspection cover and disconnect the flywheel from the converter.

  b. Remove the cable.

  c. Remove the converter housing-to-cylinder block bolts and the adapter plate-to-converter housing bolt.

17b. On vehicles equipped with a manual transmission, remove the clutch linkage.

18. Lower the vehicle.

19. Attach an engine lifting sling and hoist to the lifting brackets at the exhaust manifolds.

20. Position a jack under the transmission.

21. Raise the engine slightly and carefully pull it from the transmission. Carefully lift the engine out of the engine compartment. Install the engine on a work stand.

To install:

If clutch pressure plate and disc have been removed, install by following procedures in Chapter 7.

22. Attach an engine lifting sling and hoist to the lifting brackets at the exhaust manifolds.

23. Lower the engine carefully into the engine compartment. Make sure the exhaust manifolds are properly aligned with the muffler inlet pipes.

On a vehicle with a manual transmission, start the transmission in relation to the engine if the input shaft will not enter the clutch disc. If the engine hangs up after the shaft enters, turn the crankshaft slowly (transmission in gear) until the shaft splines mesh with the clutch disc splines. On a vehicle with an automatic transmission, start the converter pilot into the crankshaft.

24. Install the clutch housing or converter housing upper bolts, making sure that the dowels in the cylinder block engage the flywheel housing. Remove the jack from under the transmission.

25. Remove the lifting sling from the engine.

26. On a vehicle with an automatic transmission, position the kickdown rod on the transmission and engine.

27. Raise the vehicle and secure with jackstands.

28. On a vehicle with an automatic transmission, position the transmission linkage bracket and install the remaining converter housing bolts. Install the adapter plate-to-converter housing bolt. Install the converter-to-flywheel nuts and install the inspection cover. Connect the kickdown rod on the transmission.

29. Install the starter and connect the cable.

30. Connect the muffler inlet pipes at the exhaust manifolds.

31. Install the engine front support nuts and washer attaching it to the crossmember or through bolts.

32. Lower the vehicle.

33. Install the battery ground cable.

34. Connect the ignition coil primary wires, then connect the coolant temperature sending unit and oil pressure sending unit. Connect the brake booster vacuum hose.

35. Install the throttle linkage.

36. Connect fuel tank line at the fuel rail.

37. Connect the ground cable at the cylinder block.

38. Connect the heater hoses to the water pump and cylinder block.

39. Install the alternator and bracket. Con-

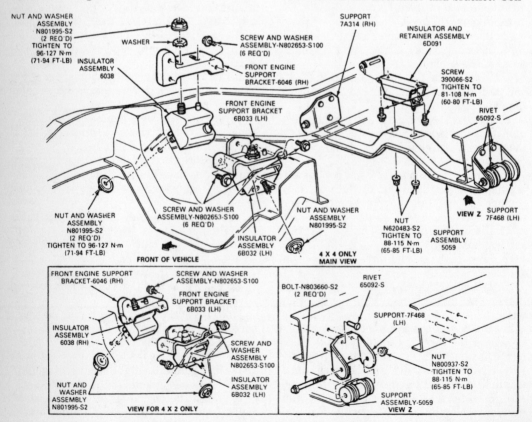

Engine mounting supports for the 2.9L engine

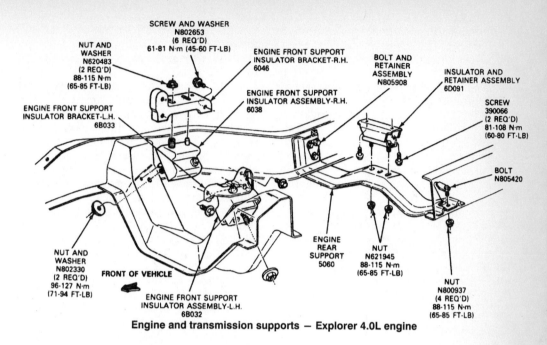

SCREW AND WASHER
N802653
(6 REQ'D)
61-81 N·m (45-60 FT-LB)

NUT AND
WASHER
N620483
(2 REQ'D)
88-115 N·m
(65-85 FT-LB)

ENGINE FRONT SUPPORT
INSULATOR BRACKET-R.H.
6046

ENGINE FRONT SUPPORT
INSULATOR ASSEMBLY-R.H.
6038

BOLT AND
RETAINER
ASSEMBLY
N805908

INSULATOR AND
RETAINER ASSEMBLY
6D091

SCREW
390066
(2 REQ'D)
81-108 N·m
(60-80 FT-LB)

ENGINE FRONT SUPPORT
INSULATOR BRACKET-L.H.
6B033

BOLT
N805420

NUT AND
WASHER
N802330
(2 REQ'D)
96-127 N·m
(71-94 FT-LB)

FRONT OF VEHICLE

ENGINE FRONT SUPPORT
INSULATOR ASSEMBLY-L.H.
6B032

ENGINE
REAR
SUPPORT
5060

NUT
N621945
88-115 N·m
(65-85 FT-LB)

NUT
N800937
(4 REQ'D)
88-115 N·m
(65-85 FT-LB)

Engine and transmission supports — Explorer 4.0L engine

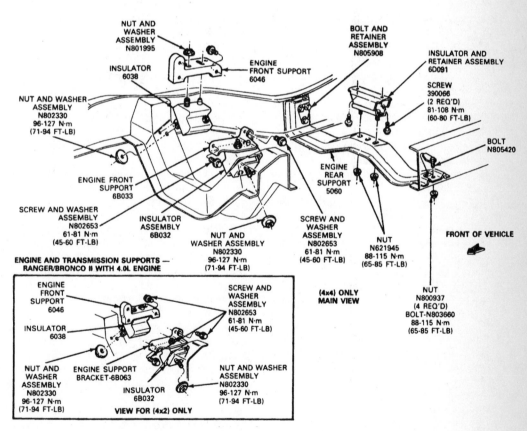

NUT AND
WASHER
ASSEMBLY
N801995

INSULATOR
6038

ENGINE
FRONT SUPPORT
6046

BOLT AND
RETAINER
ASSEMBLY
N805908

INSULATOR AND
RETAINER ASSEMBLY
6D091

SCREW
390066
(2 REQ'D)
81-108 N·m
(60-80 FT-LB)

NUT AND WASHER
ASSEMBLY
N802330
96-127 N·m
(71-94 FT-LB)

ENGINE FRONT
SUPPORT
6B033

ENGINE
REAR
SUPPORT
5060

BOLT
N805420

SCREW AND WASHER
ASSEMBLY
N802653
61-81 N·m
(45-60 FT-LB)

INSULATOR
ASSEMBLY
6B032

NUT AND
WASHER ASSEMBLY
N802330
96-127 N·m
(71-94 FT-LB)

SCREW AND
WASHER
ASSEMBLY
N802653
61-81 N·m
(45-60 FT-LB)

NUT
N621945
88-115 N·m
(65-85 FT-LB)

FRONT OF VEHICLE

ENGINE AND TRANSMISSION SUPPORTS —
RANGER/BRONCO II WITH 4.0L ENGINE

(4x4) ONLY
MAIN VIEW

NUT
N800937
(4 REQ'D)
BOLT-N803660
88-115 N·m
(65-85 FT-LB)

ENGINE
FRONT
SUPPORT
6046

SCREW AND
WASHER
ASSEMBLY
N802653
61-81 N·m
(45-60 FT-LB)

INSULATOR
6038

NUT AND
WASHER
ASSEMBLY
N802330
96-127 N·m
(71-94 FT-LB)

ENGINE SUPPORT
BRACKET-6B063

INSULATOR
6B032

NUT AND WASHER
ASSEMBLY
N802330
96-127 N·m
(71-94 FT-LB)

VIEW FOR (4x2) ONLY

Engine and transmission supports — Ranger 4.0L engine

nect the alternator ground wire to the cylinder block. Install the drive belt and adjust the belt tension, refer to Chapter 1 Belt Tension Adjustment.

40. Install A/C compressor and power steering pump, if so equipped.

41. Position the fan shroud over the fan. Install the radiator and connect the radiator upper and lower hoses. Install the fan shroud attaching bolts.

42. Fill and bleed the cooling system. Fill the crankcase with the proper grade and quantity of oil.

43. Reconnect the battery ground cable.

44. Operate the engine at fast idle until it reaches normal operating temperature and check all gaskets and hose connections for leaks. Adjust the ignition timing and the idle speed.

45. Install the intake hose. Install and align the hood.

3.0L and 4.0L Engines

1. Disconnect the negative battery cable. Drain the cooling system. Relieve fuel system pressure.

CAUTION: *When draining the coolant, keep in mind that cats and dogs are attracted by the ethylene glycol antifreeze, and are quite likely to drink any that is left in an uncovered container or in puddles on the ground. This will prove fatal in sufficient quantity. Always drain the coolant into a sealable container. Coolant should be reused unless it is contaminated or several years old.*

2. Remove the hood (matchmark hinges for correct installation).

3. Remove the air cleaner and intake hose.

4. Disconnect the radiator upper and lower hoses at the radiator.

5. Remove the fan shroud attaching bolts and position the shroud over the fan. Remove the radiator and shroud.

6. Remove the alternator and bracket. Position the alternator out of the way. Disconnect the alternator ground wire from the cylinder block.

7. Remove A/C compressor and power steering and position them out of the way, if so equipped. DO NOT disconnect the A/C refrigerant lines.

8. Disconnect the heater hoses at the block and water pump.

9. Remove the ground wires from the cylinder block.

10. On the 3.0L engine disconnect both fuel lines at the chassis to engine connections. On 4.0L engine disconnect the fuel tank to fuel rail lines at the fuel rail.

11. Disconnect the throttle cable shield and linkage at the throttle body and intake manifold. Disconnect all vacuum connections from the rear vacuum fitting in upper intake manifold.

12. Label and disconnect the primary wires from the EDIS ignition coil/primary wires from the ignition coil. Disconnect the brake booster vacuum hose. Label and disconnect the wiring from the oil pressure and engine coolant temperature senders. Also the injector harness, air charge temperature sensor, throttle position sensor. On the 3.0L engine remove the distributor assembly (mark assembly before removal) from the engine and disconnect the wiring from the low oil level sensor and oil pressure sending unit.

13. Raise the vehicle and secure with jackstands.

14. Disconnect the muffler inlet pipes at the exhaust manifolds. Disconnect the starter cable and remove the starter.

15. If equipped with manual transmission, remove the clutch housing attaching bolts. Remove the hydraulic clutch hose.

16. Remove the engine front support to crossmember attaching nuts or through bolts.

17a. If equipped with automatic transmission:

a. Remove the converter inspection cover and disconnect the flywheel from the converter.

b. Remove the cable.

c. Remove the converter housing-to-cylinder block bolts and the adapter plate-to-converter housing bolt.

17b. On vehicles equipped with a manual transmission, remove the clutch linkage.

18. Lower the vehicle.

19. Attach an engine lifting sling and hoist to the lifting brackets at the exhaust manifolds.

20. Position a jack under the transmission.

21. Raise the engine slightly and carefully pull it from the transmission. Carefully lift the engine out of the engine compartment. Install the engine on a work stand.

To install:

If clutch pressure plate and disc have been removed, install by following procedures in Chapter 7.

22. Attach an engine lifting sling and hoist to the lifting brackets at the exhaust manifolds.

23. Lower the engine carefully into the engine compartment. Make sure the exhaust manifolds are properly aligned with the muffler inlet pipes.

On a vehicle with a manual transmission, start the transmission in relation to the engine if the input shaft will not enter the clutch disc. If the engine hangs up after the shaft enters, turn the crankshaft slowly (transmission in gear) until the shaft splines mesh with the clutch disc splines. On a vehicle with an automatic transmission, start the converter pilot into the crankshaft.

24. Install the clutch housing or converter housing upper bolts, making sure that the dowels in the cylinder block engage the flywheel housing. Remove the jack from under the transmission.

25. Remove the lifting sling from the engine.

26. On a vehicle with an automatic transmission, position the kickdown rod on the transmission and engine.

27. Raise the vehicle and secure with jackstands.

28. On a vehicle with an automatic transmission, position the transmission linkage bracket and install the remaining converter housing bolts. Install the adapter plate-to-converter housing bolt. Install the converter-to-flywheel nuts and install the inspection cover. Connect the kickdown rod on the transmission.

29. Install the starter and connect the cable.

30. Connect the muffler inlet pipes at the exhaust manifolds.

31. Install the engine front support nuts and washer attaching it to the crossmember or through bolts.

32. Lower the vehicle.

33. Install the battery ground cable.

34. Connect the EDIS ignition coil primary wires/ignition coil primary wires, then connect the coolant temperature sending unit and oil pressure sending unit. Connect the brake booster vacuum hose. On the 3.0L engine install the distributor assembly to the engine and reconnect the wiring to the low oil level sensor and oil pressure sending unit.

35. Install the throttle linkage.

36. On the 3.0L engine connect both fuel lines at the chassis to engine connections. On the 4.0L engine connect the fuel tank line at the fuel rail.

37. Connect the ground cable at the cylinder block.

38. Connect the heater hoses to the water pump and cylinder block.

39. Install the alternator and bracket. Connect the alternator ground wire to the cylinder block. Install the drive belt and adjust the belt tension, refer to Chapter 1 Belt Tension Adjustment.

40. Install A/C compressor and power steering pump, if so equipped.

41. Position the fan shroud over the fan. Install the radiator and connect the radiator upper and lower hoses. Install the fan shroud attaching bolts.

42. Fill and bleed the cooling system. Fill the crankcase with the proper grade and quantity of oil.

43. Reconnect the battery ground cable.

44. Operate the engine at fast idle until it reaches normal operating temperature and check all gaskets and hose connections for leaks. On the 3.0L engine adjust ignition timing and idle speed.

45. Install the intake hose. Install and adjust the hood.

2.2L Diesel Engine

1. Open hood and install protective fender covers. Mark location of hood hinges and remove hood.

2. Disconnect battery ground cables from both batteries. Disconnect battery ground cables at engine.

3. Drain coolant from radiator.

CAUTION: *When draining the coolant, keep in mind that cats and dogs are attracted by the ethylene glycol antifreeze, and are quite likely to drink any that is left in an uncovered container or in puddles on the ground. This will prove fatal in sufficient quantity. Always drain the coolant into a sealable container. Coolant should be reused unless it is contaminated or several years old.*

4. Disconnect air intake hose from air cleaner and intake manifold.

5. Disconnect upper and lower radiator hoses from engine. Remove engine cooling fan. Remove radiator shroud screws. Remove radiator upper supports and remove radiator and shroud.

6. Disconnect radio ground strap, if so equipped.

7. Remove No. 2 glow plug relay from firewall, with harness attached, and lay on engine.

8. Disconnect engine wiring harness at main connector located on left fender apron. Disconnect starter cable from starter.

9. Disconnect accelerator cable and speed control cable, if so equipped, from injection pump.

10. Remove cold start cable from injection pump.

CAUTION: *Do not disconnect air conditioning lines or discharge the system. Have the system discharged by a qualified mechanic prior to start of engine removal.*

11. Discharge A/C system and remove A/C refrigerant lines and position out of the way.

12. Remove pressure and return hoses from power steering pump, if so equipped.

13. Disconnect vacuum fitting from vacuum pump and position fitting and vacuum hoses out of the way.

14. Disconnect and cap fuel inlet line at fuel

line heater and fuel return line at injection pump.

15. Disconnect heater hoses from engine.

16. Loosen engine insulator nuts. Raise vehicle and safely support on jackstands.

17. Drain engine oil from oil pan and remove primary oil filter.

CAUTION: *The EPA warns that prolonged contact with used engine oil may cause a number of skin disorders, including cancer! You should make every effort to minimize your exposure to used engine oil. Protective gloves should be worn when changing the oil. Wash your hands and any other exposed skin areas as soon as possible after exposure to used engine oil. Soap and water, or waterless hand cleaner should be used.*

18. Disconnect oil pressure sender hose from oil filter mounting adapter.

19. Disconnect muffler inlet pipe at exhaust manifold.

20. Remove bottom engine insulator nuts. Remove transmission bolts. Lower vehicle. Attach engine lifting sling and chain hoist.

21. Carefully lift engine out of vehicle to avoid damage to components.

22. Install engine on work stand, if necessary.

To install:

23. When installing the engine; Carefully lower engine into engine compartment to avoid damage to components.

24. Install two top transmission-to-engine attaching bolts. Remove engine lifting sling.

25. Raise vehicle and safely support on jackstands.

26. Install engine insulator nuts and tighten to specification.

27. Install remaining transmission-to-engine attaching bolts and tighten all bolts to specification.

28. Connect muffler inlet pipe to exhaust manifold and tighten to specification.

29. Install oil pressure sender hose and install new oil filter as described in Chapter 1.

30. Lower vehicle.

31. Tighten upper engine insulator nuts to specification.

32. Connect heater hoses to engine. Connect fuel inlet line to fuel line heater and fuel return line to injection pump. Connect vacuum fitting and hoses to vacuum pump. Connect pressure and return hoses to power steering pump, if so equipped. Check and add power steering fluid.

33. Install A/C refrigerant lines and charge system, if so equipped.

NOTE: *System can be charged after engine installation is complete.*

34. Install A/C drive belt, and tighten to specification.

35. Connect cold start cable to injection pump. Connect accelerator cable and speed control cable, if so equipped, to injection pump.

36. Connect engine wiring harness to main wiring harness at left fender apron. Connect radio ground strap, if so equipped.

37. Position radiator in vehicle, install radiator upper support brackets and tighten to specification. Install radiator fan shroud and tighten to specification. Install radiator fan and tighten to specification.

38. Connect upper and lower radiator hoses to engine and tighten clamps to specification. Connect air intake hose to air cleaner and intake manifold.

39. Fill and bleed cooling system.

40. Fill crankcase with specified quantity and quality of oil.

41. Connect battery ground cables to engine. Connect battery ground cables to both batteries.

42. Run engine and check for oil, fuel and coolant leaks. Close hood.

2.3L Diesel Engine

1. Mark the location of the hood hinges and remove the hood.

2. Disconnect the battery ground cables from both batteries.

3. Disconnect the battery ground cables at engine.

4. Drain the engine coolant.

CAUTION: *When draining the coolant, keep in mind that cats and dogs are attracted by the ethylene glycol antifreeze, and are quite likely to drink any that is left in an uncovered container or in puddles on the ground. This will prove fatal in sufficient quantity. Always drain the coolant into a sealable container. Coolant should be reused unless it is contaminated or several years old.*

5. Remove the crankcase breather hose at the rocker cover.

6. Remove the intake hose between the air cleaner and turbocharger.

NOTE: *Cap the turbocharger inlet.*

7. Remove the A/C compressor and position out of the way.

NOTE: *It is not necessary to disconnect A/C hoses from compressor.*

8. Disconnect the heater hoses from heater core inlet and outlet.

9. Remove the cooling fan.

10. Disconnect the radiator hoses and remove the radiator.

11. Disconnect the electrical connector at the fuel conditioner.

12. Disconnect the fuel supply line at the fuel conditioner.

from the filler neck.

16. Disconnect the throttle cable at the injection pump.

17. Disconnect the engine harness from the chassis harness at the alternator bracket.

18. Disconnect the wires from the glow plug bus bar.

19. Disconnect the starter motor wiring.

20. Remove the 2 starter motor attaching bolts and the 1 bolt at the brace attached to the starter. Remove the starter.

21. Raise the vehicle part way up and remove the right hand wheel and the right hand inner fender.

22. Disconnect the oil pressure switch wire.

23. Disconnect the oil cooler lines at the oil filter adapter.

24. Raise the vehicle all the way up.

25. Remove the nut attaching the engine insulator to the engine support brackets. Disconnect the oil level switch wire from the switch on the right hand side of the oil pan.

26. Disconnect the muffler inlet pipe from the turbo exhaust outlet pipe.

27. Disconnect the power steering pump hoses at the pump.

28. Disconnect the clutch servo hydraulic line (red hose) at the clutch housing and position it out of the way.

29. Remove the transmission attaching bolts (except top 2 bolts).

30. Lower the vehicle.

31. Attach an engine lifting sling or equivalent to the engine lifting brackets.

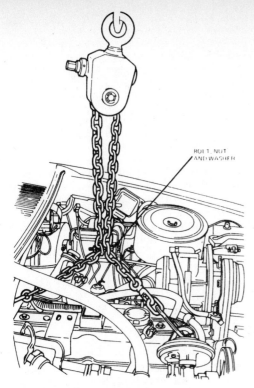

Removing the 2.2L diesel engine

13. Disconnect the fuel return line at the injection pump.

14. Disconnect the vacuum lines at the vacuum pump fitting.

15. Disconnect the coolant overflow hose

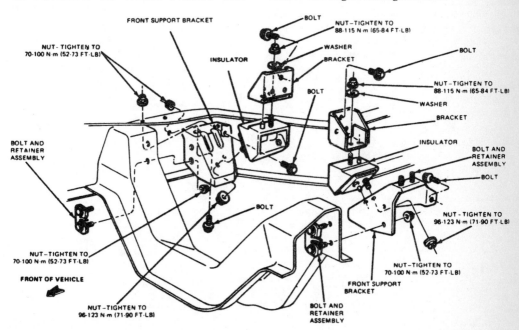

Engine mounting supports for the 2.2L diesel engine

32. Remove the top 2 transmission attaching bolts.

33. Carefully lift the engine out of vehicle by first lifting approximately 3 in. and sliding forward to avoid damage to components.

34. Install the engine on work stand, if necessary.

35. Carefully lower the engine into engine compartment to avoid damage to components.

36. Install the 2 top transmission bolts.

37. Remove the engine lifting sling.

38. Raise the vehicle.

39. Install the 2 engine insulator-to-engine support bracket bolts and tighten to specification.

40. Install the remaining transmission bolts and tighten to specification.

41. Connect the clutch servo hydraulic line (red hose) at the clutch housing.

42. Connect the power steering hoses at pump.

43. Connect the muffler inlet pipe to the turbo exhaust outlet and tighten to specification.

44. Connect the oil level switch wire.

45. Lower the vehicle part way down.

46. Connect the oil cooler lines at the oil filter adapter and tighten to specification.

47. Connect the oil pressure sender wire.

48. Install the inner fender and right hand wheel assembly.

49. Lower the vehicle all the way down.

50. Install the starter motor. Tighten the

bolts to specification, including the alternator mounting bracket brace.

51. Connect the starter motor wiring.

52. Connect the coolant temperature sensor at the left hand rear of the cylinder head.

53. Connect the chassis harness to the engine harness at the alternator bracket.

54. Connect the throttle cable and speed control cable, if so equipped, at the injection pump.

55. Connect the coolant overflow hose at the radiator filler neck.

56. Connect the vacuum lines at the vacuum pump fitting.

57. Connect the fuel return line at the injection pump.

58. Connect the fuel supply line at the fuel conditioner.

59. Connect the electrical connector at the fuel conditioner.

60. Install the radiator and radiator hoses.

61. Install the cooling fan.

62. Connect the heater hoses to the heater core inlet and outlet.

63. Install the A/C compressor.

64. Connect the intake hose between the air cleaner and turbo inlet.

65. Connect the breather hose to rocker cover.

66. Fill and bleed the cooling system.

67. Fill the engine with specified quantity and quality of oil.

68. Connect the battery ground cables to engine.

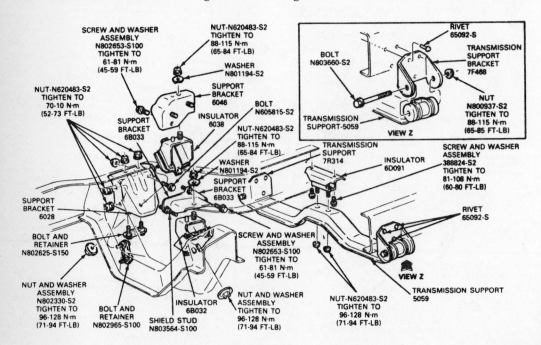

Engine mounting supports for the 2.3L turbo diesel engine

69. Start the engine and check for oil, fuel and coolant leaks.

70. Stop the engine. Check oil and coolant levels. Add if necessary.

71. Fill and bleed the power steering pump, if necessary.

72. Install the hood.

Valve Rocker Arm Cover

REMOVAL AND INSTALLATION

2.0L, 2.3L, 2.8L and 2.9L Engines

NOTE: *To service the valve rocker cover on the 2.3L EFI engine the throttle body assembly and EGR supply tube must first be removed. Refer to the necessary service procedures.*

1. Disconnect the negative battery cable. Remove the air cleaner and attaching parts. Label each spark plug wire prior to its removal in order to ease the installation of the wires on the correct spark plugs.

2. Remove the spark plug wires.

3. Remove the PCV valve and hose.

4. Remove the carburetor choke air deflector plate (shield).

5. Remove the rocker arm cover attaching screws and the load distribution washers (patch pieces). Be sure the washers are installed in their original position.

6. Remove the transmission fluid level indicator tube and bracket, which is attached to rocker arm cover.

7. Disconnect the kickdown linkage and the carburetor (automatic transmission only).

8. Position the Thermactor air hose and the wiring harness away from the right hand rocker arm cover.

9. Remove the engine oil fill cap.

10. Disconnect the vacuum line at the canister purge solenoid and disconnect the line routed from the canister to the purge solenoid (disconnect the power brake booster hose, if so equipped).

11. With a light plastic hammer, tap the rocker arm covers to break the seal.

12. Remove the rocker arm covers.

To install:

13. Clean all gasket material from the cylinder heads and rocker arm cover gasket surfaces.

14. Install the rocker arm covers, using new gaskets and install the attaching screw and rocker arm cover reinforcement pieces.

15. Install the transmission fluid level indicator tube and the bracket (attaches to rocker arm cover).

16. Connect the kickdown linkage (automatic transmission only).

17. After ensuring all rocker arm cover reinforcement washers are installed in their original position, tighten the rocker arm cover screws.

18. Install the spark plug. wires.

19. Install the PCV valve and hose.

20. Install the carburetor choke air deflector plate (shield).

21. Reposition the Thermactor air hose and the wiring harness in their original places.

22. Install the engine oil fill cap.

23. Connect the vacuum line at the canister purge (connect power brake hose, if so equipped) solenoid and connect the line routed from canister to the purge solenoid.

24. Install the air cleaner and the attaching parts.

25. Reconnect the negative battery cable. Start the engine and check for oil leaks.

3.0L Engine

NOTE: *The rocker covers installed on the 3.0L engine incorporate integral (built in) gaskets which should last the life of the vehicle. Replacement gaskets are available if required.*

1. Disconnect the negative battery cable. Disconnect the ignition wires from the spark plugs, but leave them attached to their wire looms.

2. Remove the ignition wire separators from the rocker arm cover attaching bolt studs with the wires attached, then lay the wires out of the way.

3. If the left hand cover is being removed,

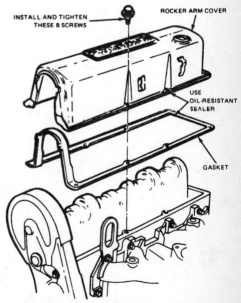

Rocker arm cover installation — 2.0L, 2.3L carbureted engines

remove the throttle body assembly remove the PCV valve and fuel injector harness stand-offs. If the right hand cover is being removed, remove the engine harness connectors, fuel injector harness stand-offs and air cleaner closure hose from oil fill adapter.

4. Using caution, slide a sharp thin blade knife between cylinder head gasket surface and rocker cover gasket at four RTV junctions. CUT ONLY THE RTV SEALER AND AVOID CUTTING INTEGRAL GASKET.

5. Remove the integral gasket from the rocker cover gasket channel. Note bolt/stud fasteners locations before removing gasket for correct installation. Clean gasket channel and remove any traces of RTV sealant.

6. Align fastener holes, lay new gasket onto channel and install by hand. Install gasket to each fastener, seat fastener against cover and at the same time roll gasket around fastener collar. If installed correctly all fasteners will be secured by gasket and not fall out.

7. To install valve cover to the engine, lightly oil all bolts and stud threads. Apply a bead of RTV sealant at the cylinder head to intake manifold rail step (two places per rail).

8. Place the rocker cover on the cylinder head and install attaching bolts and studs. Tighten the attaching bolts to 9 ft. lbs.

9. Install all remaining components in reverse order of removal procedure. Connect the ignition wires to the spark plugs and reconnect the negative battery cable. Start the engine and run to normal operating temperature and check for oil and vacuum leaks.

4.0L Engine

NOTE: *Failure to install new rocker cover gaskets and rocker cover reinforcement pieces will result in oil leaks.*

1. Disconnect the negative battery cable. Tag and remove the spark plug wires.

2. Disconnect and remove the fuel supply and return lines. See Chapter 5.

3. For left rocker cover removal, remove the upper intake manifold.

4. For right rocker cover removal, remove air inlet duct and hose to oil fill tube, drive belt from alternator, alternator. Drain cooling system remove the upper radiator hose from the engine. Remove the EDIS ignition coil and bracket assembly. Remove the A/C low pressure hose bracket if so equipped. Remove the PCV valve hose and breather.

CAUTION: *When draining the coolant, keep in mind that cats and dogs are attracted by the ethylene glycol antifreeze, and are quite likely to drink any that is left in an uncovered container or in puddles on the ground. This will prove fatal in sufficient quantity. Always drain the coolant into a sealable con-*

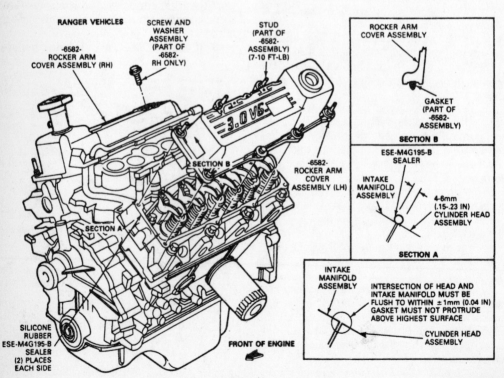

Rocker arm installation — 3.0L engine

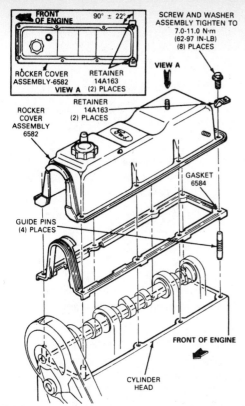

Rocker arm cover installation — 2.3L EFI engine

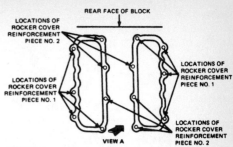

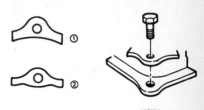

Rocker arm cover reinforcement washer locations
— 2.8L and 2.9L engines

tainer. *Coolant should be reused unless it is contaminated or several years old.*

5. Remove the rocker cover bolts and load distribution pieces. The washers must be installed in their original positions, so keep track of them.

6. Remove the rocker cover. It will probably be necessary to tap the cover loose with a plastic or rubber mallet.

7. Remove the rocker covers.

8. Clean all gasket material from the cover and head.

9. Installation is the reverse of removal. Always use a new gasket coated with sealer. If any of the RTV silicone gasket material was removed from the mating area of the head(s) and intake manifold, replace it. Torque the bolts to 3–5 ft. lbs.

10. Reconnect the negative battery cable. Start the engine and run to normal operating temperature and check for oil and fuel leaks.

Rocker Arms

REMOVAL AND INSTALLATION

2.0L, 2.3L Engines

NOTE: *A special tool is required to compress the lash adjuster.*

1. Remove the valve cover and associated parts as required.

2. Rotate the camshaft so that the base circle of the cam is against the cam follower you intend to remove.

3. Remove the retaining spring from the cam follower, if so equipped.

4. Using special tool T74P-6565-B or a valve spring compressor tool, collapse the lash adjuster and/or depress the valve spring, as necessary, and slide the cam follower over the lash adjuster and out from under the camshaft.

5. Install the cam follower in the reverse order of removal. Make sure that the lash adjuster is collapsed and released before rotating the camshaft.

Rocker Arm Shaft Assembly

REMOVAL AND INSTALLATION

2.2L Diesel Engine

1. Remove the valve cover.

2. Remove the bolts attaching the rocker shaft to the cylinder head and remove the rocker shaft.

3. Remove the push rods, if necessary.

NOTE: *Note position of push rods so they may be returned to their original positions.*

To install:

4. Install the push rods, if removed.

NOTE: *Ball end goes toward tappet.*

5. Position the rocker shaft on the cylinder head and install the retaining bolts.

NOTE: *Before tightening rocker shaft bolts, make sure the rocker arms are fully seated in the push rod cups.*

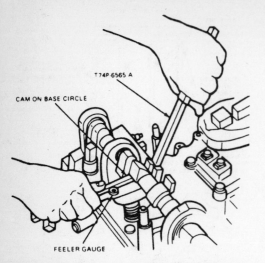

Using the special tool to collapse the lash adjuster

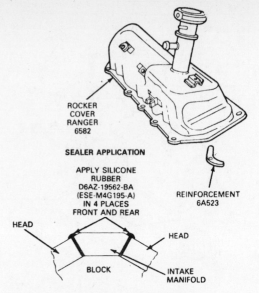

Rocker arm installation — 4.0L engine

6. Tighten the rocker shaft bolts alternately, two to three turns at a time, working from the center to the ends until all rocker shaft brackets are seated.

7. Adjust valve rocker arms as described in Chapter 2 under Valve Lash Adjustment.

8. Install the valve cover.

9. Connect the heater tube assembly to valve cover.

10. Run the engine and check for oil leaks.

2.3L Diesel Engine

1. Remove the valve cover.

2. Remove the bolts attaching the rocker shaft to the cylinder head, 1 turn at a time from the front to the rear and remove the rocker shaft.

To install:

3. Position the rocker shaft on the cylinder head.

NOTE: *Be certain the end of the rocker shaft with the single oil hole is toward the front of the engine. Also, ensure the rocker shaft is installed with the oil holes DOWN.*

4. Install the rocker shaft retaining bolts and tighten one turn at a time from front to rear, repeating the sequence until all the bolts are seated. Tighten the bolts to 25–28 ft. lbs.

5. Adjust valve rocker arms as described in Chapter 2 under Valve Lash Adjustment.

6. Install the valve cover.

7. Run the engine and check for oil leaks.

2.8L, 2.9L Engines

1. Remove the valve rocker arm covers following the procedure given above.

2. Remove the rocker arm shaft stand attaching bolts by loosening the bolts two turns at a time, in sequence (from the end of shaft to middle shaft).

3. Lift off the rocker arm and shaft assembly and the oil baffle.

To install:

4. Loosen the valve lash adjusting screws a few turns. Apply the engine oil to the assembly to provide the initial lubrication.

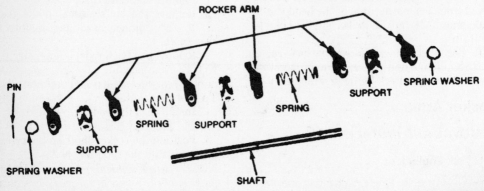

Rocker arm shaft assembly — 2.8L and 2.9L engines

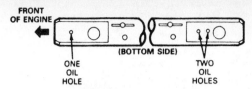

Rocker arm assembly oil hole positioning — 2.3L turbo diesel engine

5. Install the oil baffle and rocker arm shaft assembly to the cylinder head and guide adjusting screws on to the push rods.

6. Install and tighten rocker arm stand attaching bolts to 43–50 ft. lbs., two turns at a time, in sequence (from middle of shaft to the end of shaft). Adjust valve lash to cold specified setting.

7. Adjust the valve lash to the cold specified setting. Refer to Chapter 2 under Valve Lash Adjustment for adjustment procedures.

8. Install the valve rocker arm covers following the procedure given above.

DISASSEMBLY AND REASSEMBLY

1. Remove the spring washer and pin from each end of the valve rocker arm shaft.

2. Slide the rocker arms, springs and rocker arm shaft supports off the shaft. Be sure to mark the parts for re-assembly in the same locations.

3. If it is necessary to remove the plugs from each end of the shaft, drill or pierce the plug on one end. Use a steel rod to knock out the plug on the opposite end. Working from the open end, knock out the remaining plug.

4. The oil holes in the rocker arm shaft must point down when the shaft is installed. This position of the shaft can be recognized by a notch on the front face of the shaft.

5. If the plugs were removed from the shaft, use a blunt tool and install a plug, cup side out, in each end of the shaft.

6. Install a spring washer and pin on one end of the shaft, coat the rocker arm shaft with heavy engine oil and install the parts in the same sequence they were removed.

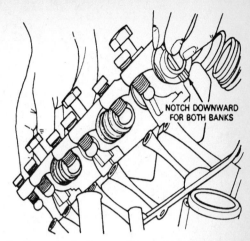

Rocker arm shaft assembly — 2.8L and 2.9L engines

3.0L Engine

1. Remove the rocker arm covers.

2. Removing the single retaining bolt at each rocker arm.

3. The rocker arm and pushrod may then be removed from the engine. Keep all rocker arms and pushrods in order so they may be installed in their original locations.

4. Installation is the reverse of removal. Tighten the rocker arm fulcrum bolts in two stages, first to 5–11 ft. lbs. (7–15 Nm), then to 18–26 ft. lbs. (25–35 Nm). Refer to the illustration for initial valve adjustment.

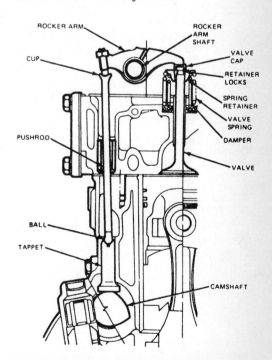

2.2L diesel engine valve train assembly

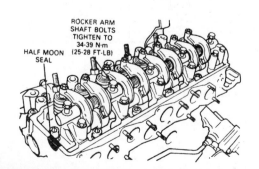

Rocker arm assembly — 2.3L turbo diesel engine

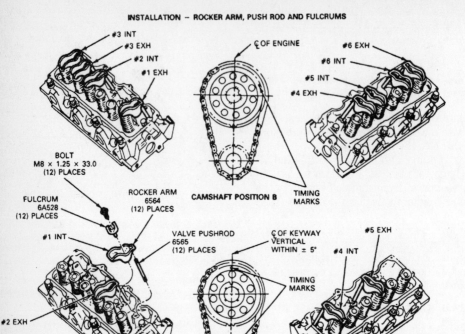

INSTALLATION – ROCKER ARM, PUSH ROD AND FULCRUMS

ASSEMBLY PROCEDURE

1. ROTATE CAMSHAFT TO POSITION "A" AS SHOWN.
2. INSTALL PUSH RODS (6565) (12) PLACES- PUSH RODS MUST BE SEATED PROPERLY ON TAPPET ASSEMBLY
3. INSTALL ROCKER ARMS (6564), FULCRUMS (6A528) AND BOLTS IN LOCATIONS AS SPECIFIED IN CAMSHAFT POSITION "A", TORQUE BOLTS TO 11 N·m AS REQ'D TO SEAT FULCRUMS IN CYLINDER HEAD
4. ROTATE CRANKSHAFT 120° TO POSITION "B"
5. INSTALL ROCKER ARMS (6564), FULCRUMS (6A528), AND BOLTS IN LOCATIONS AS SPECIFIED IN CAMSHAFT POSITION "B", TORQUE BOLTS TO 11 N·m AS REQ'D TO SEAT FULCRUMS IN CYLINDER HEAD

NOTE: FULCRUMS MUST BE FULLY SEATED IN CYLINDER HEADS AND PUSH RODS MUST BE FULLY SEATED IN ROCKER ARM SOCKETS PRIOR TO FINAL TORQUE.

6. APPLY ESE-M2C39-F OIL TO ROCKER ARM ASSEMBLIES.
7. FINAL TORQUE BOLTS TO 32.0 N·m (CAMSHAFT MAY BE IN ANY POSITION).

NOTE: CAMSHAFT POSITIONS "A" AND "B" ARE REQUIRED TO PLACE TAPPET ASSEMBLY ON BASE CIRCLE OF CAMSHAFT LOBE TO CHECK COLLAPSED TAPPET GAP.

FULCRUM AND BOLT MUST BE FULLY SEATED AFTER FINAL TORQUE

4.69-2.15 WITH TAPPET FULLY COLLAPSED ON BASE CIRCLE OF CAM LOBE AFTER ASSEMBLY REF. QUALITY AUDIT ONLY.

CYL. NO.	CAMSHAFT POSITION	
	A	B
	SET GAP OF VALVES NOTED	
1	INT.	EXH.
2	EXH.	INT.
3	NONE	INT.-EXH.
4	INT.	EXH.
5	EXH.	INT.
6	NONE	INT.-EXH.

Initial valve adjustment — 3.0L engine

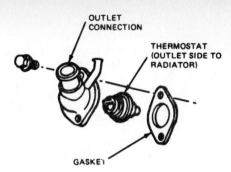

Thermostat and housing — exploded view

4.0L Engine

1. Remove the rocker cover.
2. Loosen the rocker arm shaft stand bolts, 2 turns at a time, front-to-rear, until they are free.
3. Lift off the rocker arm shaft assembly. If the pushrods are to be removed, tag them, since they have to be installed in their original positions.
4. Installation is the reverse of removal procedure. Tighten the rocker arm shaft bolts, 2 turns at a time, front to rear, until the specified torque of 52 ft. lbs. is reached. Install the rocker cover.

Thermostat

REMOVAL AND INSTALLATION

2.0L and 2.2L Engines

1. Drain the cooling system below the level of the coolant outlet housing.

CAUTION: *When draining the coolant, keep in mind that cats and dogs are attracted by the ethylene glycol antifreeze, and are quite likely to drink any that is left in an uncovered container or in puddles on the ground. This will prove fatal in sufficient quantity. Always drain the coolant into a sealable con-*

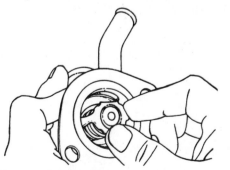

Thermostat spring always faces 'down' in all engines

tainer. *Coolant should be reused unless it is contaminated or several years old.*

2. Disconnect the heater return hose at the thermostat housing located on the left front lower side of engine.
3. Remove the coolant outlet housing retaining bolts and slide the housing with the hose attached to one side.
4. Turn the thermostat counterclockwise to unlock it from the outlet.
5. Remove the gasket from the engine block and clean both mating surfaces.

NOTE: *It is good practice to check the operation of a new thermostat before it is installed in an engine. Place the thermostat in a pan of boiling water. If it does not open more than $1/4$ in., do not install it in the engine.*

6. To install the thermostat, coat a new gasket with water resistant sealer and position it on the outlet of the engine. The gasket must be in place before the thermostat is installed.
7. Install the thermostat with the bridge (opposite end from the spring) inside the elbow connection and turn it clockwise to lock it in position, with the bridge against the flats cast into the elbow connection.
8. Position the elbow connection onto the mounting surface of the outlet, so that the thermostat flange is resting on the gasket and install the retaining bolts.
9. Connect the heater hose to the thermostat housing.
10. Fill the radiator and operate the engine until it reaches operating temperature. Check the coolant level and adjust as necessary.

2.3L Engine

1. Drain the cooling system (engine cold).

CAUTION: *When draining the coolant, keep in mind that cats and dogs are attracted by the ethylene glycol antifreeze, and are quite likely to drink any that is left in an uncovered container or in puddles on the ground. This will prove fatal in sufficient quantity. Always drain the coolant into a sealable container. Coolant should be reused unless it is contaminated or several years old.*

2. Remove the retaining bolts for the thermostat housing. Lift the housing clear and remove the thermostat. It may be easier to clean the gasket mating surfaces with the heater and radiator hoses removed from the thermostat housing.
3. Clean all gasket mating surfaces and make sure the thermostat is in the housing properly. Always use a new gasket. Tighten the thermostat housing retaining bolts to 14–21 ft. lbs. Refill the cooling system, start the engine and check for leaks.

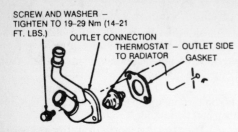

Thermostat housing assembly — 2.3L engine

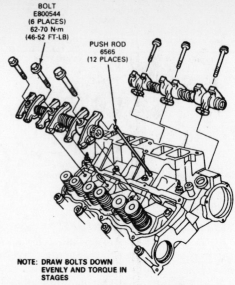

NOTE: DRAW BOLTS DOWN EVENLY AND TORQUE IN STAGES

Rocker arm shaft assembly — 4.0L engine

2.8L Engine

1. Drain the cooling system (engine cold).

CAUTION: *When draining the coolant, keep in mind that cats and dogs are attracted by the ethylene glycol antifreeze, and are quite likely to drink any that is left in an uncovered container or in puddles on the ground. This will prove fatal in sufficient quantity. Always drain the coolant into a sealable container. Coolant should be reused unless it is contaminated or several years old.*

2. Remove the retaining bolts from the thermostat housing. Move the housing out of the way, then lift out the thermostat.

3. Clean all gasket mating surfaces and make sure the new thermostat is installed correctly in the housing. Always use a new gasket. Tighten the thermostat housing bolts to 12–15 ft. lbs.

4. Refill the cooling system, start the engine and check for leaks.

3.0L Engine

1. Drain the cooling system.

CAUTION: *When draining the coolant, keep in mind that cats and dogs are attracted by the ethylene glycol antifreeze, and are quite likely to drink any that is left in an uncovered container or in puddles on the ground. This will prove fatal in sufficient quantity. Always drain the coolant into a sealable container. Coolant should be reused unless it is contaminated or several years old.*

2. Disconnect the battery ground cable.

3. Remove the upper radiator hose.

4. Remove the thermostat housing bolts.

5. Remove the housing and thermostat as an assembly.

6. Turn the thermostat counterclockwise to remove it from the housing.

7. Clean all gasket material from the housing and engine.

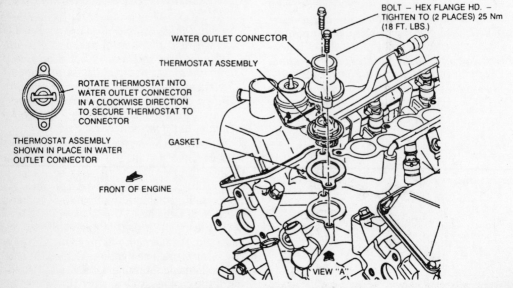

Thermostat housing assembly — 3.0L engine

8. Turn the thermostat clockwise into the housing until the thermostat bridge is perpendicular to the mounting holes.

9. Position the housing on the engine, using a new gasket coated with sealer. Tighten the bolts to 19 ft. lbs.

10. Install the hose, fill and bleed the cooling system, install the air cleaner and resonator, connect the battery ground cable and start the engine. Check for leaks.

2.9L and 4.0L Engines

1. Drain the cooling system.

CAUTION: *When draining the coolant, keep in mind that cats and dogs are attracted by the ethylene glycol antifreeze, and are quite likely to drink any that is left in an uncovered container or in puddles on the ground. This will prove fatal in sufficient quantity. Always drain the coolant into a sealable container. Coolant should be reused unless it is contaminated or several years old.*

2. Disconnect the battery ground.

3. Remove the air cleaner duct assembly.

4. Remove the upper radiator hose.

5. Remove the 3 thermostat housing attaching bolts.

6. Remove the thermostat housing. You may have to tap it loose with a plastic mallet or your hand.

To install:

7. Clean all mating surfaces thoroughly. Don't use a sharp metal tool! The housing and engine are aluminum.

8. Make sure that the sealing ring is properly installed on the thermostat rim. Position the thermostat in the housing making sure that the air release valve is in the **up** (12 o'clock) position.

9. Coat the mating surfaces of the housing and engine with an adhesive type sealer. Position the new gasket on the housing and place the housing on the engine. Torque the bolts to 7–10 ft. lbs.

Intake Manifold

REMOVAL AND INSTALLATION

2.0L, 2.3L Carbureted Engines

1. Drain the cooling system. Remove the air cleaner and duct assembly. Disconnect the negative battery cable.

CAUTION: *When draining the coolant, keep in mind that cats and dogs are attracted by the ethylene glycol antifreeze, and are quite likely to drink any that is left in an uncovered container or in puddles on the ground. This will prove fatal in sufficient quantity. Always drain the coolant into a sealable con-*

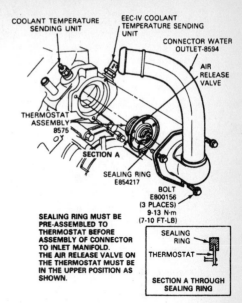

Thermostat housing assembly — 4.0L engine, 2.9L engine similar

tainer. Coolant should be reused unless it is contaminated or several years old.

2. Disconnect the accelerator cable, vacuum hoses (as required) and the hot water hose at the manifold fitting. Be sure to identify all vacuum hoses for proper reinstallation.

3. Remove the engine oil dipstick. Disconnect the heat tube at the EGR (exhaust gas recirculation) valve. Disconnect the fuel line at the carburetor fuel fitting.

4. Remove the dipstick retaining bolt from the intake manifold.

5. Disconnect and remove the PCV at the engine and intake manifold.

6. Remove the distributor cap and position the cap and wires out of the way, after removing the plastic plug connector from the valve cover.

7. Remove the intake manifold retaining bolts. Remove the manifold from the engine.

8. Clean all gasket mounting surfaces.

9. Install a new mounting gasket and intake manifold on the engine. Torque the bolts in proper sequence in two steps, first 5–7 ft. lbs., then 14–21 ft. lbs. The rest of the installation is in the reverse order of removal.

2.3L EFI And 2.3L Twin Plug Engines

The intake manifold is a two-piece (upper and lower) aluminum casting. Runner lengths are tuned to optimize engine torque and power output. The manifold provides mounting flanges for the air throttle body assembly, fuel supply manifold, accelerator control bracket and the EGR valve and supply tube. A vacuum fitting is installed to provide vacuum to various engine accessories. Pockets for the fuel injectors are machined to prevent both air and fuel leakage. The following procedure is for the removal of the intake manifold with the fuel charging assembly attached.

1. Make sure the ignition is OFF, then drain the coolant from the radiator (engine cold).

CAUTION: *When draining the coolant, keep in mind that cats and dogs are attracted by the ethylene glycol antifreeze, and are quite likely to drink any that is left in an uncovered container or in puddles on the ground. This will prove fatal in sufficient quantity. Always drain the coolant into a sealable container. Coolant should be reused unless it is contaminated or several years old.*

2. Disconnect the negative battery cable and secure it out of the way.

3. Remove the fuel filler cap to vent tank pressure. Release the pressure from the fuel system at the fuel pressure relief valve using EFI pressure gauge T80L–9974–A or equivalent. The fuel pressure relief valve is located on the fuel line in the upper right hand corner of the engine compartment. Remove the valve cap to gain access to the valve.

4. Disconnect the electrical connectors at the throttle position sensor, knock sensor, injector wiring harness, air charge temperature sensor and engine coolant temperature sensor. On the 2.3L twin plug engine disconnect TPS sensor, air bypass valve, injector wiring harness from main harness and water tempera-

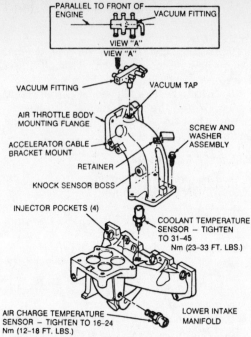

Upper and lower intake manifold assemblies on the 2.3L engine

ture indicator sensor, engine coolant temperature sensor, ignition control assembly.

5. Tag and disconnect the vacuum lines at the upper intake manifold vacuum tree, at the EGR valve and at the fuel pressure regulator and canister purge line as necessary.

6. Remove the throttle linkage shield and disconnect the throttle linkage and speed control cable (if equipped). Unbolt the accelerator cable from the bracket and position the cable out of the way.

7. Disconnect the air intake hose, air bypass hose and crankcase vent hose.

8. Disconnect the PCV hose from the fitting on the underside of the upper intake manifold.

9. Loosen the clamp on the coolant bypass line at the lower intake manifold and disconnect the hose.

10. Disconnect the EGR tube from the EGR valve by removing the flange nut.

11. Remove the upper intake manifold retaining nuts. Remove the upper intake manifold and air throttle body assembly.

12. Disconnect the push connect fitting at the fuel supply manifold and fuel return lines. Disconnect the fuel return line from the fuel supply manifold.

13. Remove the engine oil dipstick bracket retaining bolt.

14. Disconnect the electrical connectors from all four fuel injectors and move the harness aside.

15. Remove the two fuel supply manifold re-

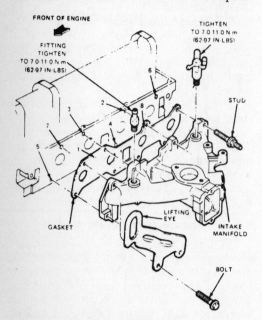

2.0L, 2.3L carbureted engines, intake manifold installation

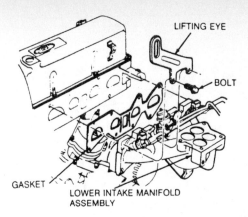

Removing the lower intake manifold on the 2.3L engine

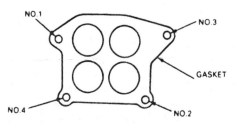

Upper intake manifold torque sequence — 2.3L engines

taining bolts, then carefully remove the fuel supply manifold and injectors. Remove the injectors by exerting a slight twisting/pulling motion.

16. Remove the four bottom retaining bolts from the lower manifold. The front two bolts also secure an engine lifting bracket. Once the bolts are removed, remove the lower intake manifold.

17. Clean and inspect the mounting faces of the lower intake manifold and cylinder head. Both surfaces must be clean and flat. If the intake manifold upper or lower section is being replaced, it will be necessary to transfer components from the old to the new part.

To install:

18. To install, first clean and oil the manifold bolt threads. Install a new lower manifold gasket.

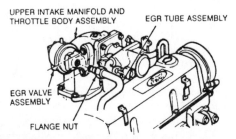

Disconnecting the EGR valve on the 2.3L engine

19. Position the lower manifold assembly to the head and install the engine lifting bracket. Install the four top manifold retaining bolts finger tight. Install the four remaining manifold bolts and tighten all bolts to 12–15 ft. lbs. and 15–22 ft. lbs. on the 2.3L twin plug engine, following the sequence illustrated.

20. Install the fuel supply manifold and injectors with two retaining bolts. Tighten the retaining bolts to 12–15 ft. lbs. and 15–22 ft. lbs. on the 2.3L twin plug engine.

21. Connect the four electrical connectors to the injectors.

22. Make sure the gasket surfaces of the upper and lower intake manifolds are clean. Place a gasket on the lower intake manifold assembly, then place the upper intake manifold in position.

23. Install the retaining bolts and tighten in sequence to 15–22 ft. lbs.

24. Install the engine oil dipstick, then con-

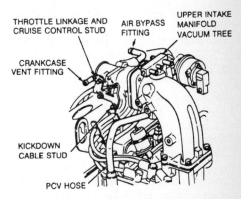

Linkage and hose location on the 2.3L engine

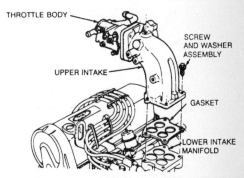

Removing the upper intake manifold on the 2.3L engine

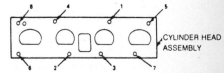

Torque sequence for the lower intake manifold — 2.3L engines

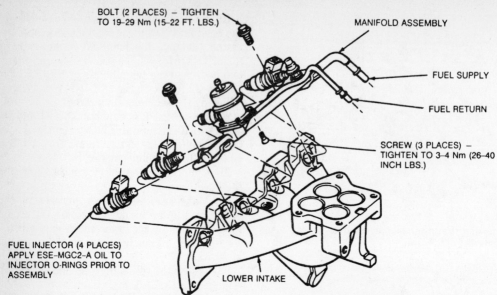

BOLT (2 PLACES) — TIGHTEN TO 19–29 Nm (15–22 FT. LBS.)

MANIFOLD ASSEMBLY

FUEL SUPPLY

FUEL RETURN

SCREW (3 PLACES) — TIGHTEN TO 3–4 Nm (26–40 INCH LBS.)

FUEL INJECTOR (4 PLACES) APPLY ESE-MGC2-A OIL TO INJECTOR O-RINGS PRIOR TO ASSEMBLY

LOWER INTAKE

Fuel supply manifold and injector mounting on the 2.3L engine

nect the fuel return and supply lines to the fuel supply manifold.

25. Connect the EGR tube to the EGR valve and tighten it to 6–9 ft. lbs. and 18 ft. lbs. on the 2.3L twin plug engine.

26. Connect the coolant bypass line and tighten the clamp. Connect the PCV system hose to the fitting on the underside of the upper intake manifold.

27. If removed, install the vacuum tee on the upper intake manifold. Use Teflon® tape on the threads and tighten to 12–18 ft. lbs. Reconnect the vacuum lines to the tee, the EGR valve and the fuel pressure regulator and canister purge line as necessary.

28. Hold the accelerator cable bracket in position on the upper intake manifold and install the retaining bolt. Tighten the bolt to 10–15 ft. lbs.

29. Install the accelerator cable to the bracket.

30. Position a new gasket on the fuel charging assembly air throttle body mounting flange. Install the air throttle body to the fuel charging assembly. Install two retaining nuts and two bolts and tighten to 12–15 ft. lbs. and 15–25 ft. lbs. on the 2.3L twin plug engine.

31. Connect the accelerator and speed control cable (if equipped), then install the throttle linkage shield.

32. Reconnect the throttle position sensor, injector wiring harness, knock sensor, air charge temperature sensor and engine coolant temperature sensor. On the 2.3L twin plug engine reconnect TPS sensor, air bypass valve, injector wiring harness to main harness and water temperature indicator sensor, engine coolant temperature sensor, ignition control assembly.

33. Connect the air intake hose, air bypass hose and crankcase ventilation hose.

34. Reconnect the negative battery cable. Refill the cooling system to specifications and pressurize the fuel system by turning the ignition switch on and off (without starting the engine) at least six times, leaving the ignition on for at least five seconds each time.

35. Start the engine and let it idle while checking for fuel, coolant and vacuum leaks. Correct as necessary. Road test the vehicle for proper operation.

2.8L Engine

1. Disconnect the negative battery cable.

2. Remove the air cleaner.

3. Disconnect the throttle cable.

4. Drain the coolant. Disconnect and remove the hose from the water outlet to the radiator and bypass hose from the intake manifold to the thermostat housing rear cover.

CAUTION: *When draining the coolant, keep in mind that cats and dogs are attracted by the ethylene glycol antifreeze, and are quite likely to drink any that is left in an uncovered container or in puddles on the ground. This will prove fatal in sufficient quantity. Always drain the coolant into a sealable container. Coolant should be reused unless it is contaminated or several years old.*

5. Remove the distributor cap and spark plug wires as an assembly.

NOTE: *Mark each plug wire with its cylinder number.*

6. Disconnect distributor wiring harness. Observe and mark the location of the distributor rotor and housing so ignition timing can be maintained at reassembly. Remove distributor

holddown screw and clamp and lift out distributor.

NOTE: *Some engines may be equipped with a security-type hold-down bolt. Use Distributor Hold-Down Wrench, Tool T82L–12270–A, or equivalent, to remove the hold-down bolt.*

7. Remove the rocker arm covers.

8. Remove the fuel line and filter.

9. Remove the intake manifold attaching bolts and nuts. Tap manifold lightly with a plastic mallet to break the gasket seal. Lift off the manifold.

10. Remove all the old gasket material and sealing compound.

To install:

11. Apply silicone sealer to the joining surfaces. Place the intake manifold gasket in position. Make sure that the tab on the right bank cylinder head gasket fits into the cutout of the manifold gasket.

12. Apply silicone sealer to the attaching bolt bosses on the intake manifold and position the intake manifold. Follow the torque sequence and torque the bolts to specifications.

13. Install the distributor so that the rotor and housing are in the same position marked at removal.

14. Install the distributor clamp and attaching bolt. Connect distributor wires.

15. Install the fuel line.

16. Replace the rocker arm cover gaskets, and reinstall the rocker arm valve covers using the procedure given under Rocker Arm Cover removal and installation.

17. Install the distributor cap. Coat the inside of each spark plug wire connector with silicone grease with a small screwdriver, and install the wires. Connect the distributor wiring harness.

18. Install and adjust the throttle linkage.

19. Install the air cleaner and the air cleaner tube at carburetor.

20. Connect the negative battery cable.

21. Connect the hoses from the water outlet to the radiator and the bypass hose from the thermostat housing rear cover to the intake manifold.

22. Refill and bleed the cooling system.

23. Recheck the ignition timing and reset the engine idle speed to specification.

24. Run the engine at fast idle and check for coolant and oil leaks.

2.9L Engine

1. Disconnect battery negative cable.

2. Remove air cleaner air intake duct from throttle body.

3. Disconnect throttle cable and bracket assembly.

4. Disconnect EGR tube at EGR valve.

5. Disconnect all vacuum hoses from fittings on upper intake manifold.

6. Disconnect electrical connections at throttle body, EGR pressure sensor, intake manifold upper and lower and distributor. Also disconnect fuel injector subharness from main EEC harness.

7. Remove upper intake manifold (plenum) assembly.

8. Drain coolant. Disconnect and remove hose from water outlet to radiator and heat supply.

CAUTION: *When draining the coolant, keep in mind that cats and dogs are attracted by the ethylene glycol antifreeze, and are quite likely to drink any that is left in an uncovered container or in puddles on the ground. This will prove fatal in sufficient quantity. Always drain the coolant into a sealable container. Coolant should be reused unless it is contaminated or several years old.*

9. Remove distributor cap and spark plug wires as an assembly.

10. Observe and mark the location of the distributor rotor and housing so ignition timing can be maintained as reassembly. Remove distributor hold-down screw and clamp and lift out distributor.

11. Remove rocker arm covers.

12. Remove intake manifold attaching bolts and nuts. Note length of manifold attaching bolts during removal so that they may be installed in their original positions. Tap manifold lightly with a plastic mallet to break gasket seal. Lift off manifold.

13. Remove all old gasket material and sealing compound.

To install:

14. Apply sealing compound to the joining surfaces. Place the intake manifold gasket in position. Ensure the tab on the right hand bank cylinder head gasket fits into the cutout of the manifold gasket.

15. Apply sealing compound to the attaching bolt bosses on the intake manifold and position the intake manifold. Follow the tightening sequence and tighten the bolts to specifications.

16. Install distributor so that rotor and housing are in the same position marked at removal.

17. Install distributor clamp and attaching bolts.

18. Replace rocker arm cover gasket, and install rocker arm valve covers using the procedure under Rocker Arm Cover and Rocker Arm.

19. Install distributor cap. Coat the inside of each spark plug wire connector with silicone grease with a small screwdriver, and install the wires. Connect distributor wiring harness.

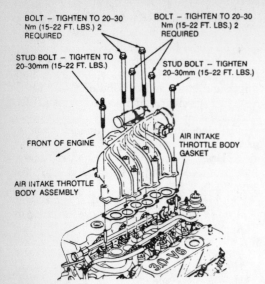

Removing the air intake throttle body on the 3.0L engine

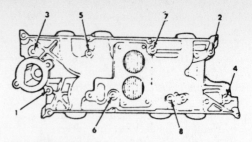

Intake manifold torque sequence on the 2.8L and 2.9L engines

20. Apply sealing compound, joining surfaces of upper and lower intake manifold. Install upper intake manifold gaskets.

21. Install upper intake manifold (plenum) assembly.

22. Connect all vacuum hoses to fittings on upper intake manifold.

23. Connect electrical connections at throttle body, EGR pressure sensor, intake manifolds sub harness to EEC main harness.

24. Install and adjust throttle linkage bracket assembly and cover.

25. Connect hoses from water outlet to radiator, and bypass hose from thermostat housing rear cover to intake manifold.

26. Connect battery negative cable.

27. Refill and bleed the cooling system.

28. Recheck ignition timing and reset engine idle speed to specification.

29. Run engine at fast idle and check for coolant and oil leaks.

3.0L Engine

1. Drain the cooling system (engine cold). Review complete service procedure before starting this repair.

CAUTION: *When draining the coolant, keep in mind that cats and dogs are attracted by the ethylene glycol antifreeze, and are quite likely to drink any that is left in an uncovered container or in puddles on the ground. This will prove fatal in sufficient quantity. Always drain the coolant into a sealable container. Coolant should be reused unless it is contaminated or several years old.*

2. Disconnect the battery ground cable.

3. Depressurize the fuel system and remove

the air intake throttle body as outlined in Chapter 5.

4. Disconnect the fuel return and supply lines.

5. Remove the fuel injector wiring harness from the engine.

6. Disconnect the upper radiator hose.

7. Disconnect the water outlet heater hose.

8. Disconnect the distributor cap with the spark plug wires attached. Matchmark and remove the distributor assembly.

9. Remove the rocker covers. Loosen retaining nut from cylinder #3 intake valve and rotate rocker arm fulcrum away from valve retainer. Remove the pushrod

10. Remove the intake manifold attaching bolts and studs (Torx type socket needed).

11. Lift the intake manifold off the engine. Use a plastic mallet to tap lightly around the intake manifold to break it loose, if necessary. Do not pry between the manifold and cylinder head with any sharp instrument. The manifold can be removed with the fuel rails and injectors in place.

12. Remove the manifold side gaskets and end seals and discard. If the manifold is being replaced, transfer the fuel injector and fuel rail components to the new manifold on a clean workbench. Clean all gasket mating surfaces.

To install:

13. First lightly oil all attaching bolts and stud threads. The intake manifold, cylinder head and cylinder block mating surfaces should be clean and free of old silicone rubber sealer. Use a suitable solvent to clean these areas.

14. Apply silicone rubber sealer (D6AZ-19562–A or equivalent) to the intersection of the cylinder block assembly and head assembly at four corners as illustrated.

NOTE: *When using silicone rubber sealer, assembly must occur within 15 minutes after sealer application. After this time, the sealer may start to set-up and its sealing effectiveness may be reduced. In high temperature/humidity conditions, the RTV will start to skin over in about 5 minutes.*

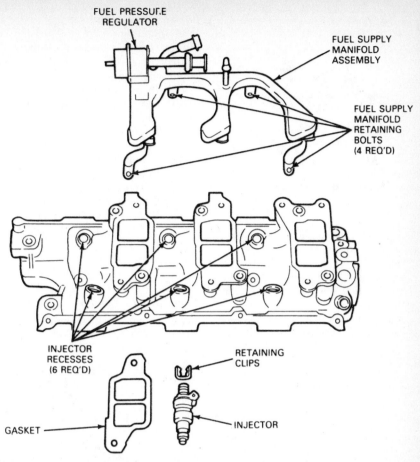

Intake manifold assembly — 2.9L engine

15. Install the front intake manifold seal and rear intake manifold seal and secure them with retaining features.

16. Position the intake manifold gaskets in place and insert the locking tabs over the tabs on the cylinder head gaskets.

17. Apply silicone rubber sealer over the gasket in the same places as in Step 14. 18. Carefully lower the intake manifold into position on the cylinder block and cylinder heads to prevent smearing the silicone sealer and causing gasketing voids.

19. Install the retaining bolts and tighten in two stages, in the sequence illustrated, first to 11 ft. lbs. and then to 18 ft. lbs.

20. If installing a new manifold, install fuel supply rail and injectors. Refer to the necessary service procedures.

21. Install #3 cylinder intake valve pushrod. Apply oil to pushrod and fulcrum prior to installation. Rotate the crankshaft to place the lifter on the heel position or base circle of camshaft. Tighten to 8 ft. lbs. to seat fulcrum in cylinder head. Final bolt torque is 24 ft. lbs.

22. Install rocker covers, fuel injector harness, throttle body assembly, hose and electrical connections.

21. Install the distributor assembly, using the matchmarks make earlier to insure correct alignment. Install the distributor cap and spark plug wires.

22. Install coolant hoses. Connect all vacuum lines. Reconnect fuel lines. Install fuel line safety clips.

23. Fill and bleed cooling system. Replace crankcase oil.

24. Install air cleaner hose. Connect battery ground cable. Start engine and check for coolant, oil, fuel and vacuum leaks.

25. Verify distributor base initial timing as outlined. Check and adjust engine idle as necessary.

4.0L Engine

The intake manifold is a 4-piece assembly, consisting of the upper intake manifold, the throttle body, the fuel supply manifold, and the lower intake manifold.

1. Disconnect the battery ground cable.
2. Remove the air cleaner and intake duct.
3. Remove the weather shield.

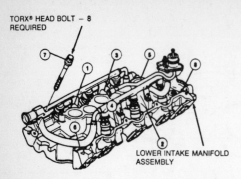

TORX® HEAD BOLT — 8
REQUIRED

LOWER INTAKE MANIFOLD
ASSEMBLY

Intake manifold torque sequence — 3.0L engine

4. Disconnect the throttle cable and bracket.

5. Tag and disconnect all vacuum lines connected to the manifold.

6. Tag and disconnect all electrical wires connected to the manifold assemblies.

7. Relieve the fuel system pressure. See Chapter 1 Fuel Filter.

8. Tag and remove the spark plug wires.

9. Remove the EDIS ignition coil and bracket.

10. Remove the throttle body. See Chapter 5.

11. Remove the 6 attaching nuts and lift off the upper manifold.

12. Remove the rocker covers.

13. Remove the lower intake manifold bolts. Tap the manifold lightly with a plastic mallet and remove it.

14. Clean all surfaces of old gasket material.

To install:

15. Apply RTV silicone gasket material at the junction points of the heads and manifold.

NOTE: *This material will set within 15 minutes, so work quickly!*

16. Install new manifold gaskets and again apply the RTV material.

17. Position the manifold and install the nuts hand tight. Torque the nuts, in 4 stages, in the sequence shown, to 18 ft. lbs.

18. Once again, apply RTV material to the manifold/head joints.

19. Install the rocker covers.

20. Install the upper manifold. Tighten the nuts to 18 ft. lbs.

21. Install the EDIS coil.

22. Connect the fuel and return lines.

23. Install the throttle body.

24. Connect all wires.

25. Connect all vacuum lines.

26. Connect the throttle linkage.

27. Install the weather shield.

28. Install the air cleaner and duct.

29. Fill and bleed the cooling system.

30. Connect the battery ground.

31. Run the engine and check for leaks.

2.2L Diesel Engine

1. Disconnect the battery ground cables from both batteries.

2. Disconnect the air inlet hose from the air

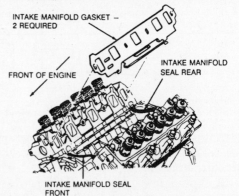

INTAKE MANIFOLD GASKET —
2 REQUIRED

INTAKE MANIFOLD
SEAL REAR

FRONT OF ENGINE

INTAKE MANIFOLD SEAL
FRONT

Installing intake manifold assembly gaskets — 3.0L engine

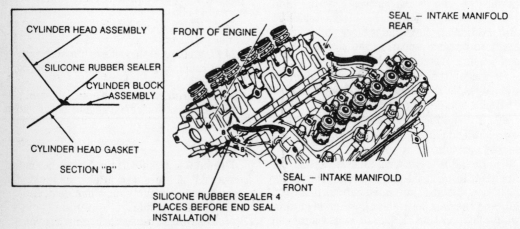

CYLINDER HEAD ASSEMBLY

SILICONE RUBBER SEALER

CYLINDER BLOCK
ASSEMBLY

CYLINDER HEAD GASKET

SECTION "B"

FRONT OF ENGINE

SEAL — INTAKE MANIFOLD
REAR

SEAL — INTAKE MANIFOLD
FRONT

SILICONE RUBBER SEALER 4
PLACES BEFORE END SEAL
INSTALLATION

Apply silicone sealer as shown intake manifold — 3.0L engine

cleaner and intake manifold. Disconnect and remove the fuel injection lines from the nozzles and injection pump. Cap all lines and fittings to prevent dirt pickup.

3. Remove the nut attaching the lower fuel return line brace to the intake manifold.

4. Disconnect and remove the lower fuel line from the injector pump and upper fuel return line.

5. Remove the air conditioner compressor with the lines attached and position out of the way. Remove the power steering pump and rear support with the lines still attached and position out of the way.

6. Remove the air inlet adapter, dropping resistor (electrical measuring device) and the gaskets.

7. Disconnect the fuel filter inlet line, remove the fuel filter mounting bracket from the cylinder head and position the filter assembly out of the way.

8. Remove the mounting nuts for the fuel line heater assembly to intake manifold and position the heater out of the way.

9. Remove the nuts that attach the intake manifold to the cylinder head. Remove the intake manifold and gasket.

To install:

10. Position intake manifold on cylinder head and install two nuts.

11. Do not tighten the mounting nuts until No. 3 lower nut that holds the fuel return line bracket is installed. After installation of the No. 3 nut, tighten all of the mounting nuts to 12–17 ft. lbs.

12. Install inlet fitting on intake manifold. Tighten bolts to specification.

13. Install A/C compressor and bracket brace.

14. Connect battery ground cables to both batteries.

15. Run engine and check for oil and intake air leaks.

2.3L Turbo Diesel Engine

1. Disconnect battery ground cables from both batteries.

2. Remove support braces from A/C compressor bracket, inlet fitting, and intake manifold.

3. Remove A/C compressor from mounting bracket and position out of the way.

4. Remove inlet fitting from intake manifold.

5. Remove turbo oil feed line from cylinder head and turbo center housing. Remove oil line clamp bolt.

6. Loosen bolts attaching turbo heat shield to exhaust manifold. Remove top bolt and position shield out of the way.

7. Remove wastegate actuator from turbo and mounting bracket.

8. Remove two top actuator mounting bracket bolts. Loosen bottom bracket bolts and position bracket out of the way.

9. Remove five remaining intake manifold bolts and two nuts and remove intake manifold.

To install:

10. Position intake manifold on cylinder head and install two nuts.

11. Rotate wastegate actuator mounting bracket and install two top mounting bolts. Install five remaining intake manifold bolts. Tighten all intake manifold and wastegate actuator mounting bracket hardware to specification.

12. Install wastegate actuator. Tighten mounting bolts to specification.

13. Install turbo heat shield on exhaust manifold.

14. Install turbo oil feed line. Tighten fittings and clamp bolt to specification.

15. Install inlet fitting on intake manifold. Tighten bolts to specification.

16. Install A/C compressor and bracket brace.

17. Connect battery ground cables to both batteries.

18. Run engine and check for oil and intake air leaks.

Exhaust Manifold

REMOVAL AND INSTALLATION

2.0L, 2.3L Engines

1. Remove the air cleaner and dust assembly. Disconnect the negative battery cable.

2. Remove the EGR line at the exhaust manifold. Loosen the EGR tube. Remove the check valve at the exhaust manifold and disconnect the hose at the end of the air by-pass valve.

3. Remove the bracket attaching the heater hoses to the valve cover. Disconnect the exhaust pipe from the exhaust manifold.

4. Remove the exhaust manifold mounting bolts/nuts and remove the manifold.

5. Install the exhaust manifold in the reverse order. Torque the manifold in sequence

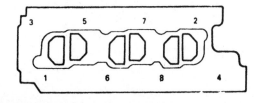

Intake manifold torque sequence — 4.0L engine

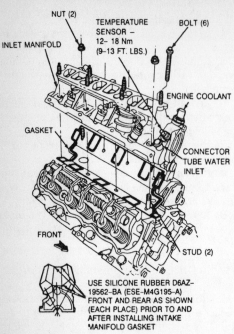

NUT (2)
TEMPERATURE SENSOR – 12– 18 Nm (9–13 FT. LBS.)
BOLT (6)
INLET MANIFOLD
ENGINE COOLANT
GASKET
CONNECTOR TUBE WATER INLET
FRONT
STUD (2)

USE SILICONE RUBBER D6AZ–19562–BA (ESE–M4G195–A) FRONT AND REAR AS SHOWN (EACH PLACE) PRIOR TO AND AFTER INSTALLING INTAKE MANIFOLD GASKET

Intake manifold gasket — 4.0L engine

in two steps, first 5–7 ft. lbs. and then 16–23 ft. lbs.

2.8L, 2.9L Engines

1. Remove the air cleaner.
2. Remove the attaching nuts from the exhaust manifold shroud (left side).
3. Disconnect the attaching nuts from the muffler inlet pipe. Remove Thermactor components as necessary to allow the removal of the exhaust manifold(s).
4. Disconnect the choke heat tubes at the carburetor.
5. Remove the manifold attaching bolts.
6. Lift the manifold from the cylinder head.

To install:
7. Position the manifold on the heads and install and tighten the attaching bolts to specification.
8. Install a new inlet pipe gasket. Install and tighten the inlet pipe attaching nuts.
9. Position the exhaust manifold shroud on the manifold and install and tighten the attaching nuts to specification (left side). Install the Thermactor components that had been removed.
10. Install the air cleaner. Reinstall the choke heat tube (if so equipped).

3.0L Engine

1. Disconnect the negative battery cable. Raise and safely support the vehicle as necessary.
2. Remove the spark plugs.
3. If removing the left side exhaust manifold remove the oil level indicator tube retaining nut, rotate the dipstick assembly out of the way.
4. Remove the manifold to exhaust pipe attaching nuts, then separate the exhaust pipe from the manifold.
5. Remove the exhaust manifold attaching bolts and the manifold.

To install:
6. Clean all gasket mating surfaces.
7. Lightly oil all bolt and stud threads before installation. If a new manifold is being installed, the oxygen sensor will have to be transferred to the new part.
8. Position the exhaust manifold on the cylinder head and install the manifold attaching bolts. Tighten them to 18 ft. lbs.
9. Connect (replace gasket if so equipped) the exhaust pipe to the manifold, then tighten the attaching nuts to 30 ft. lbs. TIGHTEN BOTH NUTS IN EQUAL AMOUNTS TO CORRECTLY SEAT INLET PIPE FLANGE.
10. Install oil tube dipstick assembly (apply sealer to tube-if removed) as necessary. Install spark plugs.
11. Connect the negative battery cable. Start the engine and check for oil and exhaust leaks.

4.0L Engine

LEFT SIDE

1. Disconnect the negative battery cable. Remove the oil level indicator tube bracket.
2. Remove the power steering pump hoses.
3. Remove the exhaust pipe-to-manifold bolts.
4. Unbolt and remove the manifold.
5. Clean and lightly oil all fastener threads.
6. Installation is the reverse of removal. Replace all gaskets if so equipped. Torque the man-

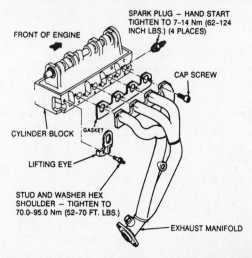

SPARK PLUG – HAND START TIGHTEN TO 7–14 Nm (62–124 INCH LBS.) (4 PLACES)
FRONT OF ENGINE
CAP SCREW
CYLINDER BLOCK
GASKET
LIFTING EYE
STUD AND WASHER HEX SHOULDER – TIGHTEN TO 70.0–95.0 Nm (52–70 FT. LBS.)
EXHAUST MANIFOLD

Exhaust manifold assembly — 2.3L engine

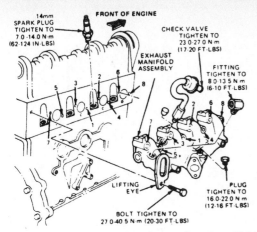

2.0L and 2.3L carbureted engines, exhaust manifold installation

ifold bolts to 19 ft. lbs.; the exhaust pipe nuts to 20 ft. lbs. TIGHTEN BOTH EXHAUST PIPE RETAINING NUTS IN EQUAL AMOUNTS TO CORRECTLY SEAT INLET PIPE FLANGE.

RIGHT SIDE

1. Drain the cooling system.

CAUTION: *When draining the coolant, keep in mind that cats and dogs are attracted by the ethylene glycol antifreeze, and are quite likely to drink any that is left in an uncovered container or in puddles on the ground. This will prove fatal in sufficient quantity. Always drain the coolant into a sealable container. Coolant should be reused unless it is contaminated or several years old.*

2. Remove the heater hose support bracket.
3. Disconnect the heater hoses.
4. Remove the exhaust pipe-to-manifold nuts.
5. Unbolt and remove the manifold.
6. Installation is the reverse of removal. Replace all gaskets if so equipped. Torque the manifold bolts to 19 ft. lbs.; the exhaust pipe nuts to 20 ft. lbs. TIGHTEN BOTH EXHAUST PIPE RETAINING NUTS IN EQUAL AMOUNTS TO CORRECTLY SEAT INLET PIPE FLANGE.

2.2L Diesel Engine

1. Disconnect the ground cables from both batteries.
2. Disconnect the exhaust pipe from the manifold.
3. Remove the heater hose bracket from the valve cover and exhaust manifold studs.
4. Remove the vacuum pump support brace and bracket. Remove the bolt that attaches the

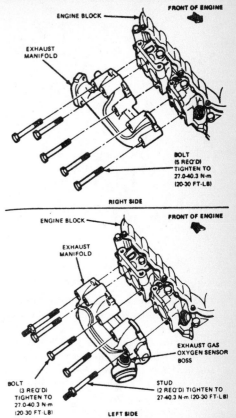

2.8L and 2.9L engine exhaust manifold torque sequence

engine oil dipstick tube support bracket to the exhaust manifold.

5. Remove the nuts that attach the exhaust manifold to the engine and remove the manifold.

6. Clean all gasket mounting surfaces. Install a new mounting gasket and install the exhaust manifold and components in the reverse order of removal. Torque the mounting bolts to 17–20 ft. lbs. After warning up engine retighten to the same torque specification.

2.3L Turbo Diesel Engine

1. Disconnect battery ground cable from both batteries.
2. Remove support brackets from A/C compressor bracket, inlet fitting and intake manifold.
3. Remove A/C compressor from mounting bracket and position out of the way.
4. Remove inlet fitting from intake manifold.
5. Remove air inlet tube from air cleaner-to-turbo inlet.
6. Remove wastegate actuator from turbocharger and mounting bracket.

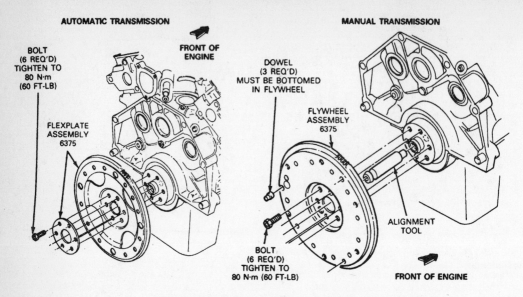

Flywheel/Flex plate assembly — 3.0L engine

7. Raise vehicle and disconnect muffler inlet pipe from turbo exhaust fitting. Lower vehicle.

8. Disconnect turbo oil feed line from cylinder head and turbo center housing.

9. Remove nuts attaching exhaust manifold to cylinder head and remove exhaust manifold and turbocharger as an assembly.

10. Remove turbocharger from exhaust manifold if necessary.

To install:

11. Install turbocharger on exhaust manifold, if removed. Tighten nuts to specification.

12. Position exhaust manifold on cylinder head and install attaching nut. Tighten nuts to specification.

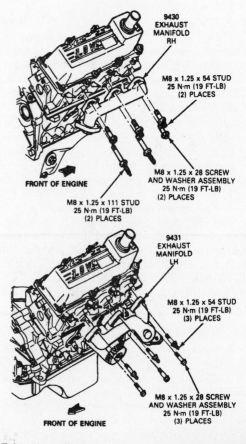

Exhaust manifold assembly — 3.0L engine

Exhaust manifold assembly — 3.0L engine

13. Install turbo oil feed line and tighten fittings and clamp bolt to specification.

14. Raise vehicle and connect muffler inlet pipe to turbo exhaust fitting. Tighten to specification. Lower vehicle.

15. Install wastegate actuator. Tighten bolts to specification.

16. Install air inlet tube between turbo inlet and air cleaner.

17. Connect inlet fitting to intake manifold and tighten to specification.

18. Install A/C compressor and compressor mounting bracket braces.

19. Connect battery ground cables to both batteries.

20. Run engine and check for oil and exhaust leaks.

Turbocharger

REMOVAL AND INSTALLATION

2.3L Turbo Diesel Engine

1. Disconnect battery ground cable from both batteries.

2. Remove support brackets from A/C compressor bracket, inlet fitting and intake manifold.

3. Remove A/C compressor from mounting bracket and position out of the way.

4. Remove inlet fitting from intake manifold.

5. Remove air inlet tube from air cleaner-to-turbo inlet.

6. Remove wastegate actuator from turbocharger and mounting bracket.

7. Raise vehicle and disconnect muffler inlet pipe from turbo exhaust fitting. Lower vehicle.

8. Disconnect turbo oil feed line from cylinder head and turbo center housing.

9. Remove nuts attaching exhaust manifold to cylinder head and remove exhaust manifold and turbocharger as an assembly.

10. Remove turbocharger from exhaust manifold.

11. Install turbocharger on exhaust manifold. Tighten nuts to specification.

12. Position exhaust manifold on cylinder head and install attaching nut. Tighten nuts to specification.

13. Install turbo oil feed line and tighten fittings and clamp bolt to specification.

14. Raise vehicle and connect muffler inlet pipe to turbo exhaust fitting. Tighten to specification. Lower vehicle.

15. Install wastegate actuator. Tighten bolts to specification.

16. Install air inlet tube between turbo inlet and air cleaner.

17. Connect inlet fitting to intake manifold and tighten to specification.

18. Install A/C compressor and compressor mounting bracket braces.

19. Connect battery ground cables to both batteries.

20. Run engine and check for oil and exhaust leaks.

Air Conditioning Compressor

REMOVAL AND INSTALLATION

1. Have the system discharged by a professional service person.

2. Disconnect the two refrigerant lines from the compressor. Cap the openings immediately!

3. Remove tension from the drive belt. Remove the belt.

4. Disconnect the clutch wire at the connector.

5. Remove the bolt attaching the support brace to the front brace and the nut attaching the support brace to the intake manifold. Remove the support brace.

6. Remove the two bolts attaching the rear support to the bracket.

7. Remove the bolt attaching the compressor tab to the front brace and the two bolts attaching the compressor front legs to the bracket.

8. Remove the compressor.

9. Installation is the reverse of removal service procedure. Use new O-rings coated with clean refrigerant oil at all fittings. Charge and leak test the system. See Chapter 1.

Radiator

REMOVAL AND INSTALLATION

1. Drain the cooling system. Remove the overflow tube from the coolant recovery bottle and from the radiator.

CAUTION: *When draining the coolant, keep in mind that cats and dogs are attracted by the ethylene glycol antifreeze, and are quite likely to drink any that is left in an uncovered container or in puddles on the ground. This will prove fatal in sufficient quantity. Always drain the coolant into a sealable container. Coolant should be reused unless it is contaminated or several years old.*

2. Disconnect the transmission cooling lines from the bottom of the radiator, if so equipped.

3. Remove the retaining bolts at the top of the shroud, and position the shroud over the fan, clear of the radiator.

4. Disconnect the upper and lower hoses from the radiator.

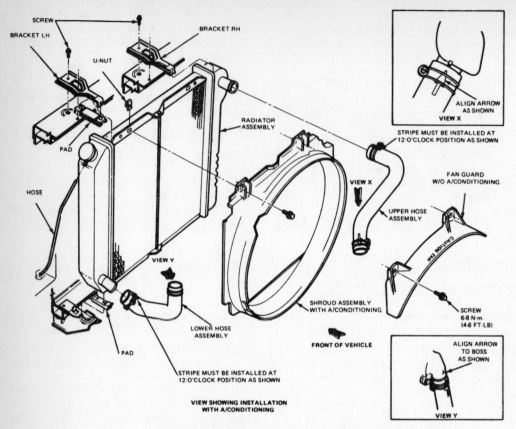

Radiator assembly — 2.8L and 2.9L engines

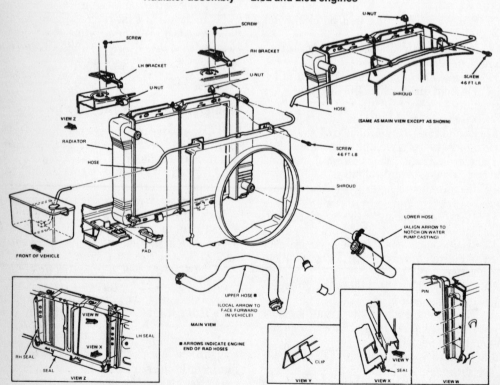

Radiator installation — 2.0L and 2.3L engines

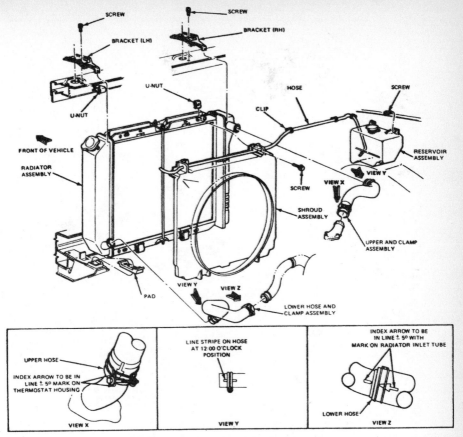

Radiator installation — 2.2L diesel engine

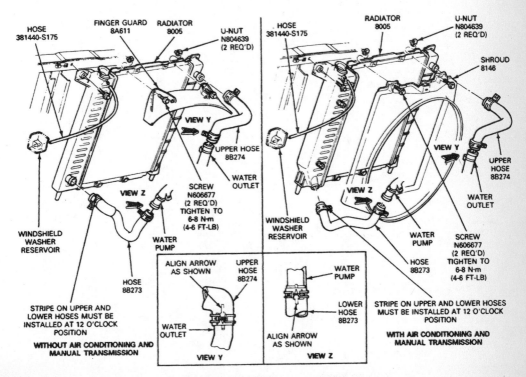

Radiator installation — 2.9L engine

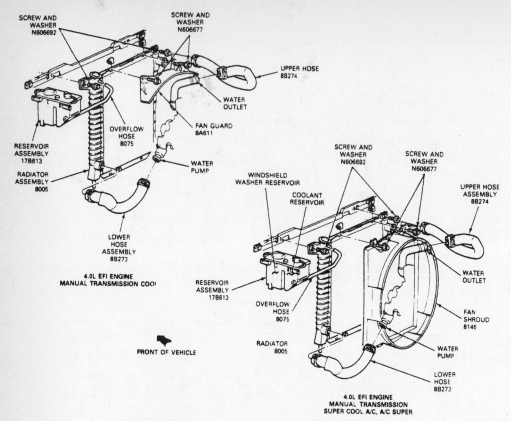

Radiator installation — Explorer 4.0L engine with M/T

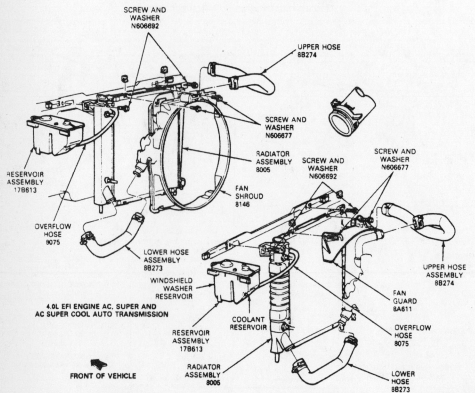

Radiator installation — Explorer 4.0L engine with A/T

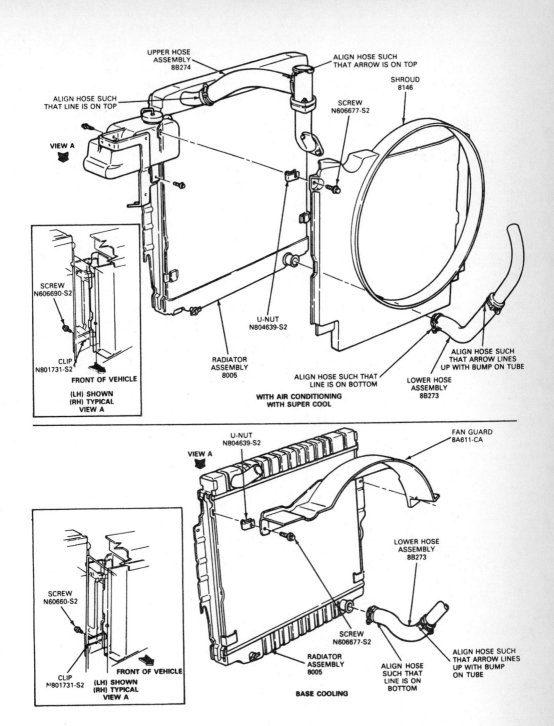

UPPER HOSE
ASSEMBLY
8B274

ALIGN HOSE SUCH
THAT ARROW IS ON TOP

SHROUD
8146

ALIGN HOSE SUCH
THAT LINE IS ON TOP

SCREW
N606677-S2

VIEW A

SCREW
N606690-S2

CLIP
N801731-S2

FRONT OF VEHICLE

(LH) SHOWN
(RH) TYPICAL
VIEW A

U-NUT
N804639-S2

RADIATOR
ASSEMBLY
8005

ALIGN HOSE SUCH THAT
LINE IS ON BOTTOM

LOWER HOSE
ASSEMBLY
8B273

ALIGN HOSE SUCH
THAT ARROW LINES
UP WITH BUMP ON TUBE

WITH AIR CONDITIONING
WITH SUPER COOL

U-NUT
N804639-S2

VIEW A

FAN GUARD
8A611-CA

SCREW
N60660-S2

CLIP
N801731-S2

FRONT OF VEHICLE

(LH) SHOWN
(RH) TYPICAL
VIEW A

RADIATOR
ASSEMBLY
8005

SCREW
N606677-S2

ALIGN HOSE
SUCH THAT
LINE IS ON
BOTTOM

LOWER HOSE
ASSEMBLY
8B273

ALIGN HOSE SUCH
THAT ARROW LINES
UP WITH BUMP
ON TUBE

BASE COOLING

Radiator installation — 2.3L turbo diesel engine

5. Remove the radiator retaining bolts or the upper supports and lift the radiator from the vehicle.

6. Install the radiator in the reverse order of removal. Fill the cooling system and check for leaks.

Air Conditioning Condenser

REMOVAL AND INSTALLATION

1. Have the system discharged by a professional service person.

2. Disconnect the refrigerant lines from the condenser using the proper spring lock tool. Cap all opening immediately!

NOTE: *The fittings are spring-lock couplings and a special tool, T81P–19623-G, should be used. The larger opening end of the tool is for $^{1}/_{2}$ in. discharge lines; the smaller end for $^{3}/_{8}$ in. liquid lines. To operate the tool, close the tool and push the tool into the open side of the cage to expand the garter spring and release the female fitting. If the tool is not inserted straight, the garter spring will cock and not release. After the garter spring is released, pull the fittings apart.*

3. Drain the cooling system.

CAUTION: *When draining the coolant, keep in mind that cats and dogs are attracted by the ethylene glycol antifreeze, and are quite likely to drink any that is left in an uncovered container or in puddles on the ground. This will prove fatal in sufficient quantity. Always drain the coolant into a sealable container. Coolant should be reused unless it is contaminated or several years old.*

4. Disconnect the upper radiator hose.

5. Remove the bolts retaining the ends of the radiator upper support to the side supports.

6. Carefully pull the top edge of the radiator rearward and remove the condenser upper support.

7. Lift out the condenser.

8. If a new condenser is being installed, add 1 fluid.oz. of new refrigerant oil to the new condenser. Installation is the reverse of removal. Always use new O-rings coated with clean refrigerant oil on the line fittings. Charge and leak test the system. See Chapter 1.

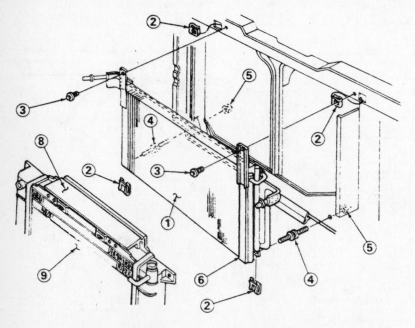

ITEM	PART NUMBER	DESCRIPTION	ITEM	PART NUMBER	DESCRIPTION
1.	19710	CONDENSER ASSY.	5.	N806046-S2	NUT & WASHER (19710 TO RADIATOR SUPPORT) (2 REQ'D.)
2.	N623342-S2	"U" NUT (19710 TO RADIATOR SUPPORT) (4 REQ'D.)	6.	19E572	SEAL (2 REQ'D. ON SOME AUTO TRANS. APPLICATIONS)
3.	N605892-S2	BOLT — (19710 TO RADIATOR SUPPORT) (2 REQ'D.)	7.	19E572	CONDENSER BOTTOM SEAL (WITH AUTO TRANS. ONLY)
4.	N806047-S2	STUD & WASHER (TO LOWER MOUNTING BRACKET) (2 REQ'D	8.	19E572	CONDENSER TOP SEAL
			9.	(REF.)	RADIATOR ASSY.

Condenser assembly

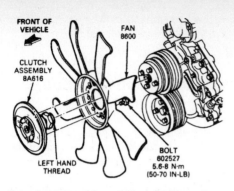

Radiator fan assembly — 2.9L and 3.0L engines

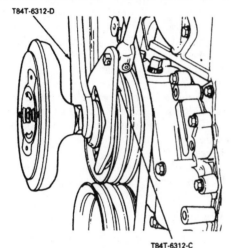

Removing the fan/clutch assembly

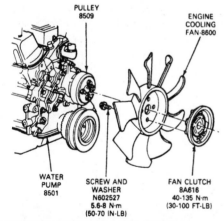

Radiator fan assembly — 4.0L engine

Engine Fan

REMOVAL AND INSTALLATION

NOTE: *Refer to exploded view illustration before starting this service procedure.*

2.0L and 2.3L Gas Engine
2.2L Diesel Engine

1. Unbolt and remove the fan finger guard.

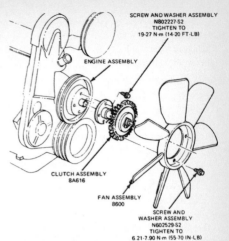

Radiator fan assembly — 2.0L and 2.3L gas engines

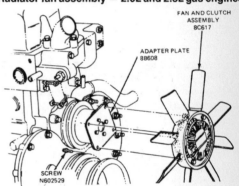

Radiator fan assembly — 2.2 diesel engine

2. Disconnect the overflow tube from the shroud, remove the mounting screws and lift the shroud off the brackets.

3. Place the shroud behind the fan.

4. Remove the 4 clutch/fan assembly-to-pulley screws and remove the clutch/fan assembly.

5. Remove the 4 fan-to-clutch screws.

6. Installation is the reverse of removal. Torque the fan-to-clutch screws to 55–70 inch lbs.; the fan/clutch assembly-to-pulley bolts to 12–18 ft. lbs.

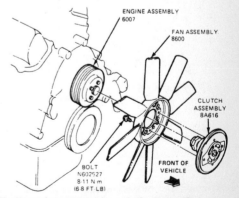

Radiator fan assembly — 2.8L gas engine

2.8L Engine
2.9L Engine
3.0L Engine
2.3 Diesel Engines

1. Remove the fan shroud.
2. Using Strap Wrench D79L–6731–A and Fan Clutch Nut Wrench T83T–6312–B, or their equivalents, loosen the large nut attaching the clutch to the water pump hub.

NOTE: *The nut is loosened clockwise.*

3. Remove the fan/clutch assembly.
4. Remove the fan-to-clutch bolts.

To install:

5. Installation is the reverse of removal. Torque the fan-to-clutch bolts to 55–70 inch lbs.; the hub nut to 50–100 ft. lbs. Don't forget, the hub is tightened counterclockwise.

4.0L Engine

1. Remove the fan shroud.
2. Using Fan Clutch Pulley Holder T84T–6312–C and Fan Clutch Nut Wrench T84T–6312–D, or their equivalents, loosen the large nut attaching the clutch to the water pump hub.

NOTE: *The nut is loosened clockwise.*

3. Remove the fan/clutch assembly.
4. Remove the fan-to-clutch bolts.

To install:

5. Installation is the reverse of removal. Torque the fan-to-clutch bolts to 55–70 inch lbs.; the hub nut to 50–100 ft. lbs. Don't forget, the hub is tightened counterclockwise.

Water Pump

REMOVAL AND INSTALLATION

2.0L, 2.3L Engines

1. Disconnect the negative battery cable.
2. Remove the two bolts that retain the fan shroud and position the shroud back over the fan.
3. Remove the four bolts that retain the cooling fan. Remove the fan and shroud.
4. Loosen and remove the power steering and A/C compressor drive belts.
5. Remove the water pump pulley and the vent hose to the emissions canister.
6. Remove the heater hose at the water pump.
7. Remove the cam belt cover. Remove the lower radiator hose from the water pump.
8. Remove the water pump mounting bolts and the water pump. Clean all gasket mounting surfaces.
9. Install the water pump in the reverse order of removal. Coat the threads of the mounting bolts with sealer before installation.

2.8L, 2.9L Engines

1. Drain the coolant from the radiator and remove the lower hose and the return hose from the water inlet housing.

CAUTION: *When draining the coolant, keep in mind that cats and dogs are attracted by the ethylene glycol antifreeze, and are quite likely to drink any that is left in an uncovered container or in puddles on the ground.*

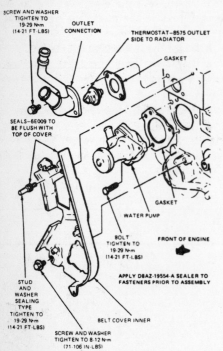

Water pump and related components — 2.0L and 2.3L engines

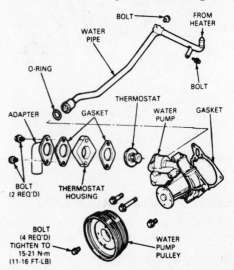

Water pump and related components — 2.3L turbo diesel engine

This will prove fatal in sufficient quantity. Always drain the coolant into a sealable container. Coolant should be reused unless it is contaminated or several years old.

2. Using Tools T83T–6312–A and B remove the fan and clutch assembly from the front of the water pump.

NOTE: *The fan clutch assembly uses a left hand thread, remove by turning the nut counterclockwise.*

3. Loosen the alternator mounting bolts and remove the alternator belt.

4. Remove the water pump pulley.

5. Remove the bolts retaining the water pump assembly and remove the water pump, water inlet housing, and the thermostat from the front cover.

6. Before installing the water pump, clean the gasket surfaces on the front cover and on the water pump assembly. Apply gasket sealer to both sides of the new gasket and install the water pump in the reverse order of removal.

2.2L Diesel and 2.3L Turbo Diesel Engines

1. Disconnect the ground cables from both batteries. Drain the cooling system.

CAUTION: *When draining the coolant, keep in mind that cats and dogs are attracted by the ethylene glycol antifreeze, and are quite likely to drink any that is left in an uncovered container or in puddles on the ground. This will prove fatal in sufficient quantity. Always drain the coolant into a sealable container. Coolant should be reused unless it is contaminated or several years old.*

2. Remove all drive belts.

3. Remove the radiator fan shroud, cooling fan and pump pulley. Disconnect the heater hose, by-pass hose and radiator hose from the water pump.

4. Remove the nuts and bolts that mount the water pump to the engine.

5. Clean all gasket mounting surfaces.

6. Install water pump in the reverse order of removal service procedure.

3.0L Engine

1. Disconnect the battery ground cable.
2. Drain the cooling system.
3. Remove the engine fan.
4. Loosen the 4 water pump pulley bolts.
5. Remove the accessory drive belts.
6. Remove the water pump pulley.
7. Remove the alternator adjusting arm and throttle body brace.
8. Remove the lower radiator hose.
9. Disconnect the heater hose at the pump.
10. Rotate the belt adjuster out of the way.
11. Remove the water pump attaching bolts. Note their location for installation.
12. Remove the pump and discard the gasket.
13. Thoroughly clean the pump and engine mating surfaces.
14. Using an adhesive type sealer, position a new gasket on the timing cover.
15. Position the water pump and start the bolts. When all the bolts are started, torque them to specifications. Refer to the necessary illustration.
16. Install the lower hose and connect the radiator hose.
17. Install the pulley and hand tighten the 4 bolts.
18. Install the alternator adjusting arm and brace.
19. Install the belts and tension them. See Chapter 1.
20. Tighten the 4 pulley bolts to 19 ft. lbs.
21. Install the fan.

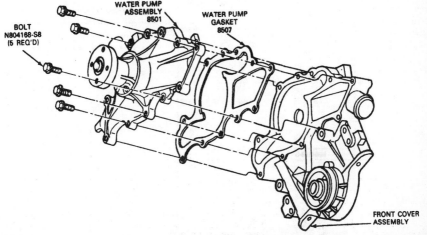

Water pump assembly — 3.0L engine

22. Fill and bleed the cooling system.

23. Connect the battery ground cable. Run the engine and check for leaks.

4.0L Engine

1. Drain the cooling system.
2. Remove the lower radiator hose.
3. Disconnect the heater hose at the pump.
4. Remove the fan and fan clutch assembly. You'll have to hold the pulley while loosening the fan clutch nut. There is a tool made for this purpose which will make the job easier, Ford tool No. T84T–6312–C.

NOTE: *The nut has left-hand threads. It is removed by turning it clockwise.*

5. Loosen the alternator mounting bolts and remove the belt. On vehicles with air conditioning, remove the alternator and bracket.
6. Remove the water pump pulley.
7. Remove the attaching bolts and remove the water pump.
8. Clean the mounting surfaces of the pump and front cover thoroughly. Remove all traces of gasket material.

9. Apply adhesive gasket sealer to both sides of a new gasket and place the gasket on the pump.

10. Position the pump on the cover and install the bolts finger-tight. When all bolts are in place, torque them to 72–108 inch lbs. (6–9 ft. lbs.).

11. Install the pulley.

12. On vehicles with air conditioning, install the alternator and bracket.

13. Install and adjust the drive belt.

14. Connect the hoses and tighten the clamps.

15. Install the fan and clutch assembly. Tighten the nut to 50–100 ft. lbs.

NOTE: *The nut is tightened counterclockwise.*

16. Fill and bleed the cooling system. Start the engine and check for leaks.

FRONT COVER, WATER PUMP — FASTENER CHART

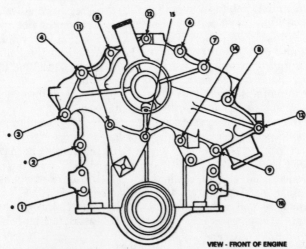

VIEW - FRONT OF ENGINE

Fastener and Hole No.	Fasteners			
	Part No.	Size	N·m	Ft-Lb
● 1	N804215	M8 x 1.25 x 72.25	25	19
● 2	N804215	M8 x 1.25 x 72.25	25	19
● 3	N606547-S8	M8 x 1.25 x 70.0	25	19
4	N606547-S8	M8 x 1.25 x 70.0	25	19
5	N605909-S8	M8 x 1.25 x 42.0	25	19
6	N804154-S8	M8 x 1.25 x 99.3	25	19
7	N606547-S8	M8 x 1.25 x 70.0	25	19
8	N606547-S8	M8 x 1.25 x 70.0	25	19
9	N606547-S8	M8 x 1.25 x 70.0	25	19
10	N605909-S8	M8 x 1.25 x 42.0	25	19
11	N804168-S8	M6 x 1.0 x 25.0	10	7
12	N804168-S8	M6 x 1.0 x 25.0	10	7
13	N804168-S8	M6 x 1.0 x 25.0	10	7
14	N804168-S8	M6 x 1.0 x 25.0	10	7
15	N804168-S8	M6 x 1.0 x 25.0	10	7

NOTE: ●Apply Pipe Sealant with Teflon D8AZ-19554-A (ESG-M4G194-A) Sealer to Fastener Threads

Water pump front cover fastener chart — 3.0L engine

Cylinder Head

REMOVAL AND INSTALLATION

2.0L, 2.3L Carbureted Engines

1. Drain the cooling system. Disconnect the negative battery cables.

CAUTION: *When draining the coolant, keep in mind that cats and dogs are attracted by the ethylene glycol antifreeze, and are quite likely to drink any that is left in an uncovered container or in puddles on the ground. This will prove fatal in sufficient quantity. Always drain the coolant into a sealable container. Coolant should be reused unless it is contaminated or several years old.*

2. Remove the air cleaner.
3. Remove the valve cover.

NOTE: *On models with air conditioning, remove the mounting bolts and the drive belt, and position the compressor out of the way. Remove the compressor upper mounting bracket from the cylinder head.*

CAUTION: *If the compressor refrigerant lines do not have enough slack to permit repositioning of the compressor without first disconnecting the refrigerant lines, the air conditioning system will have to be evacuated by a trained air conditioning serviceman. Under no circumstances should an untrained person attempt to disconnect the air conditioning refrigerant lines.*

4. Remove the intake and exhaust manifolds from the head.
5. Remove the camshaft drive belt cover. Note the location of the belt cover attaching screws that have rubber grommets.
6. Loosen the drive belt tensioner and remove the belt.
7. Remove the water outlet elbow from the cylinder head with the hose attached.
8. Remove the cylinder head attaching bolts.
9. Remove the cylinder head from the engine.

To install:

10. Clean all gasket material and carbon from the top of the cylinder block and pistons and from the bottom of the cylinder head.
11. Position a new cylinder head gasket on the engine and place the head on the engine.

NOTE: *If you encounter difficulty in positioning the cylinder head on the engine block, it may be necessary to install guide studs in the block to correctly align the head and the block. To fabricate guide studs, obtain two new cylinder head bolts and cut their heads off with a hack saw. Install the bolts in the holes in the engine block which correspond*

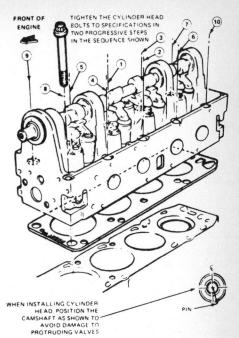

TIGHTEN THE CYLINDER HEAD BOLTS TO SPECIFICATIONS IN TWO PROGRESSIVE STEPS IN THE SEQUENCE SHOWN

FRONT OF ENGINE

WHEN INSTALLING CYLINDER HEAD, POSITION THE CAMSHAFT AS SHOWN TO AVOID DAMAGE TO PROTRUDING VALVES

PIN

Cylinder head installation — 2.0L and 2.3L carbureted engines

with cylinder head bolt holes Nos. 3 and 4, as identified in the cylinder head bolt tightening sequence illustration. Then, install the head gasket and head over the bolts. Install the cylinder head attaching bolts, replacing the studs with the original head bolts.

12. Using a torque wrench, tighten the head bolts in the sequence in two steps, first 50–60 ft. lbs., then 80–90 ft. lbs.
13. Install the camshaft drive belt.
14. Install the camshaft drive belt cover and its attaching bolts. Make sure the rubber grommets are installed on the bolts. Tighten the bolts to 6–13 ft. lbs.
15. Install the water outlet elbow and a new gasket on the engine and tighten the attaching bolts to 12–15 ft. lbs.
16. Install the intake and exhaust manifolds.
17. Assemble the rest of the components in reverse order of removal procedure.

2.3L EFI Engine

1. Drain cooling system.

CAUTION: *When draining the coolant, keep in mind that cats and dogs are attracted by the ethylene glycol antifreeze, and are quite likely to drink any that is left in an uncovered container or in puddles on the ground. This will prove fatal in sufficient quantity. Always drain the coolant into a sealable container. Coolant should be reused unless it is contaminated or several years old.*

2. Remove air cleaner assembly.

3. Remove one heater hose retaining screw to rocker cover.

4. Disconnect distributor cap and spark plug wire and remove assembly.

5. Remove spark plugs.

6. Disconnect required vacuum hoses.

7. Remove dipstick.

8. Remove rocker retaining bolts and remove cover.

9. Remove intake manifold retaining bolts.

10. Loosen alternator retaining bolts and remove belt from the pulley. Remove mounting bracket retaining bolts to the head.

11. Disconnect upper radiator hose at both ends and remove from vehicle.

12. Remove cam belt cover four bolts and remove cover. For power steering-equipped vehicles, move power steering pump bracket.

13. Loosen cam idler retaining bolts. Position idler in the unloaded position and tighten the retaining bolts.

14. Remove cam belt from the cam pulley and auxiliary pulley.

15. Remove four nuts and/or stud bolts retaining heat stove to exhaust manifold.

16. Remove the eight exhaust manifold retaining bolts.

17. Remove the cam belt idler and two bracket bolts.

18. Remove cam belt idler spring stop from the cylinder head.

19. Disconnect oil sending unit lead wire.

20. Remove cylinder head retaining bolts.

21. Remove the cylinder head.

22. Clean cylinder head gasket surface at the block.

23. Clean intake manifold gasket surface at the intake manifold.

24. Clean exhaust manifold gasket surface at the exhaust manifold.

25. Clean exhaust manifold gasket surface at the cylinder head.

26. Clean cylinder head gasket surface at the cylinder head.

27. Clean intake manifold gasket surface at the cylinder head.

28. Blow oil out of the cylinder head bolt block hoses.

29. Clean rocker cover gasket surface on the head.

30. Check cylinder head for flatness.

To install:

31. Position head gasket on the block.

32. Clean rocker arm cover (cam cover).

33. Install rocker cover gasket to the rocker cover.

34. Position cylinder head to block.

35. Install cylinder head retaining bolts and tighten to specifications.

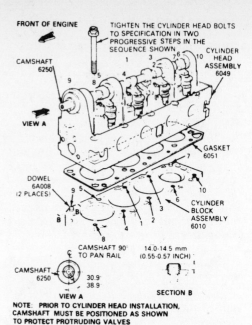

NOTE: PRIOR TO CYLINDER HEAD INSTALLATION, CAMSHAFT MUST BE POSITIONED AS SHOWN TO PROTECT PROTRUDING VALVES

Cylinder head installation — 2.3L EFI engine

36. Connect oil sending unit lead wires.

37. Install cam belt idler spring stop to the cylinder head.

38. Position cam belt idler to cylinder head, and install retaining bolts.

39. Install the eight exhaust manifold retaining bolts and/or stud bolts.

40. Install four nuts and/or stud bolts retaining heat stove to exhaust manifold.

41. Align distributor rotor with No. one plug location in the distributor cap.

42. Align cam gear with pointer.

43. Align crank pulley (TDC) with pointer on cam belt cover.

44. Position cam belt to pulleys (cam and auxiliary).

45. Loosen idler retaining bolts, rotate engine and check timing alignment.

46. Adjust belt tensioner and tighten retaining bolts.

47. Install four cam belt cover and four retaining bolts.

48. Connect upper radiator hose to engine and radiator and tighten retaining clamps.

49. Position alternator bracket to cylinder head and install retainers.

50. Position drive belt to pulley and adjust belt tension using Belt Tension Gauge Rotunda 021–00045 or equivalent.

51. Position intake manifold to head, and install retaining bolts.

52. Install rocker arm covers and retaining bolts.

53. Install spark plugs.

54. Install dipstick.

55. Connect appropriate vacuum hoses.

56. Position and connect spark plug wires and distributor.

57. Install one retaining heater/hose screw to the rocker cover.

58. Fill cooling system.

59. Start engine and check for leaks.

60. Adjust ignition timing and connect distributor vacuum line.

61. Adjust carburetor idle speed in mixture.

62. Install air cleaner.

2.8L, 2.9L Engines

1. Disconnect the battery ground cable.

2. Drain the radiator coolant.

CAUTION: *When draining the coolant, keep in mind that cats and dogs are attracted by the ethylene glycol antifreeze, and are quite likely to drink any that is left in an uncovered container or in puddles on the ground. This will prove fatal in sufficient quantity. Always drain the coolant into a sealable container. Coolant should be reused unless it is contaminated or several years old.*

3. Remove the air cleaner from the carburetor and disconnect the throttle linkage on the 2.8L. Remove the intake tube from the throttle body and disconnect the throttle linkage and cover on the 2.9L.

4. Remove the distributor. Refer to Distributor, Removal and Installation as described earlier in this Chapter.

5. Remove the radiator hose and the bypass hose from the thermostat housing and intake manifold.

6. Remove the rocker arm covers and the rocker arm shafts as described in this Chapter.

7. Remove the fuel line from carburetor and remove the carburetor on the 2.8L. Depressureize the fuel system and remove the fuel line from the fuel rail on the 2.9L.

8. Remove the intake manifold as described in this Chapter.

9. Remove and label the pushrods in order to keep them in sequence for proper assembly.

10. Remove the exhaust manifolds as described in this Chapter.

11. Remove the cylinder head attaching bolts. Remove the cylinder heads and discard the head gaskets.

To install:

12. Clean the cylinder heads, intake manifold, valve rocker arm cover and cylinder block gasket surfaces.

13. Place the cylinder head gaskets in position on the cylinder block.

NOTE: *Gaskets are marked with the words FRONT and TOP for correct positioning. Left and right cylinder head gaskets are not*

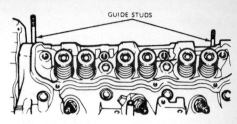

Cylinder head alignment studs — 2.8L and 2.9L engines

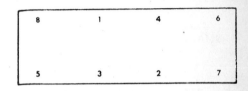

STEP 1: TIGHTEN IN SEQUENCE TO 30 N·m (22 FT-LB)
STEP 2: TIGHTEN IN SEQUENCE TO 70-75 N·m (51-55 FT-LB
STEP 3: WAIT 5 MINUTES
STEP 4: IN SEQUENCE, TURN ALL BOLTS 90 DEGREES.

Cylinder head torque sequence — 2.9L engine

interchangeable. Use new cylinder head bolts.

14. Install the fabricated alignment dowels in the cylinder block and install the cylinder head assemblies on the cylinder block, one at a time.

15. Remove the alignment dowels and install the cylinder head attaching bolts. Tighten the bolts to specification following the torque sequence.

16. Install the intake manifold as described in this Chapter.

17. Install the exhaust manifolds as described in this Chapter.

18. Apply Lubriplate®, or equivalent, to both ends of the pushrods and install the pushrods.

19. Install oil baffles and rocker arms as described in this Chapter under Rocker Arm Shaft Assembly.

20. Install the distributor as described under Distributor Removal and Installation in this Chapter.

21. Adjust the valves as described in Chapter 2 under Valve Lash adjustment.

22. Install the rocker arm covers.

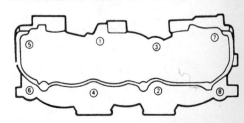

Cylinder head torque sequence — 2.8L engine

23. Install the carburetor and connect the fuel line to the carburetor on the 2.8L engine. Connect the fuel line to the fuel rail on the 2.9L engine.

24. Install the distributor cap with spark plug wires attached. Coat the inside of each spark plug boot with silicone lubricant and install them on the spark plug.

25. Install the throttle linkage and, the air cleaner or air cleaner intake tube.

26. Fill the cooling system according to instructions on the underhood decal and bleed the cooling system.

27. Connect the battery ground cable.

28. Operate the engine at fast idle and check for oil, fuel and coolant leaks.

29. Check and adjust, if necessary the ignition timing and idle speed.

3.0L Engine

NOTE: *Review the complete service procedure before starting this repair.*

1. Drain the cooling system (engine cold) into a clean container and save the coolant for reuse.

CAUTION: *When draining the coolant, keep in mind that cats and dogs are attracted by the ethylene glycol antifreeze, and are quite likely to drink any that is left in an uncovered container or in puddles on the ground. This will prove fatal in sufficient quantity. Always drain the coolant into a sealable container. Coolant should be reused unless it is contaminated or several years old.*

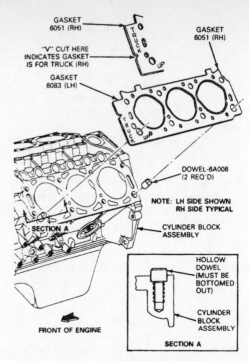

Cylinder head installation — 3.0L engine

2. Disconnect the battery ground cable.

3. Remove the air cleaner.

4. Relieve fuel pressure. Disconnect fuel lines as necessary. Mark vacuum line location and remove lines.

5. Disconnect upper and lower radiator hoses-position out of the way.

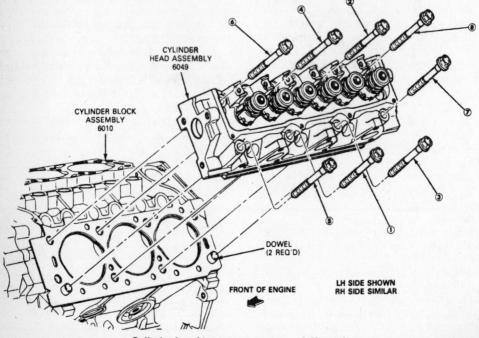

Cylinder head torque sequence — 3.0L engine

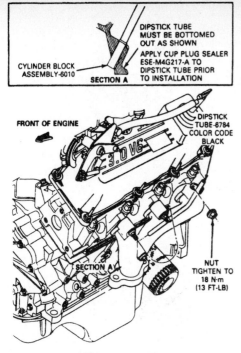

Cylinder head installation — 3.0L engine

6. Remove coil assembly. Remove the throttle body. See Chapter 5.

7. Mark distributor housing to block and note rotor position. Remove the ignition wires from the spark plugs and locating studs. Remove the distributor.

8. If the left hand cylinder head is being removed:

a. Remove the accessory drive belt.

b. Remove the power steering pump and bracket assembly. DO NOT disconnect the hoses. Tie the assembly out of the way.

c. Remove the engine oil dipstick and tube. Rotate or remove tube assembly.

d. Remove the fuel line retaining bracket bolt from the front of cylinder head.

9. If the right hand head is being removed:

a. Remove the accessory drive belt.

b. Disconnect alternator electrical harnesses.

c. Remove belt tensioner assembly.

d. Remove the alternator and bracket.

e. Remove hose from rocker cover to oil fill adapter.

10. Remove the spark plugs.

11. Remove the exhaust manifold(s).

12. Remove the rocker arm covers as previously described.

13. Loosen rocker arm fulcrum retaining bolts enough to allow the rocker arm to be lifted off the pushrod and rotate to one side.

NOTE: *Regardless of which cylinder head is being removed #3 cylinder intake valve pushrod must be removed to allow removal of the intake manifold.*

14. Remove the pushrods, keeping them in order so they may be installed in their original locations.

15. Remove the intake manifold as outlined. Refer to the necessary service procedure.

16. Loosen the cylinder head attaching bolts in reverse of the torque sequence, then remove the bolts and lift off the cylinder head(s). Remove and discard the old cylinder head gasket(s).

To install:

17. Clean the cylinder heads, intake manifold, valve rocker arm cover and cylinder block gasket surfaces of all traces of old gasket material and/or sealer. Refer to the following overhaul procedures for cylinder head component removal, valve replacement, resurfacing, etc.

18. Lightly oil all bolt and stud bolt threads except those specifying special sealant. Position the new head gasket(s) on the cylinder block, using the dowels for alignment. The dowels should be replaced if damaged.

19. Position the cylinder head(s) on the block and install the attaching bolts. Tighten the head bolts in sequence to 59 ft. lbs. Back off all bolts one full turn (360 DEGREES). Retighten the cylinder head bolts in sequence in two service steps 37 ft. lbs. and final torque specification 68 ft. lbs.

20. Install intake manifold as outlined.

21. Dip each pushrod in heavy engine oil then install the pushrods in their original locations.

22. For each valve, rotate the crankshaft until the tappet rests on the heel (base circle) of the camshaft lobe before tightening the fulcrum attaching bolts. Position the rocker arms over the pushrods, install the fulcrums (TORQUE 8 FT. LBS. TO SEAT FULCRUM) and then tighten the fulcrum attaching bolts (FINAL TORQUE) to 24 ft. lbs. (32 Nm). REFER to the necessary illustration for details if necessary.

CAUTION: *The fulcrums must be fully seated in the cylinder head and pushrods must be seated in the rocker arm sockets prior to final tightening.*

23. Lubricate all rocker arm assemblies with heavy engine oil. If the original valve train components are being installed, a valve clearance check is not required. If, however, a component has been replaced, the valve clearance should be checked.

24. Install the exhaust manifold(s).

25. Install the dipstick tube and spark plugs.

26. Position the rocker arm cover with a new gasket on the cylinder head and install the re-

INSTALLATION – ROCKER ARM, PUSH ROD AND FULCRUMS

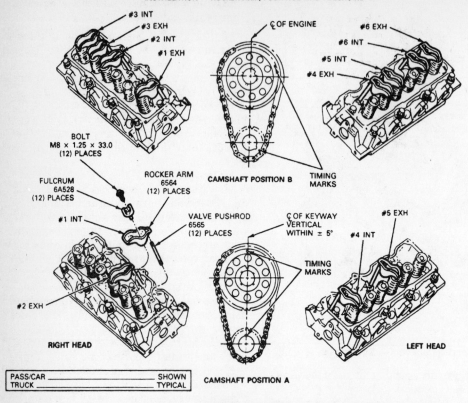

ASSEMBLY PROCEDURE

1. ROTATE CAMSHAFT TO POSITION "A" AS SHOWN.
2. INSTALL PUSH RODS (6565) (12) PLACES-PUSH RODS MUST BE SEATED PROPERLY ON TAPPET ASSEMBLY
3. INSTALL ROCKER ARMS (6564), FULCRUMS (6A528) AND BOLTS IN LOCATIONS AS SPECIFIED IN CAMSHAFT POSITION "A", TORQUE BOLTS TO 11 N·m AS REQ'D TO SEAT FULCRUMS IN CYLINDER HEAD
4. ROTATE CRANKSHAFT 120° TO POSITION "B"
5. INSTALL ROCKER ARMS (6564), FULCRUMS (6A528), AND BOLTS IN LOCATIONS AS SPECIFIED IN CAMSHAFT POSITION "B", TORQUE BOLTS TO 11 N·m AS REQ'D TO SEAT FULCRUMS IN CYLINDER HEAD

NOTE: FULCRUMS MUST BE FULLY SEATED IN CYLINDER HEADS AND PUSH RODS MUST BE FULLY SEATED IN ROCKER ARM SOCKETS PRIOR TO FINAL TORQUE.
6. APPLY ESE-M2C39-F OIL TO ROCKER ARM ASSEMBLIES.
7. FINAL TORQUE BOLTS TO 32.0 N·m (CAMSHAFT MAY BE IN ANY POSITION).
NOTE: CAMSHAFT POSITIONS "A" AND "B" ARE REQUIRED TO PLACE TAPPET ASSEMBLY ON BASE CIRCLE OF CAMSHAFT LOBE TO CHECK COLLAPSED TAPPET GAP.

FULCRUM AND BOLT MUST BE FULLY SEATED AFTER FINAL TORQUE

4.69-2.15 WITH TAPPET FULLY COLLAPSED ON BASE CIRCLE OF CAM LOBE AFTER ASSEMBLY REF. QUALITY AUDIT ONLY.

CYL. NO.	CAMSHAFT POSITION	
	A	B
	SET GAP OF VALVES NOTED	
1	INT.	EXH.
2	EXH.	INT.
3	NONE	INT.-EXH.
4	INT.	EXH.
5	EXH.	INT.
6	NONE	INT.-EXH.

Initial valve adjustment — 3.0L engine

taining bolts. Note the location of the spark plug wire routing clip stud bolts.

27. Install the injector harness.

28. Install the distributor and wires.

29. Install the throttle body and new gasket. Refer to the necessary service procedures.

30. If the left hand cylinder head was removed, perform the following:

a. Install the fuel line retaining bracket bolt to the front of cylinder head. Torque to 26 ft. lbs.

b. Install the engine oil dipstick and tube assembly.

c. Install the power steering pump and bracket assembly.

d. Install the accessory drive belt.

31. If the right hand cylinder head was removed, perform the following:

a. Install hose from rocker cover to oil fill adapter.

b. Install the alternator and bracket.

c. Install belt tensioner assembly.

d. Reconnect alternator electrical harnesses.

e. Install the accessory drive belt.

32. Connect fuel lines. Install fuel line safety clips.

33. Install all radiator hoses. Connect vacuum lines.

34. Drain and change engine oil.

CAUTION: *The EPA warns that prolonged contact with used engine oil may cause a number of skin disorders, including cancer! You should make every effort to minimize your exposure to used engine oil. Protective gloves should be worn when changing the oil. Wash your hands and any other exposed skin areas as soon as possible after exposure to used engine oil. Soap and water, or waterless hand cleaner should be used.*

35. Install the air cleaner.

36. Fill and bleed the cooling system.

37. Connect the battery ground cable.

38. Start the engine and check for leaks. Verify base ignition timing. Adjust the speed control linkage as necessary.

4.0L Engine

1. Drain the cooling system (engine cold) into a clean container and save the coolant for reuse.

CAUTION: *When draining the coolant, keep in mind that cats and dogs are attracted by the ethylene glycol antifreeze, and are quite likely to drink any that is left in an uncovered container or in puddles on the ground. This will prove fatal in sufficient quantity. Always drain the coolant into a sealable container. Coolant should be reused unless it is contaminated or several years old.*

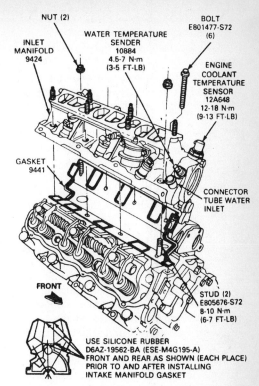

Cylinder head installation — 4.0L engine

2. Disconnect the battery ground cable.

3. Remove the air cleaner.

4. Remove the upper and lower intake manifolds as described earlier.

5. If the left cylinder head is being removed:

a. Remove the accessory drive belt.

b. Remove the air conditioning compressor.

c. Remove the power steering pump and bracket assembly. DO NOT disconnect the hoses. Tie the assembly out of the way.

d. Remove the spark plugs.

6. If the right head is being removed:

a. Remove the accessory drive belt.

b. Remove the alternator and bracket.

c. Remove the EDIS ignition coil and bracket.

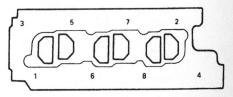

Lower intake manifold torque sequence — 4.0L engine

d. Remove the spark plugs.

7. Remove the exhaust manifold(s).

8. Remove the rocker arm covers as previously described.

9. Remove the rocker shaft assembly.

10. Remove the pushrods, keeping them in order so they may be installed in their original locations.

11. Loosen the cylinder head attaching bolts in reverse of the torque sequence, then remove the bolts and discard them. They cannot be reused.

12. Lift off the cylinder head(s).

13. Remove and discard the old cylinder head gasket(s).

To install:

14. Clean the cylinder heads, intake manifolds, valve rocker arm cover and cylinder block gasket surfaces of all traces of old gasket material and/or sealer. Refer to the following overhaul procedures for cylinder head component removal, valve replacement, resurfacing, etc.

15. Lightly oil all bolt and stud bolt threads except those specifying special sealant. Position the new head gasket(s) on the cylinder block, using the dowels for alignment. The dowels should be replaced if damaged.

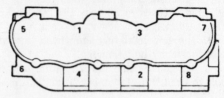

CYLINDER HEAD
BOLT TIGHTENING
SEQUENCE

Cylinder head torque sequence — 4.0L engine

NOTE: *The cylinder head(s) and intake manifold are torqued alternately and in sequence, to assure a correct fit and gasket crush.*

16. Position the cylinder head(s) on the block.

17. Apply a bead of RTV silicone gasket material to the mating joints of the head and block at the 4 corners. Install the intake manifold gasket and again apply the sealer.

NOTE: *This sealer sets within 15 minutes, so work quickly!*

18. Install the lower intake manifold and install the bolts and nuts for the manifold and head(s). Tighten all fasteners finger-tight.

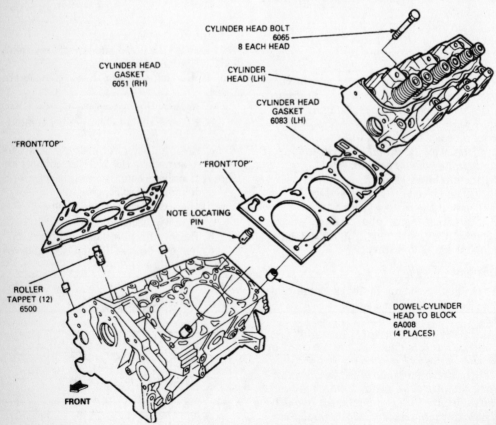

Cylinder head installation — 4.0L engine

19. Tighten the intake manifold fasteners, in sequence, to 36–72 inch lbs.

WARNING: *Do not re-use the old head bolts. ALWAYS use new head bolts!*

20. Torque the head bolts, in sequence, to 59 ft. lbs.

21. Tighten the intake manifold fasteners, in sequence, to 6–11 ft. lbs.

22. Tighten the head bolts, in sequence, an additional 80–85 DEGREES tighter. 85 degrees is a little less than ¼ turn. ¼ turn would equal 90 degrees.

23. Torque the intake manifold fasteners, in sequence, to 11–15 ft. lbs.; then, in sequence, to 15–18 ft. lbs.

24. Dip each pushrod in heavy engine oil then install the pushrods in their original locations.

25. Install the rocker shaft assembly(ies) and tighten the bolts to 46–52 ft. lbs., front to rear, in several equal stages.

26. Apply another bead of RTV sealer at the 4 corners where the intake manifold and heads meet.

27. Install the rocker covers, using new gaskets coated with sealer. Torque the bolts to 36–60 inch lbs. After 2 minutes, re-torque the cover bolts.

28. Install the upper intake manifold. Torque the nuts to 15–18 ft. lbs.

29. Install the exhaust manifold(s).

30. Install the spark plugs and wires.

31. If the left head was removed, install the power steering pump, compressor and drive belt.

32. If the right head was removed, install the EDIS coil and bracket, alternator and bracket, and the drive belt.

33. Install the air cleaner.

34. Fill the cooling system. See Chapter 1.

NOTE: *At this point, it's a good idea to change the engine oil. Coolant contamination of the engine oil often occurs during cylinder head removal.*

35. Connect the battery ground cable.

36. Start the engine and check for leaks.

2.2L Diesel Engine

1. Disconnect the ground cables from both batteries.

2. Mark the hood hinges for realignment on installation and remove the hood. Drain the cooling system.

CAUTION: *When draining the coolant, keep in mind that cats and dogs are attracted by the ethylene glycol antifreeze, and are quite likely to drink any that is left in an uncovered container or in puddles on the ground. This will prove fatal in sufficient quantity. Always drain the coolant into a sealable con-*

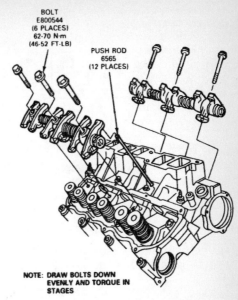

BOLT
E800544
(6 PLACES)
62-70 N·m
(46-52 FT·LB)

PUSH ROD
6565
(12 PLACES)

NOTE: DRAW BOLTS DOWN EVENLY AND TORQUE IN STAGES

Installation rocker arm shaft assemblies — 4.0L engine

tainer. Coolant should be reused unless it is contaminated or several years old.

3. Disconnect the breather hose from the valve cover and remove the intake hose and breather hose from the air cleaner and intake manifold.

4. Remove the heater hose bracket from the valve cover and exhaust manifold. Disconnect the heater hoses from the water pump and thermostat housing and position tube assembly out of the way.

5. Remove the vacuum pump support brace from the pump bracket and cylinder head.

6. Loosen and remove the alternator and vacuum pump drive belts. Loosen and remove the A/C compressor and/or power steering drive belt.

7. Disconnect the brake booster vacuum hose and remove the vacuum pump.

8. Disconnect the exhaust pipe from the exhaust manifold. Disconnect the coolant thermoswitch and coolant temperature sender wiring harness.

9. Disconnect and remove the fuel injection lines from the injector nozzles and pump. Cap all lines and fittings to prevent dirt from entering the system.

10. Disconnect the engine wire harness from the alternator, the glow plug harness and dropping resistor and position the harness out of the way.

11. Disconnect the fuel lines from both sides of the fuel heater. Remove the fuel filter assembly from the mounting bracket and position out of the way with the fuel line attached.

12. Loosen the lower No. 3 intake port nut

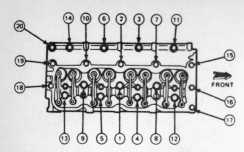

Head bolt torque sequence — 2.2L diesel engine

and the bolt on the injection pump; disconnect the lower fuel return line from the intake manifold stud and the upper fuel return line.

13. If equipped with power steering, remove the bolt that attaches the pump rear support bracket to the cylinder head.

14. Remove the upper radiator hose. Disconnect the by-pass hose from the thermostat housing.

15. Remove the A/C compressor and position out of the way with the lines still attached.

CAUTION: *Do not disconnect the compressor lines until the system has been discharged by a professional service person.*

16. Remove the valve cover, rocker arm shaft assembly and the pushrods. Identify the pushrods and keep them in order for return to their original position.

17. Remove the cylinder head attaching bolts, starting at the ends of the head, working alternately toward the center. Remove the cylinder head from the truck.

18. Clean all gasket mounting surfaces.

To install:

19. Position a new cylinder head gasket into position. Install the cylinder head attaching bolts, torque the cylinder head bolts in the proper sequence to 80–85 ft. lbs.

20. Install the pushrods, rocker arm shaft assembly and the valve cover.

21. Install the A/C compressor.

22. Install the upper radiator hose and the by-pass hose to the thermostat housing.

23. If equipped with power steering, install the bolt that attaches the pump rear support bracket to the cylinder head.

24. Connect the lower fuel return line to the intake manifold stud and the upper fuel return line. Tighten the lower No. 3 intake port nut and the bolt on the injection pump;

25. Install the fuel filter assembly. Connect the fuel lines from both sides of the fuel heater.

26. Connect the engine wire harness to the alternator, the glow plug harness and dropping resistor.

27. Connect and remove the fuel injection lines from the injector nozzles and pump.

28. Connect the exhaust pipe to the exhaust

manifold. Connect the coolant thermoswitch and coolant temperature sender wiring harness.

29. Connect the brake booster vacuum hose and install the vacuum pump.

30. Install and tighten the alternator and vacuum pump drive belts. Install and tighten the A/C compressor and/or power steering drive belt.

31. Install the vacuum pump support brace to the pump bracket and cylinder head.

32. Install the heater hose bracket from the valve cover and exhaust manifold. Connect the heater hoses to the water pump and thermostat.

33. Connect the breather hose from the valve cover and install the intake hose and breather hose to the air cleaner and intake manifold.

34. Install the hood.

35. Connect the ground cables from both batteries. Start the engine and check for leaks.

2.3L Turbo Diesel Engine

1. Disconnect battery ground cables from both batteries.

2. Mark location of hood hinges and remove hood.

3. Drain cooling system.

CAUTION: *When draining the coolant, keep in mind that cats and dogs are attracted by the ethylene glycol antifreeze, and are quite likely to drink any that is left in an uncovered container or in puddles on the ground. This will prove fatal in sufficient quantity. Always drain the coolant into a sealable container. Coolant should be reused unless it is contaminated or several years old.*

4. Disconnect breather hose from rocker cover.

5. Remove heater hose clamp from rocker cover and position hoses out of the way.

6. Remove cooling fan and shroud.

7. Remove accessory drive belts.

8. Remove upper front timing belt cover.

9. Loosen and remove camshaft/injection pump timing belt from camshaft sprocket.

10. Remove inlet hose between air cleaner and turbo inlet.

11. Raise vehicle and disconnect muffler inlet pipe from turbo exhaust fitting. Lower vehicle.

12. Remove fuel conditioner and bracket and position assembly out of the way.

13. Disconnect and remove fuel lines between injection pump and nozzles. Cap all lines and fittings using Protective Cap Set T85L–9395–A or equivalent.

14. Disconnect heater hose from fitting on LH rear of cylinder head.

15. Remove A/C compressor and mounting bracket.

16. disconnect glow plug electrical leads from No. 2 and No. 3 glow plugs.

17. Disconnect coolant temperature switch wire.

18. Remove intake and exhaust manifold.

19. Remove rocker cover.

20. Loosen cylinder head bolts using a 10mm hex-head socket. Loosen bolts in sequence as shown.

21. Remove cylinder head. Remove old head gasket.

22. Remove components as necessary.

To install:

23. Assemble components to head as necessary.

24. Clean gasket mating surfaces on cylinder head and engine block.

25. Position new cylinder head gasket on engine block.

26. Position cylinder head on engine block and install cylinder head bolts. Tighten bolts in sequence shown, as follows:

a. Tighten bolts in sequence to 38–42 ft. lbs.

b. Tighten bolts in sequence to 76–83 ft. lbs.

27. Install rocker cover.

NOTE: *Ensure half-moon gasket is installed in rear of cylinder.*

28. Install intake and exhaust manifolds.

29. Connect coolant temperature switch connector.

30. Connect glow plug connectors to No. 3 and No. 4 glow plugs.

31. Install A/C compressor bracket and A/C compressor.

32. Connect heater hose to fitting on LH rear of cylinder head.

33. Connect fuel lines to injection pump and nozzles. Tighten line nuts to specification.

34. Install fuel conditioner and bracket.

35. Raise vehicle and connect muffler inlet pipe to turbo exhaust fitting. Lower vehicle.

36. Connect inlet hose between air cleaner and turbo inlet.

37. Install and adjust injection pump/camshaft timing belt.

38. Install upper timing belt cover.

39. Install accessory drive belts.

40. Position heater hoses on rocker cover and install clamp.

41. Connect breather hose to rocker cover.

42. Change engine oil and filter. Fill engine with specified quantity and quality of oil.

43. Fill and bleed cooling system.

44. Connect battery ground cables to both batteries.

45. Run engine and check for oil, fuel and coolant leaks.

46. Install hood.

CLEANING AND INSPECTION

1. With the valves installed to protect the valve seats, remove deposits from the combustion chambers and valve heads with a scraper and a wire brush. Be careful not to damage the cylinder head gasket surface. After the valves are removed, clean the valve guide bores with a valve guide cleaning tool. Using cleaning solvent to remove dirt, grease and other deposits, clean all bolt holes; be sure the oil passage is clean.

2. Remove all deposits from the valves with a fine wire brush or buffing wheel.

3. Inspect the cylinder heads for cracks or excessively burned areas in the exhaust outlet ports.

4. Check the cylinder head for cracks and inspect the gasket surface for burrs and nicks. Replace the head if it is cracked.

5. On cylinder heads that incorporate valve seat inserts, check the inserts for excessive wear, cracks or looseness.

RESURFACING

Cylinder Head Flatness

When a cylinder head is removed because of gasket leaks, check the flatness of the cylinder head gasket surface.

1. Place a straight-edge across the gasket surface of the cylinder head. Using feeler gauges, determine the clearance at the center of the straight-edge.

2. If warpage exceeds 0.08mm in a 152mm

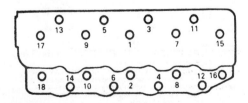

Cylinder head torque sequence — 2.3L turbo diesel engine

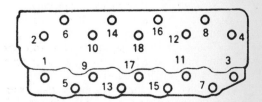

Cylinder head loosening sequence — 2.3L turbo diesel engine

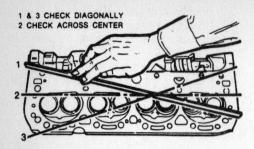

1 & 3 CHECK DIAGONALLY
2 CHECK ACROSS CENTER

Checking the cylinder head for warpage

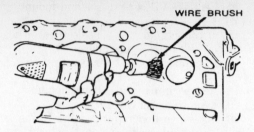

WIRE BRUSH

Remove combustion chamber carbon from the cylinder head with a wire brush and electric drill. Make sure all carbon is removed and not just burnished

span, or 0.15mm over the total length, the cylinder head must be resurfaced.

3. If necessary to refinish the cylinder head gasket surface, do not plane or grind off more than 0.25mm from the original gasket surface.

NOTE: *When milling the cylinder heads of V-6 engines, the intake manifold mounting position is altered, and must be corrected by milling the manifold flange a proportionate amount. Refer to a Machine shop as necessary.*

Valves and Springs

VALVE LASH ADJUSTMENT

Refer to Chapter 2 under Tune-Up Procedures for the Valve Lash Adjustment procedure.

Valve Spring, Retainer and Seal

REMOVAL AND INSTALLATION

Broken valve springs or damaged valve stem seals and retainers may be replaced without removing the cylinder head, provided damage to the valve or valve seat has not occurred.

NOTE: *The following procedure requires the use of special tools: air compressor, air line adapter tool to fit the spark plug hole, and a valve spring compressor tool designed to be used with the head on the engine. If the head has been removed from the engine the procedure will only require the use of a valve spring compressor tool designed to be used with the head off.*

Gasoline Engines

1. Remove the valve rocker arm cover.

2. Remove the applicable spark plug wire and spark plug.

3. Remove the valve rocker arm or shaft as described under Rocker Arm or Rocker Arm Shaft removal and installation.

4. Remove both the valve push rods from the cylinder being serviced. Remove the cam follower on overhead cam engines.

5. Install an air line with an adapter in the

spark plug hole and apply air pressure to hold the valve(s) in the closed position. Failure to hold the valve(s) closed is an indication of valve seat damage and requires removal of the cylinder head.

6. Install the valve spring compressor tool T74P–6565–A & B or equivalent. Compress the valve spring and remove the retainer locks, spring retainer and valve spring.

7. Remove and discard the valve stem seal.

8. If air pressure has forced the piston to the bottom of the cylinder, any removal of air pressure will allow the valve(s) to fall into the

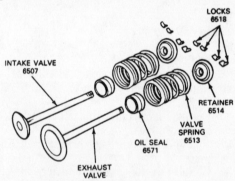

Valve train components — 2.8L and 2.9L engines

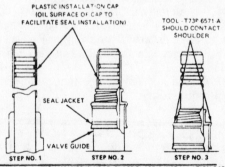

STEP NO. 1– WITH VALVES IN HEAD, PLACE PLASTIC INSTALLATION CAP OVER END OF VALVE STEM.
STEP NO. 2– START VALVE STEM SEAL CAREFULLY OVER CAP. PUSH SEAL DOWN UNTIL JACKET TOUCHES TOP OF GUIDE.
STEP NO. 3– REMOVE PLASTIC INSTALLATION CAP. USE INSTALLA TOOL—T73P-6571 A OR SCREWDRIVERS TO BOTTOM SEAL ON VALVE GUIDE.

Installing the valve stem seals — 2.0L and 2.3L engines

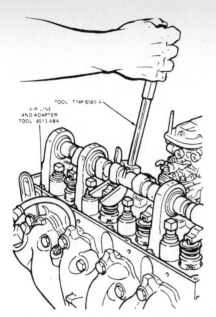

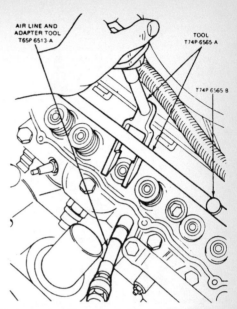

Compressing the valve spring — 2.0L and 2.3L engines

Compressing the valve spring on the cylinder head — 2.8L and 2.9L engines

cylinder. A rubber band wrapped around the end of the valve stem will prevent this condition and will still allow enough travel to check the valve for binds.

9. Inspect the valve stem for damage. Rotate the valve and check the valve stem tip for eccentric movement during rotation. Move the valve up and down through normal travel in the valve guide and check the stem for binds.

NOTE: *If the valve has been damaged, it will be necessary to remove the cylinder head.*

10. If the valve condition proves satisfactory, lubricate the valve stem with engine oil. Hold the valve in the closed position and apply air pressure within the cylinder.

11. Install a new valve stem seal. Place the spring in position over the valve and install the valve spring retainer. Compress the valve

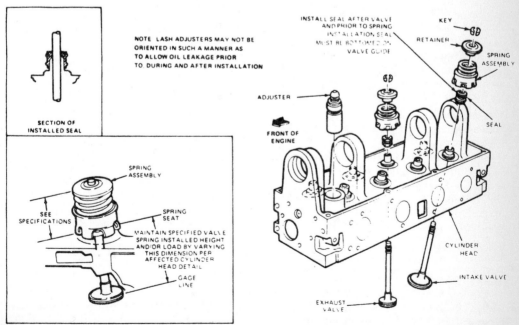

Valve train components — 2.0L and 2.3L engines

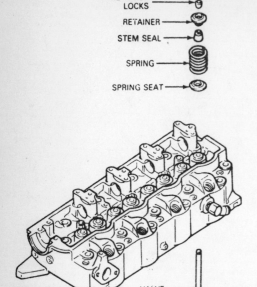

Valve train components — 2.3L turbo diesel engine

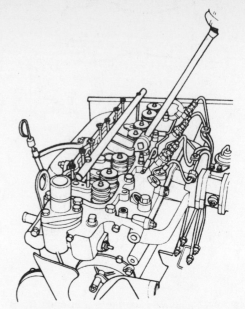

Compressing the valve spring assembly — 2.2L diesel engine

spring and install the valve spring retainer locks. Remove the valve spring compressor tools.

12. Lubricate the push rod ends with Lubriplate® or equivalent and install the push rod. Apply Lubriplate® or equivalent to the tip of the valve stem and to both ends of the rocker arm.

13. Turn off the air and remove the air line and adapter. Install the spark plug and connect the spark plug wire.

14. Clean and install the remaining valve train components and the rocker arm cover.

Diesel Engines

1. Remove valve rocker arm cover.

2. Remove the rocker arm shaft as described in this Chapter.

3. Remove the glow plug harness from glow plug and remove glow plugs.

4. Install the adapter from the compression Test kit, Rotunda 19–6001 or equivalent, in the glow plug hole, attach an airline, and turn on the air supply.

NOTE: *An alternate method of holding the valves up, is to rotate the crankshaft until the affected piston is at TDC.*

5. Install the valve spring compressor bar, Tool T83T–6513–B, and using Valve Spring compressor Tool T74P–6565–A or equivalent, compress valve the spring and remove retainer locks, spring retainer, valve spring and damper.

6. Remove valve stem seal(s).

To Install:

7. Install new valve stem seal(s).

8. Install damper, vale spring and valve spring retainer over the vale stem. Using Tool T74P–6565–A or equivalent, compress the valve spring assembly and install the retainer locks.

CAUTION: *Make sure retainer locks are fully seated in groove on valve stem.*

9. Repeat the procedure for each vale spring assembly as necessary.

10. Disconnect the air supply line and remove the adapter from glow plug hole.

11. Install the glow plugs and tighten to 11–15 ft. lbs.

12. Install glow plug harness.

13. Install the rocker arm shaft as described in this Chapter.

14. Adjust the valves as described in Chapter 2 under Diesel Engine Tune Up Procedures.

15. Install valve cover, with a new gasket.

16. Connect the heater hose tube assembly to the valve cover.

17. Run the engine and check for oil leaks.

INSPECTION

Valves

Minor pits, grooves, etc., may be removed. Discard valves that are severely damaged, or if the face runout cannot be corrected by refinishing or if the stem clearance exceeds specifications.

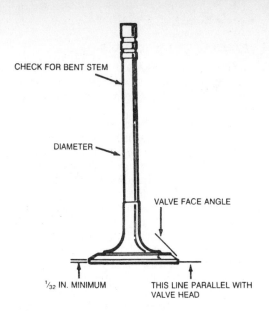

CHECK FOR BENT STEM

DIAMETER

VALVE FACE ANGLE

1/32 IN. MINIMUM

THIS LINE PARALLEL WITH VALVE HEAD

Critical valve dimensions

Discard any worn or damaged valve train parts.

REFACING VALVES

NOTE: *The valve seat refacing operation should be coordinated with the valve refacing operations so that the finished angles of the valve seat and valve face will be to specifications and provide a compression tight fit.*

If the valve face runout is excessive and/or to remove pits and grooves, reface the valves to a true 44 degree angle. Remove only enough stock to correct the runout or to clean up the grooves and pits.

If the edge of the head is less than 0.8mm from the end of the valve stem.

If the valve and/or valve seat has been refaced, it will be necessary to check the clearance between the rocker arm pad and the valve stem tip with the valve train assembly installed in the engine.

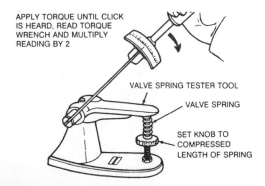

APPLY TORQUE UNTIL CLICK IS HEARD, READ TORQUE WRENCH AND MULTIPLY READING BY 2

VALVE SPRING TESTER TOOL

VALVE SPRING

SET KNOB TO COMPRESSED LENGTH OF SPRING

Checking the valve spring tension

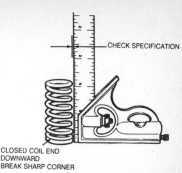

CHECK SPECIFICATION

CLOSED COIL END DOWNWARD BREAK SHARP CORNER

Checking the valve spring squareness

CHECK SPRINGS

Check the valve spring for proper pressure at the specified spring lengths using valve spring pressure tool. Weak vale springs cause poor performance; therefore, if the pressure of any spring is lower than the service limit, replace the spring. Springs should be ±5 lbs of all other springs.

Check each valve spring for squareness. Stand the spring on a flat surface next to a square. Measure the height of the spring, and rotate the spring slowly and observe the space between the top coil of the spring and the square. If the spring is out of square more than $5/64$ in. or the height varies (by comparison) by more than $1/16$ in., replace the spring.

Valve Seats

CUTTING THE SEATS

NOTE: *The valve refacing operation should be coordinated with the refacing of the valve seats so that the finished angles of the valve seat and valve face will be to specifications and provide a compression tight fit.*

Grind the valve seats of all engines to a true 45 degree angle. Remove only enough stock to

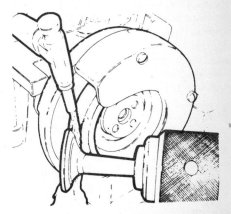

A well-equipped machine shop can handle valve refacing jobs

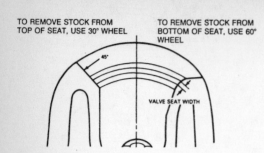

TO REMOVE STOCK FROM TOP OF SEAT, USE 30° WHEEL

TO REMOVE STOCK FROM BOTTOM OF SEAT, USE 60° WHEEL

45°

VALVE SEAT WIDTH

Refacing the valve seats

clean up pits and grooves or to correct the valve seat runout.

The finished valve seat should contact the approximate center of the valve face. It is good practice to determine where the valve seat contacts the valve face. To do this, coat the seat with Prussian blue and set the valve in place. Rotate the valve with light pressure. If the blue is transferred to the top edge of the valve face, lower the valve seat. If the blue is transferred to the bottom edge of the valve face, raise the valve seat.

LAPPING THE VALVES

When valve faces and seats have been refaced and recut, or if they are determined to be in good condition, the valves must be lapped in to ensure efficient sealing when the valve closes against the seat.

1. Invert the cylinder head so that the combustion chambers are facing up.

2. Lightly lubricate the valve stems with clean oil, and coat the valve seats with valve grinding compound. Install the valves in the head as numbered.

3. Attach the suction cup of a valve lapping tool to a valve head. You'll probably have to moisten the cup to securely attach the tool to the valve.

4. Rotate the tool between the palms. Changing position and lifting the tool often to prevent grooving. Lap the valve until a smooth, polished seat is evident (you may have to add a bit more compound after some lapping is done).

5. Remove the valve and tool, and remove ALL traces of grinding compound with solvent soaked rag, or rinse the head with solvent.

NOTE: *Valve lapping can also be done by fastening a suction cup to a piece of drill rod in a hand eggbeater type drill. Proceed as above, using the drill as a lapping tool. Due to the higher speeds involved when using the hand drill, care must be exercised to avoid grooving the seat. Lift the tool and change direction of rotation often.*

Valve Guides

REAMING VALVE GUIDES

If it becomes necessary to ream a valve guide to install a valve with an oversize stem, a reaming kit is available which contains oversize reamers and pilot tools.

When replacing a standard size valve with an oversize valve always use the reamer in sequence (smallest oversize first, then next smallest, etc.) so as not to overload the reamers. Always re-face the valve seat after the valve guide has been reamed, and use a suitable scraper to break the sharp corner at the top of the valve guide.

Knurling is a process in which the metal on the valve guide bore is displaced and raised, thereby reducing clearance. Knurling also provides excellent oil control. The option of knurling rather than reaming valve guides should be discussed with a reputable machinist or engine specialist.

Valve Lifter (Tappets)

REMOVAL AND INSTALLATION

2.8L and 2.9L Engines

1. Remove the cylinder heads.

2. Lift out the tappets with a magnet. If they are to be re-used, mark them for installation. They must be inserted in their original locations!

NOTE: *If the tappets are stuck in their bores, you'll need a claw-type removal tool.*

3. Coat the new tappets with clean engine oil and insert them in their bores.

4. Install the heads.

3.0L Engine

1. Remove the rocker covers.

2. Remove the intake manifold.

3. Loosen the rocker arm nuts and pivot

Checking valve seat concentricity with a dial gauge

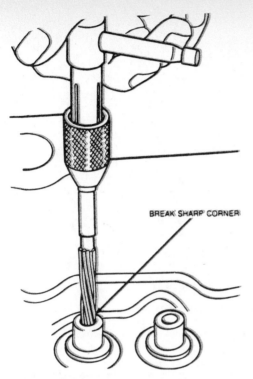

BREAK SHARP CORNER

Reaming the valve guide

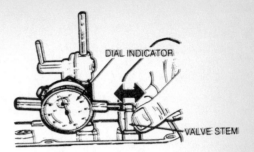

DIAL INDICATOR

VALVE STEM

Measuring the valve stem-to-guide clearance

8. Install the manifold.
9. Install the rocker covers.

4.0L Engine

1. Remove the upper and lower intake manifolds.
2. Remove the rocker covers.
3. Remove the rocker shaft assembly.
4. Remove and mark the pushrods for installation.
5. Remove the tappets with a magnet. If they are to be re-used, identify them.

NOTE: *If the tappets are stuck in their bores, you'll need a claw-type removal tool.*

6. Coat the new tappets with clean engine oil and insert them in their bores.
7. Coat the pushrods with heavy engine oil and insert them into the bores from which they came.
8. Install the rocker shaft assembly.
9. Install the rocker covers.
10. Install the upper and lower manifold.

the rocker arm out of the way. Remove and mark the pushrods for installation.

4. Remove the tappets with a magnet. If they are to be re-used, identify them.

NOTE: *If the tappets are stuck in their bores, you'll need a claw-type removal tool.*

5. Coat the new tappets with clean engine oil and insert them in their bores.
6. Coat the pushrods with heavy engine oil and insert them into the bores from which they came.
7. Replace the rocker arms. See the procedure above.

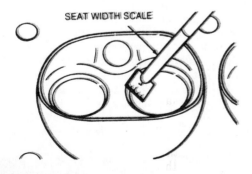

SEAT WIDTH SCALE

Measuring the valve seat width

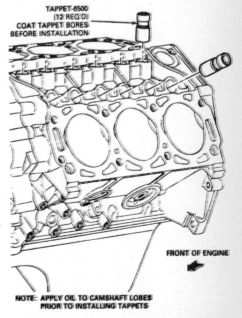

TAPPET-6500
(12 REQ'D)
COAT TAPPET BORES
BEFORE INSTALLATION

FRONT OF ENGINE

NOTE: APPLY OIL TO CAMSHAFT LOBES
PRIOR TO INSTALLING TAPPETS

Valve lifter (tappet) — 3.0L engine

Oil Pan

REMOVAL AND INSTALLATION

2.0L, 2.3L Engines

NOTE: *Before starting this repair procedure, view necessary illustrations for additional details.*

1. Disconnect the negative battery cable.
2. Remove the air cleaner assembly. Remove the oil dipstick. Remove the engine mount retaining nuts.
3. Remove the oil cooler lines at the radiator, if so equipped. Remove the (2) bolts retaining the fan shroud to the radiator and remove shroud.
4. Remove the radiator retaining bolts (automatic only). Position radiator upward and wire to the hood (automatic only).
5. Raise the vehicle and safely support on jackstands.
6. Drain the oil from crankcase.

CAUTION: *The EPA warns that prolonged contact with used engine oil may cause a number of skin disorders, including cancer! You should make every effort to minimize your exposure to used engine oil. Protective gloves should be worn when changing the oil. Wash your hands and any other exposed skin areas as soon as possible after exposure to used engine oil. Soap and water, or waterless hand cleaner should be used.*

7. Remove the starter cable from starter and remove the starter.
8. Disconnect the exhaust manifold tube to the inlet pipe bracket at the Thermactor check valve.
9. Remove the transmission mount retaining nuts to the crossmember.
10. Remove the bellcrank from the converter housing (automatic only).
11. Remove the oil cooler lines from retainer at the block (automatic only).
12. Remove the front crossmember (automatic only).
13. Disconnect the right front lower shock absorber mount (manual only).
14. Position the jack under the engine, raise and block with a piece of wood approximately $2^{1}/_{2}$ in. high. Remove the jack.
15. Position the jack under the transmission and raise slightly (automatic only).
16. Remove the oil pan retaining bolts, lower the pan to the chassis. Remove the oil pump drive and pick-up tube assembly.
17. Remove the oil pan (out the front on automatics) (out the rear on manuals).

To install:
18. Clean the oil pan and inspect for damage.

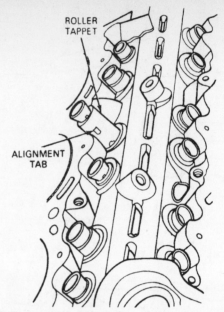

Roller tappet — 4.0L engine

Clean the oil pan gasket surface at the cylinder block. Clean the oil pump exterior and oil pump pick-up tube screen.

19. Position the oil pan gasket and end seals to the cylinder block (use contact cement to retain).
20. Position the oil pan to the crossmember.
21. Install the oil pump and pick-up tube assembly. Install the oil pan to cylinder block with retaining bolts.
22. Lower the jack under transmission (automatic only).
23. Position the jack under the engine, raise slightly, and remove the wood spacer block.
24. Replace the oil filter.
25. Connect the exhaust manifold tube to the inlet pipe bracket at the Thermactor check valve.
26. Install the transmission mount to the crossmember.
27. Install the oil cooler lines to the retainer at the block (automatic only).
28. Install the bellcrank to the converter housing (automatic only).
29. Install the right front lower shock absorber mount (manual only). Install the front crossmember (automatic only).
30. Install the starter and connect the cable. Lower vehicle.
31. Install the engine mount bolts.
32. Locate the radiator to the supports and install the (2) retaining bracket bolts (automatic only). Install the fan shroud on the radiator.
33. Connect the oil cooler lines to the radiator (automatic only).
34. Install the air cleaner assembly.

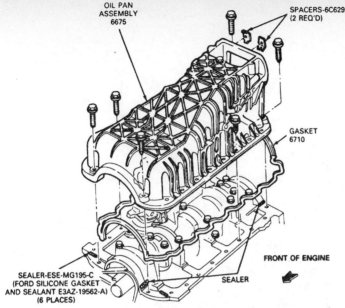

OIL PAN
ASSEMBLY
6675

SPACERS-6C629
(2 REQ'D)

GASKET
6710

FRONT OF ENGINE

SEALER-ESE-MG195-C
(FORD SILICONE GASKET
AND SEALANT E3AZ-19562-A)
(6 PLACES)

SEALER

ASSEMBLY PROCEDURE

1. APPLY SILICONE GASKET AND SEALANT E3AZ-19562-A, SIX PLACES AS SHOWN.
2. INSTALL OIL PAN GASKET IN THE OIL PAN.
3. INSTALL OIL PAN ASSEMBLY.
4. INSTALL OIL PAN FLANGE BOLTS TIGHT ENOUGH TO COMPRESS THE CORK/RUBBER OIL PAN GASKET TO THE POINT THAT THE TWO TRANSMISSION HOLES ARE ALIGNED WITH THE TWO TAPPED HOLES IN THE OIL PAN, BUT LOOSE ENOUGH TO ALLOW MOVEMENT OF THE PAN, RELATIVE TO THE BLOCK.
5. INSTALL THE TWO OIL PAN/ TRANSMISSION BOLTS AND TIGHTEN TO 40-50 N·m (30-39 FT-LB) TO ALIGN THE OIL PAN WITH THE TRANSMISSION. THEN LOOSEN BOLTS 1/2 TURN.
6. TIGHTEN ALL OIL PAN FLANGE BOLTS TO 10-13.5 N·m (90-120 IN-LB).
7. TIGHTEN THE TWO OIL PAN/ TRANSMISSION BOLTS TO 40-54 N·m (30-39 FT-LB).

Oil pan installation — 2.3L Twin Plug engine

35. Install the oil dipstick. Fill the crankcase with oil.

36. Start the engine and check for leaks.

2.8L, 2.9L Engines

1. Disconnect the battery ground cable.
2. Remove the carburetor air cleaner assembly.
3. Remove the fan shroud and position it over the fan.
4. Remove the distributor cap with the wires still attached, and position it forward of the dash panel.
5. Remove the distributor and cover the opening with a clean rag.
6. Remove the nuts attaching the front engine mounts to the cross member.
7. Remove the engine oil dipstick tube.
8. Raise the truck on a hoist and support with jackstands.
9. Drain the engine crankcase and remove the oil filter.

CAUTION: *The EPA warns that prolonged contact with used engine oil may cause a number of skin disorders, including cancer! You should make every effort to minimize your exposure to used engine oil. Protective gloves should be worn when changing the oil. Wash your hands and any other exposed skin areas as soon as possible after exposure to used engine oil. Soap and water, or waterless hand cleaner should be used.*

10. Remove the transmission fluid filler tube and plug the hole in the pan, On automatic transmission models.
11. Disconnect the muffler inlet pipes.
12. If equipped with an oil cooler, disconnect

the bracket and lower the cooler.

13. Remove the starter motor.
14. On automatic transmission models, position the cooler lines out of the way.
15. Disconnect the front stabilizer bar and position it forward.
16. Position a jack under the engine and raise the engine until it touches the dash panel. Install wooden blocks between the front motor mounts and the no. 2 crossmember.
17. Lower the engine onto the blocks and remove the jack.
18. Remove the oil pan attaching bolts and lower the pan assembly.
19. Installation is the reverse of the removal procedure

3.0L Engine

1. Disconnect the negative battery cable.
2. Remove the oil level dipstick.
3. Remove the fan shroud-leave the fan shroud over the fan assembly.
4. Remove the motor mount nuts from the frame.
5. Mark and remove the distributor assembly from the engine.
6. Raise and support the vehicle safely. Remove the oil level sensor wire.
7. Drain the engine oil from the crankcase into a suitable container and dispose of it properly.

CAUTION: *The EPA warns that prolonged contact with used engine oil may cause a number of skin disorders, including cancer! You should make every effort to minimize your exposure to used engine oil. Protective gloves should be worn when changing the oil.*

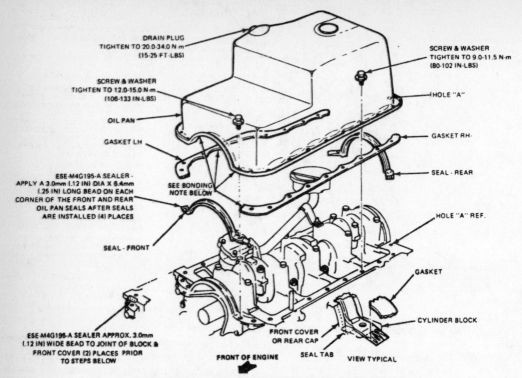

DRAIN PLUG
TIGHTEN TO 20.0-34.0 N·m
(15-25 FT·LBS)

SCREW & WASHER
TIGHTEN TO 9.0-11.5 N·m
(80-102 IN·LBS)

SCREW & WASHER
TIGHTEN TO 12.0-15.0 N·m
(106-133 IN·LBS)

HOLE "A"

OIL PAN

GASKET RH·

GASKET LH

SEAL - REAR

ESE-M4G195-A SEALER
APPLY A 3.0mm (.12 IN) DIA X 6.4mm
(.25 IN) LONG BEAD ON EACH
CORNER OF THE FRONT AND REAR
OIL PAN SEALS AFTER SEALS
ARE INSTALLED (4) PLACES

SEE BONDING
NOTE BELOW

HOLE "A" REF.

SEAL - FRONT

GASKET

CYLINDER BLOCK

ESE-M4G195-A SEALER APPROX. 3.0mm
(.12 IN) WIDE BEAD TO JOINT OF BLOCK &
FRONT COVER (2) PLACES PRIOR
TO STEPS BELOW

FRONT COVER
OR REAR CAP

SEAL TAB

FRONT OF ENGINE

VIEW TYPICAL

THERMAL BONDING INSTRUCTIONS - OIL PAN GASKETS TO BE BONDED SECURELY TO OIL PAN
USING A THERMAL PROCESS MEETING THE REQUIREMENTS OF THE (ES-DOAE-6584-A OR EQUIVALENT)
ADHESIVE COATING SPECIFICATION - IF NECESSARY IN PLACE OF THERMAL BONDING USE ADHESIVE
(ESE-M2G52-A OR B OR EQUIVALENT) APPLY EVENLY TO OIL PAN FLANGE & TO PAN SIDE OF GASKETS -
ALLOW ADHESIVE TO DRY PAST "WET" STAGE THEN INSTALL GASKETS TO OIL PAN.

1. APPLY SEALER AS NOTED ABOVE
2. INSTALL SEALS TO FRONT COVER & REAR BEARING CAP - PRESS SEAL TABS FIRMLY INTO BLOCK
3. INSTALL (2) GUIDE PINS
4. INSTALL OIL PAN OVER GUIDE PINS & SECURE WITH (4) BOLTS
5. INSTALL (18) BOLTS
6. TORQUE ALL BOLTS IN SEQUENCE CLOCKWISE FROM HOLE "A" AS NOTED ABOVE

Oil pan installation — 2.0L and 2.3L engines

Wash your hands and any other exposed skin areas as soon as possible after exposure to used engine oil. Soap and water, or waterless hand cleaner should be used.

8. Remove the starter motor from the engine.

9. Remove the transmission inspection cover.

10. Remove the right hand axle I-Beam. The brake caliper must be removed and wired out of the way. Refer to the necessary service procedures.

11. Remove the oil pan attaching bolts, using a suitable lifting device, raise the engine about 2 inches. Remove the oil pan from the engine block.

NOTE: *Oil pan fits tightly between the transmission spacer plate and oil pump pickup tube. Use care when removing the oil pan from the engine.*

12. Clean all gasket surfaces on the engine and oil pan. Remove all traces of old gasket and/ or sealer.

To install:

13. Apply a 4mm bead of RTV sealer to the junctions of the rear main bearing cap and block, and the front cover and block. The sealer sets in 15 minutes, so work quickly!

14. Apply adhesive to the gasket mating surfaces and install oil pan gasket.

15. Install the oil pan on the engine block.

16. Torque the pan bolts EVENLY to 9 ft. lbs. working from the center to the end position on the oil pan.

17. Install low-oil level sensor connector. Lower engine assembly to original position.

18. Install right hand axle I-Beam. Install the brake caliper. Refer to the necessary service procedures.

19. Install transmission inspection cover. Install starter motor.

20. Lower the vehicle and install the fan shroud.

21. Install motor mount retaining nuts. Install distributor assembly.

22. Replace the oil level dipstick. Connect

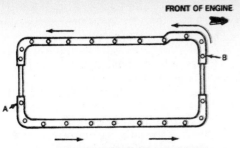

FIT THE OIL PAN BOLTS AND TIGHTEN IN TWO STEPS TO A
FINAL TORQUE OF 5-8 N·m (4-5.9 FT-LB)
STEP 1: START WITH BOLT A FOLLOW
DIRECTION OF ARROWS
STEP 2: START WITH BOLT B FOLLOW
DIRECTION OF ARROWS

Oil pan torque sequence — 2.8L and 2.9L engines

the battery ground. Fill crankcase with the correct amount of new engine oil. Start engine and check for leaks.

4.0L Engine

NOTE: *Review the complete service procedure before starting this repair.*

1. Disconnect the negative battery cable. Remove the complete engine assembly from the vehicle. Refer to the necessary service procedures in this Chapter.

2. Mount the engine on a suitable engine stand with oil pan facing up.

3. Remove the oil pan attaching bolts (note

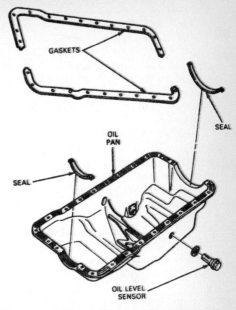

Oil pan assembly — 2.8L and 2.9L engines

location of 2 spacers) and remove the pan from the engine block.

4. Remove the oil pan gasket and crankshaft rear main bearing cap wedge seal.

5. Clean all gasket surfaces on the engine and oil pan. Remove all traces of old gasket and/or sealer.

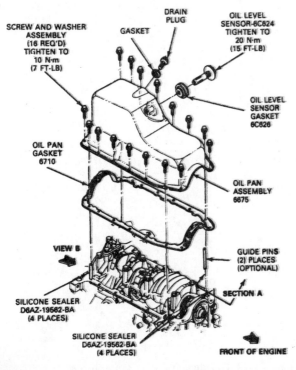

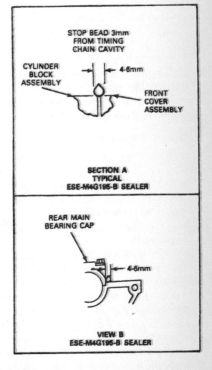

Oil pan assembly — 3.0L engine

To install:

6. Install a new crankshaft rear main bearing cap wedge seal. The seal should fit snugly into the sides of the rear main bearing cap.

7. Position the oil pan gasket to the engine block and place the oil pan in correct position on the 4 locating studs.

8. Torque the oil pan retaining bolts EVENLY to 5–7 ft. lbs.

NOTE: *The transmission bolts to the engine and oil pan. There are 2 spacers on the rear of the oil pan to allow proper mating of the transmission and oil pan. If these spacers were lost, or the oil pan was replaced, you must determine the proper spacers to install. To do this:*

a. With the oil pan installed, place a straightedge across the machined mating surface of the rear of the block, extending over the oil pan-to-transmission mounting surface.

b. Using a feeler gauge, measure the gap between the oil pan mounting pad and the straightedge.

c. Repeat the procedure for the other side.

d. Select the spacers as follows:

Gap = 0.011–0.020 in.; spacer = 0.010 in.

Gap = 0.021–0.029 in.; spacer = 0.020 in.

Gap = 0.030–0.039 in.; spacer = 0.030 in.

Failure to use the correct spacers will result in damage to the oil pan and oil leakage.

9. Install the selected spacers to the mounting pads on the rear of the oil pan before bolting the engine and transmission together. Install the engine assembly in the vehicle.

10. Connect the negative battery cable. Start the engine and check for leaks.

2.2L Diesel Engine

1. Disconnect the ground battery cables from both batteries.

2. Remove the engine oil dipstick. Disconnect the air intake hose from the air cleaner and the intake manifold.

3. Drain the coolant and remove the fan and fan shroud.

CAUTION: *When draining the coolant, keep in mind that cats and dogs are attracted by the ethylene glycol antifreeze, and are quite likely to drink any that is left in an uncovered container or in puddles on the ground. This will prove fatal in sufficient quantity. Always drain the coolant into a sealable container. Coolant should be reused unless it is contaminated or several years old.*

4. Disconnect the radiator hoses. Remove the radiator upper support brackets and remove radiator and fan shroud.

5. Disconnect and cap the fuel inlet and outlet lines at the fuel filter and the return line at the injection pump.

6. Remove the fuel filter assembly from the mounting bracket. Remove the fuel filter mounting bracket from the cylinder head.

7. Remove the nuts and washers attaching the engine brackets to the insulators.

8. Raise the vehicle and safely support on jackstands.

9. Loosen the transmission insulator bolts at the rear of the transmission. Remove the bottom engine insulator bolts.

10. Drain the engine oil from the crankcase. Remove the primary oil filter from the left side of engine.

CAUTION: *The EPA warns that prolonged contact with used engine oil may cause a number of skin disorders, including cancer! You should make every effort to minimize your exposure to used engine oil. Protective gloves should be worn when changing the oil. Wash your hands and any other exposed skin areas as soon as possible after exposure to used engine oil. Soap and water, or waterless hand cleaner should be used.*

11. Remove the by-pass filter mounting bracket and hoses.

12. Lower the vehicle.

13. Attach an engine lifting sling and hoist. Raise the engine until the insulator studs clear the insulator. Slide the engine forward, then raise the engine approximately 3 in.

14. Install a wooden block 3 in. high between the left mount and bracket. Install a wooden

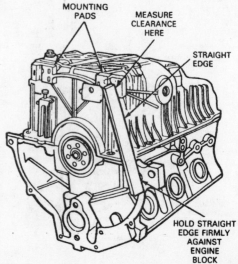

Oil pan installation — 4.0L engine

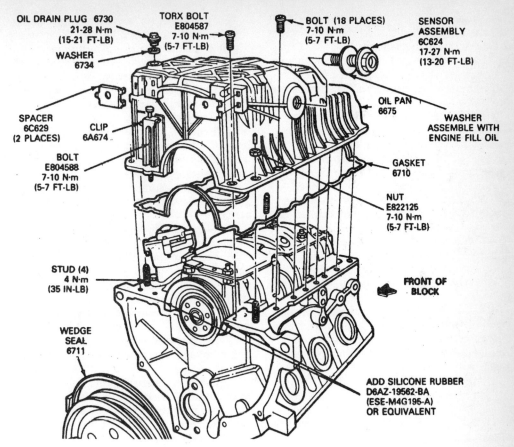

OIL DRAIN PLUG 6730
21-28 N·m
(15-21 FT-LB)

WASHER
6734

TORX BOLT
E804587
7-10 N·m
(5-7 FT-LB)

BOLT (18 PLACES)
7-10 N·m
(5-7 FT-LB)

SENSOR
ASSEMBLY
6C624
17-27 N·m
(13-20 FT-LB)

SPACER
6C629
(2 PLACES)

CLIP
6A674

OIL PAN
6675

WASHER
ASSEMBLE WITH
ENGINE FILL OIL

BOLT
E804588
7-10 N·m
(5-7 FT-LB)

GASKET
6710

NUT
E822125
7-10 N·m
(5-7 FT-LB)

STUD (4)
4 N·m
(35 IN-LB)

FRONT OF
BLOCK

WEDGE
SEAL
6711

ADD SILICONE RUBBER
D6AZ-19562-BA
(ESE-M4G195-A)
OR EQUIVALENT

Oil pan assembly — 4.0L engine

block 4¼ in. high between the right mount and bracket. Lower the engine.

15. Remove the lifting sling and raise the vehicle.

16. Remove the oil pan attaching bolts, and lower the oil pan onto the cross member.

17. Disconnect the oil pickup from the oil

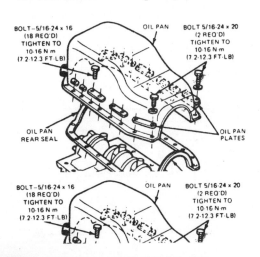

BOLT–5/16-24 x 16
(18 REQ'D)
TIGHTEN TO
10-16 N·m
(7.2-12.3 FT·LB)

OIL PAN

BOLT 5/16-24 x 20
(2 REQ'D)
TIGHTEN TO
10-16 N·m
(7.2-12.3 FT·LB)

OIL PAN
REAR SEAL

OIL PAN
PLATES

BOLT–5/16-24 x 16
(18 REQ'D)
TIGHTEN TO
10-16 N·m
(7.2-12.3 FT·LB)

OIL PAN

BOLT 5/16-24 x 20
(2 REQ'D)
TIGHTEN TO
10-16 N·m
(7.2-12.3 FT·LB)

Oil pan installation — 2.2L diesel engine

pump and bearing cap, and lay in the oil pan.

18. Move the oil pan forward and up between the front of engine and the front body sheet metal. If additional clearance is needed, move the A/C condenser forward.

To install:

19. Clean the gasket mating surfaces of the oil pan and engine block with a suitable solvent and dry thoroughly. Apply 3mm bead of Silicone Sealer on the split line between the engine block and the engine front cover and along the side rails.

20. Locate the oil pan gaskets in position with Gasket Cement and make sure that the gasket tabs are seated in seal cap grooves.

21. Press the front and rear oil pan seals in the seal cap grooves with both ends of the seals contacting oil pan gaskets.

22. Apply the 3mm bead of sealer at the ends of the oil pan seals where they meet the oil pan gaskets.

23. Position the oil pan with the pickup tube on the No. 1 crossmember.

24. Install the oil pickup tube, with a new gasket, and tighten bolts to 6–9 ft. lbs. Install the oil pan with attaching bolts and plates. Tighten bolts to 7–12 ft. lbs.

25. Lower the vehicle.

26. Install a lifting sling, raise the engine and remove the wooden blocks.

27. Lower the engine onto the insulators and install and tighten the nuts and washers.

28. Raise the vehicle and safely support on jackstands.

29. Install the transmission mount nuts.

30. Install the by-pass filter bracket and hoses. Install the by-pass oil filter.

31. Install the oil pan drain plug. Install the new primary oil filter.

32. Lower the vehicle.

33. Install the fuel filter bracket on engine.

34. Install the fuel filter and adapter on mounting bracket.

35. Install the fuel return line on the injection pump and the fuel lines on fuel filter.

36. Position the radiator in the vehicle, install the radiator hoses and upper support brackets.

37. Install the radiator fan shroud. Install the radiator fan and tighten.

38. Fill and bleed the cooling system.

39. Fill the crankcase with the specified quantity and quality of oil.

40. Install the engine oil dipstick.

41. Install the air intake hose on the air cleaner and intake manifold.

42. Connect the battery ground cables to both batteries.

43. Run the engine and check for oil, fuel and coolant leaks.

2.3L Turbo Diesel Engine

1. Disconnect battery ground cable from both batteries.

2. Remove engine oil dipstick.

3. Remove cooling fan and fan shroud.

4. Drain cooling system and remove radiator.

CAUTION: *When draining the coolant, keep in mind that cats and dogs are attracted by the ethylene glycol antifreeze, and are quite likely to drink any that is left in an uncovered container or in puddles on the ground. This will prove fatal in sufficient quantity. Always drain the coolant into a sealable container. Coolant should be reused unless it is contaminated or several years old.*

5. Remove alternator belt.

6. Remove bolts securing A/C condenser to radiator support and position condenser up and out of the way.

7. Raise vehicle.

8. Disconnect oil level switch wire.

9. Drain engine oil.

CAUTION: *The EPA warns that prolonged contact with used engine oil may cause a number of skin disorders, including cancer!*

You should make every effort to minimize your exposure to used engine oil. Protective gloves should be worn when changing the oil. Wash your hands and any other exposed skin areas as soon as possible after exposure to used engine oil. Soap and water, or waterless hand cleaner should be used.

10. Remove oil filter.

11. Remove bolts securing stabilizer bar brackets to frame and lower stabilizer bar.

12. Disconnect power steering lines from power steering pump.

13. Remove clamp securing power steering line to crossmember; position line out of the way.

14. Remove nuts securing motor mounts to support brackets.

15. Position a jack under transmission housing and raise engine until it contacts dash panel. Install wedges between motor mounts and crossmembers.

16. Remove oil pan bolts and let pan rest on crossmember.

17. Remove two bolts and one nut securing pickup tube to engine and lower pickup into oil pan.

18. Rotate crankshaft until crankshaft main bearing throws are parallel to bottom of engine to provide clearance to remove oil pan.

19. Remove oil pan through the front by first raining it up between the engine and radiator support. Then bring it out through the bottom.

To Install:

20. Clean oil an and engine block gasket mating surfaces.

21. Place oil pickup tube in oil pan and install oil pan with new gasket in position under engine. 22. Install oil pickup tube and tighten nuts and bolts to specification.

23. Apply a 3mm bead of Silicone Sealer D6AZ-19562-B or equivalent, along split line between cylinder block and front lower case and rear oil seal retainer.

24. Install oil pan and tighten bolts to specification.

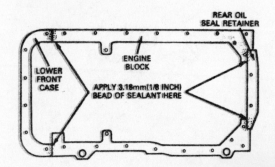

Oil pan gasket mounting — 2.3L turbo diesel engine

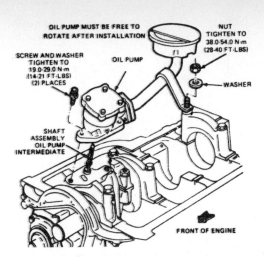

OIL PUMP MUST BE FREE TO
ROTATE AFTER INSTALLATION

SCREW AND WASHER
TIGHTEN TO
19.0-29.0 N·m
(14-21 FT-LBS)
(2) PLACES

OIL PUMP

NUT
TIGHTEN TO
38.0-54.0 N·m
(28-40 FT-LBS)

WASHER

SHAFT
ASSEMBLY
OIL PUMP
INTERMEDIATE

FRONT OF ENGINE

Oil pump installation — 2.0L and 2.3L engines

25. Remove wedges and lower engine.

26. Install motor mount retaining nuts and tighten to specification.

27. Connect power steering lines to power steering pump and install line clamp.

28. Raise stabilizer bar into position and install retaining bolts. Tighten to specification.

29. Install No. 1A crossmember and tighten to specification.

30. Connect wire to oil level switch.

31. Lower vehicle.

32. Install A/C condenser.

33. Install alternator belt.

34. Install radiator, cooling fan and shroud.

35. Fill and bleed cooling system.

36. Fill engine with specified quantity and quality of oil.

37. install engine oil dipstick.

38. Connect battery ground cables to both batteries.

39. Run engine and check for oil, coolant and power steering fluid brakes.

Oil Pump

REMOVAL AND INSTALLATION

All Gasoline Engines

Follow the service procedures under Oil Pan Removal and remove the oil pan assembly. Remove the oil pump retainer bolts and remove the oil pump. Prime the oil pump with clean engine oil by filling either the inlet or outlet port with clean engine oil. Rotate the pump shaft to distribute the oil within the pump body. Install the pump and tighten the mounting bolts to 14–21 ft. lbs. on 2.3L engines; 6–10

ft. lbs. on 2.8L & 2.9L engines; 30–40 ft. lbs. on 3.0L engines; 13–15 ft. lbs on 4.0L engines. Install the oil pan as previously described. The oil pumps are not serviceable. If defective, they must be replaced.

Do not force the oil pump if it does not seat readily. The oil pump driveshaft may be misaligned with the distributor shaft assembly. To align, rotate the intermediate driveshaft into a new position.

2.2L Diesel Engine

1. Disconnect the battery ground cables from both batteries.

2. Remove the oil pan.

3. Disconnect the oil pump outlet tube from cylinder block.

4. Remove the oil pump set screw and remove oil pump.

To install:

5. Install the oil pump.

6. Apply Teflon tape, or equivalent, to the threads of the oil pump set screws. Install the set screw and tighten.

7. Install a new gasket on the oil pump outlet tube and tighten the bolts to 6–9 ft. lbs.

8. Install the oil pan.

9. Fill the crankcase with specified quantity and quality of oil.

10. Fill and bleed the cooling system.

11. Connect the battery ground cables to both batteries.

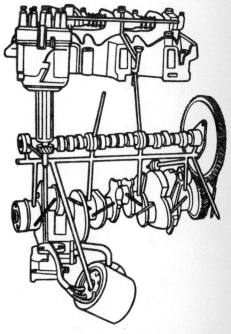

Oil pump and oil pressure lubrication system — 2.8L and 2.9L engines

2.3L Turbo Diesel Engine

1. Disconnect battery ground cables from both batteries.

2. Remove cooling fan and fan shroud.

3. Remove water pump pulley, crankshaft pulley, upper and lower timing belt covers, timing belts, and crankshaft sprockets.

4. Loosen oil pan bolts and remove six front oil pan-to-front case bolts.

5. Remove pipe plug in right hand side of engine block, Insert cross point screwdriver into hole to prevent right hand silent shaft from rotating. Remove nut attaching silent shaft sprocket to drive gear and remove sprocket.

6. Remove bolts attaching front case to engine block and remove front case.

7. Remove front case and gasket.

8. Remove silent shaft reverse rotation gear cover and remove silent shaft and gears.

9. Remove oil pump cover and remove oil pump drive gear, and inner and outer gears.

10. Remove silent shaft reverse rotation drive gear oil seal using Seal Remove T58L–101–B or equivalent.

11. Remove crankshaft front oil seal.

To install:

12. Install silent shaft oil seal using a 21mm socket.

13. Install silent shaft reverse rotation gears with marks aligned.

14. Install oil pump gears in front housing.

NOTE: *Align marks on oil pump gears when installing.*

15. Install oil pump cover and tighten to specification.

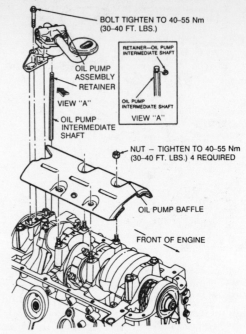

Oil pump installation — 3.0L engine

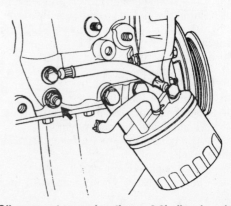

Oil pump set screw location — 2.2L diesel engine

16. Install silent shaft in reverse rotation drive gear. Position front cover and new gasket on engine block using care not to damage silent shaft bearing. Install bolts and tighten to specification.

17. Install silent shaft sprocket. Insert suitable tool in hole in block to prevent silent shaft from rotating. Tighten sprocket nut to specification.

18. Remove screwdriver and install pipe plug.

NOTE: *When installing silent shaft sprocket, ensure "D" flat on sprocket is aligned with "D" flat on shaft.*

19. Install crankshaft front oil seal.

20. Install crankshaft sprocket.

21. Apply a 3mm bead of Silicone Sealant D6A2–19562–B or equivalent along split lines

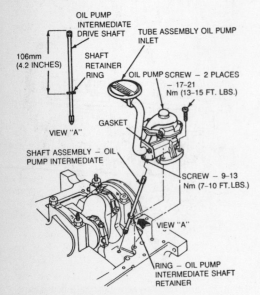

Oil pump installation — 4.0L engine

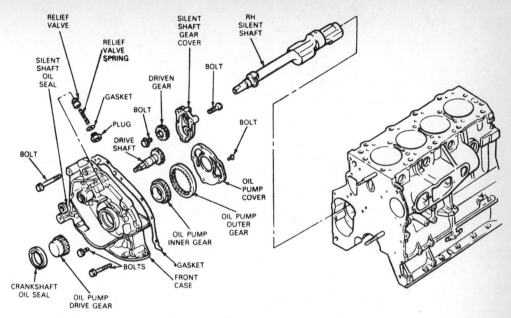

Oil pump assembly and front case — 2.3L turbo diesel engine

between lower front case cover and rear oil seal retainer and engine block.

22. Install oil pan bolts and tighten to specification.

23. Install and adjust timing belts.

24. Install upper and lower timing belt covers.

25. Install crankshaft and water pump pulleys.

26. Install accessory drive belts.

27. Install cooling fan and fan shroud.

28. Connect battery ground cables to both batteries.

29. Run again and check for oil leaks.

Camshaft Drive Belt/Timing Belt And Cover

The correct installation and adjustment of the camshaft drive belt/timing belt is mandatory if the engine is to run properly. The camshaft controls the opening of the camshaft and the crankshaft. When any given piston is on the intake stroke the corresponding intake valve must be open to admit air/fuel mixture into the cylinder. When the same piston is on the compression and power strokes, both valves in that cylinder must be closed. When the piston is on the exhaust stroke, the exhaust valve for that cylinder must be open. If the opening and closing of the valves is not coordinated with the movements of the pistons, the engine will run very poorly, if at all.

The camshaft drive belt/timing belt also turns the engine auxiliary shaft. The distributor is driven by the engine auxiliary shaft.

Since the distributor controls ignition timing, the auxiliary shaft must be coordinated with the camshaft and the crankshaft, since both valves in any given cylinder must be closed and the piston in that cylinder near the top of the compression stroke when the spark plug fires.

Due to this complex interrelationship between the camshaft, the crankshaft and the auxiliary shaft, the cogged pulleys on each component must be aligned when the camshaft drive belt/timing belt is installed.

TROUBLESHOOTING

Should the camshaft drive belt/timing belt jump timing by a tooth or two, the engine could still run; but very poorly. To visually check for correct timing of the crankshaft, auxiliary shaft, and the camshaft follow this procedure:

NOTE: *There is an access plug provided in the cam drive belt cover so that the camshaft timing cam be checked without moving the drive belt cover.*

1. Remove the access plug.

2. Turn the crankshaft until the timing marks on the crankshaft indicate TDC.

3. Make sure that the timing mark on the camshaft drive sprocket is aligned with the pointer on the inner belt cover. Also, the rotor of the distributor must align with the No. 1 cylinder firing position.

NOTE: *Never turn the crankshaft of any of the overhead cam engines in the opposite direction of normal rotation. Backward rotation of the crankshaft may cause the timing belt to slip and alter the timing.*

REMOVAL AND INSTALLATION

2.0L and 2.3L Engines

1. Rotate the engine so that No. 1 cylinder is at TDC on the compression stroke. Check that the timing marks are aligned on the camshaft and crankshaft pulleys. An access plug is provided in the cam belt cover so that the camshaft timing can be checked without removal of the cover or any other parts. Set the crankshaft to TDC by aligning the timing mark on the crank pulley with the TC mark on the belt cover. Look through the access hole in the belt cover to make sure that the timing mark on the cam drive sprocket is lined up with the pointer on the inner belt cover.

NOTE: *Always turn the engine in the normal direction of rotation. Backward rotation may cause the timing belt to jump time, due to the arrangement of the belt tensioner.*

2. Drain cooling system. Remove the upper radiator hose as necessary. Remove the fan blade and water pump pulley bolts.

CAUTION: *When draining the coolant, keep in mind that cats and dogs are attracted by the ethylene glycol antifreeze, and are quite likely to drink any that is left in an uncovered container or in puddles on the ground. This will prove fatal in sufficient quantity. Always drain the coolant into a sealable container. Coolant should be reused unless it is contaminated or several years old.*

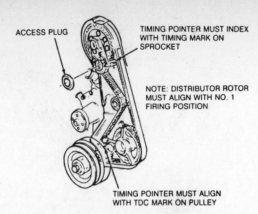

ACCESS PLUG

TIMING POINTER MUST INDEX WITH TIMING MARK ON SPROCKET

NOTE: DISTRIBUTOR ROTOR MUST ALIGN WITH NO. 1 FIRING POSITION

TIMING POINTER MUST ALIGN WITH TDC MARK ON PULLEY

Timing mark alignment — 2.3L engine

3. Loosen the alternator retaining bolts and remove the drive belt from the pulleys. Remove the water pump pulley.

4. Loosen and position the power steering pump mounting bracket and position it aside.

5. Remove the four timing belt outer cover retaining bolts and remove the cover. Remove the crankshaft pulley and belt guide.

6. Loosen the belt tensioner pulley assembly, then position a camshaft belt adjuster tool (T74P–6254–A or equivalent) on the tension spring rollpin and retract the belt tensioner away from the timing belt. Tighten the adjustment bolt to lock the tensioner in the retracted position.

7. Remove the timing belt.

To install:

8. Install the new belt over the crankshaft

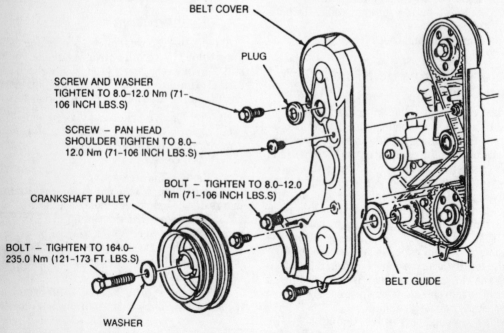

BELT COVER

PLUG

SCREW AND WASHER TIGHTEN TO 8.0–12.0 Nm (71–106 INCH LBS.S)

SCREW – PAN HEAD SHOULDER TIGHTEN TO 8.0–12.0 Nm (71–106 INCH LBS.S)

BOLT – TIGHTEN TO 8.0–12.0 Nm (71–106 INCH LBS.S)

CRANKSHAFT PULLEY

BOLT – TIGHTEN TO 164.0–235.0 Nm (121–173 FT. LBS.S)

BELT GUIDE

WASHER

Timing belt cover — 2.3L engine

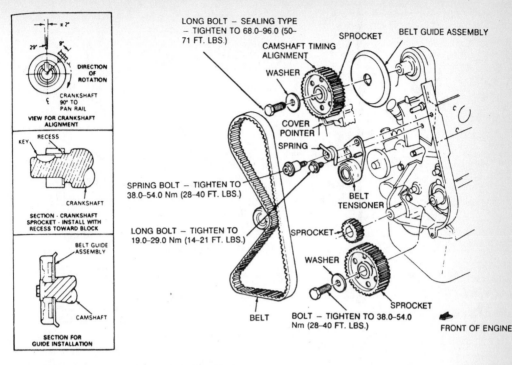

Timing belt assembly — 2.3L engine

sprocket and then counterclockwise over the auxiliary and camshaft sprockets, making sure the lugs on the belt properly engage the sprocket teeth on the pulleys. Be careful not to rotate the pulleys when installing the belt.

9. Release the timing belt tensioner pulley, allowing the tensioner to take up the belt slack. If the spring does not have enough tension to move the roller against the belt (belt hangs loose), it might be necessary to manually push the roller against the belt and tighten the bolt.

NOTE: *The spring cannot be used to set belt tension; a wrench must be used on the tensioner assembly.*

10. Rotate the crankshaft two complete turns by hand (in the normal direction of rotation) to remove the slack from the belt, then

tighten the tensioner adjustment and pivot bolts to specifications. Refer to the necessary illustrations. Make sure the belt is seated properly on the pulleys and that the timing marks are still in alignment when No. 1 cylinder is again at TDC/compression.

11. Install the crankshaft pulley and belt guide.

12. Install the timing belt cover.

13. Install the water pump pulley and fan blades. Install upper radiator hose if necessary. Refill the cooling system.

14. Position the alternator and drive belts, then adjust and tighten it to specifications.

15. Start the engine and check the ignition timing. Adjust the timing, if necessary.

2.3L Turbo Diesel Engine

1. Disconnect battery ground cables from both batteries.

2. Remove cooling fan and fan shroud.

3. Remove accessory drive belts.

4. Rotate crankshaft in direction of engine rotation to bring No. 1 piston to TDC of compression stroke.

5. Remove crankshaft pulley.

6. Remove upper and lower front covers.

7. Loosen belt tensioners from timing belts. Remove belt(s), as necessary.

To install:

8. Align crankshaft timing marks.

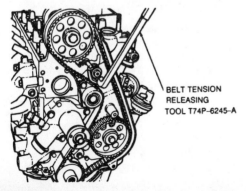

Releasing the timing belt tensioner with special tool

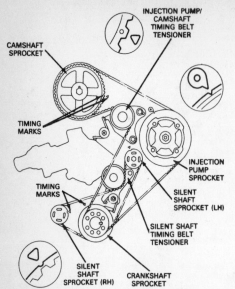

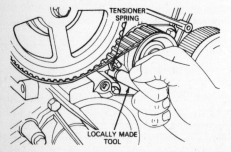

Timing belt alignment — 2.3L turbo diesel engine

Timing belt tension adjustment — 2.3L turbo diesel engine

9. Align LH and right hand silent shaft timing marks.

10. Install silent shaft belt.

NOTE: *Install belt in original direction of rotation. For ease of installation, pry on tensioner spring to reduce load on tensioner.*

11. Align camshaft timing marks.

12. Install injection pump/camshaft timing belt as follows.

NOTE: *To ease installation, locally manufacture the following tool. Using a pivot nut from a rear brake shoe adjuster, weld a piece of bar stock on the end.*

    a. Using the tensioner spring tool, release the tension on the tension spring for the injection pump/camshaft timing belt.

    b. After releasing spring tension, rotate tensioner toward water pump and tighten top bolts.

    c. Install the belt.

13. Adjust silent shaft belt and camshaft/injection pump belt tensions.

14. Install upper and lower front timing covers.

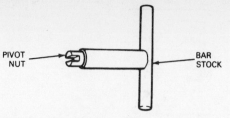

Timing belt tension tool — 2.3L turbo diesel engine

15. Install crankshaft pulley.

16. Install accessory drive belts.

17. Install cooling fan and fan shroud.

18. Connect battery ground cables to both batteries.

INJECTION PUMP/CAMSHAFT BELT ADJUSTMENT

1. Remove timing belt upper cover.

2. Rotate engine until No. 1 piston is at TDC on compression stroke.

3. Ensure crankshaft pulley, injection pump sprocket and camshaft sprocket are aligned with their timing marks.

4. Loosen top belt tensioner bolt one or two turns and loosen bottom bolt one complete turn. This allows tensioner spring to automatically adjust belt tension.

5. Rotate crankshaft clockwise to that alignment pointer on timing cover aligns with second tooth from alignment mark on camshaft sprocket.

CAUTION: *Rotate crankshaft smoothly by two camshaft sprocket teeth. Failure to do so will result in an incorrect belt tension and possible engine damage.*

6. Tighten top belt tensioner mounting bolt to specification, then tighten bottom bolt to specification.

7. Rotate the crankshaft counterclockwise until timing marks are aligned. Push belt down halfway between injection pump sprocket and camshaft sprocket and check deflection. If properly tensioned, belt should deflect 4–5mm.

SILENT SHAFT BELT ADJUSTMENT

1. Rotate crankshaft until No. 1 piston is at TDC on compression stroke.

2. Remove access cover for top belt tensioner bolt by inserting a suitable tool in slot shown and prying out.

3. Loosen top belt tension mounting bolt one complete turn. Then, loosen bottom bolt one to two turns. This allows tensioner spring to automatically adjust belt tension.

4. Tighten bottom tensioner bolt to specification, then tighten top bolt to specification.

CAUTION: *Tighten bottom bolt first. Tighten top bolt first can cause tensioner to*

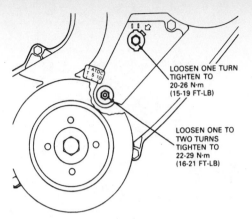

LOOSEN ONE TURN TIGHTEN TO 20-26 N·m (15-19 FT-LB)

LOOSEN ONE TO TWO TURNS TIGHTEN TO 22-29 N·m (16-21 FT-LB)

Silent shaft belt tensioner — 2.3L turbo diesel engine

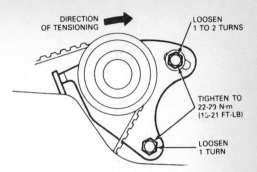

DIRECTION OF TENSIONING

LOOSEN 1 TO 2 TURNS

TIGHTEN TO 22-29 N·m (16-21 FT-LB)

LOOSEN 1 TURN

Injection pump/camshaft belt tensioner — 2.3L turbo diesel engine

rotate and over-tension the timing belt.

5. Install access cover for top tensioner bolt by sliding down along two guide lines embossed on front lower cover.

Timing Gear Cover & Oil Seal

REMOVAL AND INSTALLATION

2.8L, 2.9L Engines

1. Remove the oil pan as described under Oil Pan removal and installation.

2. Drain the coolant. Remove the radiator.

CAUTION: *When draining the coolant, keep in mind that cats and dogs are attracted by the ethylene glycol antifreeze, and are quite likely to drink any that is left in an uncovered container or in puddles on the ground. This will prove fatal in sufficient quantity. Always drain the coolant into a sealable container. Coolant should be reused unless it is contaminated or several years old.*

3. Remove the A/C compressor and the power steering bracket, if so equipped, and po-

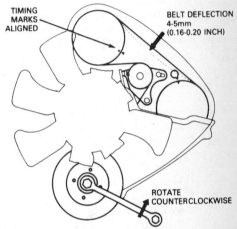

TIMING MARKS ALIGNED

BELT DEFLECTION 4-5mm (0.16-0.20 INCH)

ROTATE COUNTERCLOCKWISE

Camshaft belt deflection — 2.3L turbo diesel engine

sition then out of the way. DO NOT disconnect the A/C refrigerant lines.

4. Remove the alternator, Thermactor pump and drive belt(s).

5. Remove the fan.

6. Remove the water pump and the heater and radiator hoses.

7. Remove the drive pulley from the crankshaft.

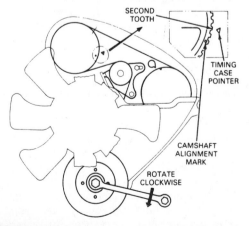

SECOND TOOTH

TIMING CASE POINTER

CAMSHAFT ALIGNMENT MARK

ROTATE CLOCKWISE

Camshaft belt alignment — 2.3L turbo diesel engine

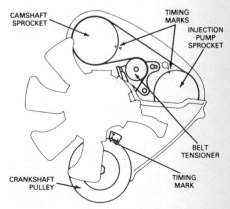

CAMSHAFT SPROCKET

TIMING MARKS

INJECTION PUMP SPROCKET

BELT TENSIONER

TIMING MARK

CRANKSHAFT PULLEY

Injection pump/camshaft belt alignment — 2.3L turbo diesel engine

8. Remove the front cover retaining bolts. If necessary, tap the cover lightly with a plastic hammer to break the gasket seal. Remove the front cover. If the front cover plate gasket needs replacement, remove the two screws and remove the plate. If necessary, remove the guide sleeves from the cylinder block.

9. If the front cover oil seal needs replacement use the following procedure:

a. Support the front cover to prevent damage while driving out the seal.

b. Drive out the seal from front cover with Front Cover Aligner, T74P-6019-A, or equivalent.

c. Support the front cover to prevent damage while installing the seal.

d. Coat the new front cover oil seal with Lubriplate® or equivalent. Install the new seal in the front cover.

To install:

10. Clean the front cover mating surfaces of gasket material. Apply sealer to the gasket surfaces on the cylinder block and back side of the front cover plate. Install the guide sleeves, with new seal rings, with the chamfered end toward the front cover, if removed. Position the gasket and the front cover plate on the cylinder block. Temporarily install the four front cover screws to position the gasket and cover plate in plate. Install and tighten the two cover plate attaching bolts, then remove the four screws that were temporarily installed.

11. Apply gasket sealer to the front cover gasket surface. Place the gasket in position on the front cover.

12. Place the front cover on the engine and

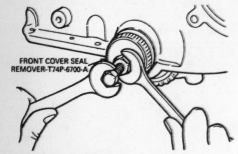

Installing the front oil seal

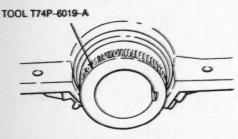

Front cover alignment special tool

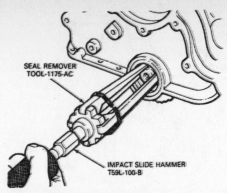

Removing the front oil seal

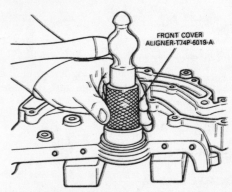

Removing and installing front oil seal with front cover assembly removed

start all the retaining screws two or three turns. Center the cover by inserting Front Cover Aligner, Tool T74P-6019-A, or equivalent in oil seal.

13. Torque the front cover attaching screws to 13-16 ft. lbs.

14. Install the belt drive pulley.

15. Install the oil pan as described under Oil Pan removal and installation.

16. Install the water pump, heater hose, A/C compressor, alternator, Thermactor pump and drive belt(s). Adjust drive belt tension.

17. Fill and bleed the cooling system.

18. Operate the engine at fast idle speed and check for coolant and oil leaks.

Timing Gears

REMOVAL AND INSTALLATION

2.8L Engine

1. Drain the cooling system and crankcase. Remove the oil pan and radiator.

CAUTION: *When draining the coolant, keep in mind that cats and dogs are attracted by the ethylene glycol antifreeze, and are quite likely to drink any that is left in an uncovered container or in puddles on the ground. This will prove fatal in sufficient quantity.*

Always drain the coolant into a sealable container. Coolant should be reused unless it is contaminated or several years old.

2. Remove the cylinder front cover and water pump, drive belt, and camshaft timing gear.

3. Use the gear puller T71P–19703–B and Shaft Protector T71P–7137–H or equivalent and remove the crankshaft gear.

To install:

4. Align the keyway in the gear with the key, then slide the gear onto the shaft, making sure that it seats tight against the spacer.

5. Check the camshaft end play. Refer to checking Camshaft procedure. If not within specifications, replace the thrust plate.

6. Align the keyway in the crankshaft gear with key in the crankshaft, and align the timing marks. Install the gear, using Crankshaft Sprocket Replacer Tool.

7. Install the cylinder front cover following the procedures in this Chapter. Install the oil pan and radiator.

8. Fill and bleed the cooling system and crankcase.

9. Start the engine and adjust the ignition timing.

10. Operate the engine at fast idle and check all hose connections and gaskets for leaks.

Timing Sprockets and Chain

REMOVAL AND INSTALLATION

2.9L Engine

1. Drain the cooling system and crankcase. Remove the oil pan and radiator.

CAUTION: *When draining the coolant, keep in mind that cats and dogs are attracted by the ethylene glycol antifreeze, and are quite likely to drink any that is left in an uncovered container or in puddles on the ground.*

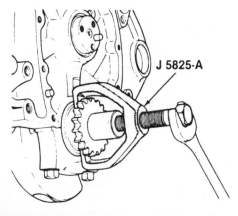

J 5825-A

Removing the crankshaft gear — 2.8L and 2.9L engines

This will prove fatal in sufficient quantity. Always drain the coolant into a sealable container. Coolant should be reused unless it is contaminated or several years old.

2. Remove the cylinder front cover and water pump, drive belt, and camshaft timing gear.

3. Use the clutch aligner T71P–P–7137–H or equivalent and remove the crankshaft sprocket.

To install:

4. Align the keyway in the gear with the key, then slide the gear onto the shaft, making sure that it seats tight against the spacer.

NOTE: *Feed the timing chain around the crankshaft sprocket and then around the camshaft sprocket. Install the camshaft sprocket together with timing chain as an assembly. Align all necessary timing marks.*

5. Check the camshaft end play. Refer to checking Camshaft. If not within specifications, replace the thrust plate.

6. Align the keyway in the crankshaft gear with key in the crankshaft, and align the timing marks. Install the gear, using Crankshaft Sprocket Replacer Tool.

7. Install the cylinder front cover following the procedures in this Chapter. Install the oil pan and radiator.

8. Fill and bleed the cooling system and crankcase.

9. Start the engine and adjust the ignition timing.

10. Operate the engine at fast idle and check all hose connections and gaskets for leaks.

TIMING CHAIN DEFLECTION

2.9L Engine

1. Remove the timing chain tensioner.

2. Rotate the crankshaft counterclockwise (as viewed from the front of the engine) to take up the slack on the left hand side of the chain.

3. Mark a reference point on a block approx-

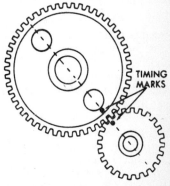

TIMING MARKS

Correct alignment of the timing marks — 2.8L and 2.9L engines

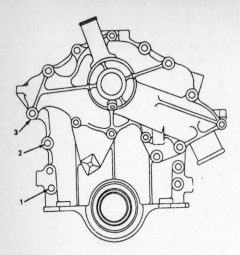

FASTENERS

Ref. No.	Part No.	Size	N-m	Ft-Lb
1	N804215-S100	M8 x 1.25 x 72.25	25	19
2	N804215-S100	M8 x 1.25 x 72.25	25	19
3	N804811-S100	M8 x 1.25 x 70.0	25	19

NOTE: Apply Pipe Sealant ESG-M4G194-A to Bolt Threads A10107-1C

Front cover bolt installation chart — 3.0L engine

imately at mid-point of the chain. Measure from this point to the chain.

4. Rotate the crankshaft in the opposite direction to take up the slack on the right hand side of the chain. Force the left hand side of the chain out with your fingers and measure the distance between the reference point and the chain. The deflection is the difference between the two measurements.

5. If the deflection measurement exceeds specification, replace the timing chain and sprockets.

6. If the wear on the tensioner face exceeds 1.5mm, replace the tensioner.

7. When installing the crankshaft sprocket, fill the keyway chamfer cavity with EOAZ–19554–AA Threadlock and Sealer or equivalent, flush with the front face of the sprocket.

Timing Cover and Chain

REMOVAL AND INSTALLATION

3.0L Engine

1. Disconnect the negative battery cable.
2. Drain the cooling system and crankcase. CAUTION: *When draining the coolant, keep in mind that cats and dogs are attracted by the ethylene glycol antifreeze, and are quite likely to drink any that is left in an uncovered container or in puddles on the ground. This will prove fatal in sufficient quantity. Always drain the coolant into a sealable container. Coolant should be reused unless it is contaminated or several years old.*
3. Remove the cooling fan.
4. Loosen the water pump pulley bolts.

Loosen and remove the accessory drive belts. Remove the water pump pulley.

5. Remove the alternator adjusting arm and brace assembly. Remove the heated air intake duct from the engine.

6. Remove the upper motor mount retaining nuts. Remove the A/C compressor upper bolts, then remove the front cover front nuts on vehicles with automatic transmission and A/C.

7. Mark and remove the distributor assembly from the vehicle.

8. Raise the vehicle. Remove the A/C compressor bolts and bracket if so equipped and position the assembly aside.

9. Remove the crankshaft pulley and damper assembly. Remove the oil pan. Refer to the necessary service procedures in this Chapter.

10. Lower the vehicle. Remove the lower radiator hose. Remove the water pump.

11. Remove the timing cover to cylinder block attaching bolts. Carefully remove the timing cover from the cylinder block.

12. Rotate crankshaft until NO. 1 piston is at TDC and timing marks are aligned in the correct position.

13. Remove the camshaft sprocket retaining bolt and washer. Check timing chain deflection for excessive wear.

14. Slide sprockets and timing chain forward and remove as assembly.

To install:

15. Clean timing cover and oil pan sealing surfaces. Clean and inspect all parts. The camshaft retaining bolt has a drilled oil passage for timing chain assembly lubrication. Clean oil passage with solvent. Do not replace with standard bolt.

16. Slide sprockets and timing chain on as assembly with timing marks in the correct location. Install camshaft retaining bolt and

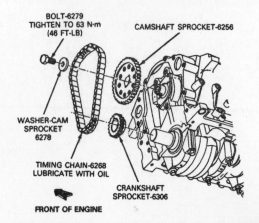

Timing chain assembly — 3.0L engine

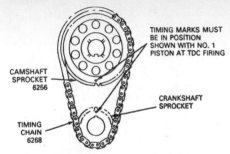

Timing marks installation — 3.0L engine

washer. Torque bolt to 46 ft. lbs. Lubricate the timing chain assembly.

17. Install timing cover assembly. Install retaining bolts with pipe sealant and tighten as outlined. Refer to the necessary illustration.

18. Install oil pan (install distributor assembly in correct position) and water pump. Refer to the necessary procedures in this Chapter.

19. Install crankshaft damper and pulley assembly.

20. Install drive belt components. Install drive belts and adjust.

21. Fill crankcase. Refill and bleed cooling system. Connect the negative battery cable. Start engine check for coolant, oil and exhaust leaks.

4.0L Engine

NOTE: *Review the complete service procedure before starting this repair. Refer to the necessary service procedures in this Chapter.*

1. Disconnect the negative battery cable. Remove/lower the oil pan.

2. Drain the cooling system.

CAUTION: *When draining the coolant, keep in mind that cats and dogs are attracted by the ethylene glycol antifreeze, and are quite likely to drink any that is left in an uncovered container or in puddles on the ground. This will prove fatal in sufficient quantity. Always drain the coolant into a sealable container. Coolant should be reused unless it is contaminated or several years old.*

3. Remove the air conditioning compressor and position it out of the way. DO NOT disconnect the refrigerant lines!

4. Remove the power steering pump and position it out of the way. DO NOT disconnect the hoses!

5. Remove the alternator.

6. Remove the fan.

7. Remove the water pump.

8. Remove the drive pulley/damper from the crankshaft.

9. Remove the crankshaft timing sensor.

10. Remove the front cover attaching bolts. It may be necessary to tap the cover loose with a plastic mallet.

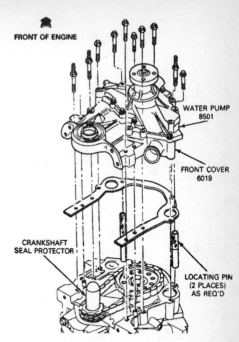

Front cover assembly — 3.0L engine

11. Remove the radiator.

12. Rotate the engine by hand until the No.1 cylinder is at TDC compression, and the timing marks are aligned.

13. Remove the camshaft sprocket bolt and sprocket retaining key.

14. Remove the camshaft and crankshaft sprockets with the timing chain.

15. If necessary, remove the tensioner and guide.

To install:

16. Install the timing chain guide. Make sure the pin of the guide is in the hole in the block. Tighten the bolts to 84–96 inch lbs.

17. Align the timing marks on the crankshaft and camshaft sprockets and install the sprockets and chain.

18. Install the camshaft sprocket bolt and sprocket retaining key. Make sure that the timing marks are still aligned.

19. Install the tensioner with the clip in place to keep it retracted.

20. Install the crankshaft key. Make sure the timing marks are still aligned.

21. Make sure the tensioner side of the chain is held inward and the other side is straight and tight.

22. Install the camshaft sprocket bolt and tighten it to 50 ft. lbs.

23. Remove the tensioner clip.

24. Check camshaft endplay.

25. Install the front cover and attaching bolts. Refer to the necessary illustration.

26. Install the radiator.

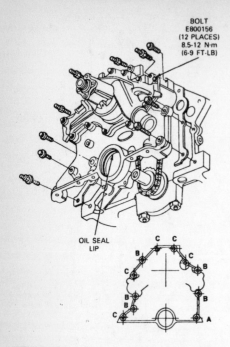

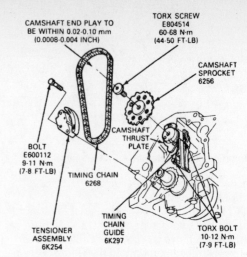

Timing chain tensioner assembly — 4.0L engine

FRONT COVER BOLTS				
FASTENER	LOCATION	SIZE	QUANTITY	TORQUE N·M (FT-LB)
BOLT	A	M8 × 47	(1)	17-21 (13-15)
BOLT	B	M8 × 25	(5)	17-21 (13-15)
STUD	C	M8 × 25	(5)	17-21 (13-15)

Front cover assembly/bolt location — 4.0L engine

27. Install the crankshaft timing sensor.
28. Install the drive pulley/damper.
29. Install the water pump.
30. Install the fan.
31. Install the alternator.
32. Install the power steering pump.
33. Install the air conditioning compressor.
34. Fill the cooling system.
35. Install the oil pan.
36. Fill the crankcase to the proper level. Connect the negative battery cable. Start engine check for leaks and roadtest the vehicle for proper operation.

Timing Cover/Seal and Timing Chain/Gears

REMOVAL AND INSTALLATION

2.2L Diesel Engine

1. Bring the engine to No. 1 piston at TDC on the compression stroke.
2. Disconnect the ground cables from the batteries. Drain the cooling system.

CAUTION: *When draining the coolant, keep in mind that cats and dogs are attracted by the ethylene glycol antifreeze, and are quite likely to drink any that is left in an uncovered container or in puddles on the ground.*

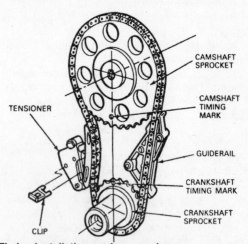

Timing installation marks — engine

This will prove fatal in sufficient quantity. Always drain the coolant into a sealable container. Coolant should be reused unless it is contaminated or several years old.

3. Remove the radiator fan shroud and cooling fan. Drain the engine oil from the crankcase.

CAUTION: *The EPA warns that prolonged contact with used engine oil may cause a number of skin disorders, including cancer! You should make every effort to minimize your exposure to used engine oil. Protective gloves should be worn when changing the oil. Wash your hands and any other exposed skin areas as soon as possible after exposure to used engine oil. Soap and water, or waterless hand cleaner should be used.*

4. Loosen the idler pulley and remove the A/C compressor belt. Remove the power steering belt. Remove the power steering pump and

mounting bracket, position out of the way with the hoses attached.

5. Loosen and remove the alternator and vacuum pump drive belts.

6. Remove the water pump. Using a suitable puller, remove the crankshaft pulley.

7. Remove the nuts and bolts retaining the timing case cover to the engine block. Remove the timing case cover.

8. Remove the engine oil pan.

9. Verify that all timing marks are aligned. Rotate the engine, if necessary, to align marks.

10. Remove the bolt attaching the camshaft gear and remove the washer and friction gear.

11. Remove the bolt attaching the injection pump gear and remove the washer and friction gear.

12. Install Ford tool T83T6306A or equivalent on to the camshaft drive gear and remove the gear. Attach the puller to the injection pump drive gear and remove the gear.

13. Remove the nuts attaching the idler gears after marking reference points on the idler gears for reinstallation position. Remove the idler gear assemblies.

14. Remove the nuts attaching the injection pump to the timing gear case. Support the injection pump in position.

15. Remove the bolts that attaching the timing gear case to the engine block and remove the case if necessary.

16. Clean all gasket mounting surfaces. Clean all parts, replace as necessary.

17. Remove the old oil seal from the front cover and replace.

18. Position the timing gear cover case with a new mounting gasket and install.

19. Install the timing gears as follows:

   a. Verify that the crankshaft and right idler pulley timing marks align and install the right idler gear assembly.

   b. Install the camshaft gear so that the timing marks align with the timing mark on the right idler gear.

   c. Install the left idler gear assembly so that the timing marks align with the timing marks align with the timing mark on the right idler gear.

   d. Install the injection pump gear so that the timing marks align with the timing mark on the left idler gear.

   e. Install all friction gears, washers, nuts and bolts on the gears.

20. Install the timing case covers using a new mounting gasket.

21. Install the remaining components in the reverse order of removal.

Camshaft and Auxiliary Shaft Sprockets and Seals

REMOVAL AND INSTALLATION

The cylinder front cover, camshaft and auxiliary shaft seals are replaced in the same manner with the same tools after the respec-

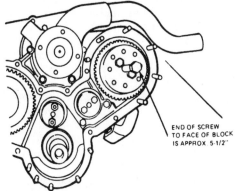

Remove the injection pump gear — 2.2L diesel engine

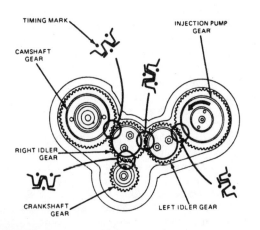

Timing gear alignment — 2.2L diesel engine

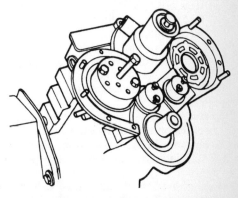

Remove the camshaft gear — 2.2L diesel engine

tive gear has been removed. Always use a new attaching bolt when replacing the camshaft sprocket or use new Teflon® sealing tape on the threads of the old bolt. To remove the sprockets, first remove the timing cover and belt, then use tool T74P–6256–B, or equivalent to pull the cam drive sprocket. The same tool is used in exactly the same manner to remove the auxiliary shaft sprocket, as well as to hold the sprockets while the attaching bolts are installed and tightened.

A front cover seal remover tool T74P–6700–B or equivalent is used to remove all the seals. When positioning this tool, make sure that the jaws are gripping the thin edge of the seal very tightly before operating the jack-screw portion of the tool.

To install the seals, a cam and auxiliary shaft seal replacer T74P–6150–A or equivalent with a stepped, threaded arbor is used. The tool acts as a press, using the internal threads of the various shafts as a pilot.

Camshaft

REMOVAL AND INSTALLATION

2.0L, 2.3L Engine

NOTE: *The following procedure covers camshaft removal and installation with the cylinder head on or off the engine. If the cylinder head has been removed start at Step 9.*

1. Drain the cooling system. Remove the air cleaner assembly and disconnect the negative battery cable.

CAUTION: *When draining the coolant, keep in mind that cats and dogs are attracted by the ethylene glycol antifreeze, and are quite likely to drink any that is left in an uncovered container or in puddles on the ground. This will prove fatal in sufficient quantity. Always drain the coolant into a sealable container. Coolant should be reused unless it is contaminated or several years old.*

2. Remove the spark plug wires from the plugs, disconnect the retainer from the valve cover and position the wires out of the way. Disconnect rubber vacuum lines as necessary.

3. Remove all drive belts. Remove the alternator mounting bracket-to-cylinder head mounting bolts, position bracket and alternator out of the way.

4. Disconnect and remove the upper radiator hose. Disconnect the radiator shroud.

5. Remove the fan blades and water pump pulley and fan shroud. Remove cam belt and valve covers.

6. Align engine timing marks at TDC for No. 1 cylinder. Remove cam drive belt.

7. Jack up the front of the vehicle and support on jackstands. Remove the front motor mount bolts. Disconnect the lower radiator hose from the radiator. Disconnect and plug the automatic transmission cooler lines.

8. Position a piece of wood on a floor jack and raise the engine carefully as far as it will go. Place blocks of wood between the engine mounts and crossmember pedestals.

9. Remove the rocker arms (camshaft followers).

10. Remove the camshaft drive gear and belt guide using a suitable puller. Remove the front oil seal with a sheet metal screw and slide hammer.

11. Remove the camshaft retainer located on the rear mounting stand by unbolting the two bolts.

12. Remove the camshaft by carefully withdrawing toward the front of the engine. Caution should be used to prevent damage to cam bearings, lobes and journals.

13. Check the camshaft journals and lobes for wear. Inspect the cam bearings, if worn (unless the proper bearing installing tool is on hand), the cylinder head must be removed for new bearings to be installed by a machine shop.

14. Camshaft installation is in the reverse order of service removal procedure. See following notes.

NOTE: *Coat the camshaft with heavy SG oil before sliding it into the cylinder head. Install a new front seal. Apply a coat of sealer or Teflon tape to the cam drive gear bolt before installation. After any procedure requiring removal of the rocker arms, each lash adjuster must be fully collapsed after assembly, then released. This must be done before the camshaft is turned.*

15. Refill cooling system. Start engine and check for leaks. Roadtest the vehicle for proper operation.

2.8L, 2.9L Engines

1. Disconnect the battery ground cable from the battery.

2. Drain the oil from the crankcase.

CAUTION: *The EPA warns that prolonged contact with used engine oil may cause a number of skin disorders, including cancer! You should make every effort to minimize your exposure to used engine oil. Protective gloves should be worn when changing the oil. Wash your hands and any other exposed skin areas as soon as possible after exposure to used engine oil. Soap and water, or waterless hand cleaner should be used.*

3. Remove the radiator, fan and spacer, drive belt and pulley.

4. Label and remove the spark plug wires from the spark plugs.

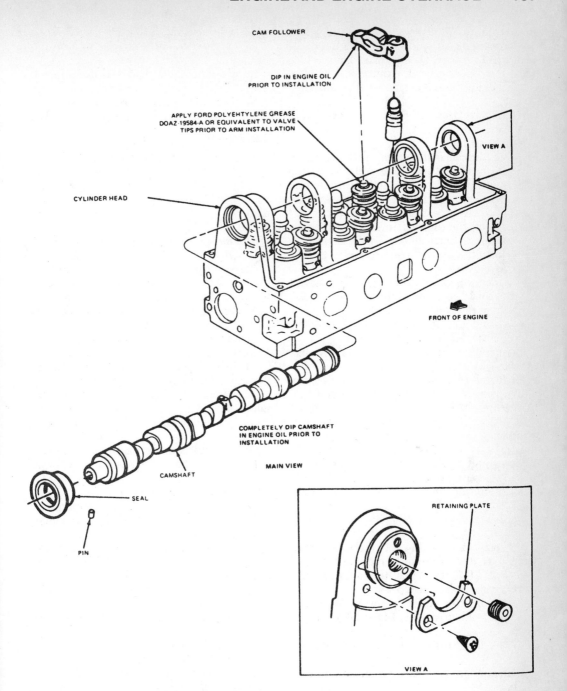

Camshaft installation — 2.0L and 2.3L engines

5. Remove the distributor cap with spark plug wires as an assembly.

6. Disconnect the distributor wiring harness and remove the distributor.

7. Remove the alternator.

8. Remove the Thermactor pump.

9. Remove the fuel lines, fuel filter and carburetor.

10. Remove the intake manifold as described earlier.

11. Remove the rocker arm covers and rocker arm and shaft assemblies as described in this Chapter. Label and remove the push rods and the tappets, so they can be reinstalled in the same location.

12. Remove the oil pan as described in this Chapter.

13. Remove the crankshaft damper.

14. Remove the engine front cover and water pump as an assembly.

15. Remove the camshaft gear attaching bolt and washer, and slide gear off camshaft.

16. Remove the camshaft thrust plate.

17. Carefully remove the camshaft from the block, avoiding any damage to the camshaft bearings.

18. Remove the camshaft drive gear and spacer ring.

To install:

19. Oil the camshaft journals with heavy SG grade engine oil and apply Lubriplate® or equivalent lubricant to the cam lobes. Install the spacer ring with the chamfered side toward the camshaft. Insert the camshaft key.

20. Install the camshaft in the block, carefully avoiding damage to the bearing surfaces.

21. Install the thrust plate so that it covers the main oil gallery.

22. Check the camshaft end play. The spacer ring and thrust plate are available in two thicknesses to permit adjusting the end play.

23. Install camshaft gear as described under Timing Gear removal and installation.

24. Install the engine front cover and water pump as an assembly.

25. Install the crankshaft pulley and secure with washer and attaching bolt. Torque the bolt to 85–96 ft. lbs.

26. Install the oil pan, as described in this Chapter.

27. Position the tappets in their original locations. Apply Lubriplate or equivalent to both ends of the push rods.

NOTE: *Install the push rods in same location as removed.*

28. Install the intake manifold, as described earlier.

29. Install the oil baffles and rocker arm and shaft assemblies. Tighten the rocker arm stand bolts to 43–50 ft. lbs. Adjust the valves and install the valve rocker arm covers.

30. Install the water pump pulley, fan spacer, fan, and drive belt. Adjust the belt tension.

31. Install the carburetor, fuel filter and fuel line.

32. Install the Thermactor pump and the alternator.

33. Install the distributor, distributor wiring harness and distributor cap and plug wires. Connect the plug wires to the spark plugs. Refer to Distributor Removal and Installation earlier in this Chapter.

NOTE: *Before installing plug wires, coat inside of each boot with silicone lubricant using a small screwdriver.*

34. Install the radiator.

35. Fill the cooling system to the proper level with a 50–50 mix of antifreeze and bleed cooling system.

36. Fill the crankcase with oil.

37. Connect the battery ground cable to the battery.

38. Run the engine and check and adjust the engine timing and idle speed.

39. Run the engine at fast idle speed and check for coolant, fuel, vacuum and oil leaks.

3.0L Engine

1. Disconnect the negative battery cable.

2. Remove the air cleaner hoses.

3. Remove the fan and spacer, and shroud.

4. Drain the cooling system. Remove the radiator.

CAUTION: *When draining the coolant, keep in mind that cats and dogs are attracted by the ethylene glycol antifreeze, and are quite likely to drink any that is left in an uncovered container or in puddles on the ground. This will prove fatal in sufficient quantity. Always drain the coolant into a sealable container. Coolant should be reused unless it is contaminated or several years old.*

5. Remove the condenser.

6. Relieve the fuel system pressure. See Chapter 1 Fuel Filter.

7. Remove the fuel lines at the fuel supply manifold.

8. Tag and disconnect all vacuum hoses in the way.

9. Tag and disconnect all wires in the way.

10. Remove the engine front cover and water pump.

11. Remove the alternator.

12. Remove the power steering pump and secure it out of the way. DO NOT disconnect the hoses!

13. Remove the air conditioning compressor and secure it out of the way. DO NOT disconnect the hoses!

14. Remove the throttle body. See Chapter 5.

15. Remove the fuel injection harness. See Chapter 5.

16. Drain the engine oil into a suitable container and dispose of it properly.

CAUTION: *The EPA warns that prolonged contact with used engine oil may cause a number of skin disorders, including cancer! You should make every effort to minimize your exposure to used engine oil. Protective gloves should be worn when changing the oil. Wash your hands and any other exposed skin areas as soon as possible after exposure to used engine oil. Soap and water, or waterless hand cleaner should be used.*

17. Turn the engine by hand to 0 BTDC of the power stroke on No. 1 cylinder.

18. Disconnect the spark plug wires from the plugs.

19. Remove the distributor cap with the spark plug wires as an assembly.

20. Matchmark the rotor, distributor body and engine. Disconnect the distributor wiring harness and remove the distributor.

21. Remove the rocker arm covers.

22. Remove the intake manifold as previously described.

23. Loosen the rocker arm bolts enough to pivot the rocker arms out of the way and remove the pushrods. Identify them for installation. They must be installed in their original positions!

24. Remove the tappets. Identify them for installation.

25. Remove the crankshaft pulley/damper.

26. Remove the starter.

27. Remove the oil pan as previously described.

28. Turn the engine by hand until the timing marks align at TDC of the power stroke on No.1 piston.

29. Check the camshaft endplay. If excessive, you'll have to replace the thrust plate.

30. Remove the camshaft gear attaching bolt and washer, then slide the gear off the camshaft.

31. Remove the camshaft thrust plate.

32. Carefully slide the camshaft out of the engine block, using caution to avoid any damage to the camshaft bearings.

To install:

33. Oil the camshaft journals and cam lobes with heavy SG engine oil (50W). Install the spacer ring with the chamfered side toward the camshaft, then insert the camshaft key.

34. Install the camshaft in the block, using caution to avoid any damage to the camshaft bearings.

35. Install the thrust plate. Tighten the attaching screws to 84 inch lbs.

36. Rotate the camshaft and crankshaft as necessary to align the timing marks. Install the camshaft gear and chain. Tighten the attaching bolt to 46 ft. lbs.

30. Coat the tappets with 50W engine oil and place them in their original locations.

31. Apply 50W engine oil to both ends of the pushrods. Install the pushrods in their original locations.

32. Pivot the rocker arms into position. Tighten the fulcrum bolts to 8 ft. lbs.

33. Rotate the engine until both timing marks are at the tops of their sprockets and aligned. Tighten the following fulcrum bolts to 18 ft. lbs.:
  - No.1 intake
  - No.2 exhaust
  - No.4 intake
  - No.5 exhaust

34. Rotate the engine until the camshaft timing mark is at the bottom of the sprocket and the crankshaft timing mark is at the top of the sprocket, and both are aligned. Tighten the following fulcrum bolts to 18 ft. lbs.:
  - No.1 exhaust
  - No.2 intake
  - No.3 intake and exhaust
  - No.4 exhaust
  - No.5 intake
  - No.6 intake and exhaust

35. Now, tighten all the bolts to 24 ft. lbs.

36. Turn the engine by hand to 0 BTDC of the power stroke on No. 1 cylinder.

37. Install the engine front cover and water pump assembly.

38. Install the oil pan.

39. Install the crankshaft damper/pulley and tighten the retaining bolt to 107 ft. lbs.

40. Install the intake manifold and tighten the mounting bolts to the specifications and in the sequence described under Intake Manifold Removal And Installation.

41. Install the rocker covers.

42. Install the injector harness.

43. Install the distributor.

44. Install the cap and wires.

45. Install the throttle body.

46. Install the alternator.

47. Install the power steering pump.

48. Install the compressor.

49. Connect all wires.

50. Connect all vacuum lines.

51. Install the radiator and condenser.

52. Install the fan and clutch.

53. Install the fuel lines.

54. Install the starter.

55. Refill the cooling system.

56. Replace the oil filter and refill the crankcase with the specified amount of engine oil.

57. Reconnect the battery ground cable.

58. Start the engine and check the ignition timing and idle speed. Adjust if necessary. Run the engine at fast idle and check for coolant, fuel, vacuum or oil leaks.

4.0L Engine

NOTE: *Review the complete service procedure before starting this repair. Refer to the necessary service procedures in this Chapter.*

1. Disconnect the negative battery cable.

2. Drain the engine oil into a suitable container and dispose of it properly.

CAUTION: *The EPA warns that prolonged contact with used engine oil may cause a number of skin disorders, including cancer! You should make every effort to minimize your exposure to used engine oil. Protective gloves should be worn when changing the oil. Wash your hands and any other exposed skin areas as soon as possible after exposure to used engine oil. Soap and water, or waterless hand cleaner should be used.*

3. Drain the cooling system.

CAUTION: *When draining the coolant, keep in mind that cats and dogs are attracted by the ethylene glycol antifreeze, and are quite likely to drink any that is left in an uncovered container or in puddles on the ground. This will prove fatal in sufficient quantity. Always drain the coolant into a sealable container. Coolant should be reused unless it is contaminated or several years old.*

4. Remove the radiator.

5. Remove the condenser.

6. Remove the fan and spacer, and shroud.

7. Remove the air cleaner hoses.

8. Tag and remove the spark plug wires.

9. Remove the EDIS ignition coil and bracket.

10. Remove the crankshaft pulley/damper.

11. Remove the clamp. bolt and oil pump drive from the rear of the block.

12. Remove the alternator.

13. Relieve the fuel system pressure. See Chapter 1 Fuel Filter.

14. Remove the fuel lines at the fuel supply manifold.

15. Remove the upper and lower intake manifolds as previously described.

16. Remove the rocker arm covers.

17. Remove the rocker shaft assemblies.

18. Remove the pushrods. Identify them for installation. They must be installed in their original positions!

19. Remove the tappets. Identify them for installation.

20. Remove the oil pan as previously described.

21. Remove the engine front cover and water pump.

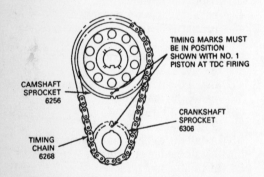

Camshaft installation — 3.0L engine

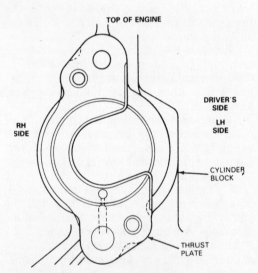

Camshaft thrust plate — 2.9L engine

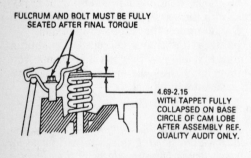

CYL. NO.	CAMSHAFT POSITION	
	A	B
	SET GAP OF VALVES NOTED	
1	INT.	EXH.
2	EXH.	INT.
3	NONE	INT.-EXH.
4	INT.	EXH.
5	EXH.	INT.
6	NONE	INT.-EXH.

Camshaft assembly installation — 3.0L engine

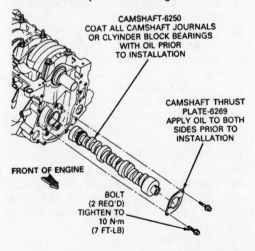

Camshaft assembly installation — 3.0L engine

22. Place the timing chain tensioner in the retracted position and install the retaining clip.

23. Turn the engine by hand until the timing marks align at TDC of the power stroke on No.1 piston.

24. Check the camshaft endplay. If excessive, you'll have to replace the thrust plate.

25. Remove the camshaft gear attaching bolt and washer, then slide the gear off the camshaft.

26. Remove the camshaft thrust plate.

27. Carefully slide the camshaft out of the engine block, using caution to avoid any damage to the camshaft bearings.

To install:

28. Oil the camshaft journals and cam lobes with heavy SG engine oil (50W).

29. Install the camshaft in the block, using caution to avoid any damage to the camshaft bearings.

30. Install the thrust plate. Make sure that it covers the main oil gallery. Tighten the attaching screws to 96 inch lbs.

31. Rotate the camshaft and crankshaft as necessary to align the timing marks. Install the camshaft gear and chain. Tighten the attaching bolt to 50 ft. lbs.

32. Remove the clip from the chain tensioner.

33. Install the engine front cover and water pump assembly. Refer to the necessary service procedures in this Chapter.

34. Install the crankshaft damper/pulley and tighten the retaining bolt to 107 ft. lbs.

35. Install the oil pan.

36. Coat the tappets with 50W engine oil and place them in their original locations.

37. Apply 50W engine oil to both ends of the pushrods. Install the pushrods in their original locations.

38. Install the upper and lower intake manifolds.

39. Install the rocker shaft assemblies.

40. Install the rocker covers.

41. Install the fan and clutch.

42. Install the fuel lines.

43. Install the oil pump drive.

44. Install the alternator.

45. Install the EDIS coil and plug wires. Coat the inside of each wire boot with silicone lubricant.

46. Install the radiator and condenser.

47. Refill the cooling system.

48. Replace the oil filter and refill the crankcase with the specified amount of engine oil.

49. Reconnect the battery ground cable.

50. Start the engine and check the ignition timing and idle speed. Adjust if necessary. Run the engine at fast idle and check for coolant, fuel, vacuum or oil leaks.

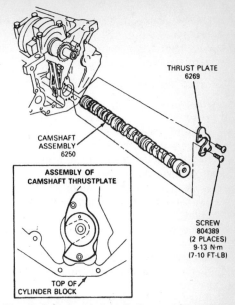

Camshaft assembly installation — 4.0L engine

2.2L Diesel Engine

1. Ford recommends that the engine be removed from the vehicle when camshaft replacement is necessary.

2. With the engine removed; remove the valve cover, rocker arms and shaft assembly and the pushrods. Remove the lifters, identify and keep in order if they are to be reused.

3. Remove the front timing case cover and camshaft gear.

4. Remove the engine oil pan and oil pump.

5. Remove the camshaft thrust plate and the camshaft. Take care when removing the camshaft not to damage lobes or bearings.

6. Apply oil to the camshaft bearings and bearing journals. Apply Polyethylene grease to

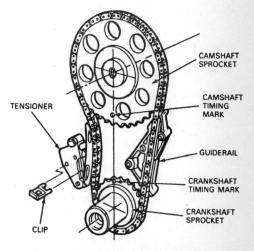

Camshaft installation — 4.0L engine

the camshaft lobes and install the camshaft into the engine.

7. Reinstall components in the reverse order of removal.

2.3L Turbo Diesel Engine

1. Disconnect battery ground cables from both batteries.
2. Remove rocker cover.
3. Remove upper front timing cover.
4. Rotate crankshaft until No. 1 piston is at TDC on compression stroke.
5. Loosen camshaft/injection pump drive belt tensioner and remove timing belt from camshaft pulley.
6. Remove camshaft pulley bolt and remove pulley.
7. Remove rocker arm shaft.
8. Remove camshaft bearing caps and remove camshaft.
9. Remove and discard camshaft oil seal.
10. Inspect camshaft and bearings.

To install:
11. Position camshaft on cylinder head and install bearing caps. Tighten bolts to specification.

CAUTION: *Ensure bearing caps are installed in their original positions.*

12. Coat sealing lip of new camshaft seal with engine oil and install seal using Camshaft Oil Seal Replacer T85T–6250–A or equivalent.

CAUTION: *Ensure seal installer is positioned with hole over spring pin on camshaft.*

13. Install rocker arm.
14. Install camshaft pulley and tighten bolt to specification.
15. Install camshaft/injection pump drive belt. Adjust drive belt.
16. Adjust valves.
17. Install upper front timing cover.
18. Install rocker cover.
19. Fill cooling system.
20. Connect battery ground cable to both batteries.
21. Run engine and check for oil leaks.

CAMSHAFT INSPECTION

Camshaft Lobe Lift

2.0L, 2.3L ENGINES

Check the lift of each lobe in consecutive order and make a note of the readings. Camshaft assembly specifications are sometimes modify by Ford after production. Refer to a local reputable machine shop as necessary.

1. Remove the air cleaner and the valve rocker arm cover.
2. Measure the distance between the major (A-A) and minor (B-B) diameters of each cam

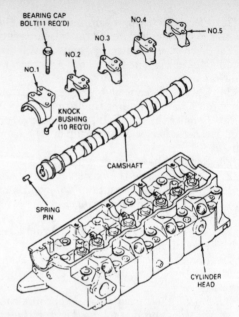

Camshaft assembly — 2.3L turbo diesel engine

lobe with a Vernier caliper and record the readings. The difference in the readings on each cam diameter is the lobe lift.

3. If the readings do not meet specifications, replace the camshaft and all rocker arms.

4. Install the valve rocker arm cover and the air cleaner.

2.8L, 2.9L, 3.0L, 4.0L AND 2.2L DIESEL ENGINES

Check the lift of each lobe in consecutive order and make a note of the reading. Camshaft assembly specifications are sometimes modify by Ford after production. Refer to a local reputable machine shop as necessary.

1. Remove the fresh air inlet tube and the air cleaner. Remove the heater hose and crankcase ventilation hoses. Remove valve rocker arm cover(s).
2. Remove the rocker arm stud nut or fulcrum bolts, fulcrum seat and rocker arm.
3. Make sure the push rod is in the valve tappet socket. Install a dial indicator D78P–

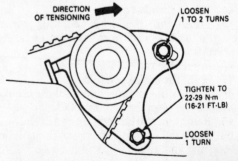

Camshaft belt tensioner — 2.3L turbo diesel engine

4201–B (or equivalent) so that the actuating point of the indicator is in the push rod socket (or the indicator ball socket adapter Tool 6565–AB is on the end of the push rod) and in the same plane as the push rod movement.

4. Disconnect the I terminal and the S terminal at the starter relay. Install an auxiliary starter switch between the battery and S terminals of the starter relay. Crank the engine with the ignition switch off. Turn the crankshaft over until the tappet is on the base circle of the camshaft lobe. At this position, the push rod will be in its lowest position.

5. Zero the dial indicator. Continue to rotate the crankshaft slowly until the push rod is in the fully raised position.

6. Compare the total lift recorded on the dial indicator with the specification.   To check the accuracy of the original indicator reading, continue to rotate the crankshaft until the indicator reads zero. If the lift on any lobe is below specified wear limits, the camshaft and the valve tappet operating on the worn lobe(s) must be replaced.

7. Remove the dial indicator and auxiliary starter switch.

8. Install the rocker arm, fulcrum seat and stud nut or fulcrum bolts. Check the valve clearance. Adjust if required (refer to procedure in Chapter 2).

9. Install the valve rocker arm covers and the air cleaner.

Camshaft End Play

2.0L, 2.3L ENGINES

Remove the camshaft drive belt cover. Push the camshaft toward the rear of the engine. Install a dial indicator so that the indicator point is on the camshaft sprocket attaching screw or gear hub. Zero the dial indicator. Position a prybar between the camshaft sprocket or gear and the cylinder head. Pull the camshaft forward and release it. Compare the dial indicator reading with specifications. If the end play is excessive, replace the thrust plate at the rear of the cylinder head. Remove the dial indicator and install the camshaft drive belt cover. The camshaft endplay specification is 0.001–0.007 inch and the service limit is 0.003 inch. Camshaft specifications are sometimes modify by Ford after production.

2.8L, 2.9L, 3.0L AND 4.0L ENGINES

1. Push the camshaft toward the rear of the engine. Install a dial indicator (Tool D78P–4201–C or equivalent so that the indicator point is on the camshaft sprocket attaching screw.

2. Zero the dial indicator. Position a prybar

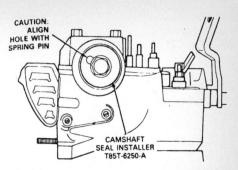

Camshaft seal installation — 2.3L turbo diesel engine

between the camshaft gear and the block. Pull the camshaft forward and release it. Compare the dial indicator reading with the specification. The camshaft endplay specification is 0.0008–0.004 inch and the service limit is 0.009 inch (0.007 inch on 3.0L engine). Camshaft specifications are sometimes modify by Ford after production.

3. If the end play is excessive, check the spacer for correct installation before it is removed. If the spacer is correctly installed, replace the thrust plate.

NOTE: *The spacer ring and thrust plate are available in two thicknesses to permit adjusting the end play.*

4. Remove the dial indicator.

2.2L DIESEL ENGINE

1. Remove the camshaft as described earlier in this Chapter.

2. Mount the thrust plate. Camshaft gear and the friction gear on the camshaft.

3. Install and tighten the lock bolt.

4. Measure the end play by inserting a feeler gauge between the thrust plate and the cam gear.

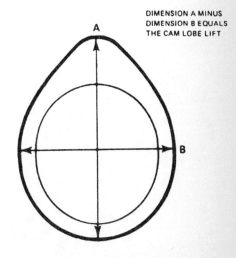

Checking OHC camshaft lobe lift

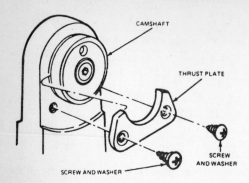

Camshaft thrust plate installation — 2.0L and 2.3L engines

5. If the end play exceeds specification replace the thrust plate. Refer to a local reputable machine shop as necessary. Camshaft specifications are sometimes modify by Ford after production.

Camshaft Bearings

REMOVAL AND INSTALLATION

If excessive camshaft wear is found, or if the engine is completely rebuilt, the camshaft bearings should be replaced. Use these service repair procedures as a guide-modify as necessary for Diesel engines.

2.0L And 2.3L Engines

1. Remove the head and place it on a work stand.
2. Remove the camshaft.

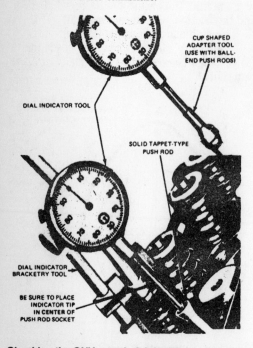

Checking the OHV camshaft lobe lift

3. Using a tool such as Bearing Replacer T71P–6250–A, remove the bearings.
4. Coat the new bearings with clean 50W engine oil and install them with the tool.

2.8L And 2.9L Engines

1. Remove the engine and place it on a work stand.
2. Remove the flywheel.
3. Remove the camshaft.
4. Using a sharp punch and hammer, drive a hole in the rear bearing bore plug and pry it out.
5. Using the special tools and instructions in Cam Bearing Replacer Kit T71P–6250–A, or their equivalents, remove the bearings.
6. To remove the front and rear bearings, use the special adapter tube T72C–6250, or equivalent.
   To install:
7. Following the instructions in the tool kit, install the bearings. Make sure that you follow the instructions carefully. Failure to use the correct expanding collets can cause severe bearing damage!

NOTE: *Make sure that the oil holes in the bearings and block are aligned!*

8. Install a new bearing bore plug coated with sealer.
9. Install the camshaft.
10. Install the flywheel.
11. Install the engine.

3.0L And 4.0L Engines

1. Remove the engine and place it on a work stand.
2. Remove the flywheel.
3. Remove the camshaft.
4. Using a sharp punch and hammer, drive a hole in the rear bearing bore plug and pry it out.
5. Using the special tools and instructions

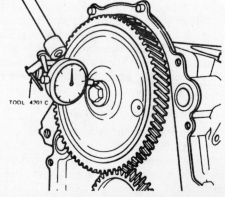

Checking camshaft endplay — 2.2L diesel engine

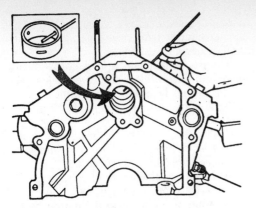

Checking oil hole alignment — No. 2 & 3 camshaft bearings — 2.9L engine

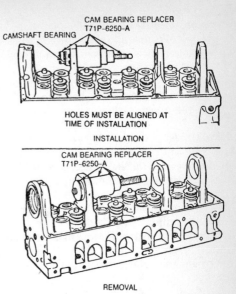

Camshaft bearing procedures — 2.3L engine

in Cam Bearing Replacer Kit T65L–6250–A, or their equivalents, remove the bearings.

6. To remove the front bearing, install the tool from the rear of the block.

To install:

7. Following the instructions in the tool kit, install the bearings. Make sure that you follow the instructions carefully. Failure to use the correct expanding collets can cause severe bearing damage!

NOTE: *Make sure that the oil holes in the bearings and block are aligned! Make sure that the front bearing is installed 0.51–0.89mm below the face of the block.*

8. Install a new bearing bore plug coated with sealer.

9. Install the camshaft.
10. Install the flywheel.
11. Install the engine.

Auxiliary Shaft

REMOVAL AND INSTALLATION

2.0L, 2.3L Engines

1. Remove the camshaft drive belt cover.
2. Remove the drive belt. Remove the auxiliary shaft sprocket. A puller may be necessary to remove the sprocket.
3. Remove the distributor and fuel pump.
4. Remove the auxiliary shaft cover and thrust plate.
5. Withdraw the auxiliary shaft from block.

NOTE: *The distributor drive gear and the fuel pump eccentric on the auxiliary shaft*

Checking camshaft endplay — 2.8L and 2.9L engines

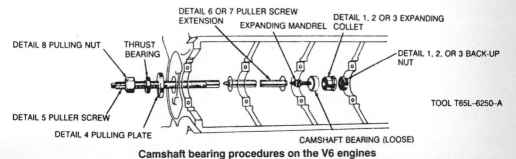

Camshaft bearing procedures on the V6 engines

must not be allowed to touch the auxiliary shaft bearings during removal and installation. Completely coat the shaft with oil before sliding it into place.

6. Slide the auxiliary shaft into the housing and insert the thrust plate to hold the shaft.

7. Install a new gasket and auxiliary shaft cover.

NOTE: *The auxiliary shaft cover and cylinder front cover share a gasket. Cut off the old gasket around the cylinder cover and use half of the new gasket on the auxiliary shaft cover.*

8. Fit a new gasket into the fuel pump and install the pump.

9. Insert the distributor and install the auxiliary shaft sprocket.

10. Align the timing marks and install the drive belt.

11. Install the drive belt cover.

12. Check the ignition timing.

2.3L Turbo Diesel Engine

RIGHT HAND SILENT SHAFT AND OIL PUMP

1. Disconnect battery ground cables from both batteries.

2. Remove cooling fan and fan shroud.

3. Remove water pump pulley, crankshaft pulley, upper and lower timing belt covers, timing belts, and crankshaft sprockets.

4. Loosen oil pan bolts and remove six front oil pan-to-front case bolts.

5. Remove pipe plug in right hand side of engine block, Insert cross point screwdriver into hole to prevent right hand silent shaft from rotating. Remove nut attaching silent shaft sprocket to drive gear and remove sprocket.

6. Remove bolts attaching front case to engine block and remove front case.

7. Remove front case and gasket.

8. Remove silent shaft reverse rotation gear cover and remove silent shaft and gears.

9. Remove oil pump cover and remove oil pump drive gear, and inner and outer gears.

10. Remove silent shaft reverse rotation drive gear oil seal using Seal Remove T58L–101–B or equivalent.

11. Remove crankshaft front oil seal.

To install:

12. Install silent shaft oil seal using a 21mm socket.

13. Install silent shaft reverse rotation gears with marks aligned.

14. Install oil pump gears in front housing.

NOTE: *Align marks on oil pump gears when installing.*

15. Install oil pump cover.

16. Install silent shaft in reverse rotation

drive gear. Position front cover and new gasket on engine block using care not to damage silent shaft bearing. Install bolts.

17. Install silent shaft sprocket. Insert suitable tool in hole in block to prevent silent shaft from rotating. Tighten sprocket nut.

18. Remove screwdriver and install pipe plug.

NOTE: *When installing silent shaft sprocket, ensure "D" flat on sprocket is aligned with "D" flat on shaft.*

19. Install crankshaft front oil seal.

20. Install crankshaft sprocket.

21. Apply a 3mm bead of Silicone Sealant D6A2–19562–B or equivalent along split lines between lower front case cover and rear oil seal retainer and engine block.

22. Install oil pan bolts.

23. Install and adjust timing belts.

24. Install upper and lower timing belt covers.

25. Install crankshaft and water pump pulleys.

26. Install accessory drive belts.

27. Install cooling fan and fan shroud.

28. Connect battery ground cables to both batteries.

29. Run again and check for oil leaks.

LEFT HAND SILENT SHAFT

1. Disconnect battery ground cables from both batteries.

2. Remove cooling fan and fan shroud.

3. Remove accessory drive belts.

4. Remove alternator and bracket.

5. Remove water pump and crankshaft pulleys.

6. Remove upper and lower timing belt covers, timing belts and injection pump.

7. Remove access plate on LH side of engine and insert a socket extension tool or equivalent in hole to prevent LH silent shaft from rotating.

8. Remove bolt attaching sprocket to silent shaft and remove sprocket.

9. Remove bolts attaching front case to engine block and remove case.

10. Remove silent shaft.

11. Remove silent shaft seal using Seal Remover Tool–1175–AC or equivalent.

To install:

12. Drive in a new silent shaft seal using an appropriate size socket.

13. Install silent shaft.

14. Install front cover and new gasket on engine block.

CAUTION: *Front cover bolts are different lengths.*

15. Insert socket extension in access hole in LH side of engine.

16. Install silent shaft sprocket on silent shaft and tighten bolt.

17. Remove extension from access hole and install cover.

18. Install crankshaft sprockets.

19. Install injection pump and sprocket.

20. Install and adjust timing belts.

21. Install upper and lower timing belt covers, water pump pulley and crankshaft pulley. 22. Install accessory drive belts.

23. Install cooling fan and shroud.

24. Connect battery ground cables to both batteries.

25. Run engine and check for oil leaks.

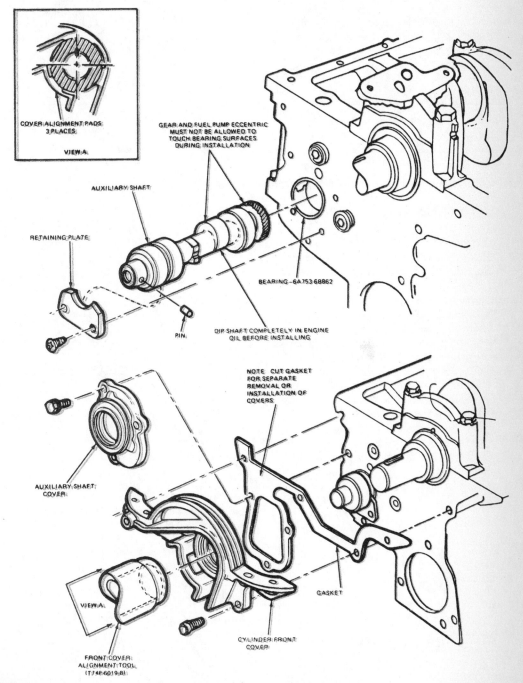

Auxiliary shaft installation — 2.0L and 2.3L engines

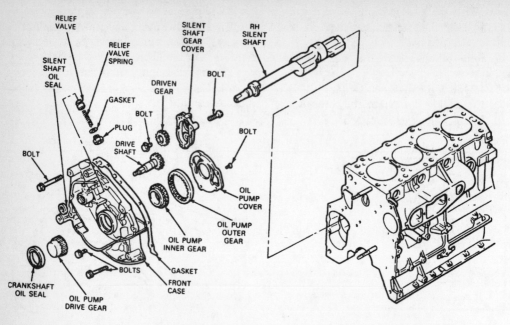

Lower front case cover and right hand silent shaft — 2.3L turbo diesel engine

Pistons and Connecting Rods

REMOVAL AND INSTALLATION

1. Drain the cooling system and the crankcase. Remove the intake manifold, cylinder heads, oil pan and the oil pump.

CAUTION: *When draining the coolant, keep in mind that cats and dogs are attracted by the ethylene glycol antifreeze, and are quite likely to drink any that is left in an uncovered container or in puddles on the ground. This will prove fatal in sufficient quantity. Always drain the coolant into a sealable container. Coolant should be reused unless it is contaminated or several years old.*

2. Turn the crankshaft until the piston to be removed is at the bottom of its travel, then place a cloth on the piston head to collect fil-

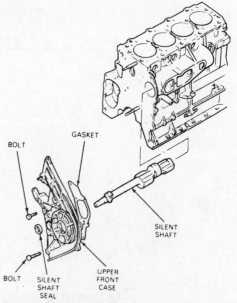

Upper front case cover and left hand silent shaft — 2.3L turbo diesel engine

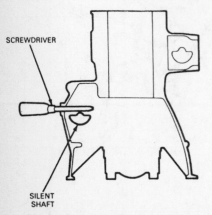

Tool positioning for holding left hand silent shaft — 2.3L turbo diesel engine

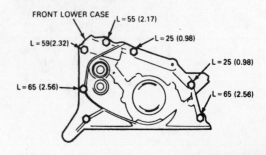

Front lower case bolts — 2.3L turbo diesel engine

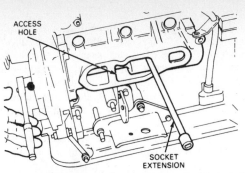

Tool positioning for holding right hand silent shaft — 2.3L turbo diesel engine

Connecting rod and bearing cap numbering

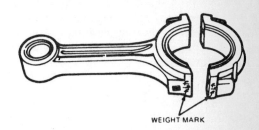

Connecting rod weight marks — 2.2L diesel engine

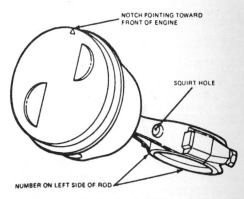

Connecting rod, piston and ring installation — 2.0L and 2.3L engines

ings. Remove any ridge of deposits at the end of the piston travel from the upper cylinder bore, using a ridge reaming tool. Do not cut into the piston ring travel area more than $\frac{1}{32}$ in. when removing the ridge.

3. Make sure that all of the connecting rod bearing caps can be identified, so they will be reinstalled in their original positions.

4. Turn the crankshaft until the connecting rod that is to be removed is at the bottom of its stroke and remove the connecting rod nuts and bearing cap.

5. Push the connecting rod and piston assembly out the top of the cylinder bore with the wooden end of a hammer handle. Be careful not to damage the crankshaft bearing journal or the cylinder wall when removing the piston and rod assembly.

6. Remove the bearing inserts from the connecting rod and cap if the bearings are to be replaced, and place the cap onto the piston/rod assembly from which it was removed.

NOTE: *On the diesel engines, be sure to install pistons in same cylinders from which they were removed or to which they were fitted. Connecting rod and bearing caps have weight marks stamped on one side of main bearing bore boss. If rod replacement is necessary, all rods should be the same weight to maintain proper balance. Numbers on connecting rod and bearing cap must be on same*

side when installed in cylinder bore. If a connecting rod is ever transposed from one block or cylinder to another, new bearings should be fitted and connecting rod should be numbered to correspond with new cylinder number.

7. Before installing the piston/connecting rod assembly, be sure to clean all gasket mating surfaces, oil the pistons, piston rings and the cylinder walls with light engine oil.

8. Be sure to install the pistons in the cylinders from which they were removed. The connecting rod and bearing caps are numbered from 1 to 3 in the right bank and from 4 to 6 in the left back on the V6 engine, beginning at the front of the engine. The numbers on the connecting rod and bearing cap must be on the same side when installed in the cylinder bore. If a connecting rod is ever transposed from one engine or cylinder to another, new bearings

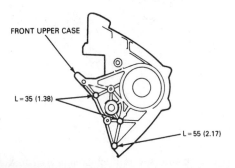

Front upper case bolts — 2.3L turbo diesel engine

should be fitted and the connecting rod should be numbered to correspond with the new cylinder number. The notch on the piston head goes toward the front of the engine.

9. Make sure the ring gaps are properly spaced around the circumference of the piston. Fit a piston ring compressor around the piston and slide the piston and connecting rod assembly down into the cylinder bore, pushing it in with the wooden hammer handle. Push the piston down until it is only slightly below the top of the cylinder bore. Guide the connecting rods onto the crankshaft bearing journals carefully, to avoid damaging the crankshaft.

10. Check the bearing clearance of all the rod bearings, fitting them to the crankshaft bearing journals.

11. After the bearings have been fitted, apply a light coating of engine oil to the journals and bearings.

12. Turn the crankshaft until the appropriate bearing journal is at the bottom of its stroke, then push the piston assembly all the way down until the connecting rod bearing seats on the crankshaft journal. Be careful not to allow the bearing cap screws to strike the crankshaft bearing journals and damage them.

13. After the piston and connecting rod assemblies have been installed, check the connecting rod side clearance on each crankshaft journal.

14. Prime and install the oil pump and the oil pump intake tube, then install the oil pan.

15. Reassemble the rest of the engine in the reverse order of disassembly.

PISTON RING REPLACEMENT

1. Select the proper ring set for the size cylinder bore.

2. Position the ring in the bore in which it is going to be used.

3. Push the ring down into the bore area where normal ring wear is not encountered.

4. Use the head of the piston to position the ring in the bore so that the ring is square with the cylinder wall. Use caution to avoid damage to the ring or cylinder bore.

5. Measure the gap between the ends of the ring with a feeler gauge. Ring gap in a worn cylinder is normally greater than specification. If the ring gap is greater than the specified limits, try an oversize ring set.

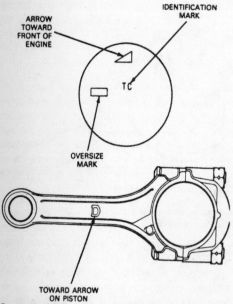

Correct piston and rod positioning — 2.3L turbo diesel engine

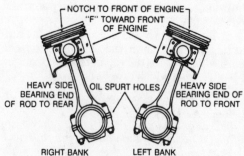

Correct piston and rod positioning — 2.8L and 2.9L engines

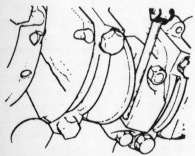

Checking the connecting rod side clearance on the crankshaft bearing journal

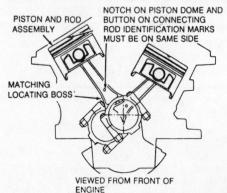

Correct piston and rod positioning — 3.0L & 4.0L engines

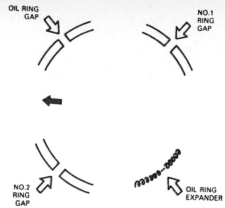

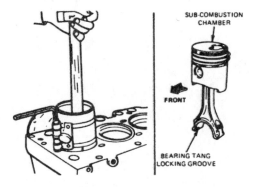

Proper spacing of the piston ring gaps — 2.3L turbo diesel engine

Installing the piston assembly — 2.2L engine

6. Check the ring side clearance of the compression rings with a feeler gauge inserted between the ring and its lower land according to specification. The gauge should slide freely around the entire ring circumference without binding. Any wear that occurs will form a step at the inner portion of the lower land. If the lower lands have high steps, the piston should be replaced.

CLEANING AND INSPECTION

Connecting Rods

1. Remove the bearings from the rod and cap. Identify the bearings if they are to be used again. Clean the connecting rod in solvent, including the rod bore and the back of the bearing inserts. Do not use a caustic cleaning solution. Blow out all passages with compressed air.

2. The connecting rods and related parts should be carefully inspected and checked for conformance to specifications. Various forms of engine wear caused by these parts can be readily identified.

3. A shiny surface on the pin boss side of the piston usually indicates that a connecting rod is bent or the piston pin hole is not in proper relation to the piston skirt and ring grooves.

4. Abnormal connecting rod bearing wear can be caused by either a bent connecting rod, an improperly machined journal, or a tapered connecting rod bore.

5. Twisted connect rods will not create an easily identifiable wear pattern, but badly twisted rods will disturb the action of the entire piston, rings, and connecting rod assembly and may be the cause of excessive oil consumption.

6. Inspect the connecting rods for signs of fractures and the bearing bores for out-of-round and taper. If the bore exceeds the maximum limit and/or if the rod is fractured, it should be replaced.

7. Check the ID of the connecting rod piston pin bore. Install oversize piston pin if the pin bore is not within specifications. Replace worn or damaged connecting rod nuts and bolts.

8. After the connecting rods are assembled to the piston, check the rods for bends or twists on a suitable alignment fixture. Follow the instructions of the fixture manufacturer. If the bend and/or twist exceeds specifications, the rod must be straightened or replaced.

Pistons, Pins and Rings

1. Remove deposits from the piston surfaces. Clean gum or varnish from the piston skirt, piston pins and rings with solvent. Do not use a caustic cleaning solution or a wire brush to clean pistons. Clean the ring groove with a ring groove cleaner. Make sure the oil ring slots (or holes) are clean.

2. Carefully inspect the pistons for fractures at the ring lands, skirts, and pin bosses, and for scuffed, rough, or scored skirts. If the lower inner portion of the ring grooves have high steps, replace the piston. The step will interfere with ring operation and cause excessive ring side clearance.

3. Spongy, eroded ares near the edge of the piston top are usually caused by detonation or pre-ignition. A shiny surface on the thrust sur-

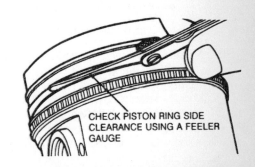

Measuring the ring side clearance

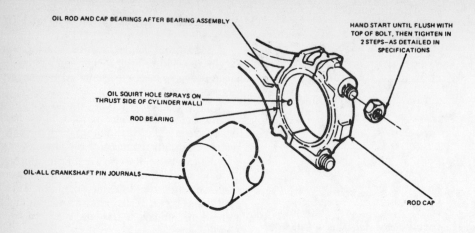

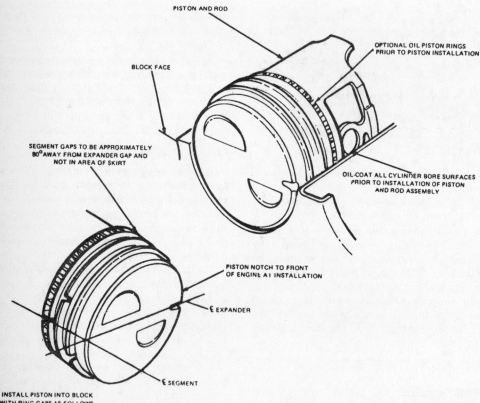

OIL ROD AND CAP BEARINGS AFTER BEARING ASSEMBLY

HAND START UNTIL FLUSH WITH
TOP OF BOLT, THEN TIGHTEN IN
2 STEPS—AS DETAILED IN
SPECIFICATIONS

OIL SQUIRT HOLE (SPRAYS ON
THRUST SIDE OF CYLINDER WALL)

ROD BEARING

OIL-ALL CRANKSHAFT PIN JOURNALS

ROD CAP

PISTON AND ROD

OPTIONAL OIL PISTON RINGS
PRIOR TO PISTON INSTALLATION

BLOCK FACE

SEGMENT GAPS TO BE APPROXIMATELY
80° AWAY FROM EXPANDER GAP AND
NOT IN AREA OF SKIRT

OIL-COAT ALL CYLINDER BORE SURFACES
PRIOR TO INSTALLATION OF PISTON
AND ROD ASSEMBLY

PISTON NOTCH TO FRONT
OF ENGINE AT INSTALLATION

€ EXPANDER

€ SEGMENT

INSTALL PISTON INTO BLOCK
WITH RING GAPS AS FOLLOWS
EXPANDER—TO FRONT OF PISTON
SEGMENT—TO REAR OF PISTON

Correct piston and rod positioning — 2.0L and 2.3L engines

face of the piston, offset from the centerline between the piston pin holes, can be caused by a bent connecting rod. Replace pistons that show signs of excessive wear, wavy ring lands or fractures, or damage from detonation or pre-ignition.

4. Check the piston to cylinder bore clearance by measuring the piston and bore diameters. Measure the OD of the piston with micrometers at the centerline of the piston pin bore

and at 90 degrees to the pin bore axis. Check the ring side clearance following the procedure under Piston Ring Replacement in this Chapter.

5. Replace piston pins showing signs of fracture, etching or wear. Check the piston pin fit in the piston and rod.

6. Check the OD of the piston pin and the ID of the pin bore in the piston. Replace any

piston pin or piston that is not within specifications.

7. Replace all rings that are scored, chipped or cracked. Check the end gap and side clearance. It is good practice to always install new rings when overhauling an engine. Rings should not be transferred from one piston to another regardless of mileage.

PISTON PIN REPLACEMENT

1. Remove the bearing inserts from the connecting rod and cap.

2. Mark the pistons to assure assembly with the same rod, rod position and installation in the same cylinders from which they were removed.

3. Using an Arbor press and tool T68P–6135–A or equivalent, press the piston pin from the piston and connecting rod. Remove the piston rings if they are to be replaced.

NOTE: *Check the fit of a new piston in the cylinder bore before assembling the piston and piston pin to the connecting rod.*

4. Apply a light coat of engine oil to all parts. Assemble the piston to the connecting rod with the indentation or notch in the original position.

5. Start the piston pin in the connecting rod (this may require a very light tap with a mallet). Using an Arbor press and tool T68P–6135–A or equivalent, press the piston pin through the piston and connecting rod until the pin is centered in the piston.

6. install the piston rings using a piston ring installation tool of the proper size (refer to Piston Ring Replacement in this Chapter).

7. Be sure the bearing inserts and the bearing bore in the connect rod and cap are clean. Foreign material under the inserts will distort the bearing and cause it to fail.

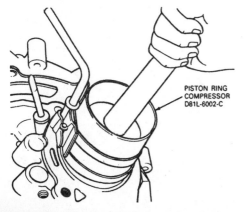

Installing the piston assembly — gas engines

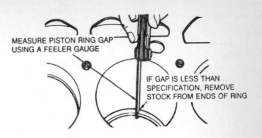

Measuring the ring end gap

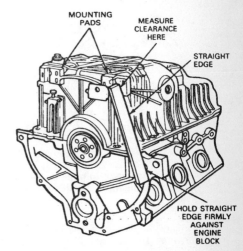

Make connecting rod bolt guides out of rubber tubing; these also protect the cylinder walls and crank journal from scratches

ROD BEARING REPLACEMENT

1. Drain the crankcase. Remove the oil level dipstick. Remove the oil pan and related parts, following the procedure under Oil Pan removal and installation in this Chapter.

CAUTION: *The EPA warns that prolonged contact with used engine oil may cause a number of skin disorders, including cancer! You should make every effort to minimize your exposure to used engine oil. Protective gloves should be worn when changing the oil. Wash your hands and any other exposed skin areas as soon as possible after exposure to used engine oil. Soap and water, or waterless hand cleaner should be used.*

2. Remove the oil pump inlet tube assembly and the oil pump.

3. Turn the crankshaft until the connecting rod to which new bearings are to be fitted is down. Remove the connecting rod cap. Remove the bearing inserts from the rod and cap.

4. Be sure the bearing inserts and the bearing bore in the connecting rod and cap are clean. Foreign material under the inserts will distort the bearing and cause failure.

5. Clean the crankshaft journal. Inspect

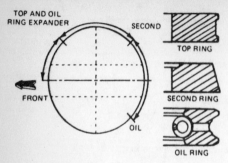

Proper spacing of the piston ring gaps around the circumference of the piston — 2.2L diesel engine

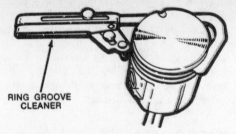

Clean the ring grooves with this tool or the edge of an old ring

Remove and install the rings with a ring expander

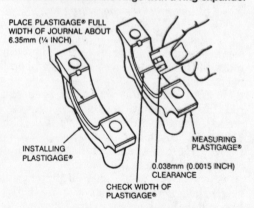

Measuring bearing clearance with Plastigage®

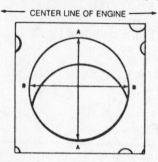

journals for nicks, burrs or bearing pick-up that would cause premature bearing wear.

6. Install the bearing inserts in the connect god and cap with the tangs fitting in slots provided.

7. Pull the connecting rod assembly down firmly on the crankshaft journal.

8. Select fit the bearing using the following procedures:

a. Place a piece of Plastigage® or it's equivalent, or the bearing surface across the full width of the bearing cap and about 6mm off center.

b. Install cap and tighten bolts to specifications. Do not turn crankshaft while Plastigage® is in place.

c. Remove cap. Using Plastigage® scale, check width of Plastigage® at widest point to get minimum clearance. Check at narrowest point to get maximum clearance. Difference between readings is taper of journal.

d. If clearance exceeds specified limits, try a 0.001 in. or 0.002 in. undersize bearing in combination with the standard bearing. Bearing clearance must be within specified limits. If standard and 0.002 in. undersize bearing does not bring clearance within desired limits, refinish crankshaft journal, then use undersize bearings.

9. After bearing has been fitted, apply light coat of engine oil to journal and bearings. Install bearing cap. Tighten cap bolts to specifications.

1. OUT OF ROUND = DIFFERENCE BETWEEN "A" AND "B"
2. TAPER = DIFFERENCE BETWEEN THE "A" MEASUREMENT AT TOP OF CYLINDER BORE AND THE "A" MEASUREMENT OF CYLINDER BORE

"A" AT RIGHT ANGLE TO CENTER LINE OF ENGINE
"B" PARALLEL TO CENTER LINE OF ENGINE

Measure the cylinder bore at the points indicated

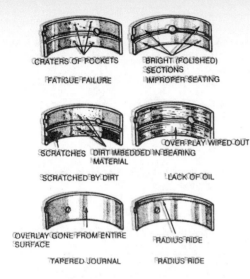

CRATERS OF POCKETS

FATIGUE FAILURE

BRIGHT (POLISHED) SECTIONS
IMPROPER SEATING

SCRATCHES   DIRT IMBEDDED IN BEARING MATERIAL

OVER-PLAY WIPED OUT

SCRATCHED BY DIRT   LACK OF OIL

OVERLAY GONE FROM ENTIRE SURFACE

RADIUS RIDE

TAPERED JOURNAL   RADIUS RIDE

Inspecting the bearings for damage

10. Repeat procedures for remaining bearings that require replacement.

11. Clean the oil pump inlet tube screen. Prime the oil pump by filing the inlet opening with oil and rotating the pump shaft until oil emerges from the outlet opening. Install the oil pump and inlet tube assembly.

12. Install the oil pan and related parts, following the procedure under Oil Pan removal and installation in this Chapter. Install the oil level dipstick.

13. Fill the crankcase with engine oil. Start the engine and check for oil pressure. Operate the engine at fast idle and check for oil leaks.

Freeze (Core) Plugs

REMOVAL AND INSTALLATION

All Engines

1. Drain the complete cooling system and engine block.

CAUTION: *When draining the coolant, keep in mind that cats and dogs are attracted by the ethylene glycol antifreeze, and are quite likely to drink any that is left in an uncovered container or in puddles on the ground. This will prove fatal in sufficient quantity. Always drain the coolant into a sealable container. Coolant should be reused unless it is contaminated or several years old.*

2. Drill or punch a hole in the center of the freeze plug and pull it out from the engine block with a slide hammer or equivalent. Note stay away from the freeze plug location when working, as coolant will flow from the engine block when the plug is removed.

3. Check the bore for roughness or burrs. If the bore is damaged, hone it and use an oversized freeze plug.

4. Coat the new freeze plug with sealer and drive into the correct position.

5. Refill the cooling system. Start engine and check for coolant leaks.

Rear Main Oil Seal

REMOVAL AND INSTALLATION

Gasoline Engines

If the crankshaft rear oil seal replacement is the only operation being performed, it can be done in the vehicle as detailed in the following procedure. If the oil seal is being replaced in conjunction with a rear main bearing replacement, the engine must be removed from the vehicle and installed on a work stand.

1. Remove the starter.

2. Remove the transmission from the vehicle, following the procedures in Chapter 7.

3. On a manual shift transmission, remove the pressure plate and cover assembly and the clutch disc following the procedure in Chapter 7.

4. Remove the flywheel attaching bolts and remove the flywheel and engine rear cover plate.

5. Use an awl to punch two holes in the crankshaft rear oil seal. Punch the holes on opposite sides of the crankshaft and just above the bearing cap to cylinder block split line. Install a sheet metal screw in each hole. Use two large screwdrivers or small pry bars and pry against both screws at the same time to remove the crankshaft rear oil seal. It may be necessary to place small blocks of wood against the cylinder block to provide a fulcrum point for the pry bars. Use caution throughout this procedure to avoid scratching or otherwise damaging the crankshaft oil seal surface.

To install:

6. Clean the oil seal recess in the cylinder block and main bearing cap.

7. Clean, inspect and polish the rear oil seal rubbing surface on the crankshaft. Coat a new oil seal and the crankshaft with a light film of engine oil. Start the seal in the recess with the seal lip facing forward and install it with a seal driver. Keep the tool, T82L-6701-A (4-cyl. engines) or T72C-6165 (6-cyl. engine) straight with the centerline of the crankshaft and install the seal until the tool contacts the cylinder block surface. Remove the tool and inspect the seal to be sure it was not damaged during installation.

8. Install the engine rear cover plate. Position the flywheel on the crankshaft flange. Coat the threads of the flywheel attaching bolts

with oil-resistant sealer and install the bolts. Tighten the bolts in sequence across from each other to the specifications listed in the Torque chart at the beginning of this Chapter.

9. On a manual shift transmission, install the clutch disc and the pressure plate assembly following the procedure in Chapter 7.

10. Install the transmission, following the procedure in Chapter 7.

2.2L Diesel Engine

1. Disconnect the battery ground cables from both batteries.

2. Raise the vehicle.

3. Remove the transmission and clutch assemblies, following the procedures in Chapter 7.

4. Remove the flywheel.

5. Remove the crankshaft rear cover assembly.

6. Remove the rear oil seal from the rear cover using a suitable tool.

To install:

7. Install a new rear oil seal into rear cover assembly using Tool, T83T-6701-C, and Handle, T80T-4000-W.

NOTE: *If the crankshaft is worn, use ring supplied with Tool, T83T-6701-C to seat seal over a new wear area.*

8. Install the crankshaft rear cover assembly and tighten bolts to 11–15 ft. lbs.

9. Install the clutch and transmission, following the procedures in Chapter 7.

10. Lower the vehicle.

11. Connect the battery ground cables to both batteries.

12. Start the engine and check for oil leaks.

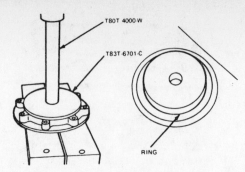

Installing the crankshaft rear main oil seal — 2.2L diesel engine

2.3L Turbo Diesel Engine

1. Disconnect battery ground cable from both batteries.

2. Raise vehicle.

3. Remove transmission. Refer to Chapter 7, Clutch and Manual Transmission.

4. Remove clutch assembly. Refer to Chapter 7, Clutch and Linkage.

5. Remove six bolts attaching flywheel to crankshaft and remove flywheel.

6. Drain engine oil.

CAUTION: *The EPA warns that prolonged contact with used engine oil may cause a number of skin disorders, including cancer! You should make every effort to minimize your exposure to used engine oil. Protective gloves should be worn when changing the oil. Wash your hands and any other exposed skin areas as soon as possible after exposure to used engine oil. Soap and water, or waterless hand cleaner should be used.*

7. Loosen oil pan retaining bolts.

8. Remove two oil pan bolts from rear seal retainer.

9. Remove five bolts attaching rear seal re-

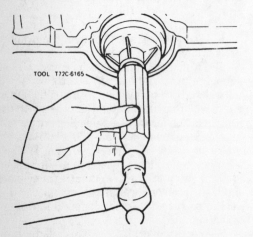

Installing the crankshaft rear main oil seal — 2.8L and 2.9L engines

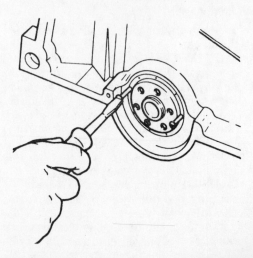

Removing the rear oil seal

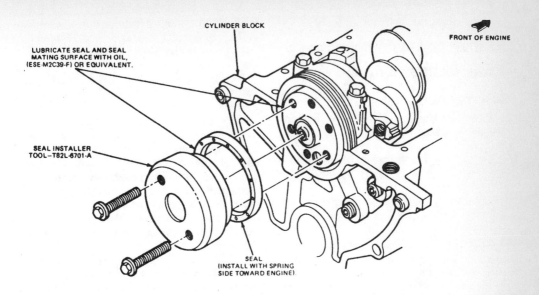

NOTE: REAR FACE OF SEAL MUST BE WITHIN 0.127mm (0.005-INCH) OF THE REAR FACE OF THE BLOCK.

Installing the crankshaft rear oil seal — 2.0L and 2.3L engines other engines similar

tainer to engine block and remove retainer and gasket.

10. Remove oil separator from rear seal retainer.

11. Remove seal from retainer using a suitable drift and a hammer.

To install:

12. Position seal retainer face down on arbor press plate.

CAUTION: *Be sure lip on seal retainer is positioned on plate with flange over the edge.*

13. Lubricate oil seal with clean engine oil and press seal into retainer (from back side of retainer) using Rear Seal Replacer T85T–6701–A or equivalent.

14. Position oil separator in seal retainer with drain hole at bottom.

15. Position oil seal retainer on engine block and install five attaching bolts. Tighten bolts to specification. Apply a 3mm bead of Silicone Sealant along split lines between engine block and rear oil seal retainer and lower front case.

16. Install two oil pan bolts and tighten all oil pan bolts to specification.

17. Install flywheel and tighten bolts to specification.

18. Install clutch assembly. Refer to Chapter 7, Clutch.

19. Install transmission. Refer to Chapter 7, Clutch and Manual Transmission.

20. Lower vehicle.

21. Fill crankcase with specified quantity and quality of oil.

22. Connect battery ground cables to both batteries.

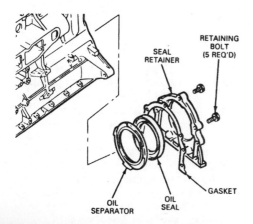

Rear main oil seal — 2.3L turbo diesel engine

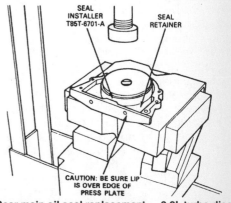

Rear main oil seal replacement — 2.3L turbo diesel engine

23. Run engine and check for oil leaks.

Crankshaft and Main Bearings

REMOVAL AND INSTALLATION

Gasoline Engines

1. Remove the engine from the vehicle as previously described, then place it on a work stand.

2. Remove the transmission (if attached), bell housing, flywheel or flex plate and rear plate.

3. Drain the crankcase and remove the oil pan with the engine in a normal upright position.

CAUTION: *The EPA warns that prolonged contact with used engine oil may cause a number of skin disorders, including cancer! You should make every effort to minimize your exposure to used engine oil. Protective gloves should be worn when changing the oil. Wash your hands and any other exposed skin areas as soon as possible after exposure to used engine oil. Soap and water, or waterless hand cleaner should be used.*

4. Remove the components from the front of the engine and the front cover.

5. Invert the engine and remove the oil pump, pickup tube and baffle, if equipped.

6. Make sure all main and connecting rod bearing caps are marked so they can be installed in their original locations.

7. Remove the connecting rod nuts and lift off the cap with its bearing insert. Install short pieces of rubber hose over the connecting rod studs to protect the crankshaft journals, then carefully push the piston and rod assemblies down into the cylinder bores.

8. Remove the main bearing caps with their bearing inserts. Inspect the crankshaft journals for nicks, burrs or bearing pickup that would cause premature bearing wear. When replacing standard bearings with new bearings, it is good practice to fit the bearing to minimum specified clearance. If the desired clearance cannot be obtained with a standard bearing, try one half of a 0.001 in. (0.025mm) or 0.002 in. (0.050mm) undersize in combination with a standard bearing to obtain the proper clearance.

9. Place a piece of Plastigage® on the bearing surface across the full width of the bearing cap, about ¼ in. (6mm) off center. Install the cap and tighten the bolts to the specified torque given in the General Engine Specifications Chart. Do not rotate the crankshaft with the Plastigage® in place. Remove the cap and use the scale provided with the kit to check the Plastigage width at its widest and narrowest points.

Widest point is minimum clearance, narrowest point is maximum clearance; the difference between the two is the taper reading of the journal.

10. Bearing clearance must be within specified limits. If standard 0.002 in. (0.050mm) undersize bearings do not bring the clearance within desired limits, the crankshaft will have to be refinished or replaced. Remove the remaining main bearing caps and lift out the crankshaft, being careful not to damage the thrust bearing surfaces. Discard the rear main oil seal. The crankshaft should be refinished at a machine shop to give the proper clearance with the next undersize bearing. If the journal will not clean up to the maximum undersize bearing, the crankshaft will have to be replaced.

11. Clean the bearing bores in the block and caps. Foreign material under the inserts or on the bearing surfaces may distort the insert and cause bearing failure.

12. Assemble the main bearing inserts in their correct location in the bearing caps and cylinder block. Check the oil hole alignment between the bearing inserts and block. Apply a liberal coating of clean heavy SG engine oil to the bearing surfaces, then carefully lower the crankshaft into position.

13. Insert the remaining bearing shells into the main bearing caps and coat the bearings with clean heavy SG engine oil, then install the caps with the arrows pointing toward the front of the engine. Apply a thin even coating of sealing compound to the rear sealing surface of the rear main bearing cap before installing. Install and tighten all main bearing cap bolts finger tight after lightly oiling the threads.

14. Tighten all bearing cap bolts, except for the thrust bearing cap, to the specifications given in the Torque Specifications Chart.

15. Align the thrust bearing surfaces by forcing the crankshaft forward and the thrust bearing cap rearward. While holding in this position, tighten the thrust bearing cap to specifications.

16. Install a new rear main oil seal as previously described.

17. On some engines, use a flat tool such as a large blunt end screwdriver to push the two wedge shaped seals between the cylinder block and rear main bearing cap. Position the seals with the round side facing the main bearing cap.

18. Pull the connecting rods up one at a time and install rod caps after applying a liberal coating of heavy SG engine oil to the bearings. Tighten all bearing caps to specifications. On V6 engines, check the connecting rod side clearance as previously described. Check the crankshaft end play with a dial indicator.

19. Install the oil pump, pickup tube and baffle, if equipped. Prime the oil pump before installation as described under Oil Pump Removal and Installation.

20. Install the front cover and timing chain, belt or gears. Replace the front cover oil seal.

21. Install the rear cover plate (if equipped) and the flywheel or flex plate. Tighten the mounting bolts to specifications.

22. Install the clutch disc, pressure plate and bell housing on manual transmission models.

23. Install the oil pan and tighten the bolts to specifications. See Oil Pan Removal and Installation for gasket and sealer placement.

24. Invert the engine to its normal, upright position and fill the crankcase with the specified amount and type of engine oil. Replace the oil filter.

25. Install the transmission, if removed with the engine.

26. Install the engine in the vehicle as previously described. Roadtest the vehicle for proper operation.

2.2L, 2.3L Diesel Engines

1. Remove the engine assembly from the vehicle as described in this Chapter, and install in work stand.

2. Remove the water pump pulley, crankshaft pulley, timing gear case cover, timing gears, fuel injection pump and timing gear case.

3. Remove the starter, flywheel, and engine-to-transmission adapter plate.

4. Remove the oil pan and oil pump.

5. Remove the rear oil seal assembly as described in this Chapter under Rear Main Oil Seal.

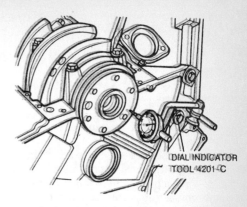

DIAL INDICATOR TOOL 4201-C

Checking crankshaft endplay

6. Remove the crankshaft main bearing caps.

NOTE: *Main bearing caps are numbered 1 through 5, front to rear, and must be returned to their original positions.*

7. Carefully lift the crankshaft out of block so the thrust bearing surfaces are not damaged.

To install:

8. Remove the main bearing inserts from the block and bearing caps.

9. Remove the connecting rod bearing inserts from the connecting rods and caps.

10. If the crankshaft main bearing journals have been refinished to a definite undersize, install the correct undersize bearing. Be sure that the bearing inserts and bearing bores are clean. Foreign material under inserts will distort bearing and cause failure.

11. Place the upper main bearing inserts in bores with tang in slot.

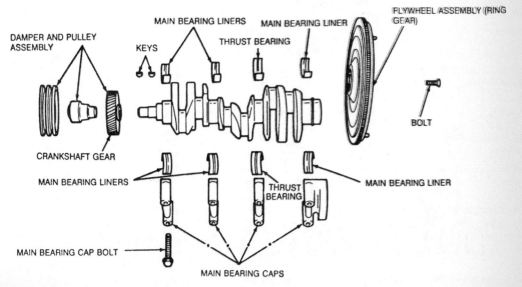

Crankshaft and bearing assembly-2.8L engine

NOTE: *The oil holes in the bearing inserts must be aligned with the oil holes in the cylinder block.*

12. Install the lower main bearing inserts in bearing caps.

13. lean the mating surfaces of block and rear main bearing cap.

14. Carefully lower the crankshaft into place. Be careful not to damage bearing surfaces.

15. Check the clearance of each main bearing by using the following procedure:

    a. Place a piece of Plastigage® or it's equivalent, on bearing surface across full width of bearing cap and about ¼ in. off center.

    b. Install cap and tighten bolts to specifi-

cations. Do not turn crankshaft while Plastigage® is in place.

    c. Remove the cap. Using Plastigage® scale, check width of Plastigage® at widest point to get maximum clearance. Difference between readings is taper of journal.

    d. If clearance exceeds specified limits, try a 0.001 in. or 0.002 in. undersize bearing in combination with the standard bearing. Bearing clearance must be within specified limits. If standard and 0.002 in. undersize bearing does not bring clearance within desired limits, refinish crankshaft journal, then install undersize bearings.

16. After the bearings have been fitted, apply a light coat of engine oil to the journals and bear-

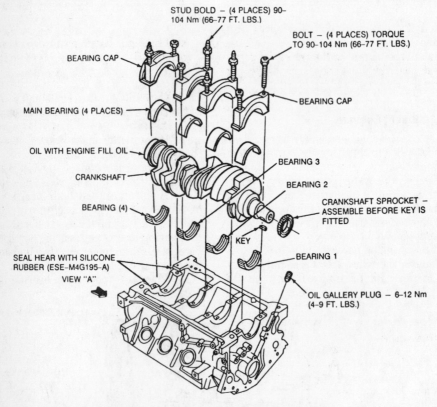

Crankshaft and bearing assembly-4.0L engine

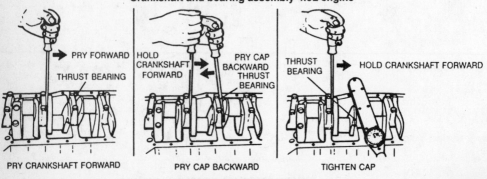

Aligning the thrust bearing

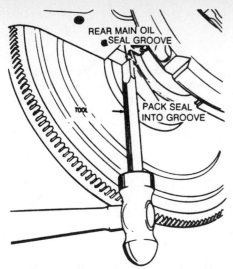

Applying RTV sealer to the rear main bearing cap — 2.8L and 2.9L engines

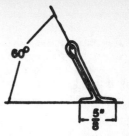

Installing the upper main bearing inserts

ings. Install the rear main bearing cap. Install all bearing caps except the thrust bearing cap (No. 3 bearing). Be sure that main bearing caps are installed in original locations. Tighten the bearing cap bolts to; 80–85 ft. lbs. on the 2.2L engine, 55–61 ft. lbs. on the 2.3L engine.

17. Install the thrust bearing cap with bolts finger tight.

18. Pry the crankshaft forward against the thrust surface of upper half of bearing.

19. Hold the crankshaft forward and pry the thrust bearing cap to the rear. This aligns the thrust surfaces of both halves of the bearing.

20. Retain the forward pressure on the crankshaft. Tighten the cap bolts to; 80–85 ft. lbs. on the 2.2L engine, 55–61 ft. lbs. on the 2.3L engine.

21. Force the crankshaft toward the rear of engine.

22. Install new bearing inserts in the connecting rods and caps. Check the clearance of each bearing, following procedure described under step 15. 23. After the connecting rod bearings have been fitted, apply light coat of engine oil to the journals and bearings.

24. Turn the crankshaft throw to bottom of its stroke. Push the piston all the way down until the rod bearing seats on crankshaft journal.

25. Install the connecting rod cap. Be sure that the connecting rod bolt heads are properly seated in the connecting rod. Tighten nuts to 50–54 ft. lbs.

26. After piston and connecting rod assemblies have been installed, check side clearance (refer to Crankshaft and Connecting Rod Specifications) between connecting rods on each connecting rod crankshaft journal.

27. Install a new rear main oil seal in oil seal adapter as described in this Chapter under Rear Main Oil Seal.

28. Install rear main oil seal adapter.

29. Install the oil pump and oil pan.

30. Install the engine-to-transmission adapter plate, flywheel and starter.

31. Install the timing gear case, fuel injection pump, timing gears, timing gear case cover, new crankshaft front oil seal, and crankshaft pulley.

32. Install the engine assembly in vehicle as described in this Chapter.

CLEANING AND INSPECTION

Crankshaft

NOTE: *Handle the crankshaft carefully to avoid damage to the finished surfaces.*

1. Clean the crankshaft with solvent, and blow out all oil passages with compressed air. Clean the oil seal contact surface at the rear of the crankshaft with solvent to remove any corrosion, sludge or varnish deposits.

2. Use crocus cloth to remove any sharp edges, burrs or other imperfections which might damage the oil seal during installation or cause premature seal wear.

NOTE: *Do not use crocus cloth to polish the seal surfaces. A finely polished surface many produce poor sealing or cause premature seal wear.*

3. Inspect the main and connecting rod journals for cracks, scratches, grooves or scores.

4. Measure the diameter of each journal at least four places to determine out-of-round, taper or undersize condition.

5. On an engine with a manual transmission, check the fit of the clutch pilot bearing in the bore of the crankshaft. A needle roller bearing and adapter assembly is used as a clutch pilot bearing. It is inserted directly into the engine crankshaft. The bearing and adapter assembly cannot be serviced separately. A new bearing must be installed whenever a bearing is removed.

6. Inspect the pilot bearing, when used, for roughness, evidence of overheating or loss of lu-

bricant. Replace if any of these conditions are found.

7. Inspect the rear oil seal surface of the crankshaft for deep grooves, nicks, burrs, porosity, or scratches which could damage the oil seal lip during installation. Remove all nicks and burrs with crocus cloth.

Main Bearings

1. Clean the bearing inserts and caps thoroughly in solvent, and dry them with compressed air.

NOTE: *Do not scrape varnish or gum deposits from the bearing shells.*

2. Inspect each bearing carefully. Bearings that have a scored, chipped, or worn surface should be replaced.

3. The copper/lead bearing base may be visible through the bearing overlay in small localized areas. This may not mean that the bearing is excessively worn. It is not necessary to replace the bearing if the bearing clearance is within recommended specifications.

4. Check the clearance of bearings that appear to be satisfactory with Plastigage® or it's equivalent. Fit the new bearings following the procedure Crankshaft and Main Bearing removal and installation in this Chapter.

REGRINDING JOURNALS

1. Dress minor scores with an oil stone. If the journals are severely marred or exceed the for the next undersize bearing.

2. Regrind the journals to give the proper clearance with the next undersize bearing. If the journal will not clean up to maximum undersize bearing available, replace the crankshaft.

3. Always reproduce the same journal shoulder radius that existed originally. Too small a

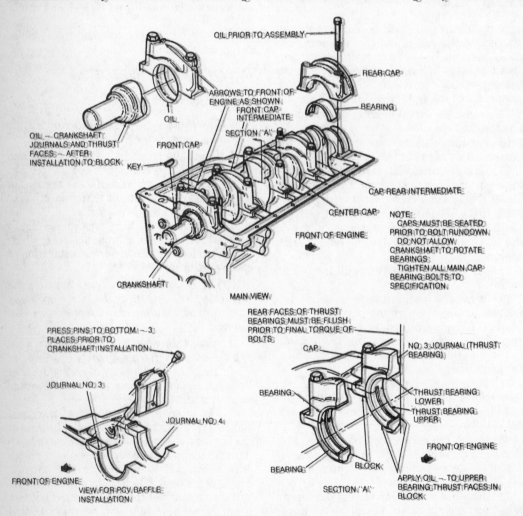

Crankshaft and bearing installation — 2.3L engine

radius will result in fatigue failure of the crank-shaft. Too large a radius will result in bearing failure due to radius ride of the bearing.

4. After regrinding the journals, chamfer the oil holes; then polish the journals with a No. 320 grit polishing cloth and engine oil. Crocus cloth may also be used as a polishing agent.

Flywheel and Ring Gear

REMOVAL AND INSTALLATION

1. Remove the transmission, following procedures in Chapter 7, Clutch and Transmission.

2. On a manual shift transmission, remove the clutch pressure plate and cover assembly and clutch disc, following the procedures in Chapter 7, Clutch and Transmission.

3. Remove the flywheel attaching bolts and remove the flywheel.

To install:

4. Position the flywheel on the crankshaft flange. Coat the threads of the flywheel attaching bolts with Loctite® or equivalent and install the bolts. Tighten the bolts in sequence across from each other to specifications.

5. On a manual shift transmission, install the clutch disc and pressure plate and cover assembly following the procedures in Chapter 7, Clutch and Transmission.

6. Install the transmission following the procedure in Chapter 7, Clutch and Transmission.

RING GEAR REPLACEMENT

NOTE: *This procedure is for manual shift transmission only. On automatic transmis-*

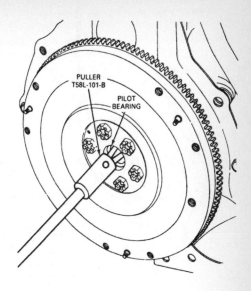

Clutch pilot bearing removal

sion if the ring gear has worn, chipped or cracked teeth, replace the flywheel assembly.

1. Heat the ring gear with a blow torch on the engine side of the gear, and knock it off the flywheel. Do not hit the flywheel when removing the ring gear.

2. Heat the new ring gear evenly until the gear expands enough to slip onto the flywheel. Make sure the gear is properly seated against the shoulder. Do not heat any part of the gear more than 500 degrees F (260 degrees C). If this limit is exceeded, the hardness will be removed from the ring gear teeth.

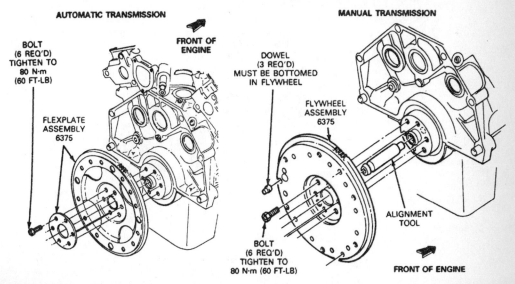

Flywheel/Flex plate assembly — 3.0L engine

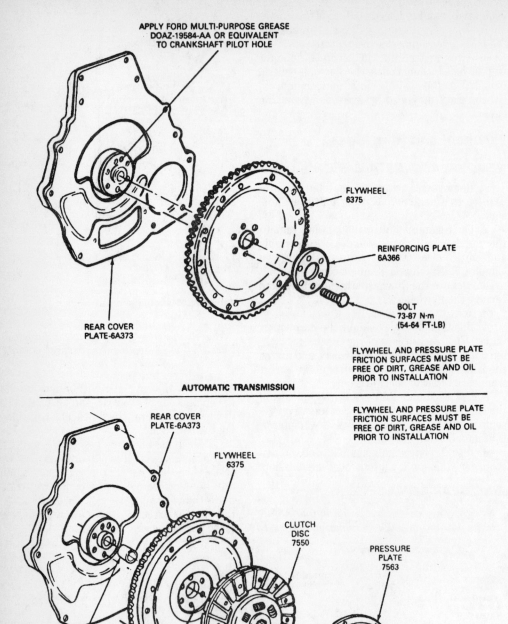

APPLY FORD MULTI-PURPOSE GREASE
DOAZ-19584-AA OR EQUIVALENT
TO CRANKSHAFT PILOT HOLE

FLYWHEEL
6375

REINFORCING PLATE
6A366

BOLT
73-87 N·m
(54-64 FT-LB)

REAR COVER
PLATE-6A373

FLYWHEEL AND PRESSURE PLATE
FRICTION SURFACES MUST BE
FREE OF DIRT, GREASE AND OIL
PRIOR TO INSTALLATION

AUTOMATIC TRANSMISSION

FLYWHEEL AND PRESSURE PLATE
FRICTION SURFACES MUST BE
FREE OF DIRT, GREASE AND OIL
PRIOR TO INSTALLATION

REAR COVER
PLATE-6A373

FLYWHEEL
6375

CLUTCH
DISC
7550

PRESSURE
PLATE
7563

ROLLER PILOT
BEARING-7600
INSTALL WITH SEAL TOWARD
TRANSMISSION

DOWEL

BOLT
73-87 N·m
(54-64 FT-LB)

BOLT
21-32 N·m
(15-24 FT-LB)

MANUAL TRANMISSION

Flywheel/Flex plate assembly — 2.3L engine

EXHAUST SYSTEM

Safety Precautions

For a number of reasons, exhaust system work can be the most dangerous type of work you can do on your vehicle. Always observe the following precautions:

• Support the vehicle extra securely. Not only will you often be working directly under it, but you'll frequently be using a lot of force, say, heavy hammer blows, to dislodge rusted parts. This can cause a vehicle that's improperly supported to shift and possibly fall.

• Wear goggles. Exhaust system parts are always rusty. Metal chips can be dislodged, even when you're only turning rusted bolts. Attempting to pry pipes apart with a chisel makes the chips fly even more frequently.

• If you're using a cutting torch, keep it a great distance from either the fuel tank or lines. Stop what you're doing and feel the temperature of the fuel bearing pipes on the tank frequently. Even slight heat can expand and/or vaporize fuel, resulting in accumulated vapor, or even a liquid leak, near your torch.

• Watch where your hammer blows fall and make sure you hit squarely. You could easily tap a brake or fuel line when you hit an exhaust system part with a glancing blow. Inspect all lines and hoses in the area where you've been working.

CAUTION: *Be very careful when working on or near the catalytic converter. External temperatures can reach 1,500°F (816°C) and more, causing severe burns. Removal or installation should be performed only on a cold exhaust system.*

Special Tools

A number of special exhaust system tools can be rented from auto supply houses or local stores that rent special equipment. A common one is a tail pipe expander, designed to enable you to join pipes of identical diameter.

It may also be quite helpful to use solvents designed to loosen rusted bolts or flanges. Soaking rusted parts the night before you do the job can speed the work of freeing rusted parts considerably. Remember that these solvents are often flammable. Apply only to parts after they are cool!

System Inspection

Inspect inlet pipes, outlet pipes and mufflers for cracked joints, broken welds and corrosion damage that would result in a leaking exhaust system. It is normal for a certain amount of

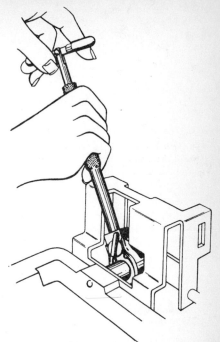

Special tool to remove exhaust mounting brackets retaining bolts in confine areas

moisture and staining to be present around the muffler seams. The presence of soot, light surface rust or moisture does not indicate a faulty muffler. Inspect the clamps, brackets and insulators for cracks and stripped or badly corroded bolt threads. When flat joints are loosened and/or disconnected to replace a shield pipe or muffler, replace the bolts and flange nuts if there is reasonable doubt that its service life is limited.

The exhaust system, including brush shields, must be free of leaks, binding, grounding and excessive vibrations. These conditions are usually caused by loose or broken flange bolts, shields, brackets or pipes. If any of these conditions exist, check the exhaust system components and alignment. Align or replace as necessary. Brush shields are positioned on the underside of the catalytic converter and should be free from bends which would bring any part of the shield in contact with the catalytic converter or muffler. The shield should also be clear of any combustible material such as dried grass or leaves.

Muffler, Catalytic Converter, Inlet and Outlet Pipes

REMOVAL AND INSTALLATION

NOTE: *The following applies to exhaust systems using clamped joints. Some models, use welded joints at the muffler. These joints will, of course, have to be cut.*

1. Raise and support the truck on jack-stands.

2. Remove the U-clamps securing the muffler and outlet pipe.

3. Disconnect the muffler and outlet pipe bracket and insulator assemblies.

4. Remove the muffler and outlet pipe assembly. It may be necessary to heat the joints to get the parts to come off. Special tools are available to aid in breaking loose the joints.

5. On Super Cab and Crew Cab models, remove the extension pipe.

6. Disconnect the catalytic converter bracket and insulator assembly.

NOTE: *For rod and insulator type hangers, apply a soap solution to the insulator surface and rod ends to allow easier removal of the insulator from the rod end. Don't use oil-based or silicone-based solutions since they will allow the insulator to slip back off once it's installed.*

7. Remove the catalytic converter.

8. On models with Managed Thermactor Air, disconnect the MTA tube assembly.

9. Remove the inlet pipe assembly.

10. Install the components making sure that all the components in the system are properly aligned before tightening any fasteners. Make sure all tabs are indexed and all parts are clear of surrounding body panels. See the accompanying illustrations.

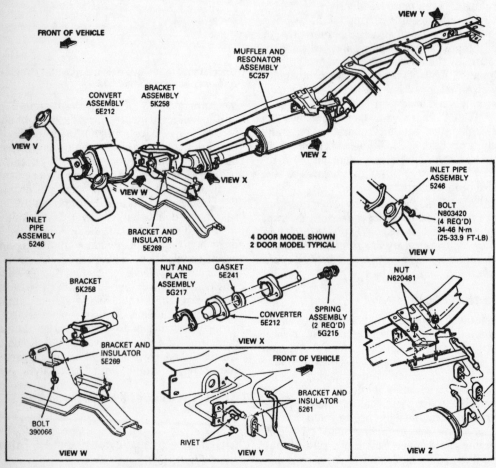

Exhaust system assembly — Explorer (4.0L engine)

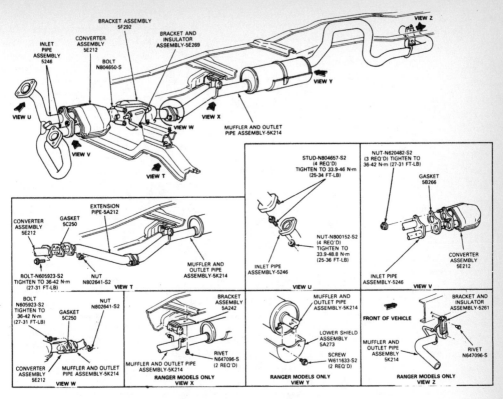

Exhaust system assembly — Ranger (6 cylinder engine)

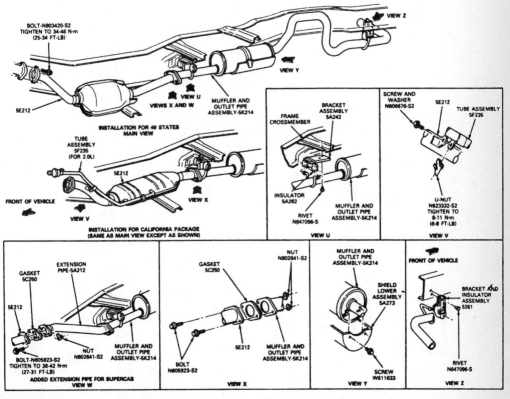

Exhaust system assembly — Ranger (4 cylinder engine)

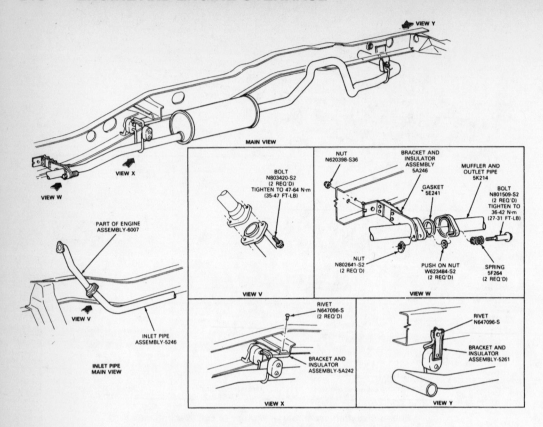

Exhaust system assembly — Ranger (4 cylinder diesel engine)

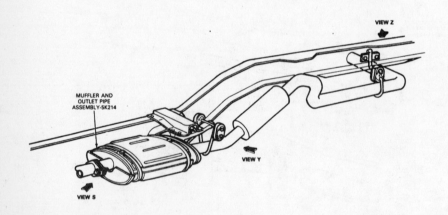

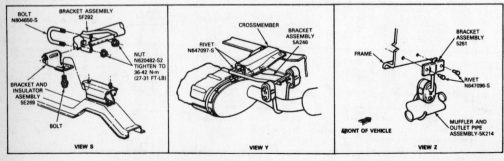

Exhaust system assembly — Bronco II (6 cylinder engine)

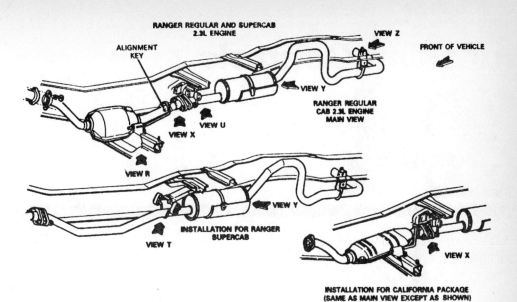

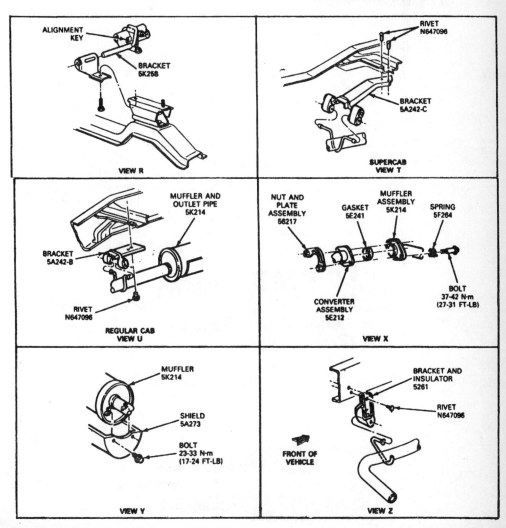

Exhaust system assembly — Ranger (4 cylinder diesel engine) regular and Supercab models

Emission Controls

EMISSION CONTROLS

NOTE: *Some emission components may be covered under Ford Dealer Emission Warranty (free of charge) see your local dealership.*

There are three types of automobile pollutants that concern automotive engineers: crankcase fumes, exhaust gases and gasoline vapors from evaporation. The devices and systems used to limit these pollutants are commonly called emission control equipment.

Crankcase Emission Controls

The crankcase emission control equipment consists of a positive crankcase ventilation (PCV) valve, a closed oil filler cap and the hoses that connect this equipment.

When the engine is running, a small portion of the gases which are formed in the combustion chamber leak by the piston rings and enter the crankcase. Since these gases are under pressure they tend to escape from the crankcase and enter into the atmosphere. If these gases were allowed to remain in the crankcase for any length of time, they would contaminate the engine oil and cause sludge to build up. If the gases are allowed to escape into the atmosphere, they would pollute the air, as they contain unburned hydrocarbons. The crankcase emission control equipment recycles these gases back into the engine combustion chamber, where they are burned.

Crankcase gases are recycled in the following manner. While the engine is running, clean filtered air is drawn into the crankcase either directly through the oil filler cap or through the carburetor air filter and then through a hose leading to the oil filler cap. As the air passes through the crankcase it picks up the combustion gases and carries them out of the crankcase up through the PCV valve and into the

FROM CRANKCASE AND/OR ROCKER ARM COVER — TO INTAKE MANIFOLD

LOW SPEED OPERATION—HIGH MANIFOLD VACUUM

HIGH SPEED OPERATION—LOW MANIFOLD VACUUM

FROM CRANKCASE AND/OR ROCKER ARM COVER — TO INTAKE MANIFOLD

A cutaway section of a PCV valve showing its operation

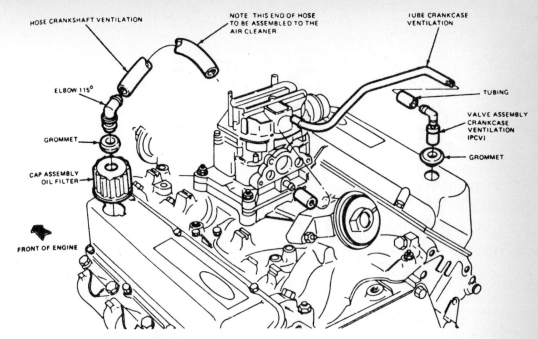

A cutaway of a typical PCV valve system

intake manifold. After they enter the intake manifold they are drawn into the combustion chamber and are burned.

The most critical component of the system is the PCV valve. This vacuum-controlled valve regulates the amount of gases which are recycled into combustion chamber. At low engine speeds the valve is partially closed, limiting the flow of gases into the intake manifold. As engine speed increases, the valve opens to admit greater quantities of the gasses into the intake manifold. If the valve should become blocked or plugged, the gases will bee prevented from escaping the crankcase by the normal route. Since these gases are under pressure, they will find their own way out of the crankcase. This alternate route is usually a weak oil seal or gasket in the engine. As the gas escapes by the gasket, it also creates an oil leak. Besides causing oil leaks, a clogged PCV valve also allows these gases to remain in the crankcase for an extended period of time, promoting the formation of sludge in the engine.

TROUBLESHOOTING

With the engine running, pull the PCV valve and hose from the valve rocker cover rubber grommet. Block off the end of the valve with your finger. A strong vacuum should be felt. Shake the valve; a clicking noise indicates it is free. Replace the valve if it is suspected of being blocked. REPLACE THE PCV VALVE INSTEAD OF TRYING TO CLEAN IT-ALSO CHECK PCV VALVE HOSE FOR CRACKS OR WEAR.

REMOVAL AND INSTALLATION

1. Pull the PCV valve and hose from the rubber grommet in the rocker cover.

2. Remove the PCV valve from the hose. Inspect the inside of the PCV valve. If it is dirty, disconnect it from the intake manifold and clean it in a suitable, safe solvent.

To install, proceed as follows:

1. If the PCV valve hose was removed, connect it to the intake manifold.

2. Connect the PCV valve to its hose.

3. Install the PCV valve into the rubber grommet in the valve rocker cover.

Evaporative Emission Controls

All gasoline powered vehicles are equipped with fuel evaporative emission control. The system is designed to limit fuel vapors released into the atmosphere.

Changes in atmospheric temperature cause fuel tanks to breathe that is, the air within the tank expands and condenses with outside temperature changes. As the temperature rises, air escapes through the tank vent tube or the vent in the tank cap. The air which escapes contains gasoline vapors. In a similar manner, the gasoline which fills the carburetor float bowl expands when the engine is stopped. Engine heat causes this expansion. The vapors escape through the carburetor and air cleaner.

The Evaporative Emission Control System

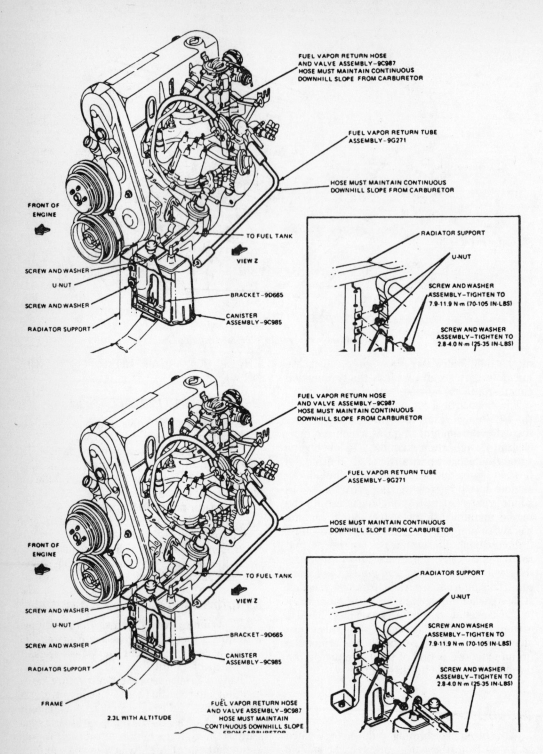

FUEL VAPOR RETURN HOSE
AND VALVE ASSEMBLY–9C987
HOSE MUST MAINTAIN CONTINUOUS
DOWNHILL SLOPE FROM CARBURETOR

FUEL VAPOR RETURN TUBE
ASSEMBLY–9G271

HOSE MUST MAINTAIN CONTINUOUS
DOWNHILL SLOPE FROM CARBURETOR

FRONT OF
ENGINE

TO FUEL TANK

VIEW Z

RADIATOR SUPPORT

U-NUT

SCREW AND WASHER
U-NUT

SCREW AND WASHER
ASSEMBLY–TIGHTEN TO
7.9-11.9 N·m (70-105 IN·LBS)

SCREW AND WASHER

BRACKET–9D665

RADIATOR SUPPORT

CANISTER
ASSEMBLY–9C985

SCREW AND WASHER
ASSEMBLY–TIGHTEN TO
2.8-4.0 N·m (25-35 IN·LBS)

FUEL VAPOR RETURN HOSE
AND VALVE ASSEMBLY–9C987
HOSE MUST MAINTAIN CONTINUOUS
DOWNHILL SLOPE FROM CARBURETOR

FUEL VAPOR RETURN TUBE
ASSEMBLY–9G271

HOSE MUST MAINTAIN CONTINUOUS
DOWNHILL SLOPE FROM CARBURETOR

FRONT OF
ENGINE

TO FUEL TANK

VIEW Z

RADIATOR SUPPORT

U-NUT

SCREW AND WASHER
U-NUT

SCREW AND WASHER
ASSEMBLY–TIGHTEN TO
7.9-11.9 N·m (70-105 IN·LBS)

SCREW AND WASHER

BRACKET–9D665

RADIATOR SUPPORT

CANISTER
ASSEMBLY–9C985

SCREW AND WASHER
ASSEMBLY–TIGHTEN TO
2.8-4.0 N·m (25-35 IN·LBS)

FRAME

2.3L WITH ALTITUDE

FUEL VAPOR RETURN HOSE
AND VALVE ASSEMBLY–9C987
HOSE MUST MAINTAIN
CONTINUOUS DOWNHILL SLOPE
FROM CARBURETOR

Carburetor and evaporative canister venting — 2.0L and 2.3L engines

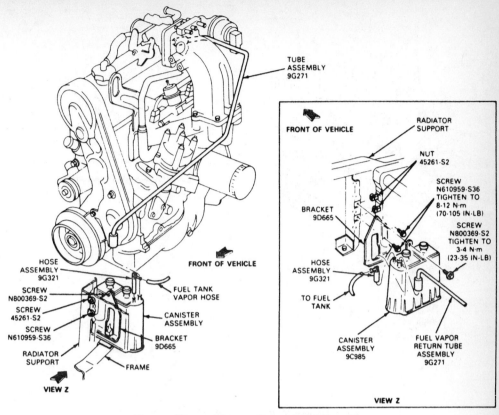

Evaporative canister venting — 2.3L EFI engine

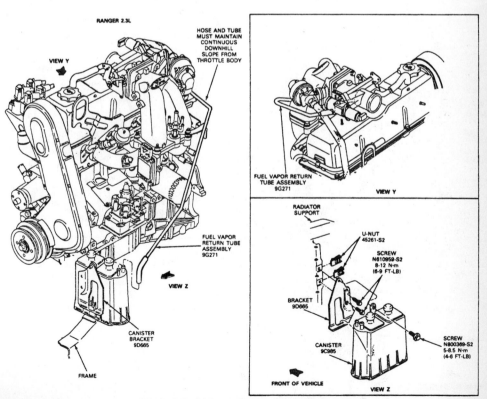

Evaporative canister venting — 2.3L EFI engine

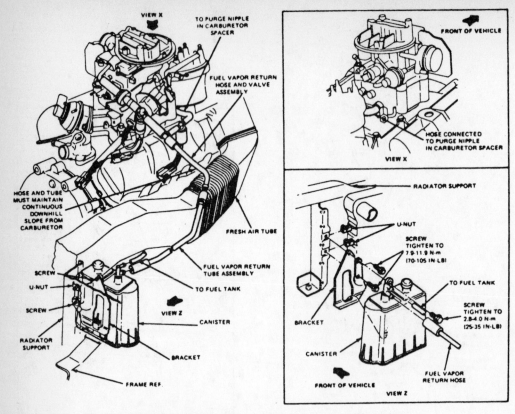

Carburetor and evaporative canister venting — 2.8L engine

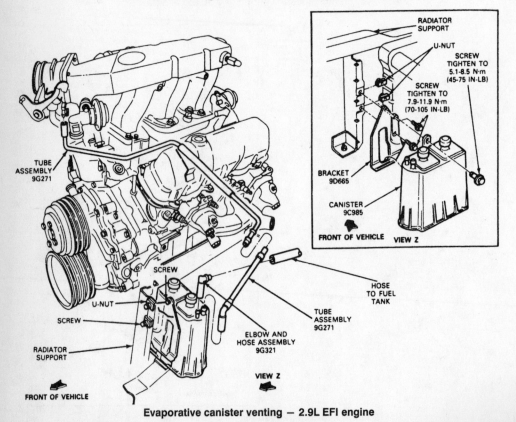

Evaporative canister venting — 2.9L EFI engine

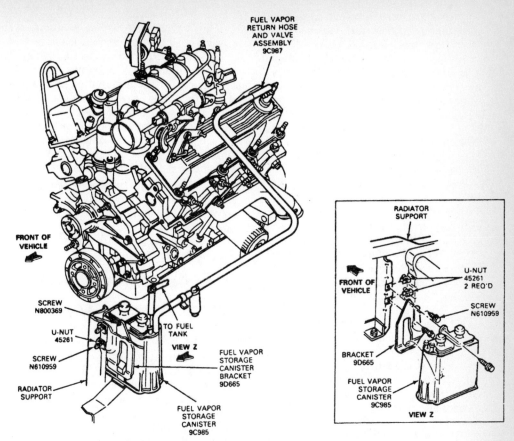

Evaporative canister venting — 3.0L EFI engine

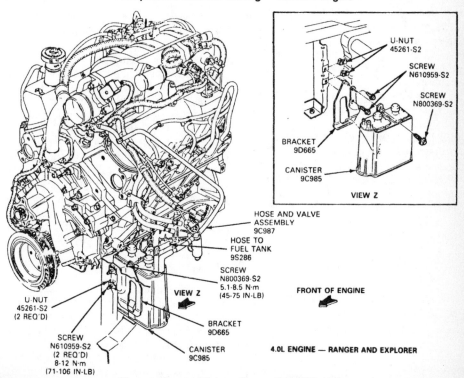

Evaporative canister venting — 4.0L EFI engine

provides a sealed fuel system with the capability to store and condense fuel vapors. The system has three parts: a fill control vent system; a vapor vent and storage system; and a pressure and vacuum relief system (special fill cap).

The fill control vent system is a modification to the fuel tank. It uses an air space within the tank which is 10–12% of the tank's volume. The air space is sufficient to provide for the thermal expansion of the fuel. The space also serves as part of the in-tank vapor vent system.

The in-tank vent system consists of the air space previously described and a vapor separator assembly. The separator assembly is mounted to the top of the fuel tank and is secured by a cam-lockring, similar to the one which secures the fuel sending unit. Foam material fills the vapor separator assembly. The foam material separates raw fuel and vapors, thus retarding the entrance of fuel into the vapor line.

The sealed filler cap has a pressure vacuum relief valve. Under normal operating conditions, the filler cap operates as a check valve, allowing air to enter the tank to replace the fuel consumed. At the same time, it prevents vapors from escaping through the cap. In case of excessive pressure within the tank, the filler cap valve opens to relieve the pressure.

Because the filler cap is sealed, fuel vapors have but one place through which they may escape-the vapor separator assembly at the top of the fuel tank. The vapors pass through the foam material and continue through a single vapor line which leads to a canister in the engine compartment. The canister is filled with activated charcoal.

Another vapor line runs from the top of the carburetor float chamber to the charcoal canister.

As the fuel vapors (hydrocarbons), enter the charcoal canister, they are absorbed by the charcoal. The air is dispelled through the open bottom of the charcoal canister, leaving the hydrocarbons trapped within the charcoal. When the engine is started, vacuum causes fresh air to be drawn into the canister from its open bottom. The fresh air passes through the charcoal picking up the hydrocarbons which are trapped there and feeding them into the carburetor for burning with the fuel mixture.

EVAPORATIVE EMISSION CONTROL SYSTEM CHECK/SERVICE

Other than a visual check to determine that none of the vapor lines are broken, there is no test for this equipment.

The only maintenance on the evaporative system is to periodically check all hoses and connections for leaks and deterioration. Replace any hoses which are found to be damaged in any way. Under normal circumstances, the charcoal canister is expected to last the life of the vehicle, but it should be periodically inspected for any damage or contamination by raw gasoline. Replace any gasoline soaked canister found. Refer to the illustrations for canister mounting and evaporative hose routing on the various engines. Filler cap damage or contamination that clogs the pressure/vacuum valve may result in deformation of the fuel tank.

NOTE: *Evaporative emission components are designed (warranted) and tested to exceed 120,000 miles/10 years of vehicle use. Some components may be covered under Ford Dealer Emission Warranty see your local dealership for details.*

Carbon Canister/Vapor Hoses

REMOVAL AND INSTALLATION

All Engines

1. Disconnect the negative battery cable.
2. Mark and disconnect the vapor hoses from the canister assembly.
3. Remove the screw securing the canister to the bracket or fender apron.
4. Lift up on the canister assembly to disengage the tab on the back side and remove the canister.
5. Installation is the reverse of the service removal procedure. Always install vapor hose in correct location. Refer to the necessary illustrations in this Chapter.

To disconnect a vapor hose from any component securely grip component with one hand and vapor hose with the other hand as close as possible to connection. Sharply twist hose along its axis to break the connection. No adhesive is used to make hose connections during vehicle assembly, but aging of the connections causes a temporary bond to exist.

If the connection is stubborn and the above method does not work, grip the hose with a pair of small pliers directly over the joint and twist again. Remove the vapor hose from the component.

Thermactor System

The Thermactor emission control system makes use of a belt-driven air pump to inject fresh air into the hot exhaust stream through the engine exhaust ports. The result is the extended burning of those fumes which were not completely ignited in the combustion chamber, and the subsequent reduction of some of the hydrocarbon and carbon monoxide content of

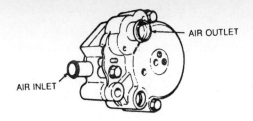

Thermactor® air pump — 19 cu. in.

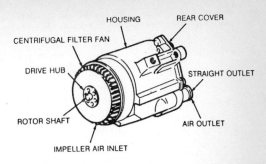

Typical Thermactor® System

the exhaust emissions into harmless carbon dioxide and water.

The Thermactor system is composed of the following components:

1. Air supply pump (belt-driven)
2. Air by pass valve
3. Check valves
4. Air manifolds (internal or external)
5. Air supply tubes (on external manifolds only)

Air for the Thermactor system is cleaned by means of a centrifugal filter fan mounted on the air pump driveshaft. The air filter does not require a replaceable element.

To prevent excessive pressure, the air pump is equipped with a pressure relief valve which uses a replaceable plastic plug to control the pressure setting.

The Thermactor air pump has sealed bearings which are lubricated for the life of the unit, and pre-set rotor vane and bearing clearances, which do not require any periodic adjustments.

The air supply from the pump is controlled by the air by-pass valve, sometimes called a dump valve. During deceleration, the air by-pass valve opens, momentarily diverting the air supply through a silencer and into the atmosphere, thus preventing backfires within the exhaust system.

A check valve is incorporated in the air inlet side of the air manifolds. Its purpose is to prevent exhaust gases from backing up into the Thermactor system. This valve is especially important in the event of drive belt failure, and during deceleration, when the air by-pass valve is dumping the air supply.

The air manifolds and air supply tubes channel the air from the Thermactor air pump into the exhaust ports of each cylinder, thus completing the cycle of the Thermactor system.

REPLACEMENT

Air By-Pass Valve

1. Disconnect the air and vacuum hoses at the air by-pass valve body.
2. Position the air by-pass valve and connect the respective hoses.

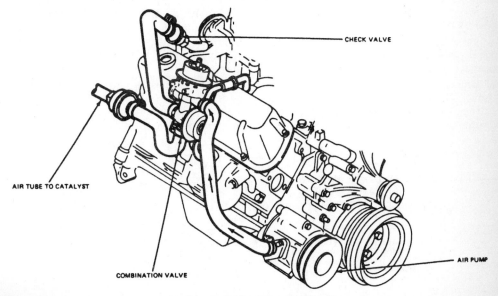

Thermactor® air pump — 11 cu. in.

Check Valve

1. Disconnect the air supply hose at the valve. Use $1^{1}/_{4}$ in. crowfoot wrench. The valve has a standard, right-hand pipe thread.

2. Clean the threads on the air supply tube with a wire brush. Do not blow compressed air through the check valve in either direction.

3. Install the check valve and tighten.

4. Connect the air supply hose.

Air Pump and Filter Fan

1. Loosen the air pump attaching bolts.

2. Remove the drive pulley attaching bolts and pull the pulley off the air pump shaft.

3. Pry the outer disc loose, then remove the centrifugal filter fan. Care must be used to prevent foreign matter from entering the air intake hole, especially if the fan breaks during removal. Do not attempt to remove the metal drive hub.

4. Install the new filter fan by drawing it into position with the pulley bolts.

Air Pump

1. Disconnect the air outlet hose at the air pump.

2. Loosen the pump belt tension adjuster.

3. Disengage the drive belt.

4. Remove the mounting bolt and air pump.

5. Position the air pump on the mounting bracket and install the mounting bolt.

6. Place the drive belt in the pulley and attach the adjusting arm to the air pump.

7. Adjust the drive belt tension and tighten the adjusting arm and mounting bolts.

8. Connect the air outlet hose to the air pump.

Relief Valve

Do not disassemble the air pump on the truck to replace the relief valve, but remove the pump from the engine.

1. Remove the relief valve on the pump housing and hold it in position with a block of wood.

2. Use a hammer to lightly tap the wood block until the relief valve is seated.

Relief Valve Pressure-Setting Plug

1. Compress the locking tabs inward (together) and remove the plastic pressure-setting plug.

2. Before installing the new plug, be sure that the plug is the correct one. The plugs are color-coded.

3. Insert the plug in the relief vale hose and push in until it snaps into place.

SYSTEM TESTING

Air Pump Functional Check

Check the air pump belt tension and adjust it, if necessary. Disconnect the air supply hose from the bypass control valve. The pump is operating properly if air flow is felt at the pump outlet and the flow increases as the engine speed is increased. Do not pry on the pump to adjust the belt as the aluminum housing is likely to collapse.

Normally Closed Bypass Valve Check

1. Disconnect the air supply hose at the valve outlet.

2. Remove the vacuum line to check to see that a vacuum signal is present at the vacuum nipple. Remove or bypass any restrictors or delay valves in the vacuum line. There must be a vacuum present at the nipple before proceeding.

3. With the engine at 1,500 rpm and the vacuum line connected to the vacuum nipple, air pump supply air should be heard and felt at the air bypass valve outlet.

4. With the engine at 1,500 rpm, disconnect the vacuum line. Air at the outlet should be significantly decreased or shut off. Air pump supply air should be heard or felt at the silencer ports.

5. If the normally closed air bypass valve does not successfully complete the above tests, check the air pump. If the pump is operating properly, replace the air bypass valve.

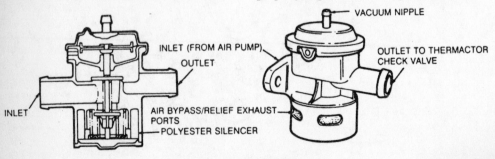

Normally closed air bypass valve

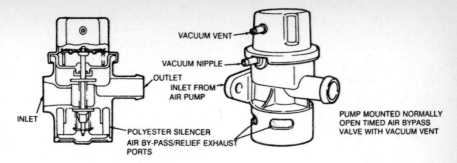

Normally open air bypass valve with vacuum vents

Normally Open Bypass Valve Check

1. Disconnect the air pump supply line at the outlet.

2. Disconnect all vacuum lines from the vacuum nipple and the vacuum vent.

3. Start the engine and raise the engine speed to 1,500 rpm. The air pump supply air should be heard and felt at the outlet.

4. Using a length of vacuum hose with no restrictors or devices, connect the vacuum nipple to one of the manifold vacuum fittings on the intake manifold. With the vacuum vent open to the atmosphere and the engine at 1,500 rpm, virtually no air should be felt at the valve outlet and virtually all air should be bypassed through the silencer ports.

5. Using the same direct vacuum line to an intake manifold vacuum source, cap the vacuum vent. Accelerate the engine speed to 2,000 rpm and suddenly release the throttle. A momentary interruption of air pump supply air should be felt at the valve outlet.

6. Reconnect all vacuum and Thermactor lines. If any of the above tests are not satisfactorily completed, check the air pump. If the air pump is operating properly, replace the bypass valve.

Normally Open Bypass Valve Without Vacuum Vent Check

1. Disconnect the air supply line at the valve outlet.

2. Disconnect the vacuum line at the vacuum nipple.

3. With the engine at 1,500 rpm, air should be heard and felt at the valve outlet.

4. Connect a direct vacuum line that is free from restrictions from any manifold vacuum source to the vacuum nipple on the air bypass valve. Air at the outlet should be momentarily decreased or shut off.

5. Air pump supply air should be heard or felt at the silencer ports during the momentary dump. Restore all original connections. If any of the above tests are not as described, check the air pump. If the air pump is operating properly, replace the bypass valve.

Air Supply Control Valve Check

1. Verify that air flow is being supplied to the valve inlet by disconnecting the air supply hose at the inlet and verifying the presence of air flow with the engine at 1,500 rpm. Reconnect the air supply hose to the valve inlet.

2. Disconnect the air supply hoses at outlets **A** and **B**.

3. Remove the vacuum line at the vacuum nipple.

4. Accelerate the engine speed to 1,500 rpm. Air flow should be heard and felt at outlet **B** with little or no air flow at outlet **A**.

5. With the engine at 1,500 rpm, connect a direct vacuum line from any manifold vacuum fitting to the air control valve vacuum nipple. Air flow should be heard and felt at outlet **A** with little or no air flow at outlet **B**.

6. If the valve is the bleed type, less air will flow from outlet **A** or **B** and the main discharge

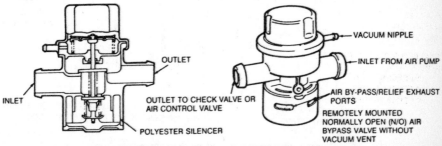

Normally open air bypass valve without vacuum vents

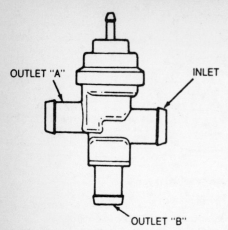

Air supply control valve

will change when vacuum is applied to the vacuum nipple.

7. Restore all connections. If the test results are not as described, replace the air control valve.

Combination Air Bypass/Air Control Valve Check

The combination air bypass/air control valve combines the functions of the air bypass and air control valve into a single unit. There are two normally closed valves; the non-bleed and bleed type, both of which look alike. One distinguishing feature will be that the bleed type will have the percent of bleed molded into the plastic case.

1. Disconnect the hoses from outlets **A** and **B**.

2. Disconnect and plug the vacuum line to port **D**.

3. With the engine operating at 1,500 rpm, air flow should be noted coming out of the bypass vents.

4. Reconnect the vacuum line to port **D** and disconnect and plug the vacuum line to port **S**. Make sure vacuum is present in the line to vacuum port **D**.

5. With the engine operating at 1,500 rpm, air flow should be noted coming out of outlet **B** and no air flow should be coming from outlet **A**.

6. With the engine at 1,500 rpm, apply 8–10 in.Hg of vacuum to port **S**. Air should now flow from outlet **A**.

7. If the valve is the bleed type, some lesser amount of air will flow from outlet **A** or **B** and the main discharge will change when vacuum is applied to port **S**.

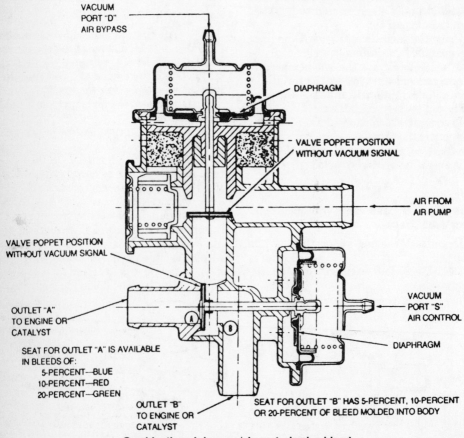

Combination air bypass/air control valve bleed

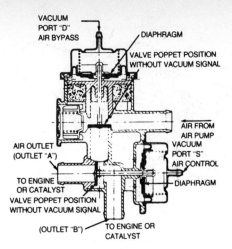

Combination air bypass/air control valve without bleed

NOTE: *If there is a small air tap attached to the inlet tube from the air pump, air flow should be present during engine operation.*

Air Check Valve/Pulse Air Valve Test

1. Inspect all hoses, tubes and the air valve for leaks.

2. Disconnect the hose on the inlet side if the air valve and attempt to blow through the valve. Air should pass freely.

3. Repeat the test, only this time attempt to suck air through the valve. No air should pass.

4. If any other results are obtained, replace the check valve.

Catalytic Converter

The converter is in the exhaust system ahead of the muffler. It contains a catalytic agent made of platinum and palladium, used to oxidize hydrocarbons (HC) and carbon monoxide (CO). The catalyst is expected to function without service of any kind for at least 50,000 miles. Use of leaded fuel would quickly cause catalyst

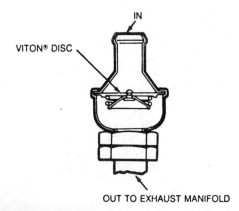

Typical air check valve

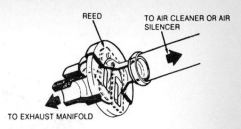

Typical pulse air valve

failure; for this reason, a tank filler restriction prevents the entry of service station leaded fuel nozzles.

Exhaust Gas Recirculation (EGR) System

The exhaust gas recirculation (EGR) system is designed to reintroduce inert exhaust gas into the combustion chamber, thereby lowering peak combustion temperatures and reducing the formation of Nitrous Oxide (NOx). The amount of exhaust gas recirculated and the timing of the cycle varies by calibration and is controlled by various factors, such as engine speed, engine vacuum, exhaust system backpressure, coolant temperature and throttle angle depending on the calibration. All EGR valves are vacuum actuated, but controlled by the EEC-IV on-board computer. The electronic EGR valve is not serviceable, however the EGR valve position (EVP) sensor and EGR valve can be replaced as individual components.

SYSTEM SERVICE

The EGR valve assembly (including the EVP sensor) should be replaced/serviced every 60,000 miles. Disconnect the vacuum hose, electrical connector and EGR line (if equipped), then remove the mounting bolts and lift off the EGR valve assembly. When replacing the EGR valve, the exhaust gas passages should be cleaned of carbon deposits. Excessive carbon deposits may require the removal of the mounting plate or intake manifold for cleaning. Excessive carbon deposits should not be pushed into the intake manifold where they can be drawn into the combustion chambers when the engine is started.

EGR SUPPLY PASSAGES AND CARBURETOR SPACE CLEANING

Remove the carburetor and carburetor spacer on engines so equipped. Clean the supply tube with a small power-driven rotary type wire brush or blast cleaning equipment. Clean the exhaust gas passages in the spacer using a suitable wire brush and/or scraper. The machined holes in the spacer can be cleaned by

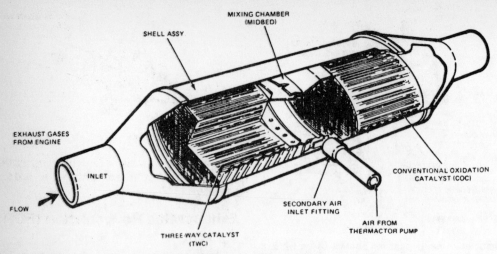

SHELL ASSY

MIXING CHAMBER
(MIDBED)

EXHAUST GASES
FROM ENGINE

INLET

FLOW

CONVENTIONAL OXIDATION
CATALYST (COC)

SECONDARY AIR
INLET FITTING

AIR FROM
THERMACTOR PUMP

THREE-WAY CATALYST
(TWC)

Catalytic converter assembly

using a suitable round wire brush. Hard encrusted material should be probed loose first, then brushed out.

EGR EXHAUST GAS CHANNEL CLEANING

Clean the exhaust has channel, where applicable, in the intake manifold, using a suitable carbon scraper. Clean the exhaust gas entry port in the intake manifold by hand passing a suitable drill bit through the holes to auger out the deposits. Do not use a wire brush. The manifold riser bore(s) should be suitably plugged during the above action to prevent any of the residue from entering the induction system.

Emission Maintenance Warning Light

The emission maintenance warning light system (starting 1985 model year) consists of an instrument panel mounted amber lens (with EGR or EMISS printed on it that is electrically connected to a sensor module located under the instrument panel. The purpose of the system is to alert the driver that emission system main-

tenance is required. Specific maintenance requirements are listed in the Emission System Scheduled Maintenance Charts. Note for your vehicle use these charts as a guide for recommended service.

The system actually measures accumulated vehicle ignition key on-time and is designed to

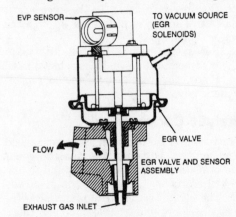

EVP SENSOR

TO VACUUM SOURCE
(EGR SOLENOIDS)

EGR VALVE

FLOW

EGR VALVE AND SENSOR
ASSEMBLY

EXHAUST GAS INLET

Cross section of the side entry type EGR valve

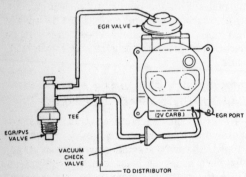

EGR VALVE

TEE

EGR PORT

(2V CARB.)

EGR/PVS
VALVE

VACUUM
CHECK
VALVE

TO DISTRIBUTOR

Typical EGR valve

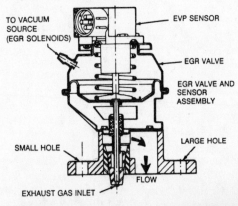

TO VACUUM
SOURCE
(EGR SOLENOIDS)

EVP SENSOR

EGR VALVE

EGR VALVE AND
SENSOR
ASSEMBLY

SMALL HOLE

LARGE HOLE

EXHAUST GAS INLET

FLOW

Cross section of the base entry type EGR valve

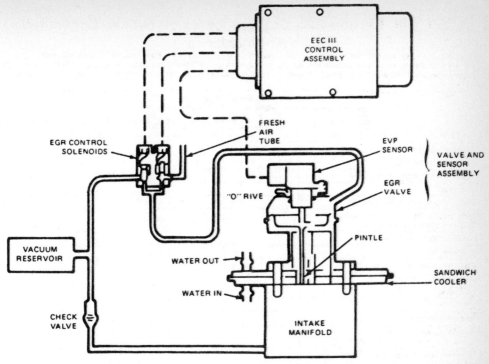

EGR system on vehicles equipped with electronic engine control

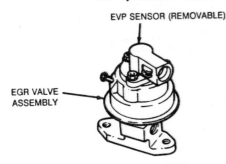

Location of the EGR valve position (EVP) sensor on the EGR valve

continuously close an electrical circuit to the amber lens after 2000 hours of vehicle operation. Assuming an average vehicle speed of 30 mph, the 2000 hours equates to approximately 60,000 miles of vehicle operation. Actual vehicle mileage intervals will vary considerably as individual driving habits vary.

Every time the ignition is switched on, the warning light will glow for 2–5 seconds as a bulb check and to verify that the system is operating properly. When approximately 60,000 miles is reached, the warning light will remain on continuously to indicate that service is required. After the required maintenance is performed, the sensor must be reset for another 60,000 mile period. The sensor module is located above the right front corner of the glove box assembly.

EMISSION WARNING LIGHT RESET PROCEDURE

1. Make sure the ignition key is OFF.
2. Locate the sensor (above the right front corner of the glove box), and lightly push a Phillips screwdriver or small rod tool through the 0.2 in. (5mm) diameter hole with the sticker labeled "RESET" and lightly press down and hold.
3. While lightly holding the screwdriver or tool down, turn the ignition switch to the RUN position. The emission warning light will then light and should remain on for as long as the screwdriver is held down. Hold the screwdriver down for approximately 5 seconds.
4. Remove the screwdriver or tool. The lamp should go out within 2–5 seconds, indicating that a reset has occurred. If the light remains on, begin again at Step 1. If the light goes out, turn the ignition off and go to the next Step.
5. Turn the ignition to the RUN position. The warning light should illuminate for 2–5 seconds and then go out. This verifies that a proper reset of the module has been accomplished. If the light remains on, repeat the reset procedure.

NOTE: *Some models (Non-EEC 2.0L engine) use a non-resettable control unit. When reset has occurred, replace it with a resettable type if available.*

2.3L EFI, 3.0L EFI and 2.8L Engines Emission System Scheduled Maintenance

All items designated with a B code are required to be performed in all states and Canada. (B) coded items are required for Canada and all states except California, and recommended only for California: b coded items are required in all states except California, and recommended only for California and Canada vehicles: (B) coded items are recommended for all vehicles. However, Ford recommends that you perform maintenance on all designated items to achieve best vehicle operation.

NORMAL DRIVING SERVICE INTERVALS Perform at the months or distances shown, whichever comes first.																
MILES (Thousands)	7.5	15	22.5	30	37.5	45	52.5	60	67.5	75	82.5	90	97.5	105	112.5	120
MAINTENANCE OPERATION　KILOMETERS (Thousands)	12	24	36	48	60	72	84	96	108	120	132	144	156	168	181	193
Emission Control Systems																
Change engine oil — every 12 months OR	B	B	B	B	B	B	B	b	b	b	b	b	b	b	b	b
Change engine oil filter — every 12 months OR	B	B	B	B	B	B	B	b	b	b	b	b	b	b	b	b
Replace spark plugs				B				b				b				b
Replace engine coolant — every 36 months OR				B				b				b				b
Check engine coolant condition & protection, hoses and clamps annually — prior to cold weather	ANNUALLY															
Inspect drive belt condition and tension				B				b				b				b
Replace air cleaner filter				B				b				b				b
Replace crankcase emission filter — if equipped				B				b				b				b
Inspect and clean injector tips — (2.3L EFI)								(b)								b
Replace PCV valves								b								b
Replace ignition wires								b								b
Check thermactor hoses and clamps								b								b
Clean choke linkages and external controls and inspect function of carburetor "hang on" devices — (2.8L only)				B				b				b				b
Replace EGR valve assembly (including EVP sensor on electronic EGR valve)*								b								b
Replace EGR vacuum solenoid(s) and filter (2.3L and 2.8L)								b								b
Replace EGO/HEGO sensor*								b								b
Check engine valve clearance (2.8L)	B			B				b				b				b

*This vehicle may be equipped with an Emissions Maintenance Warning Light. If so equipped, these parts are to be replaced either at 60,000 miles or when the Emissions Maintenance Warning Light remains on continuously with the key in the "On" position, whichever occurs first.

NOTES:
Unique Driving Conditions
If your driving habits FREQUENTLY include:
- Operating when outside temperatures remain below freezing and most trips are less than 8 km (5 miles).
- Operating during HOT WEATHER (above +90°F or +32°C) and
  — Driving continuously in excess of normal highway speeds;
  — Driving in stop-and-go "rush hour" traffic.
- Towing a trailer, using a camper or car-top carrier, or carrying maximum loads.
- Operating in severe dust conditions.
- Extensive idling, such as police, taxi or door-to-door delivery use.
- High speed operation with a fully loaded vehicle.

Change ENGINE OIL and OIL FILTER every 3 months or 4 800 km (3,000 miles) whichever occurs first.
Check/Regap SPARK PLUGS every 9 600 km (6,000 miles).
AIR CLEANER and CRANKCASE EMISSION AIR FILTERS — If operating in severe dust conditions.
Replace EGR SOLENOID FILTER(S) at 48 000 km (30,000 miles) and 144 000 km (90,000 miles) if operating in severe dust conditions. (2.3L and 2.8L)

Extreme Service Items
If vehicle is operated off-highway, perform the following items every 1 600 km (1,000 miles). If vehicle is operated in mud and or water perform the following items daily:
- Inspect disc brake system.
- Inspect front wheel bearings and lubrication.
- Inspect exhaust system for leaks, damage or loose parts.

Oxygen Sensor

TESTING

Because of the complexity of this component no attempt to repair or test it should be made. It should only be serviced/tested by a qualified (ASE) mechanic.

REMOVAL AND INSTALLATION

NOTE: *This service is a general procedure modify service steps as necessary.*

1. Disconnect the negative battery cable. Locate the oxygen sensor.
2. Disconnect the electrical connector from the sensor.

B — Required for all vehicles.
b — Required for 49 States vehicles and recommended only for California and Canada vehicles.
(b) — This item not required to be performed. However, Ford recommends that you also perform maintenance on items designated by a "(b)" in order to achieve best vehicle operation. Failure to perform this recommended maintenance will not invalidate the vehicle emissions warranty or manufacturer recall liability.

MAINTENANCE OPERATION	MILES (Thousands)	7.5	15	22.5	30	37.5	45	52.5	60	67.5	75	82.5	90	97.5	105	112.5	120
	KILOMETERS (Thousands)	12	24	36	48	60	72	84	96	108	120	132	144	156	168	181	193
Emission Control Systems																	
Change Engine Oil and Oil Filter — every 6 months OR		B	B	B	B	B	B	B	B	B	B	B	B	B	B	B	b
Replace Spark Plugs — Standard					B				B				B				b
— Platinum Type 3.0L									B								b
Replace Engine Coolant — every 36 months OR					B				B				B				b
Check Engine Coolant Condition and Protection, Hoses and Clamps Annually — Prior to Cold Weather								ANNUALLY									
Replace Air Cleaner Filter					B				b				b				b
Replace Crankcase Emission Filter					B				b				b				b
*Check/Clean Throttle Body									(b)								(b)
Replace PCV Valve (1)									b/1								b
Replace Ignition Wires									b								b

* Wheel lug nuts must be retightened to proper torque specifications at 500 miles/800 km of new vehicle operation. See your Owner Guide for proper torque specification. Also retighten to proper torque specification at 500 miles/800 km after (1) any wheel change or (2) any other time the wheel lug nuts have been loosened.

/1 At 60,000 miles your dealer will replace the PCV Valve at no cost on 3.0L and 4.0L engines except California and Canada vehicles. NOTE: Refer to page 2 of the Maintenance Schedule Record Book for "NO COST PCV VALVE REPLACEMENT".

NOTES:
Unique Driving Conditions
If your driving habits **FREQUENTLY** include one or more of the following conditions:
• Operating when outside temperatures remain **below freezing** and most trips are less than 16 km (10 miles).
• Operating during **HOT WEATHER** in stop-and-go "rush hour" traffic.
• Towing a trailer, using a camper or roof-top carrier, or carrying maximum loads.
• Operating in severe dust conditions.
• Extensive idling, such as police, taxi or door-to-door delivery use.
• High speed operation with a fully loaded vehicle (MAX. GVW).
Change ENGINE OIL and OIL FILTER every 3 months or 3,000 miles (4 800 km) whichever occurs first.
Check/Regap SPARK PLUGS every 30,000 miles (48 000 km).

AIR CLEANER AND CRANKCASE EMISSION AIR FILTERS.
If operating in severe dust conditions, ask your dealer for proper replacement intervals.
AUTOMATIC TRANSMISSION FLUID — Change each 30,000 miles (48 000 km) — if your driving habits FREQUENTLY include one or more of the following conditions.
• Operating during hot weather (above 90°F, 32°C) and carrying heavy loads and driving hilly terrain.
• Towing a trailer.
• Door-to-door delivery, police or taxi.
Extreme Service Items
If vehicle is operated off-highway, perform the following items every 1 600 km (1,000 miles). If vehicle is operated in mud and or water perform the following items daily:
• Inspect disc brake system.
• Inspect drum brake system, hoses, and lines.
• Inspect front wheel bearings and lubrication.
• Inspect exhaust system for leaks, damage or loose parts.
• Lubricate driveshaft U-joint if equipped with grease fittings.

Emission system scheduled maintenance for the 4.0L engine

3. Spray a commercial solvent onto the sensor threads and allow it to soak in for about 5 minutes.

4. Carefully remove the oxygen sensor.

To install:

5. First coat the new sensor's threads with anti-seize compound made for this purpose only. This is NOT a conventional anti-seize paste. The use of a regular compound may electrically insulate the sensor, rendering it inoperative. You must coat ONLY the threads with an electrically conductive anti-seize compound.

6. Install the sensor (installation torque is about 30 ft. lbs. most vehicles) reconnect the electrical connector. Be careful not to damage the electrical connector.

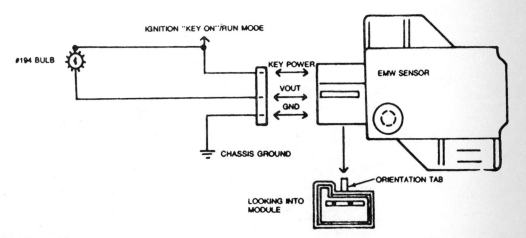

Ford emission maintenance light system schematic

Fuel System

CARBURETED FUEL SYSTEM

Mechanical Fuel Pump

The carbureted engines use a camshaft eccentric-actuated combination fuel pump located on the lower left side of the engine block.

REMOVAL

1. Disconnect the fuel inlet and outlet lines at the fuel pump. Discard the fuel inlet retaining clamp.

2. Remove the pump retaining bolts then remove the pump assembly and gasket from the engine. Discard the gasket.

INSTALLATION

1. If a new pump is to be installed, remove the fuel line connector fitting from the old pump and install it in the new pump (if so equipped).

2. Remove all gasket material from the mounting pad and pump flange. Apply oil resistant sealer to both sides of a new gasket.

3. Position the new gasket on the pump flange and hold the pump in position against the mounting pad. Make sure that the rocker arm is riding on the camshaft eccentric.

4. Press the pump tight against the pad, install the retaining bolts and alternately torque them to 14–21 ft. lbs. Connect the fuel lines. Use a new clamp on the fuel inlet line.

5. Operate the engine and check for leaks.

TESTING

Incorrect fuel pump pressure and low volume (flow rate) are the two most likely fuel pump troubles that will affect engine performance. Low pressure will cause a lean mixture and fuel starvation at high speeds and excessive pressure will cause high fuel consumption and carburetor flooding.

To determine that the fuel pump is in satisfactory operating condition, tests for both fuel pump pressure and volume should be performed.

The tests are performed with the fuel pump installed on the engine and the engine at normal operating temperature and at idle speed.

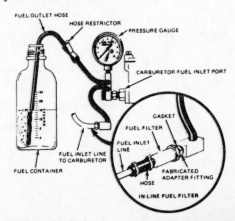

Fuel pump installation

Fuel pump volume and pressure test equipment

Before the test, make sure that the replaceable fuel filter has been changed at the proper mileage interval. If in doubt, install a new filter.

Pressure Test

1. Remove the air cleaner assembly. Disconnect the fuel inlet line of the fuel filter at the carburetor. Use care to prevent fire, due to fuel spillage. Place an absorbent cloth under the connection before removing the line to catch any fuel that might flow out of the line.
2. Connect a pressure gauge, a restrictor and a flexible hose between the fuel filter and the carburetor.
3. Position the flexible hose and the restrictor so that the fuel can be discharged into a suitable, graduated container.
4. Before taking a pressure reading, operate the engine at the specified idle rpm and vent the system into the container by opening the hose restrictor momentarily.
5. Close the hose restrictor, allow the pressure to stabilize and note the reading.

If the pump pressure is not within 4.5–6.5 psi and the fuel lines and filter are in satisfactory condition, the pump is defective and should be replaced.

If the pump pressure is within the proper range, perform the test for fuel volume.

Volume Test

1. Operate the engine at the specified idle rpm.
2. Open the hose restrictor and catch the fuel in the container while observing the time it takes to pump 1 pint. It should take 30 seconds for 1 pint to be expelled. If the pump does not pump to specifications, check for proper fuel tank venting or a restriction in the fuel line leading from the fuel tank to the carburetor before replacing the fuel pump.

Carburetor

The carburetor identification tag is attached to the carburetor. To obtain replacement parts, it is necessary to know the part number prefix, suffix and, in some cases, the design change code. If the carburetor is ever replaced by a new unit, make sure that the identification tag stays with the new carburetor and the vehicle.

REMOVAL AND INSTALLATION

1. Remove the air cleaner.
2. Remove the throttle cable and transmission linkage from the throttle lever. Disconnect all vacuum lines, emission hoses, the fuel line and electrical connections.

3. Remove the carburetor retaining nuts then remove the carburetor. Remove the carburetor mounting gasket, spacer (if so equipped), and the lower gasket from the intake manifold.
4. Before installing the carburetor, clean the gasket mounting surfaces of the spacer and carburetor. Place the spacer between two new gaskets and position the spacer and the gaskets on the intake manifold. Position the carburetor on the spacer and gasket and secure it with the retaining nuts. To prevent leakage, distortion or damage to the carburetor body flange, snug the nuts, then alternately tighten each nut in a criss-cross pattern.
5. Connect the inline fuel line, throttle cable, transmission linkage and all electrical connections and vacuum lines on the carburetor.
6. Adjust the engine idle speed, the idle fuel mixture and install the air cleaner.

FLOAT AND FUEL LEVEL ADJUSTMENTS

Aisan Model Y Feedback 1–bbl (Dry Adjustment)

Stabilize engine temperature. With vehicle parked on a level surface and running at curb idle, check that fuel level is within the limits on sight glass as shown, If not, proceed as follows.

1. Remove carburetor air horn from carburetor. Remove and discard air horn gasket.
2. Remove power valve piston and spring.
3. Invert air horn assembly. Using a drill of the specified diameter, check the clearance between the top of the float and bottom surface of air horn.

NOTE: *The float lever should be resting on needle pin when checking clearance.*

4. If required, bend float air as shown to adjust float level.

CAUTION: *Do not load the needle when adjusting the float. Also, do not bend the tab at the end of the float arm. This tab prevents the float from striking the bottom of the fuel bowl when empty. Refer to float drop adjustments.*

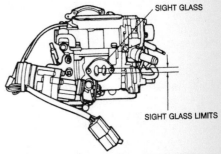

SIGHT GLASS

SIGHT GLASS LIMITS

Float level sight glass check — Aisan model Y carburetor

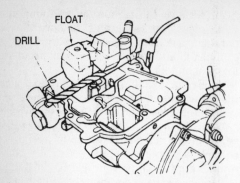

Float level adjustment — Aisan model Y carburetor

5. Install power valve piston and spring.

6. install air horn on carburetor, using a new air horn gasket.

7. Install carburetor on engine.

8. check ISC motor maximum extension rpm, adjust as necessary.

Carter Model YFA & YFA Feedback 1–bbl (Dry Adjustment)

1. Remove the air cleaner.

2. Disconnect the choke heat tube at the carburetor air horn. Disconnect the fuel inlet line at the filter.

3. Disconnect the electric choke wire at the connector.

4. Remove the wire clip retaining the link joining the fast idle choke lever to the fast idle cam and remove the link. Remove the air horn assembly attaching screws, dashpot and bracket assembly and air horn gasket. Discard the gasket.

5. Fabricate a float level gauge to the specified float level dimension. Refer to the Carburetor Specification chart for dimensions.

6. Invert the air horn assembly, and check the clearance from the float indentation on the top of the float to the bottom of the air horn with the float level gauge. Hold the air horn at eye level when gauging the float level. The float arm (lever) should be resting on the needle pin. Do not load the needle when adjusting the float. Bend the float arm as necessary to adjust the float level (clearance). Do not bend the tab at the end of the float arm. It prevents the float from striking the bottom of the fuel bowl when empty.

7. Install a new air horn to main body gasket. Make sure all holes in the new gasket have been properly punched and that no foreign material has adhered to the gasket. Install the air horn assembly, connect vent line to canister (if so equipped), and bracket assembly and air horn attaching screws and tighten to 27–37 in. lbs. Position the link and plastic bushing joining the fast idle cam to the fast idle choke lever

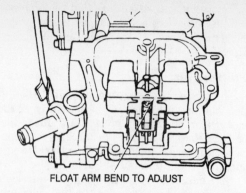

FLOAT ARM BEND TO ADJUST

Float arm adjustment — Aisan model Y carburetor

and retain in place on the fast idle cam with the plastic bushing and wire clip. Make sure the mechanical fuel bowl vent rod is engaged with the forked actuating lever (if so equipped).

8. Connect the fuel inlet line to the fuel filter.

9. Connect the electric choke wire.

10. Install the air cleaner. Starter the engine and run it until normal operating temperature is reached. Adjust the idle fuel mixture and idle speed.

Motorcraft Model 2150 2–bbl (Wet Adjustment)

1. Operate the engine until it reaches normal operating temperature. Place the vehicle on a level surface and stop the engine.

2. Remove the carburetor air cleaner assembly.

3. Remove the air horn attaching screws and the carburetor identification tag. Temporarily, leave the air horn and gasket in position on the carburetor main body and start the engine. Let the engine idle for a few minutes, then rotate the air horn out of the way and remove the air horn gasket to provide access to the float assembly.

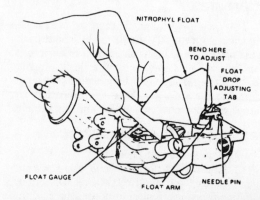

Float level adjustment — Carter YFA & YFA Feedback carburetor

4. While the engine is idling, use a scale to measure the vertical distance from the top machined surface of the carburetor main body to the level of the fuel in the fuel bowl. The measurement must be made at least $1/4$ in. away from any vertical surface to assure an accurate reading, because the surface of the fuel is concave, being higher at the edges than the center. Care must be exercised to measure the fuel level at the point of contact with the float.

5. If any adjustment is required, stop the engine to minimize the hazard of fire due to spilled gasoline. To adjust the fuel level, bend the float tab contacting the fuel inlet valve upward in relation to the original position to raise the fuel level, and downward to lower it. Each time the float is adjusted, the engine must be started and permitted to idle for a few minutes to stabilize the fuel level. Check the fuel level after each adjustment, until the specified level is obtained.

6. Assemble the carburetor in the reverse order of disassembly, using a new gasket between the air horn and the main carburetor body.

FLOAT DROP ADJUSTMENT

Aisan Model Y Feedback 1–bbl Carburetor

1. Remove carburetor air horn from carburetor. Remove and discard air horn gasket.

2. Hold air horn upright and let float hang free. Using vernier calipers, measure the maximum dimension from toe end of float to casting surface. Hold air horn at eye level when gauging the dimension.

3. The float drop dimension should be as shown in the Carburetor Chart. Adjust to specification by bending tab as shown.

4. Install air horn on carburetor, using a new air horn gasket.

5. Check ISC motor maximum extension rpm and adjust as necessary.

Carter Model YFA & YFA Feedback 1–bbl

1. Remove the air cleaner.

2. Disconnect the choke heat tube at the carburetor air horn. Disconnect the fuel inlet line at the filter.

3. Disconnect the electric choke wire at the connector.

4. Remove the wire clip retaining the link joining the fast idle choke lever to the fast idle cam and remove the link. Remove the air horn assembly attaching screws, dashpot and bracket assembly and air horn gasket. Discard the gasket.

5. Fabricate a float drop gauge to the specified dimension 38mm minimum.

6. Hold the air horn upright and let the float hang free. Measure the maximum clearance from the foe end of the float to the casting surface. Hold the air horn at eye level when gauging the dimension.

7. To adjust, bend the tab at the end of the float arm to obtain the specified setting.

8. Install a new air horn to main body gasket. Make sure all holes in the new gasket have been properly punched and that no foreign material has adhered to the gasket. Install

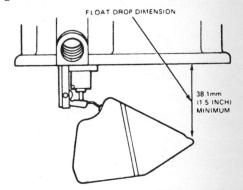

Float drop adjustment — Carter YFA & YFA Feedback carburetor

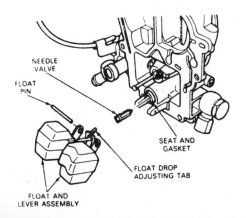

Float drop adjustment — Aisan model Y carburetor

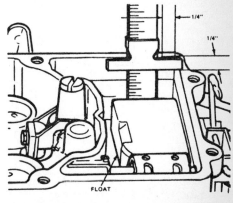

Float level adjustment — Motorcraft 2150A 2-bbl. carburetor

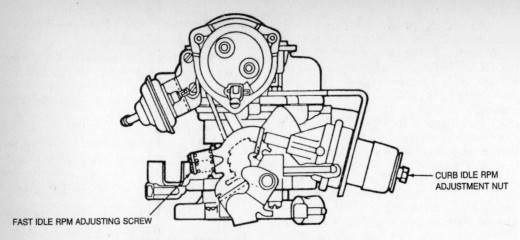

Carter YFA & YFA Feedback fast idle speed control

the air horn assembly, connect vent line to canister (if so equipped, and bracket assembly and air horn attaching screws and tighten to 27–37 in. lbs. Position the link and plastic bushing joining the fast idle cam to the fast idle choke lever and retain in place on the fast idle cam with the plastic bushing and wire clip. Make sure the mechanical fuel bowl vent rod is engaged with the forked actuating lever (if so equipped).

9. Connect the fuel inlet line to the fuel filter.

10. Connect the electric choke wire.

11. Install the air cleaner. Start the engine and run it until normal operating temperature is reached. Adjust the idle fuel mixture and idle speed.

FAST IDLE SPEED ADJUSTMENT

Carter YFA & YFA Feedback 1–bbl

1. Place the transmission in Neutral or Park.

2. Bring the engine to normal operating temperature.

3. Turn the ignition key to the Off position.

4. Put the air conditioner selector in the Off position.

5. Disconnect the vacuum hose at the EGR valve and plug.

6. Place the fast idle RPM adjusting screw on the specified step of the fast idle cam.

7. Start the engine without touching the accelerator pedal: Check/adjust fast idle RPM to specification. Refer to the under hood sticker for specifications.

8. Rev the engine momentarily, allowing the engine to return to idle and turn the ignition key to the Off position.

9. Remove the plug from the EGR vacuum hose and reconnect it.

Motorcraft Model 2150A 2–bbl

1. Place the transmission in park or neutral.

2. Bring the engine to normal operating temperature.

3. Disconnect the plug the vacuum hose at the EGR and purge valves.

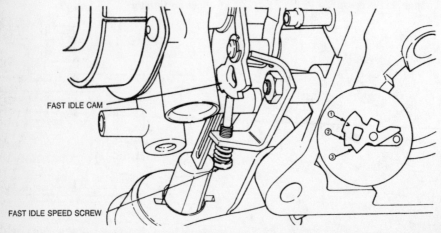

Motorcraft 2150A 2-bbl. carburetor fast idle speed adjustment

4. Place the fast idle lever on the **V** step of the fast idle cam.

5. Adjust the fast idle rpm to specifications.

6. Reconnect the EGR and purge vacuum hoses.

ACCELERATING PUMP STROKE ADJUSTMENT

Motorcraft Model 2150A 2–bbl

The accelerating pump stroke has been factory set for a particular engine application and should not be readjusted. If the stroke has been changed from the specified hole reset to specifications by following these procedures

1. Using a blunt-tipped punch, remove and retain the roll pin from the accelerator pump cover.

NOTE: *Support the area under the roll pin when removing the pin.*

2. Rotate the pump link and rod assembly until the keyed end of the assembly is aligned with the keyed hole in the pump over-travel lever.

3. Reposition the rod and swivel assembly in the specified hole and reinstall the pump link in the accelerator pump cover.

NOTE: *A service accelerator rod and swivel assembly is available (9F687) and must be used if replacement is necessary.*

Adjustment holes are not provided on the temperature compensated accelerator pump carburetors.

4. Reinstall the rod pin.

CHOKE PULLDOWN ADJUSTMENT

Carter YFA & YFA Feedback

1. Remove the air cleaner assembly.

2. Hold the throttle plate fully open and close the choke plate as far as possible without forcing it. Use a drill of the proper diameter to check the clearance between the choke plate

and air horn. Refer to the Carburetor Specification chart for specifications.

3. If the clearance is not within specification, adjust by bending the arm on the choke trip lever of the throttle lever. Bending the arm downward will decrease the clearance, and bending it upward will increase the clearance. Always recheck the clearance after making any adjustment.

Motorcraft 2150A

1. Set throttle on fast idle cam top step.

2. Note index position of choke bimetallic cap. Loosen retaining screws and rotate cap 90° in the rich (closing) direction.

3. Activate pulldown motor by manually forcing pulldown control diaphragm link in the direction of applied vacuum or by applying vacuum to external vacuum tube.

4. Measure vertical hard gauge clearance between choke plate and center of carburetor air horn wall nearest fuel bowl.

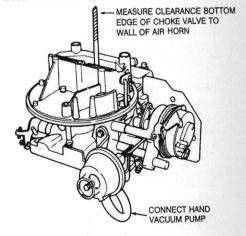

— MEASURE CLEARANCE BOTTOM EDGE OF CHOKE VALVE TO WALL OF AIR HORN

CONNECT HAND VACUUM PUMP

Motorcraft 2150A 2-bbl. carburetor choke plate pulldown adjustment

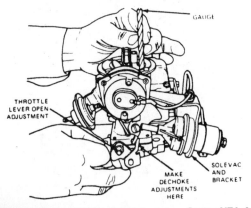

GAUGE

THROTTLE LEVER OPEN ADJUSTMENT

MAKE DECHOKE ADJUSTMENTS HERE

SOLEVAC AND BRACKET

Choke plate pulldown adjustment — Carter YFA & YFA Feedback carburetor

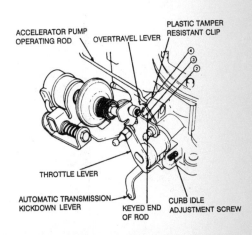

PLASTIC TAMPER RESISTANT CLIP

ACCELERATOR PUMP OPERATING ROD   OVERTRAVEL LEVER

THROTTLE LEVER

AUTOMATIC TRANSMISSION KICKDOWN LEVER

KEYED END OF ROD

CURB IDLE ADJUSTMENT SCREW

Accelerator pump stroke adjustment

Pulldown setting should be within specifications for minimum choke plate opening.

If choke plate pulldown is found to be out of specification, reset by adjusting diaphragm stop on end of choke pulldown diaphragm.

If pulldown is reset, cam clearance should be checked and reset if required.

After pulldown check is completed, reset choke bimetallic cap to recommended index position as specified in the Carburetor Specifications Chart. Check and reset fast idle speed to specifications if necessary.

SECONDARY TOUCH CLEARANCE

Aisan Model Y Carburetor

1. Remove carburetor from vehicle, as described.
2. Check and adjust secondary touch clearance as follows:

    a. Open throttle until secondary touch adjustment tang just touches secondary kicker lever.

    b. Using a drill of the specified diameter,

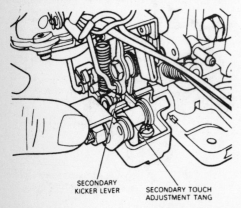

SECONDARY
KICKER LEVER

SECONDARY TOUCH
ADJUSTMENT TANG

Secondary touch clearance adjustment — Aisan model Y carburetor

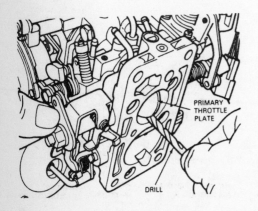

PRIMARY
THROTTLE
PLATE

DRILL

Accelerator pump stroke adjustment

check the clearance between the primary throttle plate and the wall of the bore.

    c. If required, adjustment is made by bending secondary touch adjustment tang located on the primary throttle lever.
3. Install carburetor onto engine.

SECONDARY KICK CLEARANCE

Aisan Model Y Carburetor

1. Remove carburetor from vehicle as described.
2. Check and adjust secondary kick clearance as follows:

Open primary throttle to wide-open throttle. Using a drill of the specified diameter, check the clearance between the secondary throttle plate and the wall of the bore. If required, adjustment is made by bending the secondary kick tang on the secondary throttle lever.
3. Install carburetor onto engine.

OVERHAUL

Efficient carburetion depends greatly on careful cleaning and inspection during overhaul since dirt, gum, water or varnish in or on the carburetor parts are often responsible for poor performance.

Overhaul the carburetor in a clean, dust free area. Carefully disassemble the carburetor, referring often to the exploded views. Keep all similar and look-alike parts segregated during disassembly and cleaning to avoid accidental interchange during assembly. Make a note of all jet sizes.

When the carburetor is disassembled, wash all parts (except diaphragms, electric choke unit, pump plunger and any other plastic, leather, fiber, or rubber parts) in clean carburetor solvent. Do not leave the parts in the solvent any longer than is necessary to sufficiently loosen the dirt and deposits. Excessive cleaning

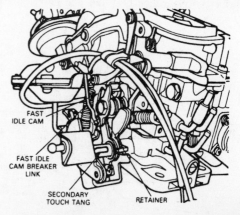

FAST
IDLE CAM

FAST IDLE
CAM BREAKER
LINK

SECONDARY
TOUCH TANG

RETAINER

Adjusting secondary touch clearance adjustment — Aisan model Y carburetor

may remove the special finish from the float bowl and choke valve bodies, leaving these parts unfit for service. Rinse all parts in clean solvent and blow them dry with compressed air or allow them to air dry, while resting on clean, lint less paper. Wipe clean all cork, plastic, leather and fiber parts with a clean, lint-free cloth.

Blow out all passages and jets with com-

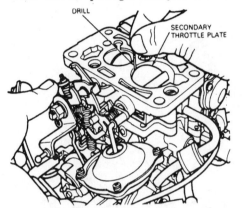

Checking secondary kick clearance adjustment — Aisan model Y carburetor

pressed air and be sure that there are no restrictions or blockages. Never use wire or similar tools to clean jets, fuel passages or air bleeds. Clean all jets and valves separately to avoid accidental interchange.

Examine all parts for wear or damage. If wear or damage is found, replace the defective parts. Especially, inspect the following:

1. Check the float needle and seat for wear. If wear is found, replace the complete assembly.

2. Check the float hinge pin for wear and the float(s) for dents or distortion. Replace the float if fuel has leaked into it.

3. Check the throttle and choke shaft bores for wear or an out-of-round condition. Damage or wear to the throttle arm, shaft or shaft bore will often require replacement of the throttle body. These parts require a close tolerance of fit; wear may allow air leakage, which could affect starting and idling.

NOTE: *Throttle shafts and bushings are not normally included in overhaul kits. They can be purchased separately.*

4. Inspect the idle mixture adjusting needles for burrs or grooves. Any such condition

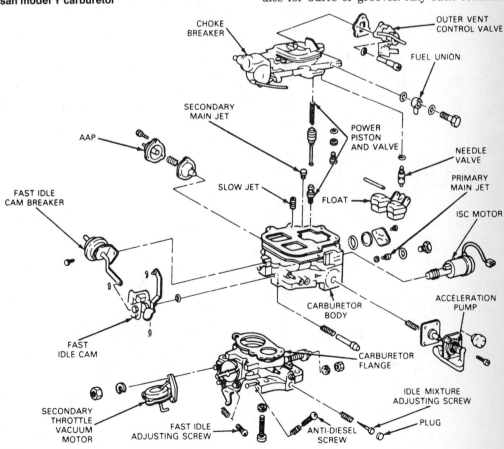

Aisan model Y 1-bbl. carburetor

requires replacement of the needle, since you will not be able to obtain a satisfactory idle.

5. Test the accelerator pump check valves. They should pass air one way, but not the other. Test for proper seating by blowing and sucking on the valve. Replace the valve as necessary. If the valve is satisfactory, wash the valve again to remove moisture.

6. Check the bowl cover for warped surfaces with a straightedge.

7. Closely inspect the valves and seats for wear and damage, replacing as necessary.

8. After the carburetor is assembled, check the choke valve for freedom of operation.

Carburetor overhaul kits are recommended for each overhaul. These kits contain all gas-

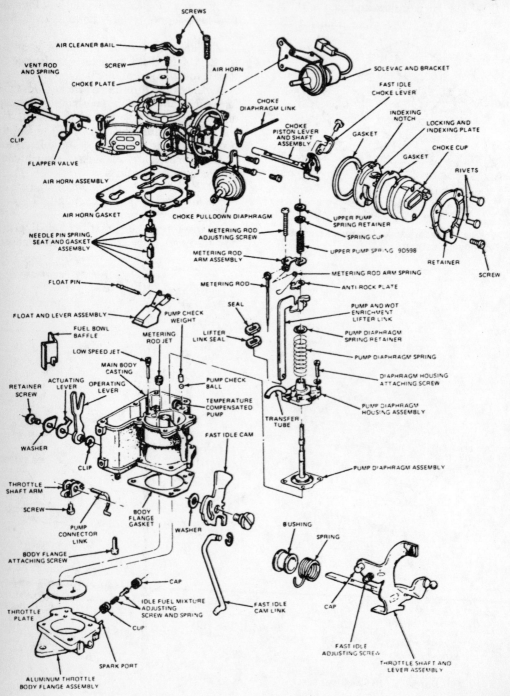

Carter YFA 1-bbl. carburetor — all except California models

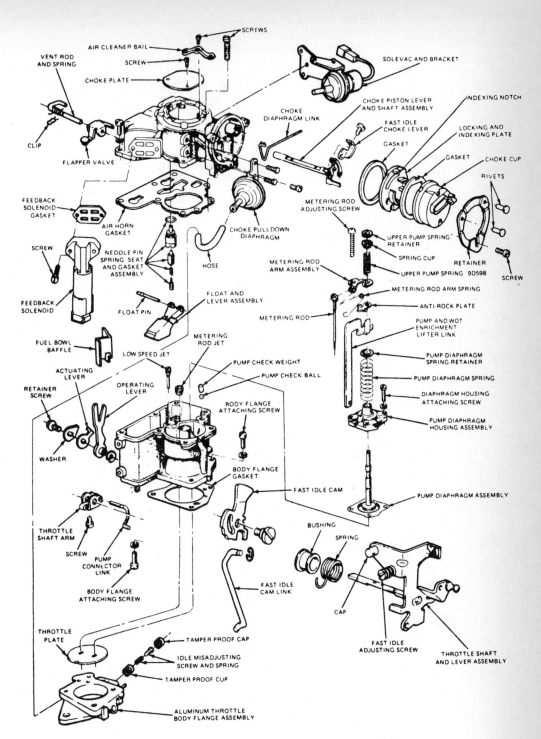

Carter YFA 1-bbl. carburetor — California models

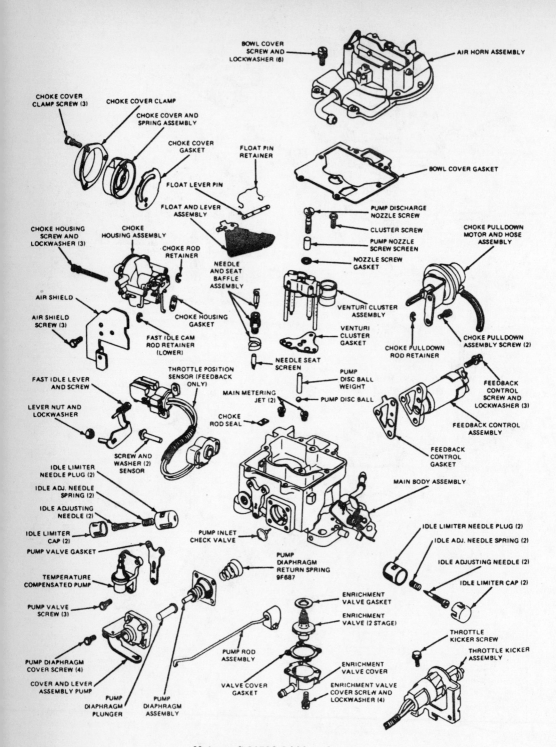

BOWL COVER SCREW AND LOCKWASHER (6)

AIR HORN ASSEMBLY

CHOKE COVER CLAMP SCREW (3)

CHOKE COVER CLAMP

CHOKE COVER AND SPRING ASSEMBLY

CHOKE COVER GASKET

FLOAT PIN RETAINER

BOWL COVER GASKET

FLOAT LEVER PIN

FLOAT AND LEVER ASSEMBLY

PUMP DISCHARGE NOZZLE SCREW

CLUSTER SCREW

CHOKE PULLDOWN MOTOR AND HOSE ASSEMBLY

CHOKE HOUSING SCREW AND LOCKWASHER (3)

CHOKE HOUSING ASSEMBLY

CHOKE ROD RETAINER

PUMP NOZZLE SCREW SCREEN

NEEDLE AND SEAT BAFFLE ASSEMBLY

NOZZLE SCREW GASKET

VENTURI CLUSTER ASSEMBLY

AIR SHIELD

AIR SHIELD SCREW (3)

CHOKE HOUSING GASKET

VENTURI CLUSTER GASKET

CHOKE PULLDOWN ROD RETAINER

CHOKE PULLDOWN ASSEMBLY SCREW (2)

FAST IDLE CAM ROD RETAINER (LOWER)

NEEDLE SEAT SCREEN

PUMP DISC BALL WEIGHT

FAST IDLE LEVER AND SCREW

THROTTLE POSITION SENSOR (FEEDBACK ONLY)

MAIN METERING JET (2)

PUMP DISC BALL

FEEDBACK CONTROL SCREW AND LOCKWASHER (3)

LEVER NUT AND LOCKWASHER

CHOKE ROD SEAL

FEEDBACK CONTROL ASSEMBLY

SCREW AND WASHER (2) SENSOR

FEEDBACK CONTROL GASKET

IDLE LIMITER NEEDLE PLUG (2)

MAIN BODY ASSEMBLY

IDLE ADJ. NEEDLE SPRING (2)

IDLE ADJUSTING NEEDLE (2)

IDLE LIMITER NEEDLE PLUG (2)

IDLE LIMITER CAP (2)

PUMP INLET CHECK VALVE

IDLE ADJ. NEEDLE SPRING (2)

PUMP VALVE GASKET

PUMP DIAPHRAGM RETURN SPRING 9F687

IDLE ADJUSTING NEEDLE (2)

TEMPERATURE COMPENSATED PUMP

ENRICHMENT VALVE GASKET

IDLE LIMITER CAP (2)

PUMP VALVE SCREW (3)

ENRICHMENT VALVE (2 STAGE)

THROTTLE KICKER SCREW

THROTTLE KICKER ASSEMBLY

PUMP DIAPHRAGM COVER SCREW (4)

PUMP ROD ASSEMBLY

ENRICHMENT VALVE COVER

COVER AND LEVER ASSEMBLY PUMP

VALVE COVER GASKET

ENRICHMENT VALVE COVER SCREW AND LOCKWASHER (4)

PUMP DIAPHRAGM PLUNGER

PUMP DIAPHRAGM ASSEMBLY

Motorcraft 2150A 2-bbl. carburetor

kets and new pars to replace those which deteriorate most rapidly. Failure to replace all of the parts supplied with the kit (especially gaskets) can result in poor performance later.

NOTE: *Most carburetor rebuilding kits include specific procedures which should be followed during overhaul.*

Most carburetor manufacturers supply overhaul kits of these basic types: minor repair; major repair; and gasket kits. Basically, they contain the following:

Minor Repair Kits:
- All gaskets
- Float needle valve
- Mixture adjusting screws
- All Diaphragms
- Spring for the pump diaphragm

Major Repair Kits:
- All jets and gaskets

Carter YFA Carburetor Specification

Check the carburetor part number tag to determine which specifications to use for your vehicle.

Year	Model	Engine	Part Number	Choke Pulldown Setting	Fast Idle Cam Setting	Dechoke Setting	Float Setting (Dry)	Choke Cap Setting	Fast Idle
1983	Ranger	2.0/122	E27E-9510-CC	.320	.140	.220	.650	Orange	2000 ①
			E27E-9510-CB	.320	.140	.220	.650	Yellow	2000 ①
			E27E-9510-GB	.320	.140	.220	.650	Yellow	2000 ①
			E37E-9510-EA	.320	.140	.270	.650	Orange	2000 ①
			E37E-9510-FA	.320	.140	.270	.650	Gray	2000 ①
		2.3/140	E27E-9510-BB	.320	.140	.270	.650	Yellow	2000 ①
			E27E-9510-FB	.320	.140	.270	.650	Yellow	2000 ①
			E37E-9510-BA	.320	.140	.270	.650	Yellow	2000 ①
			E27E-9510-EB	.320	.140	.220	.650	Black	2000 ①
			E27E-9510-HA	.320	.140	.220	.650	Black	2000 ①
			E27E-9510-HB	.320	.140	.220	.650	Black	2000 ①
			E27E-9510-FA	.320	.140	.270	.650	Yellow	2000 ①
			E37E-9510-LA	.320	.140	.270	.650	Grey	2000 ①
			E37E-9510-LB	.320	.140	.270	.650	Grey	2000 ①
			E37E-9510-NA	.320	.140	.270	.650	Grey	2000 ①
			E37E-9510-NB	.320	.140	.270	.650	Grey	2000 ①
			E37E-9510-RA	.320	.140	.270	.650	Grey	2000 ①
			E37E-9510-RB	.320	.140	.270	.650	Grey	2000 ①
			E37E-9510-TA	.320	.140	.270	.650	Grey	2000 ①
			E37E-9510-TB	.320	.140	.270	.650	Grey	2000 ①
1984	Ranger	2.0/122	E37E-9510-EB	.320	.140	.270	.650	Orange	2000 ①
			E37E-9510-FB	.320	.140	.270	.650	Grey	2000 ①
		2.3/140	E37E-9510-BB	.320	.140	.270	.650	Yellow	2000 ①
			E37E-9510-LB	.320	.140	.270	.650	Grey	2000 ①
			E37E-9510-NB	.320	.140	.270	.650	Grey	2000 ①
			E37E-9510-RB	.320	.140	.270	.650	Grey	2000 ①
			E37E-9510-TB	.320	.140	.270	.650	Grey	2000 ①
1985	Ranger	2.0/122	E57E-9510-DA	.320	.140	.270	.650	Grey	1700 ②
1986	Ranger	2.0/122	E57E-9510-DA	.320	.140	.270	.650	Grey	1700 ②
			E57E-9510-DB	.320	.140	.270	.650	Grey	1700 ②

① 1900 rpm for vehicles with less than 100 miles.   ② 1600 rpm for vehicles with less than 100 miles.

Motorcraft 2150A Carburetor Specification

Check the carburetor part number tag to determine which specifications to use for your vehicle.

Year	Model	Engine	Part Number	Choke Pulldown Setting	Fast Idle Cam Setting	Dechoke Setting	Float Setting (Wet)	Float Setting (Dry)	Accelerator Pump Lever Location	Choke Cap Setting	Fast Idle
1984	Bronco II	2.8/173	E37E-9510-AAA	.136	V-notch	.250	.810	7/16"	#4	V-notch	3000 ①
	Ranger		E37E-9510-ABA	.136	V-notch	.250	.810	7/16"	#4	V-notch	3000 ①
			E37E-9510-ADA	.136	V-notch	.250	.810	7/16"	#4	V-notch	3000 ①
			E37E-9510-AEA	.136	V-notch	.250	.810	7/16"	#4	V-notch	3000 ①
			E47E-9510-TA	.136	V-notch	.250	.810	7/16"	#4	V-notch	3000 ①
			E47E-9510-VA	.136	V-notch	.250	.810	7/16"	#4	V-notch	3000 ①
1985	Bronco II	2.8/173	E57E-9510-BA	.136	Hi-Cam	.250	.810	1/16"	#4	3NR	3000 ①
	Ranger		E57E-9510-CA	.136	Hi-Cam	.250	.810	1/16"	#4	3NR	3000 ①

① 2800 rpm for vehicles with less than 100 miles.

Aisan Model Y Carburetor Specification

Check the carburetor part number tag to determine which specifications to use for your vehicle.

Year	Model	Engine	Part Number	Choke Pulldown Setting	Fast Idle Cam Setting	Dechoke Setting	Float Setting (Dry)	Choke Cap Setting	Fast Idle
1987	Ranger	2.0 122	E77E-9510-AA	18°	14.5° ①	195 sec.	47.1 mm	20°C	3200 ②
1988	Ranger	2.0 122	E87E-9510-AA	18°	14.5° ①	195 sec.	47.1 mm	20°C	3200 ②

① On step #1
② 3100 rpm for vehicles with less than 100 miles.

- All diaphragms
- Float needle valve
- Mixture adjusting screws
- Pump ball valve
- Main jet carrier
- Float
- Some float bowl cover holddown screws and washers

Gasket Kits:
- All gaskets

After cleaning and checking all components, reassemble the carburetor, using new parts and referring to the exploded view. When reassembling, make sure that all screws and jets are tight in their seats, but do not overtighten, as the tips will be distorted. Tighten all screws gradually, in rotation. Do not tighten needle valves into their seats; uneven jetting will result. Always use new gaskets. Be sure to adjust the float level.

GASOLINE FUEL INJECTION SYSTEM

NOTE: *This book contains testing and service procedures for your vehicle's fuel injec-* tion system. More comprehensive testing and diagnostic procedures may be found in CHILTONS'S GUIDE TO FUEL INJECTION AND FEEDBACK CARBURETORS, available at your local retailer.
CAUTION: *BEFORE SERVICING ANY COMPONENTS OF THE FUEL SYSTEM, PERFORM THE FOLLOWING PROCEDURE FOR RELEASING THE FUEL SYSTEM PRESSURE. THE FUEL INJECTION SYSTEMS MAY BE UNDER PRESSURE EVEN WHEN THE ENGINE IS NOT RUNNING.*

BLEEDING THE FUEL SYSTEM
RELIEVE FUEL PRESSURE

1. Remove the fuel tank cap and the air filter.
2. Disconnect the negative battery cable.
3. Using the Fuel Pressure Gauge tool No. T80L–9974–A, connect it to the pressure relief valve (remove the valve cap) on the fuel injection manifold/fuel rail assembly.
NOTE: *Some 2.3L EFI engines have a pressure relief valve located on the throttle body. On later model 2.3L EFI engines the fuel pressure relief valve is located on the fuel injec-*

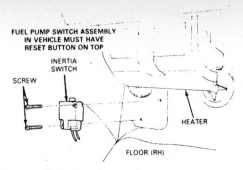

Inertia switch assembly

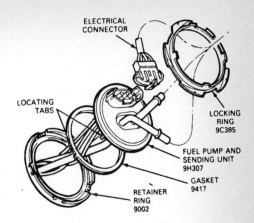

Low pressure fuel pump assembly

tion supply manifold assembly in the upper RH corner of the engine compartment. To gain access to the pressure relief valve, the valve cap must be removed.

4. Open the pressure relief valve and reduce the fuel pressure.

5. To pressurize the fuel system, perform the following:

  a. Tighten the pressure relief valve and remove the pressure gauge.

  b. Install fuel tank cap and the air filter. Reinstall the negative battery cable.

  c. Turn ignition ON/OFF several times (leave key ON position---15 seconds each time) without starting the engine to pressurize the fuel system. Check for fuel leaks at pressure regulator, fuel injectors and fuel connect fittings.

  d. Start the engine.

Inertia Switch

A safety inertia switch is installed to shut off the electric fuel pump in case of collision. The switch is located on the toe-board to the right of the transmission hump. If the pump shuts off, or if the vehicle has been hit and will not start, check for leaks-then reset the switch. The switch is reset by pushing down on the button provided. To relieve the fuel system pressure disconnect the electrical connection to inertia switch crank the engine for about 20 seconds.

Electric Fuel Pump

2.3L AND 2.9L ENGINES/TILL 1988

On the 2.3L and the 2.9L engines to model year 1988 the electric fuel pump system used on these EFI engines consisted of two fuel pumps: a low pressure boost pump mounted in the fuel tank, and a high pressure fuel pump mounted on the frame rail.

The low pressure electric fuel pump is located in the fuel tank and is a part of the fuel gauge sending unit.

REMOVAL AND INSTALLATION

External Frame Mounted Pump Assembly

The high pressure fuel pump is frame mounted and can be accessed from under the vehicle. The fuel pump assembly is retained to the frame with 3 bolts. Remove the fuel pump and bracket assembly (disconnect electrical con-

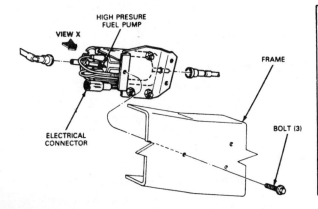

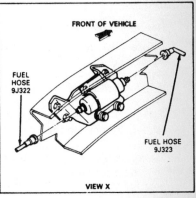

High pressure fuel pump assembly

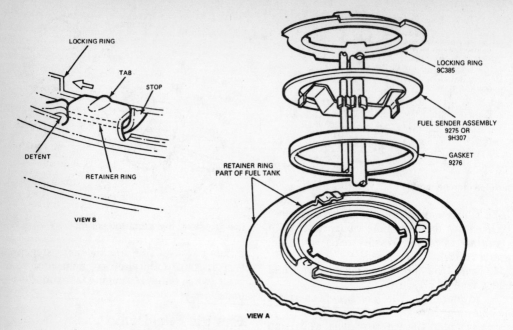

Fuel tank Sender installation (metal lockring type)

nector) from the frame of the vehicle. Before removing the fuel pump assembly, disconnect the negative battery cable and relieve the system pressure. Refer to "BLEEDING THE FUEL SYSTEM/RELIEVE FUEL PRESSURE" procedure in this Chapter.

Clean all dirt and/or grease from the fuel line fittings. "Quick Connect" fittings are used on all models equipped with a pressurized fuel system. These fittings must be disconnected using the proper procedure or the fittings may be damaged. Remove the fuel pump assembly from the metal mounting bracket. Remove the fuel pump. Install the fuel pump to mounting bracket and install the assembly to frame of the vehicle. Connect all electrical and fuel line connections, connect battery cable, pressurize the fuel system. Start engine and check for leaks.

Internal Pump In Fuel Tank

The low pressure fuel pump is located in the fuel tank and may require removal of the fuel tank assembly. Refer to Fuel Tank Removal and Installation procedures in This Chapter as necessary.

1. Disconnect the negative battery cable. Remove the fuel from the tank or remove the tank assembly.

2. Disconnect all electrical connections to the fuel system sender unit.

3. Remove any dirt around the fuel sender assembly.

4. Loosen the Quick Connect Fittings. Turn the fuel sender locking ring counterclock-

wise with special tool or equivalent (brass drift pin) remove the locking ring, sender assembly and sealing gasket. Remove the fuel pump from the fuel sender assembly.

To install:

5. Install the fuel pump to sender assembly. Place a new sealing gasket in the groove of the fuel tank. Install the fuel sender assembly in the fuel tank so that the tabs of the sender are positioned into the slots of the fuel tank. The sealing gasket must remain in place during and after the fuel sender installation.

6. Holding the fuel sender and sealing gasket in place, install and rotate the locking ring clockwise until the stop is against the retainer ring tab.

7. Install the tank assembly as necessary. Connect all electrical and fuel line connections.

8. Refill the tank, connect battery cable, pressurize the fuel system. Start engine and check for leaks.

2.3L TWIN PLUG
2.9L, 3.0L AND 4.0L ENGINES

On the 2.3L twin plug engine and the 2.9L, 3.0L and 4.0L engines starting in model year 1989 the electric fuel injection system uses a fuel tank and fuel pump/sender assembly.

REMOVAL AND INSTALLATION

1. Disconnect the negative battery cable. Depressurize the fuel system. Refer to the necessary service procedure in this Chapter.

NOTE: *On Ranger vehicles the fuel pump/ sender unit may be serviced by removing the pick-up box from the chassis, instead of removing the fuel tank assembly.*

CAUTION: *The fuel system is under pressure. Release pressure slowly and contain spillage. Observe no smoking/no open flame precautions. Have a Class B–C (dry powder) fire extinguisher within arm's reach at all times.*

2. Drain the fuel tank. Drain the gasoline into a suitable safety container and take precautions to avoid the risk of fire. Remove the fuel filler tube.

3. Support the fuel tank assembly and remove the fuel tank supports straps. Lower fuel tank partially and remove all other connections. Remove the bolt from the front strap and remove the front strap. Remove the bolt from the rear strap and remove the rear strap.

4. Remove the fuel feed hose at the fuel gauge sender push connector.

5. Remove the fuel hose from the sender unit push connector.

6. Remove the fuel vapor hose from the vapor valve.

7. Lower the fuel tank from the chassis.

8. Remove the shield from the fuel tank.

9. Remove any dirt from the fuel pump flange.

10. Turn the fuel pump locking ring counterclockwise to remove it. There is a special wrench for this purpose, but you can loosen the ring by tapping it around with a wood dowel and plastic or rubber mallet.

CAUTION: *Never hammer on or near the fuel tank with metal tools! The risk of spark and explosion is always present!*

11. Remove the fuel pump and bracket assembly.

12. Remove and discard the seal ring gasket.

WARNING: *Do not attempt to apply battery voltage to the pump to check its operation while removed from the vehicle, as running the pump dry will destroy it!*

To install:

13. Clean the area thoroughly.

14. Coat the new seal ring with multi-purpose grease to hold it in place and install it in the fuel ring groove.

15. Position the pump/sender assembly in the tank making sure that all keyways align and the seal ring stays in place.

16. Hold the fuel sender and sealing gasket in place, install and rotate the locking ring. Find the fuel tank part number on the front bottom of the tank, for vehicles equipped with E59A–9002–CAE tank: tighten the ring to 60–85 ft. lbs. wait 5 minutes and tighten again to 60–85 ft. lbs. For this tank assembly use the same ring that was removed from the tank. Do not replace the ring with a ring from another tank.

17. For tanks equipped with plastic retaining rings E99A–9A307–D, tighten nuts to 40–55 ft. lbs. use the same ring that was removed from the tank. If a new tank is installed, use a new ring.

18. For E69A–9002–PA tanks: tighten the locknut ring once to 80–113 ft. lbs. and for some vehicles tighten the polyethylene lock ring to 40–45 ft. lbs.

19. Support the tank assembly while connecting the fuel lines, vent line and electrical connectors.

20. Install the tank in the vehicle and tighten the retaining straps evenly. Make sure all gasket/rubber insulation if so equipped for retaining straps is in correct position.

21. Install filler tube.

22. Refill tank, pressurize the fuel system. Refer to the necessary service procedure in this Chapter. Check complete system for fuel leaks at fittings.

23. Start engine and recheck for fuel leaks.

Quick Connect Fuel Line Fittings

REMOVAL AND INSTALLATION

NOTE: *Quick Connect (push) type fuel line fittings must be disconnected using proper procedures or the fitting may be damaged. Two types of retainers are used on the push connect fittings. Line sizes of $3/8$ in. and $5/16$ in. use a "hairpin" clip retainer. $1/4$ in. line connectors use a "duck bill" clip retainer. In addition, some engines use spring lock connections secured by a garter spring which requires a special tool (T81P–19623–G) for removal.*

Hairpin Clip

1. Clean all dirt and/or grease from the fitting. Spread the two clip legs about $1/8$ in. (3mm) each to disengage from the fitting and pull the clip outward from the fitting. Use finger pressure only, do not use any tools.

2. Grasp the fitting and hose assembly and pull away from the steel line. Twist the fitting and hose assembly slightly while pulling, if necessary, when a sticking condition exists.

3. Inspect the hairpin clip for damage, replace the clip if necessary. Reinstall the clip in position on the fitting.

4. Inspect the fitting and inside of the connector to insure freedom of dirt or obstruction. Install fitting into the connector and push together. A click will be heard when the hairpin snaps into proper connection. Pull on the line to insure full engagement.

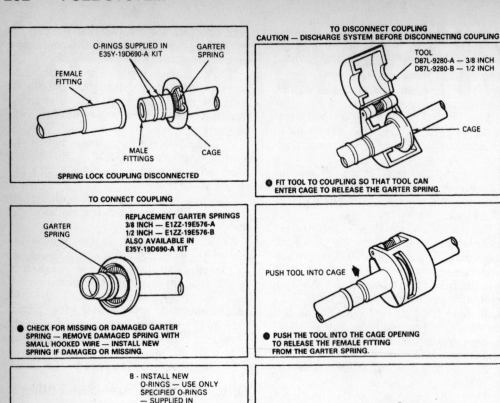

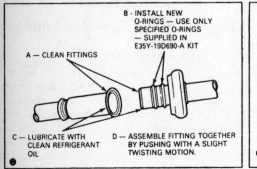

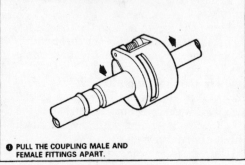

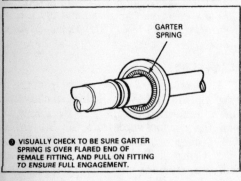

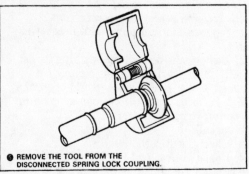

Fuel line removal and installation procedures

Duck Bill Clip

1. A special tool is available from Ford for removing the retaining clips (Ford Tool No. T82L–9500–AH). If the tool is not on hand see Step 2. Align the slot on the push connector disconnect tool with either tab on the retaining clip. Pull the line from the connector.

2. If the special clip tool is not available, use a pair of narrow 6 in. (152mm) channel lock pliers with a jaw width of 0.2 in. (5mm) or less. Align the jaws of the pliers with the openings of the fitting case and compress the part of the retaining clip that engages the case. Compressing the retaining clip will release the fitting

CHILTON'S
FUEL ECONOMY
& TUNE-UP TIPS

55 WAYS TO IMPROVE FUEL ECONOMY

Tune-up • Spark Plug Diagnosis • Emission Controls

Fuel System • Cooling System • Tires and Wheels

General Maintenance

CHILTON'S FUEL ECONOMY & TUNE-UP TIPS

Fuel economy is important to everyone, no matter what kind of vehicle you drive. The maintenance-minded motorist can save both money and fuel using these tips and the periodic maintenance and tune-up procedures in this Repair and Tune-Up Guide.

There are more than 130,000,000 cars and trucks registered for private use in the United States. Each travels an average of 10-12,000 miles per year, and, and in total they consume close to 70 billion gallons of fuel each year. This represents nearly ⅔ of the oil imported by the United States each year. The Federal government's goal is to reduce consumption 10% by 1985. A variety of methods are either already in use or under serious consideration, and they all affect you driving and the cars you will drive. In addition to "down-sizing", the auto industry is using or investigating the use of electronic fuel delivery, electronic engine controls and alternative engines for use in smaller and lighter vehicles, among other alternatives to meet the federally mandated Corporate Average Fuel Economy (CAFE) of 27.5 mpg by 1985. The government, for its part, is considering rationing, mandatory driving curtailments and tax increases on motor vehicle fuel in an effort to reduce consumption. The government's goal of a 10% reduction could be realized — and further government regulation avoided — if every private vehicle could use just 1 less gallon of fuel per week.

How Much Can You Save?

Tests have proven that almost anyone can make at least a 10% reduction in fuel consumption through regular maintenance and tune-ups. When a major manufacturer of spark plugs sur-

TUNE-UP

1. Check the cylinder compression to be sure the engine will really benefit from a tune-up and that it is capable of producing good fuel economy. A tune-up will be wasted on an engine in poor mechanical condition.

2. Replace spark plugs regularly. New spark plugs alone can increase fuel economy 3%.

3. Be sure the spark plugs are the correct type (heat range) for your vehicle. See the Tune-Up Specifications.

Heat range refers to the spark plug's ability to conduct heat away from the firing end. It must conduct the heat away in an even pattern to avoid becoming a source of pre-ignition, yet it must also operate hot enough to burn off conductive deposits that could cause misfiring.

The heat range is usually indicated by a number on the spark plug, part of the manufacturer's designation for each individual spark plug. The numbers in bold-face indicate the heat range in each manufacturer's identification system.

Manufacturer	Typical Designation
AC	R **45** TS
Bosch (old)	WA **145** T30
Bosch (new)	HR **8** Y
Champion	RBL **15** Y
Fram/Autolite	**415**
Mopar	P-**62** PR
Motorcraft	BRF-**42**
NGK	BP **5** ES-15
Nippondenso	W **16** EP
Prestolite	14GR **5** 2A

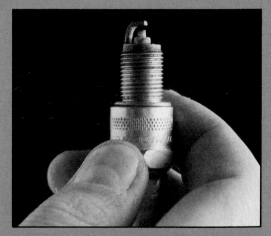

Periodically, check the spark plugs to be sure they are firing efficiently. They are excellent indicators of the internal condition of your engine.

On AC, Bosch (new), Champion, Fram/Autolite, Mopar, Motorcraft and Prestolite, a higher number indicates a hotter plug. On Bosch (old), NGK and Nippondenso, a higher number indicates a colder plug.

4. Make sure the spark plugs are properly gapped. See the Tune-Up Specifications in this book.

5. Be sure the spark plugs are firing efficiently. The illustrations on the next 2 pages show you how to "read" the firing end of the spark plug.

6. Check the ignition timing and set it to specifications. Tests show that almost all cars have incorrect ignition timing by more than 2°.

veyed over 6,000 cars nationwide, they found that a tune-up, on cars that needed one, increased fuel economy over 11%. Replacing worn plugs alone, accounted for a 3% increase. The same test also revealed that 8 out of every 10 vehicles will have some maintenance deficiency that will directly affect fuel economy, emissions or performance. Most of this mileage-robbing neglect could be prevented with regular maintenance.

Modern engines require that all of the functioning systems operate properly for maximum efficiency. A malfunction anywhere wastes fuel. You can keep your vehicle running as efficiently and economically as possible, by being aware of your vehicle's operating and performance characteristics. If your vehicle suddenly develops performance or fuel economy problems it could be due to one or more of the following:

PROBLEM	POSSIBLE CAUSE
Engine Idles Rough	Ignition timing, idle mixture, vacuum leak or something amiss in the emission control system.
Hesitates on Acceleration	Dirty carburetor or fuel filter, improper accelerator pump setting, ignition timing or fouled spark plugs.
Starts Hard or Fails to Start	Worn spark plugs, improperly set automatic choke, ice (or water) in fuel system.
Stalls Frequently	Automatic choke improperly adjusted and possible dirty air filter or fuel filter.
Performs Sluggishly	Worn spark plugs, dirty fuel or air filter, ignition timing or automatic choke out of adjustment.

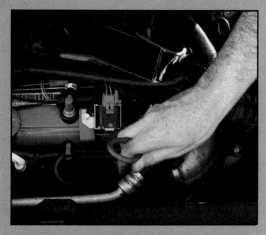

Check spark plug wires on conventional point type ignition for cracks by bending them in a loop around your finger.

Be sure that spark plug wires leading to adjacent cylinders do not run too close together. (Photo courtesy Champion Spark Plug Co.)

7. If your vehicle does not have electronic ignition, check the points, rotor and cap as specified.

8. Check the spark plug wires (used with conventional point-type ignitions) for cracks and burned or broken insulation by bending them in a loop around your finger. Cracked wires decrease fuel efficiency by failing to deliver full voltage to the spark plugs. One misfiring spark plug can cost you as much as 2 mpg.

9. Check the routing of the plug wires. Misfiring can be the result of spark plug leads to adjacent cylinders running parallel to each other and too close together. One wire tends to

pick up voltage from the other causing it to fire "out of time".

10. Check all electrical and ignition circuits for voltage drop and resistance.

11. Check the distributor mechanical and/or vacuum advance mechanisms for proper functioning. The vacuum advance can be checked by twisting the distributor plate in the opposite direction of rotation. It should spring back when released.

12. Check and adjust the valve clearance on engines with mechanical lifters. The clearance should be slightly loose rather than too tight.

SPARK PLUG DIAGNOSIS

Normal

APPEARANCE: This plug is typical of one operating normally. The insulator nose varies from a light tan to grayish color with slight electrode wear. The presence of slight deposits is normal on used plugs and will have no adverse effect on engine performance. The spark plug heat range is correct for the engine and the engine is running normally.

CAUSE: Properly running engine.

RECOMMENDATION: Before reinstalling this plug, the electrodes should be cleaned and filed square. Set the gap to specifications. If the plug has been in service for more than 10-12,000 miles, the entire set should probably be replaced with a fresh set of the same heat range.

Oil Deposits

APPEARANCE: The firing end of the plug is covered with a wet, oily coating.

CAUSE: The problem is poor oil control. On high mileage engines, oil is leaking past the rings or valve guides into the combustion chamber. A common cause is also a plugged PCV valve, and a ruptured fuel pump diaphragm can also cause this condition. Oil fouled plugs such as these are often found in new or recently overhauled engines, before normal oil control is achieved, and can be cleaned and reinstalled.

RECOMMENDATION: A hotter spark plug may temporarily relieve the problem, but the engine is probably in need of work.

Incorrect Heat Range

APPEARANCE: The effects of high temperature on a spark plug are indicated by clean white, often blistered insulator. This can also be accompanied by excessive wear of the electrode, and the absence of deposits.

CAUSE: Check for the correct spark plug heat range. A plug which is too hot for the engine can result in overheating. A car operated mostly at high speeds can require a colder plug. Also check ignition timing, cooling system level, fuel mixture and leaking intake manifold.

RECOMMENDATION: If all ignition and engine adjustments are known to be correct, and no other malfunction exists, install spark plugs one heat range colder.

Photos Courtesy Fram Corporation

Carbon Deposits

APPEARANCE: Carbon fouling is easily identified by the presence of dry, soft, black, sooty deposits.

CAUSE: Changing the heat range can often lead to carbon fouling, as can prolonged slow, stop-and-start driving. If the heat range is correct, carbon fouling can be attributed to a rich fuel mixture, sticking choke, clogged air cleaner, worn breaker points, retarded timing or low compression. If only one or two plugs are carbon fouled, check for corroded or cracked wires on the affected plugs. Also look for cracks in the distributor cap between the towers of affected cylinders.

RECOMMENDATION: After the problem is corrected, these plugs can be cleaned and reinstalled if not worn severely.

MMT Fouled

APPEARANCE: Spark plugs fouled by MMT (Methycyclopentadienyl Maganese Tricarbonyl) have reddish, rusty appearance on the insulator and side electrode.

CAUSE: MMT is an anti-knock additive in gasoline used to replace lead. During the combustion process, the MMT leaves a reddish deposit on the insulator and side electrode.

RECOMMENDATION: No engine malfunction is indicated and the deposits will not affect plug performance any more than lead deposits (see Ash Deposits). MMT fouled plugs can be cleaned, regapped and reinstalled.

High Speed Glazing

APPEARANCE: Glazing appears as shiny coating on the plug, either yellow or tan in color.

CAUSE: During hard, fast acceleration, plug temperatures rise suddenly. Deposits from normal combustion have no chance to fluff-off; instead, they melt on the insulator forming an electrically conductive coating which causes misfiring.

RECOMMENDATION: Glazed plugs are not easily cleaned. They should be replaced with a fresh set of plugs of the correct heat range. If the condition recurs, using plugs with a heat range one step colder may cure the problem.

Ash (Lead) Deposits

APPEARANCE: Ash deposits are characterized by light brown or white colored deposits crusted on the side or center electrodes. In some cases it may give the plug a rusty appearance.

CAUSE: Ash deposits are normally derived from oil or fuel additives burned during normal combustion. Normally they are harmless, though excessive amounts can cause misfiring. If deposits are excessive in short mileage, the valve guides may be worn.

RECOMMENDATION: Ash-fouled plugs can be cleaned, gapped and reinstalled.

Detonation

APPEARANCE: Detonation is usually characterized by a broken plug insulator.

CAUSE: A portion of the fuel charge will begin to burn spontaneously, from the increased heat following ignition. The explosion that results applies extreme pressure to engine components, frequently damaging spark plugs and pistons.

Detonation can result by over-advanced ignition timing, inferior gasoline (low octane) lean air/fuel mixture, poor carburetion, engine lugging or an increase in compression ratio due to combustion chamber deposits or engine modification.

RECOMMENDATION: Replace the plugs after correcting the problem.

EMISSION CONTROLS

13. Be aware of the general condition of the emission control system. It contributes to reduced pollution and should be serviced regularly to maintain efficient engine operation.

14. Check all vacuum lines for dried, cracked or brittle conditions. Something as simple as a leaking vacuum hose can cause poor performance and loss of economy.

15. Avoid tampering with the emission control system. Attempting to improve fuel econ-

FUEL SYSTEM

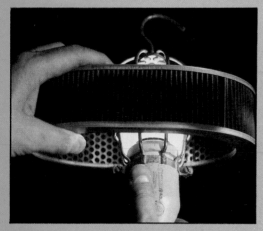

Check the air filter with a light behind it. If you can see light through the filter it can be reused.

Extremely clogged filters should be discarded and replaced with a new one.

18. Replace the air filter regularly. A dirty air filter richens the air/fuel mixture and can increase fuel consumption as much as 10%. Tests show that ⅓ of all vehicles have air filters in need of replacement.

19. Replace the fuel filter at least as often as recommended.

20. Set the idle speed and carburetor mixture to specifications.

21. Check the automatic choke. A sticking or malfunctioning choke wastes gas.

22. During the summer months, adjust the automatic choke for a leaner mixture which will produce faster engine warm-ups.

COOLING SYSTEM

29. Be sure all accessory drive belts are in good condition. Check for cracks or wear.

30. Adjust all accessory drive belts to proper tension.

31. Check all hoses for swollen areas, worn spots, or loose clamps.

32. Check coolant level in the radiator or expansion tank.

33. Be sure the thermostat is operating properly. A stuck thermostat delays engine warm-up and a cold engine uses nearly twice as much fuel as a warm engine.

34. Drain and replace the engine coolant at least as often as recommended. Rust and scale

TIRES & WHEELS

38. Check the tire pressure often with a pencil type gauge. Tests by a major tire manufacturer show that 90% of all vehicles have at least 1 tire improperly inflated. Better mileage can be achieved by over-inflating tires, but never exceed the maximum inflation pressure on the side of the tire.

39. If possible, install radial tires. Radial tires deliver as much as ½ mpg more than bias belted tires.

40. Avoid installing super-wide tires. They only create extra rolling resistance and decrease fuel mileage. Stick to the manufacturer's recommendations.

41. Have the wheels properly balanced.

omy by tampering with emission controls is more likely to worsen fuel economy than improve it. Emission control changes on modern engines are not readily reversible.

16. Clean (or replace) the EGR valve and lines as recommended.

17. Be sure that all vacuum lines and hoses are reconnected properly after working under the hood. An unconnected or misrouted vacuum line can wreak havoc with engine performance.

23. Check for fuel leaks at the carburetor, fuel pump, fuel lines and fuel tank. Be sure all lines and connections are tight.

24. Periodically check the tightness of the carburetor and intake manifold attaching nuts and bolts. These are a common place for vacuum leaks to occur.

25. Clean the carburetor periodically and lubricate the linkage.

26. The condition of the tailpipe can be an excellent indicator of proper engine combustion. After a long drive at highway speeds, the inside of the tailpipe should be a light grey in color. Black or soot on the insides indicates an overly rich mixture.

27. Check the fuel pump pressure. The fuel pump may be supplying more fuel than the engine needs.

28. Use the proper grade of gasoline for your engine. Don't try to compensate for knocking or "pinging" by advancing the ignition timing. This practice will only increase plug temperature and the chances of detonation or pre-ignition with relatively little performance gain.

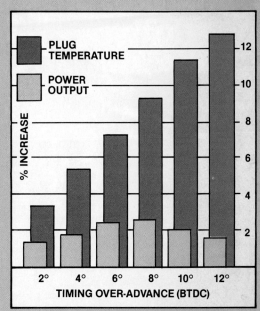

Increasing ignition timing past the specified setting results in a drastic increase in spark plug temperature with increased chance of detonation or preignition. Performance increase is considerably less. (Photo courtesy Champion Spark Plug Co.)

that form in the engine should be flushed out to allow the engine to operate at peak efficiency.

35. Clean the radiator of debris that can decrease cooling efficiency.

36. Install a flex-type or electric cooling fan, if you don't have a clutch type fan. Flex fans use curved plastic blades to push more air at low speeds when more cooling is needed; at high speeds the blades flatten out for less resistance. Electric fans only run when the engine temperature reaches a predetermined level.

37. Check the radiator cap for a worn or cracked gasket. If the cap does not seal properly, the cooling system will not function properly.

42. Be sure the front end is correctly aligned. A misaligned front end actually has wheels going in differed directions. The increased drag can reduce fuel economy by .3 mpg.

43. Correctly adjust the wheel bearings. Wheel bearings that are adjusted too tight increase rolling resistance.

Check tire pressures regularly with a reliable pocket type gauge. Be sure to check the pressure on a cold tire.

GENERAL MAINTENANCE

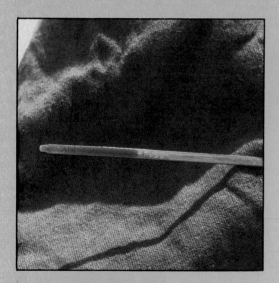

Check the fluid levels (particularly engine oil) on a regular basis. Be sure to check the oil for grit, water or other contamination.

A vacuum gauge is another excellent indicator of internal engine condition and can also be installed in the dash as a mileage indicator.

44. Periodically check the fluid levels in the engine, power steering pump, master cylinder, automatic transmission and drive axle.

45. Change the oil at the recommended interval and change the filter at every oil change. Dirty oil is thick and causes extra friction between moving parts, cutting efficiency and increasing wear. A worn engine requires more frequent tune-ups and gets progressively worse fuel economy. In general, use the lightest viscosity oil for the driving conditions you will encounter.

46. Use the recommended viscosity fluids in the transmission and axle.

47. Be sure the battery is fully charged for fast starts. A slow starting engine wastes fuel.

48. Be sure battery terminals are clean and tight.

49. Check the battery electrolyte level and add distilled water if necessary.

50. Check the exhaust system for crushed pipes, blockages and leaks.

51. Adjust the brakes. Dragging brakes or brakes that are not releasing create increased drag on the engine.

52. Install a vacuum gauge or miles-per-gallon gauge. These gauges visually indicate engine vacuum in the intake manifold. High vacuum = good mileage and low vacuum = poorer mileage. The gauge can also be an excellent indicator of internal engine conditions.

53. Be sure the clutch is properly adjusted. A slipping clutch wastes fuel.

54. Check and periodically lubricate the heat control valve in the exhaust manifold. A sticking or inoperative valve prevents engine warm-up and wastes gas.

55. Keep accurate records to check fuel economy over a period of time. A sudden drop in fuel economy may signal a need for tune-up or other maintenance.

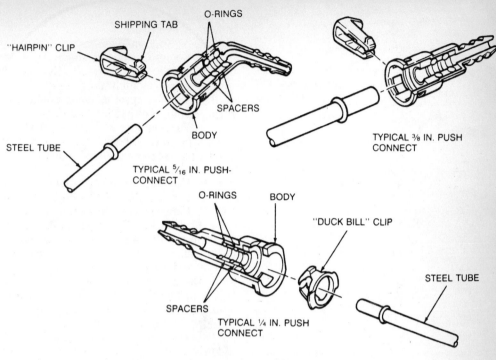

O-RINGS

SHIPPING TAB

"HAIRPIN" CLIP

STEEL TUBE

SPACERS

BODY

TYPICAL 5/16 IN. PUSH-
CONNECT

TYPICAL 3/8 IN. PUSH
CONNECT

O-RINGS   BODY

"DUCK BILL" CLIP

STEEL TUBE

SPACERS

TYPICAL 1/4 IN. PUSH
CONNECT

Various types of quick connect fuel line fittings

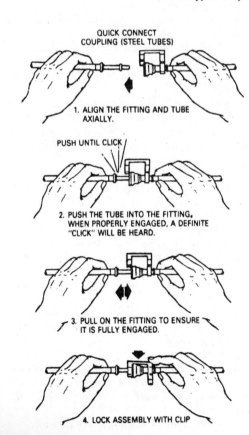

QUICK CONNECT
COUPLING (STEEL TUBES)

1. ALIGN THE FITTING AND TUBE
AXIALLY.

PUSH UNTIL CLICK

2. PUSH THE TUBE INTO THE FITTING.
WHEN PROPERLY ENGAGED, A DEFINITE
"CLICK" WILL BE HEARD.

3. PULL ON THE FITTING TO ENSURE
IT IS FULLY ENGAGED.

4. LOCK ASSEMBLY WITH CLIP

Fuel line removal and installation procedures

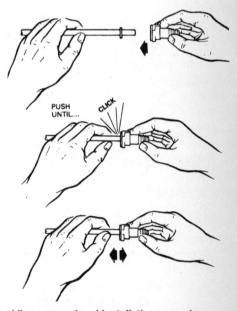

PUSH
UNTIL....   CLICK

Fuel line removal and installation procedures

which may be pulled from the connector. Both
sides of the clip must be compressed at the
same time to disengage.

3. Inspect the retaining clip, fitting end and
connector. Replace the clip if any damage is ap-
parent.

4. Push the line into the steel connector
until a click is heard, indicting the clip is in
place. Pull on the line to check engagement.

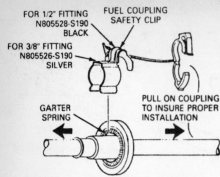

FOR 1/2" FITTING
N805528-S190
BLACK

FUEL COUPLING
SAFETY CLIP

FOR 3/8" FITTING
N805526-S190
SILVER

GARTER
SPRING

PULL ON COUPLING
TO INSURE PROPER
INSTALLATION

**SPRING LOCK COUPLING – FOR FUEL LINE TO
ENGINE FUEL RAIL CONNECTIONS**

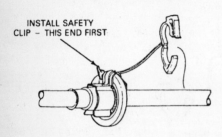

INSTALL SAFETY
CLIP – THIS END FIRST

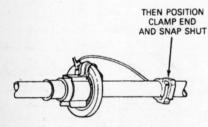

THEN POSITION
CLAMP END
AND SNAP SHUT

Fuel line removal and installation procedures

Fuel Charging Assembly

REMOVAL AND INSTALLATION

2.3L EFI Engine

1. Drain coolant from the radiator. Disconnect the negative battery cable and secure it out of the way. Relieve the fuel system pressure. Refer to the necessary service procedure in this Chapter.

CAUTION: *When draining the coolant, keep in mind that cats and dogs are attracted by the ethylene glycol antifreeze, and are quite likely to drink any that is left in an uncovered container or in puddles on the ground. This will prove fatal in sufficient quantity. Always drain the coolant into a sealable container. Coolant should be reused unless it is contaminated or several years old.*

2. Disconnect electrical connectors at:

  a. Throttle Position Sensor
  b. Injector Wiring Harness at main engine harness and at water temperature indicator sensor.
  c. Knock Sensor
  d. Air Charge Temperature Sensor
  e. Engine Coolant Temperature Sensor
  f. Disconnect air bypass valve and ignition control assembly as equipped.

3. Disconnect upper intake manifold vacuum fitting connections by disconnecting:

  a. Vacuum lines at upper intake manifold vacuum tree. Labeling the hose locations with tape is recommended to aid reinstallation.
  b. Vacuum line to EGR valve.
  c. Vacuum line to fuel pressure regulator.
  d. Canister purge line as equipped.

4. Remove throttle linkage shield, and disconnect throttle linkage, cruise control, and kickdown cable. Unbolt accelerator cable from bracket and position cable out of the way.

5. Disconnect air intake hose, air bypass hose, and crankcase vent hose. Disconnect PCV system by disconnecting hose from fitting on underside of upper intake manifold.

6. Loosen hose clamp on water bypass line at lower intake manifold, and disconnect hose.

7. Disconnect EGR tube from EGR valve by removing flange nut.

8. Remove upper intake manifold retaining nuts.

9. Remove upper intake manifold and air throttle body assembly.

10. Remove engine oil dipstick bracket retaining bolt.

11. Disconnect the push connect fitting at the fuel supply manifold and fuel return lines.

12. Disconnect the electrical connectors from all four fuel injectors and move harness aside.

13. Remove fuel supply manifold retaining bolts. Carefully remove fuel supply manifold and injectors.

NOTE: *Injectors can be removed from the fuel supply manifold at this time by exerting a slight twisting/pulling motion.*

14. Remove four bottom retaining bolts from lower manifold.

15. Remove four upper retaining bolts from lower manifold.

NOTE: *The front two bolts also secure an engine lift bracket. Remove lower intake manifold assembly.*

To install:

16. Clean and inspect the mounting faces of the fuel charging manifold assembly and the cylinder head. Both surfaces must be clean and flat.

17. Clean and oil manifold bolt threads.

18. Install a new gasket.

19. Position the lower manifold assembly to

head and install engine lift bracket. Install four upper manifold retaining bolts finger tight.

20. Install four remaining manifold bolts. Tighten all bolts to 15–22 ft. lbs. following the tightening sequence.

21. Install the fuel supply manifold and injectors with two retaining bolts. Tighten bolts to 15–22 ft. lbs.

NOTE: *Refer to Fuel Injector Installation procedure in this Chapter.*

22. Connect four electrical connectors to injectors.

23. Ensure that gasket surfaces of upper and lower intake manifolds are clean.

24. Place a new service gasket on the lower intake manifold assembly and place the upper intake manifold in position.

25. Install retaining bolts and tighten in sequence to 15–22 ft. lbs. Refer to the necessary illustration.

26. Install engine oil dipstick.

27. Connect the fuel supply and fuel return lines to fuel supply manifold.

28. Connect EGR tube to the EGR valve. Tighten to 18–28 ft. lbs.

29. Connect the water bypass line.

30. Connect the PCV system hose to the fitting on the underside of the upper intake manifold.

31. Connect upper intake manifold vacuum fitting connections by reconnecting:

    a. Vacuum lines at upper intake manifold vacuum tree.

    b. Vacuum line to EGR valve.

    c. Vacuum line to fuel pressure regulator.

    d. Canister purge line if equipped.

32. Hold accelerator cable bracket in position on upper manifold and install retaining bolts. Tighten bolt to 10–15 ft. lbs.

33. Install accelerator cable to bracket.

34. Connect accelerator cable and cruise control. Install throttle linkage shield.

35. Connect electrical connectors to:

    a. Throttle position sensor
    b. Injector wiring harness
    c. Injector wiring harness at water temperature indicator sensor.
    d. Knock sensor
    e. Air charge temperature sensor
    f. Engine coolant temperature sensor
    e. Air bypass valve and ignition control assembly if equipped.

36. Connect air intake hose, air bypass hose, and crankcase vent hose.

37. Connect negative battery cable.

38. Install engine coolant.

39. Replace fuel pressure relief cap, then build up fuel pressure as follows: without starting the engine, turn key back and forth at least six times from ON to OFF position, leaving key ON for 15 seconds each time; then check for fuel leaks.

40. Use EEC self-test connector to check proper EEC-IV system functioning.

41. Start engine and allow to run at idle until engine temperature stabilizes. Check for cooling system leaks.

42. Verify correct engine idle.

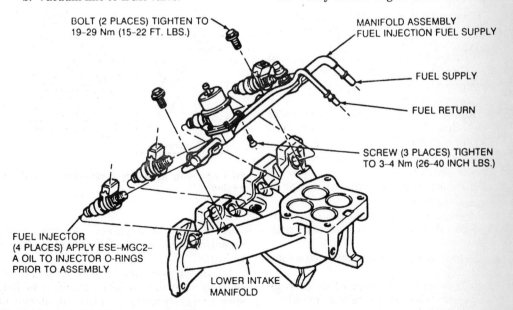

Location of the fuel lines — 2.3L EFI engine

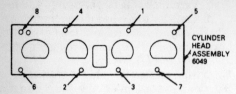

Lower manifold tightening sequence — 2.3L EFI engine

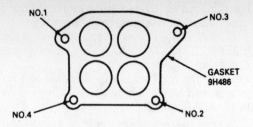

Upper manifold tightening sequence — 2.3L EFI engine

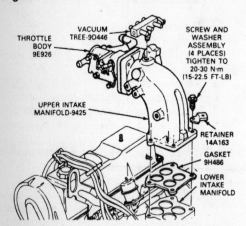

Upper manifold assembly installation — 2.3L EFI engine

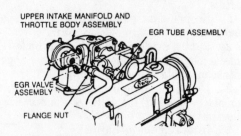

Disconnecting the EGR valve — 2.3L EFI engine

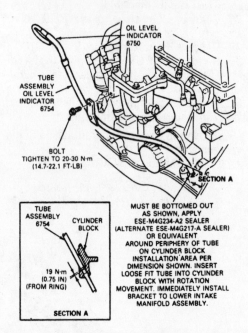

Fuel charging assembly installation — 2.3L EFI engine

2.9L Engine

1. Disconnect electrical connectors at air bypass valve, throttle position sensor, EGR sensor and air charge temperature sensor (ACT).

2. Remove air inlet tube from air cleaner to throttle body.

3. Remove snow/ice shield to expose throttle linkage. Disconnect throttle cable from ball stud.

4. Disconnect upper intake manifold vacuum connectors; both the front and rear fittings including the EGR valve and vacuum line to fuel pressure regulator.

5. Disconnect PCV closure tube from under throttle body and disconnect PCV vacuum tube from under the manifold.

6. Remove canister purge line from fitting near power steering pump.

7. Disconnect EGR tube from EGR valve by removing flange nut.

8. Loosen bolt which retains A/C line at the upper rear of the upper manifold and disengage retainer.

9. Remove six upper intake manifold retaining bolts.

10. Remove upper intake and throttle body as an assembly from lower intake manifold.

To install:

11. Clean and inspect mounting faces of the lower and upper intake manifold.

12. Position new gasket on lower intake mounting face. The use of alignment studs may be helpful.

13. Install upper intake manifold and throttle body assembly to lower manifold making sure gasket remains in place (if alignment studs aren't used). Align EGR tube in valve.

14. Install six upper intake manifold retaining bolts. Tighten to 11–15 ft. lbs.

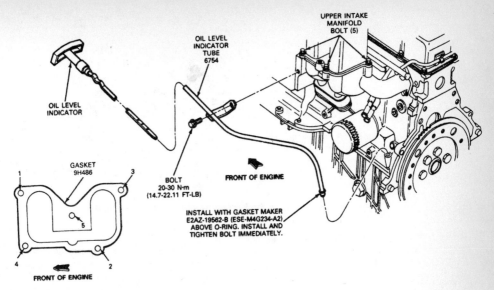

OIL LEVEL
INDICATOR TUBE
6754

UPPER INTAKE
MANIFOLD
BOLT (5)

OIL LEVEL
INDICATOR

FRONT OF ENGINE

GASKET
9H486

BOLT
20-30 N·m
(14.7-22.11 FT-LB)

INSTALL WITH GASKET MAKER
E2AZ-19562-B (ESE-M4G234-A2)
ABOVE O-RING. INSTALL AND
TIGHTEN BOLT IMMEDIATELY.

FRONT OF ENGINE

NOTE: The three bolts with stud heads go in hole
positions 2, 3 and 4.

Dipstick installation — 2.3L EFI engine

15. Engage A/C line retainer cup and tighten bolt to specification.

16. Tighten EGR tube and flare fitting. Tighten lower retainer nut at the exhaust manifold.

17. Install canister purge line to fitting.

18. Connect PCV vacuum hose to bottom of upper manifold and PCV closure hose to throttle body.

19. Connect vacuum lines to vacuum tree, EGR valve, and fuel pressure regulator.

20. Connect throttle cable to throttle body and install snow/ice shield.

21. Connect electrical connector at air bypass valve, TPS sensor, EGR sensor, and ACT sensor.

NOTE: *If lower intake manifold assembly was removed, fill and bleed the cooling system.*

3.0L Engine

1. Disconnect the negative battery cable.

2. Remove the fuel cap to vent tank pressure, then depressurize the fuel system as previously described.

CAUTION: *The fuel system is under pressure. Release pressure slowly and contain spillage. Observe no smoking/no open flame precautions. Have a Class B–C (dry powder) fire extinguisher within arm's reach at all times.*

3. Disconnect the push connect fitting at the fuel supply line.

4. Disconnect the wiring harness at the throttle position sensor, air bypass valve and air charge temperature sensor.

5. Remove the air cleaner outlet tube between the air cleaner and throttle body by loosening the two clamps.

6. Remove the snow shield by removing the retaining nut on top of the shield and the two bolts on the side.

7. Tag and disconnect the vacuum hoses at the vacuum fittings on the intake manifold.

8. Disconnect and remove the accelerator and speed control cables (if equipped) from the accelerator mounting bracket and throttle lever.

9. Remove the transmission valve (TV) linkage from the throttle lever on automatic transmission models.

10. Remove the six retaining bolts and lift the air intake/throttle body assembly off the guide pins on the lower intake manifold and remove the assembly from the engine.

11. Remove and discard the gasket from the lower intake manifold assembly.

12. Carefully disconnect the wiring harness from the fuel injectors.

13. Disconnect the vacuum line from the fuel pressure regulator.

14. Remove the four fuel injector manifold retaining bolts, two on each side.

15. Carefully disengage the fuel rail assembly from the fuel injectors by lifting and gently rocking the rail.

To install:

16. Carefully install the fuel rail assembly and injectors into the lower intake manifold, one side at a time, pushing down on the fuel rail to make sure the O-rings are seated.

17. Hold the fuel rail assembly in place and

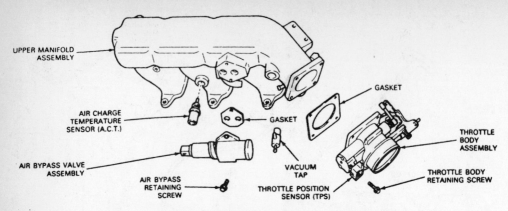

UPPER MANIFOLD
ASSEMBLY

GASKET

AIR CHARGE
TEMPERATURE
SENSOR (A.C.T.)

GASKET

THROTTLE
BODY
ASSEMBLY

AIR BYPASS VALVE
ASSEMBLY

VACUUM
TAP

AIR BYPASS
RETAINING
SCREW

THROTTLE POSITION
SENSOR (TPS)

THROTTLE BODY
RETAINING SCREW

Upper manifold and related components — 2.9L EFI engine

install the retaining bolts finger tight. Tighten the retaining bolts to 6–8 ft. lbs.

18. Connect the fuel supply and return lines.

19. Connect the fuel injector wiring harness at the injectors.

20. Connect the vacuum line to the fuel pressure regulator.

21. Clean and inspect the mounting faces of the air intake/throttle body assembly and the lower intake manifold. Both surfaces must be clean and flat.

22. Clean and oil the manifold stud threads.

23. Install a new gasket on the lower intake manifold.

24. Using the guide pins as locators, install the air intake/throttle body assembly to the lower intake manifold.

25. Install the stud bolt and five retaining bolts as illustrated finger tight, then tighten them to 19 ft.lb in the numbered sequence illustrated.

26. Connect the fuel supply and return lines

to the fuel rail.

27. Connect the wiring harness to the throttle position sensor, air charge temperature sensor and air bypass valve.

28. Install the accelerator cable and speed control cable, if equipped.

29. Install the vacuum hoses to the vacuum fittings, making sure the hoses are installed in their original locations.

30. Install the throttle valve linkage to the throttle lever, if equipped with automatic transmission.

31. Reconnect the negative battery cable.

32. Install the fuel tank cap.

33. Install the snow shield and air cleaner outlet tube.

34. Build up fuel pressure by turning the ignition switch ON and OFF at least 6 times, leaving the ignition on for at least five seconds each time. Check for fuel leaks.

35. Start the engine and adjust the idle speed, if necessary.

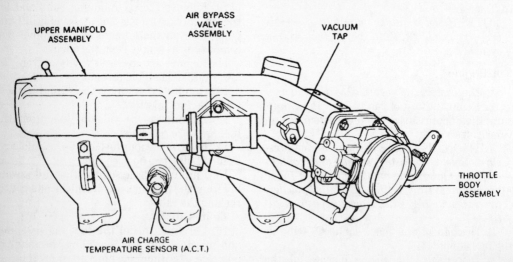

UPPER MANIFOLD
ASSEMBLY

AIR BYPASS
VALVE
ASSEMBLY

VACUUM
TAP

THROTTLE
BODY
ASSEMBLY

AIR CHARGE
TEMPERATURE SENSOR (A.C.T.)

Upper manifold and related components — 2.9L EFI engine

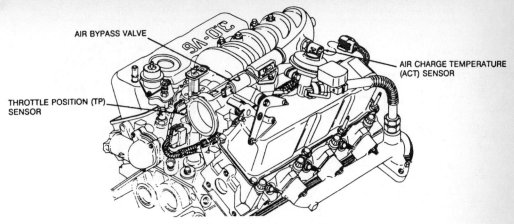

Wiring connections — 3.0L engine

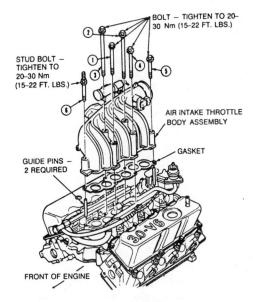

Removing the air intake/throttle body assembly. Tighten the bolts in the numbered sequence when installing

4.0L Engine

1. Disconnect the battery ground cable.

2. Remove the air cleaner and intake duct.

3. Remove the weather shield.

4. Disconnect the throttle cable and bracket.

5. Tag and disconnect all vacuum lines connected to the manifold.

6. Tag and disconnect all electrical wires connected to the manifold assemblies.

7. Relieve the fuel system pressure. Refer to the necessary service procedure in this Chapter.

CAUTION: *The fuel system is under pressure. Release pressure slowly and contain spillage. Observe no smoking/no open flame*

precautions. Have a Class B–C (dry powder) fire extinguisher within arm's reach at all times.

8. Tag and remove the spark plug wires.

9. Remove the EDIS ignition coil and bracket.

10. Remove the 4 screws retaining the throttle body to the upper manifold. Lift off the throttle body and discard the gasket.

11. Remove the 6 attaching nuts and lift off the upper manifold.

12. Remove the rocker covers.

13. Disconnect the fuel supply line at the fuel manifold.

14. Disconnect the fuel return line at the pressure regulator as follows:

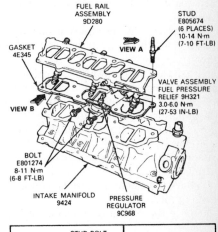

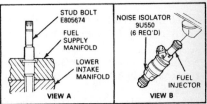

Fuel charging assembly installation — 4.0L engine

NOTE: If the fitting has been properly disengaged, the fitting should slide off the regulator with minimum effort.

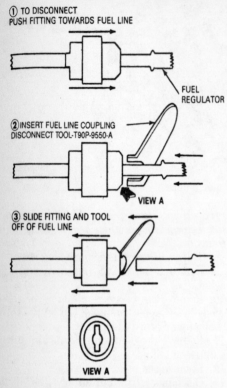

① TO DISCONNECT
PUSH FITTING TOWARDS FUEL LINE

FUEL REGULATOR

② INSERT FUEL LINE COUPLING DISCONNECT TOOL-T90P-9550-A

VIEW A

③ SLIDE FITTING AND TOOL OFF OF FUEL LINE

VIEW A

Fuel line removal and installation procedures

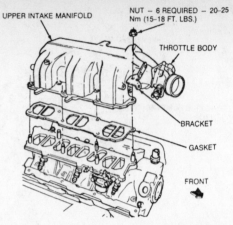

UPPER INTAKE MANIFOLD

NUT — 6 REQUIRED — 20-25 Nm (15-18 FT. LBS.)

THROTTLE BODY

BRACKET

GASKET

FRONT

Removing the air intake/throttle body assembly

a. Disengage the locking tabs on the connector retainer and separate the retainer halves.

b. Check the visible, internal portion of the fitting for dirt. Clean the fitting thoroughly.

c. Push the fitting towards the regulator, insert the fingers on Fuel Line Coupling Key T90P–9550–A, or equivalent, into the slots in the coupling. Using the tool, pull the fitting from the regulator. The fitting should slide off easily, if properly disconnected.

15. Remove the 6 Torx® head stud bolts retaining the manifold and remove the manifold.

16. Remove the electrical harness connector from each injector.

17. Remove the retaining clip from each injector.

18. Grasp the injector body and pull upward while gently rocking the injector from side-to-side.

19. Remove the lower intake manifold bolts. Tap the manifold lightly with a plastic mallet and remove it.

20. Clean all surfaces of old gasket material.

To install:

21. Apply RTV silicone gasket material at the junction points of the heads and manifold.

NOTE: *This material will set within 15 minutes, so work quickly!*

22. Install new manifold gaskets and again apply the RTV material.

23. Position the manifold and install the nuts hand tight. Torque the nuts, in 4 stages, in the sequence shown, to 18 ft. lbs. Refer to Chapter 3 for the necessary illustrations.

24. Once again, apply RTV material to the manifold/head joints.

25. Install the rocker covers.

26. Inspect the O-rings for each injector. There should be 2 for each. Replace them as required.

27. Inspect, and if necessary, replace the plastic cap covering the injector pintle. If there is no plastic cap, it may have fallen into the manifold.

28. Coat the O-rings with 5W engine oil and push/twist each injector into the fuel manifold.

29. Install the retainers and electrical harness connectors.

30. Position the fuel supply manifold and press it down firmly until the injectors are fully seated in the fuel supply manifold and lower intake manifold.

31. Install the 6 Torx® head bolts and tighten them to 7–10 ft. lbs.

32. Install the fuel supply line and tighten the fitting to 15–18 ft. lbs.

33. Install the fuel return line on the regulator by pushing it onto the fuel pressure regulator line of to the shoulder.

WARNING: *The connector should grip the line securely!*

34. Install the connector retainer and snap the two halves of the retainer together.

35. Install the upper manifold. Tighten the nuts to 18 ft. lbs.

36. Install the EDIS coil.

37. Connect the fuel and return lines.

38. Ensure that the mating surfaces of the throttle body and upper manifold are clean and free of gasket material.

39. Install a new gasket on the manifold and position the throttle body on the manifold. Tighten the bolts to 76–106 inch lbs.

40. Connect all wires.

41. Connect all vacuum lines.

42. Connect the throttle linkage.

43. Install the weather shield.

44. Install the air cleaner and duct.

45. Fill and bleed the cooling system.

46. Connect the battery ground.

47. Run the engine and check for leaks.

Air Throttle Body

REMOVAL AND INSTALLATION

2.3L EFI Engine

1. Disconnect the negative battery cable. Remove throttle linkage shield and throttle cable and cruise control.

2. Remove throttle position sensor electrical connector.

3. Remove air intake hose, air bypass hose, and crankcase vent hose.

4. Remove two throttle body nuts (lower) and two bolts (upper).

5. Carefully separate air throttle body from upper intake manifold.

6. Remove and discard gasket between throttle body and upper intake manifold.

WARNING: *If scraping is necessary, be careful not to damage gasket surfaces of throttle body and upper manifold assemblies, or allow material to drop into manifold.*

To install:

7. Ensure that both throttle body and upper intake manifold gasket surfaces are clean.

8. Install throttle body gasket on the two lower studs of the upper intake manifold.

9. Install throttle body to upper intake manifold and secure with two retaining nuts and two bolts (hand start all first-then evenly tighten) Tighten to 12–25 ft. lbs.

10. Connect throttle position sensor electrical connectors, throttle cable, cruise control, air intake hose, air bypass hose, and crankcase vent hose.

11. Connect throttle linkage shield. Connect battery cable start engine and check for proper operation.

2.9L EFI Engine

1. Disconnect the negative battery cable. Disconnect throttle position sensor electrical connector.

2. Remove air inlet duct.

3. Remove snow/ice shield and disconnect throttle cable from ball stud.

4. Disconnect air bypass hose, PCV closure hose, and canister purge hose from the fittings beneath throttle body.

5. Remove four screws retaining throttle body to upper intake manifold.

6. Carefully separate air throttle body from upper intake manifold.

7. Remove and discard gasket between throttle body and upper intake manifold.

To install:

8. Ensure that both throttle body and upper intake manifold gasket surfaces are clean.

9. Install throttle body and gasket to the upper intake manifold. Tighten retaining screws to 6–9 ft. lbs.

10. Reconnect all electrical, vacuum and battery connections. Start engine and check for proper operation.

3.0L Engine

1. Disconnect the negative battery cable. Remove the air cleaner outlet tube.

2. Remove the snow shield by removing the three plastic retainers.

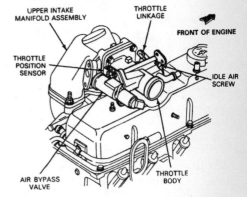

Throttle body replacement — 2.3L EFI engine

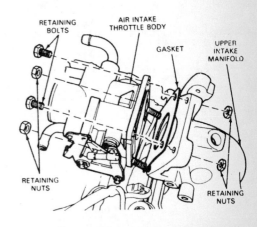

Throttle body assembly — 2.3L EFI engine

3. Matchmark and disconnect the vacuum and PCV hoses.

4. Disconnect and remove the accelerator and speed control cables (if equipped) from the accelerator mounting bracket and throttle lever.

5. Disconnect the wiring harness at the throttle position sensor, air bypass valve and air charge temperature sensor.

6. Remove the 4 retaining bolts and 2 stud bolts and lift the air intake/throttle body assembly off the lower intake manifold.

7. Remove and discard the gasket.

To install:

8. Clean and inspect the mounting faces of the throttle body assembly and the lower intake manifold. Both surfaces must be clean and flat.

9. Install a new gasket on the lower intake manifold.

10. Install the air throttle body assembly on the lower intake manifold.

11. Install the bolts finger tight, then tighten them evenly in sequence from the center outward (see illustration in this Chapter) to 19 ft. lbs.

12. Connect the wiring harness to the throttle position sensor, air charge temperature sensor and air bypass valve.

13. Install the accelerator cable and speed control cable, if equipped.

14. Install the vacuum hoses to the vacuum fittings, making sure the hoses are installed in their original locations.

15. Install the snow shield and air cleaner outlet tube. Reconnect the battery cable, start engine and check for proper operation.

4.0L Engine

1. Disconnect the negative battery cable. Remove the air cleaner inlet tube.

2. Remove the snow shield.

3. Disconnect the throttle cable at the ball stud.

4. Disconnect the canister purge hose from under the throttle body.

5. Disconnect the wiring harness at the throttle position sensor.

6. Remove the 4 retaining bolts and lift the throttle body assembly off the upper intake manifold.

7. Remove and discard the gasket.

To install:

8. Clean and inspect the mounting faces of the throttle body assembly and the upper intake manifold. Both surfaces must be clean and flat.

9. Install a new gasket on the manifold.

10. Install the air throttle body assembly on the intake manifold.

11. Install the bolts finger tight, then tighten them evenly to 76–106 inch lbs.

12. Connect the wiring harness to the throttle position sensor.

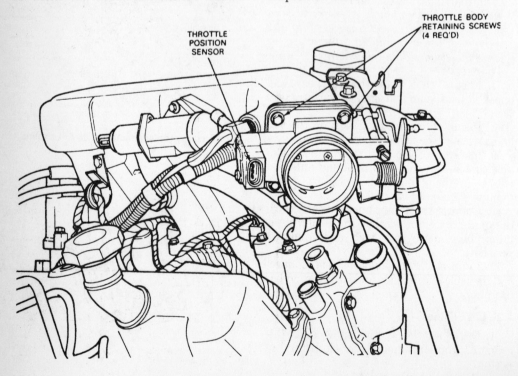

Throttle body replacement — 2.9L EFI engine

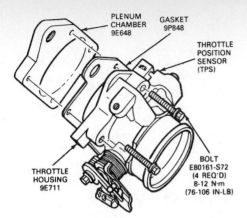

Throttle body assembly — 4.0L EFI engine

13. Install the canister purge hose.

14. Install the snow shield and air cleaner outlet tube. Reconnect the battery cable. Start engine, check for proper operation.

Air Bypass Valve

REMOVAL AND INSTALLATION

2.3L Engine

1. Disconnect the electrical connector at the air bypass valve.

2. Remove the air cleaner cover.

3. Separate the air bypass valve and gasket from the air cleaner by removing the three mounting bolts.

4. Install the air bypass valve and gasket to the air cleaner cover and tighten the retaining bolts to 6–8 ft. lbs.

5. Install the air cleaner cover.

6. Reconnect the air bypass valve electrical connector.

2.9L And 3.0L Engines

1. Disconnect the air bypass valve connector.

2. Remove the air bypass valve retaining screws.

3. Remove the air bypass valve and gasket from the air intake/throttle body assembly. If scraping is necessary to remove old gasket material, be careful not to damage the air bypass valve or throttle body gasket mounting surfaces. Do not allow any foreign material to drop into the throttle body during service.

4. Installation is the reverse of removal. Tighten the mounting bolts to 6–8 ft. lbs.

4.0L

1. Disconnect the air bypass valve connector.

2. Remove the air bypass valve retaining screws.

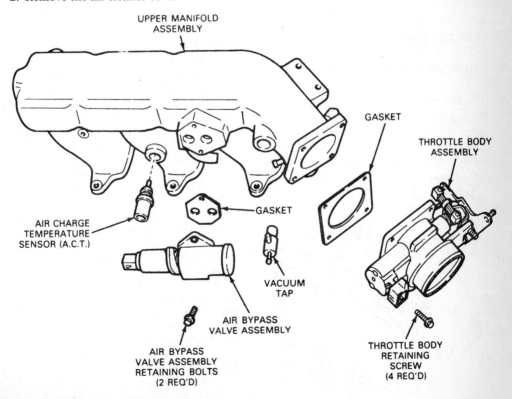

Air bypass valve assembly — 3.0L engine

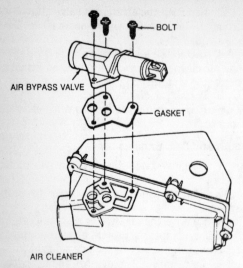

Air bypass valve mounting — 2.3L engine

3. Remove the air bypass valve and gasket from the air intake/throttle body assembly. If scraping is necessary to remove old gasket material, be careful not to damage the air bypass valve or throttle body gasket mounting surfaces. Do not allow any foreign material to drop into the throttle body during service.

4. Installation is the reverse of removal procedure. Tighten the mounting bolts to 6–8 ft. lbs.

Fuel Supply Manifold Assembly

REMOVAL AND INSTALLATION

2.3L EFI Engine

1. Remove fuel tank cap and release pressure from the fuel system by opening the pressure relief valve on the fuel line in the upper RH corner of the engine compartment using

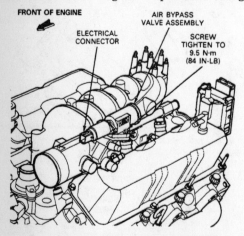

Air bypass valve assembly — 2.9L engine

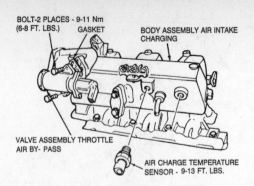

Air bypass valve — 4.0L engine

EFI Pressure Gauge T80L–9974–B or equivalent.

NOTE: *The cap on the relief valve must be removed.*

2. Remove the upper intake manifold as outlined in this Chapter as necessary. Remove injector electrical connector.

3. Disconnect spring lock coupling retainer clips from the fuel inlet and return fittings. Disconnect push connect fitting at the fuel supply manifold and return lines. Remove two fuel supply manifold retaining bolts.

4. Carefully disengage manifold and fuel injectors from engine and remove manifold and injectors.

NOTE: *The injectors may be removed from the manifold at this point, following instructions outlined under Fuel Injector Removal.*

To install:

5. Lubricate new O-rings with light grade oil ESF–M6C2–A or equivalent and install two on each injector (one per injector if injectors were not removed from fuel supply manifold).

6. Install the fuel injector supply manifold and injectors into the intake manifold, making sure the injectors are well seated.

7. Secure the fuel manifold assembly using two retaining bolts. Tighten to 15–22 ft. lbs.

8. Connect fuel supply and return lines to fuel supply manifold. Reinstall spring lock coupling retainer clips on fuel inlet and return fittings.

9. Install the upper intake manifold assembly as outlined.

10. Connect injector electrical connectors. Start the engine and let idle for 2 minutes. Turn engine OFF and check for fuel leaks where the fuel injector is installed in the fuel rail, intake manifold or cylinder head.

2.9L EFI Engine

1. Thoroughly clean the engine.
2. Depressurize the fuel system.
3. Remove upper manifold assembly.

4. Disconnect the fuel supply and return line connections at the fuel supply manifold.

5. Remove four fuel supply manifold retaining bolts.

6. Using Spring Lock coupling Tools D87L–

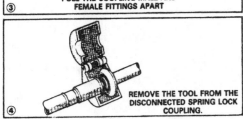

Fuel line removal and installation procedures

9280–A or B or equivalent, disconnect the cross-over fuel hose from the fuel supply manifold.

7. Carefully disengage fuel supply manifold from lower intake manifold. The fuel injectors are retained in the fuel supply manifold with clips.

8. Installation is the reverse of the service removal procedure. Make sure the injectors are fully seated in the fuel rail cups and intake manifold all fuel line connections are connected properly. Start the engine and let idle for 2 minutes. Turn engine OFF and check for fuel leaks where the fuel injector is installed in the fuel rail and intake manifold.

6-3.0L Engine

1. Remove the air intake/throttle body assembly as previously described. Be sure to depressurize the fuel system before disconnecting any fuel lines.

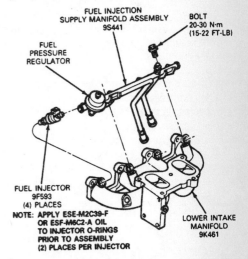

Fuel supply manifold installation — 2.3L EFI engine

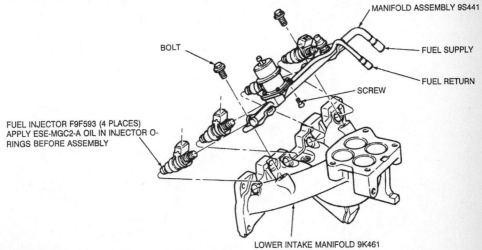

Fuel supply manifold — 2.3L EFI engine

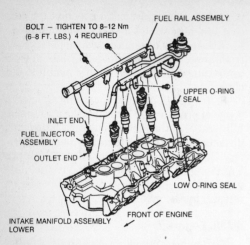

Fuel rail and injectors — 3.0L engine

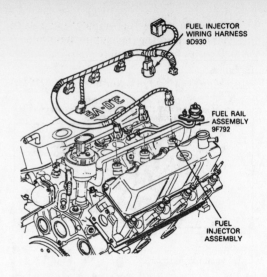

Fuel rail assembly — 3.0L engine

CAUTION: *The fuel system is under pressure. Release pressure slowly and contain spillage. Observe no smoking/no open flame precautions. Have a Class B–C (dry powder) fire extinguisher within arm's reach at all times.*

2. Carefully disconnect the wiring harness from the fuel injectors.

3. Disconnect the vacuum line from the fuel pressure regulator.

4. Remove the four fuel injector manifold retaining bolts, two on each side.

5. Carefully disengage the fuel rail assembly from the fuel injectors by lifting and gently rocking the rail.

6. Remove the fuel injectors from the intake manifold by lifting while gently rocking from side to side. Place all removed components on a clean surface to prevent contamination by dirt or grease.

CAUTION: *Injectors and fuel rail must be handles with extreme care to prevent damage to sealing areas and sensitive fuel metering orifices.*

7. Examine the injector O-rings for deterioration or damage and install new O-rings, if required (two per injector).

To install:

8. Make sure the injector caps are clean and free from contamination or damage.

9. Lubricate all O-rings with clean engine oil, then install the injectors in the fuel rail using a light twisting/pushing motion.

10. Carefully install the fuel rail assembly and injectors into the lower intake manifold, one side at a time, pushing down on the fuel rail to make sure the O-rings are seated.

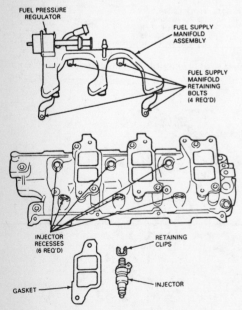

Fuel supply manifold — 2.9L EFI engine

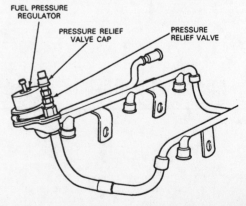

Fuel pressure relief valve — 3.0L engine

11. Hold the fuel rail assembly in place and install the retaining bolts finger tight. Tighten the retaining bolts to 6–8 ft. lbs.

12. Connect the fuel supply and return lines.

13. Connect the fuel injector wiring harness at the injectors.

14. Connect the vacuum line to the fuel pressure regulator.

15. Install the air intake/throttle body as previously described.

4.0L Engine

1. Disconnect the battery ground cable.

2. Remove the air cleaner and intake duct.

3. Remove the weather shield.

4. Disconnect the throttle cable and bracket.

5. Tag and disconnect all vacuum lines connected to the manifold.

6. Tag and disconnect all electrical wires connected to the manifold assemblies.

7. Relieve the fuel system pressure.

CAUTION: *The fuel system is under pressure. Release pressure slowly and contain spillage. Observe no smoking/no open flame precautions. Have a Class B–C (dry powder) fire extinguisher within arm's reach at all times.*

8. Tag and remove the spark plug wires.

9. Remove the EDIT ignition coil and bracket.

10. Remove the 4 screws retaining the throttle body to the upper manifold. Lift off the throttle body and discard the gasket.

11. Remove the 6 attaching nuts and lift off the upper manifold.

12. Disconnect the fuel supply line at the fuel manifold.

13. Disconnect the fuel return line at the pressure regulator as follows:

    a. Disengage the locking tabs on the connector retainer and separate the retainer halves.

    b. Check the visible, internal portion of the fitting for dirt. Clean the fitting thoroughly.

    c. Push the fitting towards the regulator, insert the fingers on Fuel Line Coupling Key T90P–9550–A, or equivalent, into the slots in the coupling. Using the tool, pull the fitting from the regulator. The fitting should slide off easily, if properly disconnected.

14. Remove the 6 Torx® head stud bolts retaining the manifold and remove the manifold.

To install:

15. Position the fuel supply manifold and press it down firmly until the injectors are fully seated in the fuel supply manifold and lower intake manifold.

16. Install the 6 Torx® head bolts and tighten them to 7–10 ft. lbs.

17. Install the fuel supply line and tighten the fitting to 15–18 ft. lbs.

18. Install the fuel return line on the regulator by pushing it onto the fuel pressure regulator line of to the shoulder.

WARNING: *The connector should grip the line securely!*

19. Install the connector retainer and snap the two halves of the retainer together.

20. Install the upper manifold. Tighten the nuts to 18 ft. lbs.

21. Install the EDIS coil.

22. Connect the fuel and return lines.

23. Ensure that the mating surfaces of the throttle body and upper manifold are clean and free of gasket material.

24. Install a new gasket on the manifold and position the throttle body on the manifold. Tighten the bolts to 76–106 inch lbs.

25. Connect all wires.

26. Connect all vacuum lines.

27. Connect the throttle linkage.

28. Install the weather shield.

29. Install the air cleaner and duct.

30. Fill and bleed the cooling system.

31. Connect the battery ground.

32. Run the engine and check for leaks.

Fuel Pressure Regulator

REMOVAL AND INSTALLATION

4-2.3L EFI Engine

1. Ensure assembly is depressurized by removing fuel tank cap and releasing pressure from fuel system by opening the pressure relief valve on the fuel line in the upper RH corner of the engine compartment. Use EFI Pressure Gauge T80L–9974–B or equivalent.

2. Remove vacuum line at pressure regulator.

3. Remove three Allen retaining screws from regulator housing.

4. Remove pressure regulator assembly, gasket and O-ring. Discard gasket and inspect O-ring for signs of cracks or deterioration.

5. If scraping is necessary, be careful not to damage fuel pressure regulator or fuel supply line gasket surfaces.

To install:

6. Lubricate fuel pressure regulator O-ring with light oil ESF–M6C2–A or equivalent.

NOTE: *Never use silicone grease. It will clog the injectors.*

7. Make sure gasket surfaces of fuel pressure regulator and fuel injection manifold are clean.

8. Install O-ring and new gasket on regulator.

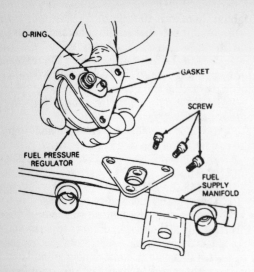

Fuel pressure regulator — 2.3L EFI engine

9. Install fuel pressure regulator on injector manifold. Tighten three retaining screws to 26–40 in. lbs.

10. Install vacuum line at pressure regulator.

2.9L EFI Engine

1. Depressurize the fuel system as described earlier.

2. Remove the vacuum line at the pressure regulator.

3. Disconnect the fuel return line from the fuel pressure regulator. See illustration.

4. Remove the 2 retaining screws from the regulator housing.

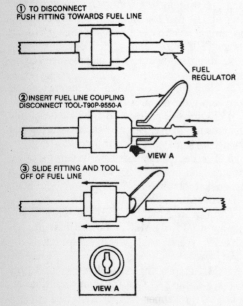

Disconnect fuel pressure regulator line

5. Remove the pressure regulator assembly, washer and O-ring. Discard the washer and check the O-ring for signs of cracks or deterioration.

To install:

6. Clean the gasket mating surfaces. If scraping is necessary, be careful not to damage the fuel pressure regulator or supply line gasket mating surfaces.

7. Lubricate the pressure regulator O-ring with light engine oil. Do not use silicone grease; it will clog the injectors.

8. Install the O-ring and a new gasket on the pressure regulator.

9. Install the pressure regulator on the fuel manifold and tighten the retaining screws to 71–102 in. lbs. (8–11 Nm).

10. Install all fuel line connections. Make sure all fuel line connections are properly connected.

11. Install the vacuum line at the pressure regulator. Build up fuel pressure by turning the ignition switch ON and OFF at least 6 times, leaving the ignition on for at least 5 seconds each time. Check for fuel leaks.

3.0L And 4.0L Engines

1. Depressurize the fuel system as described earlier in this Chapter.

CAUTION: *The fuel system is under pressure. Release pressure slowly and contain spillage. Observe no smoking/no open flame precautions. Have a Class B–C (dry powder) fire extinguisher within arm's reach at all times.*

2. Remove the vacuum and fuel lines at the pressure regulator. See illustration in this Chapter.

NOTE: *On 3.0L engine in order to gain access to pressure regulator screws, loosen or remove fuel rail to intake manifold mounting bolt(s) as required and carefully lift pressure regulator side of the fuel rail.*

3. Remove the 2 or 3 allen retaining screws from the regulator housing.

4. Remove the pressure regulator assembly, gasket and O-ring. Discard the gasket and check the O-ring for signs of cracks or deterioration.

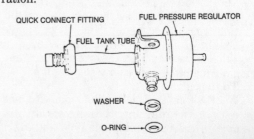

Fuel pressure regulator — 2.9L EFI engine

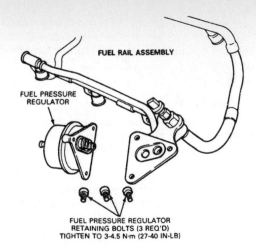

FUEL RAIL ASSEMBLY

FUEL PRESSURE REGULATOR

FUEL PRESSURE REGULATOR RETAINING BOLTS (3 REQ'D) TIGHTEN TO 3-4.5 N·m (27-40 IN-LB)

Fuel pressure regulator — 3.0L EFI engine

To install:

5. Clean the gasket mating surfaces. If scraping is necessary, be careful not to damage the fuel pressure regulator or supply line gasket mating surfaces.

6. Lubricate the pressure regulator O-ring with light engine oil. Do not use silicone grease; it will clog the injectors.

7. Install the O-ring and a new gasket on the pressure regulator.

8. Install the pressure regulator on the fuel manifold and tighten the retaining screws to 27–40 inch lbs. on the 3.0L engine and 6–8 ft. lbs. on the 4.0L engine.

NOTE: *On 3.0L engine install pressure regulator side of the fuel rail to injectors and intake manifold. Ensure that the fuel rail is fully seated and injectors are installed correctly. Tighten fuel rail to manifold bolts to 7 ft. lbs.*

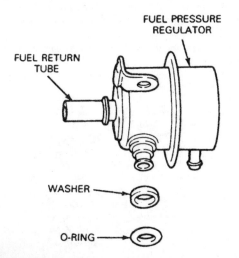

FUEL PRESSURE REGULATOR

FUEL RETURN TUBE

WASHER

O-RING

Fuel pressure regulator — 4.0L EFI engine

9. Install the vacuum and fuel lines at the pressure regulator. Build up fuel pressure by turning the ignition switch ON and OFF at least 6 times, leaving the ignition on for at least 5 seconds each time. Check for fuel leaks.

Fuel Injector

REMOVAL AND INSTALLATION

2.3L EFI Engine

1. Remove fuel tank cap and release pressure from fuel system by opening the fuel pressure relief valve using EFI Pressure Gauge T80L–9974–B or equivalent.

NOTE: *The cap on the relief valve must be removed.*

2. Carefully remove electrical connectors from individual injectors.

3. Remove fuel supply manifold as outlined.

4. Grasping injector body, pull up while gently rocking injector from side-to-side.

5. Inspect injector O-rings (two per injector) for signs of deterioration. Replace as required.

WARNING: *Do not attempt to clean the injector pintle or metering orifice with tools or brushes. Use Rotunda Injector Cleaner/ Tester 113–80001 or equivalent.*

To install:

6. Lubricate new O-rings with light grade oil ESF–M6C2–A or equivalent and install two on each injector.

NOTE: *Never use silicone grease. It will clog the injectors.*

7. Install injector(s) into fuel supply manifold. Use a light, twisting, pushing motion to install them.

8. Carefully seat fuel supply manifold assembly and injectors. Secure manifold with two attaching bolts. Tighten to 15–22 ft. lbs.

9. Connect fuel supply and return lines to fuel supply manifold. Reinstall spring lock coupling retainer clips on fuel inlet and return fittings.

10. Install the upper intake manifold assembly as outlined. Install cap on relief valve as necessary.

11. Connect injector electrical connectors. Start the engine and let idle for 2 minutes. Turn engine OFF and check for fuel leaks where the fuel injector is installed in the fuel rail and intake manifold.

6-2.9L EFI Engine

1. Depressurize the fuel system. Refer to the necessary service procedure in this Chapter.

2. Remove upper intake manifold as outlined.

3. Remove fuel supply manifold as outlined.

4. Carefully remove electrical harness connectors from individual injectors as required.

5. Remove injector retaining clips as required.

6. Grasping injector body, pull up while gently rocking injector from side-to-side.

7. Inspect injector O-rings (two per injector) for signs of deterioration. Replace as required.

8. Inspect injector "plastic hat" (covering the injector pintle) and washer for signs of deterioration. Replace as required. If hat is missing, look for it in intake manifold.

To install:

9. Lubricate new O-rings with light grade oil ESP–M6C2–A or equivalent and install two on each injector.

NOTE: *Never use silicone grease. It will clog the injector(s).*

10. Install injector(s), using a light, twisting, pushing motion.

11. Install injector retainer clip noting engagement with groove injector and flared edge of the cup. Install fuel supply manifold as outlined. Replace retainer clips if distorted.

12. Install electrical harness connectors to injectors.

13. Install upper intake manifold.

14. Make sure the injectors are fully seated in the fuel rail cups and intake manifold all fuel

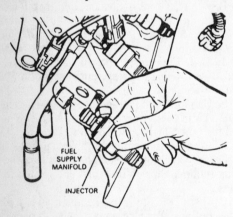

Fuel injector replacement — 2.3 EFI engine

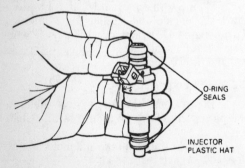

Fuel injector assembly — 2.3 EFI engine

line connections are connected properly. Start the engine and let idle for 2 minutes. Turn engine OFF and check for fuel leaks where the fuel injector is installed in the fuel rail and intake manifold.

6-3.0L Engine

For fuel injector removal and installation procedures refer to Fuel Supply Manifold Assembly service procedures in this Chapter.

4.0L Engine

1. Depressurize the fuel system. Refer to the necessary service procedure in this Chapter.

2. Remove upper intake manifold as outlined.

3. Remove fuel supply manifold as outlined.

4. Carefully remove electrical harness connectors from individual injectors as required.

5. Remove injector retaining clips as required.

6. Grasping injector body, pull up while gently rocking injector from side-to-side.

7. Inspect injector O-rings (two per injector) for signs of deterioration. Replace as required.

8. Inspect injector "plastic hat" (covering the injector pintle) and washer for signs of deterioration. Replace as required. If hat is missing, look for it in intake manifold.

To install:

9. Lubricate new O-rings with light grade oil ESP–M6C2–A or equivalent and install two on each injector.

NOTE: *Never use silicone grease. It will clog the injector(s).*

10. Install injector(s), using a light, twisting, pushing motion.

11. Install injector retainer clip noting engagement with groove injector and flared edge of the cup. Install fuel supply manifold as outlined. Replace retainer clips if distorted.

12. Install electrical harness connectors to injectors.

13. Install upper intake manifold assembly.

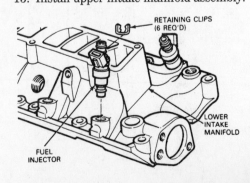

Fuel injector replacement — 2.9 EFI engine

14. Make sure the injectors are fully seated in the fuel rail cups and intake manifold all fuel line connections are connected properly. Start the engine and let idle for 2 minutes. Turn engine OFF and check for fuel leaks where the fuel injector is installed in the fuel rail and intake manifold.

DIESEL ENGINE FUEL SYSTEM

Injector Timing

2.2L Diesel Engine

NOTE: *Special tools Ford 14–0303, Static Timing Gauge Adapter and D82L4201A, Metric Dial Indicator, or the equivalents are necessary to set or check the injector timing.*

1. Disconnect both battery ground cables. Remove the air inlet hose from the air cleaner and intake manifold.

2. Remove the distributor head plug bolt and washer from the injector pump.

3. Install the Timing Gauge Adapter and Metric Dial Indicator so that the indicator pointer is in contact with the injector pump plunger and gauge reads approximately 2.0mm.

4. Align the 2°ATDC (after top dead center) on the crankshaft pulley with the indicator on the timing case cover.

5. Slowly turn the engine counterclockwise until the dial indicator pointer stops moving (approximately 30°–50°).

6. Adjust the dial indicator to 0 (Zero). Confirm that the dial indicator does not move from Zero, by rotating the crankshaft slightly right and left.

7. Turn the crankshaft clockwise until the timing mark aligns with the cover indicator. The dial indicator should read 1mm ± 0.02mm. If the reading is not within specifications, adjust the timing as follows:

a. Loosen the injection pump mounting nuts and bolts.

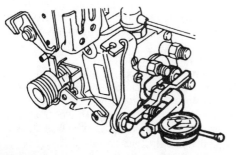

Installation of the injection pump timing gauge — 2.2L diesel engine

b. Rotate the injection pump counterclockwise (reverse direction of engine rotation) past the correct timing position, then clockwise until the timing is correct. This procedure will eliminate gear backlash.

c. Repeat Steps 5, 6, and 7 to check that the timing is properly adjusted.

8. Remove the dial indicator and adapter. Install the injector head gasket and plug. Install all removed parts.

9. Run engine, check and adjust idle RPM. Check for fuel leaks.

2.3L Engine

1. Remove top timing belt cover.

2. Rotate engine until No. 1 piston is at TDC on the compression stroke. Verify this by checking timing marks.

3. If engine temperature is below 122°F (50°C), bypass the cold start mechanism as follows:

• Insert a suitable tool and rotate the fast idle lever.

• Insert a spacer or a wrench at least 7mm thick between cold start advance lever and the cold start device.

4. Loosen, but do not remove, the two mounting bolts and two nuts attaching the injection pump to the mounting bracket and front cover.

5. To prevent the delivery valve holders from turning with the fuel line nuts, loosen, but do not remove, the nuts securing the fuel lines to the injection pump using a backup wrench.

6. Remove the timing plug bolt from the center of the fuel injection pump hydraulic head.

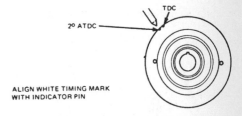

ALIGN WHITE TIMING MARK
WITH INDICATOR PIN

Aligning the timing mark — 2.2L diesel engine

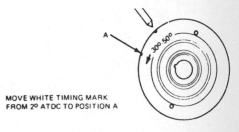

MOVE WHITE TIMING MARK
FROM 2° ATDC TO POSITION A

Moving the crankshaft pulley timing mark — 2.2L diesel engine

7. Install adapter Rotunda model 014–00303 or equivalent, into the port in the hydraulic head.

8. Mount Tool D82L-1201-A or equivalent dial indicator, in timing adapter with a minimum preload of 0.010 in. (0.25mm).

9. Rotate the crankshaft approximately 30° counterclockwise. The, set the dial indicator to zero.

10. Rotate the crankshaft clockwise to 5° ATDC and check that the dial indicator indicates 1mm ± 0.03mm.

11. If the timing is out of specification, rotate the injection pump body until the dial indicator indicates specification. Rotate the pump clockwise if the reading is more than specification, or counterclockwise if less than specification. Tighten the injection pump mounting nuts to 11–15 ft. lbs. and tighten the bolts to 15–19 ft. lbs.

12. After tightening injection pump mounting bolts and nuts, repeat Steps 9 and 10 to ensure that the injection timing has not changed.

13. Tighten the fuel line nuts at the injection pump to 17–26 ft. lbs.

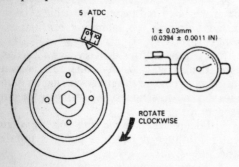

Injection timing check — 2.3L diesel engine

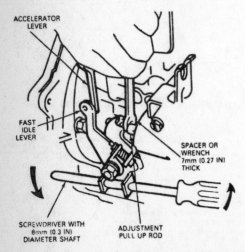

Bypassing the cold start device — 2.3L diesel engine

14. Using a new copper gasket, install the injection timing plug bolt and tighten to 10–14 ft. lbs.

15. Install the upper timing belt cover.

16. Run the engine and check for fuel leaks at the injection pump.

Fuel Filter

REMOVAL AND INSTALLATION

2.2L Engine

1. Disconnect both battery ground cables.

2. Disconnect and cap the fuel filter inlet and outlet lines.

3. Remove the two bolts/nuts attaching the priming pump to the bracket an remove the pump.

4. Remove the two bolts attaching the bracket to the engine and remove the bracket.

5. Install the fuel filter mounting bracket on the engine.

6. Install the priming pump assembly on the bracket.

7. Install the fuel filter lines and clamps.

8. Connect both battery ground cables.

9. Run the engine and check for fuel leaks.

2.3L Engine

The 2.3L diesel engine fuel filter is the paper element cartridge type and the conditioner housing includes an air vent screw to bleed air from the fuel lines.

1. Remove the rear bracket shield, attaching bolts, and unplug the electrical connectors attached to the shield. These connectors pull apart by pulling on the wire bundle on each side. Be resting the shield on the engine valve cover, the electrical connector halves leading to the fuel conditioner can be left attached to the shield.

2. Remove the rectangular filter element cartridge by unlatching holddown clamps by hand or with suitable tool, and pull element cartridge rear ward until it clears the base.

3. Clean the filter mounting pad.

4. Install the new element by pushing straight on after lining up filter element grommet holes with corresponding inlet/outlet tubes on the base.

5. Snap on the clamps.

6. Install the rear bracket shield, tighten the bolts to specification and plug the electrical connections back together. If the connectors were pulled away from the shield, push the locators back in the holes provided in the shield to secure the electrical connectors.

NOTE: *To avoid fuel contamination do not add fuel directly to the new filter.*

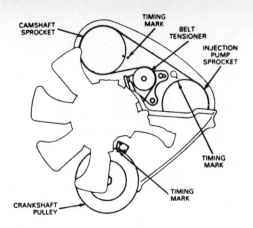

Timing mark alignment — 2.3L diesel engine

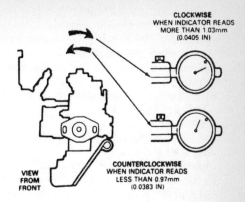

Injection timing adjustment — 2.3L diesel engine

2.3L ENGINE
FRAME-MOUNTED INLINE FUEL FILTER

The inline fuel filter is a molded plastic mesh type designed to protect the electrical fuel boost pump from contamination. It is located on the left hand side frame rail about tow feet rear of the fuel boost pump.

1. Pinch off the fuel hose to the rear of the inline filter using a rubber coated clamp or other suitable device to prevent fuel from siphoning from the tank. Care must be taken not to damage the fuel hose.
2. Remove the two hose clamps closest to the inline filter and remove filter.
3. Install replacement filter and two new clamps. Remove the hose pinch-off clamp.

2.3L ENGINE — PURGING AIR AND PRIMING FUEL FILTER

1. Turn the ignition switch **ON** to activate the electric fuel boost pump.
2. Loosen the air vent plug on the condi-

tioner housing until fuel flows from the air vent plug hole free of bubbles.
3. Tighten the air vent plug securely.
4. Start the engine and check for leaks.
WARNING: *DO NOT OPEN AIR VENT PLUG WITH THE ENGINE RUNNING!*

Injection Pump

REMOVAL AND INSTALLATION

2.2L Engine

1. Disconnect both battery ground cables.
2. Remove the radiator fan and shroud. Loosen and remove the A/C compressor/power steering pump drive belt and idler pulley, if so equipped. Remove the injection pump drive gear cover and gasket.
3. Rotate the engine until the injection pump drive gear keyway is at TDC.
4. Remove the large nut and washer attaching the drive gear to the injection pump.
NOTE: *Care should be taken not to drop the washer into timing gear case.*

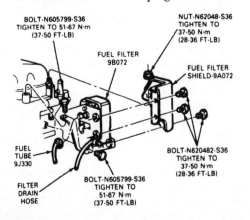

Fuel conditioner filter replacement — 2.3L diesel engine

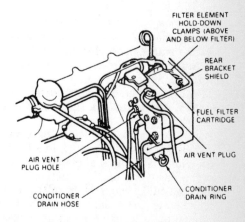

Purging and priming the fuel filter — 2.3L diesel engine

5. Disconnect the intake hose from the air cleaner and intake manifold.

6. Disconnect the throttle cable and the speed control cable, if so equipped.

7. Disconnect and cap the fuel inlet line at injection pump.

8. Disconnect the fuel shut-off solenoid lead at the injection pump.

9. Disconnect and remove the fuel injection lines from the nozzles and injection pump. Cap all the fuel lines and fittings.

10. Disconnect the lower fuel return line from the injection pump and the fuel hoses. Loosen the lower No. 3 intake port nut and remove the fuel return line.

11. Remove the two nuts attaching the injection pump to the front timing gear cover and one bolt attaching the pump to the rear support bracket.

12. Install a Gear and Hub Remover, Tool T83T-6306-A or equivalent, in the drive gear cover and attach to the injection pump drive gear. Rotate the screw clockwise until the injection pump disengages from the drive gear. Remove the injection pump.

NOTE: *Carefully remove the injection pump to avoid dropping the key into the timing gear case. Disconnect the cold start cable before removing the injection pump from the vehicle.*

Connect the cold start cable to pump before positioning the injection pump in the timing gear case.

13. Install the injection pump in position in the timing gear case aligning the key with keyway in the drive gear in the TDC position.

NOTE: *Use care to avoid dropping the key in the timing gear case.*

14. Install the nuts and washers attaching the injection pump to the timing gear case and tighten to draw the injection pump into position.

NOTE: *Do not tighten at this time.*

15. Install the bolt attaching the injection pump to the rear support. Install the washer and nut attaching the injection drive gear to the injection pump and tighten.

16. Install the injection pump drive gear cover, with a new gasket, on the timing gear case cover and tighten.

17. Adjust the injection timing at this time.

18. Install the lower fuel return line to the injection pump and intake manifold stud. Tighten the Banjo bolt on the injection pump and nut on the intake manifold. Install the connecting fuel hoses and clamps. Install the fuel injection lines to the injection pump an nozzles.

19. Connect the lead to fuel shut-off solenoid on the injection pump Connect the fuel inlet line to the injection pump and install the hose clamp.

20. Install the throttle cable and speed control cable, if so equipped.

21. Air bleed the fuel system.

22. Install the intake hose on the air cleaner and intake manifold.

23. Install the A/C compressor/power steering pump drive belt and idler pulley, if so equipped.

24. Install the radiator shroud and radiator fan.

25. Connect both battery ground cables.

26. Run the engine and check for oil and fuel leaks.

2.3L Engine

1. Disconnect battery ground bales from both batteries.

2. Remove radiator fan and shroud.

3. Loosen and remove accessory drive belts.

4. Rotate crankshaft in direction of engine rotation to bring No. 1 piston to TDC on compression stroke.

5. Remove upper front timing cover as outlined.

6. Loosen and remove timing belt from injection pump.

7. Remove nut attaching sprocket to injection pump.

8. Install puller T77F-4220-B1, or equivalent and remove sprocket.

9. Disconnect throttle cable and speed control cables, if so equipped.

10. Disconnect coolant hoses from injection pump wax element.

11. Disconnect hoses from boost compensator and A/C throttle kicker.

12. Disconnect fuel return line at injection pump from injection return pipe.

13. Disconnect chassis fuel return line from injection pump.

14. Disconnect and cap fuel supply line from fuel conditioner.

15. Disconnect and remove fuel lines at injection pump and nozzles. Cap all lines and fittings using Protective Cap Set, T85T-9395-A or equivalent.

16. Remove two nuts attaching injection pump to rear front case. Then remove two injection pump bracket-to-engine bracket bolts and two engine bracket-to-engine block bolts, and remove pump.

17. Position injection pump on engine and install two nuts attaching injection pump to engine rear front cover. Position injection pump bracket-to-engine bracket on engine block and install two bolts.

18. Install two injection pump bracket-to-

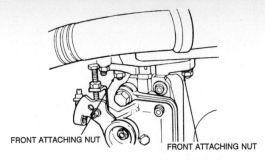

FRONT ATTACHING NUT

FRONT ATTACHING NUT

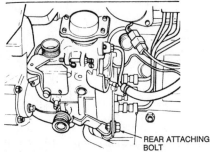

REAR ATTACHING BOLT

Injection pump attaching locations

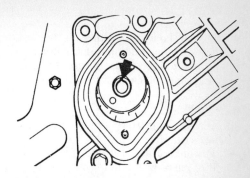

Aligning the key and keyway in the TDC position

engine bracket bolts. Tighten all nuts and bolts to specification.

19. Install injection pump sprocket. Tighten nut to 40–50 ft. lbs.

20. Install and adjust timing belt as outlined in Chapter 3.

21. Adjust injection pump timing.

22. Tighten the two injection pump retaining nuts and four bolts to specification.

23. Install injection lines on injection pump and nozzles. Tighten line nuts to specification.

24. Install fuel supply line and fuel return line on injection pump.

25. Connect nozzle returning line to injection pump.

26. Connect hoses to boost compensator and A/C throttle kicker.

27. Connect coolant hoses to injection pump wax element.

28. Connect throttle cable and speed control cable, if so equipped.

29. Install upper front cover as outlined.

30. Install accessory drive belts.

31. Install radiator fan and shroud.

32. Connect battery ground cables to both batteries.

33. Run engine and check for fuel and coolant leaks.

Fuel Injectors

REMOVAL AND INSTALLATION

2.2L Engine

1. Disconnect both battery ground cables.

2. Disconnect and remove the injection

lines from the nozzles and injection pump. Cap all lines and fittings.

3. Remove the fuel return line and gaskets.

4. Remove the bolts attaching the fuel line heater clamp to the cylinder head and position the heater out of the way.

5. Remove the nozzles, using a 27mm deepwell socket.

6. Remove the nozzle washer (copper) and nozzle gasket (steel), using Tool T71P–19703–C or equivalent.

7. Clean the nozzle assemblies with Nozzle Cleaning Kit, Rotunda 14–0301 or equivalent, and a suitable solvent, and dry thoroughly. Clean the nozzle seats in the cylinder head with Nozzle Seat Cleaner, T83T–9527–B or equivalent.

8. Position the new nozzle washers and gaskets in the nozzle seats, install the nozzles and tighten.

NOTE: *Install the nozzle gaskets with blue side face up (toward nozzle).*

9. Position the fuel line heater clamps and install attaching bolts.

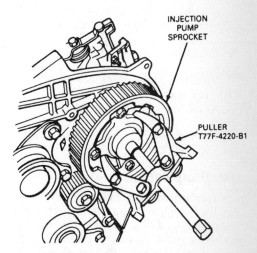

INJECTION PUMP SPROCKET

PULLER T77F-4220-B1

Removing the injection pump sprocket — 2.3L diesel engine

10. Install the fuel return line with new gaskets on nozzles.

11. Install the injection lines on the nozzles and injection pump and tighten the line nuts.

12. Connect both battery ground cables. Run the engine and check for fuel leaks.

2.3L Engine

1. Disconnect battery ground cables from both batteries.

2. Disconnect and remove injection lines from injection nozzles and injection pump. Cap all lines and fittings using Protective Cap Set, T85T–9395–A, or equivalent.

3. Remove fuel return pipe and gaskets.

4. Remove nozzles, using a 21mm deep well socket. Remove holder gasket and nozzles gasket, using O-ring Tool T71P–19703–C or equivalent.

To install:

5. Clean exterior of nozzle assemblies using brass brush from Nozzle Clean Kit, 014–00301, or equivalent, and a suitable solvent, and dry thoroughly.

6. Install new nozzle gasket and holder gasket in cylinder. Install nozzles and tighten to specification, using a 21mm deep well socket.

7. Install fuel return pipe using new gaskets. Tighten nuts to specification.

8. Install injection lines on nozzle and fuel injection pump and tighten line nuts to specification.

9. Connect battery ground cables to both batteries.

10. Run engine and check for fuel leaks.

Fuel Cut-Off Solenoid

REMOVAL AND INSTALLATION

1. Disconnect both battery ground cables.

2. Remove the connector from the fuel cut-off solenoid.

3. Remove the fuel cut-off solenoid assembly.

4. Install the fuel cut-off solenoid, with a new O-ring, and tighten.

5. Install the connector on the fuel cut-off solenoid.

6. Connect both battery ground cables. Run the engine and check for fuel leaks.

Glow Plug System

The **quick start; afterglow** system is used to enable the engine to start more quickly when the engine is cold. It consists of the four glow plugs, the control module, two relays, a glow plug resistor assembly, coolant temperature switch, clutch and neutral switches and connecting wiring. Relay power and feedback circuits

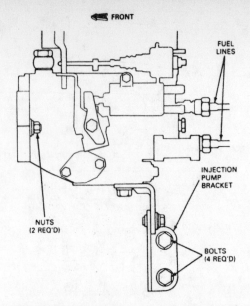

Installing the injection pump — 2.3L diesel engine

are protected by fuse links in the wiring harness. The control module is protected by a separate 10A fuse in the fuse panel.

When the ignition switch is turned to the ON position, a Wait-to-Start signal appears near the cold-start knob on the panel. When the signal appears, relay No. 1 also closes and full system voltage is applied to the glow plugs. If engine coolant temperature is below 30°C (86°F), relay No. 2 also closes at this time. After three seconds, the control module turns off the Wait-to-Start light indicating that the engine is ready for starting. If the ignition switch is left in the ON position about three seconds more without cranking, the control opens relay No. 1 and current to the plugs stops to prevent overheating. However, if coolant temperature is below 30°C (86°F) when relay No. 1 opens, relay no. 2 remains closed to apply reduced voltage to the plugs through the glow plug resistor until the ignition switch is turned off.

When the engine is cranked, the control module cycles relay No. 1 intermittently. Thus, glow plug voltage will alternate between 12 and four volts, during cranking, with relay No. 2 closed, or between 12 and zero volts with relay No. 2 open. After the engine starts, alternator output signals the control module to stop the No. 1 relay cycling and the afterglow function takes over.

If the engine coolant temperature is below 30°C (86°F), the No. 2 relay remains closed. This applies reduced (4.2 to 5.3) voltage to the glow plugs through the glow plug resistor. When the vehicle is under way (clutch and neutral switches closed), or coolant temperature is above 30°C (86°F), the control module opens

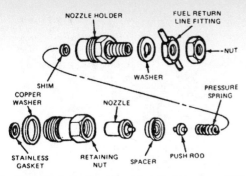

Fuel injection nozzle assembly components — 2.2L diesel engine

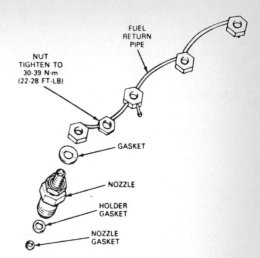

Fuel injection nozzle assembly — 2.3L diesel engine

relay No. 2, cutting off all current to the glow plugs.

TESTING THE GLOW PLUGS

1. Disconnect the leads from each glow plug. Connect one lead of the ohmmeter to the glow plug terminal and the other lead to a good ground. Set the ohmmeter on the ×1 scale. Test each glow plug in the like manner.
2. If the ohmmeter indicates less than 1 ohm, the problem is not with the glow plug.
3. If the ohmmeter indicates 1 or more ohms, replace the glow plug and retest.

REMOVAL AND INSTALLATION

1. Disconnect both battery ground cables.
2. Disconnect the glow plug harness from the glow plugs. On the 2.3L diesel engine remove the nuts attaching the bus bar to the glow plugs.
3. Using a 12mm deepwell socket, remove the glow plugs.
4. Install the glow plugs, using a 12mm deepwell socket, and tighten to 11–15 ft. lbs.
5. Install the glow plug harness on the glow

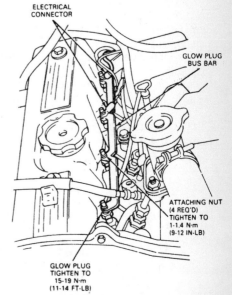

Glow plug harness and buss bar — 2.3L diesel engine

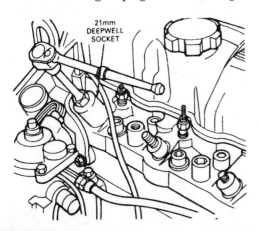

Removing the fuel injector nozzle — 2.3L diesel engine

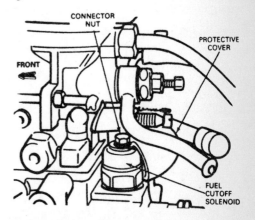

Fuel cutoff solenoid — 2.3L diesel engine

plugs. On the 2.3L diesel engine install the nuts attaching the bus bar to the glow plugs.

6. Connect both battery ground cables.

FUEL TANK

REMOVAL AND INSTALLATION

Ranger Models

MIDSHIP FUEL TANK

1. Drain the fuel from the fuel tank.
2. Loosen the fill pipe clamp.
3. Remove the bolts securing the skid plate and brackets to the frame, if so equipped. Remove the skid plate and brackets as an assembly.
4. Remove the bolt and nut from the rear strap and remove the rear strap.
5. Remove the nut from the front strap and remove the front strap.
6. Remove the clamp from the feed hose at the sender unit.
7. Remove the fuel hose from sender unit.
8. Remove the fuel vapor hose from the vapor valve.
9. Lower the tank from vehicle.
10. Remove the shield from tank.

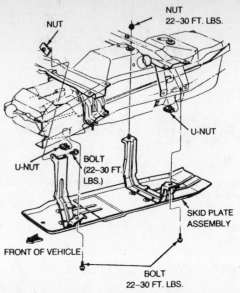

Midship fuel tank skid plate installation — Ranger models

11. Remove the front mounting bolt from the vehicle by drilling a hole in the cab floor over the bolt hole (drill dimple in floor pan).

To install:

12. Install the front mounting bolt to vehicle.
13. Attach the lower insulators to the front

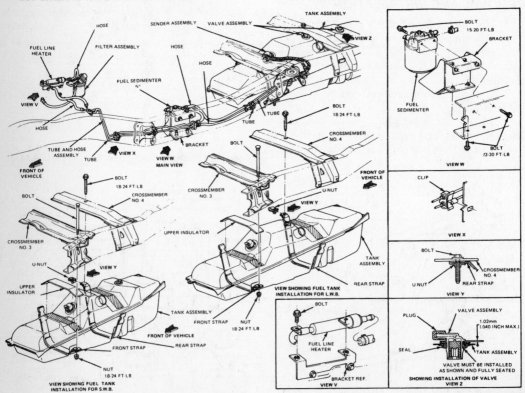

Midship fuel tank installation — diesel engine

and rear strap using adhesive ESB–M2G115–A or equivalent.

14. Attach the rear strap to the vehicle.
15. Install the shield on tank.
16. Position the tank to the vehicle. Attach the front strap to vehicle.
17. Attach the fuel vapor hose to the vapor valve.
18. Attach the fuel hose to the sender unit.
19. Install the clamps to feed and return hoses at the sender unit.
20. Install the filler pipe in position. Tighten the fill pipe clamp.
21. Install the nut to the front mounting bolt and tighten to 18–20 ft. lbs.
22. Install the bolt to the rear strap and tighten.
23. Install the skid plate and bracket assembly, if so equipped. Tighten the screws to 25–30 ft. lbs.

REAR FUEL TANK (DUAL TANKS)

1. Insert a siphon through the filler neck and drain the fuel into a suitable container.
2. Raise the rear of the vehicle. Remove the skid plate, if so equipped.
3. To avoid any chance of sparking at or near the tank, disconnect the ground cable from the vehicle battery. Disconnect the fuel gauge sending unit wire at the fuel tank.
4. Loosen the clamp on the fuel filler pipe hose at the filler pipe and disconnect the hose from the pipe.
5. Loosen the hose clamps, slide the clamps

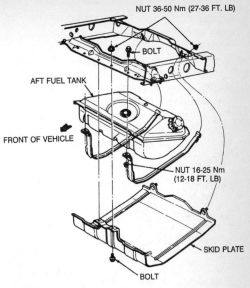

Fuel tank installation — Bronco II models

forward and disconnect the fuel line at the fuel gauge sending unit.
6. If the fuel gauge sending unit is to be removed, turn the unit retaining ring, and gasket, and remove the unit from the tank.
7. Remove the strap attaching nut at each tank mounting strap, swing the strap down, and lower the tank enough to gain access to the tank vent hose.
8. Disconnect the fuel tank vent hose at the top of the tank. Disconnect the fuel tank-to-separator tank lines at the fuel tank.

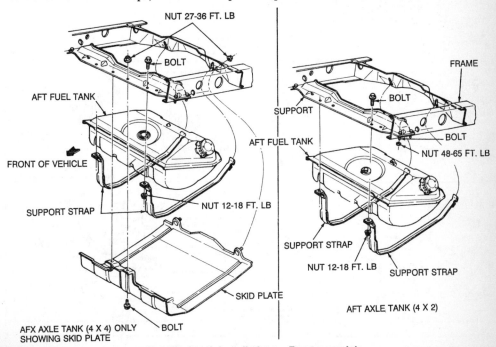

Rear fuel tank installation — Ranger models

9. Lower the fuel tank and remove it from under the vehicle

To install the fuel tank:

10. Position the forward edge of the tank to the frame crossmember, and connect the vent hose to the top of the tank. Connect the fuel tank-to-separator tank lines at the fuel tank.

11. Position the tank and mounting straps, and install the attaching nuts and flat washers.

12. If the fuel gauge sending unit was re-moved, make sure that all of the old gasket material has been removed from the unit mounting surface on the fuel tank. Using a new gasket, position the fuel gauge sending unit to the fuel tank and secure it with the retaining ring.

13. Connect the fuel line at the fuel gauge sending unit and tighten the hose clamps securely. Install the drain plug, if so equipped.

14. Connect the fuel gauge sending unit wire

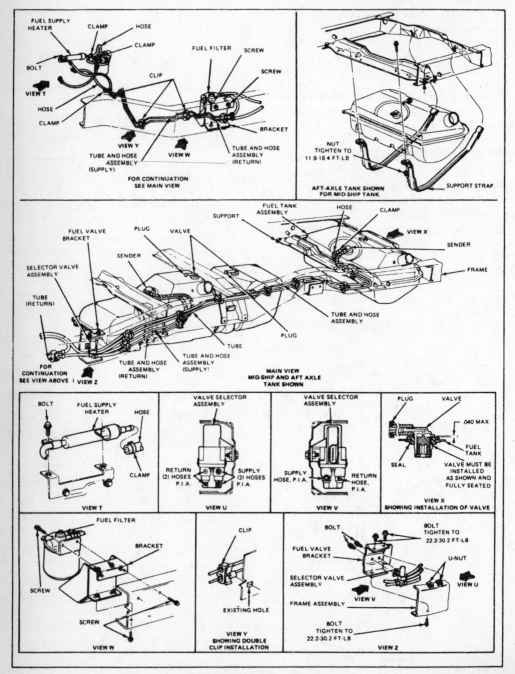

Dual fuel tank installation — diesel engine

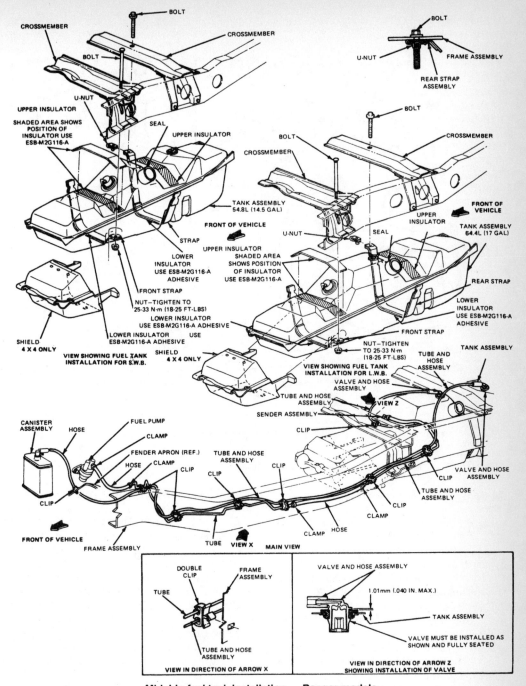

Midship fuel tank installation — Ranger models

to the sending unit.

15. Install the skid plate and tighten the mounting nuts, if so equipped.

16. Connect the filler pipe-to-tank hose at the filler pipe and install the hose clamp.

17. Connect the vehicle battery ground cable.

18. Fill the tank and check all connections for leaks.

19. Lower the vehicle.

Bronco II And Explorer Models

NOTE: *Read the entire service procedure and refer to the illustrations before starting repair--modify the service steps as necessary. Always replace all gas line hoses and retaining clamps if necessary.*

1. Insert a siphon through the filler neck and drain the fuel into a suitable container.

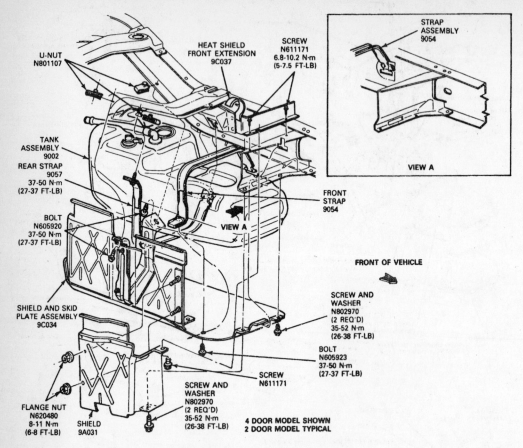

Fuel tank installation — Explorer

Drain the fuel tank by removing drain plug if so equipped.

2. Raise the rear of the vehicle and safely support. Remove the skid plate, if so equipped.

3. To avoid any chance of sparking at or near the tank, disconnect the ground cable from the vehicle battery. Disconnect the fuel gauge sending unit wire at the fuel tank.

4. Loosen the clamp on the fuel filler pipe hose at the filler pipe and disconnect the hose from the pipe.

5. Loosen the hose clamps, slide the clamps forward and disconnect the fuel line at the fuel gauge sending unit.

6. Support the fuel tank assembly. Remove the strap attaching nut at each tank mounting strap.

7. Swing the strap down, and lower the tank enough to gain access to the tank vent hose.

8. Disconnect the fuel tank vent hose at the top of the tank. Disconnect the fuel tank-to-separator tank lines at the fuel tank.

9. Lower the fuel tank and remove it from under the vehicle

10. Position the forward edge of the tank to the frame crossmember, and connect the vent hose to the top of the tank. Connect the fuel tank-to-separator tank lines at the fuel tank.

11. Position the tank and mounting straps, and install the attaching nuts and flat washers. Tighten mounting strap retaining nuts evenly.

12. Connect the fuel line at the fuel gauge sending unit and tighten the hose clamps securely. Install the drain plug, if so equipped.

13. Connect the fuel gauge sending unit wire to the sending unit.

14. Install the skid plate and tighten the mounting nuts, if so equipped.

15. Connect the filler pipe-to-tank hose at the filler pipe and install the hose clamp.

16. Connect the vehicle battery ground cable.

17. Fill the tank and check all connections for leaks.

18. Lower the vehicle.

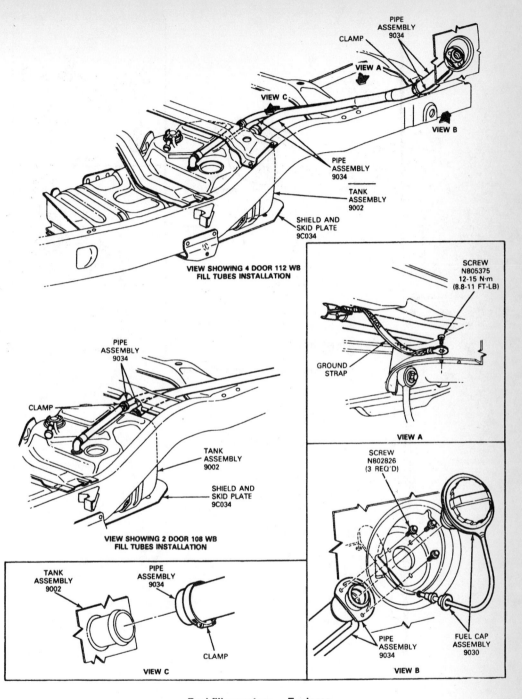

Fuel filler system — Explorer

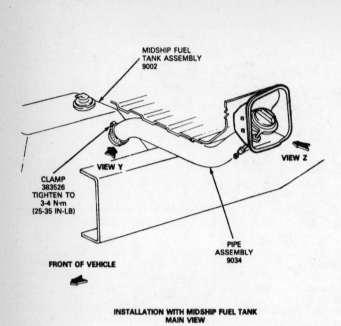

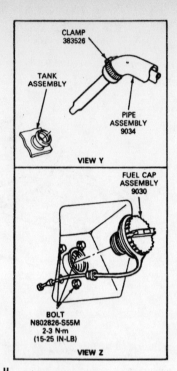

MIDSHIP FUEL
TANK ASSEMBLY
9002

CLAMP
383526
TIGHTEN TO
3-4 N·m
(25-35 IN-LB)

VIEW Y

FRONT OF VEHICLE

PIPE
ASSEMBLY
9034

INSTALLATION WITH MIDSHIP FUEL TANK
MAIN VIEW

VIEW Z

CLAMP
383526

TANK
ASSEMBLY

PIPE
ASSEMBLY
9034

VIEW Y

FUEL CAP
ASSEMBLY
9030

BOLT
N802826-S55M
2-3 N·m
(15-25 IN-LB)

VIEW Z

Fuel filler system — Ranger/Bronco II

Chassis Electrical

6

HEATING AND AIR CONDITIONING

Blower Motor

REMOVAL AND INSTALLATION

Without Air Conditioning

1. Disconnect the negative battery cable.
2. Remove the air cleaner or air inlet duct, as necessary.

3. Remove the 2 screws attaching the vacuum reservoir to the blower assembly and remove the reservoir.
4. Disconnect the wire harness connector from the blower motor by pushing down on the connector tabs and pulling the connector off of the motor.
5. Disconnect the blower motor cooling tube at the blower motor.
6. Remove the 3 screws attaching the blower motor and wheel to the heater blower assembly.

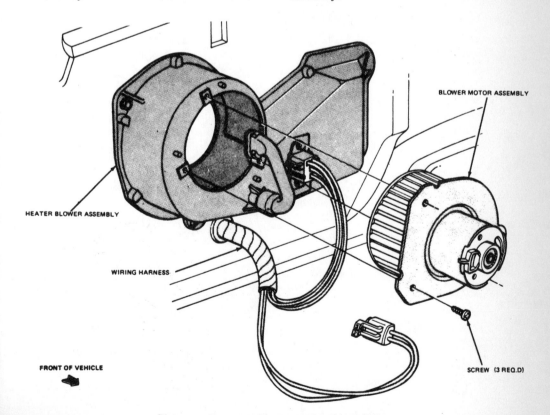

BLOWER MOTOR ASSEMBLY

HEATER BLOWER ASSEMBLY

WIRING HARNESS

FRONT OF VEHICLE

SCREW (3 REQ.D)

Blower motor assembly removal and installation

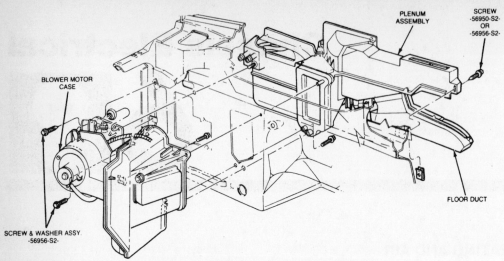

Heater blower motor case and plenum assembly

7. Holding the cooling tube aside, pull the blower motor and wheel from the heater blower assembly and remove it from the vehicle.

8. Remove the blower wheel push-nut or clamp from the motor shaft and pull the blower wheel from the motor shaft.

9. Install the blower wheel on the blower motor shaft.

10. Install the hub clamp or push-nut.

11. Holding the cooling tube aside, position the blower motor and wheel on the heater blower assembly and install the 3 attaching screws.

12. Connect the blower motor cooling tube and the wire harness connector.

13. Install the vacuum reservoir on the hoses with the 2 screws.

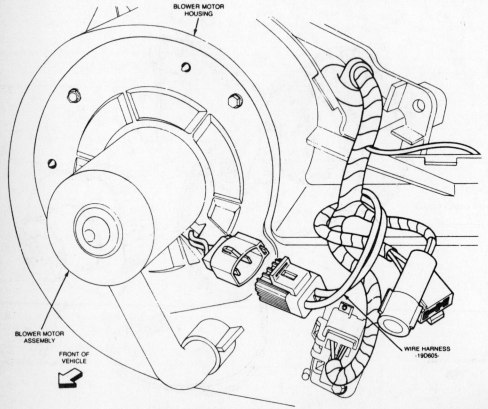

Blower motor electrical connections

14. Install the air cleaner or air inlet duct, as necessary.

15. Connect the negative battery cable and check the system for proper operation.

With Air Conditioning

1. Disconnect the negative battery cable.

2. In the engine compartment, disconnect the wire harness from the motor by pushing down on the tab while pulling the connection off at the motor.

3. Remove the air cleaner or air inlet duct, as necessary.

4. On Bronco II, Explorer and Ranger, remove the solenoid box cover retaining bolts and the solenoid box cover, if equipped.

5. Disconnect the blower motor cooling tube from the blower motor.

6. Remove the 3 blower motor mounting

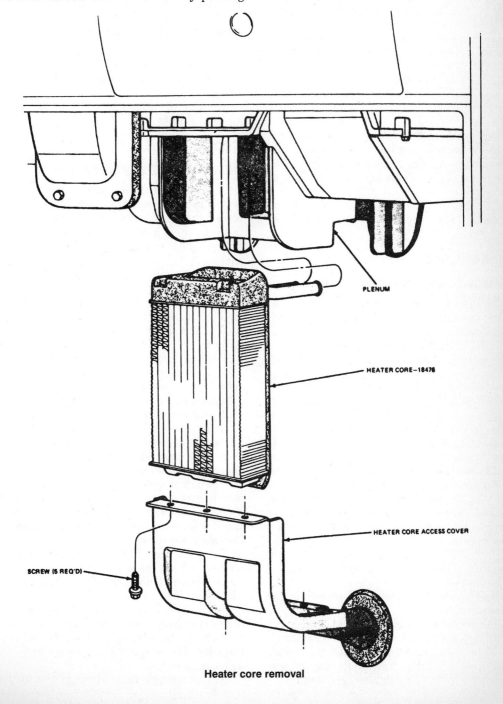

PLENUM

HEATER CORE—18476

HEATER CORE ACCESS COVER

SCREW (5 REQ'D)

Heater core removal

plate attaching screws and remove the motor and wheel assembly from the evaporator assembly blower motor housing.

7. Remove the blower motor hub clamp from the motor shaft and pull the blower wheel from the shaft.

To install:

8. Install the blower motor wheel on the blower motor shaft and install a new hub clamp.

9. Install a new motor mounting seal on the blower housing before installing the blower motor.

10. Position the blower motor and wheel assembly in the blower housing and install the 3 attaching screws.

11. Connect the blower motor cooling tube.

12. Connect the electrical wire harness hardshell connector to the blower motor by pushing into place.

13. On Bronco II, Explorer and Ranger, position the solenoid box cover, if equipped, into place and install the 3 retaining screws.

14. Install the air cleaner or air inlet duct, as necessary.

15. Connect the negative battery cable and check the blower motor in all speeds for proper operation.

Heater Core

REMOVAL AND INSTALLATION

1. Disconnect the negative battery cable. Allow the engine to cool down. Drain the cooling system.

CAUTION: *When draining the coolant, keep in mind that cats and dogs are attracted by the ethylene glycol antifreeze, and are quite likely to drink any that is left in an uncovered container or in puddles on the ground. This will prove fatal in sufficient quantity. Always drain the coolant into a sealable container. Coolant should be reused unless it is contaminated or several years old.*

2. Disconnect the heater hoses from the heater core tubes and plug hoses.

3. In the passenger compartment, remove the five screws attaching the heater core access cover to the plenum assembly and remove the access cover.

4. Pull the heater core rearward and down, removing it from the plenum assembly.

To install:

5. Position the heater core and seal in the plenum assembly.

6. Install the heater core access cover to the plenum assembly and secure with five screws.

7. Install the heater hoses to the heater core tubes at the dash panel in the engine compartment. Do not over-tighten hose clamps.

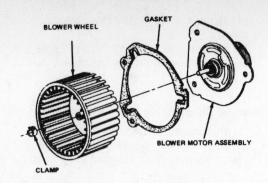

Blower wheel removed from motor

8. Check the coolant level and add coolant as required. Connect the negative battery cable.

9. Start the engine and check the system for coolant leaks.

Control Head

REMOVAL AND INSTALLATION

1. Disconnect the negative battery cable.

2. Open the ash tray and remove the 2 screws that hold the ash tray drawer slide to the instrument panel. Remove the ash tray and drawer slide bracket from the instrument panel.

3. Gently pull the finish panel away from the instrument panel and the cluster. The finish panel pops straight back for approximately 1 in., then up to remove. Be careful not to trap the finish panel around the steering column.

NOTE: *If equipped with the electronic 4×4 shift-on-the-fly module, disconnect the wire from the rear of the 4×4 transfer switch before trying to remove the finish panel from the instrument panel.*

4. Remove the 4 screws attaching the control assembly to the instrument panel.

5. Pull the control through the instrument panel opening far enough to allow removal of the electrical connections from the blower switch and control assembly illumination lamp. Using a suitable tool, remove the 2 hose vacuum harness from the vacuum switch on the side of the control.

6. At the rear of the control, using a suitable tool, release the temperature and function cable snap-in flags from the white control bracket.

7. On the bottom side of the control, remove the temperature cable from the control by rotating the cable until the T-pin releases the cable. The temperature cable is black with a blue snap-in flag.

8. Pull enough cable through the instru-

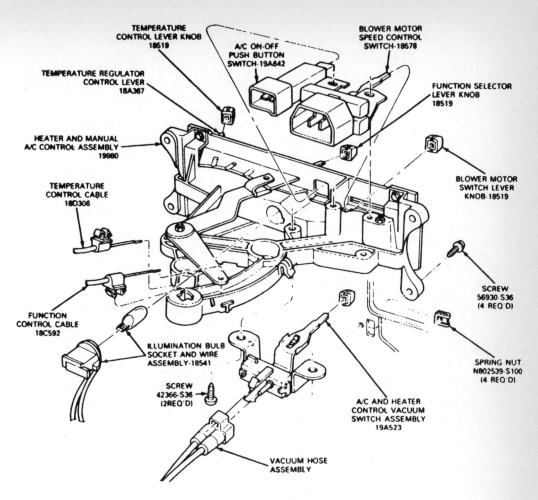

TEMPERATURE
CONTROL LEVER KNOB
18519

A/C ON-OFF
PUSH BUTTON
SWITCH-19A642

BLOWER MOTOR
SPEED CONTROL
SWITCH-18578

TEMPERATURE REGULATOR
CONTROL LEVER
18A367

FUNCTION SELECTOR
LEVER KNOB
18519

HEATER AND MANUAL
A/C CONTROL ASSEMBLY
19980

BLOWER MOTOR
SWITCH LEVER
KNOB-18519

TEMPERATURE
CONTROL CABLE
18D306

FUNCTION
CONTROL CABLE
18C592

SCREW
56930-S36
(4 REQ'D)

ILLUMINATION BULB
SOCKET AND WIRE
ASSEMBLY-18541

SPRING NUT
N802539-S100
(4 REQ'D)

SCREW
42366-S36
(2REQ'D)

A/C AND HEATER
CONTROL VACUUM
SWITCH ASSEMBLY
19A523

VACUUM HOSE
ASSEMBLY

Control head — exploded view

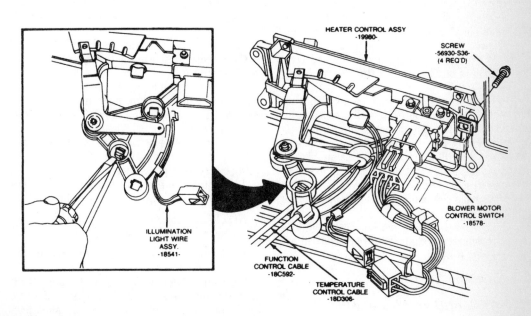

HEATER CONTROL ASSY
-19980

SCREW
-56930-S36-
(4 REQ'D)

ILLUMINATION
LIGHT WIRE
ASSY.
-18541-

BLOWER MOTOR
CONTROL SWITCH
-18578-

FUNCTION
CONTROL CABLE
-18C592-

TEMPERATURE
CONTROL CABLE
-18D306-

Control head removal

ment panel opening until the function cable can be held vertical to the control, then remove the control cable from the function lever. The function cable is white with a black snap-in flag.

9. Remove the control assembly from the instrument panel.

To install:

10. Pull the control cables through the control assembly opening in the instrument panel for a distance of approximately 8 in. (203mm).

11. Hold the control assembly up to the instrument panel with it's face directed toward the floor of the vehicle. This will locate the face of the control in a position that is 90 degrees out of it's installed position.

12. Carefully bend and attach the function cable that has a white color code and a black snap-in terminal to the white plastic lever on the control assembly. Rotate the control assembly back to it's normal position for installation, then snap the black cable flag into the control assembly bracket.

13. On the opposite side of the control assembly, attach the black temperature control cable with the blue plastic snap-in flag to the blue plastic lever on the control. Make sure the end of the cable is seated securely with the T-top pin on the control. Rotate the cable to it's operating position and snap the blue cable flag into the control assembly bracket.

14. Connect the wiring harness to the blower switch and the illumination lamp to it's receptacle on the control assembly. Connect the dual terminal on the vacuum hose to the vacuum switch on the control assembly.

15. Position the control assembly into the instrument panel opening and install the 4 mounting screws.

16. If equipped, reconnect the 4 × 4 electric shift harness on the rear of the cluster finish panel.

17. Install the cluster finish panel with integral push-pins. Make sure that all pins are fully seated around the rim of the panel.

18. Reinsert the ash tray slide bracket and reconnect the illumination connection circuit. Reinstall the 2 screws that retain the ash tray retainer bracket and the finish panel.

19. Replace the ash tray and reconnect the cigarette lighter.

20. Connect the negative battery cable and check the heater system for proper control assembly operation.

Evaporator Core

REMOVAL AND INSTALLATION

1. Disconnect the negative battery cable.
2. Discharge the refrigerant from the air

conditioning system according to the proper procedure. See Chapter 1, for the procedure.

3. Disconnect the electrical connector from the pressure switch located on top of the accumulator/drier. Remove the pressure switch.

4. Disconnect the suction hose from the accumulator/drier using the spring-lock coupling disconnect procedure. Cap the openings to prevent the entrance of dirt and moisture.

5. Disconnect the liquid line from the evaporator core inlet tube using a backup wrench to loosen the fitting. Cap the openings to prevent the entrance of dirt and moisture.

6. Remove the screws holding the evaporator case service cover and vacuum reservoir to the evaporator case assembly.

7. Store the vacuum reservoir in a secure position to avoid vacuum line damage.

8. Remove the 2 dash panel mounting nuts.

9. Remove the evaporator case service cover from the evaporator case assembly.

10. Remove the evaporator core and accumulator/drier assembly from the vehicle.

To install:

NOTE: *Add 3 oz. (90ml) of clean refrigerant oil to a new replacement evaporator core to maintain the total system oil charge.*

11. Position the evaporator core and accumulator/drier assembly into the evaporator case out-board half.

12. Position the evaporator case service cover into place on the evaporator case assembly.

13. Install the 2 dash panel mounting nuts.

14. Install the screws holding the evaporator service case half to the evaporator case assembly.

15. Place the vacuum reservoir in it's installed position. Attach the reservoir to the case with 2 screws.

16. Connect the liquid line to the evaporator inlet tube using a backup wrench to tighten the fitting. Use a new O-ring lubricated with clean refrigerant oil.

17. Connect the suction hose to the accumulator/drier according to the spring-lock coupling connection procedure.

18. Install the pressure switch on the accumulator/drier and tighten finger-tight.

NOTE: *Do not use a wrench to tighten the pressure switch.*

19. Connect the electrical connector to the pressure switch.

20. Connect the negative battery cable. Leak test, evacuate and charge the system according to the proper procedure. Observe all safety precautions.

21. Check the system for proper operation.

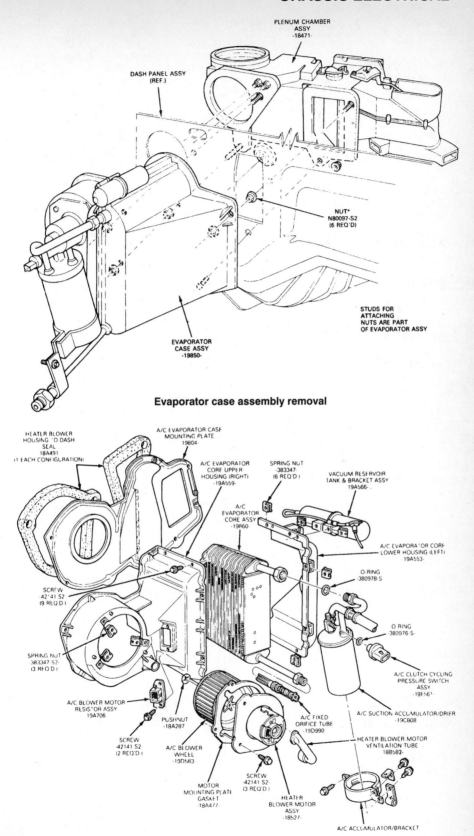

PLENUM CHAMBER
ASSY
-18471-

DASH PANEL ASSY
(REF.)

NUT*
N80097-S2
(6 REQ'D)

STUDS FOR
ATTACHING
NUTS ARE PART
OF EVAPORATOR ASSY

EVAPORATOR
CASE ASSY
-19850-

Evaporator case assembly removal

HEATER BLOWER
HOUSING TO DASH
SEAL
18A491
(1 EACH CONFIGURATION)

A/C EVAPORATOR CASE
MOUNTING PLATE
19804

A/C EVAPORATOR
CORE UPPER
HOUSING (RIGHT)
-19A559-

SPRING NUT
-383347-
(6 REQ'D)

VACUUM RESERVOIR
TANK & BRACKET ASSY
19A566-

A/C
EVAPORATOR
CORE ASSY
-19860-

A/C EVAPORATOR CORE
LOWER HOUSING (LEFT)
19A553-

O-RING
-380978-S

SCREW
-42141 S2
(9 REQ'D)

O RING
-380976-S

SPRING NUT
-383347 S2
(3 REQ'D)

A/C CLUTCH CYCLING
PRESSURE SWITCH
ASSY
-19E561-

A/C BLOWER MOTOR
RESISTOR ASSY
19A706

A/C SUCTION ACCUMULATOR/DRIER
-19C808-

PUSHNUT
-18A287

A/C FIXED
ORIFICE TUBE
-19D990

HEATER BLOWER MOTOR
VENTILATION TUBE
18B582-

SCREW
-42141 S2
(2 REQ'D)

A/C BLOWER
WHEEL
-19D583-

SCREW
-42141 S2
(3 REQ'D)

MOTOR
MOUNTING PLATE
GASKET
-18A477-

HEATER
BLOWER MOTOR
ASSY
-18527-

A/C ACCUMULATOR/BRACKET

Evaporator case assembly — exploded view

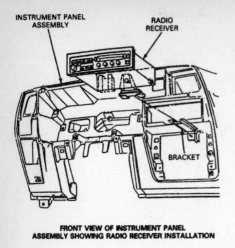

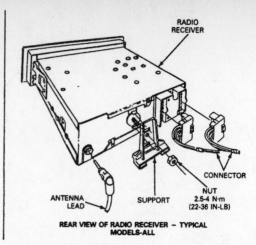

FRONT VIEW OF INSTRUMENT PANEL
ASSEMBLY SHOWING RADIO RECEIVER INSTALLATION

REAR VIEW OF RADIO RECEIVER – TYPICAL
MODELS-ALL

Radio removal and installation — ETR type

AUDIO SYSTEMS

Knob Type Radio

REMOVAL AND INSTALLATION

1. Disconnect the battery ground cable.
2. Remove the knobs and discs from the radio control shafts.
3. Remove the two steering column shroud-to-panel retaining screws and remove the shroud.
4. Detach the cluster trim cover or appliques from the instrument panel by removing the eight screws.
6. Remove the four screws securing the mounting plate assembly to the instrument panel and remove the radio with the mounting plate and rear bracket.
7. Disconnect the antenna lead-in cable, speaker wires and the radio (power) wire.
8. Remove the nut and washer assembly attaching the radio rear support.

9. Remove the nuts and washers from the radio control shafts and remove the mounting plate from the radio.

To install:

10. Install the radio rear support using the nut and washer assembly.
11. Install the mounting plate to the radio using the two lock washers and two nuts.
12. Connect the wiring connectors to the radio and position the radio with the mounting plate to the instrument panel.

NOTE: *Make sure that the hair pin area of the rear bracket is engaged to the instrument panel support.*

13. Secure the mounting plate to the instrument panel with the four screws.

NOTE: *Make sure the mounting plate is fully seated on the instrument panel.*

14. Install the panel trim covers and steering column shroud.
15. Install the panel knobs and discs to the radio control shafts.
16. Connect the battery ground cable.

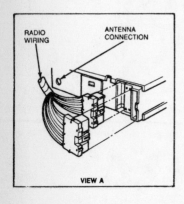

VIEW A

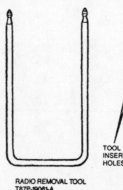

RADIO REMOVAL TOOL
T87P-19061-A

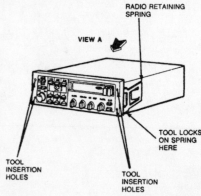

Radio removal tool and use — ETR type

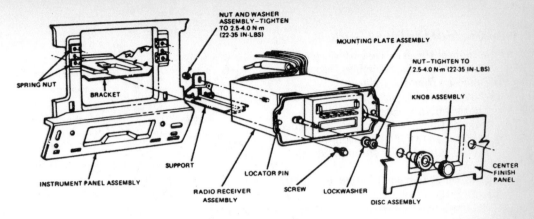

NUT AND WASHER ASSEMBLY–TIGHTEN TO 2.5-4.0 N·m (22-35 IN-LBS)

MOUNTING PLATE ASSEMBLY

NUT–TIGHTEN TO 2.5-4.0 N·m (22-35 IN-LBS)

KNOB ASSEMBLY

SPRING NUT

BRACKET

CENTER FINISH PANEL

INSTRUMENT PANEL ASSEMBLY

SUPPORT

LOCATOR PIN

RADIO RECEIVER ASSEMBLY

SCREW

LOCKWASHER

DISC ASSEMBLY

Radio removal — knob style

Electronically Tuned Radio (ETR)

REMOVAL AND INSTALLATION

1. Disconnect the negative battery cable.
2. Remove the finish panel from around the radio assembly.
3. Insert the radio removal tool T87P-19061-A or equivalent, into the radio face.
4. Pull the radio out of the instrument panel.
5. Disconnect the wiring connectors and antenna from the radio.
6. Connect the wiring and slide the radio into the instrument panel.
7. Install the finish panel and connect the battery cable.
8. Check the operation of the radio.

Equalizer

REMOVAL AND INSTALLATION

1. Disconnect the negative battery cable.
2. Remove the finish panel from around the equalizer assembly.
3. Remove the 4 equalizer mounting screws.
4. Pull the equalizer from the instrument panel and disconnect the electrical connector.
5. Connect the electrical lead and install the equalizer into the instrument panel. Install the mounting screws.
6. Install the finish panel and connect the negative battery cable.
7. Check the operation of the stereo system.

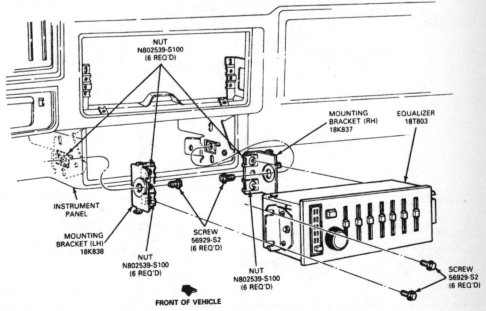

NUT N802539-S100 (6 REQ'D)

MOUNTING BRACKET (RH) 18K837

EQUALIZER 18T803

INSTRUMENT PANEL

MOUNTING BRACKET (LH) 18K838

NUT N802539-S100 (6 REQ'D)

SCREW 56929-S2 (6 REQ'D)

NUT N802539-S100 (6 REQ'D)

SCREW 56929-S2 (6 REQ'D)

FRONT OF VEHICLE

Equalizer removal and installation

Antenna

REMOVAL AND INSTALLATION

1. Disconnect the negative battery cable.
2. Remove the radio assembly. Disconnect the antenna lead from the radio.
3. Remove the antenna mast and lift the cover from the antenna base.
4. Remove the antenna base mounting screws or bolt. Remove the mounting gasket.
5. Pull the antenna wire through the opening.
6. Install the antenna in position, be sure to place the gasket properly.
7. Route antenna cable so as to avoid interference with heater operation.
8. Install the radio assembly. Connect the battery cable and check the operation of the radio.

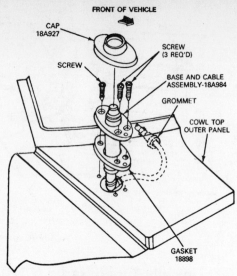

VIEW SHOWING INSTALLATION OF ANTENNA
ON COWL TOP OUTER PANEL (RH SIDE)

Antenna removal and installation

WINDSHIELD WIPERS

Wiper Arm And Blade

REPLACEMENT

To remove the arm and blade assembly, raise the blade end of the arm off of the windshield and move the slide latch away from the pivot shaft. The wiper arm can now be removed from the shaft without the use of any tools. To install, push the main head over the pivot shaft. Be sure the wipers are in the parked position, and the blade assembly is in its correct position. Hold the main arm head onto the pivot shaft while raising the blade end of the wiper arm and push the slide latch into the lock under the pivot shaft head. Then, lower the blade to the windshield. If the blade does not lower to the windshield, the slide latch is not completely in place.

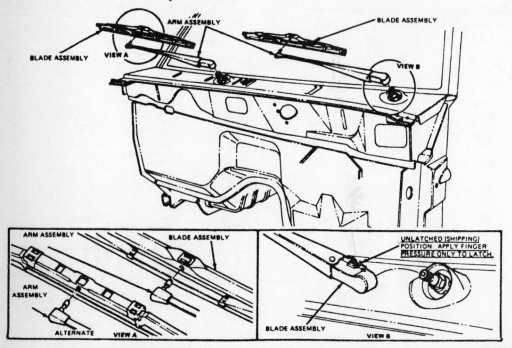

Windshield wiper arm and blade assembly installation

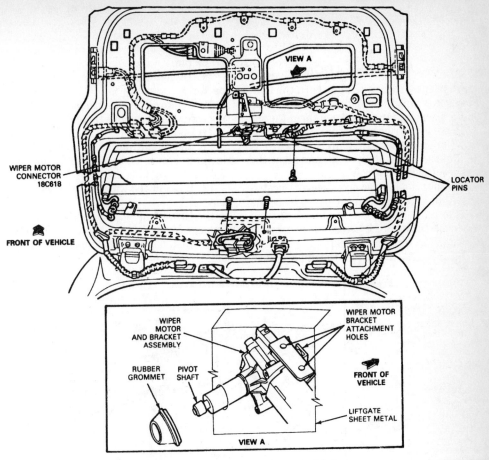

Rear wiper motor mounting — Explorer

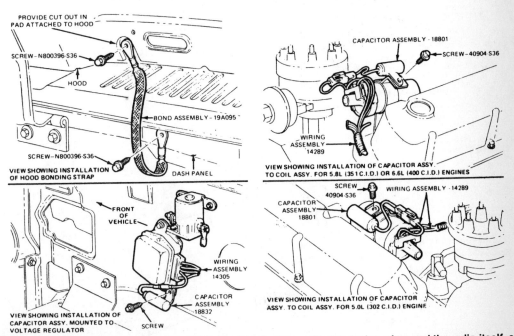

Typical radio suppression equipment, pickups. These, along with spark plug wires and the radio itself, are the areas to check when the radio reception becomes poor

Windshield Wiper Motor

REMOVAL AND INSTALLATION

1. Turn the wiper switch on. Turn the ignition switch on until the blades are straight up and then turn ignition off to keep them there.

2. Remove the right wiper arm and blade.

3. Remove the negative battery cable.

4. Remove the right pivot nut and allow the linkage to drop into the cowl.

5. Remove the linkage access cover, located on the right side of the dash panel near the wiper motor.

6. Reach through the access cover opening and unsnap the wiper motor clip.

7. Push the clip away from the linkage until it clears the nib on the crank pin. Then, push the clip off the linkage.

8. Remove the wiper linkage from motor crank pin.

9. Disconnect the wiper motor's wiring connector.

10. remove the wiper motor's three attaching screws and remove the motor.

To install:

11. Install the motor and attach the three attaching screws. Tighten to 60-65 inch lbs. (6.7-7.3 Nm).

12. Connect the wiper motor's wiring connector.

13. Install the clip completely on the right linkage. Make sure the clip is completely on.

14. Install the left linkage on the wiper motor crank pin.

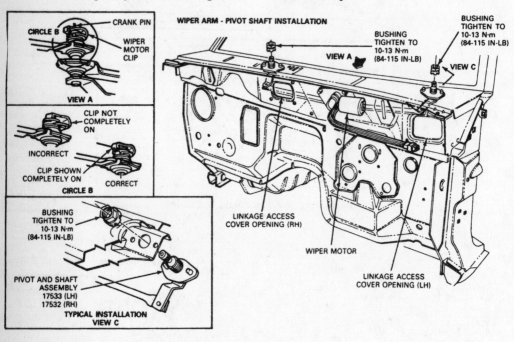

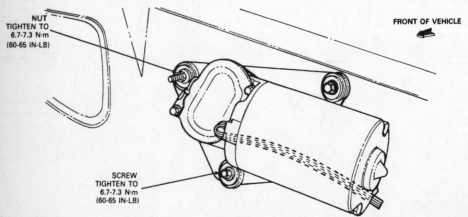

Windshield wiper motor and linkage mounting

15. Install the right linkage on the wiper motor crank pin and pull the linkage on to the crank pin until it snaps.

NOTE: *The clip is properly installed if the nib is protruding through the center of the clip.*

16. Reinstall the right wiper pivot shaft and nut.

17. Reconnect the battery and turn the ignition **ON**. Turn the wiper switch off so the wiper motor will park, then turn the ignition **OFF**. Replace the right linkage access cover.

18. Install the right wiper blade and arm.

19. Check the system for proper operation.

Pivot Shaft and Linkage

REMOVAL AND INSTALLATION

1. Perform steps 1 through 8 of the wiper motor removal procedure.

2. Slide the right pivot shaft and linkage assembly out through the R.H. access opening.

3. If the left linkage is to be serviced, remove the L.H. wiper arm and blade assembly.

4. Remove the left linkage access cover.

5. Remove the left pivot nut, lower the linkage and slide it out through the L.H. access opening.

NOTE: *The left and right pivot and linkage assemblies are serviced separately.*

6. Installation is the reverse of the removal procedure above.

Rear Window Wiper Motor

REMOVAL AND INSTALLATION

1. Disconnect the negative battery cable.

2. Remove the wiper arm and blade.

3. Remove the liftgate interior trim.

4. Remove the motor attaching bolts (3). Disconnect the electrical leads.

5. Remove the wiper motor from the vehicle.

6. Install the wiper motor in position and connect the electrical leads.

7. Install the liftgate trim. Connect the negative battery cable.

INSTRUMENTS AND SWITCHES

Instrument Cluster

REMOVAL AND INSTALLATION

1. Disconnect the battery ground cable.

2. Remove the two steering column shroud-to-panel retaining screws and remove the shroud.

3. Remove the lower instrument panel

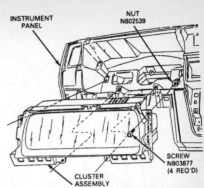

Instrument cluster removal and installation — Explorer

trim.

4. Remove the cluster trim cover from the instrument panel by removing the eight screws.

5. Remove the four instrument cluster to panel retaining screws.

6. Position the cluster slightly away from the panel for access to the back of the cluster to disconnect the speedometer.

NOTE: *If there is not sufficient access to disengage the speedometer cable from the speedometer, it may be necessary to remove the speedometer cable at the transmission and pull cable through cowl, to allow room to reach the speedometer quick disconnect.*

7. Disconnect the wiring harness connector from the printed circuit, and any bulb-and-socket assemblies from the wiring harness to the cluster assembly and remove the cluster assembly from the instrument panel.

To install:

8. Apply approximately 1/8 in. diameter ball of D7AZ-19A331–A Silicone Dielectric compound or equivalent in the drive hole of the speedometer head.

9. Position the cluster near its opening in the instrument panel.

10. Connect the wiring harness connector to the printed circuit, and any bulb-and-socket assemblies from the wiring harness to the cluster assembly.

11. Position the cluster to the instrument panel and install the four cluster to panel retaining screws.

13. Install the panel trim covers and the steering column shroud.

14. Connect the battery ground cable.

15. Check operation of all gauges, lamps and signals.

Fuel, Oil Pressure, Voltage and Coolant Temperature Gauges

Each of the gauges can be removed in the

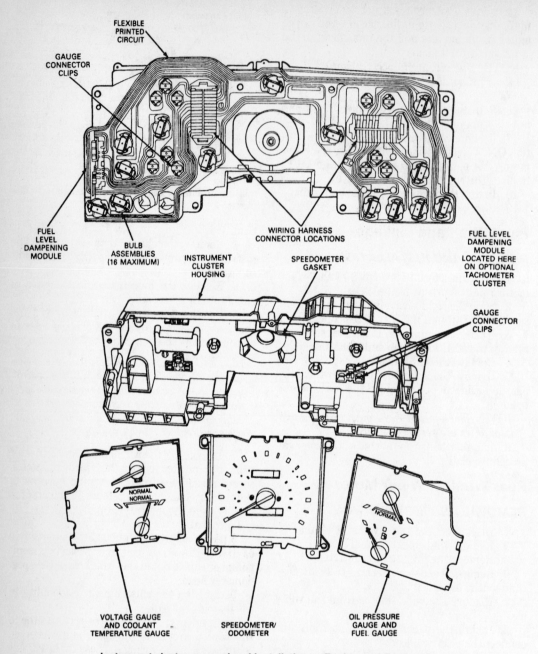

FLEXIBLE PRINTED CIRCUIT

GAUGE CONNECTOR CLIPS

FUEL LEVEL DAMPENING MODULE

BULB ASSEMBLIES (16 MAXIMUM)

INSTRUMENT CLUSTER HOUSING

WIRING HARNESS CONNECTOR LOCATIONS

SPEEDOMETER GASKET

FUEL LEVEL DAMPENING MODULE LOCATED HERE ON OPTIONAL TACHOMETER CLUSTER

GAUGE CONNECTOR CLIPS

VOLTAGE GAUGE AND COOLANT TEMPERATURE GAUGE

SPEEDOMETER/ ODOMETER

OIL PRESSURE GAUGE AND FUEL GAUGE

Instrument cluster removal and installation — Ranger and Bronco II

same manner, once the instrument cluster is removed.

1. Disconnect the negative battery cable.
2. Remove the instrument cluster assembly.
3. Remove the lens from the instrument cluster.
4. Pull the gauge from the cluster.
5. Install the gauge, by pushing it firmly into position.
6. Install the cluster lens and install the cluster into the instrument panel.

Speedometer Cable

REMOVAL AND INSTALLATION

1. Raise and safely support the vehicle.
2. Disengage the cable from the transmission.

NOTE: *Disconnect the cable by pulling it out of the speed sensor. Do not attempt to remove the spring retainer clip with the cable and the sensor.*

3. Disconnect the cable from its retaining clips.

4. Push the cable through the grommet in the floor and pull it into the passenger compartment.

5. Disconnect the cable from the speedometer, cluster removal may be necessary.

6. Install the speedometer in position and route it through the floor.

7. Connect it at the speedometer and at the transmission.

Speedometer Cable Core

REMOVAL AND INSTALLATION

1. Reach up behind the cluster and disconnect the cable by depressing the quick disconnect tab and pulling the cable away.

2. Remove the cable from the casing. If the cable is broken, raise the vehicle on a hoist and disconnect the cable from the transmission.

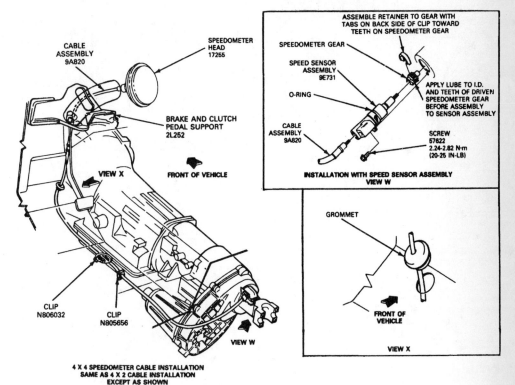

Speedometer cable routing and mounting

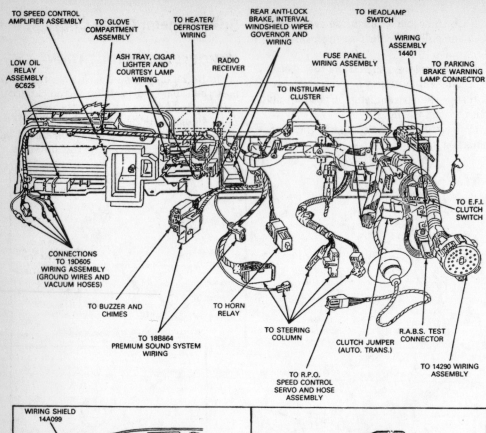

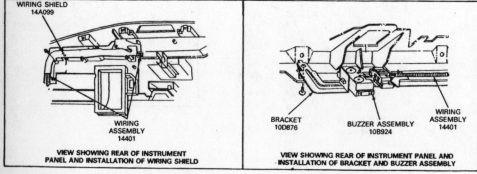

Instrument panel wiring — rear of instrument panel

3. Remove the cable from the casing.

4. To remove the casing from the vehicle, pull it through the floor pan.

5. To replace the cable, slide the new cable into the casing and connect it at the transmission.

6. Route the cable through the floor pan and position the grommet in its groove in the floor.

7. Push the cable onto the speedometer head.

Instrument Panel

REMOVAL AND INSTALLATION

1. Disconnect the negative battery cable.

2. Disconnect the instrument panel wiring connectors in the engine compartment.

3. Remove the 2 screws retaining the lower steering column cover and remove the cover.

4. Remove the ashtray and retainer.

5. Remove the upper and lower steering column shrouds.

6. Remove the instrument cluster finish panel. Remove the radio assembly and equalizer, if equipped.

7. Remove the screws retaining the instrument cluster. Remove the cluster, making sure to disconnect the electrical leads.

8. Remove the screw that attaches the instrument panel to the brake and clutch pedal support.

9. Disconnect the wiring from the switches on the steering column.

10. Remove the front inside pillar moldings.

11. Remove the right side cowl trim cover.

12. Remove the lower right insulator from under the instrument panel.

13. Remove the 2 bolts retaining the instrument panel to the lower right side of the cowl.

14. Remove the 2 screw retaining the instrument panel to the parking brake bracket, on the drivers side.

15. Remove the 4 screw retaining the top of the instrument panel.

16. Reach through the openings in the instru-

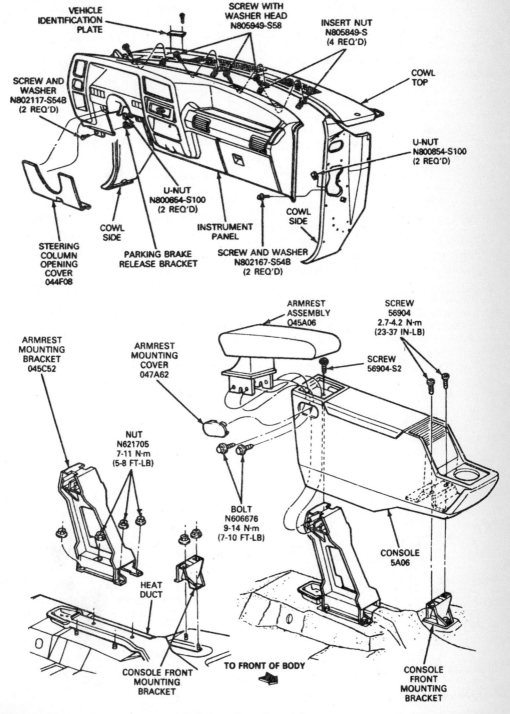

Instrument panel mounting

ment panel and disconnect any remaining electrical connectors. Disconnect the heater/air conditioning controls.

NOTE: *Removing the instrument panel will be much easier with the help of an assistant, as it is extremely bulky and difficult to maneuver.*

17. Carefully tilt the instrument panel forward and remove it from the vehicle. Work the instrument panel around the steering wheel.
To install:
18. If the instrument panel is being replaced, transfer all mounting brackets and switches to the new panel.
19. Position the instrument panel inside the vehicle and install the 4 screw that retain it along the top.
20. Install the retaining screws on the left and right sides. Make sure the instrument panel is properly mounted.

NOTE: *Making sure the instrument panel is positioned correctly at this point, will avoid problems with fit and rattles, after its installed. Also check for pinched or cut wires.*

21. Install the moldings and the trim panels.
22. Connect the heater/air conditioning controls and all of the instrument panel switches.
23. Connect the wiring to the steering column switches.
24. Install the instrument cluster, radio and ashtray assemblies.
25. Install the instrument cluster finish panel.
26. Install the steering column shrouds.
27. Reconnect all wiring connectors in the engine compartment.
28. Connect the negative battery cable.

29. Check the operation of ALL accessories.

Center Console

REMOVAL AND INSTALLATION

1. Remove the small arm rest screw covers.
2. Remove the 4 arm rest retaining bolts.
3. Remove the 2 rear arm rest retaining screws and the 2 screws in the front utility tray.
4. Remove the entire assembly, by lifting it from its mounting bracket.
5. Install the console in position and install all mounting screws.

Windshield Wiper Switch

REMOVAL AND INSTALLATION

NOTE: *The switch handle is an integral part of the switch and cannot be replaced separately.*

1. Disconnect the negative battery cable from the battery.
2. Remove the steering column trim shrouds.
3. Disconnect the quick connect electrical connector.
4. Peel back the foam sight shield, remove the two hex-head screws holding the switch, and remove the windshield wiper switch.
5. Position the switch on the column and install the two hex head screws. Replace the foam sight shield over the witch.
6. Connect the quick connect electrical connector.
7. Install the upper and lower trim shrouds.

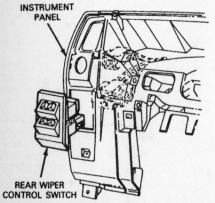

FRONT VIEW OF INSTRUMENT PANEL ASSEMBLY

Rear window wiper control switch removal

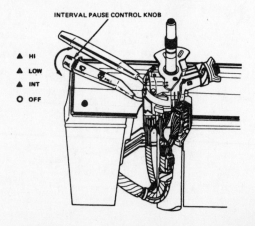

Windshield wiper switch mounting

Rear Wiper Switch

REMOVAL AND INSTALLATION

1. Disconnect the negative battery cable.
2. Remove the instrument cluster finish panel.
3. Remove the switch from the instrument panel, by carefully prying upward.
4. Disconnect the electrical lead from the switch.
5. Connect the wiring and install the switch in the instrument panel.
6. Install the cluster finish panel.
7. Connect the negative battery cable. Check the operation of the switch.

Headlight Switch

REMOVAL AND INSTALLATION

1. Disconnect the battery ground cable.
2. Pull the headlight switch knob to the headlight on position.
3. Depress the shaft release button and remove the knob and shaft assembly.
4. Remove the instrument panel finish panel.
5. Unscrew the mounting nut and remove the switch from the instrument panel, then remove the wiring connector from the switch.
   To install:
6. Connect the wiring connector to the headlamp switch, position the switch in the instrument panel and install the mounting nut.
7. Install the instrument panel finish panel.
8. Install the headlamp switch knob and shaft assembly by pushing the shaft into the switch until it locks into position.
9. Connect the battery ground cable, and check the operation of the headlight switch.

Ignition Switch

REMOVAL AND INSTALLATION

1. Rotate the ignition key to the **LOCK** position.
2. Disconnect the negative battery cable.
3. Remove the upper and lower steering column trim panels.
4. On models equipped with tilt steering, remove the trim ring from around the steering column.
5. Disconnect the ignition switch electrical connector.
6. Drill out the break-off head bolts connecting the ignition switch to the lock cylinder housing. This can be done with an 1/8 in. drill bit.
7. Remove the remaining pieces of the bolt

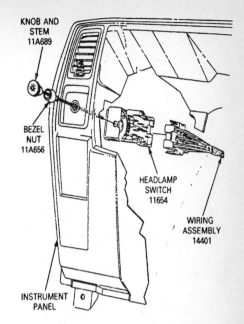

Headlight switch removal and installation

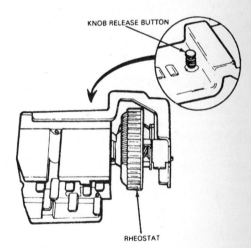

Headlight switch knob — release button location

with and Easy-Out® tool or equivalent, bolt extractor.
8. Disengage the switch from the actuator pin.
9. Remove the switch from the column.
   To install:
10. Rotate the ignition switch to the **RUN** position.
11. Install the replacement switch, by aligning the holes on the switch casting base with the holes in the lock cylinder housing. Note that the replacement switch is supplied with the switch in the **RUN** position.

NOTE: *Minor movement of the switch might be required to align the actuator pin with the slot in the carrier.*

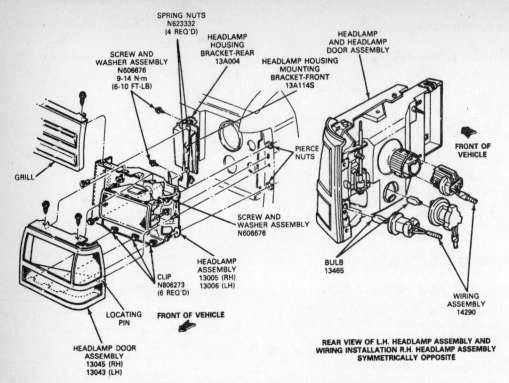

SPRING NUTS
N623332
(4 REQ'D)

HEADLAMP
HOUSING
BRACKET-REAR
13A004

HEADLAMP
AND HEADLAMP
DOOR ASSEMBLY

SCREW AND
WASHER ASSEMBLY
N606676
9-14 N·m
(6-10 FT-LB)

HEADLAMP HOUSING
MOUNTING
BRACKET-FRONT
13A114S

FRONT OF
VEHICLE

GRILL

PIERCE
NUTS

SCREW AND
WASHER ASSEMBLY
N606676

BULB
13465

CLIP
N806273
(6 REQ'D)

HEADLAMP
ASSEMBLY
13005 (RH)
13006 (LH)

WIRING
ASSEMBLY
14290

LOCATING
PIN

FRONT OF VEHICLE

HEADLAMP DOOR
ASSEMBLY
13045 (RH)
13043 (LH)

REAR VIEW OF L.H. HEADLAMP ASSEMBLY AND
WIRING INSTALLATION R.H. HEADLAMP ASSEMBLY
SYMMETRICALLY OPPOSITE

Headlight door and bulb removal — late model vehicles

12. Install new break-off head bolts and tighten them until the heads shear off. This will take approximately 35-50 inch lbs. of torque.

13. Connect the electrical lead to the switch.

14. Connect the negative battery cable and check the operation of the switch in all positions.

15. Install the steering column trim.

LIGHTING

Headlights

REMOVAL AND INSTALLATION

1. Remove the headlamp door attaching screws and remove the headlamp door. On the Explorer, remove the grille.

2. Remove the headlight retaining ring screws, and remove the retaining ring. Do not disturb the adjusting screw settings.

3. Pull the headlight bulb forward and disconnect the wiring assembly plug from the bulb.

4. Connect the wiring assembly plug to the new bulb. Place the bulb in position, making sure that the locating tabs of the bulb are fitted in the positioning slots.

5. Install the headlight retaining ring.

6. Place the headlight trim ring or door into position, and install the retaining screws. Install the grille on Explorer.

HEADLIGHT ADJUSTMENT

NOTE: *Before making any headlight adjustments, preform the following steps for preparation:*

1. Make sure all tires are properly inflated.

2. Take into consideration any faulty wheel alignment or improper rear axle tracking.

3. Make sure there is no load in the truck other than the driver.

4. Make sure all lenses are clean.

Each headlight is adjusted by means of two screws located at the 12 o'clock and 9 o'clock positions on the headlight underneath the trim ring. Always bring each beam into final position by turning the adjusting screws clockwise so that the headlight will be held against the tension springs when the operation is completed.

Signal and Marker Lights

REMOVAL AND INSTALLATION

Front Marker and Turn Signal

1. Remove the screws retaining the headlight door. On Explorer, remove the grille.

2. Carefully rotate the headlight door away

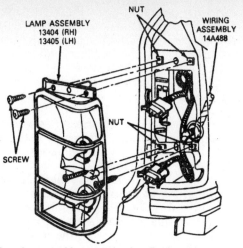

Rear lamp and lens removal — Explorer

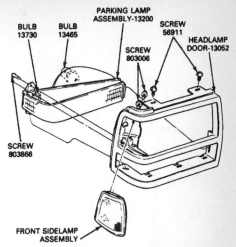

Turn signal, marker, and parking light lens removal — late model vehicles

from the vehicle, rotating the inboard side away from the vehicle.

3. Remove the side marker, parking and turn signal bulbs and sockets from the headlamp door assembly. They can be removed by turning them.

4. Remove the retaining screws for the lens to be changed and remove it from the headlight door.

5. Install the removed lens assembly and install the bulbs and sockets.

6. Install the headlight door assembly.

7. Check the operation of the lights.

Rear Marker, Brake and Turn Signal Lamps

1. Remove the 4 screws retaining the lamp assembly to the vehicle.

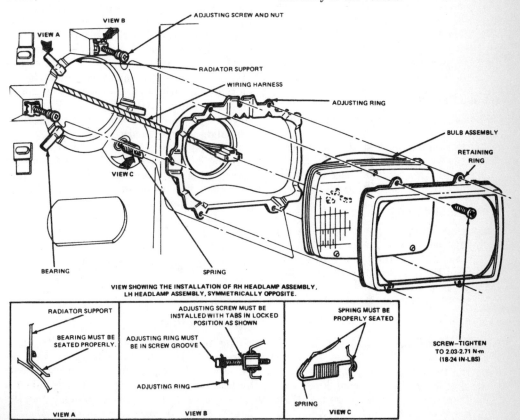

Headlight and bezel removal — earlier models

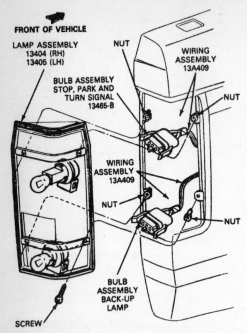

FRONT OF VEHICLE
LAMP ASSEMBLY
13404 (RH)
13405 (LH)
NUT
WIRING ASSEMBLY 13A409
BULB ASSEMBLY
STOP, PARK AND
TURN SIGNAL
13465-B
NUT
WIRING ASSEMBLY 13A409
NUT
NUT
BULB ASSEMBLY BACK-UP LAMP
SCREW

Rear lamp and lens removal — Ranger and Bronco II

2. Remove the lamp assembly from the vehicle by pulling it outward. On the Explorer, make sure the 2 retainers at the bottom of the assembly release.

3. Remove the bulbs and sockets.

4. Install the lamp assembly in position, on the Explorer, make sure the bottom of the assembly seats properly.

High Mount Brake Light

1. Remove the screws retaining the lamp to the tailgate.

2. Pull the lamp away from the vehicle and disconnect the wiring connector.

3. Install the lamp assembly back into position, making sure it is seated properly.

Dome and Cargo Lamps

The dome and cargo lamps can be removed by, removing their plastic covers and then removing the mounting screws. Pull the assembly away from the vehicle and disconnect the wiring. Use care when installing the dome lamps, so as not to damage the interior trim.

TRAILER WIRING

Wiring the truck for towing is fairly easy. There are a number of good wiring kits available and these should be used, rather than trying to design your own. All trailers will need brake lights and turn signals as well as tail lights and side marker lights. Most states require extra marker lights for overly wide trailers. Also, most states have recently required back-up lights for trailers, and most trailer manufacturers have been building trailers with back-up lights for several years.

Additionally, some Class I, most Class II and just about all Class III trailers will have electric brakes.

Add to this number an accessories wire, to operate trailer internal equipment or to charge the trailer's battery, and you can have as many as seven wires in the harness.

Determine the equipment on your trailer and buy the wiring kit necessary. The kit will contain all the wires needed, plus a plug adapter set which included the female plug, mounted on the bumper or hitch, and the male plug, wired into, or plugged into the trailer harness.

When installing the kit, follow the manufacturer's instructions. The color coding of the wires is standard throughout the industry.

One point to note, some domestic vehicles, and most imported vehicles, have separate turn signals. On most domestic vehicles, the brake lights and rear turn signals operate with the same bulb. For those vehicles with separate turn signals, you can purchase an isolation unit so that the brake lights won't blink whenever the turn signals are operated, or, you can go to your local electronics supply house and buy four diodes to wire in series with the brake and turn signal bulbs. Diodes will isolate the brake and turn signals. The choice is yours. The isolation units are simple and quick to install, but far more expensive than the diodes. The diodes, however, require more work to install properly, since they require the cutting of each bulb's wire and soldering in place of the diode.

One final point, the best kits are those with a spring loaded cover on the vehicle mounted socket. This cover prevents dirt and moisture from corroding the terminals. Never let the vehicle socket hang loosely. Always mount it securely to the bumper or hitch.

CIRCUIT PROTECTION

Fusible Links

The fusible link is a short length of special, Hypalon (high temperature) insulated wire, integral with the engine compartment wiring harness and should not be confused with standard wire. It is several wire gauges smaller than the circuit which it protects. Under no circumstances should a fuse link replacement repair be made using a length of standard wire cut from bulk stock or from another wiring harness.

REPLACEMENT

To repair any blown fusible link use the following procedure:

1. Determine which circuit is damaged, its location and the cause of the open fusible link. If the damaged fuse link is one of three fed by a common No. 10 or l2 gauge feed wire, determine the specific affected circuit.

2. Disconnect the negative battery cable.

3. Cut the damaged fusible link from the wiring harness and discard it. If the fusible link is one of three circuits fed by a single feed wire, cut it out of the harness at each splice end and discard it.

4. Identify and procure the proper fusible

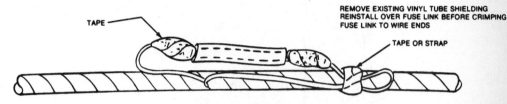

TYPICAL REPAIR USING THE SPECIAL #17 GA. (9.00" LONG-YELLOW) FUSE LINK REQUIRED FOR THE AIR/COND. CIRCUITS (2) #687E and #261A LOCATED IN THE ENGINE COMPARTMENT

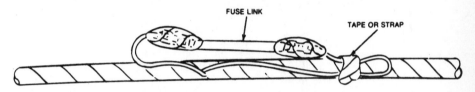

TYPICAL REPAIR FOR ANY IN-LINE FUSE LINK USING THE SPECIFIED GAUGE FUSE LINK FOR THE SPECIFIC CIRCUIT

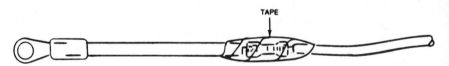

TYPICAL REPAIR USING THE EYELET TERMINAL FUSE LINK OF THE SPECIFIED GAUGE FOR ATTACHMENT TO A CIRCUIT WIRE END

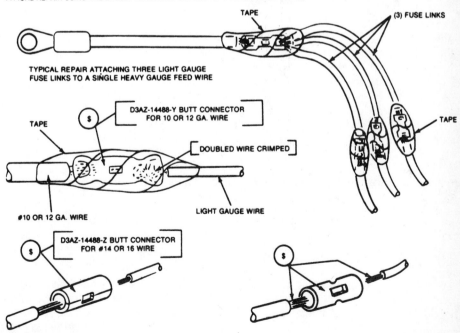

Fusible link repair

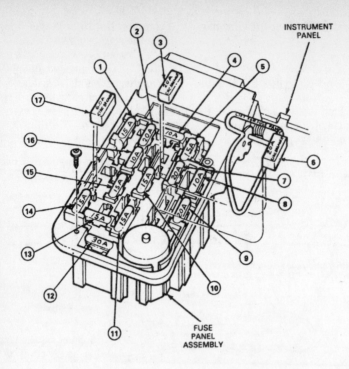

1. 15 Amp Fuse — Four-Way Flash, Stoplamps, Speed Control Inhibit
2. 20 Amp Fuse — Horns
3. 20 Amp C.B. — Cigar Lighter, Flash to Pass
4. 10 Amp Fuse — Instrument Panel Illumination, Park/H Lamp Hot
5. 20 Amp Fuse — Premium Radio Amplifier
6. 30 Amp C.B. — Power Windows, Lumbar
7. 20 Amp Fuse — R.A.B.S. Module
8. 10 Amp Fuse — Hego Heater
9. 20 Amp Fuse — Cluster Warning Lamps, Electronic All Wheel Drive
10. 15 Amp Fuse — Speed Control Amplifier, Radio
11. 15 Amp Fuse — Park/License Lamps
12. 30 Amp Fuse — Blower Motor
13. 15 Amp Fuse — Turn Lamps, B/U Lamps, Turn Indicator, R. Def. Control
14. 15 Amp Fuse — Dome/Courtesy Lamp
15. 15 Amp Fuse — Rear Window Wash/Wipe
16. 10 Amp Fuse — Air Conditioning Switches, Clutch Coil
17. 6 Amp C.B. — Front Wash/Wipe

Fuse panel and fuse identification — Ranger and Bronco II. The fuse location can vary with year and model

link and butt connectors for attaching the fusible link to the harness.

5. To repair any fusible link in a 3–link group with one feed:

    a. After cutting the open link out of the harness, cut each of the remaining undamaged fusible links close to the feed wire weld.

    b. Strip approximately 1/2 in. of insulation from the detached ends of the two good fusible links. Then insert two wire ends into one end of a butt connector and carefully

push one stripped end of the replacement fuse link into the same end of the butt connector and crimp all three firmly together.

NOTE: *Care must be taken when fitting the three fusible links into the butt connector as the internal diameter is a snug fit for three wires. Make sure to use a proper crimping tool. Pliers, side cutters, etc. will not apply the proper crimp to retain the wires and withstand a pull test.*

c. After crimping the butt connector to the three fusible links, cut the weld portion from the feed wire and strip approximately ½ in. of insulation from the cut end. Insert the stripped end into the open end of the butt connector and crimp very firmly.

d. To attach the remaining end of the replacement fusible link, strip approximately ½ in. of insulation from the wire end of the circuit from which the blow fusible link was removed, and firmly crimp a butt connector or equivalent to the stripped wire. Then, insert the end of the replacement link into the other end of the connector and crimp firmly.

e. Using rosin core solder with a consistency of 60 percent tin and 40 percent lead,

solder the connectors and the wires at the repairs and insulate with electrical tape.

7. To repair any fusible link which has an eyelet terminal on one end such as the charging circuit, cut off the open fusible link behind the weld, strip approximately ½ in. of insulation from the cut end and attach the appropriate new eyelet fusible link to the cut stripped wire with an appropriate size butt connector. Solder the connectors and wires at the repair and insulate with tape.

8. Connect the negative battery cable to the battery and test the system for proper operation.

NOTE: *Do not mistake a resistor wire for a fusible link. The resistor wire is generally longer and has print stating, "Resistor—don't cut or splice". When attaching a*

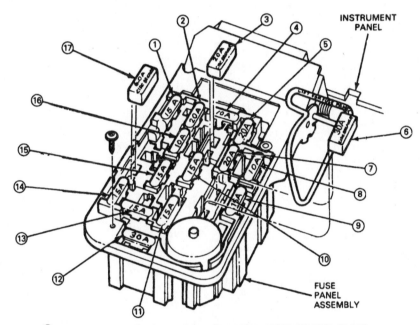

① 15 AMP FUSE — FOUR-WAY FLASH, STOPLAMPS, SPEED CONTROL INHIBIT
② 20 AMP FUSE — HORNS
③ 20 AMP C.B. — CIGAR LIGHTER, FLASH TO PASS, POWER LUMBAR, MULTI-FUNCTION SWITCH
④ 10 AMP FUSE — INSTRUMENT PANEL ILLUMINATION
⑤ 20 AMP FUSE — PREMIUM RADIO AMPLIFIER, TRAILER TOW
⑥ 30 AMP C.B. — POWER WINDOWS
⑦ 20 AMP FUSE — R.A.B.S. MODULE
⑧ 10 AMP FUSE — HEGO HEATER
⑨ 15 AMP FUSE — CLUSTER WARNING LAMPS, ELECTRONIC ALL WHEEL DRIVE
⑩ 15 AMP FUSE — SPEED CONTROL AMPLIFIER, RADIO
⑪ 15 AMP FUSE — PARK/LICENSE LAMPS
⑫ 30 AMP FUSE — BLOWER MOTOR
⑬ 15 AMP FUSE — TURN LAMPS, B/U LAMPS, TURN INDICATOR, R. DEF. CONTROL
⑭ 15 AMP FUSE — DOME/COURTESY LAMP
⑮ 15 AMP FUSE — REAR WINDOW WASH/WIPE
⑯ 10 AMP FUSE — AIR CONDITIONING SWITCHES, CLUTCH COIL
⑰ 6 AMP C.B. — FRONT WASH/WIPE

Fuse panel and fuse identification — Explorer

single No. 16, 17, 18 or 20 gauge fusible link to a heavy gauge wire, always double the stripped wire end of the fusible link before inserting and crimping it into the butt connector for positive wire retention.

Turn Signal and Hazard Flasher Locations

Both the turn signal flasher and the hazard warning flasher are mounted on the fuse panel on the truck. To gain access to the fuse panel, remove the cover from the lower edge of the instrument panel below the steering column. First remove the two fasteners from the lower edge of the cover. Then pull the cover downward until the spring clips disengage from the instrument panel.

The turn signal flasher unit is mounted on the front of the fuse panel, and the hazard warning flasher is mounted on the rear of the fuse panel.

MANUAL TRANSMISSION

Identification

All manual transmissions are equipped with an identification tag which must be used when servicing the unit. The 4-speed manual transmissions are designated code X and the 5-speed overdrive transmissions are code 5 or M/D.

The 4-speed manual transmission and the Mitsubishi 5-speed overdrive transmission service tags are located toward the right front side of the transmission case. The Mazda M5OD 5-speed overdrive transmission service tag is located on the left hand side of the transmission case.

Some early Ranger and Bronco II are equipped with a 4-speed manual transmission. The 4-speed manual transmission used on the 2.2L diesel engines and gasoline engines are fully synchronized with all gears, except reverse, in constant mesh. All forward speed gears are helically cut for quiet operation. The reverse gear and reverse idler gear are spur-cut. Gear shifting is directly control by a floor shift mechanism, which is built into the extension housing. When fitted to the diesel engine, the transmission features an integral clutch housing and gear case and a separate extension housing.

The Mazda (Toyo Kogyo) 5-speed overdrive transmission is fully synchronized with all gears, except reverse gear, which is in constant mesh. All forward speed gears are helically cut for quiet operation. The reverse gear and reverse idler gear are spur-cut. Gear shifting is directly control by a floor shift mechanism, which is built into the extension housing. The 5-speed overdrive transmission used on the gasoline engines is very similar to the 4-speed transmission used on the Ranger gasoline engine. When fitted to the diesel engine, the 5-speed

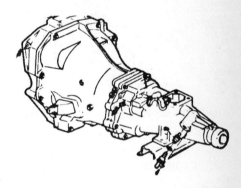

4-speed manual transmission assembly — diesel engine

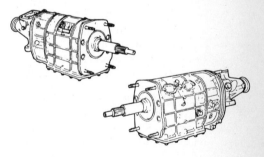

Mazda (Toyo Kogyo) 5-speed transmission assembly

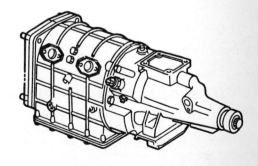

Transmission service tag — Mitsubishi

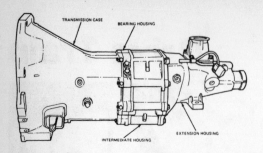

5-speed manual transmission assembly — diesel engine

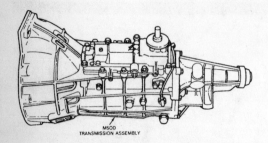

Mazda M50D 5-speed transmission assembly

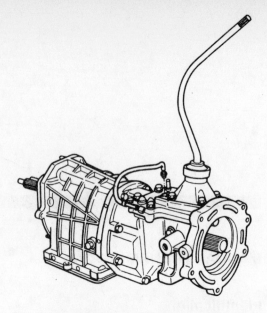

Mitsubishi FM145 5-speed transmission assembly

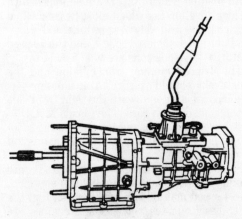

Mitsubishi FM146 5-speed transmission assembly

overdrive transmission features a bearing housing, intermediate housing and extension housing.

The Mazda M5OD 5-speed overdrive transmission is a top shift, fully synchronized transmission. The M5OD transmission comes in both a M5OD-R1 and a ZF M5OD-HD version. Its main case, top cover and extension housing are constructed of aluminum alloy.

The Mitsubishi 5-speed overdrive transmissions are fully synchronized in all forward gears and reverse. The Mitsubishi transmission includes the FM132, FM145 and the FM146 versions. These transmissions are equipped with top mounted shifter, which operates shift rails through a set of shift forks. The shift forks operates the synchronizer sleeves and allow shifts through 1-2, 3-4 and overdrive-reverse. A shift interlock system, located in the side of the transmission case, prevents the shift rails from engaging 2 gears at the same time.

Adjustments

SHIFTER AND LINKAGE ADJUSTMENTS

Both the 4-speed and 5-speed transmissions are directly controlled with a floor shift mechanism built into the transmission extension housing. There are no adjustments necessary on these transmissions.

Shift Handle

REMOVAL AND INSTALLATION

1. Disconnect the negative battery cable.

NOTE: *Do not remove the shift ball, unless the shift ball or boot is to be replaced. Otherwise, remove the shift ball, boot and lever as an assembly.*

2. Remove the plastic shift pattern insert from the shift ball.

3. Heat the shift ball to 140–180°F (60–82°C), using a heat gun.

4. Position a block of wood beneath the shift ball and carefully hammer the ball from the lever. Be careful not to damage the finish on the shift lever.

5. Place the gearshift lever in **N** position.

6. Remove the rubber boot retainer screws.

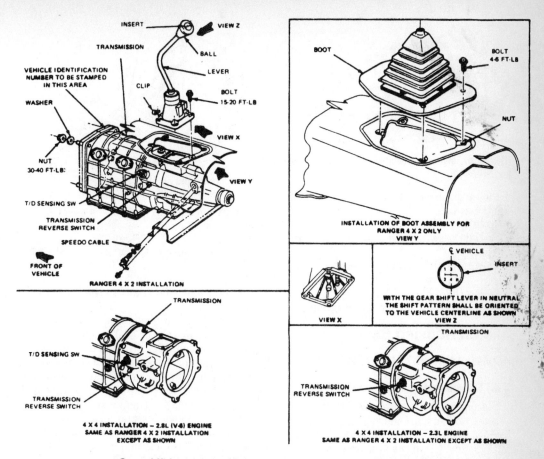

Gear shift lever assembly, gasoline engine shown, diesel similar

7. Remove the shift lever-to-extension housing/transfer case adapter housing retaining bolts. Pull the gearshift lever straight up and away from the gearshift lever retainer.

To install:

8. Prior to installing the shift lever, lubricate the shift lever ball stud, using C1AZ-19590-B (ESA-M1C75-B) or equivalent.

9. Fit the shift lever into place and install the retaining bolts. Tighten and torque the retaining bolts 20–27 ft. lbs. (28–36 Nm).

10. Install the rubber boot and retaining screws.

11. If the shift ball was removed, heat the shift ball to 140°–180°F (60°–82°C), using a heat gun. Tap the ball onto the shift lever, using a $\frac{7}{16}$ in. (11mm will work) socket and mallet.

12. Place the shift lever in **N** position. Then, align the shift pattern plastic insert with the vehicle centerline and install it to the shift ball.

Neutral Sensing Switch

All manual transmission vehicles are equipped with a neutral sensing switch. The neutral sensing switch signals the vehicle on-board computer, which allows the vehicle to start only when the transmission is in **N**.

REMOVAL AND INSTALLATION

1. Disconnect the negative battery cable.
2. Raise and support the vehicle safely.
3. Place the transmission in any position other than **N**.
4. Clean the area around the switch, then remove the switch.

To install:

5. Install the switch and tighten 8–12 ft. lbs (11–16Nm).
6. Reconnect the harness connector to the switch.
7. Lower the vehicle.
8. Reconnect the negative battery cable.

Back-up Lamp Switch

REMOVAL AND INSTALLATION

1. Disconnect the negative battery cable.
2. Raise and support the vehicle safely.
3. Place the transmission in any position other than **R** or **N**.

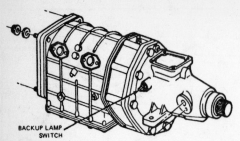

Transmission switch location — Mazda (Toyo Kogyo) 5-speed

4. Clean the area around the switch, then remove the switch.

To install:

5. Install the switch and tighten 8–12 ft. lbs (11–16Nm).

6. Reconnect the harness connector to the switch.

7. Lower the vehicle.

8. Reconnect the negative battery cable.

Extension Housing Seal

REMOVAL AND INSTALLATION

4-Speed Transmission and 5-speed

1. Disconnect the negative battery cable.

2. Raise and support the vehicle safely.

3. Place a suitable drain pan beneath the extension housing. Clean the area around the extension housing seal.

4. Matchmark the driveshaft to the rear axle flange. Disconnect the driveshaft and pull it rearward from the transmission.

5. Using an oil seal removal tool, T71P–

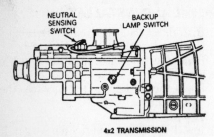

4x2 TRANSMISSION

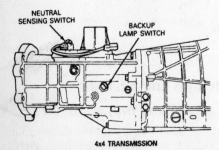

4x4 TRANSMISSION

Transmission switches location — Mitsubishi 5-speed

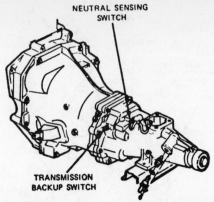

Transmission switches location — 4-speed (diesel) shown

7657–A or equivalent, remove the extension housing seal.

To install:

6. Apply gear lubricant to the lip of the oil seal.

7. Fit the replacement seal to the extension housing and install the seal, using the oil seal installation tool, T71P–7095–A or equivalent.

8. Install the driveshaft to the transmission extension housing. Connect the driveshaft to the rear axle flange. Make sure the marks made during removal are in alignment. Fit the attaching washer, lockwasher and nuts.

9. Check and adjust the transmission fluid level, using Ford manual transmission lube D8DZ–19C547–A (ESP–M2C83–C) or equivalent.

10. Lower the vehicle.

11. Reconnect the negative battery cable.

Mitsubishi 5-Speed Transmission

1. Disconnect the negative battery cable.

2. Raise and support the vehicle safely.

3. Place a suitable drain pan beneath the extension housing. Clean the area around the extension housing seal.

4. Matchmark the driveshaft to the rear axle flange. Disconnect the driveshaft and pull it rearward from the unit.

5. Remove the extension housing seal using tool T74P–77248–A or equivalent, remove the extension housing seal.

To install:

6. Lubricate the inside diameter of the oil seal and install the seal into the extension housing using tool T74P–77052–A. Check to ensure that the oil seal drain hole faces downward.

7. Install the driveshaft to the extension housing. Connect the driveshaft to the rear axle flange. Make sure the marks made during removal are in alignment. Fit the attaching washer, lockwasher and nuts.

8. Check and adjust the transmission fluid

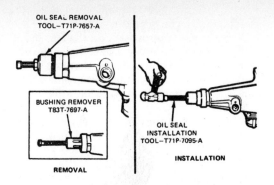

Extension housing oil seal, removal and installation — 4-Speed and Toyo Kogyo transmissions

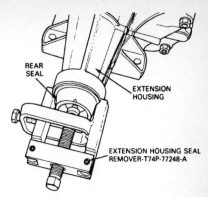

Extension housing oil seal removal — Mitsubishi 2WD transmission

level, using Ford manual transmission lube D8DZ–19C547–A (ESP–M2C83–C) or equivalent.

9. Lower the vehicle.

10. Reconnect the negative battery cable.

M5OD 5-Speed Transmission

1. Disconnect the negative battery cable.

2. Raise and support the vehicle safely.

3. Place a suitable drain pan beneath the extension housing. Clean the area around the transfer extension housing seal.

4. Matchmark the driveshaft to the rear axle flange. Disconnect the driveshaft and pull it rearward from the unit.

5. Remove the extension housing seal using tool T74P–77248–A or equivalent, remove the extension housing seal.

To install:

6. Lubricate the inside diameter of the oil seal and install the seal into the extension housing using tool T61L–7657–A. Check to ensure that the oil seal drain hole faces downward.

7. Install the driveshaft to the extension housing. Connect the driveshaft to the rear axle flange. Make sure the marks made during

removal are in alignment. Fit the attaching washer, lockwasher and nuts.

8. Check and adjust the transmission fluid level, using Ford manual transmission lube D8DZ–19C547–A (ESP–M2C83–C) or equivalent.

9. Lower the vehicle.

10. Reconnect the negative battery cable.

Transmission

REMOVAL AND INSTALLATION

4-Speed Transmission And Mazda (Toyo Kogyo) 5-Speed Transmission

1. Disconnect the negative battery cable.

2. Remove the gearshift lever, shim and bushing from the unit. Cover the opening in the housing with a cloth to prevent dirt from falling into the unit.

3. Disconnect the clutch master cylinder pushrod from the clutch pedal.

4. Raise the vehicle and support it safely.

5. Matchmark the driveshaft to the rear axle flange. Disconnect the driveshaft and pull

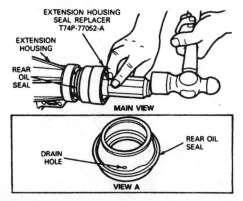

Extension housing oil seal installation — Mitsubishi 2WD and M50D 2WD transmissions

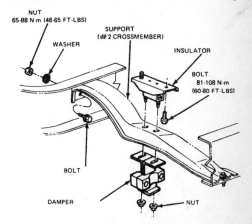

Crossmember installation — 4-speed diesel engines

it rearward from the transmission. Plug the extension housing to prevent leakage.

6. Remove the dust shield and slave cylinder from the clutch housing. Secure it to the side, using a piece of wire.

7. Disconnect the starter motor and back-up lamp wiring harness.

8. Remove the starter motor and speedometer cable.

9. Place a wood block on a service jack and position the jack under the engine oil pan.

10. Position a transmission jack under the transmission assembly.

11. On 4 × 4 vehicles, remove the transfer case.

12. Remove the transmission-to-engine retaining bolts and washers.

13. Remove the transmission mount and damper retaining bolts/nuts.

14. Remove the crossmember-to-frame retaining nuts and remove the crossmember from the vehicle.

15. Carefully lower the transmission jack, while working the transmission off the dowel pins. Slide the transmission rearward and remove it from the vehicle.

To install:

16. Check that the mating surfaces of the clutch housing, engine rear and dowel holes are free of burrs, dirt and paint.

17. Place the transmission on the transmission jack. Place the transmission under the vehicle, then raise it into position. Align the input shaft splines with the clutch disc splines and work the transmission forward into the locating dowels.

18. Install the transmission-to-engine retaining bolts and washers. Tighten and torque the retaining bolts 28–38 ft. lbs. (38–52Nm). Remove the transmission jack.

NOTE: *Always place flat washers between the retaining bolts to avoid damaging the aluminum surface.*

19. Install the starter motor. Tighten and torque the retaining bolts 15–20 ft. lbs. (20–27Nm).

20. Raise the engine and install the crossmember, transmission mount and damper. Torque the retaining to specifications.

21. Remove the service jack from supporting the engine.

22. On 4WD vehicles, install the transfer case.

23. Install the driveshaft to the transmission extension housing.

24. Connect the driveshaft to the rear axle

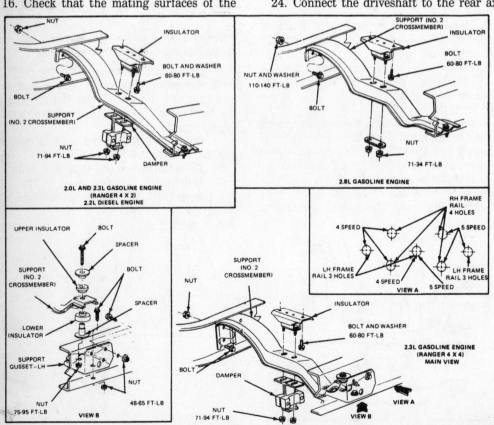

Crossmember installation — 4-speed gasoline engines

flange. Make sure the marks made during removal are in alignment. Fit the attaching washer, lockwasher and nuts. Torque the driveshaft-to-flange retaining nuts to 61–87 ft. lbs. on all except the Ranger w/4WD, which gets a torque of 41–55 ft. lbs.

25. Install the dust shield and slave cylinder to the clutch housing. Torque the slave cylinder-to-clutch housing bolts 15–20 ft. lbs. (21–27Nm) and the dust shield bolts 5–10 ft. lbs. (7–13Nm).

26. Reconnect the starter motor and back-up lamp wiring harness.

27. Install the speedometer cable.

28. Check and adjust the transmission fluid level, using Ford manual transmission lube D8DZ–19C547–A (ESP–M2C83–C) or equivalent.

29. Lower the vehicle.

30. Remove the cloth and avoid getting dirt in the unit. Install the gearshift lever, shim and bushing into the gearshift lever retainer.

31. Install the gearshift lever-to-cover retaining bolts and boot retaining screws.

32. Reconnect the clutch master cylinder pushrod to the clutch pedal.

33. Reconnect the negative battery cable.

34. Check for proper shifting and operation of the transmission.

Mitsubishi 5-speed Transmissions

1. Disconnect the negative battery cable.

2. Remove the gearshift lever assembly from the control housing.

3. Cover the opening in the control housing with a cloth to prevent dirt from falling into the unit.

4. Raise the vehicle and support it safely.

5. Matchmark the driveshaft to the rear axle and transfer case flange, as required. Disconnect the rear driveshaft at both the rear axle and transfer case flanges.

6. Disconnect the forward driveshaft from the front axle and remove by sliding forward. Install a suitable plug in the transfer case adapter to prevent fluid leakage.

7. Disconnect the hydraulic fluid line from the clutch slave cylinder.

8. Disconnect the speedometer from the transfer case/extension housing.

9. Disconnect the starter motor cable, the back-up lamp switch wire and the neutral safety switch wire.

10. Place a wood block on a service jack and position the jack under the engine oil pan.

11. Support the transfer case using the proper equipment. Carefully remove the transfer case from the vehicle.

12. Remove the starter. Place a transmission jack under the transmission.

13. Remove the transmission-to-engine retaining bolts and washers.

14. Remove the nuts and bolts attaching the transmission mount and damper to the crossmember.

15. Remove the nuts and bolts attaching the crossmember to the frame side rails and remove the crossmember.

16. Lower the engine jack. Work the clutch housing off the locating dowels and slide the clutch housing and the transmission rearward until the input shaft clears the clutch disc.

17. Remove the transmission from the vehicle.

18. Remove the clutch housing from the transmission.

To install:

19. Install the clutch housing to the transmission.

20. Check that the mating surfaces of the clutch housing, engine rear and dowel holes are free of burrs, dirt and paint.

21. Place the transmission on the transmission jack. Position the transmission under the

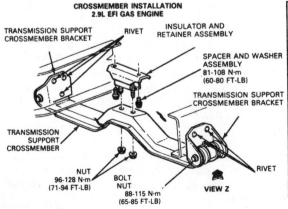

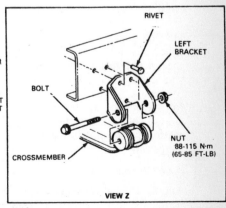

Crossmember installation — 2.9L EFI gasoline engine

vehicle, then raise it into position. Align the input shaft splines with the clutch disc splines and work the transmission forward into the locating dowels.

22. Install the transmission-to-engine retaining bolts and washers. Tighten and torque the retaining bolts 28–38 ft. lbs. (38–52Nm). Remove the transmission jack.

NOTE: *Always place flat washers between the retaining bolts to avoid damaging the aluminum surface.*

23. Install the starter motor. Tighten the attaching nuts to 15–20 ft. lbs. (21–27 Nm).

24. Raise the engine and install the rear crossmember, insulator and damper and attaching nuts and bolts. Tighten and torque the bolts to specification.

25. Install the transfer case.

26. Install the rear driveshaft in the transfer case adapter and attach it to the rear axle flange. Make sure the marks made during removal are in alignment. Install the attaching nuts and bolts. Torque circular flange bolts to 61–87 ft. lbs.; all others to 41–55 ft. lbs.

27. Install the front driveshaft in the transfer case adapter and attach it to the front axle flange. Make sure the marks made during removal are in alignment. Install the attaching nuts and bolts. Torque the nuts to 50 ft. lbs.

28. Connect the starter cable, back-up lamp switch wire, shift indicator wire and the neutral safety switch.

29. Connect the clutch hydraulic line to slave cylinder on the input shaft. Bleed the hydraulic clutch system.

30. Install the speedometer cable.

31. Remove the fill plug and check the fluid level. The fluid level should be level with the bottom of the fill hole. Ford manual transmission lube SAE 80W, D8DZ–19C547–A (ESP–M2C83–C) or equivalent is recommended.

32. Lower the vehicle.

33. Remove the cloth over the transfer case adapter opening. Avoid getting dirt in the adapter.

34. Install the gearshift lever assembly in the control housing. Make sure the ball on the lever is in the socket in the unit. Install the attaching bolts and tighten to 6–10 ft. lbs. (8–14 Nm).

35. Install the boot cover and bolts.

36. Reconnect the negative battery cable.

37. Check for proper shifting and operation of the transmission.

M5OD 5-speed Transmissions

1. Disconnect the negative battery cable.

2. Remove the gearshift lever assembly from the control housing.

3. Cover the opening in the control housing with a cloth to prevent dirt from falling into the unit.

4. Raise the vehicle and support it safely.

5. Matchmark the driveshaft to the rear axle flange. Pull the driveshaft rearward and disconnect it from the transmission.

6. Disconnect the clutch hydraulic line a the clutch housing. Plug the lines.

7. Disconnect the speedometer from the transfer case/extension housing.

8. Disconnect the starter motor and back-up lamp switch harness connector.

9. Place a wood block on a service jack and position the jack under the engine oil pan.

10. On 4WD vehicles, remove the transfer case from the vehicle.

11. Remove the starter motor.

12. Position a transmission jack, under the transmission.

13. Remove the transmission-to-engine retaining bolts and washers.

14. Remove the nuts and bolts attaching the transmission mount and damper to the crossmember.

15. Remove the nuts and bolts attaching the crossmember to the frame side rails and remove the crossmember.

16. Lower the engine jack. Work the clutch housing off the locating dowels and slide the clutch housing and the transmission rearward until the input shaft clears the clutch disc.

17. Remove the transmission from vehicle.

To install:

18. Check that the mating surfaces of the clutch housing, engine rear and dowel holes are free of burrs, dirt and paint.

19. Place the transmission on the transmission jack. Position the transmission under the vehicle, then raise it into position. Align the input shaft splines with the clutch disc splines and work the transmission forward into the locating dowels.

20. Install the transmission-to-engine retaining bolts and washers. Tighten and torque the retaining bolts 28–38 ft. lbs. (38–52Nm). Remove the transmission jack.

21. Install the starter motor. Tighten the attaching nuts to 15–20 ft. lbs. (21–27 Nm).

22. Raise the engine and install the rear crossmember, insulator and damper and attaching nuts and bolts. Tighten and torque the bolts to specification.

23. On 4WD vehicles, install the transfer case.

24. Insert the driveshaft into the transmission extension housing and install the center bearing attaching nuts, washers and lockwashers.

25. Connect the driveshaft to the rear axle drive flange.

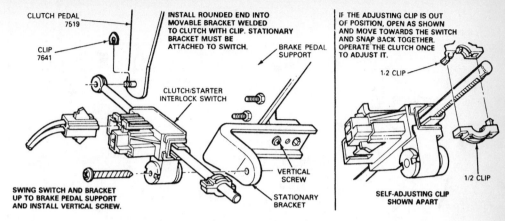

Clutch/starter interlock switch assembly

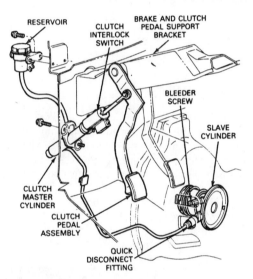

Typical hydraulic clutch system

26. Connect the starter motor and back-up lamp switch connectors.

27. Connect the hydraulic clutch line and bleed the system.

28. Install the speedometer cable.

29. Check and adjust the fluid level.

30. Lower the vehicle.

33. Install the gearshift lever assembly. Install the boot cover and bolts.

34. Reconnect the negative battery cable.

35. Check for proper shifting and operation of the transmission.

CLUTCH

Adjustments

NOTE: *The clutch system is hydraulically activated. The hydraulic clutch system locates*

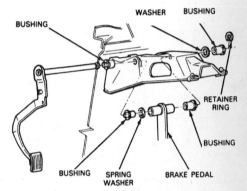

Clutch pedal removal and installation

the clutch pedal and provides automatic clutch adjustment. No adjustment of the clutch linkage or pedal position is required.

Master Cylinder and Reservoir

REMOVAL AND INSTALLATION

1983–84

NOTE: *The clutch hydraulic system is serviced as a complete unit; it has been bled of air and filled with fluid. Individual components of the system are not available separately.*

1. Remove the lock pin and disconnect the master cylinder push rod from the clutch pedal.

2a. 4–2.0L, 2.3L gasoline engines: Remove the bolt attaching the dust shield to the clutch housing and remove the dust shield. Push the slave cylinder rearward to disengage from the recess in the housing lugs, then slide outward to remove.

2b. 6–2.8L gasoline engine and 4–2.2L diesel engine: Remove the bolts attaching the slave cylinder to the clutch housing and remove the slave cylinder. Disengage the push rod from the release lever as the cylinder is removed.

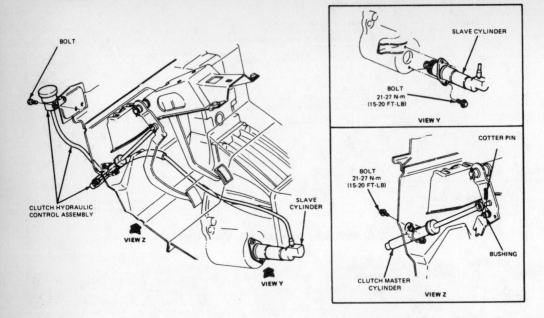

Hydraulic clutch system components — 1984 2.8L engine

Retain the push rod to release lever plastic bearing inserts.

3. Remove the two bolts attaching the master cylinder to the firewall.

4. Remove the two bolts attaching the fluid reservoir to the cowl access cover.

5. Remove the master cylinder from the opening in the firewall and remove the hydraulic system assembly upward and out of the engine compartment.

To install:

6. Position the hydraulic system downward into the engine compartment. The slave to master cylinder tube routing is to be above the brake tubes and below the steering column shaft.

NOTE: *On 6–2.8L vehicles, the tube must lay on top of the clutch housing.*

7. Insert the master cylinder push rod through the opening in the firewall, position

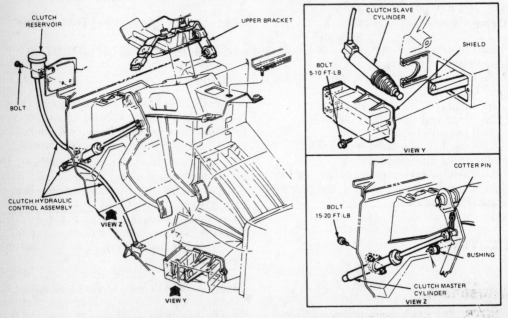

Hydraulic clutch system components — 1983–84 2.0L and 2.3L engines

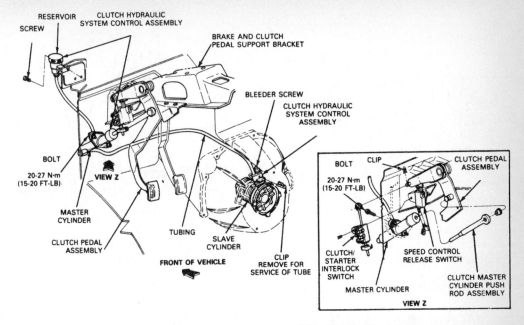

Hydraulic clutch system components — 1983–84 2.2L diesel engine

the master cylinder on the firewall, and install the attaching bolts. Torque the bolts to 15–20 ft. lbs.

8. Position the fluid reservoir on the cowl opening cover and install the attaching bolts. Torque the attaching bolts to 15–20 ft. lbs.

9. Install the slave cylinder by pushing the slave cylinder push rod into the cylinder, engage the push rod and plastic bearing inserts into the release lever, and attach the cylinder to the clutch housing.

NOTE: *With a new system, the slave cylinder contains a shipping strap that pre-positions the push rod for installation, and also provides a bearing insert. Following installation of the slave cylinder, the first actuation of the clutch pedal will break the shipping strap and give normal system operation.*

10a. 4–2.0L,2.3L engines: Snap the dust shield into position. Install the retaining bolt and tighten to 5–10 ft. lbs.

10b. 6–2.8L gasoline and 4–2.2L diesel engines: Install the bolts attaching the slave cylinder to the clutch housing and torque them to 15–20 ft. lbs.

11. Clean and apply a light film of oil to the master cylinder push rod bushing and install the bushing and push rod to the clutch pedal. Retain with the lock pin.

12. Depress the clutch pedal at least 10 times to verify smooth operation and proper clutch release.

1985–91

1. Disconnect the negative battery cable.

2. Disconnect the clutch master cylinder pushrod from the clutch pedal.

3. Remove the switch from the master cylinder assembly, if equipped.

4. Remove the screw retaining the fluid reservoir to the cowl access cover.

5. Disconnect the tube from the slave cylinder and plug both openings.

6. Remove the bolts retaining the clutch master cylinder to the dash panel and remove the clutch master cylinder assembly.

To install:

7. Install the pushrod through the hole in the engine compartment. Make certain it is located on the correct side of the clutch pedal. Place the master cylinder assembly in position and install the retaining bolts. Tighten to 8–12 ft. lbs. (11–16Nm).

8. Insert the coupling end into the slave cylinder and install the tube into the clips.

9. Fit the reservoir on the cowl access cover and install the retaining screws.

10. Replace the retainer bushing in the clutch master cylinder pushrod if worn or damaged. Install the retainer and pushrod on the clutch pedal pin. Make certain the bushing is fitted correctly with the flange of the bushing against the pedal blade.

11. Install the switch.

12. Bleed the system.

13. Reconnect the negative battery cable.

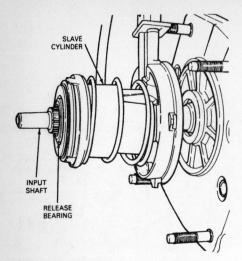

Slave cylinder assembly — 1983–85

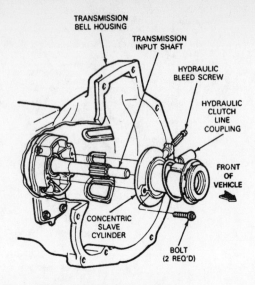

Slave cylinder assembly — 1986–91

Slave Cylinder

REMOVAL AND INSTALLATION

NOTE: *Before performing any service that requires removal of the slave cylinder, the master cylinder and pushrod must be disconnected from the clutch pedal. If not disconnected, permanent damage to the master cylinder assembly will occur if the clutch pedal is depressed while the slave cylinder is disconnected.*

1983–84

The clutch hydraulic system is serviced as a complete unit; it has been bled of air and filled with fluid. Individual components of the system are not available separately. Refer to Clutch Master Cylinder and Reservoir removal and installation.

1985

1. Disconnect the negative battery cable.
2. Remove the transmission assembly.
3. Remove the clutch housing-to-transmission retaining nuts and remove the housing assembly.
4. Remove the slave cylinder from the transmission input shaft.
To install:
5. Fit the slave cylinder over the transmission input shaft with the tower portion facing the transmission.
6. Install the clutch housing to the transmission. Make certain the slave cylinder is properly located in the notches of the clutch housing.
7. Install the transmission.
8. Bleed the hydraulic system.

1986–91

1. Disconnect the negative battery cable.
2. Disconnect the coupling at the transmission, using the clutch coupling removal tool T88T–70522–A or equivalent. Slide the white plastic sleeve toward the slave cylinder while applying a slight tug on the tube.
3. Remove the transmission assembly.

NOTE: *On the 2.9L (4WD) vehicles, the clutch housing must be removed with the transmission assembly.*

4. Remove the slave cylinder-to-transmission retaining bolts.
5. Remove the slave cylinder from the transmission input shaft.
To install:
6. Fit the slave cylinder over the transmission input shaft with the bleed screws and coupling facing the left side of the transmission.
7. Install the slave cylinder retaining bolts. Torque to 13–19 ft. lbs. (18–26Nm).
8. Install the transmission.
9. Reconnect the coupling to the slave cylinder.
10. Bleed the system.
11. Reconnect the negative battery cable.

Bleeding the System

The following procedure is recommended for bleeding a hydraulic system installed on the vehicle. The largest portion of the filling is carried out by gravity. It is recommended that the original clutch tube with quick connect be replaced when servicing the hydraulic system because air can be trapped in the quick connect and prevent complete bleeding of the system. The replacement tube does not include a quick connect.

1. Clean the dirt and grease from the dust cap.

2. Remove the cap and diaphragm and fill the reservoir to the top with approved brake fluid C6AZ–19542–AA or BA, (ESA–M6C25–A) or equivalent.

NOTE: *To keep brake fluid from entering the clutch housing, route a suitable rubber tube of appropriate inside diameter from the bleed screw to a container.*

3. Loosen the bleed screw, located in the slave cylinder body, next to the inlet connection. Fluid will now begin to move from the master cylinder down the tube to the slave cylinder.

NOTE: *The reservoir must be kept full at all time during the bleeding operation, to ensure no additional air enters the system.*

4. Notice the bleed screw outlet. When the slave is full, a steady stream of fluid comes from the slave outlet. Tighten the bleed screw.

5. Depress the clutch pedal to the floor and hold for 1–2 seconds. Release the pedal as rapidly as possible. The pedal must be released completely. Pause for 1–2 seconds. Repeat 10 times.

6. Check the fluid level in the reservoir. The fluid should be level with the step when the diaphragm is removed.

7. Repeat Step 5 and 6 five times. Replace the reservoir diaphragm and cap.

8. Hold the pedal to the floor, crack open the bleed screw to allow any additional air to escape. Close the bleed screw, then release the pedal.

9. Check the fluid in the reservoir. The hydraulic system should now be fully bled and should release the clutch.

10. Check the vehicle by starting, pushing the clutch pedal to the floor and selecting reverse gear. There should be no grating of gears. If there is, and the hydraulic system still contains air, repeat the bleeding procedure from Step 5.

Driven Disc and Pressure Plate

CAUTION: *The clutch driven disc contains asbestos, which has been determined to be a cancer causing agent. Never clean clutch surfaces with compressed air! Avoid inhaling any dust from any clutch surface! When cleaning clutch surface, use a commercially available brake cleaning fluid.*

REMOVAL AND INSTALLATION

1983–84

1. Disconnect the negative battery cable.

2. Disconnect the clutch master cylinder from the clutch pedal and remove.

3. Raise the vehicle and support it safely.

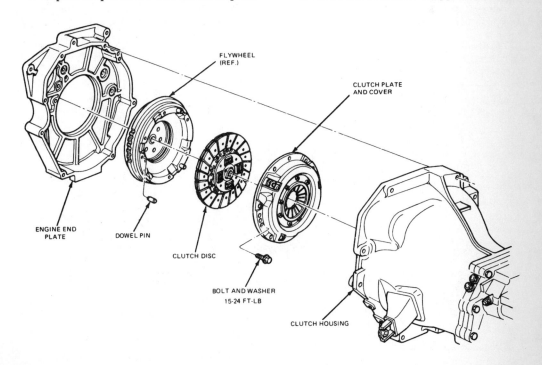

FLYWHEEL (REF.)

CLUTCH PLATE AND COVER

ENGINE END PLATE

DOWEL PIN

CLUTCH DISC

BOLT AND WASHER 15-24 FT-LB

CLUTCH HOUSING

Clutch housing installation — 1983–84 2.2L I-4 diesel engine

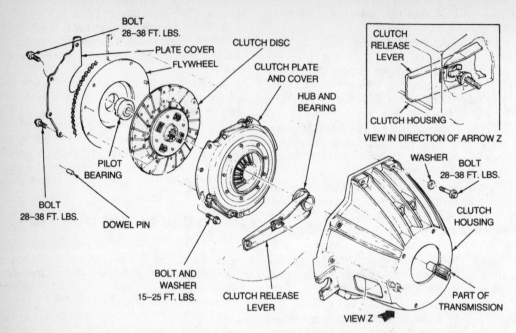

Clutch housing installation — 1983–84 2.0L and 2.3L I-4 gasoline engines

4. Remove the dust shield from the clutch housing. Disconnect the hydraulic clutch linkage from the housing and release lever.

5. Remove the starter.

6. Remove the transmission from the vehicle.

7. Mark the assembled position of the pressure plate and cover the flywheel, to aid during re-assembly.

8. Loosen the pressure plate and cover attaching bolts evenly until the pressure plate springs are expanded, and remove the bolts.

9. Remove the pressure plate and cover assembly and the clutch disc from the flywheel. Remove the pilot bearing only for replacement.

To install:

10. Position the clutch disc on the flywheel so that the Clutch Alignment Shaft D79T–

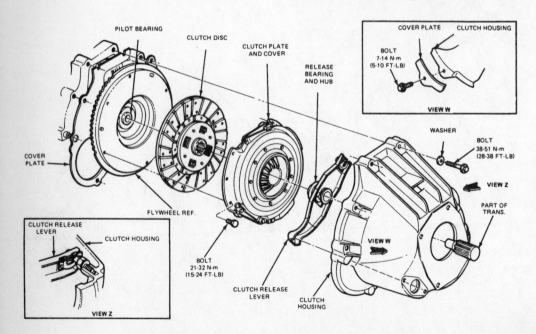

Clutch housing installation — 1983–84 2.8L V-6 gasoline engine

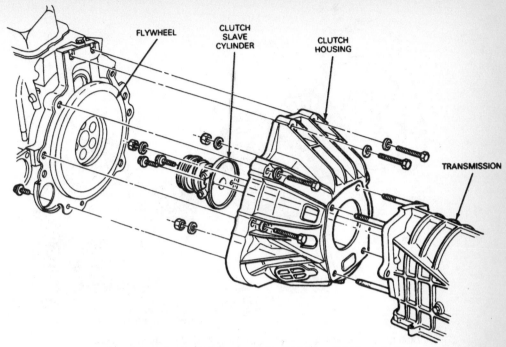

FLYWHEEL   CLUTCH SLAVE CYLINDER   CLUTCH HOUSING   TRANSMISSION

Clutch housing installation — 1985–88 2.8L and 2.9L engines

7550–A or equivalent can enter the clutch pilot bearing and align the disc.

11. When installing the original pressure plate and cover assembly, align the assembly and flywheel according to the marks made during the removal operations. Position the pressure plate and cover assembly on the flywheel, align the pressure plate and disc, and install the retaining bolts that fasten the assembly to the flywheel. Torque the bolts to 15–24 ft. lbs., and remove the clutch disc alignment tool.

12. Install the transmission into the vehicle.

13. Install the hydraulic clutch linkage on the housing in position with the release lever. Install the dust shield and install the starter.

14. Lower the vehicle and connect the clutch hydraulic system master cylinder to the clutch pedal. Check the clutch for proper operation.

15. Reconnect the negative battery cable.

1985–88

1. Disconnect the negative battery cable.

2. Disconnect the clutch hydraulic system master cylinder from the clutch pedal and remove.

3. Raise the vehicle and support it safely.

4. Remove the starter.

5. Disconnect the hydraulic coupling at the transmission.

NOTE: *Clean the area around the hose and slave cylinder to prevent fluid contamination.*

6. Remove the transmission from the vehicle.

7. Mark the assembled position of the pressure plate and cover the flywheel, to aid during re-assembly.

8. Loosen the pressure plate and cover attaching bolts evenly until the pressure plate springs are expanded, and remove the bolts.

9. Remove the pressure plate and cover assembly and the clutch disc from the flywheel. Remove the pilot bearing only for replacement.

To install:

10. Position the clutch disc on the flywheel so that the Clutch Alignment Shaft Tool T74P–

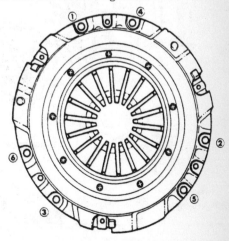

Pressure plate bolt tightening sequence

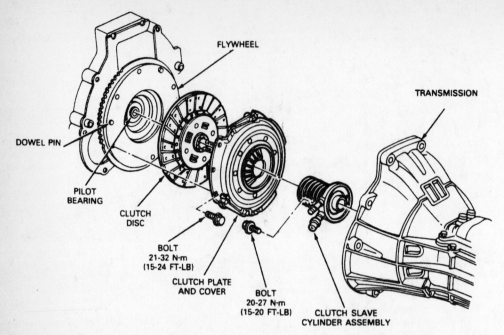

Clutch housing installation — 1985–91 2.0L, 2.3L, 3.0L and 4.0L engines

7137–K or equivalent can enter the clutch pilot bearing and align the disc.

11. When reinstalling the original pressure plate and cover assembly, align the assembly and flywheel according to the marks made during the removal operations. Position the pressure plate and cover assembly on the flywheel, align the pressure plate and disc, and install the retaining bolts that fasten the assem-bly to the flywheel. Tighten the bolts to 15–25 ft.lbs. (21–35 Nm) in the proper sequence. Remove the clutch disc pilot tool.

12. Install the transmission into the vehicle.

13. Connect the coupling by pushing the male coupling into the slave cylinder.

14. Connect the hydraulic clutch master cylinder pushrod to the clutch pedal.

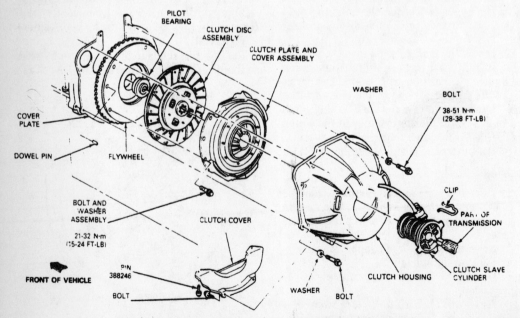

Clutch housing installation — 1985–87 2.3L turbo diesel engine

AUTOMATIC TRANSMISSION

Identification

There are 3 optional automatic transmissions used in the Ford Ranger/Bronco II/Explorer. They may be identified by checking the transmission code on the Safety Standard Certification Label attached to the driver's side door post, in the space marked **Trans.** The transmissions can also be identified by a tag attached to the lower left hand extension attaching bolt. The transmission codes are as follows:

- C3 transmission is code V
- C5 transmission is code W
- A4LD (4-speed overdrive) transmission is code T

Fluid Pan and Filter

REMOVAL AND INSTALLATION

NOTE: *For the C5 Automatic Transmission (Code W) use fluid that meets Ford Specification ESP-M2C166–H (Type H) or equivalent. The C3 Automatic Transmission (Code V) and the A4LD Automatic Transmission (Code T) use Dexron II® or equivalent automatic transmission fluid.*

1. Disconnect the negative battery cable.
2. Raise and support the vehicle safely.
3. Loosen the transmission pan attaching bolts to drain the fluid from the transmission.
4. When all the fluid has drained from the transmission, remove and thoroughly clean the pan and screen. Discard the pan gasket.

To install:

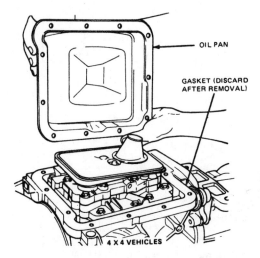

OIL PAN

GASKET (DISCARD AFTER REMOVAL)

4 X 4 VEHICLES

C-5 automatic transmission, sectional view

5. Place a new gasket on the pan, and install the pan on the transmission.
6. Add 3 quarts of fluid to the transmission through the filler tuber.
7. Check the fluid level. Adjust, if required.

NOTE: *If it is necessary to perform a complete drain and refill, it will be necessary to remove the remaining fluid from the torque converter and the cooler lines.*

To drain the torque converter:

a. Remove the converter housing lower cover.

b. Rotate the torque converter until the drain plug comes into view.

c. Remove the drain plug and allow the transmission fluid to drain.

d. Flush the cooler lines completely.

Adjustments

SHIFT/MANUAL LINKAGE

Before the linkage is adjusted, be sure the engine idle speed and anti-stall dashpot are properly adjusted.

1. Position the transmission selector control lever in **D** position and loosen the trunion bolt. On 4ALD transmission, do not use the overdrive **D** position.

NOTE: *Make sure that the shift lever detent pawl is held against the rearward Drive detent stop during the linkage adjustment procedure.*

2. Position the transmission manual lever in the **D** position, by moving the bellcrank lever all the way rearward, then forward 3 detents.

3. With the transmission selector lever/manual lever in the **D** position, apply light forward pressure to the shifter control tower arm while tightening the trunion bolt to 12–23 ft. lbs. Forward pressure on the shifter lower arm

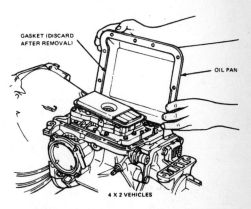

GASKET (DISCARD AFTER REMOVAL)

OIL PAN

4 X 2 VEHICLES

C-3 automatic transmission, sectional view

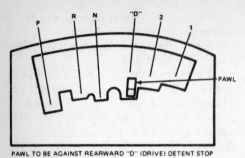

PAWL TO BE AGAINST REARWARD "D" (DRIVE) DETENT STOP

Pawl Positioning for linkage adjustment — C-3 and C-5 transmission

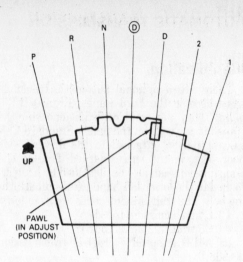

Pawl Positioning for linkage adjustment — A4LD transmission

will ensure correct positioning within the **D** detent as noted in Step 1.

After adjustment, check for Park engagement. The control lever must move to the right when engaged in Park. Check the transmission control lever in all detent positions with the engine running to ensure correct detent transmission action. Readjust if necessary.

KICKDOWN ROD ADJUSTMENT

C3 and C5 Transmissions

NOTE: *The engine should be at operating temperature whenever kickdown rod adjustments are made.*

1. Place a 6 lb. weight on the kickdown lever.

2. Rotate the throttle to the wide open position.

3. Insert a 0.06 in. (1.5mm) feeler gauge between the throttle lever and the adjusting screw.

4. Rotate the adjusting screw until it makes

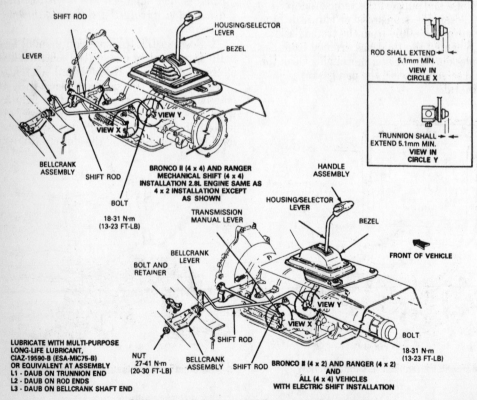

Shift control linkage — A4LD transmission shown

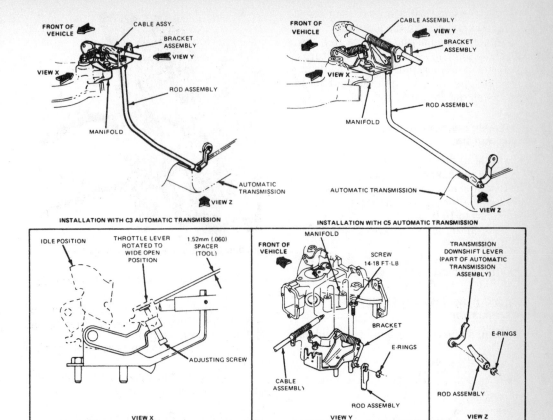

Kickdown rod installation and adjustment — C-3 and C-5 transmissions

contact with the feeler gauge. Remove the feeler gauge.

5. After the adjustment has been made, a clearance of 0.001–0.008 in. (0.025–0.203mm) is acceptable.

6. Remove the weight from the kickdown lever.

KICKDOWN CABLE

A4LD transmission

The kickdown cable is self-adjusting over a tolerance range of 1 in. (25mm). If the cable requires readjustment, reset the by depressing the semi-circular metal tab on the self-adjuster mechanism and pulling the cable forward (toward the front of the vehicle) to the "Zero" position setting. The cable will then automatically readjust to the proper length when kicked down.

BAND(S)

Front Band Adjustment (C3 Transmission Only)

1. Remove the downshift rod from the transmission downshift lever. Clean all of the dirt

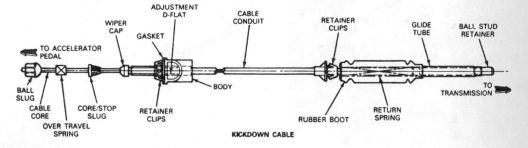

Kickdown cable — 2.3L and 2.9L EFI engine shown

away from the band adjusting nut and screw area. Remove and discard the locknut.

2. Tighten the adjusting screw to 10 ft. lbs. Back off the adjusting screw exactly two turns.

3. Install a new locknut, hold the adjusting screw in position and tighten the locknut 35–45 ft. lbs. Install the downshift rod.

Intermediate Band Adjustment
C5 Transmission

1. Clean all dirt from the adjusting screw and remove and discard the locknut.

2. Install a new locknut on the adjusting screw. Using a torque wrench, tighten the adjusting screw to 10 ft. lbs.

3. Back off the adjusting screw EXACTLY 4 $\frac{1}{4}$ TURNS.

4. Hold the adjusting screw steady and tighten the locknut to 40 ft. lbs.

Rear Band (Low-Reverse) Adjustment
C5 Transmission

1. Clean all dirt from around the band ad-

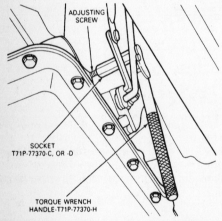

Adjusting intermediate band — C-5 transmission

Adjusting low-reverse band — C-5 transmission

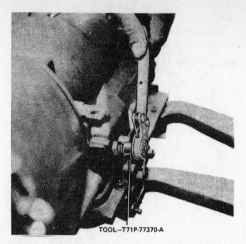

Adjusting front band — C-3 transmission

justing screw and remove and discard the locknut.

2. Install a new locknut on the adjusting screw. Using a torque wrench, tightening the adjusting screw to 10 ft.lbs.

3. Back off the adjusting screw EXACTLY 3 FULL TURNS.

4. Hold the adjusting screw steady and tighten the locknut to 40 ft. lbs.

Neutral Start Switch/Back-up Switch

The neutral start switch, mounted on the transmission, allows the vehicle to start only in **P** or **N**. The switch has a dual purpose, in that it is also the back-up lamp switch.

REMOVAL AND INSTALLATION

C3 and A4LD Transmissions

1. Disconnect the negative battery cable.
2. Raise and support the vehicle safely.
3. Disconnect the harness connector from the neutral start switch.

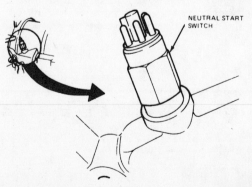

Neutral start switch installation — C-3 and A4LD transmission

4. Clean the area around the switch. Remove the switch and O-ring, using a thin wall socket (tool T74P–77247–A or equivalent).

To install:

5. Fit a new O-ring to the switch. Install the switch.

6. Reconnect the harness connector to the switch.

7. Lower the vehicle.

8. Reconnect the negative battery cable.

9. Check the operation of the switch, with the parking brake engaged. The engine should only start in **N** or **P**. The back-up lamps should come ON only in **R**.

C5 Transmission

1. Disconnect the negative battery cable.
2. Raise and support the vehicle safely.
3. Remove the downshift linkage rod from the transmission downshift lever.
4. Apply rust penetrant to the outer lever attaching nut to prevent breaking the inner lever shaft. Remove the transmission downshift outer lever attaching nut and lever.
5. Remove the two neutral start switch retaining bolts.
6. Disconnect the multiple wire connector.
7. Remove the neutral start switch from the transmission.

To install:

8. Install the neutral start switch on the transmission. Install the two retaining bolts.
9. Adjust the neutral safety switch following the above procedure.
10. Install the outer downshift lever and retaining nut, and tighten the nut. Install the downshift linkage rod with the retaining clips.
11. Connect the wire multiple connector. Check the operation of the switch. The engine should start only with the transmission selector lever in **N** or **P**.

ADJUSTMENT

C5 Transmission

1. With the automatic transmission linkage properly adjusted, loosen the two switch attaching bolts.
2. Place the transmission selector lever in neutral. Rotate the switch and insert the gauge pin (No. 43, $\frac{3}{32}$ in. drill shank end) fully into the gauge pin holes of the switch. The gauge pin has to be inserted a full $\frac{1}{2}$ in. (13mm) into the three holes of the switch. Move the switch as necessary to allow the drill to rest against the case.
3. Tighten the two switch attaching bolts 55–75 inch lbs. Remove the drill from the switch.
4. Check the operation of the switch. The

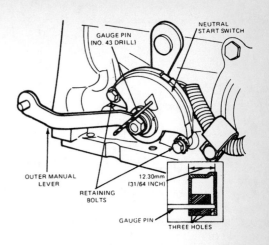

Adjusting neutral safety switch — C-5 transmission

engine should start only with the transmission selector lever in **N** or **P**.

Vacuum Diaphragm

REMOVAL AND INSTALLATION

A4LD Transmission

1. Disconnect the negative battery cable.
2. Raise and support the vehicle safely.
3. Disconnect the hose from the vacuum diaphragm.
4. Remove the vacuum diaphragm retaining clamp bolt and clamp. Do not pry on the clamp.
5. Pull the vacuum diaphragm from the transmission case and remove the vacuum diaphragm control rod from the transmission case.

To install:

6. Install the vacuum diaphragm control rod from the transmission case.

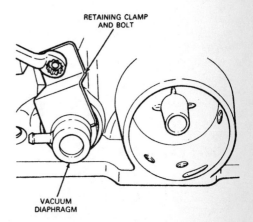

Vacuum diaphragm, installation — A4LD transmission

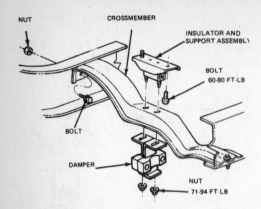

Crossmember removal and installation — C-3 transmission

7. Push the vacuum diaphragm into the case and secure it with the clamp and bolt. Tighten to 80–106 inch lbs. (9–12Nm).

8. Fit the vacuum hose to the diaphragm.

9. Lower the vehicle.

10. Reconnect the negative battery cable.

Extension Housing Seal

REMOVAL AND INSTALLATION

1. Disconnect the negative battery cable.

2. Raise and support the vehicle safely.

3. Matchmark the driveshaft end yoke and rear axle companion flange to assure proper positioning during assembly. Remove the driveshaft.

4. Remove the oil seal from the extension housing, using seal remover T71P–7657–A or equivalent.

To install:

Before install the replacement seal, inspect the sealing surface of the universal joint yoke for scores. If scoring is found, replace the yoke.

5. Install the new seal, using seal installer T74P–77052–A or equivalent. Coat the inside diameter at the end of the rubber boot portion of the seal with long-life lubricant (C1AZ–19590–BA or equivalent).

6. Align the matchmarks and install the driveshaft.

7. Lower the vehicle.

8. Reconnect the negative battery cable.

Transmission

REMOVAL AND INSTALLATION

C3 Transmission

1. Raise the vehicle and safely support on jackstands. Place a drain pan under the transmission fluid pan. Starting at the rear of the pan and working toward the front, loosen the attaching bolts and allow the fluid to drain. Then remove all of the pan attaching bolts except two at the front, to allow the fluid to further drain. After all the fluid has drained, install two bolts on the rear side of the pan to temporarily hold it in place.

2. Remove the converter drain plug access cover and adapter plate bolts from the lower end of the converter housing.

3. Remove the 4 flywheel to converter attaching nuts. Crank the engine to turn the converter to gain access to the nuts, using a wrench on the crankshaft pulley attaching bolt. On belt driven overhead camshaft engines, never turn the engine backwards.

4. Crank the engine until the converter drain plug is accessible and remove the plug. Place a drain pan under the converter to catch the fluid. After all the fluid has been drained from the converter, reinstall the plug and tighten to 20–30 ft. lbs. Remove the driveshaft. Install cover, plastic bag etc. over end of extension housing.

5. Remove the speedometer cable from the extension housing. Disconnect the shift rod at the transmission manual lever.Disconnect the downshift rod at the transmission downshift lever.

6. Remove the starter-to-converter housing attaching bolts and position the starter out of the way.

7. Disconnect the neutral safety switch wires from the switch. Remove the vacuum line from the transmission vacuum modulator.

8. Position a suitable jack under the transmission and raise it slightly.

9. Remove the engine rear support-to-crossmember bolts. Remove the crossmember-to-frame side support attaching bolts and remove the crossmember insulator and support and damper.

10. Lower the jack under the transmission and allow the transmission to hang.

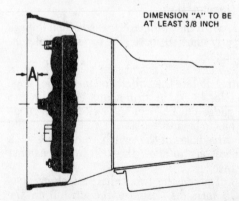

Positioning of converter hub to bell housing flange — C-3 transmission

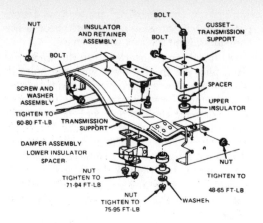

Crossmember removal and installation — C-5 transmission

11. Position a jack to the front of the engine and raise the engine to gain access to the two upper converter housing-to-engine attaching bolts.

12. Disconnect the oil cooler lines at the transmission. Plug all openings to keep out dirt.

13. Remove the lower converter housing-to-engine attaching bolts. Remove the transmission filler tube.

14. Secure the transmission to the jack with a safety chain.

15. Remove the two upper converter housing-to-engine attaching bolts. Move the transmission to the rear and down to remove it from under the vehicle.

To install:

16. Position the converter to the transmission making sure the converter hub is fully engaged in the pump. With the converter properly installed, place the transmission on the jack and secure with safety chain.

17. Rotate the converter so the drive studs and drain plug are in alignment with their holes in the flywheel. With the transmission mounted on a transmission jack, move the converter and transmission assembly forward into position being careful not to damage the flywheel and the converter pilot.

WARNING: *During this move, to avoid damage, do not allow the transmission to get into a nosed down position as this will cause the converter to move forward and disengage from the pump gear. The converter must rest squarely against the flywheel. This indicates that the converter pilot is not binding in the engine crankshaft.*

18. Install the two upper converter housing-to-engine attaching bolts and tighten to 28–38 ft. lbs.

19. Remove the safety chain from the transmission. Insert the filler tube in the stub tube

and secure it to the cylinder block with the attaching bolt. Tighten the bolt to 28–38 ft. lbs. If the stub tube is loosened or dislodged, it should be replaced. Install the oil cooler lines in the retaining clip at the cylinder block. Connect the lines to the transmission case.

20. Remove the jack supporting the front of the engine. Raise the transmission. Position the crossmember, insulator and support and damper to the frame side supports and install the attaching bolts. Tighten the bolt to 60–80 ft. lbs.

21. Lower the transmission and install the rear engine support-to-crossmember nut. Tighten the bolt to 60–80 ft. lbs.

22. Remove the transmission jack. Install the vacuum hose on the transmission vacuum unit. Install the vacuum line into the retaining clip.

23. Connect the neutral safety switch plug to the switch. Install the starter and tighten the attaching bolts to 15–20 ft. lbs.

24. Install the 4 flywheel-to-converter attaching nuts. When assembling the flywheel to the converter, first install the attaching nuts and tighten to 20–34 ft. lbs.

25. Install the converter drain plug access cover and adaptor plate bolts. Tighten the bolts to 12–16 ft. lbs.

26. Connect the muffler inlet pipe to the exhaust manifold.

27. Connect the transmission shift rod to the manual lever. Connect the downshift rod to the downshift lever.

28. Connect the speedometer cable to the extension housing. Install the driveshaft. Tighten the companion flange U-bolt attaching nuts to 70–95 ft.lbs.

29. Adjust the manual and downshift linkage as required.

30. Lower the vehicle. Fill the transmission to the correct level with the specified fluid.

31. Start the engine and shift the transmission to all ranges, then recheck the fluid level.

C5 Transmission
2WD Vehicles

1. Raise the vehicle and safely support on jackstands. Place the drain pan under the transmission fluid pan. Starting at the rear of the pan and working toward the front, loosen the attaching bolts and allow the fluid to drain. Finally remove all of the pan attaching bolts except two at the front, to allow the fluid to further drain. With fluid drained, install two bolts on the rear side of the pan to temporarily hold it in place.

2. Remove the converter drain plug access cover from the lower end of the converter housing.

3. Remove the converter-to-flywheel attaching nuts. Place a wrench on the crankshaft pulley attaching bolt to turn the converter to gain access to the nuts.

4. Place a drain pan under the converter to catch the fluid. With the wrench on the crankshaft pulley attaching bolt, turn the converter to gain access to the converter drain plug and remove the plug. After the fluid has been drained, reinstall the plug.

5. Disconnect the driveshaft from the rear axle and slide shaft rearward from the transmission. Install a suitable cover or plug in the extension housing to prevent fluid leakage. Mark the rear driveshaft yoke and axle flange so they can be installed in their original position.

6. Disconnect the cable from the terminal on the starter motor. Remove the three attaching bolts and remove the starter motor. Disconnect the neutral start switch wires at the plug connector.

7. Remove the rear mount-to-crossmember attaching nuts and the two crossmember-to-frame attaching bolts. Remove the right and left gusset.

8. Remove the two engine rear insulator-to-extension housing attaching bolts.

9. Disconnect the TV linkage rod from the transmission TV lever. Disconnect the manual rod from the transmission manual lever at the transmission.

10. Remove the two bolts securing the bellcrank bracket to the converter housing.

11. Raise the transmission with a suitable jack to provide clearance to remover the crossmember. Remove the rear mount from the crossmember and remove the crossmember from the side supports. Lower the transmission to gain access to the oil cooler lines. Disconnect each oil line from the fittings on the transmission.

12. Disconnect the speedometer cable from the extension housing.

13. Remove the bolt that secures the transmission fluid filler tube to the cylinder block. Lift the filler tube and the dipstick from the transmission.

14. Secure the transmission to the jack with the chain. Remove the converter housing-to-cylinder block attaching bolts.

15. Carefully move the transmission and converter assembly away from the engine and, at the same time, lower the jack to clear the underside of the vehicle.

To install:

16. Tighten the converter drain plug to specifications. Position the converter on the transmission, making sure the converter drive flats are fully engaged in the pump gear by rotating the converter.

17. With the converter properly installed, place the transmission on the jack. Secure the transmission to the jack with a chain.

18. Rotate the converter until the studs and drain plug are in alignment with the holes in the flywheel. Move the converter and transmission assembly forward into position, using care not to damage the flywheel and the converter pilot. The converter must rest squarely against the flywheel. This indicates that the converter pilot is not binding in the engine crankshaft.

19. Install and tighten the converter housing-to-engine attaching bolts to specification.

20. Remove the safety chain from around the transmission.

21. Install the new O-ring on the lower end of the transmission filler tube. Insert the tube in the transmission case and secure the tube to the engine with the attaching bolt.

22. Connect the speedometer cable to the extension housing.

23. Connect the oil cooler lines to the right side of transmission case.

24. Secure the engine rear support to the extension housing and tighten the bolts to specification.

25. Position the crossmember on the side supports. Lower the transmission and remove the jack. Secure the crossmember to the side supports with the attaching bolts.

26. Position the damper assembly over the engine rear support studs. (The painted face of the damper is facing forward when installed in the vehicle.) Secure the rear engine support to the crossmember.

27. Position the bellcrank to the converter housing and install the two attaching bolts.

28. Connect the TV linkage rod to the transmission TV lever. Connect the manual linkage rod to the manual lever at the transmission.

29. Secure the converter-to-flywheel attaching nuts and tighten them to specification.

30. Install the converter housing access cover and secure it with the attaching bolts.

31. Secure the starter motor in place with the attaching bolts. Connect the cable to the terminal on the starter. Connect the neutral start switch wires at the plug connector.

32. Connect the driveshaft to the rear axle so the index marks on the companion flange and the rear yoke are aligned. Lubricate the slip yoke with grease. Adjust the shift linkage as required.

33. Adjust throttle linkage.

34. Lower the vehicle. Fill the transmission to the correct level with the specified fluid.

33. Start the engine and shift the transmission to all ranges, then recheck the fluid level.

C5 Transmission
4WD Vehicles

1. Remove the bolt securing the fluid filler tube to the engine valve cover bracket.

2. Raise the vehicle on a hoist and support with jackstands.

3. Place a drain pan under the transmission fluid pan.

4. Starting at the rear of the pan and working towards the front, loosen the attaching bolts and allow the fluid to drain. Finally, remove all of the pan attaching bolts except two at the front, to allow the fluid to drain further. With fluid drained, install two bolts on the rear side of the pan to temporarily hold it in place.

5. Remove the converter drain plug access cover from the lower end of the converter housing.

6. Remove the converter-to-flywheel attaching nuts.

7. Place a wrench on the crankshaft pulley attaching bolt to turn the converter to gain access to the nuts.

8. Place a drain pan under the converter to catch the fluid. With the wrench on the crankshaft pulley attaching bolt, turn the converter to gain access to the converter drain plug and remove the plug. After the fluid has been drained, reinstall the plug.

9. Disconnect the cable from the terminal at the starter motor. Remove the three attaching bolts and remove the starter motor. Disconnect the neutral safety switch wires at the plug connector.

10. Remove the two engine rear insulator-to-extension housing attaching bolts.

11. Disconnect the TV linkage rod from the transmission TV lever. Disconnect the manual rod from the transmission manual lever at the transmission. Disconnect the downshift and manual linkage rods from the levers on the transmission.

12. Remove the vacuum hose from the vacuum diaphragm unit. Remove the vacuum line from the retaining clip.

13. Remove the two bolts securing the bellcrank bracket to the converter housing.

14. Remove the transfer case. Refer to Transfer Case in this chapter for the correct procedure.

15. Raise the transmission with a transmission jack to provide clearance to remove the crossmember. Remove the rear mount from the crossmember and remove the crossmember from the side supports.

16. Lower the transmission to gain access to the oil cooler lines.

17. Disconnect each oil line from the fittings on the transmission.

18. Disconnect the speedometer cable from the extension housing.

19. Secure the transmission to the jack with the chain.

20. Secure the converter housing-to-cylinder block attaching bolts.

21. Carefully move the transmission and converter assembly away from the engine and, at the same time, lower the jack to clear the underside of the vehicle.

22. Remove the converter and mount the transmission in a holding fixture.

To install:

23. Tighten the converter drain plug to 15–28 ft. lbs.

24. Position the converter on the transmission, making sure the converter drive flats are fully engaged in the pump gear by rotating the converter.

25. With the converter properly installed, place the transmission on the jack. Secure the transmission to the jack with a chain.

26. Rotate the converter until the studs and drain plug are in alignment with the holes in the flywheel.

27. Move the converter and transmission assembly forward into position using care not to damage the flywheel and the converter pilot. The converter must rest squarely against the flywheel. This indicates that the converter pilot is not binding in the engine crankshaft.

28. Install and tighten the converter housing-to-engine attaching bolts to 22–32 inch lbs.

29. Remove the safety chain from around the transmission.

30. Install a new O-ring on the lower end of the transmission filler tube. Insert the tube in the transmission case.

31. Connect the speedometer cable to the extension housing.

32. Connect the oil cooler lines to the right of the transmission case.

33. Position the crossmember on the side supports.

34. Position the rear mount insulator on the crossmember and install the attaching bolts and nuts.

35. Install the transfer case. Refer to Transfer Case in this chapter.

36. Secure the engine rear support to the extension housing and tighten the bolts.

37. Lower the transmission and remove the jack.

38. Secure the crossmember to the side supports with the attaching bolts and tighten the bolts.

39. Position the bellcrank to the converter housing and install the two attaching bolts.

40. Connect the downshift and manual link-

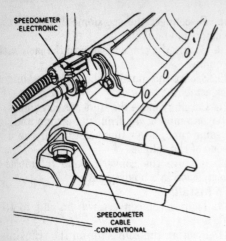

Speedometer cable connection

age rods to their respective levers on the transmission.

41. Connect the vacuum line to the vacuum diaphragm making sure that the line is in the retaining clip.

42. Secure the converter-to-flywheel attaching nuts and tighten them to 20–34 ft. lbs.

43. Install the converter housing access cover and secure it with the attaching bolts.

44. Secure the starter motor in place with the attaching bolts. Connect the cable to the terminal on the starter. Connect the neutral safety switch wires at the plug connector.

45. Adjust the shift linkage as required. Refer to shift linkage adjustment, shown earlier in this chapter.

46. Remove the jackstands and lower the vehicle.

47. Position the transmission fluid filler tube to the valve cover bracket and secure with the attaching bolt.

48. Fill the transmission to the correct level with the specified fluid.

49. Start the engine and shift the transmission to all ranges, then recheck the fluid level.

A4LD Transmission

1. Disconnect the negative battery cable.

2. Raise the vehicle and support it safely.

3. Position a drain pan under the transmission pan.

4. Starting at the rear, loosen, but do not remove the pan bolts.

5. Loosen the pan from the transmission and allow the fluid to drain gradually.

6. Remove all of the pan bolts except 2 at the front or rear and allow the fluid to continue draining.

7. Remove the converter access cover from the lower right side of the converter housing on the 3.0L engine. Remove the cover from the bottom of the engine oil pan on the 2.3L engine. Remove a bolt on the access cover of the 2.9L engine and swing the cover open. Remove the access cover and adapter plate bolts from the lower left side of the converter housing on all other applications.

8. Remove the flywheel to converter attaching nuts. Use a socket and breaker bar on the crankshaft pulley attaching bolt. Rotate the pulley clockwise as viewed from the front to gain access to each of the nuts.

NOTE: *On belt driven overhead cam engines, never rotate the pulley in a counterclockwise direction as viewed from the front.*

9. Scribe a mark indexing the driveshaft to the rear axle flange. Remove the driveshaft.

10. Remove the speedometer cable from the extension housing.

11. Disconnect the shift rod or cable at the transmission manual lever and retainer bracket.

12. Disconnect the downshift cable from the downshift lever. Depress the tab on the retainer and remove the kickdown cable from the bracket.

13. Disconnect the neutral start switch wires, converter clutch solenoid and the 3–4 shift solenoid connector.

14. Remove the starter mounting bolts and the ground cable. Remove the starter.

15. Remove the vacuum line from the transmission vacuum modulator.

16. Remove the filler tube from the transmission.

17. Position a transmission jack under the transmission and raise it slightly.

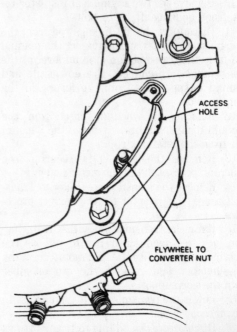

Torque converter nut access hole

18. Remove the engine rear support to crossmember bolts.

19. Remove the crossmember to frame side support attaching nuts and bolts. Remove the crossmember.

20. Remove the converter housing to engine bolts.

21. Slightly lower the jack to gain access to the oil cooler lines. Disconnect the oil cooler lines at the transmission. Plug all openings to keep dirt and contamination out.

22. Move the transmission to the rear so it disengages from the dowel pins and the converter is disengaged from the flywheel. Lower the transmission from the vehicle.

23. Remove the torque converter from the transmission.

NOTE: *If the transmission is to be removed for a period of time, support the engine with a safety stand and wood block.*

To install:

Proper installation of the converter requires full engagement of the converter hub in the pump gear. To accomplish this, the converter must be pushed and at the same time rotated through what feels like 2 notches or bumps. When fully installed, rotation of the converter will usually result in a clicking noise heard, caused by the converter surface touching the housing to case bolts.

This should not be a concern, but an indication of proper converter installation since, when the converter is attached to the engine flywheel, it will be pulled slightly forward away from the bolt heads. Besides the clicking sound, the converter should rotate freely with no binding.

For reference, a properly installed converter will have a distance from the converter pilot nose from face to converter housing outer face of 11–14mm.

1. Install the converter on the transmission.

2. With the converter properly installed, position the transmission on the jack.

3. Rotate the converter so that the drive studs are in alignment with the holes in the flywheel.

4. Move the converter and transmission assembly forward into position, being careful not to damage the flywheel and converter pilot. The converter housing is piloted into position by the dowels in the rear of the engine block.

NOTE: *During this move, to avoid damage, do not allow the transmission to get into a nose down position as this will cause the converter to move forward and disengage from the pump gear.*

5. Install the converter housing to engine attaching bolts and tighten to 28–38 ft. lbs. (38–51 Nm). The 2 longer bolts are located at the dowel holes.

6. Remove the jack supporting the engine.

7. Raise the transmission. Position the crossmember to the frame side supports. Install the attaching bolts and tighten to 20–30 ft. lbs. (27–41 Nm).

8. Lower the transmission and install the rear engine to crossmember nut and tighten to 60–80 ft. lbs. (82–108 Nm). Remove the transmission jack.

9. Install the filler tube in the transmission.

10. Install the oil cooler lines in the retaining clip at the cylinder block. Connect the lines to the transmission case.

11. Install the vacuum hose on the transmission vacuum unit. Install the vacuum line into the retaining clip.

12. Connect the neutral start switch plug to the neutral start switch. Connect the converter clutch solenoid wires and the 3–4 shift solenoid wires.

13. Install the starter and tighten the bolts to 15–20 ft. lbs. (20–27 Nm).

14. Install the flywheel to converter attaching nuts and tighten to 20–34 ft. lbs. (27–46 Nm).

15. Connect the muffler inlet pipe to the exhaust manifold.

16. Connect the transmission shift rod or cable to the manual lever.

17. Connect the downshift cable to the downshift lever.

18. Install the speedometer cable or sensor.

19. Install the driveshaft making sure to line up the scribe marks made during removal on the driveshaft and axle flange. Tighten the companion flange U-bolt attaching nuts to 70–95 ft. lbs. (95–130 Nm).

20. Adjust the manual and downshift linkages.

21. Lower the vehicle. Connect the negative battery cable.

22. Fill the transmission to the proper level with the specified fluid.

23. Check the transmission, converter and oil cooler lines for leaks.

TRANSFER CASE

Identification

There are 4 transfer cases used on the Ranger/Bronco II/Explorer. There are 2 versions of the 13-50 (Mechanical shift and Electronic shift), the 13-54 and the 13-59.

The Borg Warner 13-50, mechanical shift

transfer case, is a 3-piece aluminum part time unit. It transfers power from the transmission to the rear axle and when actuated, also the front drive axle. The unit is lubricated by a positive displacement oil pump that channels oil flow through drilled holes in the rear output shaft. The pump turns with the rear output shaft and allows towing of the vehicle at maximum legal road speeds for extended distances without disconnecting the front and/or rear driveshaft.

The Borg Warner 13-50, electronic shift transfer case, transfers power from the transmission to the rear axle and also the front drive axle, when electronically actuated.

This system consists of a pushbutton control, an electronic control module, an electric shift motor with an integral shift position sensor and a speed sensor.

The electric shift motor, mounted externally at the rear of the transfer case, drives a rotary helical cam. The cam moves the 2WD–4WD shift fork and 4H–4L reduction shift fork to the selected vehicle drive position.

The Borg Warner 13-54 is a 3-piece aluminum part time transfer case. It transfers power from the transmission to the rear axle and when actuated, also the front drive axle. The unit is lubricated by a positive displacement oil pump that channels oil flow through drilled

holes in the rear output shaft. The pump turns with the rear output shaft and allows towing of the vehicle at maximum legal road speeds for extended distances without disconnecting the front and/or rear driveshaft.

The Borg Warner 13-59 transfer drive case is a 3-piece aluminum assembly. It consists of a front mounting adapter, a front case and a rear cover that transmits power from the transmission to the rear axle. The input shaft and the output shaft are connected together by a coupling sleeve providing direct drive between the 2 shafts. The case assembly contains no lubricant and none should be installed.

Adjustments

Manual Shift 13-50 and 13-54

The following procedure should be used, if a partial or incomplete engagement of the transfer case shift lever detent is experienced or if the control assembly requires removal.

1. Disconnect the negative battery cable.
2. Raise the shift boot to expose the top surface of the cam plates.
3. Loosen the 1 large and 1 small bolt, ap-

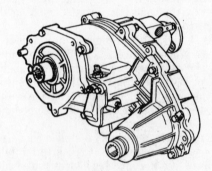

Borg-Warner 13-50 — mechanical shift

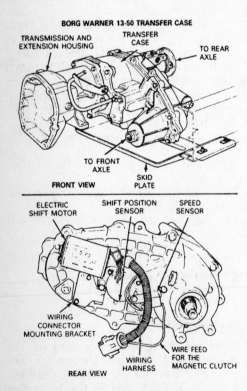

BORG WARNER 13-50 TRANSFER CASE

TRANSMISSION AND EXTENSION HOUSING
TRANSFER CASE
TO REAR AXLE
TO FRONT AXLE
SKID PLATE
FRONT VIEW

ELECTRIC SHIFT MOTOR
SHIFT POSITION SENSOR
SPEED SENSOR
WIRING CONNECTOR MOUNTING BRACKET
WIRING HARNESS
WIRE FEED FOR THE MAGNETIC CLUTCH
REAR VIEW

Borg-Warner 13-50 — electronic shift

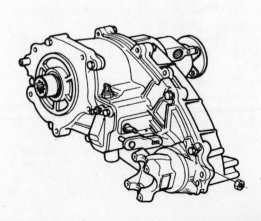

Borg-Warner 13-54 — mechanical shift

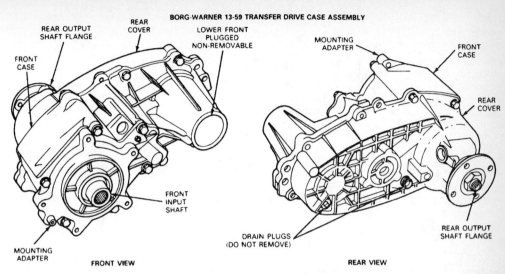

BORG-WARNER 13-59 TRANSFER DRIVE CASE ASSEMBLY

REAR OUTPUT SHAFT FLANGE — REAR COVER — LOWER FRONT PLUGGED NON-REMOVABLE — FRONT CASE — MOUNTING ADAPTER — FRONT CASE — REAR COVER — FRONT INPUT SHAFT — MOUNTING ADAPTER — FRONT VIEW — DRAIN PLUGS (DO NOT REMOVE) — REAR VIEW — REAR OUTPUT SHAFT FLANGE

Borg-Warner 13-59 transfer drive case

proximately 1 turn. Move the transfer case shift lever to the **4L** position (lever down).

4. Move the cam plate rearward until the bottom chamfered corner of the neutral lug just contacts the forward right edge of the shift lever.

5. Hold the cam plate in this position and torque the larger bolt first to 70–90 ft. lbs. (95–122 Nm) and torque the smaller bolt to 31–42 ft. lbs. (42–57 Nm).

6. Move the transfer case in cab shift lever to all shift positions to check for positive engagement. There should be a clearance between the shift lever and the cam plate in the **2H** front and **4H** rear (clearance not to exceed 3.3mm) and **4L** shift positions.

7. Install the shift boot assembly.

8. Reconnect the negative battery cable.

Borg Warner 13-59

The Borg Warner 13–59 does not require adjustment.

Transfer Case

REMOVAL AND INSTALLATION

Borg Warner 13-50 Manual Shift

CAUTION: *The catalytic converter is located beside the transfer case. Be careful when working around the catalytic converter because of the extremely high temperatures generated by the converter!*

1. Disconnect the negative battery cable.

2. Raise the vehicle and support it safely.

3. Remove the skid plate from frame, if so equipped.

4. Place a drain pan under transfer case,

remove the drain plug and drain the fluid from the transfer case.

5. Disconnect the 4-wheel drive indicator switch wire connector at the transfer case.

6. Disconnect the front driveshaft from the axle input yoke.

7. Loosen the clamp retaining the front driveshaft boot to the transfer case, and pull the driveshaft and front boot assembly out of the transfer case front output shaft.

8. Disconnect the rear driveshaft from the transfer case output shaft yoke.

9. Disconnect the speedometer drive gear from the transfer case rear cover.

10. Disconnect the vent hose from the control lever.

11. Loosen or remove the large bolt and the small bolt retaining the shifter to the extension housing. Pull on the control lever until the bushing slides off the transfer case shift lever pin. If necessary, unscrew the shift lever from the control lever.

12. Remove the heat shield from the transfer case.

13. Support the transfer case with a transmission jack.

14. Remove the five bolts retaining the transfer case to the transmission and the extension housing.

15. Slide the transfer case rearward off the transmission output shaft and lower the transfer case from the vehicle. Remove the gasket from between the transfer case and extension housing.

To install:

16. Place a new gasket between the transfer case and the extension housing.

17. Raise the transfer case with the transmis-

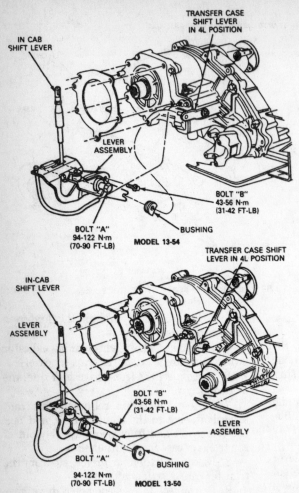

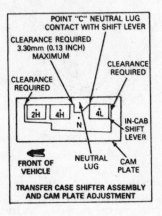

Linkage adjustment — manual shift 13-50 and 13-54 transfer casec

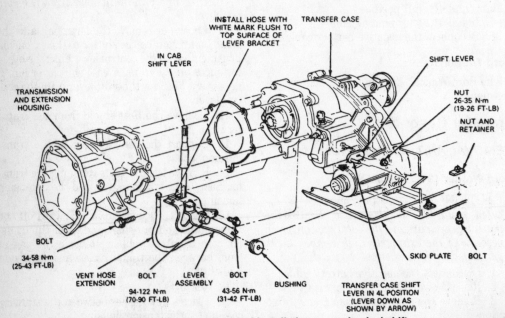

Borg-Warner 13-50, removal and installation — mechanical shift

sion jack so that the transmission output shaft aligns with the splined transfer case input shaft. Slide the transfer case forward onto the transmission output shaft and onto the dowel pin. Install the five bolts retaining the transfer case to the extension housing. Torque the bolts to 25–35 ft. lbs. in the sequence shown in the diagram.

18. Remove the transmission jack from the transfer case.

19. Install the heat shield on the transfer case. Torque the bolts to 27–37 ft. lbs.

20. Move the control lever until the bushing is in position over the transfer case shift lever pin. Install and hand start the attaching bolts. First, tighten the large bolt retaining the shifter to the extension housing to 70–90 ft. lbs. then the small bolt to 31–42 ft. lbs.

NOTE: *Always tighten the large bolt retaining the shifter to the extension housing before tightening the small bolt.*

21. Install the vent assembly so the white marking on the hose is in position in the notch in the shifter.

NOTE: *The upper end of the vent hose should be 2 in. (51mm) above the top of the shifter and positioned inside of the shift lever boot.*

22. Connect the speedometer drive gear to the transfer case rear cover. Torque the screw to 20–25 inch lbs.

23. Connect the rear driveshaft to the transfer case output shaft yoke. Torque the bolts to 12–15 ft. lbs.

24. Clean the transfer case front output shaft female splines. Apply 5–8 grams of Lubriplate® or equivalent to the splines. Insert the front driveshaft male spline.

25. Connect the front driveshaft to the axle input yoke. Torque the bolts to 12–15 ft.lbs.

26. Push the driveshaft boot to engage the external groove on the transfer case front output shaft. Secure with a clamp.

27. Connect the 4-wheel drive indicator switch wire connector at the transfer case.

28. Install the drain plug and torque to 14–22 ft. lbs. Remove the fill plug and install 3 U.S. pints of DEXRON® II, automatic transmission fluid. Install fill plug and torque to 14–22 ft. lbs.

29. Install the skid plate to the frame. Torque the nuts and bolts to 22–30 ft. lbs.

30. Remove the jackstands and lower the vehicle from the hoist.

31. Reconnect the negative battery cable.

Borg Warner 13-50 Electric Shift

CAUTION: *The catalytic converter is located beside the transfer case. Be careful when working around the catalytic converter because of the extremely high temperatures generated by the converter.*

1. Disconnect the negative battery cable.

2. Raise the vehicle and support it safely.

3. If so equipped, remove the skid plate from frame.

4. Place a drain pan under transfer case, remove the drain plug and drain fluid from the transfer case.

5. Remove the wire connector from the feed wire harness at the rear of the transfer case. Be sure to squeeze the locking tabs, then pull the connectors apart.

6. Disconnect the front driveshaft from the axle input yoke.

7. Loosen the clamp retaining the front driveshaft boot to the transfer case, and pull the driveshaft and front boot assembly out of the transfer case front output shaft.

8. Disconnect the rear driveshaft from the transfer case output shaft yoke.

9. Disconnect the speedometer driven gear from the transfer case rear cover.

10. Disconnect the vent hose from the control lever.

11. Loosen or remove the large bolt and the small bolt retaining the shifter to the extension housing. Pull on the control lever until the bushing slides off the transfer case shift lever pin. If necessary, unscrew the shift lever from the control lever.

12. Remove the heat shield from the transfer case.

13. Support the transfer case with a transmission jack.

14. Remove the 5 bolts retaining the transfer case to the transmission and the extension housing.

15. Slide the transfer case rearward off the transmission output shaft and lower the transfer case from the vehicle. Remove the gasket from between the transfer case and extension housing.

To install:

16. Install the heat shield onto the transfer case and place a new gasket between the transfer case and adapter.

17. Raise the transfer case with a suitable transmission jack or equivalent, raise it high enough so that the transmission output shaft aligns with the splined transfer case input shaft.

18. Slide the transfer case forward on to the transmission output shaft and onto the dowel pin. Install transfer case retaining bolts and torque them to 26–43 ft. lbs. (35–58 Nm).

19. Connect the rear driveshaft to the rear output shaft yoke and torque the retaining bolts to 20–28 ft. lbs. (27–38 Nm). Attach the shift rod to the transfer case shift lever and

transfer case control rod and attach with retaining rings.

20. Connect the speedometer driven gear to the transfer case. Connect the 4WD indicator switch wire connector at the transfer case.

21. Connect the front driveshaft to the front output yoke and torque the yoke nut to 8–15 ft. lbs. (11–20 Nm). Attach the heat shield to the engine mounting bracket and mounting lug on the transfer case.

22. Install the skid plate to the frame. Connect the wire connectors on the rear of the transfer case, making sure the retaining tabs lock.

23. Fill the transfer case with 6.5 pints of Dexron®II transmission fluid or equivalent. Torque the fill plug to 14–22 ft. lbs. (19–32 Nm). Lower the vehicle. Start the engine and check the transfer case for correct operation. Stop the engine and check the fluid level, add as necessary.

24. Reconnect the negative battery cable.

Borg Warner 13-54 Mechanical Shift

CAUTION: *The catalytic converter is located beside the transfer case. Be careful when working around the catalytic converter because of the extremely high temperatures generated by the converter!*

1. Disconnect the negative battery cable.
2. Raise the vehicle and support it safely.
3. Remove the skid plate from frame, if so equipped.
4. Remove the damper from the transfer case, if so equipped.
5. Place a drain pan under transfer case,

remove the drain plug and drain the fluid from the transfer case.

6. Disconnect the 4WD drive indicator switch wire connector at the transfer case.

7. Disconnect the front driveshaft from the transfer case output shaft flange and wire the shaft out of the way.

8. Disconnect the rear driveshaft from the transfer case output shaft flange and wire the shaft out of the way.

9. Disconnect the speedometer drive gear from the transfer case rear cover.

10. Disconnect the vent hose from the control lever.

11. Remove the shift lever retaining nut and remove the lever.

12. Remove the bolts that retains the shifter to the extension housing. Note the size and location of the bolts to aid during installation. Remove the lever assembly and bushing.

13. Support the transfer case with a suitable jack and remove the 5 bolts retaining the transfer case to the transmission and the extension housing.

14. Slide the transfer case rearward off the transmission output shaft and lower the transfer case from the vehicle. Remove and discard the gasket between the transfer case and extension housing.

To install:

15. Fit a new gasket to the front mounting surface of the transfer case assembly. It may be necessary to use a small daub of sealant to hold the gasket down.

16. Raise the transfer case with the transmis-

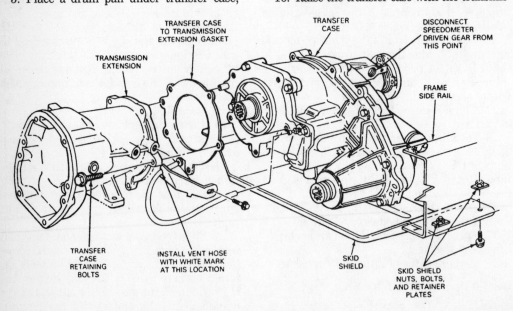

Borg-Warner 13-50, removal and installation — electrical shift

sion jack so that the transmission output shaft aligns with the splined transfer case input shaft. Slide the transfer case forward onto the transmission output shaft and onto the dowel pin. Install the five bolts retaining the transfer case to the extension housing. Torque the bolts to 25–35 ft. lbs. (34–48Nm) in the sequence shown in the diagram.

17. Remove the transmission jack from the transfer case.

18. Install and adjust the shifter, as required.

NOTE: *Always tighten the large bolt retaining the shifter to the extension housing before tightening the small bolt.*

19. Install the vent assembly so the white marking on the hose is in position in the notch in the shifter.

NOTE: *The upper end of the vent hose should be $3/4$ in. (19mm) above the top of the shifter and positioned inside of the shift lever boot.*

20. Connect the speedometer drive gear to the transfer case rear cover. Torque the screw to 20–25 inch lbs. (2.3–2.8Nm).

21. Connect the rear driveshaft to the transfer case output shaft yoke. Torque the bolts to 61–87 ft. lbs. (83–118Nm).

22. Connect the front driveshaft to the transfer case output shaft yoke. Torque the bolts to 12–16 ft.lbs. (16–22Nm).

23. Connect the 4WD indicator switch wire connector at the transfer case.

24. Install the drain plug and torque to 14–22 ft. lbs. Remove the fill plug and install 3 U.S. pints of DEXRON® II, automatic transmission fluid. Install fill plug and torque to 14–22 ft. lbs.

25. Install the damper to the transfer case, if so equipped. Using new damper bolts, tighten the bolts to 25–35 ft. lbs. (34–48Nm).

26. Install the skid plate to the frame. Torque the nuts and bolts to 15–20 ft. lbs. (20–27Nm).

27. Lower the vehicle.

28. Reconnect the negative battery cable.

Borg Warner 13-59

CAUTION: *The catalytic converter is located beside the heat shield. Be careful when working around the converter because of the extremely high temperatures generated by the converter!*

1. Disconnect the negative battery cable.

2. Raise the vehicle and support safely.

3. Disconnect the rear driveshaft from the transfer case output shaft flange.

4. Disconnect the speedometer driven gear from the transfer case rear cover.

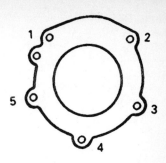

Case to extension — bolt torque sequence

5. Support the transfer case with a transmission jack.

6. Remove the 5 bolts retaining the transfer case to the transmission and the extension housing.

7. Slide the transfer case rearward off the transmission output shaft and lower the transfer case from the vehicle. Remove the gasket from between the transfer case and extension housing.

To Install:

8. Place a new gasket between the transfer case and adapter.

9. Raise the transfer case with a suitable transmission jack or equivalent, raise it high enough so that the transmission output shaft aligns with the splined transfer case input shaft.

10. Slide the transfer case forward on to the transmission output shaft and onto the dowel pin. Install transfer case retaining bolts and torque them to 25–43 ft. lbs.

11. Remove the transmission jack from the transfer case.

12. Connect the speedometer cable assembly to the transfer case rear cover. Tighten the screw to 20–25 inch lbs.

13. Connect the rear driveshaft to the output shaft flange and torque the yoke nut to 61–87 ft. lbs. (83–118 Nm).

14. Lower the vehicle.

15. Reconnect the negative battery cable.

DRIVELINE

General Description

The driveshaft is a steel tubular or aluminum shaft which is used to transfer the torque from the engine, through the transmission output shaft, to the differential in the axle, which in turn transmits torque to the wheels.

The splined slip yoke and transmission output shaft permit the driveshaft to move forward and rearward as the axle moves up and

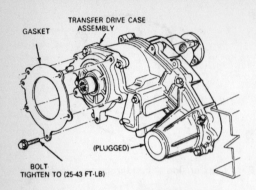

Borg-Warner 13-59, removal and installation

down. This provides smooth performance during vehicle operation.

The front driveshaft connects the power flow from the transfer case to the front drive axle.

Some vehicles may be equipped with a Double Cardan type driveshaft. This driveshaft incorporates 2 U-joints, a centering socket yoke and a center slip at the transfer case end of each shaft. A single U-joint is used at the axle end of the shaft.

The Constant Velocity (CV) type U-joint allows the driveline angel to be adjusted according to the up-and-down movement of the vehicle without disturbing the power flow. The CV U-joint is composed of an outer bearing retainer and flange, sprig, cap, circlip, inner bearing assembly and wire ring. The inner bearing

assembly is composed of a bearing cage, 6 ball bearings and an inner race.

The driveshafts used on Ranger/Bronco II/ Explorer may be 1 of 3 types. They are as follows:

• Front and rear driveshaft – Single Cardan type U-joint
• Front and rear driveshaft – Double Cardan type U-joint
• Rear driveshaft – CV (Constant Velocity) type U-joint

Front Driveshaft
Single Cardan Type

REMOVAL AND INSTALLATION

1. Disconnect the negative battery cable.
2. Raise and support the vehicle safely.

NOTE: *The driveshaft is a balanced unit. Before removing the drive shaft, matchmark the driveshaft in relationship to the end yoke so that it may be installed in its original position.*

3. Using a shop cloth or gloves, pull back on the dust slinger to remove the boot from the transfer case slip yoke.

4. Remove the bolts and straps that retains the driveshaft to the front driving axle yoke. Remove the U-joint assembly from the front driving axle yoke.

5. Slide the splined yoke assembly out of the transfer case and remove the driveshaft assembly.

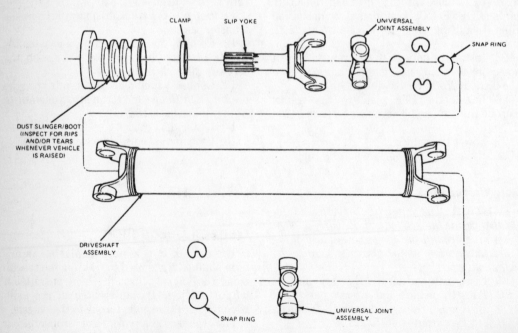

Front driveshaft and U-joint, exploded view — Single Cardan Type

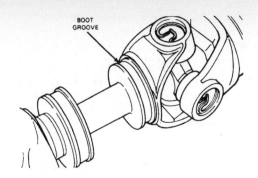

Dust slinger, boot installation

6. Inspect the boot for rips or tears. Inspect the stud yoke splines for wear or damage. Replace any damage parts.

To install:

7. Apply a light coating of Multi-purpose Long-Life lubricant C1AZ–19490–B or equivalent, to the yoke splines and the edge of the inner diameter of the rubber boot.

8. Slide the driveshaft into the transfer case front output yoke assembly. Make certain the wide tooth splines on the slip yoke are indexed to the output yoke in the transfer case.

9. Position the U-joint assembly in the front drive axle yoke in its original position. Install the retaining bolts and straps. Tighten the bolts to 10–15 ft. lbs. (14–20Nm).

10. Firmly press the dust slinger until the boot is felt to engage the output yoke in the transfer case.

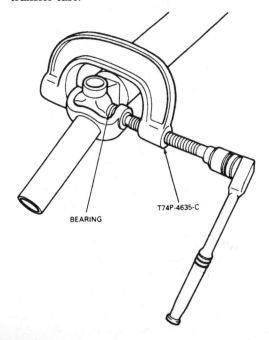

U-joint bearing removal

11. Lower the vehicle.

12. Connect the negative battery cable.

NOTE: *If replacement of the dust slinger/ boot is necessary. Use the following procedure.*

DUST SLINGER/BOOT REPLACEMENT

1. Remove the boot clamp using cutter pliers and discard the clamp. Remove the boot from the stud yoke.

2. Install a new dust slinger/boot on the stud yoke making certain the boot is seated in the groove in the yoke.

3. Install a new clamp on the boot. Position the clamp tabs in the slots so each tab fits into a slot. Then, crimp the clamp securely using a pair of clamp pliers T63P–9171–A or equivalent. Do not crimp to the point where the clamp damage the boot.

Rear Driveshaft Single Cardan Type

REMOVAL AND INSTALLATION

Except Ranger 4WD

1. Disconnect the negative battery cable.

2. Raise and support the vehicle safely.

NOTE: *The driveshaft is a balanced unit. Before removing the drive shaft, matchmark the driveshaft yoke in relationship to the axle flange so that it may be installed in its original position.*

3. On Super Cab vehicles, remove the center bearing assembly-to-frame retaining bolts. Remove the spacers under the center bearing bracket, if installed.

4. Remove the retaining bolts and disconnect the driveshaft from the axle companion flange. Pull the driveshaft rearward until the slip yoke clears the transmission extension housing and seal. Plug the extension housing to prevent lubricant leakage.

To install:

5. Lubricate the slip yoke splines with Multi-purpose Long-Life lubricant C1AZ–

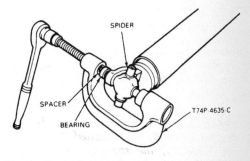

U-joint bearing installation

19490–B or equivalent. Remove the plug from the extension housing.

6. Inspect the extension housing seal. Replace, if necessary.

7. Install the driveshaft assembly. Do not allow the slip yoke assembly to bottom on the output shaft with excessive force.

8. Install the driveshaft so the index mark on the rear yoke is in line with the index mark on the axle companion flange. Tighten all circular flange bolts to 61–87 ft. lbs. (83–118Nm).

9. On Super Cab vehicles, tighten the center bearing retaining bolts to 27–37 ft. lbs. (37–50Nm).

NOTE: *Make certain the center bearing bracket assembly is reinstalled "square" to the vehicle. If the spacers were installed under the center bearing be sure to reinstall them.*

Ranger (4WD)

1. Disconnect the negative battery cable.
2. Raise and support the vehicle safely.

NOTE: *The driveshaft is a balanced unit. Before removing the drive shaft, matchmark the driveshaft yoke in relationship to the axle flange so that it may be installed in its original position.*

3. On Super Cab vehicles, remove the center bearing assembly-to-frame retaining bolts. Remove the spacers under the center bearing bracket, if installed.

4. Remove the retaining bolts and disconnect the driveshaft from the axle companion flange.

5. Remove the retaining bolts that retains the driveshaft to the rear of the transfer case.

6. Remove the driveshaft.

To install:

7. Install the driveshaft into the rear of the transfer case. Make certain that the driveshaft is positioned with the slip yoke toward the front of the vehicle. Install the bolts and tighten to 41–55 ft. lbs. (55–74Nm).

8. Install the driveshaft so the index mark on the rear yoke is in line with the index mark on the axle companion flange.

9. On Super Cab vehicles, tighten the center bearing retaining bolts to 27–37 ft. lbs. (37–50Nm).

NOTE: *Make certain the center bearing bracket assembly is reinstalled "square" to the vehicle. If the spacers were installed under the center bearing be sure to reinstall them.*

DISASSEMBLY AND ASSEMBLY

2WD

1. Prior to disassembly, mark the position of the driveshaft components relative to the driveshaft tube. All components must be re-assembled in the same relationship to maintain proper balance.

2. Place the driveshaft on a suitable workbench.

3. Remove the snaprings that retain the bearing cups.

4. Position the U-joint removal tool, T74P–4635–C or equivalent, on the slip yoke and press out the bearing. If the bearing cup cannot be pressed all the way out of the slip yoke, remove it with vise grip or channel lock pliers.

5. Reposition the tool 180° to press on the spider and remove the remaining bearing cup from the opposite side.

6. On 2WD vehicles, remove the slip yoke form the spider. On 4WD vehicles, remove the spider from the driveshaft.

7. Remove the remaining bearing cups and spiders from the driveshaft in the same manner.

8. Clean the yoke area at each end of the driveshaft.

9. Four Wheel Drive (4WD) vehicles only:

   a. Remove the clamps on the driveshaft boot seal. Discard the clamp.

   b. Note the orientation of the slip yoke to the driveshaft tube for installation during assembly. Mark the position of the slip yoke to the driveshaft tube.

   c. Carefully pull the slip yoke from the driveshaft. Be careful not to damage the boot seal.

   d. Clean and inspect the spline area of the driveshaft.

To assemble:

10. Four Wheel Drive (4WD) vehicles only:

   a. Lubricate the driveshaft slip splines with Multi-purpose Long-Life lubricant C1AZ–19490–B or equivalent.

   b. With the boot loosely installed on the driveshaft tube, install the slip yoke into the driveshaft splines in their original orientation.

   c. Using new clamps, install the driveshaft boot in its original position.

11. Start a new bearing cup into the yoke at the rear of the driveshaft.

12. Position the new spider in the rear yoke and press the bearing cup 1/4 in. (6mm) below the yoke surface, using spacer.

13. Remove the tool and install a new snapring.

14. Start a new bearing cup into the

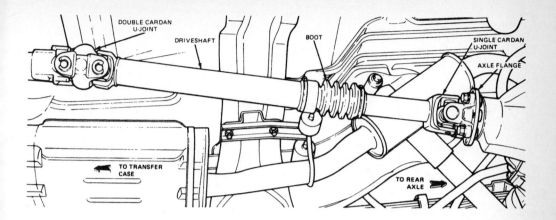

Rear driveshaft assembly — with Single Cardan and Double Cardan Type U-joint

opposite side of the yoke.

15. Position the U-joint tool and press on the bearing cup until the opposite bearing cup contacts the snapring.

16. Remove the tool and install a new snapring. It may be necessary to grind the surface of the snapring to permit easier entry.

17. Reposition the driveshaft and install the remaining bearing cups and spider in the same manner.

18. Check the universal joints for freedom of movement. If binding has resulted from misalignment during assembly, a sharp rap on the yokes with a brass hammer will seat the bearing needles. Be sure to support the shaft end during this procedure and do not strike the bearings themselves. Make certain the universal joints are free to rotate easily without binding before installing the driveshaft.

19. Lubricate the U-joint assemblies with Multi-purpose Long-Life lubricant C1AZ–19490–B or equivalent.

Center Bearing Single Cardan Type

REPLACEMENT

Super Cab

1. Remove the driveshaft from the vehicle.

2. Separate the driveshaft from the coupling shaft maintaining proper orientation.

3. Remove the nut retaining the half round yoke to the coupling shaft and remove the yoke.

4. Check the center bearing support for wear by rotating the outer area while holding the coupling shaft. If any wear or roughness is evident, replace the bearing.

5. Inspect the rubber insulator for evidence of hardness, cracking or deterioration. Replace if damaged in any way.

6. Re-install the coupling shaft yoke.

NOTE: *Be sure the yoke is re-installed on the coupling shaft in the same orientation as it was originally installed. The orientation is*

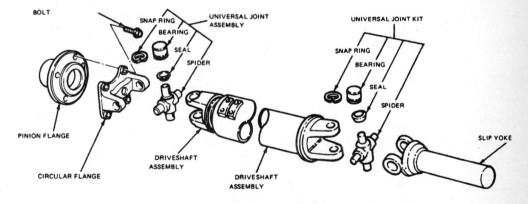

CIRCULAR FLANGE APPLICATION–TYPICAL

Rear driveshaft assembly — Single Cardan Type U-joint

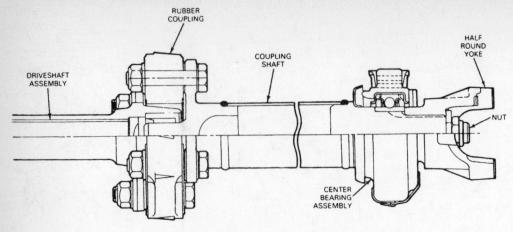

RUBBER
COUPLING

COUPLING
SHAFT

HALF
ROUND
YOKE

DRIVESHAFT
ASSEMBLY

NUT

CENTER
BEARING
ASSEMBLY

RANGER SUPERCAB (4 X 4) WITH MANUAL TRANSMISSION
ILLUSTRATED · OTHERS TYPICAL

Driveshaft and coupling assembly

critical so that proper driveshaft balance and U-joint phasing is maintained. Tighten the retaining nut to 100–120 ft. lbs. (135–162Nm).

7. Re-assemble the driveshaft to the coupling shaft, maintaining proper orientation.

Front and Rear Driveshaft Double Cardan Type

REMOVAL AND INSTALLATION

1. Disconnect the negative battery cable.
2. Raise and support the vehicle safely.

NOTE: *The driveshaft is a balanced unit. Before removing the drive shaft, matchmark the driveshaft in relationship to the axle flange so that it may be installed in its original position.*

3. Remove the bolts retaining the flange to the transfer case. Disconnect the U-joint from the flange at the transfer case.
4. Remove the bolts retaining the flange to the rear axle. Disconnect the U-joint from the flange at the rear axle.
5. Remove the driveshaft.

To install:

6. Position the single U-joint end of the driveshaft to the rear axle and install the re-taining bolts. Tighten the bolts to 61–87 ft. lbs. (83–118Nm).
7. Position the double Cardan U-joint to the transfer case and install the retaining bolts. Tighten the bolts to 12–16 ft. lbs. (17–22Nm).
8. Lower the vehicle.
9. Re-connect the negative battery cable.

DISASSEMBLY AND ASSEMBLY

1. Place the driveshaft on a suitable work-bench.
2. Matchmark the positions of the spiders, the center yoke and the centering socket yoke as related to the stud yoke which is welded to the front of the driveshaft tube.

NOTE: *The spiders must be assembled with the bosses in their original position to provide proper clearance.*

3. Remove the snaprings that secure the bearings in the front of the center yoke.
4. Position the U-joint tool, T74P–4635–C or equivalent, on the center yoke. Thread the tool clockwise until the bearing protrudes approximately $3/8$ in. (10mm) out of the yoke.
5. Position the bearing in a vice and tap on the center yoke to free it from the bearing. Lift the 2 bearing cups from the spider.
6. Re-position the tool on the yoke and move the remaining bearing in the opposite direction so that it protrudes approximately $3/8$ in. (10mm) out of the yoke.
7. Position the bearing in a vice. Tap on the center yoke to free it from the bearing. Remove the spider from the center yoke.
8. Pull the centering socket yoke off the center stud. Remove the rubber seal from the centering ball stud.
9. remove the snaprings form the center yoke and form the driveshaft yoke.
10. Position the tool on the driveshaft yoke and press the bearing outward until the inside of the center yoke almost contacts the slinger ring at the front of the driveshaft yoke. Pressing beyond this point can distort the slinger ring interference point.

11. Clamp the exposed end of the bearing in a vice and drive on the center yoke with a soft-faced hammer to free it from the bearing.

12. Reposition the tool and press on the spider to remove the opposite bearing.

13. Remove the center yoke from the spider. Remove the spider form the driveshaft yoke.

14. Clean all serviceable parts in cleaning solvent. If using a repair kit, install all of the parts supplied in the kit.

15. Remove the clamps on the driveshaft boot seal. Discard the clamps.

16. Note the orientation of the slip yoke to the driveshaft tube for installation during assembly. Mark the position of the slip yoke to the driveshaft tube.

17. Carefully pull the slip yoke from the driveshaft. Be careful not to damage the boot seal.

18. Clean and inspect the spline area of the driveshaft.

To assemble:

19. Lubricate the driveshaft slip splines with Multi-purpose Long-Life lubricant C1AZ–19490–B or equivalent.

20. With the boot loosely installed on the driveshaft tube, install the slip yoke into the driveshaft splines in their original orientation.

21. Using new clamps, install the driveshaft boot in its original position.

22. To assemble the double Cardan joint, position the spider in the driveshaft yoke. Make certain the spider bosses (or lubrication plugs on kits) will be in the same position as originally installed. Press in the bearing using the U-joint tool. Then, install the snaprings.

23. Pack the socket relief and the ball with Multi-purpose Long-Life lubricant C1AZ–19490–B or equivalent, then position the center yoke over the spider ends and press in the bearing. Install the snaprings.

24. Install a new seal on the centering ball stud. Position the centering socket yoke on the stud.

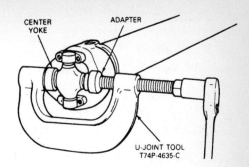

Pressing bearing from center yoke

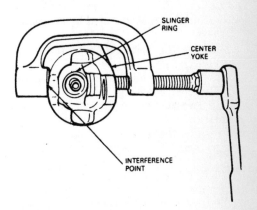

Center yoke interference point

25. Place the front spider in the center yoke. Make certain the spider bosses (or lubrication plugs on kits) are properly positioned.

26. With the spider loosely positioned on the center stop, seat the first pair of bearings into the centering socket yoke. Then, press the second pair into the centering yoke. Install the snaprings.

27. Apply pressure on the centering socket yoke and install the remaining bearing cup.

28. If a kit was used, lubricate the U-joint through the grease fitting, using Multi-purpose

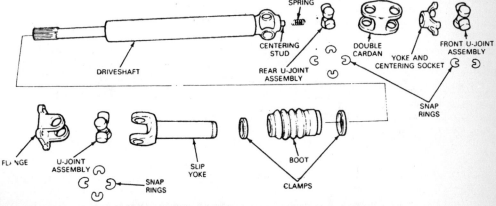

Double Cardan U-joint, disassembled — exploded view

Long-Life lubricant C1AZ–19490–B or equivalent.

Rear Driveshaft Constant Velocity (CV) Type U-joint

REMOVAL AND INSTALLATION

1. Disconnect the negative battery cable.
2. Raise and support the vehicle safely.

NOTE: *The driveshaft is a balanced unit. Before removing the drive shaft, matchmark the driveshaft in relationship to the flange on the transfer case and the flange on the rear axle so that it may be installed in its original position.*

3. Remove the bolts retaining the driveshaft to the transfer case.
4. Remove the bolts retaining the driveshaft to the rear axle flange.
5. Remove the driveshaft.

To install:

6. Position the driveshaft to the rear axle flange so that the marks made previously are line up. Install and tighten the retaining bolts to 61–87 ft. lbs. (83–118Nm).
7. Position the driveshaft to the transfer case flange so that the marks made previously are line up. Install and tighten the retaining bolts to 61–87 ft. lbs. (83–118Nm).
8. Lower the vehicle.
9. Reconnect the negative battery cable.

DISASSEMBLY AND ASSEMBLY

1. Place the driveshaft on a suitable workbench.

NOTE: *The CV joint components are matched. Extreme care should be take not to mix or substitute components.*

2. Remove the clamp retaining the shroud to the outer bearing race and flange assembly.
3. Carefully tap the shroud lightly with a

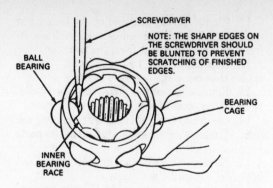

Removing ball bearings

blunt tool and remove the shroud. Be careful not to damage the shroud, dust boot or outer bearing race and flange assembly.

4. Peel the boot upward and away from the outer bearing race and flange assembly.
5. Remove the wire ring that retains the inner race to the outer race.
6. Remove the inner race and shaft assembly from the outer race and flange assembly. Remove the cap and spring from inside the outer retainer.
7. Remove the circlip retaining the inner race assembly to the shaft, using snapring pliers. Discard the clip and remove the inner race assembly.
8. If required, remove the clamp retaining the boot to the shaft and remove the boot.
9. Carefully pry the ball bearings from the cage. Be careful not to scratch or damage the cage, race or ball bearings.
10. Rotate the inner race to align with the cage windows and remove the inner race through the wider end of the cage.

To assemble:

11. Install the inner bearing race in the bearing cage. Install the race through the large end of the cage with the counterbore facing the large end of the cage.

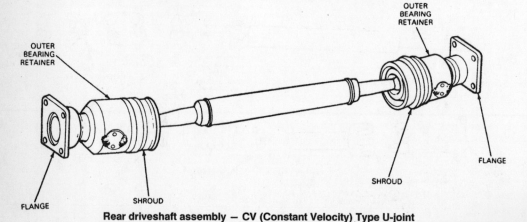

Rear driveshaft assembly — CV (Constant Velocity) Type U-joint

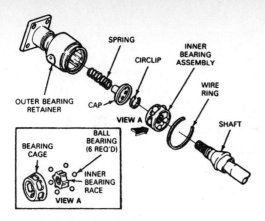

CV U-joint assembly, exploded view

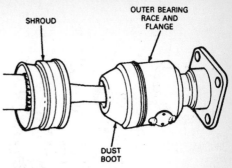

Removing shroud from outer bearing race and flange

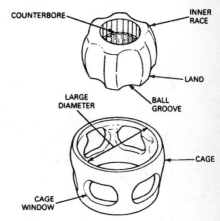

Assembling inner bearing race to cage

12. Push the race to the top of the cage and rotate the race until all the ball slots are aligned with the windows. This will lock the race to the top of the cage.

13. With the bearing cage and inner race properly aligned, install the ball bearings. The bearings can be pressed through the bearing cage with the heel of the hand. Repeat this step until the remaining ball bearings are installed.

14. If removed, install a new dust boot on the shaft, using a new clamp. Make certain the boot is seated in its groove.

NOTE: *The clamp is a fixed diameter push-on metal ring.*

15. Install the inner bearing assembly on the shaft. Make certain the circlip is exposed.

16. Install a new circlip on the shaft. Do not over-expand or twist the circlip during installation.

17. Install the spring and cap in the outer bearing retainer and flange.

18. Fill the outer bearing retainer with 3 oz. of Constant Velocity Joint Grease, D8RZ–19590–A or equivalent.

19. Insert the inner race and shaft assembly in the outer bearing retainer and flange.

20. Push the inner race down until the wire spring groove is visible and install the wire ring.

21. Fill the top of the outer bearing retainer with Constant Velocity Joint Grease, D8RZ–19590–A or equivalent. Remove all excess grease from the external surfaces.

22. Pull the dust boot over the retainer. Make certain the boot is seated in the groove and that any air pressure which may have built up in the boot is relieved.

NOTE: *Insert a dulled screwdriver blade between the boot and outer bearing retainer and allow the trapped air to escape from the boot.*

23. Install the shroud over the boot and retainer and install the clamp.

REAR AXLE

A Ford conventional, integral-carrier type rear axle or Ford Traction-Lock Limited Slip Differential is used on the Ranger/Bronco II/Explorer.

The housing assembly consists of a cast center section with 2 steel tube assemblies and a stamped rear cover. The hypoid gear set consists of a ring gear and an overhung drive pinion, which is supported by 2 opposed tapered roller bearings.

The differential case is a 1 piece design with 2 openings to allow for assembly of the internal components and lubricant flow.

The limited-slip axle assembly, except for the differential case and its internal components, is identical to the conventional axle.

The limited-slip differential employs 2 sets of multiple disc clutches to control differential action.

Identification

To identify the axle type used on this vehicle, refer to the axle code on the Safety Certification Label, or the Axle Identification label attached to one of the bolts on the housing. There

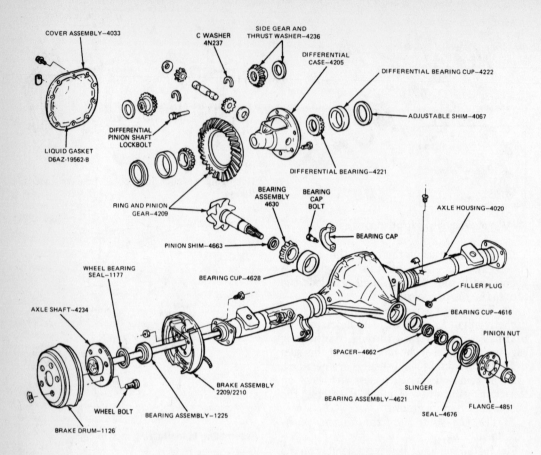

Integral carrier rear axle assembly — exploded view

are two ring gear sizes available; 7½ in. (190.5mm) ring gear axle and the 8.8 in. (223.5mm) ring gear.

Axle Shaft, Bearing and Seal

REMOVAL AND INSTALLATION

1. Disconnect the negative battery cable.
2. Raise and support the vehicle safely.
3. Remove the rear wheels and brake drums.

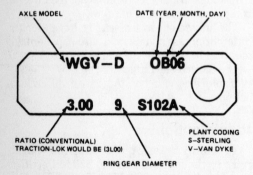

Axle identification tag

4. Drain the rear axle lubricant.
5. For all axles except 3.73:1 and 4.10:1 ratio.

   a. Remove the differential pinion shaft lock bolt and differential pinion shaft.

   NOTE: *The pinion gears may be left in place. Once the axle shafts are removed, reinstall the pinion shaft and lock bolt.*

   b. Push the flanged end of the axle shafts toward the center of the vehicle and remove the C-lockwasher from the end of the axle shaft.

   c. Remove the axle shafts from the housing. If the seals and/or bearing are not being replaced, be careful not to damage the seals with the axle shaft splines upon removal.

6. For 3.73:1 and 4.10:1 ratio axles.

   a. Remove the pinion shaft lock bolt. Place a hand behind the differential case and push out the pinion shaft until the step contacts the ring gear.

   b. Remove the C-lockwasher from the axle shafts.

   c. Remove the axle shafts from the housing. If the seals and/or bearing are not being replaced, be careful not to damage the seals with the axle shaft splines upon removal.

7. Insert the wheel bearing and seal remover, T85L–1225–AH or equivalent, and a slide hammer into the axle bore and position it behind the bearing so the tanks on the tool engage the bearing outer race. Remove the bearing and seal as a unit.

To install:

8. If removed, lubricate the new bearing with rear axle lubricant and install the bearing into the housing bore. Use axle tube bearing replacer, T78P–1225–A or equivalent.

9. Apply Multi-Purpose Long-Life Lubricant, C1AZ–19590–B or equivalent, between the lips of the axle shaft seal.

10. Install a new axle shaft seal using axle

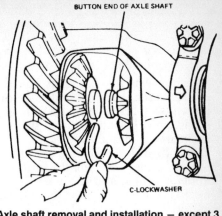

Axle shaft removal and installation — except 3.73:1 and 4.10:1 ratio axle

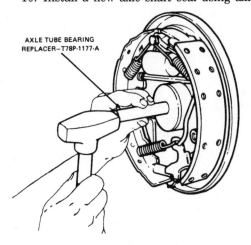

Wheel bearing and axle shaft seal installation

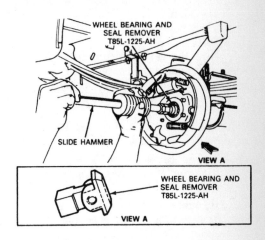

Axle shaft seal and wheel bearing removal

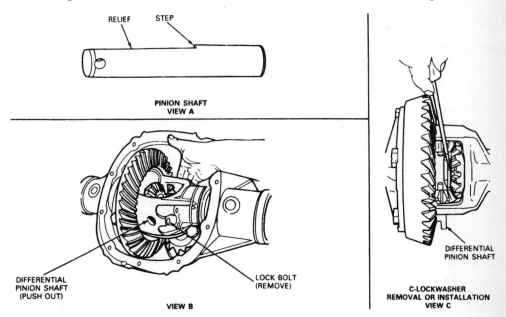

Axle shaft removal and installation — 3.73:1 and 4.10:1 ratio axle

tube seal replacer T78P–1177–A or equivalent.

NOTE: *To permit axle shaft installation on 3.73:1 and 4.10:1 ratio axles, make sure the differential pinion shaft contacts the ring gear before performing Step 11.*

11. Carefully slide the axle shaft into the axle housing, making sure not to damage the oil seal. Start the splines into the side gear and push firmly until the button end of the axle shaft can be seen in the differential case.

12. Install the C-lockwasher on the end of the axle shaft splines, then pull the shaft outboard until the shaft splines engage the C-lockwasher seats in the counterbore of the differential side gear.

13. Position the differential pinion shaft through the case and pinion gears, aligning the hole in the shaft with the lock screw hole. Install the lock bolt and tighten to 15–22 ft. lbs. (21–29Nm).

14. Clean the gasket mounting surface on the rear axle housing and cover. Apply a continuous bead of Silicone Rubber Sealant ESE–M4G195–A or equivalent to the carrier casting face.

15. Install the cover and tighten the retaining bolts to 25–35 ft. lbs. (20–34Nm).

NOTE: *The cover assembly must be installed within 15 minutes of application of the silicone sealant.*

16. Add lubricant until it is $1/4$ in. (6mm) below the bottom of the filler hole in the running position. Install the filler plug and tighten to 15–30 ft. lbs. (20–41Nm).

Pinion Oil Seal

REMOVAL AND INSTALLATION

1. Disconnect the negative battery cable.
2. Raise and support the vehicle safely. Allow the axle to drop to rebound position for working clearance.
3. Remove the rear wheels and brake drums. No drag must be present on the axle.
4. Mark the companion flanges and U-joints for correct reinstallation position.
5. Remove the driveshaft.
6. Using an inch pound torque wrench and socket on the pinion yoke nut measure the amount of torque needed to maintain differential rotation through several clockwise revolutions. Record the measurement.
7. Use a suitable tool to hold the companion flange. Remove the pinion nut.
8. Place a drain pan under the differential. Clean the area around the seal and mark the yoke-to-pinion relation.
9. Use a 2-jawed puller to remove the com-

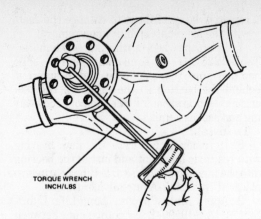

Checking drive pinion bearing preload

panion flange.

10. Remove the seal with a small prybar.

To install:

11. Thoroughly clean the oil seal bore.

NOTE: *If you are not absolutely certain of the proper seal installation depth, the proper seal driver must be used. If the seal is misaligned or damaged during installation, it must be removed and a new seal installed.*

12. Drive the new seal into place with a seal driver such as T83T–4676–A. Coat the seal lip with clean, waterproof wheel bearing grease.

13. Coat the splines with a small amount of wheel bearing grease and install the yoke, aligning the matchmarks. Never hammer the yoke onto the pinion!

14. Install a new nut on the pinion.

15. Hold the yoke with a holding tool. Tighten the pinion nut, taking frequent turning torque readings until the original preload reading is attained. If the original preload reading, that you noted before disassembly, is lower than the specified reading of 8–14 inch lbs. for used bearings; 16–29 inch lbs. for new bearings, keep tightening the pinion nut until the specified reading is reached. If the original preload reading is higher than the specified values, torque the nut just until the original reading is reached.

WARNING: *Under no circumstances should the nut be backed off to reduce the preload reading! If the preload is exceeded, the yoke and bearing must be removed and a new collapsible spacer must be installed. The entire process of preload adjustment must be repeated.*

15. Install the driveshaft using the matchmarks. Torque the nuts to 15 ft. lbs.

16. Lower the vehicle.

17. Reconnect the negative battery cable.

Axle Housing

REMOVAL AND INSTALLATION

1. Disconnect the negative battery cable.
2. Raise and support the vehicle safely.
3. Matchmark and disconnect the drive-shaft at the axle.
4. Remove the wheels and brake drums.
5. Disengage the brake line from the clips that retain the line to the housing.
6. Disconnect the vent tube from the housing.
7. Remove the axle shafts.
8. Remove the brake backing plate from the housing and support them with wire. Do not disconnect the brake line.
9. Disconnect each rear shock absorber from the mounting bracket stud on the housing.
10. Lower the axle slightly to reduce some of the spring tension. At each rear spring, remove the spring clip (U-bolt) nuts, spring clips and spring seat caps.
11. Remove the housing from under the vehicle.

To Install:
12. Position the axle housing under the rear springs. Install the spring clips (U-bolts), spring seat clamps and nuts. Tighten the spring clamps evenly to 115 ft. lbs.
13. If a new axle housing is being installed, remove the bolts that attach the brake backing plate and bearing retainer from the old housing flanges. Position the bolts in the new housing flanges to hold the brake backing plates in position. Torque the bolts to 40 ft. lbs.
14. Install the axle shafts.
15. Connect the vent tube to the housing.
16. Position the brake line to the housing and secure it with the retaining clips.
17. Raise the axle housing and springs enough to allow connecting the rear shock absorbers to the mounting bracket studs on the housing. Torque the nuts to 60 ft. lbs.
18. Connect the driveshaft to the axle. Torque the nuts to 8–15 ft. lbs.
19. Install the brake drums and wheels.
20. Lower the vehicle.
21. Reconnect the negative battery cable.

FRONT DRIVE AXLE

Identification

The Dana Model 28 and Dana Model 35 front drive axles are used on the Ranger/Bronco II/Explorer. A code of F07A will appear on the axle identification tag if the vehicle is equipped with the Dana 35 axle and a code of E87A if equipped with the Dana 28 axle. The axles may be identified by a part number stamped on the left carrier arm between the fill plug and axle end or by using the Safety Certification Label attached to the door latch edge of the driver's side door.

The Dana 28 and Dana 35 are of the integral

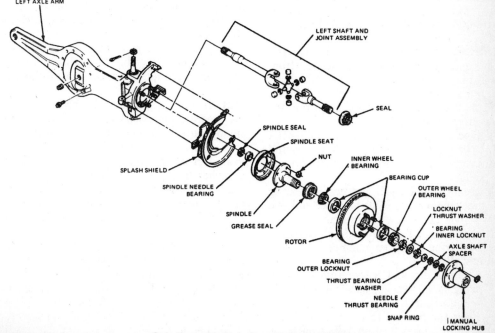

Spindle and left shaft and joint installation

carrier housing hypoid-gear type, in which the centerline of the drive pinion is mounted above the centerline of the ring gear. The differential carrier is made of aluminum and mounted directly to the left axle arm assembly. The right hand axle shaft stub shaft is retained in the carrier by a C-clip in the differential case. The cover on the front of the carrier housing is integral with the left hand axle arm assembly.

Spindle, Right and Left Shaft and Joint Assembly

REMOVAL AND INSTALLATION

1. Disconnect the negative battery cable.
2. Raise and support the vehicle safely. Remove the wheel and tire assembly.
3. Remove the disc brake calipers and support the caliper on the vehicle's frame rail.
4. Remove the hub locks, wheel bearings and lock nuts.
5. Remove the hub and rotor. Remove the outer wheel bearing cone.
6. Remove the grease seal from the rotor with the seal remover tool, 1175–AC or equivalent, and a slide hammer. Discard the seal.
7. Remove the inner wheel bearing.
8. Remove the inner and outer bearing cups from the rotor with bearing cup puller tool, D78P–1225–B or equivalent.
9. Remove the nuts retaining the spindle to the steering knuckle. Tap the spindle with a plastic or rawhide hammer to jar the spindle from the knuckle. Remove the splash shield.
10. From the right side of the vehicle, remove the shaft and joint assembly by pulling the assembly out of the carrier.
11. From the right side of the carrier, remove and discard the keystone clamp from the shaft and joint assembly and the stub shaft. Slide the rubber boot onto the stub shaft and pull the shaft and joint assembly from the splines of the stub shaft.
12. Place the spindle in a vise on the second step of the spindle. Wrap a shop towel around the spindle or use a brass-jawed vise to protect the spindle.
13. Remove the oil seal and needle bearing from the spindle with a slide hammer and seal remover tool, 1175–AC or equivalent.
14. If required, remove the seal from the shaft, by driving off with a hammer.
To install:
15. Clean all dirt and grease from the spindle bearing bore. Bearing bore must be free from nicks and burrs.
16. Place the bearing in the bore with the manufacturer's identification facing outward. Drive the bearing into the bore using spindle

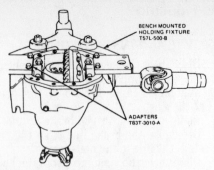

Installing carrier in holding fixture

bearing replacer tool, T83T–3123–A and drive handle T80T–4000–W or equivalent.
17. Install the grease seal in the bearing bore with the lip side of the seal facing towards the tool. Drive the seal in the bore using spindle bearing replacer tool, T83T–3123–A and drive handle T80T–4000–W or equivalent. Coat the bearing seal lip with Multi-Purpose Long Life Lubricant C1AZ–19590–B or equivalent.
18. If remove, install a new shaft seal. Place the shaft in a press and install the seal with seal installer tool, T83T–3132–A.
19. From the right side of the carrier, install the rubber boot and new keystone clamps on the stub shaft slip yoke. Since the splines on the shaft are phased, there is only 1 way to assemble the right shaft and joint assembly into the slip yoke. Align the missing spline in the slip yoke barrel with the gapless male spline on the shaft and joint assembly. Slide the right shaft and joint assembly into the slip yoke making sure the splines are fully engaged. Slide the boot over the assembly and crimp the keystone clamp.
20. From the left side of the carrier, slide the shaft and joint assembly through the knuckle and engage the splines on the shaft in the carrier.
21. Install the splash shield and spindle onto the steering knuckle. Install and tighten the spindle nuts to 35–45 ft. lbs. (47–61Nm).
22. Drive the bearing cups into the rotor, using bearing cup replacer T73T–4222–B and drive handle T80T–4000–W or equivalent.
23. Pack the inner and outer wheel bearings and the lip of the oil seal with Multi-Purpose Long Life Lubricant C1AZ–19590–B or equivalent.
24. Place the inner wheel bearing in the inner cup. Drive the grease seal into the bore with hub seal replacer tool, T83T–1175–B and drive handle T80T–4000–W or equivalent. Coat the bearing seal lip with Multi-Purpose Long Life Lubricant C1AZ–19590–B or equivalent.
25. Install the rotor on the spindle. Install the outer wheel bearing into the cup.

NOTE: *Make certain the grease seal lip totally encircles the spindle.*

26. Install the wheel bearing, locknut, thrust bearing, snapring and locking hubs.
27. Install the disc brake calipers. Install the wheel and tire assembly.
28. Lower the vehicle.
29. Reconnect the negative battery cable.

Right Hand Slip Yoke and Stub Shaft Assembly, Carrier, Carrier Oil Seal and Bearing

REMOVAL AND INSTALLATION

1. Disconnect the negative battery cable.
2. Raise and support the vehicle safely.
3. Remove the nuts and U-bolts connecting the driveshaft to the yoke. Disconnect the driveshaft from the yoke. Wire the driveshaft aside.
4. Remove the spindles, the left and right shaft and U-joint assemblies.
5. Support the carrier with a suitable jack and remove the bolts retaining the carrier to the support arm. Separate the carrier from the support arm and drain the lubricant from the carrier. Remove the carrier from the vehicle.
6. Place the carrier in a holding fixture, T57L–500–B and adapter T83T–3010–A or equivalent.
7. Rotate the slip yoke and shaft assembly so the open side of the snapring is exposed. Remove the snapring from the shaft.
8. Remove the slip yoke and shaft assembly from the carrier.
9. Remove the oil seal and caged needle bearings at the same time, using slide hammer (T50T–100–A) and collet (D80L–100–A) or equivalent. Discard the seal and needle bearing.
   To install:

10. Check that the bearing bore is free from nicks and burrs. Install a new caged needle bearing on the needle bearing replacer tool, T83T–1244–A or equivalent, with the manufacturer's name and part number facing outward towards the tool. Drive the needle bearing until it is seated in the bore.
11. Coat the seal with Multi-Purpose Long Life Lubricant C1AZ–19590–B or equivalent. Drive the seal into the carrier using needle bearing replacer tool, T83T–1244–A or equivalent.
12. Install the slip yoke and shaft assembly into the carrier so the grooves in the shaft is visible in the differential case.
13. Install the snapring in the groove in the shaft. Force the snapring into position. Do not tap the center of the snapring. This may damage the snapring.
14. Clean all traces of gasket sealant from the surfaces of the carrier and support arm and make sure the surfaces are free from dirt and oil.
15. Apply a bead of RTV sealant to the surface of the carrier. Position the carrier on a suitable jack and install it into position on the support arm, using guide pins to align. Install the retaining bolts and hand tighten. Then, tighten the bolts in a clockwise or counterclockwise pattern to 40–50 ft. lbs. (54–68Nm).
16. Install the shear bolt retaining the carrier to the axle arm and tighten to 75–95 ft. lbs. (102–129Nm).
17. Install both spindles, the left and right shaft and joint assemblies.
18. Connect the driveshaft to the yoke. Install the nuts and U-bolts and tighten to 8–15 ft. lbs. (11–20Nm).
19. Lower the vehicle.
20. Reconnect the negative battery cable.

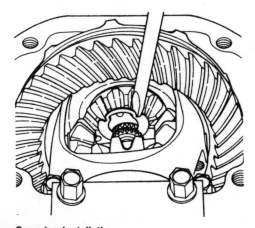

Snapring installation

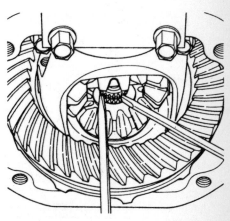

Snapring removal

Axle Housing

REMOVAL AND INSTALLATION

Ranger/Bronco II (Dana 28)

1. Disconnect the negative battery cable.
2. Raise and support the vehicle safely. Remove the wheel and tire assembly.

NOTE: *Before removing the driveshaft from the front axle yoke, mark the yoke and driveshaft so that they can be reassembled in the same relative position, thus eliminating driveshaft imbalance.*

3. Disconnect the driveshaft from the front axle yoke.
4. Remove the disc brake calipers and support the caliper on the vehicle's frame rail.
5. Remove the cotter pin and nut retaining the steering linkage to the spindle. Disconnect the linkage from the spindle.

NOTE: *The axle arm assembly must be supported on the jack throughout spring removal and installation and must not be per-*

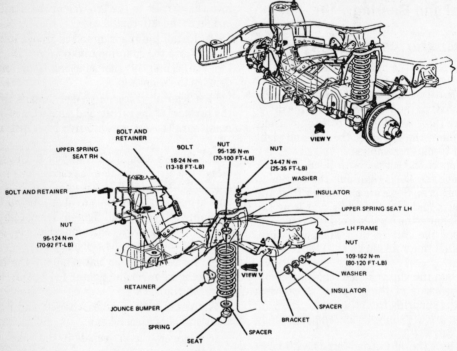

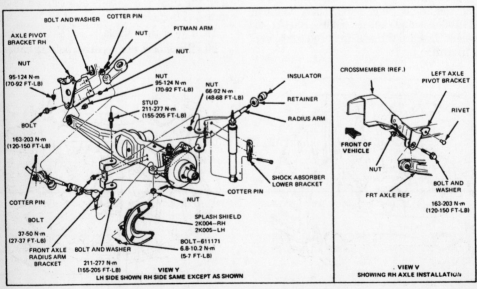

Front drive axle installation — Ranger/Bronco II

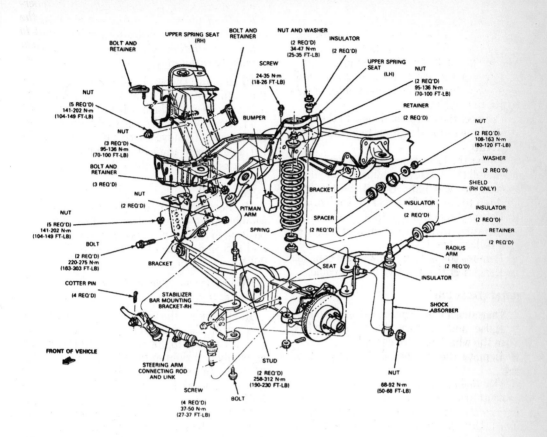

Front drive axle installation — Explorer

mitted to hang by the brake hose. If the length of the brake hose is not sufficient to provide adequate clearance for the removal and installation of the spring, the caliper must be removed.

6. Remove the bolt and nut and disconnect the shock absorber from the radius arm bracket.

7. Remove the stud and bolts that connect the radius arm bracket and radius arm to the axle arm. Remove the bracket and radius arm.

8. Remove the pivot bolt securing the right handle axle arm assembly to the crossmember. Remove the keystone clamps securing the axle shaft boot from the axle shaft slip yoke and axle shaft and slide the rubber boot over. Disconnect the right driveshaft from the slip yoke assembly. Lower the jack and remove the right axle arm assembly.

9. Position another jack under the differential housing. Remove the bolt that connects the left axle arm to the crossmember. Lower the jacks and remove the left axle arm assembly.

To install:

10. Position the under the left axle arm assembly. Raise the axle arm until the arm is in position in the left pivot bracket. Install the nut and bolt and tighten to 120–150 ft. lbs. (163–203Nm).

NOTE: *Do not remove the jack from under the differential housing at this time.*

11. Place new keystone clamps for the axle shaft boot on the axle shaft assembly. Position the right axle arm on a jack and raise the right axle arm so the right driveshaft slides onto the slip yoke stub shaft and the axle arm is in position in the right pivot bracket. Install the nut and bolt and tighten to 120–150 ft. lbs. (163–203Nm).

NOTE: *Do not remove the jack from the right axle arm at this time.*

12. Position the radius arm and front bracket on the axle arms. Install a new stud and nut on the top of the axle and radius arm assembly and tighten to 160–220 ft. lbs. (217–298Nm). Install the bolts in the front of the

bracket and tighten to 27–37 ft. lbs. (37–50Nm).

13. Install the seat, spacer retainer and coil spring on the stud and nut. Raise the jack to compress the coil spring. Install the nut and tighten to 70–100 ft. lbs. (95–135Nm).

14. Connect the shock absorber to the axle arm assembly. Install the nut and tighten to 42–72 ft. lbs. (57–97Nm).

15. Connect the tie rod ball joint to the spindle. Install the nut and tighten to 50–75 ft. lbs. (68–101Nm).

16. Lower the jacks from the axle arms.

17. Install the disc brake calipers. Install the wheel and tire assembly. Install the lug nuts and tighten to 85–115 ft. lbs. (115–155Nm).

18. Connect the front output shaft to the front axle yoke. Install the U-bolts and tighten to 8–15 ft. lbs. (11–20Nm).

19. Remove the jacks and lower the vehicle.

20. Reconnect the negative battery cable.

Explorer (Dana 35)

1. Disconnect the negative battery cable.

2. Raise and support the vehicle safely. Remove the wheel and tire assembly.

3. Remove the spindle, shaft and joint assembly.

NOTE: *Before removing the driveshaft from the front axle yoke, mark the yoke and driveshaft so that they can be reassembled in the same relative position, thus eliminating driveshaft imbalance.*

4. Disconnect the driveshaft from the front axle yoke.

5. Remove the cotter pin and nut retaining the steering linkage to the spindle. Disconnect the linkage from the spindle.

6. Remove the left stabilizer bar link lower bolt. Remove the link from the radius arm bracket.

7. Position a jack under the left axle arm assembly ad slightly compress the coil spring.

8. Remove the shock absorber lower nut and disconnect the shock absorber from the radius arm bracket.

9. Remove the nut which retains the lower portion of the spring to the axle arm. Slowly lower the jack and remove the coil spring, spacer, seat and stud.

NOTE: *The axle arm assembly must be supported on the jack throughout spring re-moval and installation and must not be permitted to hang by the brake hose. If the length of the brake hose is not sufficient to provide adequate clearance for the removal and installation of the spring, the caliper must be removed.*

10. Remove the stud and bolts that connect the radius arm bracket and radius arm to the axle arm. Remove the bracket and radius arm.

11. Position another jack under the differential housing. Remove the bolt that connects the left axle arm to the axle pivot bracket. Lower the jacks and remove the left axle arm assembly.

To install:

12. Position the under the left axle arm assembly. Raise the axle arm until the arm is in position in the left pivot bracket. Install the nut and bolt and tighten to 120–150 ft. lbs. (163–203Nm).

NOTE: *Do not remove the jack from the axle arm at this time.*

13. Position the radius arm and front bracket on the axle arms. Install a new stud and nut on the top of the axle and radius arm assembly and tighten to 190–230 ft. lbs. (258–311Nm). Install the bolts in the front of the bracket and tighten to 27–37 ft. lbs. (37–50Nm).

14. Install the seat, spacer retainer and coil spring on the stud and nut. Raise the jack to compress the coil spring. Install the nut and tighten to 70–100 ft. lbs. (95–135Nm).

15. Connect the shock absorber to the radius arm. Install the nut and tighten to 42–72 ft. lbs. (57–97Nm).

16. Connect the tie rod ball joint to the knuckle. Install the nut and tighten to 50–75 ft. lbs. (68–101Nm). Install the stabilizer bar mounting bracket and tighten to 203–240 ft. lbs. (275–325Nm).

17. Connect the front driveshaft shaft to the front axle yoke. Install the U-bolts and tighten the nuts to 8–15 ft. lbs. (11–20Nm).

NOTE: *Reassemble the yoke and driveshaft to the marks made during disassembly.*

18. Install the spindle, shaft and joint assemblies.

19. Remove the jacks and lower the vehicle.

20. Reconnect the negative battery cable.

WHEELS

Front Wheels

REMOVAL AND INSTALLATION

1. Set the parking brake. Block the diagonally opposite wheel.

2. On vehicles with automatic transmission position the selector lever in **PARK**.

3. On vehicles with manual transmission position the selector lever in **NEUTRAL**.

4. As necessary, remove the hubcap or wheel cover. Loosen the lug nuts, but do not remove them.

5. Raise the vehicle until the wheel and tire assembly clears the floor. Properly support the vehicle.

6. Remove the lug nuts. Remove the tire and wheel assembly from its mounting.

To install:

7. Position the wheel and tire assembly on its mounting.

CAUTION: *Whenever a wheel is installed be sure to remove any corrosion, dirt or foreign material that may be present on the mounting surfaces of the hub, drum or rotor that contacts the wheel.   Installing wheels with-*

out proper metal to metal contact at the wheel mounting surfaces can cause the wheel lug nuts to loosen and could allow the wheel to come off while the vehicle is in motion!

8. Install the lug nuts. Be sure that the cone end of the lug nut faces inward.

9. With the lug nuts loosely installed, turn the wheel until one nut is at the top of the bolt circle. Tighten the lug nut until snug.

10. In a criss-cross manner tighten the remaining lug nuts until snug in order to minimize runout.

11. Lower the vehicle. Torque the lug nuts to 100 ft. lbs. in the proper sequence

CAUTION: *Retighten the wheel lug nuts to specification after about 500 miles of driving. Failure to do this could result in the wheel coming off while the vehicle is in motion possibly causing loss of vehicle control or collision.*

INSPECTION

Replace wheels if they are bent, cracked, leaking air or heavily rusted or if the lug nuts often become loose. Do not use bent wheels that have been straightened or do not use inner tubes in leaking wheels. Do not replace wheels with used wheels. Wheels that have been straightened or are leaking air or are used may have structural damage and could fail without warning.

Front Wheel Lug Nut Studs

REMOVAL AND INSTALLATION

1. Raise and support the vehicle safely.

2. Remove the tire and wheel assembly.

3. Remove the disc brake rotor. Be sure to properly support the brake caliper to avoid damage to the brake line hose.

4. Position the disc brake rotor in a press so that press ram pressure is not directly exerted on the disc brake rotor surface.

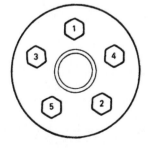

TIGHTEN LUG NUTS
IN THIS
SEQUENCE

Lug nut torque sequence — 2WD and 4WD vehicles

5. Using the proper press stock, press the lug stud from the disc brake rotor. Discard the lug stud. Remove the disc brake rotor from its mounting in the press.

To install:

6. Position a new lug stud in the disc brake rotor hole. Align the serrations of the new stud with the serration marks from the old lug stud.

7. Using a hammer tap the lug stud until the serrations on the stud are started in the hole. Be sure that the lug stud is not installed in an off centered position.

8. Reposition the disc brake rotor in the press so that the rotor is supported on the wheel mounting flange. Be sure to allow enough clearance for the stud to pass through the hole.

9. Do not apply ram pressure directly to the rotor surface. Using the proper press stock, press the lug stud in position until the stud is flush against the inner surface of the disc brake rotor hub.

10. Install the disc brake rotor. Reposition the brake caliper. Install the tire and wheel assembly. Lower the vehicle.

CAUTION: *Retighten the wheel lug nuts to specification after about 500 miles of driving. Failure to do this could result in the wheel coming off while the vehicle is in motion possibly causing loss of vehicle control or collision.*

Rear Wheels

REMOVAL AND INSTALLATION

1. Set the parking brake. Block the diagonally opposite wheel.

2. On vehicles with automatic transmission position the selector lever in **PARK**.

3. On vehicles with manual transmission position the selector lever in **NEUTRAL**.

4. As necessary, remove the hubcap or wheel cover. Loosen the lug nuts, but do not remove them.

5. Raise the vehicle until the wheel and tire assembly clears the floor. Properly support the vehicle.

6. Remove the lug nuts. Remove the tire and wheel assembly from its mounting.

To install:

7. Position the wheel and tire assembly on its mounting.

CAUTION: *Whenever a wheel is installed be sure to remove any corrosion, dirt or foreign material that may be present on the mounting surfaces of the hub, drum or rotor that contacts the wheel. Installing wheels without proper metal to metal contact at the wheel mounting surfaces can cause the wheel lug*

nuts to loosen and could allow the wheel to come off while the vehicle is in motion.

8. Install the lug nuts. Be sure that the cone end of the lug nut faces inward.

9. With the lug nuts loosely installed, turn the wheel until one nut is at the top of the bolt circle. Tighten the lug nut until snug.

10. In a criss-cross manner tighten the remaining lug nuts until snug in order to minimize runout.

11. Lower the vehicle. Torque the lug nuts to 100 ft. lbs. in the proper sequence

Retighten the wheel lug nuts to specification after about 500 miles of driving. Failure to do this could result in the wheel coming off while the vehicle is in motion possibly causing loss of vehicle control or collision.

INSPECTION

Replace wheels if they are bent, cracked, leaking air or heavily rusted or if the lug nuts often become loose. Do not use bent wheels that have been straightened or do not use inner tubes in leaking wheels. Do not replace wheels with used wheels. Wheels that have been straightened or are leaking air or are used may have structural damage and could fail without warning.

Rear Wheel Lug Nut Studs

REMOVAL AND INSTALLATION

1. Raise and support the vehicle safely.

2. Remove the tire and wheel assembly.

3. Remove the brake drum.

4. Using wheel stud removal tool T74P–3044–A1 or equivalent, press the lug stud from its seat in the hub.

WARNING: *Never use a hammer to remove the lug stud, as damage to the hub or bearing may result.*

To install:

5. Insert the new lug stud in the hole in the hub. Rotate the stud slowly to assure the serrations are aligned with those made by the old lug nut stud.

6. Place 4 flat washers over the outside end of the lug nut stud and thread the wheel lug nut with the flat washer side against the washers.

7. Tighten the wheel nut until the stud head seats against the back side of the hub. Do not use air tools as the serrations may be stripped from the stud.

8. Remove the wheel lug nut and washers. Install the brake drum. Install the tire and wheel assembly. Lower the vehicle.

CAUTION: *Retighten the wheel lug nuts to specification after about 500 miles of driving. Failure to do this could result in the wheel coming off while the vehicle is in motion possibly causing loss of vehicle control or collision.*

2-WHEEL DRIVE FRONT SUSPENSION

Coil Springs

REMOVAL AND INSTALLATION

1. Raise the front of the vehicle and place jackstands under the frame and a jack under the axle.

WARNING: *The axle must not be permitted to hang by the brake hose. If the length of the brake hoses is not sufficient to provide adequate clearance for removal and installation of the spring, the disc brake caliper must be removed from the spindle. A Strut Spring Compressor, T81P–5310–A or equivalent may be used to compress the spring sufficiently, so that the caliper does not have to be removed. After removal, the caliper must be placed on the frame or otherwise supported to prevent suspending the caliper from the caliper hose. These precautions are absolutely necessary to prevent serious damage to the tube portion of the caliper hose assembly!*

2. Disconnect the shock absorber at the lower shock stud. Remove the nut securing the

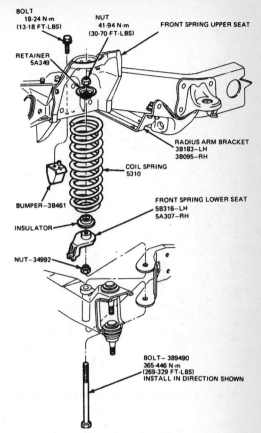

2WD Ranger coil spring and related components

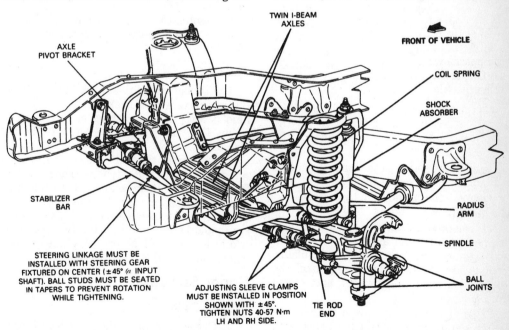

2WD Bronco II and Explorer front suspension assembly

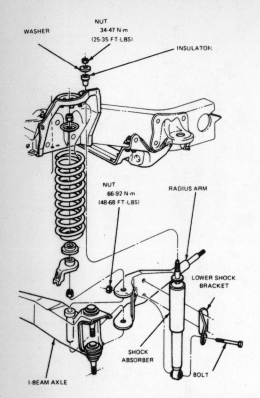

WASHER

NUT
34-47 N·m
(25-35 FT-LBS)

INSULATOR

NUT
66-92 N·m
(48-68 FT-LBS)

RADIUS ARM

LOWER SHOCK
BRACKET

SHOCK
ABSORBER

BOLT

I-BEAM AXLE

2WD Bronco II and Explorer coil spring and related components

lower retainer to spring seat. Remove the lower retainer.

3. Lower the axle as far as it will go without stretching the brake hose and tube assembly. The axle should now be unsupported without hanging by the brake hose. If not, then either remove the caliper or use Strut Spring Compressor Tool, T81P-5310-A or equivalent. Remove the spring.

4. If there is a lot of slack in the brake hose assembly, a pry bar can be used to lift the spring over the bolt that passes through the lower spring seat.

5. Rotate the spring so the built-in retainer on the upper spring seat is cleared.

6. Remove the spring from the vehicle.

To install:

7. If removed, install the bolt in the axle arm and install the nut all the way down. Install the spring lower seat and lower insulator. On the Bronco II and Explorer, also install the stabilizer bar mounting bracket and spring spacer.

8. With the axle in the lowest position, install the top of the spring in the upper seat. Rotate the spring into position.

9. Lift the lower end of the spring over the bolt.

10. Raise the axle slowly until the spring is seated in the lower spring upper seat. Install the lower retainer and nut.

11. Connect the shock absorber to the lower shock stud.

12. Remove the jack and jackstands and lower vehicle.

Shock Absorbers

REMOVAL AND INSTALLATION

NOTE: *Low pressure gas shocks are charged with Nitrogen gas. Do not attempt to open, puncture or apply heat to them. Prior to installing a new shock absorber, hold it upright and extend it fully. Invert it and fully compress and extend it at least 3 times. This will bleed trapped air.*

1. Raise the vehicle, as required to provide additional access and remove the bolt and nut attaching the shock absorber to the lower bracket on the radius arm.

2. Remove the nut, washer and insulator from the shock absorber at the frame bracket and remove the shock absorber.

3. Position the washer and insulator on the shock absorber rod and position the shock absorber to the frame bracket.

4. Position the insulator and washer on the shock absorber rod and install the attaching nut loosely.

5. Position the shock absorber to the lower bracket and install the attaching bolt and nut loosely.

6. Tighten the lower attaching bolts to 40–63 ft. lbs., and the upper attaching bolts to 25–35 ft. lbs.

TESTING

1. Visually check the shock absorbers for the presence of fluid leakage. A thin film of fluid is acceptable. Anything more than that means that the shock absorber must be replaced.

2. Disconnect the lower end of the shock absorber. Compress and extend the shock fully as fast as possible. If the action is not smooth in both directions, or there is no pressure resistance, replace the shock absorber. Shock absorbers should be replaced in pairs. In the case of relatively new shock absorbers, where one has failed, that one, alone, may be replaced.

Upper Ball Joint

INSPECTION

1. Check and adjust the front wheel bearings. Raise the vehicle and position a jackstand under the I-beam axle beneath the coil spring.

2. Have a helper grasp the lower edge of the tire and move the wheel assembly in and out.

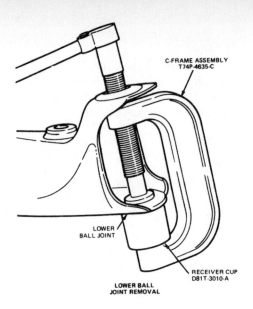

2WD Ranger, Bronco II and Explorer ball joint removal

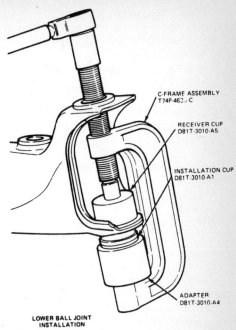

2WD Ranger, Bronco II and Explorer ball joint installation

3. While the wheel is being moved, observe the upper spindle arm and the upper part of the axle jaw.

4. A $\frac{1}{32}$ in. (0.8mm) or greater movement between the upper part of the axle jaw and the upper spindle arm indicates that the upper ball joint must be replaced

REMOVAL AND INSTALLATION

1. Raise and support the vehicle safely, with jackstands.

2. Remove the spindle and the ball joint assembly from the vehicle.

3. Remove the snapring from the ball joint. Using a ball joint removal tool, remove the ball joint from the spindle. Do not heat the ball joint or the axle to aid in removal.

4. Installation is the reverse of the removal procedure. Torque the ball joint stud nut to 85–110 ft. lbs. for 1983–89 Ranger and Bronco II.

Lower Ball Joint

INSPECTION

1. Check and adjust the front wheel bearings. Raise the vehicle and position a jackstand under the I-beam axle beneath the coil spring.

2. Have a helper grasp the upper edge of the tire and move the wheel assembly in and out.

3. While the wheel is being moved, observe the lower spindle arm and the lower part of the axle jaw.

4. A $\frac{1}{32}$ in. (0.8mm) or greater movement between the lower part of the axle jaw and the

lower spindle arm indicates that the lower ball joint must be replaced

REMOVAL AND INSTALLATION

1. Raise and support the vehicle safely, with jackstands.

2. Remove the spindle and the ball joint assembly from the vehicle.

3. Remove the snapring from the ball joint. Using a ball joint removal tool, remove the ball joint from the spindle. Do not heat the ball joint or the axle to aid in removal.

4. Installation is the reverse of the removal procedure.

5. Torque the ball joint stud nut to 104–146 ft. lbs. for 1983–88 Ranger and Bronco II.

6. Torque the stud nut to 95–110 ft. lbs. for 1989 Ranger and Bronco II and 1991 Explorer.

Spindle

REMOVAL AND INSTALLATION

1983–88

1. Raise the front of the vehicle and install jackstands.

2. Remove the wheel and tire assembly.

3. Remove the caliper assembly from the rotor and hold it out of the way with wire.

4. Remove the dust cap, cotter pin, nut, nut retainer, washer, and outer bearing, and remove the rotor from the spindle.

5. Remove inner bearing cone and seal. Discard the seal.

6. Remove brake dust shield.

7. Disconnect the steering linkage from the spindle and spindle arm by removing the cotter pin and nut.

8. Remove the cotter pin from the lower ball joint stud. Remove the nut from the upper and lower ball joint stud.

9. Strike the lower side of the spindle to pop the ball joints loose from the spindle.

WARNING: *Do not use a ball joint fork to separate the ball joint from the spindle, as this will damage the seal and the ball joint socket!*

10. Remove the spindle.

To install:

NOTE: *A 3 step sequence for tightening ball joint stud nuts must be followed to avoid excessive turning effort of spindle about axle.*

11. Prior to assembly of the spindle, make sure the upper and lower ball joints seals are in place.

12. Place the spindle over the ball joints. Apply Loctite® or equivalent to the lower ball joint stud and tighten to 35 ft. lbs. If the lower ball stud turns while the nut is being tightened, push the spindle up against the ball stud.

13. Install the camber adjuster in the upper over the upper ball joint. If camber adjustment is necessary, special adapters must be installed.

14. Apply Loctite® or equivalent to upper ball joint stud and install nut. Hold the camber adapter with a wrench to keep the ball joint stud from turning. If the ball joint stud turns, tap the adapter deeper into the spindle. Tighten the nut to 85–110 ft. lbs.

15. Finish tightening the lower ball stud nut to 104–146 ft. lbs. Advance nut to next castellation and install cotter pin.

16. Install the dust shield.

17. Pack the inner and outer bearing cones with high temperature wheel bearing grease. Use a bearing packer. If a bearing packer is unavailable, pack the bearing cone by hand working the grease through the cage behind the rollers.

18. Install the inner bearing cone and seal. Install the hub and rotor on the spindle.

19. Install the outer bearing cone, washer, and nut. Adjust bearing endplay and install the cotter pin and dust cap.

20. Install the caliper.

21. Connect the steering linkage to the spindle. Tighten the nut to 51–75 ft. lbs. and advance the nut as required for installation of the cotter pin.

22. Install the wheel and tire assembly. Lower the vehicle. Check, and if necessary, adjust the toe setting.

1989–91

1. Raise the front of the vehicle and install jackstands.

2. Remove the wheel and tire assembly.

3. Remove the caliper assembly from the rotor and hold it out of the way with wire.

4. Remove the dust cap, cotter pin, nut, nut retainer, washer, and outer bearing, and remove the rotor from the spindle.

5. Remove inner bearing cone and seal. Discard the seal.

6. Remove brake dust shield.

7. Disconnect the steering linkage from the spindle and spindle arm by removing the cotter pin and nut.

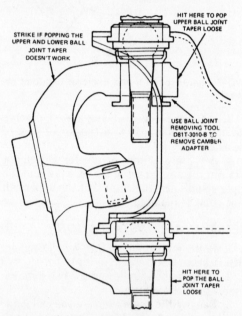

2WD Ranger, Bronco II and Explorer spindle assembly cross-section

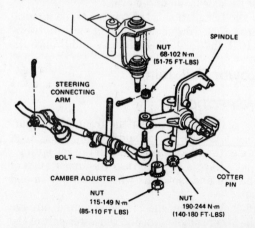

2WD Ranger spindle and ball joint assembly

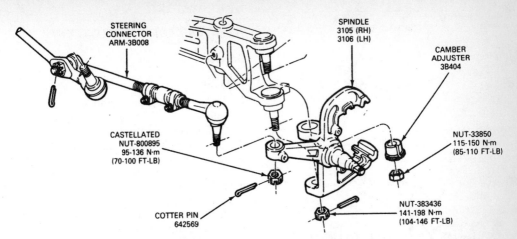

2WD Bronco II and Explorer spindle and ball joint assembly

8. With Tie Rod removal tool 3290–D or equivalent remove the tie rod end from the spindle arm.

9. Remove the cotter pin and the castellated nut from the lower ball joint stud.

10. Remove the axle clamp bolt from the axle. Remove the camber adjuster from the upper ball joint stud and axle beam.

11. Strike the area inside the top of the axle to pop the lower ball joint loose from the axle beam.

WARNING: *Do not use a ball joint fork to separate the ball joint from the spindle, as this will damage the seal and the ball joint socket!*

12. Remove the spindle and the ball joint assembly from the axle.

To install:

NOTE: *A 3 step sequence for tightening ball joint stud nuts must be followed to avoid excessive turning effort of spindle about axle.*

13. Prior to assembly of the spindle, make sure the upper and lower ball joints seals are in place.

14. Place the spindle and the ball joint assembly into the axle.

15. Install the camber adjuster in the upper over the upper ball joint. If camber adjustment is necessary, special adapters must be installed.

16. Tighten the lower ball joint stud to 104–146 ft. lbs. for the Ranger and 95–110 ft. lbs. for the Bronco II and Explorer. Continue tightening the castellated nut until it lines up with the hole in the ball joint stud. Install the cotter pin. Install the dust shield.

17. Pack the inner and outer bearing cones with high temperature wheel bearing grease. Use a bearing packer. If a bearing packer is unavailable, pack the bearing cone by hand working the grease through the cage behind the rollers.

18. Install the inner bearing cone and seal. Install the hub and rotor on the spindle.

19. Install the outer bearing cone, washer, and nut. Adjust bearing endplay and install the cotter pin and dust cap.

20. Install the caliper.

21. Connect the steering linkage to the spindle. Tighten the nut to 52–74 ft. lbs. and advance the nut as required for installation of the cotter pin.

22. Install the wheel and tire assembly. Lower the vehicle. Check, and if necessary, adjust the toe setting.

Radius Arm

REMOVAL AND INSTALLATION

1. Raise the front of the vehicle, place jackstands under the frame. Place a jack under the axle.

WARNING: *The axle must be supported on the jack throughout spring removal and installation, and must not be permitted to hang by the brake hose. If the length of the brake hose is not sufficient to provide adequate clearance for removal and installation of the spring, the disc brake caliper must be removed from the spindle. After removal, the caliper must be placed on the frame or otherwise supported to prevent suspending the caliper from the caliper hose. These precautions are absolutely necessary to prevent serious damage to the tube portion of the caliper hose assembly.*

2. Disconnect the lower end of the shock absorber from the shock lower bracket (bolt and nut).

3. Remove the front spring. Loosen the axle pivot bolt.

4. Remove the spring lower seat from the radius arm, and then remove the bolt and nut

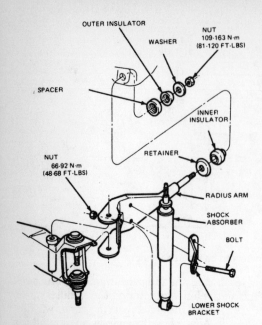

2WD Ranger, Bronco II and Explorer radius rod and related components

that attaches the radius arm to the axle and front bracket.

5. Remove the nut, rear washer and insulator from the rear side of the radius arm rear bracket.

6. Remove the radius arm from the vehicle, and remove the inner insulator and retainer from the radius arm stud.

To install:

7. Position the front end of the radius arm to the axle. Install the attaching bolt from underneath, and install the nut finger tight.

8. Install the retainer and inner insulator on the radius arm stud and insert the stud through the radius arm rear bracket.

9. Install the rear washer, insulator and nut on the arm stud at the rear side of the arm rear bracket. Tighten the nut to 81–120 ft. lbs.

10. Tighten the nut on the radius arm-to-axle bolt to 160–220 ft. lbs.

11. Install the spring lower seat and spring insulator on the radius arm so that the hole in the seat goes over the arm-to-axle bolt.

12. Install the front spring.

13. On 1983–89 vehicles connect the lower end of the shock absorber to the lower bracket on the radius arm with the attaching bolt and nut with the bolt head installed towards tire, tighten the nut to 48–68 ft. lbs.

14. On 1990–91 vehicles connect the lower end of the shock absorber to the stud on the radius arm with the retaining nut. Torque the nut to 40–63 ft. lbs.

Stabilizer Bar

REMOVAL AND INSTALLATION

Ranger

1983–89

1. As required, raise and support the vehicle safely.

2. Remove the nuts and U-bolts retaining the lower shock bracket/stabilizer bar bushing to radius arm.

3. Remove retainers and remove the stabilizer bar and bushing.

To install:

4. Place stabilizer bar in position on the radius arm and bracket.

5. Install retainers and U-bolts. Tighten retainer bolt to 35–50 ft. lbs. Tighten U-bolt nuts to 48–64 ft. lbs.

1990–91

1. As required, raise and support the vehicle safely.

2. Remove the nuts and bolts retaining the stabilizer bar to the end links.

3. Remove the retainers and the stabilizer bar and bushings from the vehicle.

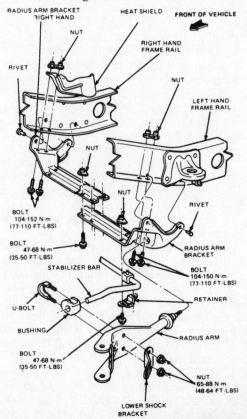

2WD Ranger front stabilizer bar and related components

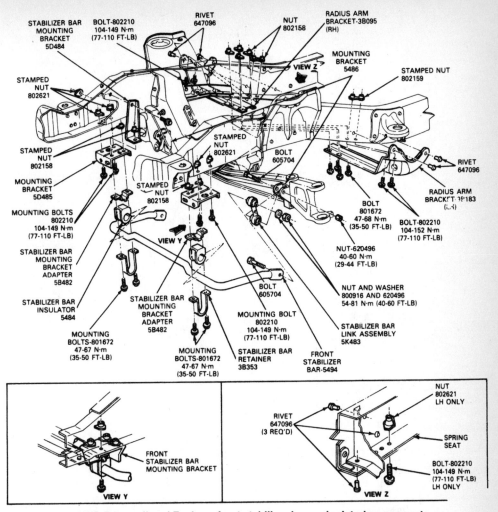

STABILIZER BAR
MOUNTING
BRACKET
5D484

BOLT-802210
104-149 N·m
(77-110 FT-LB)

RIVET
647096

NUT
802158

RADIUS ARM
BRACKET-3B095
(RH)

MOUNTING
BRACKET
5486

STAMPED NUT
802159

STAMPED
NUT
802621

STAMPED
NUT
802621

BOLT
605704

RIVET
647096

STAMPED
NUT
802158

MOUNTING
BRACKET
5D485

STAMPED
NUT
802158

RADIUS ARM
BRACKET 3B183
(LH)

MOUNTING BOLTS
802210
104-149 N·m
(77-110 FT-LB)

BOLT
801672
47-68 N·m
(35-50 FT-LB)

BOLT-802210
104-152 N·m
(77-110 FT-LB)

STABILIZER BAR
MOUNTING
BRACKET
ADAPTER
5B482

VIEW Y

NUT-620496
40-60 N·m
(29-44 FT-LB)

STABILIZER BAR
INSULATOR
5484

STABILIZER BAR
MOUNTING
BRACKET
ADAPTER
5B482

BOLT
605704

NUT AND WASHER
800916 AND 620496
54-81 N·m (40-60 FT-LB)

MOUNTING
BOLTS-801672
47-67 N·m
(35-50 FT-LB)

MOUNTING
BOLTS-801672
47-67 N·m
(35-50 FT-LB)

MOUNTING BOLT
802210
104-149 N·m
(77-110 FT-LB)

STABILIZER BAR
RETAINER
3B353

FRONT
STABILIZER
BAR-5494

STABILIZER BAR
LINK ASSEMBLY
5K483

FRONT
STABILIZER BAR
MOUNTING BRACKET

VIEW Y

RIVET
647096
(3 REQ'D)

NUT
802621
LH ONLY

SPRING
SEAT

BOLT-802210
104-149 N·m
(77-110 FT-LB)
LH ONLY

VIEW Z

2WD Bronco II and Explorer front stabilizer bar and related components

To install:

4. Position the stabilizer bar to the axles and brackets.

5. Install the retainer and the end link bolts.

6. Torque the retainer bolts to 35–50 ft. lbs. Torque the end link nuts to 30–40 ft. lbs.

Bronco II and Explorer

1. As required, raise and support the vehicle safely.

2. Remove the nuts and washer and disconnect the stabilizer link assembly from the front I-beam axle.

3. Remove the mounting bolts and remove the stabilizer bar retainers from the stabilizer bar assembly.

4. Remove the stabilizer bar from the vehicle.

To install:

5. Place stabilizer bar in position on the frame mounting brackets.

6. Install retainers and tighten retainer

bolt to 30–50 ft. lbs. If removed, install the stabilizer bar link assembly to the stabilizer bar. Install the nut and washer and tighten to 40–60 ft. lbs. on Bronco II and 30–40 ft. lbs. on Explorer.

7. Position the stabilizer bar link in the I-beam mounting bracket. Install the bolt and tighten to 30–44 ft. lbs.

I-Beam Axle

REMOVAL AND INSTALLATION

1. Raise and safely support the vehicle. Remove the front wheel spindle. Remove the front spring. On 1989–91 vehicles, remove the front stabilizer bar, if equipped.

2. Remove the spring lower seat from the radius arm, and then remove the bolt and nut that attaches the stabilizer bar bracket, if equipped on 1989–91 vehicles and the radius arm to the (I-Beam) front axle.

3. If equipped, on 1983–88 vehicles disconnect the stabilizer bar from the front I-beam

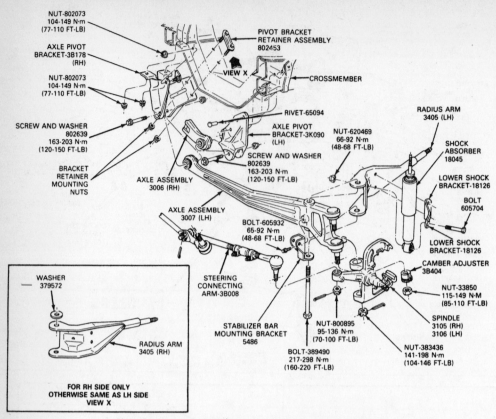

2WD Bronco II and Explorer front I-beam axle assembly

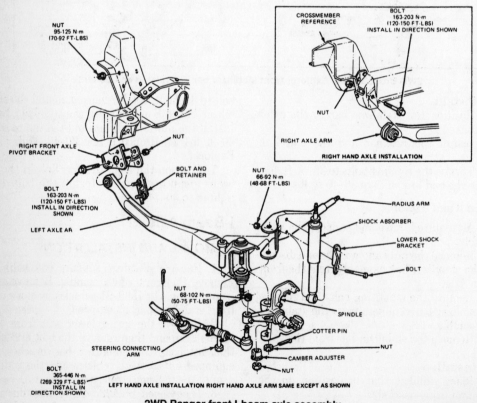

2WD Ranger front I-beam axle assembly

axle. Remove the axle-to-frame pivot bracket bolt and nut.

4. To install, position the axle to the frame pivot bracket and install the bolt and nut finger tight.

5. Position the opposite end of the axle to the radius arm, install the attaching bolt from underneath through the bracket, the radius arm,, and the axle. Install the nut and tighten to 120–150 ft. lbs.

6. Install the spring lower seat on the radius arm so that the hole in the seat indexes over the arm-to-axle bolt.

7. Install the front spring.

NOTE: *Lower the vehicle on its wheels or properly support the vehicle at the front springs before tightening the axle pivot bolt and nut.*

8. Tighten the axle-to-frame pivot bracket bolt to 120–150 ft. lbs.

9. Install the front wheel spindle.

Front Wheel Bearings

REPLACEMENT

1. Raise and support the vehicle safely. Remove the tire and wheel assembly from the hub and rotor.

2. Remove the caliper from its mounting and position it to the side with mechanics wire in order to prevent damage to the brake line hose.

3. Remove the grease cap from the hub. Remove the cotter pin, retainer, adjusting nut and flat washer from the spindle.

4. Remove the outer bearing cone and roller assembly from the hub. Remove the hub and rotor from the spindle.

5. Using seal removal tool 1175–AC or equivalent remove and discard the grease seal. Remove the inner bearing cone and roller assembly from the hub.

6. Clean the inner and outer bearing assemblies in solvent. Inspect the bearings and the cones for wear and damage. Replace defective parts, as required.

7. If the cups are worn or damaged, remove them with front hub remover tool T81P–1104–C and tool T77F–1102–A or equivalent.

8. Wipe the old grease from the spindle. Check the spindle for excessive wear or damage. Replace defective parts, as required.

To install:

9. If the inner and outer cups were removed, use bearing driver handle tool T80–4000–W or equivalent and replace the cups. Be sure to seat the cups properly in the hub.

10. Use a bearing packer tool and properly repack the wheel bearings with the proper grade and type grease. If a bearing packer is not available work as much of the grease as possible between the rollers and cages. Also, grease the cone surfaces.

11. Position the inner bearing cone and roller assembly in the inner cup. A light film of grease should be included between the lips of the new grease retainer (seal).

12. Install the retainer using the proper installer tool. Be sure that the retainer is properly seated.

13. Install the hub and rotor assembly onto the spindle. Keep the hub centered on the spindle to prevent damage to the spindle and the retainer.

14. Install the outer bearing cone and roller assembly and flat washer on the spindle. Install the adjusting nut. Adjust the wheel bearings.

15. Install the retainer, a new cotter pin and the grease cap. Install the caliper.

16. Lower the vehicle and tighten the lug nuts to 100 ft. lbs. Before driving the vehicle pump the brake pedal several times to restore normal brake pedal travel.

CAUTION: *Retighten the wheel lug nuts to specification after about 500 miles of driving. Failure to do this could result in the wheel coming off while the vehicle is in motion possibly causing loss of vehicle control or collision.*

ADJUSTMENT

1. Raise and support the vehicle safely. Remove the wheel cover. Remove the grease cap from the hub.

2. Wipe the excess grease from the end of the spindle. Remove the cotter pin and retainer. Discard the cotter pin.

3. Loosen the adjusting nut 3 turns.

CAUTION: *Obtain running clearance between the disc brake rotor surface and shoe linings by rocking the entire wheel assembly in and out several times in order to push the caliper and brake pads away from the rotor. An alternate method to obtain proper running clearance is to tap lightly on the caliper housing. Be sure not to tap on any other area that may damage the disc brake rotor or the brake lining surfaces. Do not pry on the phenolic caliper piston. The running clearance must be maintained throughout the adjustment procedure. If proper clearance cannot be maintained, the caliper must be removed from its mounting.*

4. While rotating the wheel assembly, tighten the adjusting nut to 17–25 ft. lbs. in order to seat the bearings. Loosen the adjusting nut a half turn. Retighten the adjusting nut 18–20 inch lbs.

5. Place the retainer on the adjusting nut. The castellations on the retainer must be in

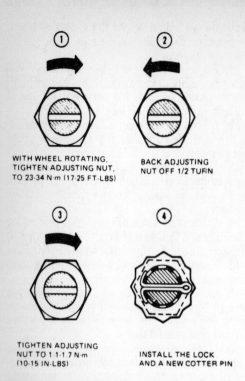

WITH WHEEL ROTATING,
TIGHTEN ADJUSTING NUT,
TO 23-34 N·m (17-25 FT-LBS)

BACK ADJUSTING
NUT OFF 1/2 TURN

TIGHTEN ADJUSTING
NUT TO 1.1-1.7 N·m
(10-15 IN-LBS)

INSTALL THE LOCK
AND A NEW COTTER PIN

2WD Ranger, Bronco II and Explorer wheel bearing adjustment procedure

alignment with the cotter pin holes in the spindle. Once this is accomplished install a new cotter pin and bend the ends to insure its being locked in place.

6. Check for proper wheel rotation. If correct, install the grease cap and wheel cover. If rotation is noisy or rough recheck your work and correct as required.

7. Lower the vehicle and tighten the lug nuts to 100 ft. lbs., if the wheel was removed. Before driving the vehicle pump the brake pedal several times to restore normal brake pedal travel.

CAUTION: *If the wheel was removed, retighten the wheel lug nuts to specification after about 500 miles of driving. Failure to do this could result in the wheel coming off while the vehicle is in motion possibly causing loss of vehicle control or collision.*

Front End Alignment

CASTER AND CAMBER

If you should start to notice abnormal tire wear patterns and handling (steering wheel is hard to return to straight ahead position after negotiating a turn on pavement), and misalign-

ment of caster and camber are suspected, make the following checks:

1. Check the air pressure in all the tires. Make sure that the pressures agree with those specified for the tires and vehicle being checked.

2. Raise the front of the vehicle off the ground and support it safely. Grasp each front tire at the front and rear, and push the wheel inward and outward. If any free-play is noticed, adjust the wheel bearings.

NOTE: *There is supposed to be a very, very small amount of free-play present where the wheel bearings are concerned. Replace the bearings if they are worn or damaged.*

3. Check all steering linkage for wear or maladjustment. Adjust and/or replace all worn parts.

4. Check the steering gear mounting bolts and tighten if necessary.

5. Rotate each front wheel slowly, and observe the amount of lateral or side runout. If the wheel runout exceeds $1/8$ in. (3mm), replace the wheel or install the wheel on the rear.

6. Inspect the radius arms to be sure they are not bent or damaged. Inspect the bushings at the radius arm-to-axle attachment and radius arm-to-frame attachment points for wear or looseness. Repair or replace parts as required.

Caster is the number of degrees of backward (positive) or forward (negative) tilt of the spindle or the line connecting the ball joint centers. Camber is the number of degrees the top of the wheel tilts outward (positive) or inward (negative) from a vertical plane.

Before checking caster or camber, perform the toe alignment check. Using alignment equipment known to be accurate and following the equipment manufacturer's instructions, measure and record the caster angle and the camber angle of both front wheels.

If the caster and camber measurements exceed the maximum variances, inspect for damaged front suspension components. Replace as required.

NOTE: *Twin-I-Beam axles are not to be bent or twisted to correct caster or camber readings.*

Both caster and camber adjustments are possible with service adjusters. These service adjusters are available in $1/2$, 1 and $1^1/2$ degree increments. On of these adjusters is used to adjust both caster and camber.

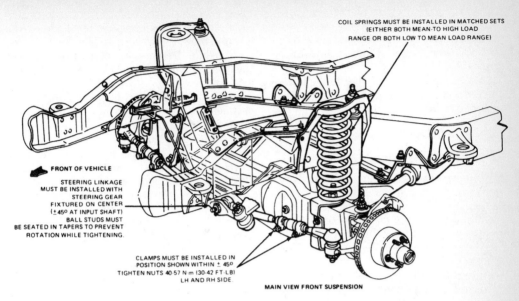

COIL SPRINGS MUST BE INSTALLED IN MATCHED SETS
(EITHER BOTH MEAN-TO HIGH LOAD
RANGE OR BOTH LOW TO MEAN LOAD RANGE)

FRONT OF VEHICLE

STEERING LINKAGE
MUST BE INSTALLED WITH
STEERING GEAR
FIXTURED ON CENTER
(± 45° AT INPUT SHAFT)
BALL STUDS MUST
BE SEATED IN TAPERS TO PREVENT
ROTATION WHILE TIGHTENING.

CLAMPS MUST BE INSTALLED IN
POSITION SHOWN WITHIN ± 45°
TIGHTEN NUTS 40-57 N·m (30-42 FT·LB)
LH AND RH SIDE

MAIN VIEW FRONT SUSPENSION

4WD Ranger, Bronco II and Explorer front suspension assembly

4-WHEEL DRIVE FRONT SUSPENSION

Coil Springs

REMOVAL AND INSTALLATION

1. Raise the vehicle and install jackstands under the frame. Position a jack beneath the spring under the axle. Raise the jack and compress the spring.

2. Remove the nut retaining the shock absorber to the radius arm. Slide the shock out from the stud.

3. Remove the nut that retains the spring to the axle and radius arm. Remove the retainer.

4. Slowly lower the axle until all spring tension is released and adequate clearance exists to remove the spring from its mounting.

5. Remove the spring by rotating the upper coil out of the tabs in the upper spring seat. Remove the spacer and the seat.

WARNING: *The axle must be supported on the jack throughout spring removal and installation, and must not be permitted to hang by the brake hose. If the length of the brake hose is not sufficient to provide adequate clearance for removal and installation of the spring, the disc brake caliper must be removed from the spindle. After removal, the caliper must be placed on the frame or otherwise supported to prevent suspending the caliper from the brake line hose.   These precautions are absolutely necessary to prevent seri-*

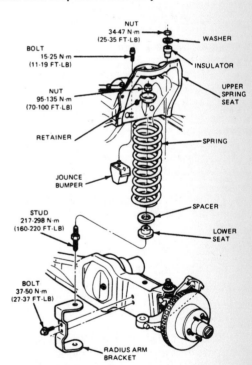

NUT
34-47 N·m
(25-35 FT·LB)

BOLT
15-25 N·m
(11-19 FT·LB)

WASHER

INSULATOR

NUT
95-135 N·m
(70-100 FT·LB)

UPPER
SPRING
SEAT

RETAINER

SPRING

JOUNCE
BUMPER

STUD
217-298 N·m
(160-220 FT·LB)

SPACER

LOWER
SEAT

BOLT
37-50 N·m
(27-37 FT·LB)

RADIUS ARM
BRACKET

4WD Ranger, Bronco II and Explorer coil spring and related components

ous damage to the tube portion of the caliper hose assembly!

6. If required, remove the stud from the axle assembly.

To install:

7. If removed, install the stud on the axle and torque to 190–230 ft. lbs. Install the lower seat and spacer over the stud.

8. Place the spring in position and slowly

raise the front axle. Ensure springs are positioned correctly in the upper spring seats.

9. Position the spring lower retainer over the stud and lower seat and torque the attaching nut to 70–100 ft. lbs.

10. Position the shock absorber to the lower stud and install the attaching nut. Tighten the nut to 41–63 ft. lbs. Lower the vehicle.

Shock Absorbers

REMOVAL AND INSTALLATION

NOTE: *Low pressure gas shocks are charged with Nitrogen gas. Do not attempt to open, puncture or apply heat to them. Prior to installing a new shock absorber, hold it upright and extend it fully. Invert it and fully compress and extend it at least 3 times. This will bleed trapped air.*

1. Raise the vehicle, as required to provide additional access and remove the bolt and nut attaching the shock absorber to the lower bracket on the radius arm.

2. Remove the nut, washer and insulator from the shock absorber at the frame bracket and remove the shock absorber.

To install:

3. Position the washer and insulator on the shock absorber rod and position the shock absorber to the frame bracket.

4. Position the insulator and washer on the shock absorber rod and install the attaching nut loosely.

5. Position the shock absorber to the lower bracket and install the attaching bolt and nut loosely.

6. Tighten the lower attaching bolts to 39–53 ft. lbs., and the upper attaching bolts to 25–35 ft. lbs.

TESTING

1. Visually check the shock absorbers for the presence of fluid leakage. A thin film of fluid is acceptable. Anything more than that means that the shock absorber must be replaced.

2. Disconnect the lower end of the shock absorber. Compress and extend the shock fully as fast as possible. If the action is not smooth in both directions, or there is no pressure resistance, replace the shock absorber. Shock absorbers should be replaced in pairs. In the case of relatively new shock absorbers, where one has failed, that one, alone, may be replaced.

Steering Knuckle and Ball Joints

INSPECTION

1. Check and adjust the front wheel bearings. Raise the vehicle and position a jackstand

under the I-beam axle beneath the coil spring.

2. Have a helper grasp the lower edge of the tire and move the wheel assembly in and out.

3. While the wheel is being moved, observe the lower spindle arm and the lower part of the axle jaw.

4. A $\frac{1}{32}$ in. (0.8mm) or greater movement between the lower part of the axle jaw and the lower spindle arm indicates that the lower ball joint must be replaced

5. To check the upper ball joints, while the wheel is being moved, observe the upper spindle arm and the upper part of the axle jaw.

4. A $\frac{1}{32}$ in. (0.8mm) or greater movement between the upper part of the axle jaw and the upper spindle arm indicates that the upper ball joint must be replaced

REMOVAL AND INSTALLATION

1983–89

1. Raise the vehicle and support on jackstands.

2. Remove the wheel and tire assembly.

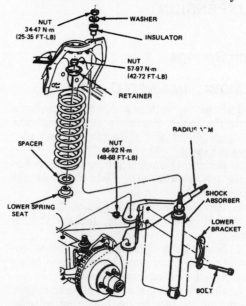

4WD Ranger, Bronco II and Explorer shock absorber and related components

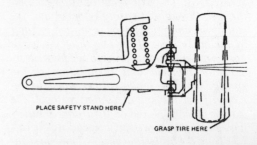

Safety stand positioning and ball joint checking

3. Remove the caliper.

4. Remove hub locks, wheel bearings, and locknuts.

5. Remove the hub and rotor. Remove the outer wheel bearing cone.

6. Remove the grease seal from the rotor with seal remover tool 1175–AC and slide hammer 750T–100–A or equivalent. Discard seal and replace with a new one upon assembly.

7. Remove the inner wheel bearing.

8. Remove the inner and outer bearing cups from the rotor with a bearing cup puller.

9. Remove the nuts retaining the spindle to the steering knuckle. Tap the spindle with a plastic or rawhide hammer to jar the spindle from the knuckle. Remove the splash shield.

10. On the left side of the vehicle remove the shaft and joint assembly by pulling the assembly out of the carrier.

11. On the right side of the carrier, remove and discard the keystone clamp from the shaft and joint assembly and the stub shaft. Slide the rubber boot onto the stub shaft and pull the shaft and joint assembly from the splines of the stub shaft.

12. Place the spindle in a vise on the second step of the spindle. Wrap a shop towel around the spindle or use a brass-jawed vise to protect the spindle.

13. Remove the oil seal and needle bearing from the spindle with slide hammer T50T–100–A and seal remover tool–1175–A–C or equivalent.

14. If required, remove the seal from the shaft, by driving off with a hammer.

15. If the tie rod has not been removed, then remove cotter pin from the tie rod nut and then remove nut. Tap on the tie rod stud to free it from the steering arm.

16. Remove the upper ball joint cotter pin and nut. Loosen the lower ball joint nut to the end of the stud.

17. Strike the inside of the spindle near the upper and lower ball joints to break the spindle loose from the ball joint studs.

18. Remove the camber adjuster sleeve. If required, use pitman arm puller, T64P–3590–F or equivalent to remove the adjuster out of the spindle. Remove the lower ball joint nut.

19. Place knuckle in vise and remove snapring from bottom ball joint socket if so equipped.

20. Assemble the C-frame, D79D–3010–AA, forcing screw, D79T–3010–AE and ball joint remover T83T–3050–A or equivalent on the lower ball joint.

21. Turn forcing screw clockwise until the lower ball joint is removed from the steering knuckle.

22. Repeat Steps 20 and 21 for the upper ball joint.

To install:
NOTE: *The lower ball joint must always be installed first.*

23. Clean the steering knuckle bore and insert lower ball joint in knuckle as straight as possible. The lower ball joint doesn't have a cotter pin hole in the stud.

24. Assemble the C-frame, D79T–3010–AA, forcing screw, D790T–3010–AE, ball joint installer, T83T–3050–A and receiver cup T80T–3010–A3 or equivalent tools, to install the lower ball joint.

25. Turn the forcing screw clockwise until the lower ball joint is firmly seated. Install the snapring on the lower ball joint.

NOTE: *If the ball joint cannot be installed to the proper depth, realignment of the receiver cup and ball joint installer will be necessary.*

26. Repeat Steps 24 and 25 for the upper ball joint.

27. Assemble the knuckle to the axle arm assembly. Install the camber adjuster on the top ball joint stud with the arrow pointing outboard for POSITIVE CAMBER and the arrow pointing inboard for NEGATIVE CAMBER and ZERO camber bushings will not have an arrow and may be rotated in either direction as long as the lugs on the yoke engage the slots in the bushing.

CAUTION: *The following torque sequence must be followed exactly when securing the spindle. Excessive spindle turning effort may result in reduced steering returnability if this procedure is not followed.*

28. Install a new nut on the bottom ball joint stud and tighten to 40 ft. lbs.

29. Install a new nut on the top ball stud and tighten to 85–100 ft. lbs., then advance nut until castellation aligns with cotter pin hole and install cotter pin.

30. Finish tightening the lower nut to 95–110 ft. lbs.

NOTE: *The camber adjuster will seat itself into the spindle at a predetermined position during the tightening sequence. Do not attempt to adjust this position.*

31. Clean all dirt and grease from the spindle bearing bore. Bearing bores must be free from nicks and burrs.

32. Place the bearing in the fore with the manufacturer's identification facing outward. Drive the bearing into the bore using spindle replacer, T83T–3123–A and driver handle T80T–4000–W or equivalent.

33. Install the grease seal in the bearing bore with the lip side of the seal facing towards the tool. Drive the seal in the bore with spindle bearing replacer, T83T–3123–A and driver handle T80–4000–W or equivalent. Coat the bearing seal lip with Lubriplate®.

34. If removed, install a new shaft seal. Place the shaft in a press, and install the seal with spindle/axle seal installer, T83T-3132-A, or equivalent.

35. On the right side of the carrier, install the rubber boot and new keystone clamps on the stub slip yoke. Since the splines on the shaft are phased, there is only one way to assemble the right shaft and joint assembly into the slip yoke. Align the missing spline in the slip yoke barrel with the gap less male spline on the shaft and joint assembly. Slide the right shaft and joint assembly into the slip yoke making sure the splines are fully engaged. Slide the boot over the assembly and crimp the keystone clamp using keystone clamp pliers, T63P-9171-A or equivalent.

36. On the left side of the carrier slide the shaft and joint assembly through the knuckle and engage the splines on the shaft in the carrier.

37. Install the splash shield and spindle onto the steering knuckle. Install and tighten the spindle nuts to 35–45 ft. lbs.

38. Drive the bearing cups into the rotor using bearing cup replacer T73T-4222-B and driver handle, T80T-4000-W or equivalent.

39. Pack the inner and outer wheel bearings and the lip of the oil seal with Multi-Purpose Long-Life Lubricant, C1AZ-19590-B or equivalent.

40. Place the inner wheel bearing in the inner cup. Drive the grease seal into the bore with hub seal replacer, T83T-1175-B and driver handle, T80T-4000-W or equivalent. Coat the bearing seal lip with multipurpose long life lubricant, C1AZ-19590-B or equivalent.

41. Install the rotor on the spindle. Install the outer wheel bearing into cup.

NOTE: *Verify that the grease seal lip totally encircles the spindle.*

42. Install the wheel bearing, locknut, thrust bearing, snapring, and locking hubs.

1990–91

1. Raise the vehicle and support on jackstands.

2. Remove the wheel and tire assembly.

3. Remove the caliper.

4. Remove hub locks, wheel bearings, and locknuts.

5. Remove the hub and rotor. Remove the outer wheel bearing cone.

6. Remove the grease seal from the rotor with seal remover tool 1175-AC and slide hammer 750T-100-A or equivalent. Discard seal and replace with a new one upon assembly.

7. Remove the inner wheel bearing.

8. Remove the inner and outer bearing cups

from the rotor with a bearing cup puller.

9. Remove the nuts retaining the spindle to the steering knuckle. Tap the spindle with a plastic or rawhide hammer to jar the spindle from the knuckle. Remove the splash shield.

10. On the left side of the vehicle remove the shaft and joint assembly by pulling the assembly out of the carrier.

11. On the right side of the carrier, remove and discard the keystone clamp from the shaft and joint assembly and the stub shaft. Slide the rubber boot onto the stub shaft and pull the shaft and joint assembly from the splines of the stub shaft.

12. Place the spindle in a vise on the second step of the spindle. Wrap a shop towel around the spindle or use a brass-jawed vise to protect the spindle.

13. Remove the oil seal and needle bearing from the spindle with slide hammer T50T-100-A and seal remover tool 1175-A-C or equivalent.

14. If required, remove the seal from the shaft, by driving off with a hammer.

15. If the tie rod has not been removed, then remove cotter pin from the tie rod nut and then remove nut. Tap on the tie rod stud to free it from the steering arm.

16. Remove the upper ball joint cotter pin and nut. Loosen the lower ball joint nut to the end of the stud.

17. Strike the inside of the spindle near the upper and lower ball joints to break the spindle loose from the ball joint studs.

18. Remove the camber adjuster sleeve. If required, use pitman arm puller, T64P-3590-F or equivalent to remove the adjuster out of the spindle. Remove the lower ball joint nut.

19. Place knuckle in vise and remove snapring from bottom ball joint socket if so equipped.

20. Assemble the C-frame, T74P-4635-C, forcing screw, D79T-3010-AE and ball joint remover T83T-3050-A or equivalent on the lower ball joint.

21. Turn forcing screw clockwise until the lower ball joint is removed from the steering knuckle.

22. Repeat Steps 20 and 21 for the upper ball joint.

NOTE: *Always remove lower ball joint first*
To install:

23. Clean the steering knuckle bore and insert lower ball joint in knuckle as straight as possible. The lower ball joint doesn't have a cotter pin hole in the stud.

24. Assemble the C-frame, T74P-4635-C, forcing screw, D790T-3010-AE, ball joint installer, T83T-3050-A and receiver cup T80T-3010-A3 or equivalent tools, to install the lower ball joint.

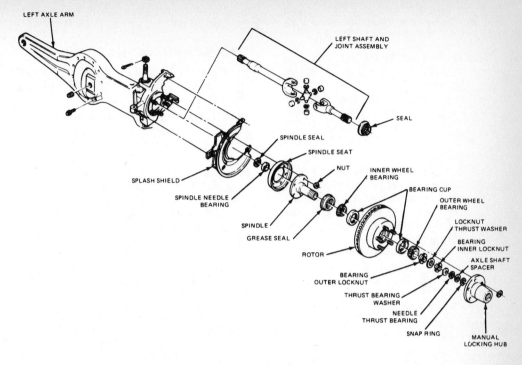

LEFT AXLE ARM

LEFT SHAFT AND
JOINT ASSEMBLY

SEAL

SPINDLE SEAL

SPINDLE SEAT

NUT

INNER WHEEL
BEARING

BEARING CUP

OUTER WHEEL
BEARING

LOCKNUT
THRUST WASHER

BEARING
INNER LOCKNUT

AXLE SHAFT
SPACER

SPLASH SHIELD

SPINDLE NEEDLE
BEARING

SPINDLE

GREASE SEAL

ROTOR

BEARING
OUTER LOCKNUT

THRUST BEARING
WASHER

NEEDLE
THRUST BEARING

SNAP RING

MANUAL
LOCKING HUB

4WD Ranger, Bronco II and Explorer spindle and left hand shaft assembly

25. Turn the forcing screw clockwise until the lower ball joint is firmly seated. Install the snapring on the lower ball joint.

NOTE: *If the ball joint cannot be installed to the proper depth, realignment of the receiver cup and ball joint installer will be necessary.*

26. Repeat Steps 24 and 25 for the upper ball joint.

27. Install the camber adjuster into the support arm. Position the slot in its original position.

CAUTION: *The following torque sequence must be followed exactly when securing the*

spindle. *Excessive spindle turning effort may result in reduced steering returnability if this procedure is not followed.*

28. Install a new nut on the bottom of the ball joint stud and torque to 90 ft. lbs. (minimum). Tighten to align the nut to the next slot in the nut with the hole in the ball joint stud. Install a new cotter pin.

29. Install the snapring on the upper ball joint stud. Install the upper ball joint pinch bolt and torque the nut to 48–65 ft. lbs.

NOTE: *The camber adjuster will seat itself into the knuckle at a predetermined position*

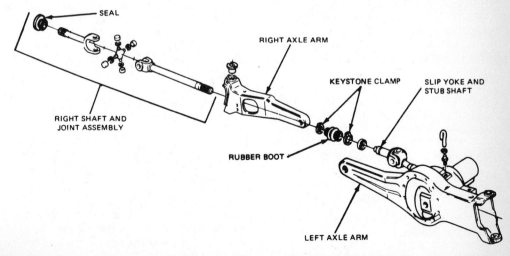

SEAL

RIGHT AXLE ARM

KEYSTONE CLAMP

SLIP YOKE AND
STUB SHAFT

RIGHT SHAFT AND
JOINT ASSEMBLY

RUBBER BOOT

LEFT AXLE ARM

4WD Ranger, Bronco II and Explorer right hand shaft assembly

during the tightening sequence. Do not attempt to adjust this position.

30. Clean all dirt and grease from the spindle bearing bore. Bearing bores must be free from nicks and burrs.

31. Place the bearing in the fore with the manufacturer's identification facing outward. Drive the bearing into the bore using spindle replacer, T80T–4000S and driver handle T80T–4000–W or equivalent.

32. Install the grease seal in the bearing bore with the lip side of the seal facing towards the tool. Drive the seal in the bore with spindle bearing replacer, T83T–3123–A and driver handle T80–4000–W or equivalent. Coat the bearing seal lip with Lubriplate®.

33. If removed, install a new shaft seal. Place the shaft in a press, and install the seal with spindle/axle seal installer, T83T–3132–A, or equivalent.

34. On the right side of the carrier, install the rubber boot and new keystone clamps on the stub slip yoke.

NOTE: *This axle does not have a blind spline. Therefore, special attention should be made to assure that the yoke ears are in line during assembly.*

35. Slide the boot over the assembly and crimp the keystone clamp using keystone clamp pliers, T63P–9171–A or equivalent.

36. On the left side of the carrier slide the shaft and joint assembly through the knuckle and engage the splines on the shaft in the carrier.

37. Install the splash shield and spindle onto the steering knuckle. Install and tighten the spindle nuts to 40–50 ft. lbs.

38. Drive the bearing cups into the rotor using bearing cup replacer T73T–4222–B and driver handle, T80T–4000–W or equivalent.

39. Pack the inner and outer wheel bearings and the lip of the oil seal with Multi–Purpose Long–Life Lubricant, C1AZ–19590–B or equivalent.

40. Place the inner wheel bearing in the inner cup. Drive the grease seal into the bore with hub seal replacer, T80T–4000–T and driver handle, T80T–4000–W or equivalent. Coat the bearing seal lip with multipurpose long life lubricant, C1AZ–19590–B or equivalent.

41. Install the rotor on the spindle. Install the outer wheel bearing into cup.

NOTE: *Verify that the grease seal lip totally encircles the spindle.*

42. Install the wheel bearing, locknut, thrust bearing, snapring, and locking hubs.

Radius Arm

REMOVAL AND INSTALLATION

1. Raise the front of the vehicle, place jackstands under the frame. Place a jack under the axle.

WARNING: *The axle must be supported on the jack throughout spring removal and installation, and must not be permitted to hang by the brake hose. If the length of the brake hose is not sufficient to provide adequate clearance for removal and installation of the spring, the disc brake caliper must be removed from the spindle. After removal, the caliper must be placed on the frame or otherwise supported to prevent suspending the caliper from the caliper hose.   These precautions are absolutely necessary to prevent serious damage to the tube portion of the caliper hose assembly.*

2. Disconnect the lower end of the shock absorber from the shock lower bracket on 1983–89 vehicles and the lower stud on 1990–91 vehicles. Remove the front spring from the vehicle.

3. Remove the spring lower seat and stud from the radius arm. Remove the bolts that attach the radius arm to the axle and front bracket.

4. Remove the nut, rear washer and insulator from the rear side of the radius arm rear bracket.

5. Remove the radius arm from the vehicle. Remove the inner insulator and retainer from the radius arm stud.

To install:

6. Position the front end of the radius arm from bracket to axle. Install the retaining bolts and stud in the bracket finger tight.

7. Install the retainer and inner insulator on the radius arm stud and insert the stud through the radius arm rear bracket.

8. Install the rear washer, insulator and nut on the arm stud at the rear side of the arm rear bracket. Tighten the nut to 80–120 ft. lbs.

9. Tighten the stud to 190–230 ft. lbs. Tighten the front bracket to axle bolts to 37–50 ft. lbs. and the lower bolt and washer to 190–230 ft. lbs.

10. Install the spring lower seat and spring insulator on the radius arm so that the hole in the seat goes over the arm to axle bolt. Tighten the axle pivot bolt to 120–150 ft. lbs.

11. Install the front spring. Connect the lower end of the shock absorber to the lower bracket on 1983–89 vehicles and to the stud 1990–91 vehicles of the radius arm and torque the retaining nut to 42–72 ft. lbs. on 1983–90 vehicles and 39–53 ft. lbs on 1991 vehicles.

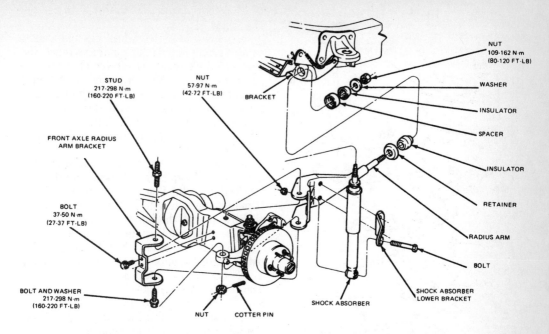

4WD Ranger, Bronco II and Explorer radius rod and related components

Stabilizer Bar

REMOVAL AND INSTALLATION

1983–88

1. As required, raise and support the vehicle safely. Remove the nuts and U-bolts retaining the lower shock bracket/stabilizer bar bushing to the radius arm.

2. Remove the retainers and remove the stabilizer bar and bushing.

3. Place the stabilizer bar in position on the radius arm and bracket.

4. Install the retainers and U-bolts. Tighten the retainer bolts to 35–50 ft. lbs. Tighten the U-bolt nuts to 48–68 ft. lbs.

1989–91

1. As required, raise and support the vehicle safely. Remove the bolts and the retainers from the center and right hand end of the stabilizer bar.

2. Remove the nut, bolt and washer retaining the stabilizer bar to the stabilizer link.

3. Remove the stabilizer bar and bushings from the vehicle.

4. Installation is the reverse of the removal procedure. Tighten the retainer bolts to 35–50 ft. lbs. Tighten the stabilizer bar to link nut to 30–44 ft. lbs.

Manual Locking Hubs

REMOVAL AND INSTALLATION

1. Raise the vehicle and install jackstands.
2. Remove the wheel and tire assembly.
3. Remove the retainer washers from the lug nut studs and remove the manual locking hub assembly.
4. To remove the internal hub lock assembly from the outer body assembly, remove the outer lock ring seated in the hub body groove.
5. The internal assembly, spring and clutch gear will now slide out of the hub body.

WARNING: *Do not remove the screw from the plastic dial!*

6. Rebuild the hub assembly in the reverse order of disassembly.

To install:

7. Install the manual locking hub assembly over the spindle and place the retainer washers on the lug nut studs.

8. Install the wheel and tire assembly. Install the lug nuts and torque to specification.

BEARING ADJUSTMENT

1. Raise the vehicle and install jackstands.
2. Remove the wheel and tire assembly.
3. Remove the retainer washers from the

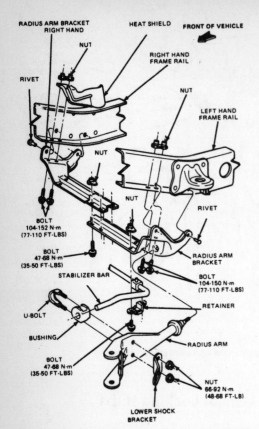

4WD Ranger, Bronco II and Explorer front stabilizer bar and related components

lug nut studs and remove the manual locking hub assembly from the spindle.

4. Remove the snapring from the end of the spindle shaft.

5. Remove the axle shaft spacer, needle thrust bearing and the bearing spacer.

6. Remove the outer wheel bearing locknut from the spindle using 4 prong spindle nut spanner wrench, T86T–1197–A or equivalent. Make sure the tabs on the tool engage the slots in the locknut.

7. Remove the locknut washer from the spindle.

8. Loosen the inner wheel bearing locknut using 4 prong spindle nut spanner wrench, tool T83T–1197–A for 1983–89 vehicles and tool T86T–1197–A for 1990–91 vehicles or equivalent. Make sure that the tabs on the tool engage the slots in the locknut and that the slot in the tool is over the pin on the locknut.

9. Tighten the inner locknut to 35 ft. lbs. to seat the bearings.

10. Spin the rotor and back off the inner locknut $1/4$ turn. Install the lockwasher on the spindle. Retighten the inner locknut to 16 inch lbs. It may be necessary to turn the inner locknut slightly so that the pin on the locknut aligns with the closest hole in the lockwasher.

11. Install the outer wheel bearing locknut using 4 prong spindle nut spanner wrench, tool T83T–1197–A for 1983–89 vehicles and tool T86T–1197–A for 1990–91 vehicles or equivalent. Tighten locknut to 150 ft. lbs.

12. Install the bearing thrust spacer and needle thrust bearing, as required. Install the axle shaft spacer.

13. Clip the snapring onto the end of the spindle.

14. Install the manual hub assembly over the spindle. Install the retainer washers.

15. Install the wheel and tire assembly. Install and torque lug nuts to specification.

16. Check the endplay of the wheel and tire assembly on the spindle. Endplay should be 0.001–0.003 in. (0.025–0.076mm). On 1990–91 vehicles the maximum torque to rotate the hub should be 25 inch lbs.

BEARING REPLACEMENT

1. Raise the vehicle and install jackstands.

2. Remove the wheel and tire assembly.

3. Remove the retainer washers and remove the manual locking hub assembly.

4. Remove the caliper and wire it to the side using mechanics wire.

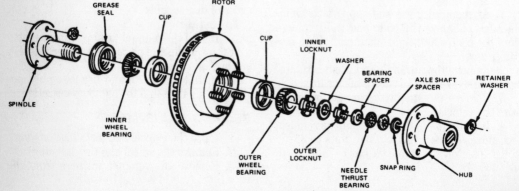

Ranger, Bronco II and Explorer manual locking hub assembly

5. Remove the snapring from the end of the spindle shaft.

6. Remove the axle shaft spacer, needle thrust bearing and the bearing spacer.

7. Remove the outer wheel bearing locknut from the spindle using 4 prong spindle nut spanner wrench, T86T–1197–A or equivalent. Make sure the tabs on the tool engage the slots in the locknut.

8. Remove the locknut washer from the spindle.

9. Remove the inner wheel bearing adjusting nut using 4 prong spindle nut spanner wrench, tool T83T–1197–A for 1983–89 vehicles and tool T86T–1197–A for 1990–91 vehicles or equivalent. Make sure that the tabs on the tool engage the slots in the locknut and that the slot in the tool is over the pin on the locknut.

10. Remove the disc brake rotor and the hub assembly. Remove the outer wheel bearing cone assembly.

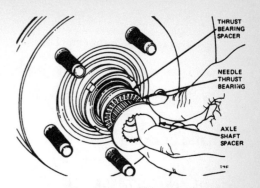

Ranger, Bronco II and Explorer manual locking hub thrust bearing and spacer removal

11. Remove the grease seal from the rotor with seal remover tool 1175–AC and slide hammer 750T–100–A or equivalent. Discard seal and replace with a new one upon assembly.

12. Remove the inner wheel bearing.

13. Inspect the bearing cups for pits or cracks. If necessary, remove them with internal puller tool D80L–943–A and slide hammer 750T–100–A. or equivalent.

NOTE: *If new cups are installed, install new cone and roller assemblies.*

To install:

14. Lubricate the bearings with disc brake wheel bearing grease. Clean all old grease from the hub. Pack the cones and rollers. If a bearing packer is not available, work as much lubricant as possible between the rollers and the cages.

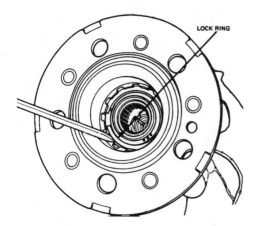

Ranger, Bronco II and Explorer manual locking hub outer ring removal

15. If bearing cups are to be installed, position cups in rotor and drive in place with bearing cup tool T73T–4222–B and driver handle T80T–4000–W.

16. Position the inner bearing in the inner cup in the rotor. Install the grease seal by driving in place with hub seal replacer tool T83T–1175–B and Driver Handle T80T–4000–W.

17. Carefully install the rotor onto the spindle. Install the outer wheel bearing in the rotor.

18. Install the inner adjusting nut with the pin facing out. Tighten the inner adjusting nut to 35 ft. lbs. to seat the bearings.

19. Spin the rotor and back off the inner nut 1/4 turn. Retighten the inner nut to 16 inch lbs. Install the locking washer. It may be necessary to turn the inner nut slightly so that the pin on the nut aligns with the closest hole in the lockwasher.

20. Install the outer wheel bearing locknut using 4 prong spindle nut spanner wrench, tool T83T–1197–A for 1983–89 vehicles and tool T86T–1197–A for 1990–91 vehicles or equivalent. Tighten locknut to 150 ft. lbs.

21. Install the bearing thrust spacer and

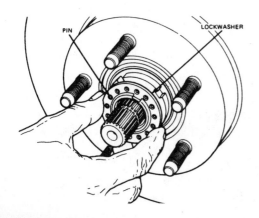

Ranger, Bronco II and Explorer manual locking hub lockwasher installation

needle thrust bearing, as required. Install the axle shaft spacer.

22. Clip the snapring onto the end of the spindle.

23. Install the caliper. Install the locking hub assembly.

24. Install the wheel assembly. Lower the vehicle.

Automatic Locking Hubs

REMOVAL AND INSTALLATION

NOTE: *The following procedures also include the bearing adjustment procedure.*

1983–90

1. Raise the vehicle and install jackstands.
2. Remove the wheel and tire assembly.
3. Remove the retainer washers from the lug nut studs and remove the automatic locking hub assembly from the spindle.
   To install:
4. Install the automatic locking hub assembly over the spindle by lining up the 3 legs in the hub assembly with 3 pockets in the cam assembly. Install the retainer washers.
5. Install the wheel and tire assembly. Torque the lug nuts to specification.

1991

1. Raise the vehicle and install jackstands.
2. Remove the wheel and tire assembly.
3. Remove the retainer washers from the lug nut studs and remove the automatic locking hub assembly from the spindle.
   To install:
4. Install the automatic locking hub assembly over the spindle by lining up the 3 legs in the hub assembly with the 3 pockets in the cam assembly. Install the retainer washers.

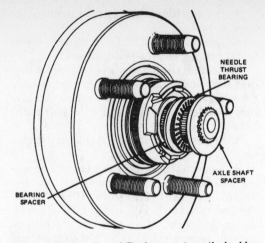

Ranger, Bronco II and Explorer automatic locking hub thrust bearing removal

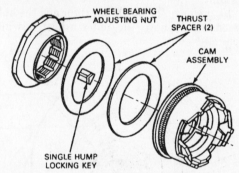

Ranger, Bronco II and Explorer automatic locking hub cam assembly 1991

5. Install the wheel and tire assembly. Torque the lug nuts to specification.

BEARING REPLACEMENT

1. Raise the vehicle and install jackstands.
2. Remove the wheel and tire assembly.
3. Remove the retainer washers and remove the automatic locking hub assembly.

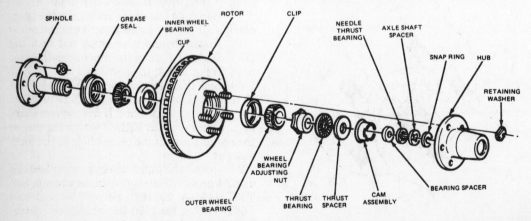

Ranger, Bronco II and Explorer automatic locking hub assembly

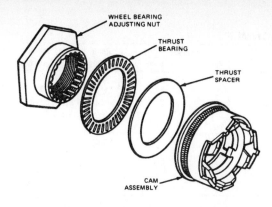

Ranger, Bronco II and Explorer automatic locking hub cam assembly 1983–90

4. Remove the caliper and wire it to the side using mechanics wire.

5. Remove the snapring from the end of the spindle shaft.

6. Remove the axle shaft spacer, needle thrust bearing and the bearing spacer.

7. Remove the outer wheel bearing locknut from the spindle using 4 prong spindle nut spanner wrench, T86T–1197–A or equivalent. Make sure the tabs on the tool engage the slots in the locknut.

8. Remove the locknut washer from the spindle.

9. Remove the inner wheel bearing adjusting nut using 4 prong spindle nut spanner wrench, tool T83T–1197–A for 1983–89 vehicles and tool T86T–1197–A for 1990–91 vehicles or equivalent. Make sure that the tabs on the tool engage the slots in the locknut and that the slot in the tool is over the pin on the locknut.

10. Remove the disc brake rotor and the hub assembly. Remove the outer wheel bearing cone assembly.

11. Remove the grease seal from the rotor with seal remover tool 1175–AC and slide hammer 750T–100–A or equivalent. Discard seal and replace with a new one upon assembly.

12. Remove the inner wheel bearing.

13. Inspect the bearing cups for pits or cracks. If necessary, remove them with internal puller tool D80L–943–A and slide hammer 750T–100–A. or equivalent.

NOTE: *If new cups are installed, install new cone and roller assemblies.*

To install:

14. Lubricate the bearings with disc brake wheel bearing grease. Clean all old grease from the hub. Pack the cones and rollers. If a bearing packer is not available, work as much lubricant as possible between the rollers and the cages.

15. If bearing cups are to be installed, position cups in rotor and drive in place with bearing cup tool T73T–4222–B and driver handle T80T–4000–W.

16. Position the inner bearing in the inner cup in the rotor. Install the grease seal by driving in place with hub seal replacer tool T83T–1175–B and Driver Handle T80T–4000–W.

17. Carefully install the rotor onto the spindle. Install the outer wheel bearing in the rotor.

18. Install the inner adjusting nut, with the pin facing out. Tighten the inner locknut to 35 ft. lbs. to seat the bearings.

19. Spin the rotor and back off the inner locknut 1/4 turn (90°). Retighten the inner locknut to 16 inch lbs. Install the locking washer. It may be necessary to turn the inner locknut slightly so that the pin on the locknut aligns with the closest hole in the lockwasher.

20. Install the outer wheel bearing locknut using 4 prong spindle nut spanner wrench, tool T83T–1197–A for 1983–89 vehicles and tool T86T–1197–A for 1990–91 vehicles or equivalent. Tighten locknut to 150 ft. lbs.

21. Install the bearing thrust spacer and needle thrust bearing, as required. Install the axle shaft spacer.

22. Clip the snapring onto the end of the spindle.

23. Install the caliper. Install the locking hub assembly.

24. Install the wheel. Lower the vehicle.

Front End Alignment

CASTER AND CAMBER

If you should start to notice abnormal tire wear patterns and handling (steering wheel is hard to return to straight ahead position after negotiating a turn on pavement), and misalignment of caster and camber are suspected, make the following checks:

1. Check the air pressure in all the tires. Make sure that the pressures agree with those specified for the tires and vehicle being checked.

2. Raise the front of the vehicle off the ground and support it safely. Grasp each front tire at the front and rear, and push the wheel inward and outward. If any free-play is noticed, adjust the wheel bearings.

NOTE: *There is supposed to be a very, very small amount of free-play present where the wheel bearings are concerned. Replace the bearings if they are worn or damaged.*

3. Check all steering linkage for wear or maladjustment. Adjust and/or replace all worn parts.

4. Check the steering gear mounting bolts and tighten if necessary.

WHEEL ALIGNMENT

Year	Model	Ride Height		Caster		Camber		Toe-in (inches)	Toe-in (Degrees)
		Min.	Max.	Min.	Max.	Min.	Max.		
1983	Ranger 2WD	$2^3/_4$	$3^1/_4$	$4^1/_2$	7	−1	1	$1/_{32}$	$1/_{16}$
		$3^1/_4$	$3^1/_2$	4	$6^1/_2$	$−^1/_2$	$1^3/_4$	$1/_{32}$	$1/_{16}$
		$3^1/_2$	4	$3^3/_8$	$5^7/_8$	0	$2^3/_8$	$1/_{32}$	$1^1/_{16}$
		4	$4^1/_4$	$2^5/_8$	$5^1/_8$	$^3/_4$	3	$1/_{32}$	$1/_{16}$
		$4^1/_4$	$4^3/_4$	2	$4^1/_2$	$1^1/_2$	$3^3/_4$	$1/_{32}$	$1/_{16}$
	Ranger 4WD	$2^3/_4$	$3^1/_4$	5	8	−1	$1/_2$	$1/_{32}$	$1/_{16}$
		$3^1/_4$	$3^1/_2$	4	7	0	$1^1/_2$	$1/_{32}$	$1/_{16}$
		$3^1/_2$	4	3	6	$1/_2$	2	$1/_{32}$	$1/_{16}$
		4	$4^1/_4$	$2^1/_2$	$5^1/_2$	$1^1/_4$	$2^3/_4$	$1/_{32}$	$1/_{16}$
		$4^1/_4$	$4^3/_4$	$1^3/_4$	5	2	$3^3/_4$	$1/_{32}$	$1/_{16}$
1984	Bronco II	$2^3/_4$	3	$5^1/_2$	$8^1/_2$	−2	$−^1/_2$	$1/_{32}$	$1/_{16}$
		$3^1/_4$	$3^1/_2$	4	7	−1	$1/_2$	$1/_{32}$	$1/_{16}$
		$3^1/_2$	$3^3/_4$	3	6	0	$1^1/_2$	$1/_{32}$	$1/_{16}$
		4	$4^1/_4$	2	5	1	$2^1/_2$	$1/_{32}$	$1/_{16}$
		$4^1/_4$	$4^3/_4$	1	4	2	$3^1/_2$	$1/_{32}$	$1/_{16}$
	Ranger 2WD (w/forged axle)	$3^1/_4$	$3^1/_2$	$5^1/_4$	$8^1/_4$	−2	$−^1/_2$	$1/_{32}$	$1/_{16}$
		$3^1/_2$	$3^3/_4$	$4^1/_2$	$7^1/_2$	$−1^5/_8$	$1/_8$	$1/_{32}$	$1/_{16}$
		$3^3/_4$	4	$3^1/_2$	$6^1/_2$	$−^1/_2$	1	$1/_{32}$	$1/_{16}$
		4	$4^1/_4$	2	6	$1/_4$	$1^3/_4$	$1/_{32}$	$1/_{16}$
		$4^1/_2$	$4^3/_4$	$1^7/_8$	$4^7/_8$	$1^1/_4$	$2^3/_4$	$1/_{32}$	$1/_{16}$
	Ranger 2WD (w/stamped axle)	3	$3^1/_4$	$5^1/_4$	$8^1/_4$	−2	$−^1/_2$	$1/_{32}$	$1/_{16}$
		$3^1/_4$	$3^1/_2$	$4^1/_2$	$7^1/_2$	$−1^5/_8$	$1/_8$	$1/_{32}$	$1/_{16}$
		$3^1/_2$	$3^3/_4$	$3^1/_2$	$6^1/_2$	$−^1/_2$	1	$1/_{32}$	$1/_{16}$
		$3^3/_4$	4	3	6	$1/_4$	$1^3/_4$	$1/_{32}$	$1/_{16}$
		$4^1/_4$	$4^1/_2$	$1^7/_8$	$4^7/_8$	$1^1/_4$	$2^3/_4$	$1/_{32}$	$1/_{16}$
	Ranger 4WD	$2^3/_4$	3	$5^1/_2$	$8^1/_2$	−2	$−^1/_2$	$1/_{32}$	$1/_{16}$
		$3^1/_4$	$3^1/_2$	4	7	−1	$1/_2$	$1/_{32}$	$1/_{16}$
		$3^1/_2$	$3^3/_4$	3	6	0	$1^1/_2$	$1/_{32}$	$1/_{16}$
		4	$4^1/_4$	2	5	1	$2^1/_2$	$1/_{32}$	$1/_{16}$
		$4^1/_4$	$4^3/_4$	1	4	2	$3^1/_2$	$1/_{32}$	$1/_{16}$
1985	Bronco II	$2^3/_4$	3	$5^1/_2$	$8^1/_2$	−2	$−^1/_2$	$1/_{32}$	$1/_{16}$
		$3^1/_4$	$3^1/_2$	4	7	−1	$1/_2$	$1/_{32}$	$1/_{16}$
		$3^1/_2$	$3^3/_4$	3	6	0	$1^1/_2$	$1/_{32}$	$1/_{16}$
		4	$4^1/_4$	2	5	1	$2^1/_2$	$1/_{32}$	$1/_{16}$
		$4^1/_4$	$4^3/_4$	1	4	2	$3^1/_2$	$1/_{32}$	$1/_{16}$
	Ranger 2WD (w/forged axle)	$3^1/_4$	$3^1/_2$	$5^1/_4$	$8^1/_4$	−2	$−^1/_2$	$1/_{32}$	$1/_{16}$
		$3^1/_2$	$3^3/_4$	$4^1/_2$	$7^1/_2$	$−1^5/_8$	$1/_8$	$1/_{32}$	$1/_{16}$
		$3^3/_4$	4	$3^1/_2$	$6^1/_2$	$−^1/_2$	1	$1/_{32}$	$1/_{16}$
		4	$4^1/_4$	2	6	$1/_4$	$1^3/_4$	$1/_{32}$	$1/_{16}$
		$4^1/_2$	$4^3/_4$	$1^7/_8$	$4^7/_8$	$1^1/_4$	$2^3/_4$	$1/_{32}$	$1/_{16}$
	Ranger 2WD (w/stamped axle)	3	$3^1/_4$	$5^1/_4$	$8^1/_4$	−2	$−^1/_2$	$1/_{32}$	$1/_{16}$
		$3^1/_4$	$3^1/_2$	$4^1/_2$	$7^1/_2$	$−1^5/_8$	$1/_8$	$1/_{32}$	$1/_{16}$
		$3^1/_2$	$3^3/_4$	$3^1/_2$	$6^1/_2$	$−^1/_2$	1	$1/_{32}$	$1/_{16}$
		$3^3/_4$	4	3	6	$1/_4$	$1^3/_4$	$1/_{32}$	$1/_{16}$
		$4^1/_4$	$4^1/_2$	$1^7/_8$	$4^7/_8$	$1^1/_4$	$2^3/_4$	$1/_{32}$	$1/_{16}$
	Ranger 4WD	$2^3/_4$	3	$5^1/_2$	$8^1/_2$	−2	$−^1/_2$	$1/_{32}$	$1/_{16}$
		$3^1/_4$	$3^1/_2$	4	7	−1	$1/_2$	$1/_{32}$	$1/_{16}$
		$3^1/_2$	$3^3/_4$	3	6	0	$1^1/_2$	$1/_{32}$	$1/_{16}$
		4	$4^1/_4$	2	5	1	$2^1/_2$	$1/_{32}$	$1/_{16}$
		$4^1/_4$	$4^3/_4$	1	4	2	$3^1/_2$	$1/_{32}$	$1/_{16}$

WHEEL ALIGNMENT

Year	Model	Ride Height Min.	Ride Height Max.	Caster Min.	Caster Max.	Camber Min.	Camber Max.	Toe-in (inches)	Toe-in (Degrees)
1986	Bronco II	$2^3/4$	3	$5^1/2$	$8^1/2$	−2	$-^1/2$	$^1/32$	$^1/16$
		$3^1/4$	$3^1/2$	4	7	−1	$^1/2$	$^1/32$	$^1/16$
		$3^1/2$	$3^3/4$	3	6	0	$1^1/2$	$^1/32$	$^1/16$
		4	$4^1/4$	2	5	1	$2^1/2$	$^1/32$	$^1/16$
		$4^1/4$	$4^3/4$	1	4	2	$3^1/2$	$^1/32$	$^1/16$
	Ranger 2WD (w/forged axle)	$3^1/4$	$3^1/2$	$5^1/14$	$8^1/4$	−2	$-^1/2$	$^1/32$	$^1/16$
		$3^1/2$	$3^3/4$	$4^1/2$	$7^1/2$	$-1^5/8$	$^1/8$	$^1/32$	$^1/16$
		$3^3/4$	4	$3^1/2$	$6^1/2$	$-^1/2$	1	$^1/32$	$^1/16$
		4	$4^1/4$	2	6	$^1/4$	$1^3/4$	$^1/32$	$^1/16$
		$4^1/2$	$4^3/4$	$1^7/8$	$4^7/8$	$1^1/4$	$2^3/4$	$^1/32$	$^1/16$
	Ranger 2WD (w/stamped axle)	3	$3^1/4$	$5^1/4$	$8^1/4$	−2	$-^1/2$	$^1/32$	$^1/16$
		$3^1/4$	$3^1/2$	$4^1/2$	$7^1/2$	$-1^5/8$	$^1/8$	$^1/32$	$^1/16$
		$3^1/2$	$3^3/4$	$3^1/2$	$6^1/2$	$-^1/2$	1	$^1/32$	$^1/16$
		$3^3/4$	4	3	6	$^1/4$	$1^3/4$	$^1/32$	$^1/16$
		$4^1/4$	$4^1/2$	$1^7/8$	$4^7/8$	$1^1/4$	$2^3/4$	$^1/32$	$^1/16$
	Ranger 4WD	$2^3/4$	3	$5^1/2$	$8^1/2$	−2	$-^1/2$	$^1/32$	$^1/16$
		$3^1/4$	$3^1/2$	4	7	−1	$^1/2$	$^1/32$	$^1/16$
		$3^1/2$	$3^3/4$	3	6	0	$1^1/2$	$^1/32$	$^1/16$
		4	$4^1/4$	2	5	1	$2^1/2$	$^1/32$	$^1/16$
		$4^1/4$	$4^3/4$	1	4	2	$3^1/2$	$^1/32$	$^1/16$
1987	Bronco II	$2^3/4$	3	$5^1/2$	$8^1/2$	−2	$-^1/2$	$^1/32$	$^1/16$
		$3^1/4$	$3^1/2$	4	7	−1	$^1/2$	$^1/32$	$^1/16$
		$3^1/2$	$3^3/4$	3	6	0	$1^1/2$	$^1/32$	$^1/16$
		4	$4^1/4$	2	5	1	$2^1/2$	$^1/32$	$^1/16$
		$4^1/4$	$4^3/4$	1	4	2	$3^1/2$	$^1/32$	$^1/16$
	Ranger 2WD (w/forged axle)	$3^1/4$	$3^1/2$	$5^1/4$	$8^1/4$	−2	$-^1/2$	$^1/32$	$^1/16$
		$3^1/2$	$3^3/4$	$4^1/2$	$7^1/2$	$-1^5/8$	$^1/8$	$^1/32$	$^1/16$
		$3^3/4$	4	$3^1/2$	$6^1/2$	$-^1/2$	1	$^1/32$	$^1/16$
		4	$4^1/4$	2	6	$^1/4$	$1^3/4$	$^1/32$	$^1/16$
		$4^1/2$	$4^3/4$	$1^7/8$	$4^7/8$	$1^1/4$	$2^3/4$	$^1/32$	$^1/16$
	Ranger 2WD (w/stamped axle)	3	$3^1/4$	$5^1/4$	$8^1/4$	−2	$-^1/2$	$^1/32$	$^1/16$
		$3^1/4$	$3^1/2$	$4^1/2$	$7^1/2$	$-1^5/8$	$^1/8$	$^1/32$	$^1/16$
		$3^1/2$	$3^3/4$	$3^1/2$	$6^1/2$	$-^1/2$	1	$^1/32$	$^1/16$
		$3^3/4$	4	3	6	$^1/4$	$1^3/4$	$^1/32$	$^1/16$
		$4^1/4$	$4^1/2$	$1^7/8$	$4^7/8$	$1^1/4$	$2^3/4$	$^1/32$	$^1/16$
	Ranger 4WD (exc. STX)	$2^3/4$	3	$5^1/2$	$8^1/2$	−2	$-^1/2$	$^1/32$	$^1/16$
		$3^1/4$	$3^1/2$	4	7	−1	$^1/2$	$^1/32$	$^1/16$
		$3^1/2$	$3^3/4$	3	6	0	$1^1/2$	$^1/32$	$^1/16$
		4	$4^1/4$	2	5	1	$2^1/2$	$^1/32$	$^1/16$
		$4^1/4$	$4^3/4$	1	4	2	$3^1/2$	$^1/32$	$^1/16$
	Ranger 4WD (STX)	$4^1/4$	$4^1/2$	$5^1/2$	$8^1/2$	−2	$-^1/2$	$^1/32$	$^1/16$
		$4^1/2$	5	4	7	−1	$^1/2$	$^1/32$	$^1/16$
		5	$5^1/4$	3	6	0	$1^1/2$	$^1/32$	$^1/16$
		$5^1/4$	$5^3/4$	2	5	1	$2^1/2$	$^1/32$	$^1/16$
		$5^3/4$	6	1	4	2	$3^1/2$	$^1/32$	$^1/16$
1988	Bronco II	$2^3/4$	3	$5^1/2$	$8^1/2$	−2	$-^1/2$	$^1/32$	$^1/16$
		$3^1/4$	$3^1/2$	4	7	−1	$^1/2$	$^1/32$	$^1/16$
		$3^1/2$	$3^3/4$	3	6	0	$1^1/2$	$^1/32$	$^1/16$
		4	$4^1/4$	2	5	1	$2^1/2$	$^1/32$	$^1/16$
		$4^1/4$	$4^3/4$	1	4	2	$3^1/2$	$^1/32$	$^1/16$

WHEEL ALIGNMENT

Year	Model	Ride Height Min.	Ride Height Max.	Caster Min.	Caster Max.	Camber Min.	Camber Max.	Toe-in (inches)	Toe-in (Degrees)
1988	Ranger 2WD (w/forged axle)	$3^1/_4$	$3^1/_2$	$5^1/_4$	$8^1/_4$	-2	$-^1/_2$	$^1/_{32}$	$^1/_{16}$
		$3^1/_2$	$3^3/_4$	$4^1/_2$	$7^1/_2$	$-1^5/_8$	$^1/_8$	$^1/_{32}$	$^1/_{16}$
		$3^3/_4$	4	$3^1/_2$	$6^1/_2$	$-^1/_2$	1	$^1/_{32}$	$^1/_{16}$
		4	$4^1/_4$	2	6	$^1/_4$	$1^3/_4$	$^1/_{32}$	$^1/_{16}$
		$4^1/_2$	$4^3/_4$	$1^7/_8$	$4^7/_8$	$1^1/_4$	$2^3/_4$	$^1/_{32}$	$^1/_{16}$
	Ranger 2WD (w/stamped axle)	3	$3^1/_4$	$5^1/_4$	$8^1/_4$	-2	$-^1/_2$	$^1/_{32}$	$^1/_{16}$
		$3^1/_4$	$3^1/_2$	$4^1/_2$	$7^1/_2$	$-1^5/_8$	$^1/_8$	$^1/_{32}$	$^1/_{16}$
		$3^1/_2$	$3^3/_4$	$3^1/_2$	$6^1/_2$	$-^1/_2$	1	$^1/_{32}$	$^1/_{16}$
		$3^3/_4$	4	3	6	$^1/_4$	$1^3/_4$	$^1/_{32}$	$^1/_{16}$
		$4^1/_4$	$4^1/_2$	$1^7/_8$	$4^7/_8$	$1^1/_4$	$2^3/_4$	$^1/_{32}$	$^1/_{16}$
	Ranger 4WD (exc. STX)	$2^3/_4$	3	$5^1/_2$	$8^1/_2$	-2	$-^1/_2$	$^1/_{32}$	$^1/_{16}$
		$3^1/_4$	$3^1/_2$	4	7	-1	$^1/_2$	$^1/_{32}$	$^1/_{16}$
		$3^1/_2$	$3^3/_4$	3	6	0	$1^1/_2$	$^1/_{32}$	$^1/_{16}$
		4	$4^1/_4$	2	5	1	$2^1/_2$	$^1/_{32}$	$^1/_{16}$
		$4^1/_4$	$4^3/_4$	1	4	2	$3^1/_2$	$^1/_{32}$	$^1/_{16}$
	Ranger 4WD (STX)	$4^1/_4$	$4^1/_2$	$5^1/_2$	$8^1/_2$	-2	$-^1/_2$	$^1/_{32}$	$^1/_{16}$
		$4^1/_2$	5	4	7	-1	$^1/_2$	$^1/_{32}$	$^1/_{16}$
		5	$5^1/_4$	3	6	0	$1^1/_2$	$^1/_{32}$	$^1/_{16}$
		$5^1/_4$	$5^3/_4$	2	5	1	$2^1/_2$	$^1/_{32}$	$^1/_{16}$
		$5^3/_4$	6	1	4	2	$3^1/_2$	$^1/_{32}$	$^1/_{16}$
1989	Bronco II	$2^3/_4$	3	$5^1/_2$	$8^1/_2$	-2	$-^1/_2$	$^1/_{32}$	$^1/_{16}$
		$3^1/_4$	$3^1/_2$	4	7	-1	$^1/_2$	$^1/_{32}$	$^1/_{16}$
		$3^1/_2$	$3^3/_4$	3	6	0	$1^1/_2$	$^1/_{32}$	$^1/_{16}$
		4	$4^1/_4$	2	5	1	$2^1/_2$	$^1/_{32}$	$^1/_{16}$
		$4^1/_4$	$4^3/_4$	1	4	2	$3^1/_2$	$^1/_{32}$	$^1/_{16}$
	Ranger 2WD (w/forged axle)	$3^1/_4$	$3^1/_2$	$5^1/_4$	$8^1/_4$	-2	$-^1/_2$	$^1/_{32}$	$^1/_{16}$
		$3^1/_2$	$3^3/_4$	$4^1/_2$	$7^1/_2$	$-1^5/_8$	$^1/_8$	$^1/_{32}$	$^1/_{16}$
		$3^3/_4$	4	$3^1/_2$	$6^1/_2$	$-^1/_2$	1	$^1/_{32}$	$^1/_{16}$
		4	$4^1/_4$	2	6	$^1/_4$	$1^3/_4$	$^1/_{32}$	$^1/_{16}$
		$4^1/_2$	$4^3/_4$	$1^7/_8$	$4^7/_8$	$1^1/_4$	$2^3/_4$	$^1/_{32}$	$^1/_{16}$
	Ranger 2WD (w/stamped axle)	3	$3^1/_4$	$5^1/_4$	$8^1/_4$	-2	$-^1/_2$	$^1/_{32}$	$^1/_{16}$
		$3^1/_4$	$3^1/_2$	$4^1/_2$	$7^1/_2$	$-1^5/_8$	$^1/_8$	$^1/_{32}$	$^1/_{16}$
		$3^1/_2$	$3^3/_4$	$3^1/_2$	$6^1/_2$	$-^1/_2$	1	$^1/_{32}$	$^1/_{16}$
		$3^3/_4$	4	3	6	$^1/_4$	$1^3/_4$	$^1/_{32}$	$^1/_{16}$
		$4^1/_4$	$4^1/_2$	$1^7/_8$	$4^7/_8$	$1^1/_4$	$2^3/_4$	$^1/_{32}$	$^1/_{16}$
	Ranger 4WD (exc. STX)	$2^3/_4$	3	$5^1/_2$	$8^1/_2$	-2	$-^1/_2$	$^1/_{32}$	$^1/_{16}$
		$3^1/_4$	$3^1/_2$	4	7	-1	$^1/_2$	$^1/_{32}$	$^1/_{16}$
		$3^1/_2$	$3^3/_4$	3	6	0	$1^1/_2$	$^1/_{32}$	$^1/_{16}$
		4	$4^1/_4$	2	5	1	$2^1/_2$	$^1/_{32}$	$^1/_{16}$
		$4^1/_4$	$4^3/_4$	1	4	2	$3^1/_2$	$^1/_{32}$	$^1/_{16}$
	Ranger 4WD (STX)	$4^1/_4$	$4^1/_2$	$5^1/_2$	$8^1/_2$	-2	$-^1/_2$	$^1/_{32}$	$^1/_{16}$
		$4^1/_2$	5	4	7	-1	$^1/_2$	$^1/_{32}$	$^1/_{16}$
		5	$5^1/_4$	3	6	0	$1^1/_2$	$^1/_{32}$	$^1/_{16}$
		$5^1/_4$	$5^3/_4$	2	5	1	$2^1/_2$	$^1/_{32}$	$^1/_{16}$
		$5^3/_4$	6	1	4	2	$3^1/_2$	$^1/_{32}$	$^1/_{16}$
1990	Bronco II	$2^3/_4$	3	$5^1/_2$	$8^1/_2$	-2	$-^1/_2$	$^1/_{32}$	$^1/_{16}$
		$3^1/_4$	$3^1/_2$	4	7	-1	$^1/_2$	$^1/_{32}$	$^1/_{16}$
		$3^1/_2$	$3^3/_4$	3	6	0	$1^1/_2$	$^1/_{32}$	$^1/_{16}$
		4	$4^1/_4$	2	5	1	$2^1/_2$	$^1/_{32}$	$^1/_{16}$
		$4^1/_4$	$4^3/_4$	1	4	2	$3^1/_2$	$^1/_{32}$	$^1/_{16}$
	Ranger 2WD (w/forged axle)	$3^1/_4$	$3^1/_2$	$5^1/_4$	$8^1/_4$	-2	$-^1/_2$	$^1/_{32}$	$^1/_{16}$
		$3^1/_2$	$3^3/_4$	$4^1/_2$	$7^1/_2$	$-1^5/_8$	$^1/_8$	$^1/_{32}$	$^1/_{16}$
		$3^3/_4$	4	$3^1/_2$	$6^1/_2$	$-^1/_2$	1	$^1/_{32}$	$^1/_{16}$
		4	$4^1/_4$	2	6	$^1/_4$	$1^3/_4$	$^1/_{32}$	$^1/_{16}$
		$4^1/_2$	$4^3/_4$	$1^7/_8$	$4^7/_8$	$1^1/_4$	$2^3/_4$	$^1/_{32}$	$^1/_{16}$

WHEEL ALIGNMENT

Year	Model	Ride Height Min.	Ride Height Max.	Caster Min.	Caster Max.	Camber Min.	Camber Max.	Toe-in (inches)	Toe-in (Degrees)
1990	Ranger 2WD	3	$3^1/_4$	$5^1/_4$	$8^1/_4$	-2	$-^1/_2$	$^1/_{32}$	$^1/_{16}$
	(w/stamped	$3^1/_4$	$3^1/_2$	$4^1/_2$	$7^1/_2$	$-1^5/_8$	$^1/_8$	$^1/_{32}$	$^1/_{16}$
	axle)	$3^1/_2$	$3^3/_4$	$3^1/_2$	$6^1/_2$	$-^1/_2$	1	$^1/_{32}$	$^1/_{16}$
		$3^3/_4$	4	3	6	$^1/_4$	$1^3/_4$	$^1/_{32}$	$^1/_{16}$
		$4^1/_4$	$4^1/_2$	$1^7/_8$	$4^7/_8$	$1^1/_4$	$2^3/_4$	$^1/_{32}$	$^1/_{16}$
	Ranger 4WD	$2^3/_4$	3	$5^1/_2$	$8^1/_2$	-2	$-^1/_2$	$^1/_{32}$	$^1/_{16}$
	(exc. STX)	$3^1/_4$	$3^1/_2$	4	7	-1	$^1/_2$	$^1/_{32}$	$^1/_{16}$
		$3^1/_2$	$3^3/_4$	3	6	0	$1^1/_2$	$^1/_{32}$	$^1/_{16}$
		4	$4^1/_4$	2	5	1	$2^1/_2$	$^1/_{32}$	$^1/_{16}$
		$4^1/_4$	$4^3/_4$	1	4	2	$3^1/_2$	$^1/_{32}$	$^1/_{16}$
	Ranger 4WD	$4^1/_4$	$4^1/_2$	$5^1/_2$	$8^1/_2$	-2	$-^1/_2$	$^1/_{32}$	$^1/_{16}$
	(STX)	$4^1/_2$	5	4	7	-1	$^1/_2$	$^1/_{32}$	$^1/_{16}$
		5	$5^1/_4$	3	6	0	$1^1/_2$	$^1/_{32}$	$^1/_{16}$
		$5^1/_4$	$5^3/_4$	2	5	1	$2^1/_2$	$^1/_{32}$	$^1/_{16}$
		$5^3/_4$	6	1	4	2	$3^1/_2$	$^1/_{32}$	$^1/_{16}$
1991	Explorer	$2^3/_4$	3	$5^1/_2$	$8^1/_2$	-2	$-^1/_2$	$^1/_{32}$	$^1/_{16}$
		$3^1/_4$	$3^1/_2$	4	7	-1	$^1/_2$	$^1/_{32}$	$^1/_{16}$
		$3^1/_2$	$3^3/_4$	3	6	0	$1^1/_2$	$^1/_{32}$	$^1/_{16}$
		4	$4^1/_4$	2	5	1	$2^1/_2$	$^1/_{32}$	$^1/_{16}$
		$4^1/_4$	$4^3/_4$	1	4	2	$3^1/_2$	$^1/_{32}$	$^1/_{16}$
	Ranger 2WD	$3^1/_4$	$3^1/_2$	$5^1/_4$	$8^1/_4$	-2	$-^1/_2$	$^1/_{32}$	$^1/_{16}$
	(w/forged	$3^1/_2$	$3^3/_4$	$4^1/_2$	$7^1/_2$	$-1^5/_8$	$^1/_8$	$^1/_{32}$	$^1/_{16}$
	axle)	$3^3/_4$	4	$3^1/_2$	$6^1/_2$	$-^1/_2$	1	$^1/_{32}$	$^1/_{16}$
		4	$4^1/_4$	2	6	$^1/_4$	$1^3/_4$	$^1/_{32}$	$^1/_{16}$
		$4^1/_2$	$4^3/_4$	$1^7/_8$	$4^7/_8$	$1^1/_4$	$2^3/_4$	$^1/_{32}$	$^1/_{16}$
	Ranger 2WD	3	$3^1/_4$	$5^1/_4$	$8^1/_4$	-2	$-^1/_2$	$^1/_{32}$	$^1/_{16}$
	(w/stamped	$3^1/_4$	$3^1/_2$	$4^1/_2$	$7^1/_2$	$-1^5/_8$	$^1/_8$	$^1/_{32}$	$^1/_{16}$
	axle)	$3^1/_2$	$3^3/_4$	$3^1/_2$	$6^1/_2$	$-^1/_2$	1	$^1/_{32}$	$^1/_{16}$
		$3^3/_4$	4	3	6	$^1/_4$	$1^3/_4$	$^1/_{32}$	$^1/_{16}$
		$4^1/_4$	$4^1/_2$	$1^7/_8$	$4^7/_8$	$1^1/_4$	$2^3/_4$	$^1/_{32}$	$^1/_{16}$
	Ranger 4WD	$2^3/_4$	3	$5^1/_2$	$8^1/_2$	-2	$-^1/_2$	$^1/_{32}$	$^1/_{16}$
	(exc. STX)	$3^1/_4$	$3^1/_2$	4	7	-1	$^1/_2$	$^1/_{32}$	$^1/_{16}$
		$3^1/_2$	$3^3/_4$	3	6	0	$1^1/_2$	$^1/_{32}$	$^1/_{16}$
		4	$4^1/_4$	2	5	1	$2^1/_2$	$^1/_{32}$	$^1/_{16}$
		$4^1/_4$	$4^3/_4$	1	4	2	$3^1/_2$	$^1/_{32}$	$^1/_{16}$
	Ranger 4WD	$4^1/_4$	$4^1/_2$	$5^1/_2$	$8^1/_2$	-2	$-^1/_2$	$^1/_{32}$	$^1/_{16}$
	(STX)	$4^1/_2$	5	4	7	-1	$^1/_2$	$^1/_{32}$	$^1/_{16}$
		5	$5^1/_4$	3	6	0	$1^1/_2$	$^1/_{32}$	$^1/_{16}$
		$5^1/_4$	$5^3/_4$	2	5	1	$2^1/_2$	$^1/_{32}$	$^1/_{16}$
		$5^3/_4$	6	1	4	2	$3^1/_2$	$^1/_{32}$	$^1/_{16}$

5. Rotate each front wheel slowly, and observe the amount of lateral or side runout. If the wheel runout exceeds $^1/_8$ in. (3mm), replace the wheel or install the wheel on the rear.

6. Inspect the radius arms to be sure they are not bent or damaged. Inspect the bushings at the radius arm-to-axle attachment and radius arm-to-frame attachment points for wear or looseness. Repair or replace parts as required.

Caster is the number of degrees of backward (positive) or forward (negative) tilt of the spindle or the line connecting the ball joint centers. Camber is the number of degrees the top of the wheel tilts outward (positive) or inward (negative) from a vertical plane.

Before checking caster or camber, perform the toe alignment check. Using alignment equipment known to be accurate and following the equipment manufacturer's instructions, measure and record the caster angle and the camber angle of both front wheels.

If the caster and camber measurements exceed the maximum variances, inspect for damaged front suspension components. Replace as required.

Both caster and camber adjustments are possible with service adjusters. These service adjusters are available in $^1/_2$, 1 and $1^1/_2$ degree increments. On of these adjusters is used to adjust both caster and camber.

REAR SUSPENSION

Leaf Springs

REMOVAL AND INSTALLATION

1. Raise the vehicle and install jackstands under the frame. The vehicle must be supported in such a way that the rear axle hangs free with the tires still touching the ground.

2. Remove the nuts from the spring U-bolts and drive the U-bolts from the U-bolt plate.

3. Remove the spring to bracket nut and bolt at the front of the spring.

4. Remove the shackle upper and lower nuts and bolts at the rear of the spring.

5. Remove the spring and shackle assembly from the rear shackle bracket.

To install:

6. Position the spring in the shackle. Install the upper shackle spring bolt and nut with the bolt head facing outward.

7. Position the front end of the spring in the bracket and install the bolt and nut.

8. Position the shackle in the rear bracket and install the nut and bolt.

9. Position the spring on top of the axle with the spring tie bolt centered in the hole provided in the seat.

10. Lower the vehicle to the floor. Torque the spring U-bolt nuts to 65–75 ft. lbs. Torque the front spring bolt to 75–115 ft. lbs. Torque the rear shackle nuts and bolts to 75–115 ft. lbs.

Shock Absorbers

REMOVAL AND INSTALLATION

1. Raise the vehicle and position jackstands under the axle or wheel, in order to take the load off of the shock absorber.

2. Remove the shock absorber lower retain-

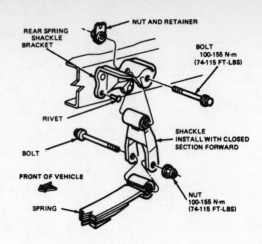

Ranger, Bronco II and Explorer spring to rear shackle assembly

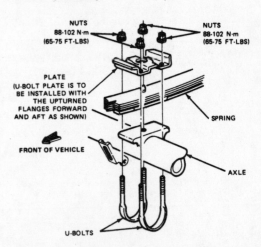

Ranger, Bronco II and Explorer U-bolt and spring plate assembly

ing nut and bolt. Swing the lower end free of the mounting bracket on the axle housing.

To install:

3. Remove the retaining nut(s) from the upper shock absorber mounting

4. Remove the shock absorber from the vehicle.

5. Installation is the reverse of the removal procedure. Torque the lower shock absorber retaining bolt to 39–53 ft. lbs.

6. On the Ranger and Bronco II torque the upper shock absorber mounting nut to 39–53 ft. lbs. On the Explorer torque the upper shock absorber retaining nuts to 15–21 ft. lbs.

TESTING

1. Visually check the shock absorbers for the presence of fluid leakage. A thin film of fluid is acceptable. Anything more than that

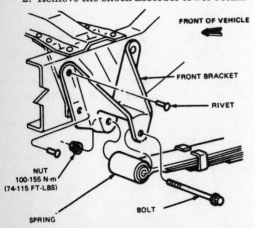

Ranger, Bronco II and Explorer spring to front bracket assembly

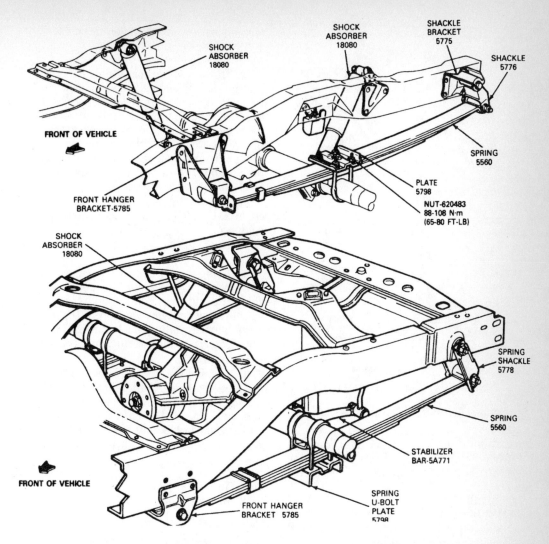

Rear suspension assembly — Ranger (top) and Bronco II and Explorer (bottom)

means that the shock absorber must be re-placed.

2. Disconnect the lower end of the shock absorber. Compress and extend the shock fully as fast as possible. If the action is not smooth in both directions, or there is no pressure resistance, replace the shock absorber. Shock absorbers should be replaced in pairs. In the case of relatively new shock absorbers, where one has failed, that one, alone, may be replaced.

Stabilizer Bar

REMOVAL AND INSTALLATION

1. As required, raise and support the vehicle.

2. Remove the nuts, bolts and washers and disconnect the stabilizer bar from the links.

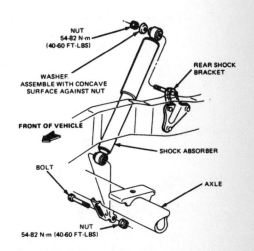

1983–91 Ranger and 1983–90 Bronco II rear shock absorber assembly

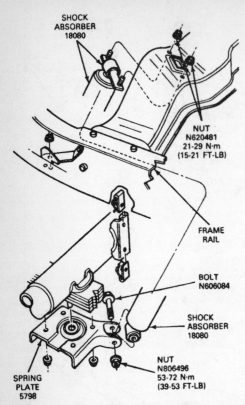

1991 Explorer rear shock absorber assembly

3. Remove the U-bolts and nuts from the mounting bracket and retainers. Remove the mounting brackets, retainers and stabilizer bars.

To install:

4. Position the U-bolts and mounting brackets on the axle with the brackets having the **UP** marking in the proper position.

5. Install the stabilizer bar and retainers on the mounting brackets with the retainers having the **UP** marking in the proper position.

6. Connect the stabilizer bar to the rear links. Install the nuts, bolts, and washers and tighten.

7. Tighten the mounting bracket U-bolt nuts to 30–42 ft. lbs.

STEERING

Steering Wheel

REMOVAL AND INSTALLATION

1983–87

1. Disconnect the negative battery cable. Remove the steering wheel hub cover by remov-

ing the screws from the spokes and lifting the steering wheel hub cover. On the deluxe wheel, pop the hub emblem off. On sport wheels, unscrew the hub emblem.

2. Disconnect the horn switch wires by pulling the spoke terminal from the blade connectors. On vehicles equipped with speed control, squeeze or pinch the **J** clip ground wire terminal firmly and pull it out of the hole in the steering wheel. Do not pull the ground terminal out of the threaded hole without squeezing the terminal clip to relieve the spring retention of the terminal in the threaded hole.

3. Remove the horn switch assembly and disconnect the horn and speed control wire, if equipped.

4. Remove the steering wheel attaching nut.

5. Using a steering wheel puller, remove the steering wheel from the upper steering shaft. Do not use a knock-off type steering wheel puller or strike the end of the steering column upper shaft with a hammer. This could cause damage to the steering shaft bearing.

To install:

6. Position the steering wheel on the end of the steering wheel shaft. Align the mark and the flats on the steering wheel with the mark and the flats on the shaft, assuring that the straight ahead steering wheel position corresponds to the straight ahead position of the front wheels.

7. Install the wheel nut. Tighten the nut to 30–40 ft. lbs.

8. Install the horn switch assembly and con-

Steering wheel alignment — 1989–91 vehicles

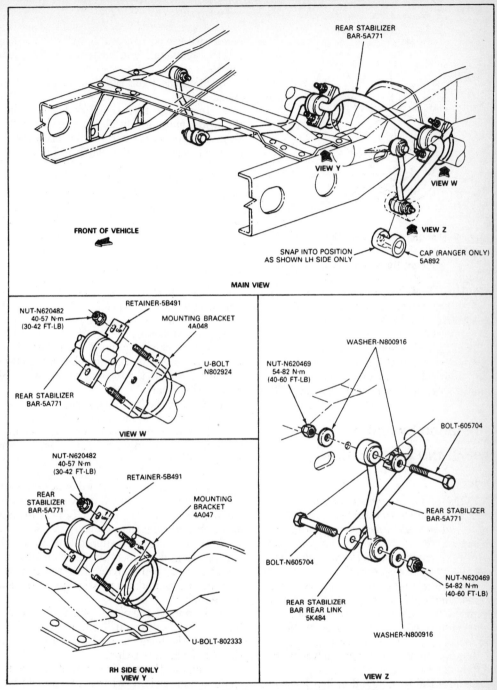

REAR STABILIZER
BAR-5A771

VIEW Y

VIEW W

VIEW Z

FRONT OF VEHICLE

SNAP INTO POSITION
AS SHOWN LH SIDE ONLY

CAP (RANGER ONLY)
5A892

MAIN VIEW

NUT-N620482
40-57 N·m
(30-42 FT-LB)

RETAINER-5B491

MOUNTING BRACKET
4A048

U-BOLT
N802924

REAR STABILIZER
BAR-5A771

VIEW W

WASHER-N800916

NUT-N620469
54-82 N·m
(40-60 FT-LB)

BOLT-605704

REAR STABILIZER
BAR-5A771

BOLT-N605704

REAR STABILIZER
BAR REAR LINK
5K484

NUT-N620469
54-82 N·m
(40-60 FT-LB)

WASHER-N800916

VIEW Z

NUT-N620482
40-57 N·m
(30-42 FT-LB)

RETAINER-5B491

REAR
STABILIZER
BAR-5A771

MOUNTING
BRACKET
4A047

U-BOLT-802333

**RH SIDE ONLY
VIEW Y**

Ranger, Bronco II and Explorer rear stabilizer assembly

nect the horn and speed control wire, if equipped.

9. Install the cover or trim emblem.

10. Check the steering column for proper operation.

1988–91

1. Disconnect the negative battery cable.

2. From the underside of the steering wheel, remove the screws that hold the steering wheel pad to the steering wheel spokes.

3. Lift up the steering wheel pad and disconnect the horn wires from the steering wheel pad by pulling the spade terminal from the blade connectors.

4. Remove the steering wheel pad. Remove the bolt from the steering shaft.

5. Using the proper steering wheel removal

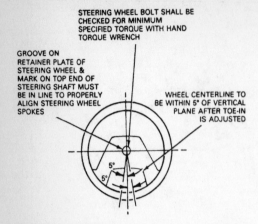

STEERING WHEEL BOLT SHALL BE CHECKED FOR MINIMUM SPECIFIED TORQUE WITH HAND TORQUE WRENCH

GROOVE ON RETAINER PLATE OF STEERING WHEEL & MARK ON TOP END OF STEERING SHAFT MUST BE IN LINE TO PROPERLY ALIGN STEERING WHEEL SPOKES

WHEEL CENTERLINE TO BE WITHIN 5° OF VERTICAL PLANE AFTER TOE-IN IS ADJUSTED

Steering wheel alignment — 1983–88 vehicles

tool, remove the steering wheel from the steering column.

WARNING: *Do not hammer on the steering wheel or the steering shaft or use a knock off type steering wheel puller as damage to the steering column will occur.*

6. Installation is the reverse of the removal procedure. Be sure that the steering wheel is properly aligned before installing the lock bolt. Torque the steering wheel lock bolt to 23–33 ft. lbs.

Combination Switch

REMOVAL AND INSTALLATION

1983–88

WARNING: *The corrugated outer tube steering shaft column upper support bracket assembly and shrouds affect energy absorption on impact. It is absolutely necessary to handle these components with care when performing any service operation!*

1. Disconnect the negative battery cable. For tilt column only, remove the upper extension shroud by squeezing it at the 6 and 12 o'clock positions and popping it free of the retaining plate at the 3 o'clock position.

2. Remove the 2 trim shroud halves by removing the 2 attaching screws.

3. Remove the turn signal switch lever by grasping the lever and by using a pulling and twisting motion of the hand while pulling the lever straight out from the switch.

4. Peel back the foam sight shield from the turn signal switch.

5. Disconnect the 2 turn signal switch electrical connectors.

6. Remove the 2 self-tapping screws attaching the turn signal switch to the lock cylinder housing. Disengage the switch from the housing.

To install:

7. Align the turn signal switch mounting holes with the corresponding holes in the lock cylinder housing, and install 2 self-tapping screws.

8. Stick the foam sight shield to the turn signal switch.

9. Install the turn signal switch lever into the switch manually, by aligning the key on the lever with the keyway in the switch and by pushing the lever toward the switch to full engagement.

10. Install the 2 turn signal switch electrical connectors to full engagement.

11. Install the steering column trim shrouds.

1989–91

1. Disconnect the negative battery cable. Remove the steering wheel.

2. On vehicles equipped with tilt wheel, remove the tilt lever.

3. On vehicles equipped with tilt wheel, remove the steering column collar by pressing on the collar from the top and bottom while removing the collar.

4. Remove the instrument panel trim cover retaining screws. Remove the trim cover.

5. Remove the 2 screws from the bottom of the steering column shroud. Remove the bottom half of the shroud by pulling the shroud down and toward the rear of the vehicle.

6. If the vehicle is equipped with automatic transmission, move the shift lever as required to aid in removal of the shroud. Lift the top half of the shroud from the column.

7. If the vehicle is equipped with automatic transmission, disconnect the selector indicator actuation cable by removing the screw from the column casting and the plastic plug at the end of the cable.

8. To remove the plastic plug from the shift lever socket casting push on the nose of the plug until the head clears the casting and pull the plug from the casting.

9. Remove the plastic clip that retains the combination switch wiring to the steering column bracket.

10. Remove the 2 self taping screws that retain the combination switch to the steering column casting. Disengage the switch from the casting.

11. Disconnect the 3 electrical connectors, using caution not to damage the locking tabs. Be sure not to damage the PRNDL cable.

12. Installation is the reverse of the removal procedure. Torque the combination switch retaining screws to 18–27 inch lbs.

Ignition Switch

REMOVAL AND INSTALLATION

1983–88

1. Rotate the lock cylinder key to the Lock position. Disconnect the negative battery cable from the battery.

2. For tilt column only, remove the upper extension shroud by squeezing it at the 6 and 12 o'clock positions and popping it free of the retaining plate at the 3 o'clock position.

3. Remove the 2 trim shroud halves by removing the 2 attaching screws.

4. Disconnect the ignition switch electrical connector.

5. Drill out the break-off head bolts connecting the switch to the lock cylinder housing by using a $1/8$ in. (3mm) drill bit.

6. Remove the 2 bolts, using an Ex-3 Easy-out® tool or equivalent.

7. Disengage the ignition switch from the actuator pin.

To install:

8. Rotate the ignition key to the **RUN** position, approximately 90° clockwise from **LOCK**.

9. Install the replacement switch by aligning the holes on the switch casting base with the holes in the lock cylinder housing. Note that the replacement switch is provided in the RUN position. Minor movement of the lock cylinder to align the actuator pin with the **U** shaped slot in the switch carrier may be required.

10. Install the new break-off head bolts and tighten until heads shear off (approximately 35–50 inch lbs.).

11. Connect the electrical connector to the ignition switch.

12. Connect the negative battery cable to the battery terminal. Check the ignition switch for proper operation in all modes.

13. Install the steering column trim shrouds.

1989–91

1. Disconnect the negative battery cable.

2. Remove the steering wheel.

3. As necessary, remove all under dash panels in order to gain access to the ignition switch.

4. As necessary, lower the steering column to gain working clearance.

5. Disconnect the ignition switch electrical connectors.

6. Remove the ignition switch retaining screws from the studs. Disengage the ignition switch from switch rod. Remove the switch from the vehicle.

To install:

7. Position the lock cylinder in the **LOCK** position.

8. To set the switch, position a wire in the opening in the outer surface of the switch through its positions until the wire drops down into the slot.

NOTE: *The slot is in the bottom of the switch where the rod must be inserted to allow full movement through the switch positions.*

9. Position the ignition switch on the column studs and over the actuating rod. Torque the retaining nuts to 3.3–5.3 ft. lbs.

10. Remove the wire from the slot in the housing. Continue the installation in the reverse order of the removal procedure.

Ignition Lock Cylinder Assembly

REMOVAL AND INSTALLATION

1983–88

1. Disconnect the negative battery cable.

2. Remove the trim shroud. Remove the electrical connector from the key warning switch.

3. Turn the lock cylinder to the **RUN** position.

4. Place a $1/8$ in. (3mm) diameter pin or small drift punch in the hole located at 4 o'clock and $1^1/4$ in. (31.75mm) from the outer edge of the lock cylinder housing. Depress the retaining pin, and pull out the lock cylinder.

To install:

5. Prior to installation of the lock cylinder, lubricate the cylinder cavity, including the drive gear, with Lubriplate® or equivalent.

6. To install the lock cylinder, turn the lock cylinder to the RUN position, depress the retaining pin, and insert it into the lock cylinder housing. Assure that the cylinder is fully seated and aligned into the interlocking washer before turning the key to the **OFF** position. This action will permit the cylinder retaining pin to extend into the hole in the lock cylinder housing.

7. Using the ignition key, rotate the lock cylinder to ensure correct mechanical operation in all positions. Install the electrical connector onto the key warning switch.

8. Connect the battery ground cable.

9. Check for proper ignition functions and verify that the column is locked in the **LOCK** position.

10. Install the trim shrouds.

1989–91

1. Disconnect the negative battery cable. Remove the steering wheel.

2. On vehicles equipped with tilt wheel, remove the tilt lever.

3. On vehicles equipped with tilt wheel, remove the steering column collar by pressing on the collar from the top and bottom while removing the collar.

4. Remove the instrument panel trim cover retaining screws. Remove the trim cover.

5. Remove the 2 screws from the bottom of the steering column shroud. Remove the bottom half of the shroud by pulling the shroud down and toward the rear of the vehicle.

6. If the vehicle is equipped with automatic transmission, move the shift lever as required to aid in removal of the shroud. Lift the top half of the shroud from the column.

7. Turn the lock cylinder with the ignition key in it to the **ON** position. On vehicles equipped with automatic transmission be sure that the selector lever is in the **PARK** position.

8. Push down on the lock cylinder retaining pin with a $1/8$ in. (3mm) diameter wire pin or small punch. Pull the lock cylinder from the column housing. Disconnect the lock cylinder wiring plug from the horn brush wiring connector.

To install:

9. Prior to installation of the lock cylinder, lubricate the cylinder cavity, including the drive gear, with Lubriplate® or equivalent.

10. To install the lock cylinder, turn the lock cylinder to the **ON** position, depress the retaining pin. Insert the lock cylinder housing into its housing in the flange casting. Be sure that the tab at the end of the cylinder aligns with the slot in the ignition drive gear.

11. Turn the key to the **OFF** position. This action will permit the cylinder retaining pin to extend into the cylinder casting housing hole.

12. Using the ignition key rotate the lock cylinder to ensure correct mechanical operation in all positions. Connect the key warning wire plug.

13. Install the steering column lower shroud. Install the steering wheel.

14. Check for proper vehicle operation in **PARK** and **NEUTRAL**. Also be sure that the start circuit cannot be actuated in **DRIVE** or **REVERSE**.

Steering Linkage

REMOVAL AND INSTALLATION

Pitman Arm

1. As required, raise and safely support the vehicle using jackstands.

2. Remove the cotter pin and nut from the drag link ball stud at the pitman arm.

3. Remove the drag link ball stud from the pitman arm using pitman arm removal tool T64P-3590-F or equivalent.

4. Remove the pitman arm retaining nut and washer. Remove the pitman arm from the steering gear sector shaft using tool T64P-3590-F or equivalent.

To install:

5. Installation is the reverse of the removal procedure. Torque the pitman arm attaching washer and nut to 170–230 ft. lbs. Torque the drag link ball stud nut to 50–70 ft. lbs. and install a new cotter pin.

6. Check and adjust front end alignment, as required.

Tie Rod

1. Raise and support the vehicle using jackstands. Be sure that the front wheels are in the straight ahead position.

2. Remove the nut and cotter pin from the ball stud on the drag link. Remove the ball stud from the drag link using pitman arm removal tool T64P-3590-F or equivalent.

3. Loosen the bolts on the tie rod adjusting sleeve. Be sure to count and record the number of turns it takes to remove the tie rod from the tie rod adjusting sleeve. Remove the tie rod from the vehicle.

To install:

4. Install the tie rod in the tie rod sleeve in the same number of turns it took to remove it. Torque the tie rod adjusting sleeve nuts to 30–42 ft. lbs.

5. Be sure that the adjusting sleeve clamps are pointed down ± 45°. Tighten the tie rod ball stud to drag link retaining bolt to 50–75 ft. lbs. Install a new cotter pin.

6. Check and adjust front end alignment, as required.

Tie Rod Ends

1. Raise and support the vehicle using jackstands. Be sure that the front wheels are in the straight ahead position.

2. Remove the nut and cotter pin from the ball stud on the drag link. Remove the ball stud from the drag link using pitman arm removal tool T64P-3590-F or equivalent.

3. Loosen the bolts on the tie rod adjusting sleeve. Be sure to count and record the number of turns it takes to remove the sleeve from the ball stud.

To install:

4. Install the adjusting sleeve on the tie rod ball stud in the same number of turns it took to remove it. Loosely assemble the ball stud in the spindle arm.

5. Torque the retaining nuts to 30–42 ft. lbs. Be sure that the adjusting sleeve clamps are pointed down ± 45°.

6. With the vehicle wheels in the straight

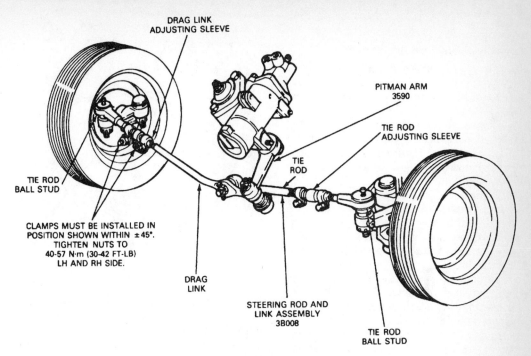

DRAG LINK
ADJUSTING SLEEVE

PITMAN ARM
3590

TIE ROD
ADJUSTING SLEEVE

TIE
ROD

TIE ROD
BALL STUD

CLAMPS MUST BE INSTALLED IN
POSITION SHOWN WITHIN ± 45°.
TIGHTEN NUTS TO
40-57 N·m (30-42 FT-LB)
LH AND RH SIDE.

DRAG
LINK

STEERING ROD AND
LINK ASSEMBLY
3B008

TIE ROD
BALL STUD

Steering linkage assembly

ahead position install and torque the nut to 50–75 ft. lbs. Install a new cotter pin.

7. Check and adjust front end alignment, as required.

Drag Link

1. Raise and support the vehicle using jackstands. Be sure that the front wheels are in the straight ahead position.

2. Remove the nuts and cotter pins from the ball stud at the pitman arm and steering tie rod. Remove the ball studs from the linkage using pitman arm removal tool T64P-3590-F or equivalent.

3. Loosen the bolts on the drag link adjusting sleeve. Be sure to count and record the number of turns it takes to remove the drag link.

To install:

4. Install the drag link in the same number of turns it took to remove it. Tighten the adjusting sleeve nuts to 30–42 ft. lbs. Be sure that the adjusting sleeve clamps are pointed down ± 45°.

5. Position the drag link ball stud in the pitman arm. Position the steering tie rod ball stud in the drag link. With the vehicle wheels in the straight ahead position install and torque the nuts to 50–75 ft. lbs. Install a new cotter pin.

6. Check and adjust front end alignment, as required.

Manual Steering Gear Pickups Only

ADJUSTMENTS

Preload and Meshload Check

1. Raise and support the front of the vehicle on jackstands.

2. Disconnect the pitman arm at the ball stud.

3. Lubricate the wormshaft seal with a drop of automatic transmission fluid.

4. Remove the horn pad from the steering wheel.

5. Turn the steering wheel slowly to one stop.

6. Using an inch-pound torque wrench on the steering wheel nut, check the amount of torque needed to rotate the steering wheel through a 1½ turn cycle. The preload should be 2–6 inch lbs. If correct, proceed with the rest of the Steps. If not perform preload and mesh adjustment.

7. Rotate the steering wheel from stop-to-stop, counting the total number of turns. Using that figure, center the steering wheel (½ the total turns).

8. Using the inch-pound torque wrench, rotate the steering wheel 90° to either side of center, noting the highest torque reading over center. The meshload should be 4–10 inch lbs.,

or at least 2 inch lbs. more than the preload figure.

Preload and Meshload Adjustment

1. Remove the steering gear from the vehicle.

2. Torque the sector cover bolts on the gear to 32–40 ft. lbs.

3. Loosen the preload adjuster nut and tighten the worm bearing adjuster nut until all endplay has been removed. Lubricate the wormshaft seal with a few drops of automatic transmission fluid.

4. Using an $^{11}/_{16}$ in., 12-point socket and an inch lbs. torque wrench, carefully turn the wormshaft all the way to the right.

5. Turn the shaft back to the left and measure the torque over a $1^1/_2$ turn cycle. This is the preload reading.

6. Tighten or loosen the adjuster nut to bring the preload into range (5–6 inch lbs.).

7. Hold the adjuster nut while torquing the locknut to 166–187 ft. lbs.

8. Rotate the wormshaft stop-to-stop counting the total number of turns and center the shaft ($^1/_2$ the total turns).

9. Using the torque wrench and socket, measure the torque required to turn the shaft 90° to either side of center.

10. Turn the sector shaft adjusting screw as needed to bring the meshload torque within the 9–11 inch lbs. range, or at least 4 inch lbs. higher than the preload torque.

11. Hold the adjusting screw while tightening the locknut to 14–25 ft. lbs.

12. Install the gear.

REMOVAL AND INSTALLATION

1. Raise and safely support the vehicle using jackstands. Disengage the flex coupling shield from the steering gear input shaft shield and slide it up the intermediate shaft.

2. Remove the bolt that retains the flex cou-

Manual steering gear — preload measurement

pling to the steering gear.

3. Remove the steering gear input shaft shield.

4. Remove the nut and washer that secures the pitman arm to the sector shaft. Remove the pitman arm using pitman arm puller tool, T64P–3590–F or equivalent. Do not hammer on the end of the puller as this can damage the steering gear.

5. Remove the bolts and washers that attach the steering gear to the side rail. Remove the gear.

To install:

6. Rotate the gear input shaft (wormshaft) from stop to stop, counting the total number of turns. Then turn back exactly half-way, placing the gear on center.

7. Slide the steering gear input shaft shield on the steering gear input shaft.

8. Position the flex coupling on the steering gear input shaft. Ensure that the flat on the gear input shaft is facing straight up and aligns with the flat on the flex coupling. Install the steering gear to side rail with bolts and washers. Torque the bolts to 66 ft. lbs.

9. Place the pitman arm on the sector shaft and install the attaching washer and nut. Align the 2 blocked teeth on the Pitman arm with 4 missing teeth on the steering gear sector shaft. Tighten the nut to 230 ft. lbs. on 1983–88 vehicles and 170–230 ft. lbs. on 1989–91 vehicles.

10. Install the flex coupling to steering gear input shaft attaching bolt and tighten to 35 ft. lbs. on 1983–88 vehicles and 50–62 ft. lbs. on 1989–91 vehicles.

11. Snap the flex coupling shield to the steering gear input shield.

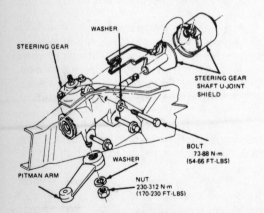

Manual steering gear and related components

12. Check the system to ensure equal turns from center to each lock position.

Power Steering Gear

ADJUSTMENTS

Meshload

1. As required, raise and support the vehicle using jackstands.

2. Disconnect the pitman arm from the sector shaft using tool T64P–3590–F or equivalent.

3. Disconnect and cap the fluid return line at the reservoir return line pipe.

4. Place the end of the return line in a clean container and turn the steering wheel from stop to stop several times to discharge the fluid from the gear. Discard the used fluid.

5. Turn the steering gear 45° from the right stop.

6. Remove the steering wheel hub cover. Attach an inch lb. torque wrench to the steering wheel nut and determine the torque required to rotate the shaft slowly about $1/8$ turn from the 45° position toward center.

7. Turn the steering wheel back to center and determine the torque required to rotate the shaft back and forth across the center position.

8. Specification for vehicles under 5000 miles is 12–24 inch lbs. If the vehicle has over 5000 miles, reset the meshload measured while rocking the input shaft over center is less than 10 inch lbs. greater than torque 45° from the right stop.

9. If reset is required loosen the adjuster locknut and turn the sector shaft adjuster screw until the reading is the specified value greater than the torque at 45° from the stop. Hold the sector shaft screw in place and tighten the locknut.

REMOVAL AND INSTALLATION

1. Disconnect the pressure and return lines from the steering gear. Plug the lines and the ports in the gear to prevent entry of dirt.

2. Remove the upper and lower steering gear shaft U-joint shield from the flex coupling. Remove the bolts that secure the flex coupling to the steering gear and to the column steering shaft assembly.

3. Raise the vehicle and remove the pitman arm attaching nut and washer.

4. Remove the pitman arm from the sector shaft using tool T64P–3590–F. Remove the tool from the pitman arm. Do not damage the seals.

5. Support the steering gear, and remove the steering gear attaching bolts.

6. Work the steering gear free of the flex coupling. Remove the steering gear from the vehicle.

To install:

7. Install the lower U–joint shield onto the steering gear lugs. Slide the upper U–joint shield into place on the steering shaft assembly.

8. Slide the flex coupling into place on the steering shaft assembly. Turn the steering

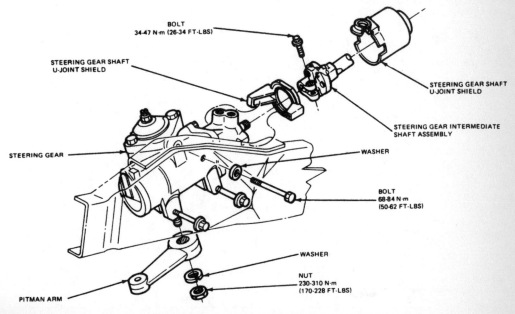

Power steering gear and related components

wheel so that the spokes are in the horizontal position. Center the steering gear input shaft.

9. Slide the steering gear input shaft into the flex coupling and into place on the frame side rail. Install the attaching bolts and tighten to 50–62 ft. lbs. Tighten the flex coupling bolt 26–34 ft. lbs.

10. Be sure the wheels are in the straight ahead position, then install the pitman arm on the sector shaft. Install the pitman arm attaching washer and nut. Tighten nut to 170–230 ft. lbs.

11. Connect and tighten the pressure and the return lines to the steering gear.

12. Disconnect the coil wire. Fill the reservoir. Turn on the ignition and turn the steering wheel from left to right to distribute the fluid.

13. Recheck fluid level and add fluid, if necessary. Connect the coil wire, start the engine and turn the steering wheel from side to side. Inspect for fluid leaks.

Power Steering Pump

REMOVAL AND INSTALLATION

1983–88

1. Disconnect the negative battery cable.
2. Remove some power steering fluid from

the reservoir by disconnecting the fluid return line hose at the reservoir. Drain the fluid into a container and discard it.

3. Remove the pressure hose from the pump. If equipped, disconnect the power steering pump pressure switch.

4. On the 2.0L and 2.3L engines, loosen the alternator pivot bolt and the adjusting bolt to remove belt tension.

5. On the 2.8L and 2.9L engines, loosen the adjusting nut and the slider bolts on the pump support to slacken the belt tension.

6. On the 2.2L diesel engine, loosen the adjustment bolt and the pivot bolt on the idler pulley to slacken belt tension.

7. Remove the drive belt from the pulley.

8. Install power steering pump pulley removal tool T69L–10300–B or equivalent. Hold the pump and rotate the tool counterclockwise to remove the pulley. Do not apply in and out pressure to the pump shaft, as internal pump damage will occur.

9. Remove the power steering retaining bolts. Remove the power steering pump from the vehicle.

10. Discard any remaining power steering fluid.

To install:

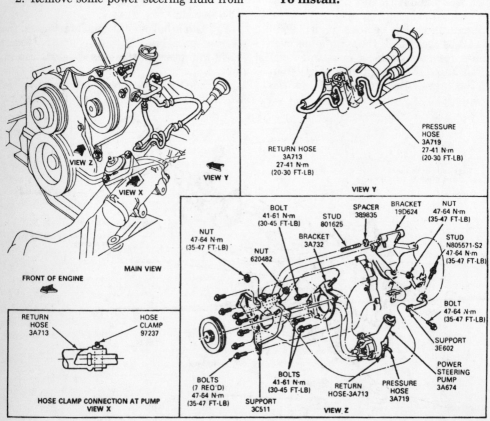

Power steering pump assembly — 1988–91 Ranger and Bronco II with 2.9L engine

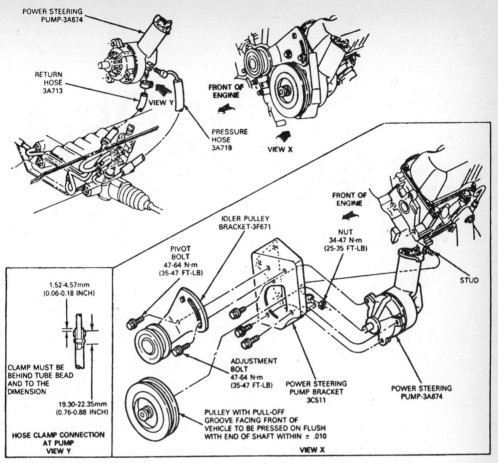

Power steering pump assembly — 1991 Ranger with 3.0L engine

11. Position the pump on the bracket. Install and tighten the retaining bolts.

12. Install the pulley removal tool and install the power steering pump pulley to the power steering pump.

NOTE: *Fore and aft location of the pulley on the power steering pump shaft is critical. Incorrect belt alignment may cause belt squeal or chirp. Be sure that the pull off groove on the pulley is facing front and flush with the end of the shaft ± 0.010 in. (0.25mm).*

13. Continue the installation in the reverse order of the removal procedure. Adjust the belt tension to specification.

14. On the 2.0L and 2.3L engines torque the adjuster bolt 22–40 ft. lbs. Torque the alternator pivot bolt to 40–50 ft. lbs.

15. On the 2.8L and 2.9L engines torque the slider bolts to 35–47 ft. lbs.

16. On the 2,2L diesel engine insert a ¹/₂ in. drive breaker bar into the slot in the idler pulley. Slide the pulley over in order to obtain proper belt tension.

1989–91

1. Disconnect the negative battery cable.

2. Remove some power steering fluid from the reservoir by disconnecting the fluid return line hose at the reservoir. Drain the fluid into a container and discard it.

3. Remove the pressure hose from the pump. If equipped, disconnect the power steering pump pressure switch.

4. On the 2.3L and 3.0L engines, loosen the idler pulley assembly pivot and adjusting bolts to slacken the belt tension.

5. On the 2.9L engine loosen the adjusting nut and the slider bolts on the pump support to slacken belt tension.

6. On the 4.0L engine, slacken belt tension by lifting the tensioner pulley in a clockwise direction. Remove the drive belt from under the tensioner pulley and slowly lower the pulley to its stop.

7. Remove the drive belt from the pulley. If necessary, remove the oil dipstick tube.

8. If equipped, remove the power steering pump bracket support brace.

9. Install power steering pump pulley re-

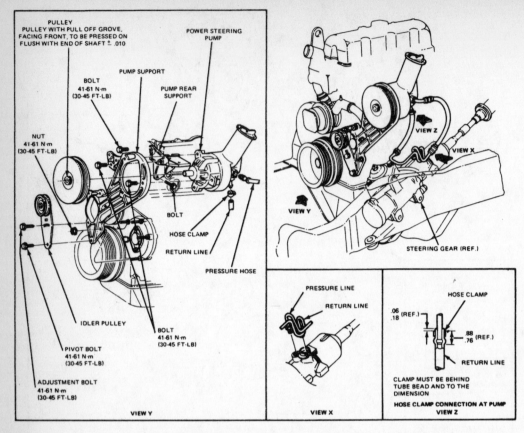

Power steering pump assembly — 1983–87 Ranger with 2.2L diesel engine

moval tool T69L–10300–B or equivalent. Hold the pump and rotate the tool counterclockwise to remove the pulley. Do not apply in and out pressure to the pump shaft, as internal pump damage will occur.

10. Remove the power steering retaining bolts. Remove the power steering pump from the vehicle.

To install:

11. Position the pump on the bracket. Install and tighten the retaining bolts.

12. Install the pulley removal tool and install the power steering pump pulley to the power steering pump.

NOTE: *Fore and aft location of the pulley on the power steering pump shaft is critical. Incorrect belt alignment may cause belt squeal or chirp. Be sure that the pull off groove on the pulley is facing front and flush with the end of the shaft ± 0.010 in. (0.25mm).*

13. Continue the installation in the reverse order of the removal procedure. Adjust the belt tension to specification.

14. On the 2.3L and 3.0L engines torque the idler pivot pulley bolts 30–40 ft. lbs. for the 2.3L engine and 35–47 ft. lbs. for the 3.0L engine

15. On the 2.9L engine torque the slider bolts to 35–47 ft. lbs.

16. On the 4.0L while lifting the tensioner pulley in a clockwise direction, slide the belt under the tensioner pulley and lower the pulley to the belt.

BLEEDING

1. Disconnect the coil wire.

2. Crank the engine and continue adding fluid until the level stabilizes.

3. Continue to crank the engine and rotate the steering wheel about 30° to either side of center.

4. Check the fluid level and add as required.

5. Connect the coil wire and start the engine. Allow it to run for several minutes.

6. Rotate the steering wheel from stop to stop.

7. Shut of the engine and check the fluid level. Add fluid as necessary.

QUICK-CONNECT PRESSURE LINE

1983–89

Some pumps will have a quick-connect fitting for the pressure line. This fitting may,

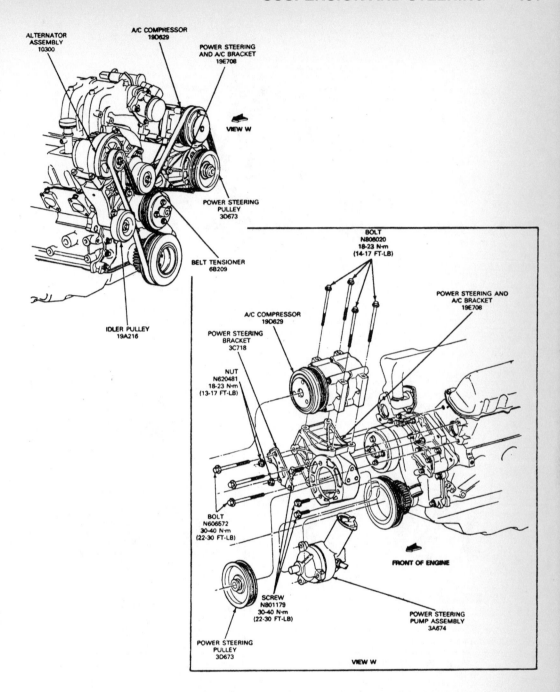

Power steering pump assembly — 1991 Ranger and Explorer with 4.0L engine

under certain circumstances, leak and/or be improperly engaged resulting in unplanned disconnection.

The leak is usually caused by a cut O-ring, imperfections in the outlet fitting inside diameter, or an improperly machined O-ring groove.

Improper engagement can be caused by an improperly machined tube end, tube nut, snapring, outlet fitting or gear port.

If a leak occurs, the O-ring should be replaced with new O-rings. Special O-rings are made for quick-disconnect fittings. Standard O-rings should never be used in their place. If the new O-rings do not solve the leak problem, replace the outlet fitting. If that doesn't work, replace the pressure line.

Improper engagement due to a missing or bent snapring, or improperly machined tube

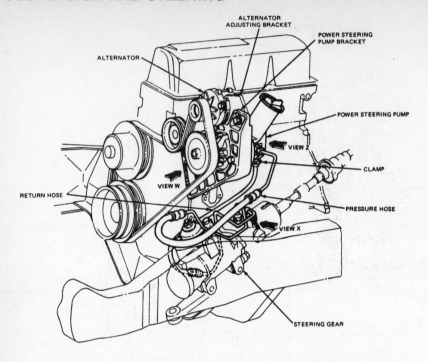

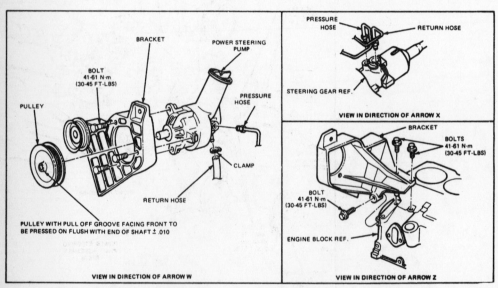

Power steering pump assembly — 1983–88 Ranger with 2.0L and 2.3L engines

nut, may be corrected with a Ford snapring kit made for the purpose. If that doesn't work, replace the pressure hose.

When tightening a quick-connect tube nut, always use a tube nut wrench; never use an open-end wrench! Use of an open-end wrench will result in deformation of the nut! Tighten quick-connect tube nuts to 15 ft. lbs. maximum.

Swivel and/or endplay of quick-connect fittings is normal.

1990–91

If a leak occurs between the tubing and the tube nut, replace the hose assembly. If a leak occurs between the tube nut and the pump outlet replace the plastic washer.

1. Check the fitting to determine whether the leak is between the tube and tube nut or between the tube nut and pump outlet.

2. If the leak is between the tube nut and pump outlet check to be sure the nut is tightened to 30–40 ft. lbs. Do not over tighten this nut.

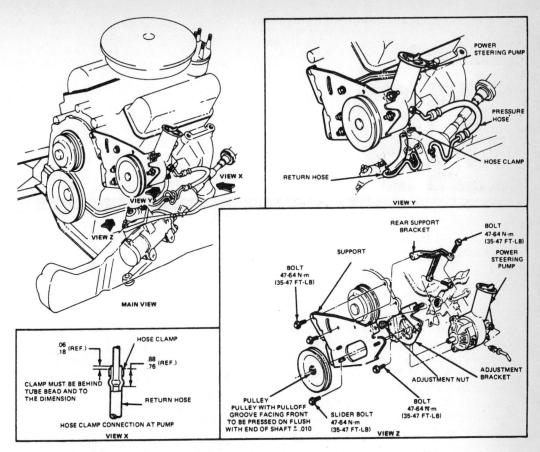

Power steering pump assembly — 1984–88 Bronco II with 2.8L engines

3. If the leak continues or if the leak is between the tube and tube nut, remove the line.

4. Unscrew the tube nut and inspect the plastic seal washer. Replace the plastic seal washer when the line is removed.

5. To aid in the assembly of the new plastic seal washer, a tapered shaft may be required to stretch the washer so that it may be slipped over the tube nut threads.

6. If the rubber O-ring is damaged it cannot be serviced and the hose assembly will have to be replaced.

7. Connect the tube nut and torque to 30–40 ft. lbs.

CAUTION: *The quick connect fitting may disengage if not fully assembled, if the snapring is missing or if the tube nut or hose end is not machined properly. If the fitting disengages replace the hose assembly. The fitting is fully engaged when the hose will not pull*

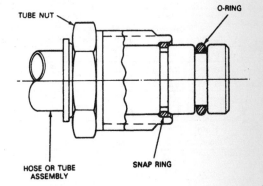

Quick connect fittings

out. *To test for positive engagement the system should be properly filled, the engine started and the steering wheel turned from stop to stop.*

Brakes

BRAKE SYSTEM

CAUTION: *Clean, high quality brake fluid is essential to the safe and proper operation of the brake system. You should always buy the highest quality brake fluid that is available. If the brake fluid becomes contaminated, drain and flush the system and fill the master cylinder with new fluid. Never reuse any brake fluid. Any brake fluid that is removed from the system should be discarded.*

Adjustment

The drum brakes are self-adjusting and require a manual adjustment only after the brake shoes have been replaced.

NOTE: *Disc brakes are not adjustable.*

To adjust the rear brakes with drums installed, follow the procedure given below:
1. Raise the vehicle and support it with safety stands.
2. Remove the rubber plug from the adjusting slot on the backing plate.
3. Turn the adjusting screw using a Brake Shoe Adjustment Tool or equivalent inside the

BRAKE SPECIFICATIONS

Year	Model	Master Cylinder Bore	Caliper Bore	Wheel Cylinder Bore Front	Wheel Cylinder Bore Rear	Rotor Diameter	Rotor Minimum Thickness	Rotor Maximum Run-out	Brake Drum Diameter Front	Brake Drum Diameter Rear	Machined Oversize Front	Machined Oversize Rear
1983	Ranger	0.9375	2.597	—	0.750	10.28①	0.810	0.003	—	9.00②	—	9.060
1984	Bronco II	0.9375	2.597	—	0.750	10.86①	0.810	0.003	—	9.00②	—	9.060
	Ranger	0.9375	2.597	—	0.750	10.28①	0.810	0.003	—	9.00②	—	9.060
1985	Bronco II	0.9375	2.597	—	0.750	10.86①	0.810	0.003	—	9.00②	—	9.060
	Ranger	0.9375	2.597	—	0.750	10.28①	0.810	0.003	—	9.00②	—	9.060
1986	Bronco II	0.9375	2.597	—	0.750	10.28①	0.810	0.003	—	9.00②	—	9.060
	Ranger	0.9375	2.597	—	0.750	10.28①	0.810	0.003	—	9.00②	—	9.060
1987	Bronco II	0.9375	2.597	—	0.750	10.28①	0.810	0.003	—	9.00②	—	9.060
	Ranger	0.9375	2.597	—	0.750	10.28①	0.810	0.003	—	9.00②	—	9.060
1988	Bronco II	0.9375	2.597	—	0.750	10.28①	0.810	0.003	—	9.00②	—	9.060
	Ranger	0.9375	2.597	—	0.750	10.28①	0.810	0.003	—	9.00②	—	9.060
1989	Bronco II	0.9375	2.597	—	0.750	10.28①	0.810	0.003	—	9.00②	—	9.060
	Ranger	0.9375	2.597	—	0.750	10.28①	0.810	0.003	—	9.00②	—	9.060
1990	Bronco II	0.9375	2.597	—	0.750	10.28①	0.810	0.003	—	9.00②	—	9.060
	Ranger	0.9375	2.597	—	0.750	10.28①	0.810	0.003	—	9.00②	—	9.060
1991	Explorer	0.9375	2.597	—	0.750	10.28①	0.810	0.003	—	9.00②	—	9.060
	Ranger	0.9375	2.597	—	0.750	10.28①	0.810	0.003	—	9.00②	—	9.060

① 4WD: 10.86
② Optional 10″ rear brakes
NOTE: Always use specifications as a service guide for brake system components

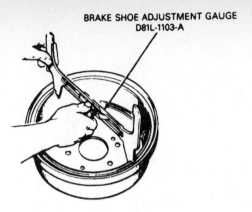

Brake shoe adjustment gauge — Step 1

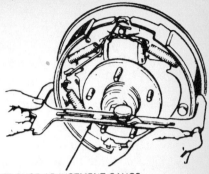

Brake shoe adjustment gauge — Step 2

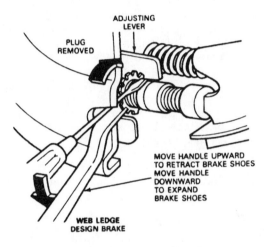

Brake shoe adjustment gauge — Step 3

hole to expand the brake shoes until they drag against the brake drum and lock the drum.

4. Insert a small screwdriver or piece of firm wire (coat hanger wire) into the adjusting slot and push the automatic adjusting lever out and free of the starwheel on the adjusting screw and hold it there.

5. Engage the topmost tooth possible on the starwheel with the brake adjusting spoon. Move the end of the adjusting spoon upward to move the adjusting screw starwheel downward and contract the adjusting screw. Back off the adjusting screw starwheel until the wheel spins FREELY with a minimum of drag about 10 to 12 notches. Keep track of the number of turns that the starwheel is backed off, or the number of strokes taken with the brake adjusting spoon.

6. Repeat this operation for the other side. When backing off the brakes on the other side, the starwheel adjuster must be backed off the same number of turns to prevent side-to-side brake pull.

7. When all drum brakes are adjusted, remove the safety stands and lower the vehicle and make several stops while backing the vehicle, to equalize the brakes at all of the wheels.

8. Road test the vehicle. PERFORM THE ROAD TEST ONLY WHEN THE BRAKES WILL APPLY AND THE VEHICLE CAN BE STOPPED SAFELY!

Brake Light Switch

REMOVAL AND INSTALLATION

1. Lift the locking tab on the switch connector and disconnect the wiring.

2. Remove the hairpin retainer, slide the stoplamp switch, pushrod and nylon washer off of the pedal. Remove the washer, then the switch by sliding it up or down.

NOTE: *On some vehicles equipped with speed control, the spacer washer is replaced by the dump valve adapter washer.*

3. To install the switch, position it so that the U-shaped side is nearest the pedal and directly over/under the pin.

4. Slide the switch up or down, trapping the

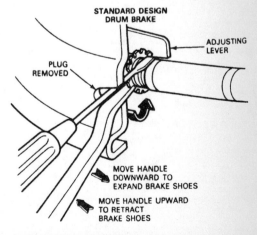

Adjusting rear brake shoes

master cylinder pushrod and bushing between the switch side plates.

5. Push the switch and pushrod assembly firmly towards the brake pedal arm. Assemble the outside white plastic washer to the pin and install the hairpin retainer.

NOTE: *Don't substitute any other type of retainer. Use only the Ford specified hairpin retainer.*

6. Assemble the connector on the switch.

7. Check stoplamp operation.

NOTE: *Make sure that the stoplamp switch wiring has sufficient travel during a full pedal stroke.*

Master Cylinder

REMOVAL AND INSTALLATION

Manual Brake System

1. Working from inside the cab below the instrument panel, disconnect the wires from the stop lamp switch.

2. Remove the retaining nut, shoulder bolt and spacers, securing the master cylinder push rod to the brake pedal assembly. Remove the stop lamp switch from the pedal.

3. Disconnect the brake hydraulic system lines (always use correct tool, a Line wrench) from the master cylinder.

4. Remove the master cylinder-to-dash panel retaining nuts, and remove the master cylinder.

5. Remove the boot from the master cylinder push rod.

To install:

6. Place the master cylinder assembly on the dash panel in the engine compartment and install the retaining bolts. Tighten the bolts to 13–25 ft. lbs.

7. Connect the hydraulic brake system lines to the master cylinder.

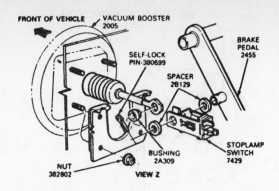

Stoplight switch mounting

8. Secure the push rod to the brake pedal assembly using the shoulder bolt. Make sure the bushings and spacers are installed properly. Install self-locking nut.

9. Connect the wires to the stop lamp switch. Bleed the brake system as described in this Chapter. Centralize the differential valve. Fill the dual master cylinder reservoirs with DOT 3 brake fluid to within 1/4 in. (6mm) of the top. Install the gasket and reservoir cover. Roadtest the vehicle.

Power Brake System

1. With the engine turned off, push the brake pedal down to expel vacuum from the brake booster system.

2. Disconnect the hydraulic lines (use correct tool, a Line Wrench) from the brake master cylinder.

3. Remove the brake booster-to-master cylinder retaining nuts and lock washers. Remove the master cylinder from the brake booster.

To install:

4. Before installing the master cylinder, check the distance from the outer end of the booster assembly push rod to the front face of

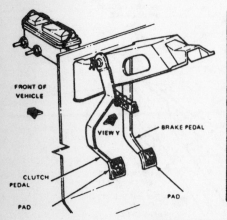

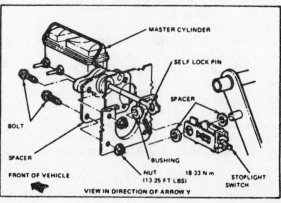

Manual brake master cylinder removal and installation

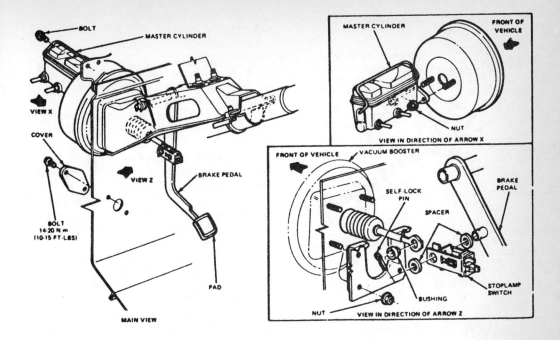

Power brake master cylinder removal and installation

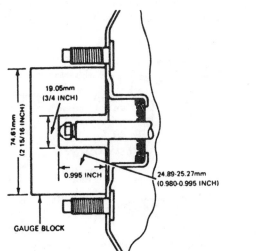

Bendix booster push rod gauge, dimensions and adjustment

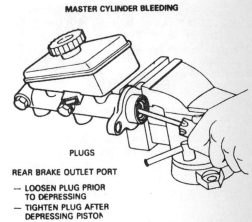

Master cylinder bleeding procedure

the brake booster assembly. Turn the push rod adjusting screw in or out as required to obtain the length shown. Refer to illustration in this Chapter.

5. Position the master cylinder assembly over the booster push rod and onto the 2 studs on the booster assembly. Install the attaching nuts and lockwashers and tighten to 13–25 ft. lbs.

6. Connect the hydraulic brake system lines to the master cylinder.

7. Bleed the hydraulic brake system (refer to procedure in this Chapter). Centralize the dif-

ferential valve. Then, fill the dual master cylinder reservoirs with DOT 3 brake fluid to within $1/4$ in. (6mm) of the top. Install the gasket and reservoir cover. Roadtest the vehicle for proper operation.

When replacing the master cylinder it is best to BENCH BLEED the master cylinder before installing it to the vehicle. Mount the master cylinder into a vise or suitable equivalent (do not damage the cylinder). Fill the cylinder to the correct level with the specified fluid. Block off all the outer brake line holes but one, then, using a long tool such as rod position it in the cylinder to actuate the brake master cylinder.

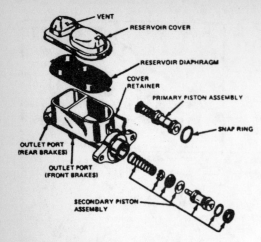

Exploded view of the master cylinder assembly

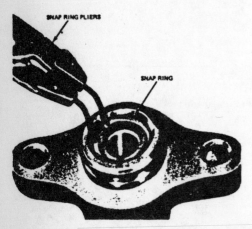

Snapring removal of the master cylinder

Pump (push tool in and out) the brake master cylinder 3 or 4 times till brake fluid is release out and no air is in the brake fluid. Repeat this procedure until all brake fluid is released out of every hole and no air is expelled.

OVERHAUL

NOTE: *Use this service procedure and exploded view diagrams as a guide for overhaul of the master cylinder assembly. If in doubt about overhaul condition or service procedure replace the complete assembly with a new master cylinder assembly.*

The most important thing to remember when rebuilding the master cylinder is cleanliness. Work in clean surroundings with clean tools and clean cloths or paper for drying purposes. Have plenty of clean alcohol and brake fluid on hand to clean and lubricate the internal components. There are service repair kits available for overhauling the master cylinder.

1. Clean the outside of the master cylinder and remove the filler cap and gasket (dia-phragm). Pour out any fluid that remains in the cylinder reservoir. Do not use any fluids other than brake fluid or alcohol to clean the master cylinder.

2. Unscrew the piston stop from the bottom of the cylinder body. Remove the O-ring seal from the piston stop. Discard the seal.

3. Remove the pushrod boot, if so equipped, from the groove at the rear of the master cylinder.

4. Remove the snapring retaining the primary and secondary piston assemblies within the cylinder body.

5. Remove the pushrod (if so equipped) and primary piston assembly from the master cylinder. Discard the piston assembly, including the boot (if so equipped).

6. Apply an air hose to the rear brake outlet port of the cylinder body and carefully blow the secondary piston out of the cylinder body.

7. Remove the return spring, spring retainer, cup protector, and cups from the secondary piston. Discard the cup protector and cups.

8. Clean all of the remaining parts in clean isopropyl alcohol and inspect the parts for chipping, excessive wear or damage. Replace them as required.

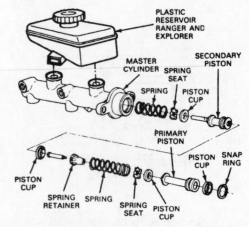

Exploded view of the master cylinder assembly

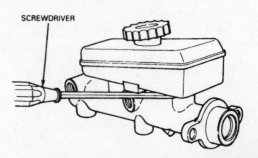

Plastic reservoir assembly

NOTE: *When using a master cylinder repair kit, install all the parts supplied in the kit.*

9. Check all recesses, reopenings and internal passages to be sure they are open and free from foreign matter. Use compressed air to blow out dirt and cleaning solvent remaining after the parts have been cleaned in the alcohol. Place all the parts on a clean pan, lint-free cloth, or paper to dry.

10. Dip all the parts, except the cylinder body, in clean brake fluid.

11. Assemble the 2 secondary cups, back-to-back, in the grooves near the end of the secondary piston.

12. Install the secondary piston assembly in the master cylinder.

13. Install a new O-ring on the piston stop, and start the stop into the cylinder body.

14. Position the boot, snapring and pushrod retainer on the pushrod. Make sure the pushrod retainer is seated securely on the ball end of the rod. Seat the pushrod in the primary piston assembly.

15. Install the primary piston assembly in the master cylinder. Push the primary piston inward and tighten the secondary piston stop to retain the secondary piston in the bore.

16. Press the pushrod and pistons inward and install the snapring in the cylinder body.

17. Before the master cylinder is installed on the vehicle, the unit must be bled: support the master cylinder body in a vise, and fill both fluid reservoirs with brake fluid.

18. Loosely install plugs in the front and rear brake outlet bores. Depress the primary piston several times until air bubbles cease to appear in the brake fluid.

19. Tighten the plugs and attempt to depress the piston. The piston travel should be restricted after all air is expelled.

20. Remove the plugs. Install the cover and

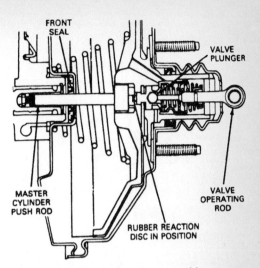

Cutaway view of brake booster assembly

gasket (diaphragm) assembly, and make sure the cover retainer is tightened securely.

21. Install the master cylinder in the vehicle and bleed the hydraulic system.

Booster

REMOVAL AND INSTALLATION

NOTE: *Make sure that the booster rubber reaction disc is properly installed if the master cylinder push rod is removed or accidentally pulled out. A dislodged disc may cause excessive pedal travel and extreme operation sensitivity. The disc is black compared to the silver colored valve plunger that will be exposed after the push rod and front seal is removed. The booster unit is serviced as an assembly and must be replaced if the reaction disc cannot be properly installed and aligned, or if it cannot be located within the unit itself.*

1. Disconnect the stop lamp switch wiring to prevent running the battery down.

2. Support the master cylinder from the underside with a prop.

3. Remove the master cylinder-to-booster retaining nuts.

4. Loosen the clamp that secures the manifold vacuum hose to the booster check valve, and remove the hose. Remove the booster check valve.

5. Pull the master cylinder off the booster and leave it supported by the prop, far enough away to allow removal of the booster assembly.

6. From inside the cab on vehicles equipped with push rod mounted stop lamp switch, remove the retaining pin and slide the stop lamp switch, push rod, spacers and bushing off the brake pedal arm.

7. From the engine compartment remove

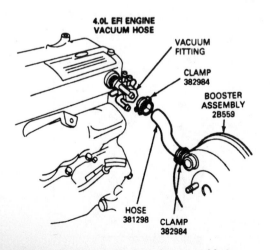

Vacuum hose for brake booster assembly

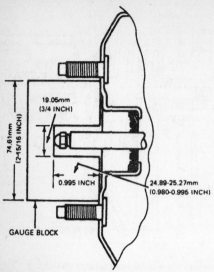

Bendix booster push rod gauge, dimensions and adjustment procedure

the bolts that attach the booster to the dash panel.

To install:

8. Mount the booster assembly on the engine side of the dash panel by sliding the bracket mounting bolts and valve operating rod in through the holes in the dash panel.

NOTE: *Make certain that the booster push rod is positioned on the correct side of the*

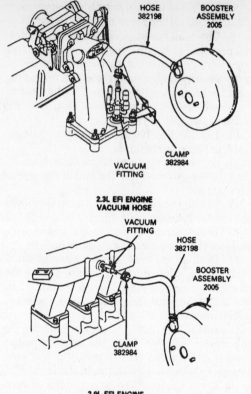

Vacuum hose for brake booster assembly

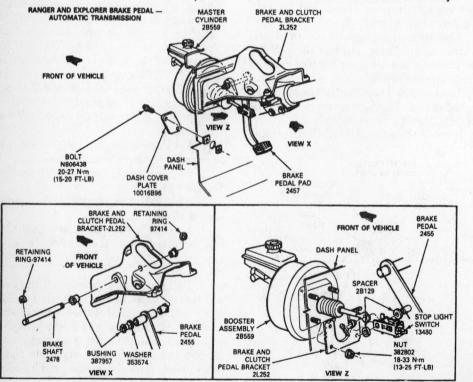

Brake booster assembly

master cylinder to install onto the push pin prior to tightening the booster assembly to the dash.

9. From inside the cab, install the booster mounting bracket-to-dash panel retaining nuts.

10. Position the master cylinder on the booster assembly, install the retaining nuts, and remove the prop from underneath the master cylinder.

11. Install the booster check valve. Connect the manifold vacuum hose to the booster check valve and secure with the clamp.

12. From inside the cab on vehicles equipped with push rod mounted stop lamp switch, install the bushing and position the switch on the end of the push rod. Then install the switch and rod on the pedal arm, along with spacers on each side, and secure with the retaining pin.

13. Connect the stop lamp switch wiring.

14. Start the engine and check brake operation.

Brake Hoses and Lines

HYDRAULIC BRAKE LINE CHECK

The hydraulic brake lines and brake linings are to be inspected at the recommended intervals in the maintenance schedule. Follow the steel tubing from the master cylinder to the flexible hose fitting at each wheel. If a section of the tubing is found to be damaged, replace the entire section with tubing of the same type (steel, not copper), size, shape, and length. When installing a new section of brake tubing, flush clean brake fluid or denatured alcohol through to remove any dirt or foreign material from the line. Be sure to flare both ends to provide sound, leak-proof connections (replacement brake lines can purchased already made up at local parts store). When bending the tubing to fit the underbody contours, be careful not to kink or crack the line.

Check the flexible brake hoses that connect the steel tubing to each wheel cylinder. Replace the hose if it shows any signs of softening, cracking, or other damage. When installing a new front brake hose, position the hose to avoid contact with other chassis parts. Place a new copper gasket over the hose fitting and thread the hose assembly into the front wheel cylinder. A new rear brake hose must be positioned clear of the exhaust pipe or shock absorber. Thread the hose into the rear brake tube connector. When installing either a new front or rear brake hose, engage the opposite end of the hose to the bracket on the frame. Install the

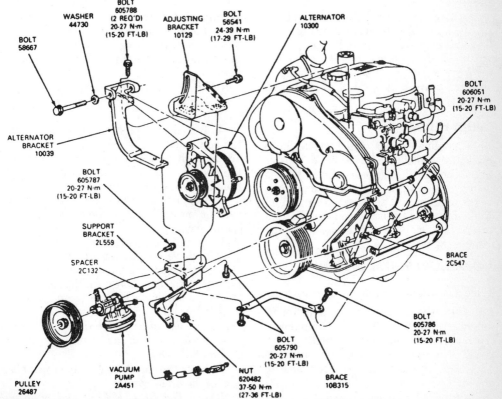

Vacuum pump removal and installation — 2.3L diesel engine

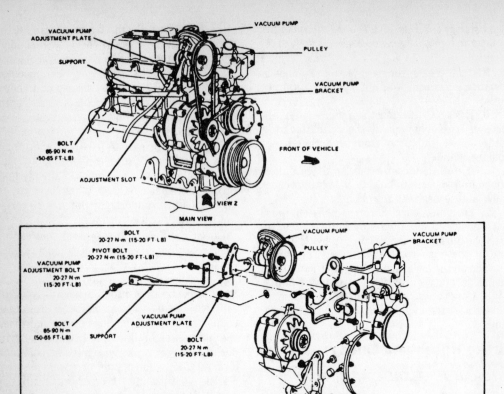

VIEW Z

Vacuum pump removal and installation — 2.2L diesel engine

horseshoe type retaining clip and connect the tube to the hose with the tube fitting nut.

Always bleed the system after hose or line replacement. Before bleeding, make sure that the master cylinder is topped up with high temperature, extra heavy duty fluid of at least SAE 70R3 quality.

Vacuum Pump

Unlike gasoline engines, diesel engines have little vacuum available to power brake booster systems. The diesel is thus equipped with a vacuum pump, which is driven by a single belt off of the alternator. This pump is located on the top right side of the engine on the 2.2L and on the bottom left side of the engine on the 2.3L diesel engine.

REMOVAL AND INSTALLATION

2.2L And 2.3L Diesel Engine

1. Loosen the vacuum pump adjustment bolt and the pivot bolt. Slide the pump downward and remove the drive belt from the pulley.

NOTE: *If the vacuum pump drive belt is to be replaced, the alternator drive belt must be removed.*

2. Remove the hose clamp and disconnect the pump from the hose on the manifold vacuum outlet fitting.

3. Remove the pivot and adjustment bolts and the bolts retaining the pump to the adjustment plate. Remove the vacuum pump and adjustment plate.

NOTE: *The vacuum pump is not to be disassembled. It is only serviced as a unit.*

To install:

4. Install the bolts attaching the pump to the adjustment plate and tighten the bolts to 15–20 ft. lbs. Position the pump and plate on the vacuum pump bracket and loosely install the pivot and adjustment bolts.

5. Connect the hose from the manifold vacuum outlet fitting to the pump and install the hose clamp.

6. Install the drive belt on the pulley. Place a $^3/_8$ in. drive breaker bar or ratchet into the slot on the vacuum pump adjustment plate. Lift up on the assembly until the specified belt tension is obtained. Tighten the pivot and adjustment bolts to 15–20 ft. lbs.

NOTE: *The alternator belt tension must be adjusted prior to adjusting the vacuum pump belt tension.*

7. Start the engine and verify proper operation of the brake system.

NOTE: *The BRAKE light will glow until vacuum builds up to the normal level.*

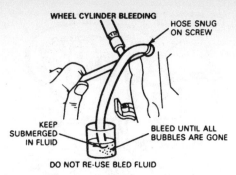

Wheel cylinder bleeding procedure

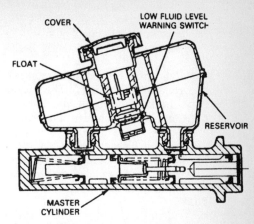

Master cylinder and reservoir assembly

Centralizing the Pressure Differential Valve

After any repair or bleeding of the primary (front brake) or secondary (rear brake) system, the dual brake system warning light will usually remain illuminated due to the pressure differential valve remaining in the off-center position.

To centralize the pressure differential valve and turn off the warning light after the systems have been bled, follow the procedure below.

1. Turn the ignition switch to the ACC or ON position.

2. Check the fluid level in the master cylinder reservoirs and fill them to within 1/4 in. (6mm) of the top with brake fluid, if necessary.

3. Depress the brake pedal and the piston should center itself causing the brake warning light to go out.

4. Turn the ignition switch to the OFF position.

5. Before driving the vehicle, check the operation of the brakes and be sure that a firm pedal is obtained.

Bleeding The Brakes

When any part of the hydraulic system has been disconnected for repair or replacement, air may get into the lines and cause spongy pedal action (because air can be compressed and brake fluid cannot). To correct this condition, it is necessary to bleed the hydraulic system after it has been properly connected to be sure all air is expelled from the brake cylinders and lines.

When bleeding the brake system, bleed one brake cylinder at a time, beginning at the cylinder with the longest hydraulic line (farthest from the master cylinder) first. ALWAYS Keep the master cylinder reservoir filled with brake fluid during the bleeding operation. Never use brake fluid that has been drained from the hydraulic system, no matter how clean it is.

It will be necessary to centralize the pressure differential value after a brake system failure has been corrected and the hydraulic system has been bled.

The primary and secondary hydraulic brake

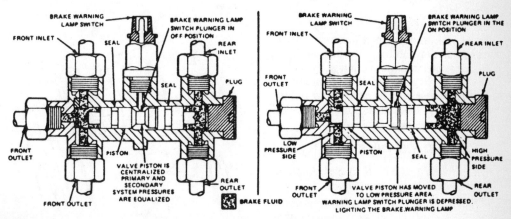

Cutaway view of typical pressure differential valve

systems are individual systems and are bled separately. During the entire bleeding operation, do not allow the reservoir to run dry. Keep the master cylinder reservoir filled with brake fluid.

1. Clean all dirt from around the master cylinder fill cap, remove the cap and fill the master cylinder with brake fluid until the level is within $1/4$ in. (6mm) of the top edge of the reservoir.

2. Clean off the bleeder screws at all 4 wheels. The bleeder screws are located on the inside of the brake backing plate, on the backside of the wheel cylinders and on the front brake calipers.

3. Attach a length of rubber hose over the nozzle of the bleeder screw at the wheel to be done first. Place the other end of the hose in a glass jar, submerged in brake fluid.

4. Open the bleeder screw valve $1/2$–$3/4$ turn.

5. Have an assistant slowly depress the brake pedal. Close the bleeder screw valve and tell your assistant to allow the brake pedal to return slowly. Continue this pumping action to force any air out of the system. When bubbles cease to appear at the end of the bleeder hose, close the bleeder valve and remove the hose.

6. Check the master cylinder fluid level and add fluid accordingly. Do this after bleeding each wheel.

7. Repeat the bleeding operation at the remaining 3 wheels, ending with the one closet to the master cylinder. Fill the master cylinder reservoir.

FRONT DISC BRAKES

Pads

INSPECTION

Replace the front pads when the pad thickness is at the minimum thickness recommended by the Ford Motor Co. which is $1/32$ in. (0.8mm), or at the minimum allowed by the applicable state or local motor vehicle inspection code. Pad thickness may be checked by removing the wheel and looking through the inspection port in the caliper assembly.

REMOVAL AND INSTALLATION

NOTE: *Always replace all disc pad assemblies on an axle. Never service one wheel only.*

1. To avoid fluid overflow when the caliper piston is pressed into the caliper cylinder bores, siphon or dip part of the brake fluid out of the larger master cylinder reservoir (connected to

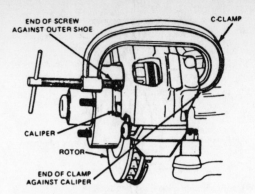

Bottoming the caliper piston

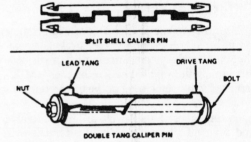

Caliper pins

Caliper pin with the bolt head on the outside of the caliper

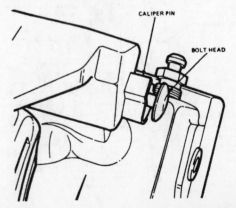

Separation between the bolt head and the caliper pin

the front disc brakes). Discard the removed fluid.

2. Raise the vehicle and install jackstands. Remove a front wheel and tire assembly.

3. Place an 8 in. (203mm) C-clamp on the caliper and tighten the clamp to bottom the caliper piston in the cylinder bore. Remove the clamp.

NOTE: *Do not use a screwdriver or similar tool to pry piston away from the rotor.*

4. There are 3 types of caliper pins used: a single tang type, a double tang type and a split-shell type. The pin removal process is depend-

Removing the bolt head

ent upon how the pin is installed (bolt head direction). Remove the upper caliper pin first.

NOTE: *On some applications, the pin may be retained by a nut and Torx® head bolt (except the split-shell type).*

5. If the bolt head is on the outside of the caliper, use the following procedure:

    a. From the inner side of the caliper, tap the bolt within the caliper pin until the bolt head on the outer side of the caliper shows a separation between the bolt head and the caliper pin.

    b. Using a hacksaw or bolt cutter, remove

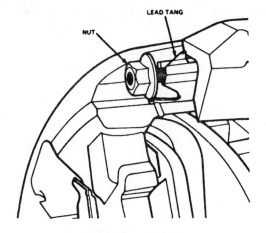

Caliper pin with nut on the outside

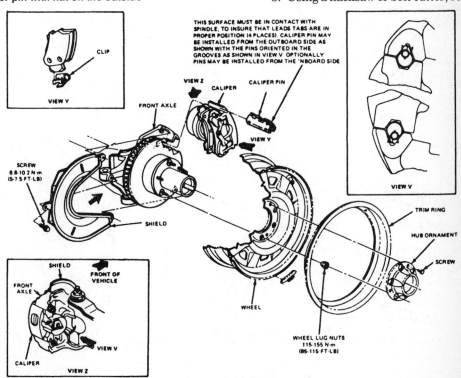

Front disc brake assembly

the bolt head from the bolt.

c. Depress the tab on the bolt head end of the upper caliper pin with a screwdriver, while tapping on the pin with a hammer. Continue tapping until the tab is depressed by the V-slot.

d. Place one end of a punch, 1/2 in.

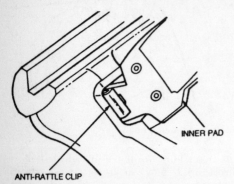

Installing the inner pad and the anti-rattle clip into the caliper

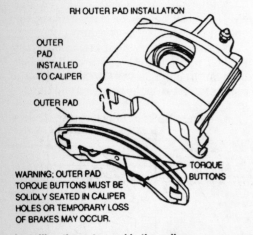

Installing the outer pad in the caliper

(13mm) or smaller, against the end of the caliper pin and drive the caliper pin out of the caliper toward the inside of the vehicle. Do not use a screwdriver or other edged tool to help drive out the caliper pin as the V-grooves may be damage.

WARNING: *Never reuse caliper pins. Always install new pins whenever a caliper is removed.*

6. If the nut end of the bolt is on the outside of the caliper, use the following procedure:

a. Remove the nut from the bolt.

b. Depress the lead tang on the end of the upper caliper pin with a screwdriver while tapping on the pin with a hammer. Continue tapping until the lead tang is depressed by the V-slot.

c. Place one end of a punch, 1/2 in. (13mm) or smaller, against the end of the caliper pin and drive the caliper pin out of the caliper toward the inside of the vehicle. Do not use a screwdriver or other edged tool to help drive out the caliper pin as the V-grooves may be damaged.

7. Repeat the procedure in Step 4 for the lower caliper pin.

8. Remove the caliper from the rotor. If the caliper is to be removed for service, remove the brake hose from the caliper.

9. Remove the outer pad. Remove the anti-rattle clips and remove the inner pad.

To install:

10. Place a new anti-rattle clip on the lower end of the inner pad. Be sure the tabs on the clip are positioned properly and the clip is fully seated.

11. Position the inner pads and anti-rattle clip in the abutment with the anti-rattle clip tab against the pad abutment and the loop-type spring away from the rotor. Compress the anti-

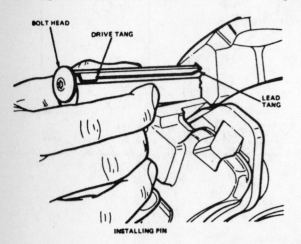

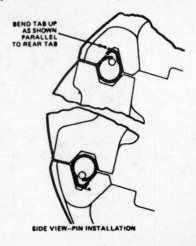

Installing the caliper pin

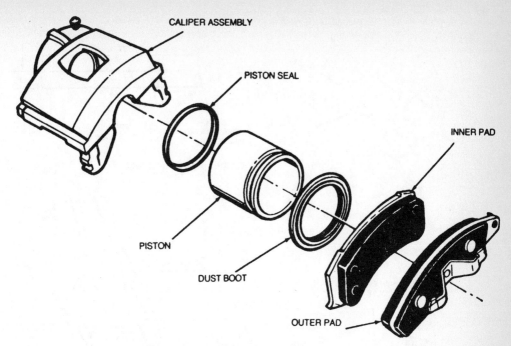

CALIPER ASSEMBLY

PISTON SEAL

INNER PAD

PISTON

DUST BOOT

OUTER PAD

Caliper assembly

rattle clip and slide the upper end of the pad in position.

12. Install the outer pad, making sure the torque buttons on the pad spring clip are seated solidly in the matching holes in the caliper.

13. Install the caliper on the spindle, making sure the mounting surfaces are free of dirt and lubricate the caliper grooves with Disc Brake Caliper Grease. Install new caliper pins, making sure the pins are installed with the fang in position as shown. The pin must be installed with the lead tang in first, the bolt head facing outward (if equipped) and the pin positioned as shown. Position the lead tang in the V-slot mounting surface and drive in the caliper until the drive tang is flush with the caliper assembly. Install the nut (if equipped) and tighten to 32–47 inch lbs.

WARNING: *Never reuse caliper pins. Always install new pins whenever a caliper is removed.*

14. If removed, install the brake hose to the caliper.

15. Bleed the brakes as described earlier in this Chapter.

16. Install the wheel and tire assembly. Torque the lug nuts to 85–115 ft. lbs.

17. Remove the jackstands and lower the ve-

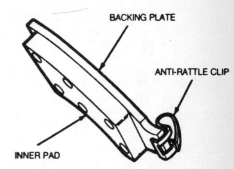

BACKING PLATE

ANTI-RATTLE CLIP

INNER PAD

Anti-rattle clip installed on the inner pad

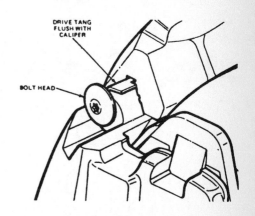

DRIVE TANG FLUSH WITH CALIPER

BOLT HEAD

Correct caliper pin installation

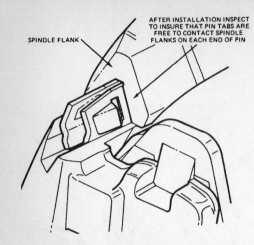

SPINDLE FLANK

AFTER INSTALLATION INSPECT
TO INSURE THAT PIN TABS ARE
FREE TO CONTACT SPINDLE
FLANKS ON EACH END OF PIN

Correct brake pad installation

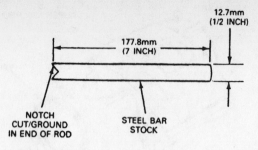

12.7mm
(1/2 INCH)

177.8mm
(7 INCH)

NOTCH
CUT/GROUND
IN END OF ROD

STEEL BAR
STOCK

Caliper pin removal tool

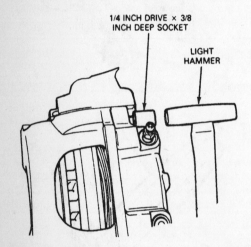

1/4 INCH DRIVE × 3/8
INCH DEEP SOCKET

LIGHT
HAMMER

Removing the caliper pin

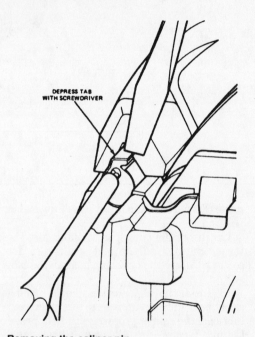

DEPRESS TAB
WITH SCREWDRIVER

Removing the caliper pin

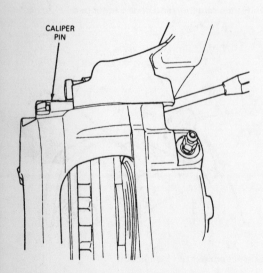

CALIPER
PIN

Using tool to remove the caliper pin

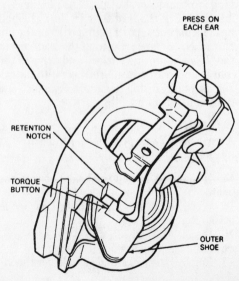

PRESS ON
EACH EAR

RETENTION
NOTCH

TORQUE
BUTTON

OUTER
SHOE

Removing the outer shoe from the caliper assembly

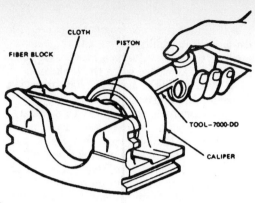

Caliper piston removal

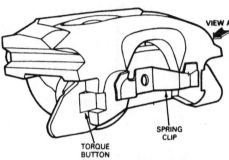

CORRECT SHOE INSTALLATION IN CALIPER

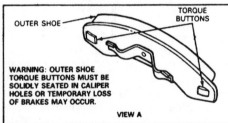

Correct brake shoe installation in caliper

CAUTION: *If high pressure air is applied, the piston will pop out with considerable force and cause damage or injury.*

5. If the piston jams, release the air pressure and tap sharply on the piston end with a soft hammer. Reapply air pressure.

6. When the piston is out, remove the boot from the piston and the seal from the bore.

7. Clean the housing and piston with denatured alcohol. Dry with compressed air.

8. Lubricate the new piston seal, boot and piston with clean brake fluid, and assemble them in the caliper.

9. The dust boot can be worked in with the fingers and the piston should be pressed straight in until it bottoms. Be careful to avoid cocking the piston in the bore.

10. A C-clamp may be necessary to bottom the piston.

11. Install the caliper using the procedure given in the pad and caliper replacement procedure above.

Rotor (Disc)

REMOVAL AND INSTALLATION

1. Jack up the front of the vehicle and support on jackstands.

2. Remove the wheel and tire.

3. Remove the caliper assembly as described earlier in this Chapter.

4. Follow the procedure given under hub and wheel bearing removal in Chapter 7 for models with manual and automatic locking hubs.

NOTE: *New rotor assemblies come protected with an anti-rust coating which should be removed with denatured alcohol or degreaser. New hubs must be packed with EP wheel bearing grease. If the old rotors are to be reused, check them for cracks, grooves or waviness. Rotors that aren't too badly scored or grooved can be resurfaced by most automotive shops. Minimum rotor thickness should be 0.81 in. (20.5mm). If refinishing exceeds that, the rotor will have to be replaced.*

hicle. Check the brake fluid level and fill as necessary. Check the brakes for proper operation.

Calipers

OVERHAUL

1. For caliper removal, see the above procedure. Disconnect the brake hose.

2. Clean the exterior of the caliper with denatured alcohol.

3. Remove the plug from the caliper inlet port and drain the fluid.

4. Air pressure is necessary to remove the piston. When a source of compressed air is found, such as a shop or gas station, apply air to the inlet port slowly and carefully until the piston pops out of its bore.

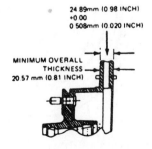

Disc brake service limits

REAR DRUM BRAKES

Brake Drums

REMOVAL AND INSTALLATION

1. Raise the vehicle so that the wheel to be worked on is clear of the floor and install jackstands under the vehicle.

2. Remove the hub cap and the wheel/tire assembly. Remove the 3 retaining nuts and remove the brake drum. It may be necessary to back off the brake shoe adjustment in order to remove the brake drum. This is because the drum might be grooved or worn from being in service for an extended period of time.

3. Before installing a new brake drum, be sure and remove any protective coating with carburetor degreaser.

4. Install the brake drum in the reverse order of removal and adjusts the brakes.

INSPECTION

After the brake drum has been removed from the vehicle, it should be inspected for runout, severe scoring cracks, and the proper inside diameter.

Minor scores on a brake drum can be removed with fine emery cloth, provided that all grit is removed from the drum before it is installed on the vehicle.

A badly scored, rough, or out-of-round (runout) drum can be ground or turned on a brake drum lathe. Do not remove any more material from the drum than is necessary to provide a smooth surface for the brake shoe to contact. The maximum diameter of the braking surface is shown on the inside of each brake drum. Brake drums that exceed the maximum braking surface diameter shown on the brake drum, either through wear or refinishing, must

be replaced. This is because after the outside wall of the brake drum reaches a certain thickness (thinner than the original thickness) the drum loses its ability to dissipate the heat created by the friction between the brake drum and the brake shoes, when the brakes are applied. Also the brake drum will have more tendency to warp and/or crack.

The maximum braking surface diameter specification, which is shown on each drum, allows for a 0.060 in. (1.5mm) machining cut over the original nominal drum diameter plus 0.030 in. (0.76mm) additional wear before reaching the diameter where the drum must be discarded. Use a brake drum micrometer to measure the inside diameter of the brake drums.

Brake Shoes

REMOVAL AND INSTALLATION

1. Raise and support the vehicle and remove the wheel and brake drum from the wheel to be worked on.

NOTE: *If you have never replaced the brakes on a car before and you are not too familiar with the procedures involved, only disassemble and assemble one side at a time, leaving the other side intact as a reference during reassembly.*

2. Install a clamp over the ends of the wheel cylinder to prevent the pistons of the wheel cylinder from coming out, causing loss of fluid.

3. Contract the brake shoes by pulling the self-adjusting lever away from the starwheel adjustment screw and turn the starwheel up and back until the pivot nut is drawn onto the starwheel as far as it will come.

4. Pull the adjusting lever, cable and automatic adjuster spring down and toward the rear to unhook the pivot hook from the large hole in the secondary shoe web. Do not attempt to pry the pivot hook from the hole.

5. Remove the automatic adjuster spring and the adjusting lever.

6. Remove the secondary shoe-to-anchor spring with a brake tool. (Brake tools are very

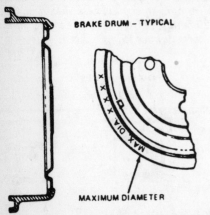

BRAKE DRUM - TYPICAL

MAX DIA

MAXIMUM DIAMETER

Rear brake drum maximum inside surface diameter marking location

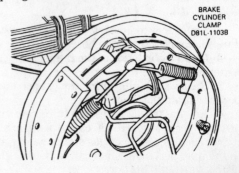

BRAKE
CYLINDER
CLAMP
D81L-1103B

Rear brake shoe removal procedure

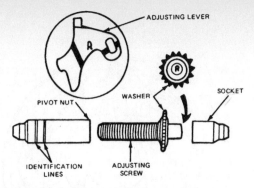

Exploded view adjusting screw assembly

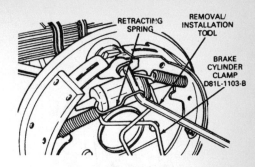

Rear brake shoe removal procedure

common and are available at auto parts stores). Remove the primary shoe-to-anchor spring and unhook the cable anchor. Remove the anchor pin plate.

7. Remove the cable guide from the secondary shoe.

8. Remove the shoe hold-down springs, shoes, adjusting screw, pivot nut, and socket. Note the color of each hold-down spring for assembly. To remove the hold-down springs, reach being the brake backing plate and place one finger on the end of one of the brake hold-down spring mounting pins. Using a pair of pliers, grasp the washer-type retainer on top of the hold-down spring that corresponds to the pin that you are holding. Push down on the pliers and turn them 90° to align the slot in the washer with the head on the spring mounting pin. Remove the spring and washer retainer and repeat this operation on the hold-down spring on the other shoe.

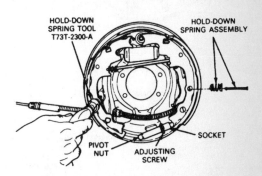

Rear brake shoe removal procedure

9. Remove the parking brake link and spring. Disconnect the parking brake cable from the parking brake lever.

10. After removing the rear brake secondary shoe, disassemble the parking brake lever from the shoe by removing the retaining clip and spring washer.

BRAKE SHOE AND ADJUSTING SCREW - EXPLODED VIEW (LH SIDE SHOWN)

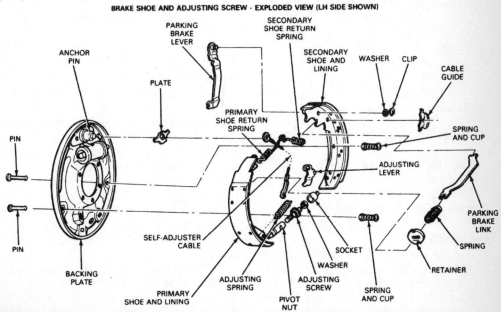

Exploded view brake shoe and adjusting screw assembly

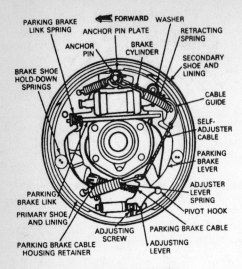

PARKING BRAKE LINK SPRING | ◄ FORWARD | WASHER
ANCHOR PIN PLATE | RETRACTING SPRING
ANCHOR PIN | BRAKE CYLINDER
BRAKE SHOE HOLD-DOWN SPRINGS | SECONDARY SHOE AND LINING
CABLE GUIDE
SELF-ADJUSTER CABLE
PARKING BRAKE LEVER
PARKING BRAKE LINK | ADJUSTER LEVER SPRING
PRIMARY SHOE AND LINING | PIVOT HOOK
ADJUSTING SCREW | PARKING BRAKE CABLE
PARKING BRAKE CABLE HOUSING RETAINER | ADJUSTING LEVER

10-INCH REAR BRAKE (LEFT SIDE)

REAR BRAKE (LEFT SIDE)

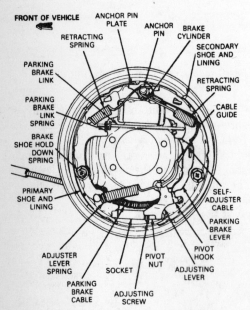

FRONT OF VEHICLE | ANCHOR PIN PLATE | ANCHOR PIN | BRAKE CYLINDER
RETRACTING SPRING | SECONDARY SHOE AND LINING
PARKING BRAKE LINK | RETRACTING SPRING
PARKING BRAKE LINK SPRING | CABLE GUIDE
BRAKE SHOE HOLD DOWN SPRING
PRIMARY SHOE AND LINING | SELF-ADJUSTER CABLE
PARKING BRAKE LEVER
PIVOT HOOK
ADJUSTER LEVER SPRING | PIVOT NUT | ADJUSTING LEVER
SOCKET
PARKING BRAKE CABLE | ADJUSTING SCREW

Exploded view rear drum brake assembly

To assemble and install the brake shoes:

11. Assemble the parking brake lever to the secondary shoe and secure it with the spring washer and retaining clip.

12. Apply a light coating of Lubriplate® at the points where the brake shoes contact the backing plate.

13. Position the brake shoes on the backing plate, and install the hold-down spring pins, springs, and spring washer-type retainers. Install the parking brake link, spring and washer. Connect the parking brake cable to the parking brake lever.

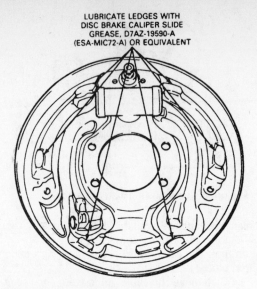

LUBRICATE LEDGES WITH DISC BRAKE CALIPER SLIDE GREASE, D7AZ-19590-A (ESA-MIC72-A) OR EQUIVALENT

Rear brake shoe installation procedures

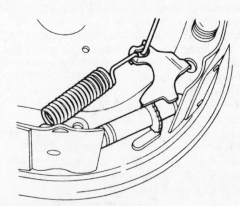

Rear brake installation procedure

14. Install the anchor pin plate, and place the cable anchor over the anchor pin with the crimped side toward the backing plate.

15. Install the primary shoe-to-anchor spring with the brake tool.

16. Install the cable guide on the secondary shoe web with the flanged holes fitted into the hole in the secondary shoe web. Thread the cable around the cable guide groove.

17. Install the secondary shoe-to-anchor (long) spring. Be sure that the cable end is not cocked or binding on the anchor pin when installed. All of the parts should be flat on the anchor pin. Remove the wheel cylinder piston clamp.

18. Apply Lubriplate® to the threads and the socket end of the adjusting starwheel screw. Turn the adjusting screw into the adjusting pivot nut to the limit of the threads and then back off $1/2$ turn.

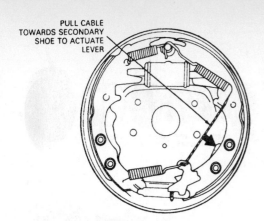

PULL CABLE
TOWARDS SECONDARY
SHOE TO ACTUATE
LEVER

Rear brake installation procedure

NOTE: *Interchanging the brake shoe adjusting screw assemblies from one side of the vehicle to the other would cause the brake shoes to retract rather than expand each time the automatic adjusting mechanism operated. To prevent this, the socket end of the adjusting screw is stamped with an R or an L for RIGHT or LEFT. The adjusting pivot nuts can be distinguished by the number of lines machined around the body of the nut; one line indicates left hand nut and 2 lines indicates a right hand nut.*

19. Place the adjusting socket on the screw and install this assembly between the shoe ends with the adjusting screw nearest to the secondary shoe.

20. Place the cable hook into the hole in the adjusting lever from the backing plate side. The adjusting levers are stamped with an **R** (right) or an **L** (left) to indicate their installation on the right or left hand brake assembly.

21. Position the hooked end of the adjuster spring in the primary shoe web and connect the loop end of the spring to the adjuster lever hole.

22. Pull the adjuster lever, cable and automatic adjuster spring down toward the rear to engage the pivot hook in the large hole in the secondary shoe web.

23. After installation, check the action of the adjuster by pulling the section of the cable between the cable guide and the adjusting lever toward the secondary shoe web far enough to lift the lever past a tooth on the adjusting screw starwheel. The lever should snap into position behind the next tooth, and release of the cable should cause the adjuster spring to return the lever to its original position. This return action of the lever will turn the adjusting screw starwheel one tooth. The lever should contact the adjusting screw starwheel one tooth above the center line of the adjusting screw.

If the automatic adjusting mechanism

does not perform properly, check the following:

1. Check the cable end fittings. The cable ends should fill or extend slightly beyond the crimped section of the fittings. If this is not the case, replace the cable.

2. Check the cable guide for damage. The cable groove should be parallel to the shoe web, and the body of the guide should lie flat against the web. Replace the cable guide if this is not so.

3. Check the pivot hook on the lever. The hook surfaces should be square with the body on the lever for proper pivoting. Repair or replace the hook as necessary.

4. Make sure that the adjusting screw starwheel is properly seated in the notch in the shoe web.

Wheel Cylinders

REMOVAL AND INSTALLATION

1. To remove the wheel cylinder, jack up the vehicle and remove the wheel, hub, and drum.

2. Disconnect the brake line at the fitting on the brake backing plate.

3. Remove the brake assemblies.

4. Remove the screws that hold the wheel cylinder to the backing plate and remove the wheel cylinder from the vehicle.

5. Installation is the reverse of the above removal procedure. After installation bleed and adjust the brakes as described earlier in this Chapter.

OVERHAUL

Wheel cylinder rebuilding kits are available for reconditioning wheel cylinders. The kits usually contain new cup springs, cylinder cups, and in some, new boots. The most important factor to keep in mind when rebuilding wheel cylinders is cleanliness. Keep all dirt away from the wheel cylinders when you are reassembling them.

1. Remove the wheel cylinder as described earlier.

2. Remove the rubber dust covers on the ends of the cylinder. Remove the pistons and piston cups and the spring. Remove the bleeder screw and make sure that it is not plugged.

3. Discard all of the parts that the rebuilding kit will replace.

4. Examine the inside of the cylinder. If it is severely rusted, pitted or scratched, then the cylinder must be replaced as the piston cups won't be able to seal against the walls of the cylinder.

5. Using a wheel cylinder hone or emery cloth and crocus cloth, polish the inside of the cylinder. The purpose of this is to put a new

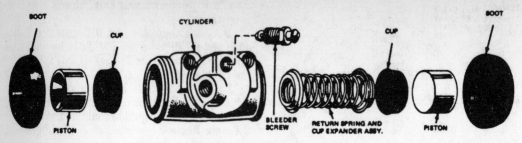

Rear wheel cylinder assembly

surface on the inside of the cylinder. Keep the inside of the cylinder coated with brake fluid while honing.

6. Wash out the cylinder with clean brake fluid after honing.

7. When reassembling the cylinder, dip all of the parts in clean brake fluid. Assemble the wheel cylinder in the reverse order of removal and disassembly.

PARKING BRAKE

Cable

ADJUSTMENT

Pre-Tension Procedure

NOTE: *This procedure is to be used when a new Tension Limiter has been installed.*

1. Depress the parking brake pedal.

2. Grip the Tension Limiter Bracket to prevent it from spinning and tighten the equalizer nut 2 1/2 in. (63.5mm) up the rod.

3. Check to make sure the cinch strap has slipped less than 1 3/8 in. (35mm) remaining.

Final Adjustment

NOTE: *This procedure is to be used to remove the slack from the system if a new Tension Limiter has not been installed.*

1. Make sure the brake drums are cold for correct adjustment.

2. Position the parking brake pedal to the fully depressed position.

3. Grip the threaded rod to prevent it from spinning and tighten the equalizer nut 6 full turns past its original position on the threaded rod.

4. Attach an appropriate cable tension gauge (Rotunda Model 21–0018 or equivalent) behind the equalizer assembly either toward the right or left rear drum assembly and meas-

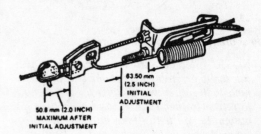

Pre-tension adjustment — parking brake assembly

ure cable tension. Cable tension should be 400–600 lbs. with the parking brake pedal fully in the last detent position. If tension is low, repeat Steps 2 and 3.

5. Release parking brake and check for rear wheel drag. The cables should be tight enough to provide full application of the rear brake shoes, when the parking brake lever or foot pedal is placed in the fully applied position, yet loose enough to ensure complete release of the brake shoes when the lever is in the released position.

NOTE: *The Tension Limiter will reset the parking brake tension any time the system is disconnected provided the distance between the bracket and the cinch strap hook is reduced during adjustment. When the cinch strap contacts the bracket, the system tension will increase significantly and over tensioning may result. If all available adjustment travel has been used, the tension limiter must be replaced.*

REMOVAL AND INSTALLATION

Equalizer-To-Control Cable

1. Raise the vehicle on a hoist and support on jackstands. Back off the equalizer nut and remove slug of front cable from the tension limiter.

2. Remove the parking brake cable from the bracket.

3. Remove the jackstands and lower the ve-

hicle. Remove the forward ball end of the parking brake cable from the control assembly clevis.

4. Remove the cable from the control assembly.

5. Using a fishing line wire leader or cord attached to the control lever end of the cable, remove the cable from the vehicle.

To install:

6. Transfer the fish wire or cord to the new cable. Position the cable in the vehicle, routing the cable through the dash panel. Remove the fish wire and secure the cable to the control.

7. Connect the forward ball end of the brake cable to the clevis of the control assembly. Raise the vehicle on a hoist.

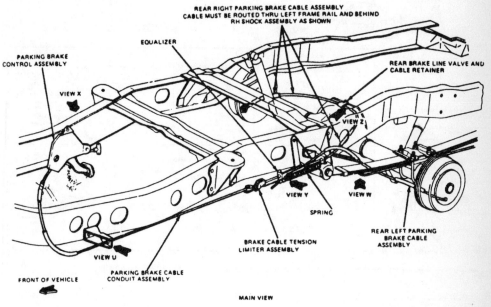

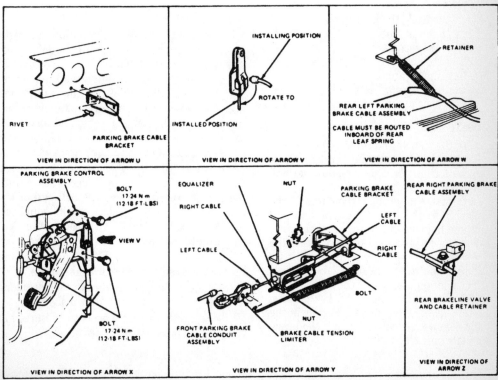

Parking brake system — Ranger models (Explorer models similar)

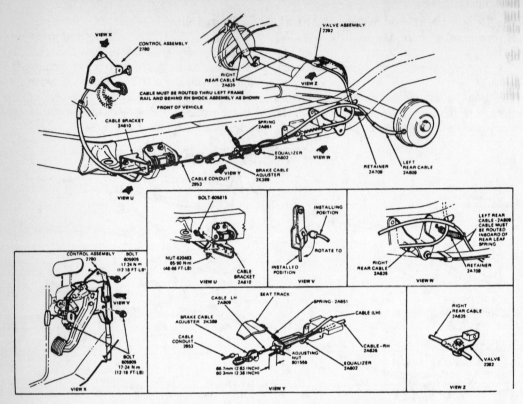

Parking brake system — Bronco II models (Explorer models similar)

8. Route the cable through the bracket.

9. Connect the slug of the cable to the Tension Limiter connector. Adjust the parking brake cable at the equalizer using the appropriate procedure shown above.

10. Rotate both rear wheels to be sure that the parking brakes are not dragging.

Equalizer-To-Rear Wheel Cables

1. Raise the vehicle and remove the hub cap wheel, Tension Limiter and brake drum. Remove the locknut on the threaded rod and disconnect the cable from the equalizer.

2. Compress the prongs that retain the cable housing to the frame bracket, and pull the cable and housing out of the bracket.

3. Working on the wheel side, compress the prongs on the cable retainer so they can pass through the hole in the brake backing plate. Draw the cable retainer out of the hole.

4. With the spring tension off the parking brake lever, lift the cable out of the slot in the lever, and remove the cable through the brake backing plate hole.

To install:

5. Route the right cable behind the right shock and through the hole in the left frame side rail. Route the left cable inboard of the leaf spring. Pull the cable through the brake backing plate until the end of the cable is inserted over the slot in the parking brake lever. Pull the excess slack from the cable and insert the cable housing into the brake backing plate access hole until the retainer prongs expand.

6. Insert the front of the cable housing through the frame crossmember bracket until the prong expands. Insert the ball end of the cable into the key hole slots on the equalizer, rotate the equalizer 90° and recouple the Tension Limiter threaded rod to the equalizer.

7. Install the rear brake drum, wheel, and hub cap, and adjust the rear brake shoes.

8. Adjust the parking brake tension using the appropriate procedure shown above.

9. Rotate both rear wheels to be sure that the parking brakes are not dragging.

REAR BRAKE DRUM

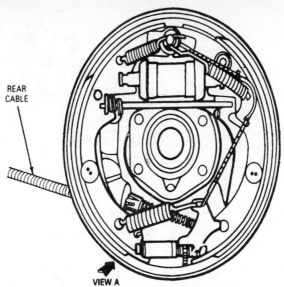

VIEW A

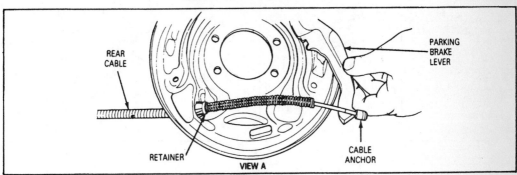

VIEW A

Parking brake cable installation

REAR ANTI-LOCK BRAKE SYSTEM (RABS)

Component Location

The RABS consists of the following components:

1. RABS module (1989–91) – located in the dash under the IP panel mount on a brace, center of panel area. The (RABS) module for 1987–88 model year is located behind an access cover in back of the driver's side door pillar.

2. Dual Solenoid Electro-Hydraulic Valve is located 5 in. (127mm) rearward of the No. 1 crossmember on the inboard side of the LH frame rail.

3. Speed Sensor and Excitor Ring – located in the rear differential housing.

4. Yellow REAR ANTI-LOCK Warning Light – located in the instrument cluster.

5. RABS Diagnostic Connector – located on the main wire bundle inside of cab under the dash, slightly rearward driver side.

6. Diode/Resistoe Element – located in the master cylinder fluid level sensor wiring harness on the left splash apron.

7. Sensor test Connector – located under the hood slightly rearward the washer bottle.

Computer (RABS) Module

REMOVAL AND INSTALLATION

The (RABS) module 1987–88 is located behind an access cover in back of the driver's side door pillar. On the 1989–91 model years start at service Step 2.

1. Remove the access cover for the module from the pillar behind the driver's seat if necessary.

2. Disconnect the wiring harness to the module.

3. Remove the retaining screws and remove the module.

REAR ANTI-LOCK BRAKE SYSTEM COMPONENT LOCATION

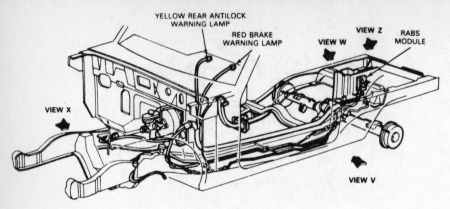

REAR ANTI-LOCK BRAKES – BRONCO II

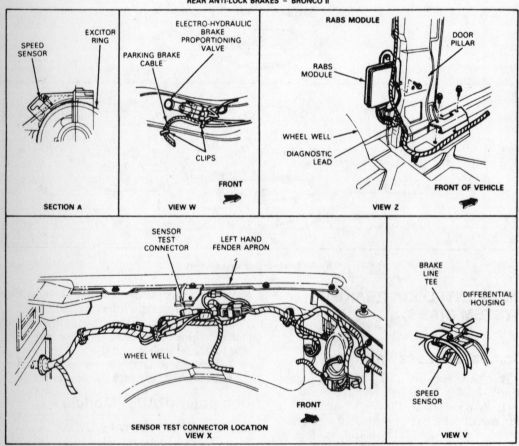

Rear anti-lock brake (RABS) system component locations 1987–88 year

To install:

4. Place the module in position against the door pillar. Install and tighten the retaining bolts.

5. Connect the wiring harness to the module.

6. Place the access cover in position.

7. Check the system for proper operation.

RABS Valve

REMOVAL AND INSTALLATION

The valve is located on the left frame rail above the rear axle.

1. Disconnect the brake lines from the valve and plug the lines.

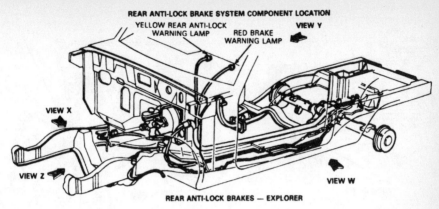

REAR ANTI-LOCK BRAKE SYSTEM COMPONENT LOCATION

YELLOW REAR ANTI-LOCK WARNING LAMP

RED BRAKE WARNING LAMP

VIEW Y

VIEW X

VIEW Z

VIEW W

REAR ANTI-LOCK BRAKES — EXPLORER

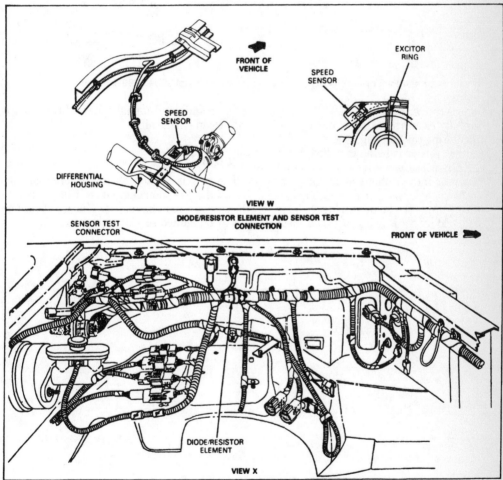

FRONT OF VEHICLE

SPEED SENSOR

EXCITOR RING

SPEED SENSOR

DIFFERENTIAL HOUSING

VIEW W

SENSOR TEST CONNECTOR

DIODE/RESISTOR ELEMENT AND SENSOR TEST CONNECTION

FRONT OF VEHICLE

DIODE/RESISTOR ELEMENT

VIEW X

Rear anti-lock brake (RABS) system component locations 1989–91 year

2. Disconnect the wiring harness at the valve.

3. Remove the 3 nuts retaining the valve to the frame rail and lift out the valve.

4. Installation is the reverse of removal. Don't overtighten the brake lines. Bleed the brakes.

RABS Sensor

REMOVAL AND INSTALLATION

The sensor is located on the rear axle housing.

1. Remove the sensor holddown bolt.

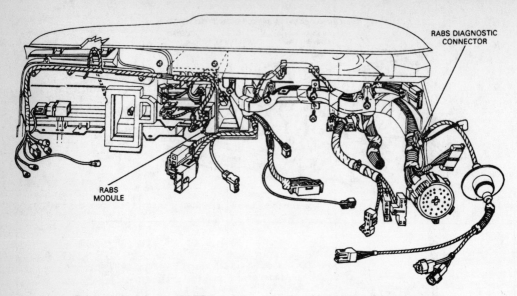

Rear anti-lock brake (RABS) module removal and installation 1989–91 year

2. Remove the sensor.

3. Carefully clean the axle surface to keep dirt from entering the housing.

4. If a new sensor is being installed, lubricate the O-ring with clean engine oil. Carefully push the sensor into the housing aligning the mounting flange hole with the threaded hole in the housing. Torque the holddown bolt to 30 ft. lbs.   If the old sensor is being installed, clean it thoroughly and install a new O-ring coated with clean engine oil.

Exciter Ring

The ring is located on the differential case inside the axle housing. Once it is pressed of the case it cannot be reused. This job should be left to a qualified service technician.

Body

10

EXTERIOR

Doors

REMOVAL AND INSTALLATION

1. If replacing the door with a stripped unit, remove all usable components from the old door.

2. If removing the rear door (Explorer), remove the scuff plate and center panel trim panel. Remove the upper and lower hinge access cover plate if equipped, and matchmark the hinge-to-body and hinge-to-door location.

Support the door either on jackstands or have somebody hold it for you.

3. Remove the lower hinge-to-door bolts.

4. Remove the upper hinge-to-door bolts and lift the door off the hinges.

5. If the hinges are being replaced, remove them from the door pillar.

To install:

6. If they were removed, install the hinges in the same position as before removal. Tighten the bolts finger tight.

7. Position the door on the hinges and install the bolts finger tight.

8. Install all previously removed hardware to the new door before adjustments are made.

9. Install the trim panel and scuff plate if they were removed.

10. Adjust the door and tighten all retaining bolts.

11. Install the hinge access cover plates.

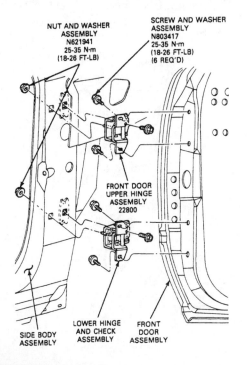

Front door hinge mounting — Explorer

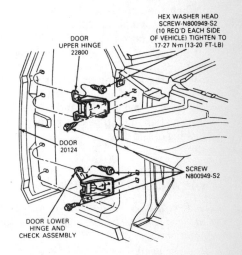

Door hinge mounting — Ranger and Bronco II

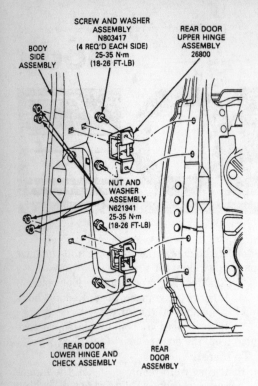

Rear door hinge mounting — Explorer

ADJUSTMENT

NOTE: *Loosen the hinge-to-door bolts for lateral adjustment only. Loosen the hinge-to-body bolts for both lateral and vertical adjustments.*

1. Determine which hinge bolts are to be loosened and back them out just enough to allow movement.

2. To move the door safely, use a padded pry bar. When the door is in the proper position, tighten the bolts to specification and check the door operation. There should be no binding or interference when the door is closed and opened.

3. Door closing adjustment can also be affected by the position of the lock striker plate. Loosen the striker plate bolts and move the striker plate just enough to permit proper closing and locking of the door.

Hood

REMOVAL AND INSTALLATION

NOTE: *It is highly recommended that you have at least one assistant helping during this operation.*

1. Open the hood.
3. Matchmark the hood-to-hinge position.
2. Have you're assistant(s) support the weight of the hood.

4. Remove the hood-to-hinge bolts and lift the hood off of the hinges.

5. Installation is the reverse of the removal. Loosely install the hood and align the matchmarks. Torque all bolts to 62–97 inch lbs.

ALIGNMENT

1. Open the hood and matchmark the hinge and latch positions.

2. Loosen the hinge-to-hood bolts just enough to allow movement of the hood.

3. Move the hood as required to obtain the proper fit and alignment between the hood and all adjoining body panels. Tighten the bolts to 62–97 inch lbs. when satisfactorily aligned.

4. Loosen the 2 latch attaching bolts.

5. Move the latch from side-to-side to align the latch with the striker. Torque the latch bolts.

6. Lubricate the latch and hinges and check the hood fit several times.

Liftgate

REMOVAL AND INSTALLATION

Bronco II and Explorer

NOTE: *On Explorer, the liftgate glass should not be open while the liftgate is open. Make sure the window is closed before opening the liftgate.*

1. Open the liftgate door.

2. Remove the upper rear center garnish molding.

3. Support the door in the open position

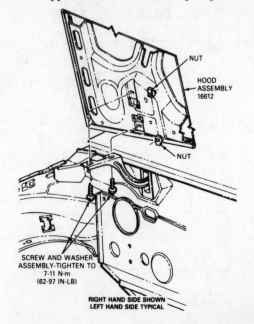

Hood, hinge and mounting hardware

and disconnect the liftgate gas cylinder assist rod assemblies.

4. Carefully move the headliner out of position and remove the hinge-to-header panel attaching nuts.

5. Remove the hinge-to-liftgate attaching bolts and remove the complete assembly.

To install:

6. Install the hinge to liftgate door and tighten the attaching bolts.

7. Install the hinge to roof header panel and tighten the nut.

8. Adjust the liftgate hinge as necessary.

9. Install the header and garnish molding.

Alignment

NOTE: *On Explorer, the liftgate glass should not be open while the liftgate is open.*

Make sure the window is closed before opening the liftgate.

The liftgate can be adjusted slightly in or out and side to side by loosening the hinge-to-header nut or bolt. Some up and down adjustment can be accomplished by loosening the hinge bolts on the liftgate and moving the gate up or down. The liftgate should be adjusted for even and parallel fit with adjoining panels.

Tailgate

REMOVAL AND INSTALLATION

Ranger

1. Remove the tailgate support strap at the pillar T-head pivot.

2. Lift off the tailgate at the right hinge.

3. Pull off the left hinge.

4. Transfer all necessary hardware to the new tailgate if necessary.

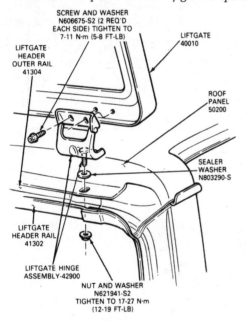

Liftgate and hinge assembly — Bronco II

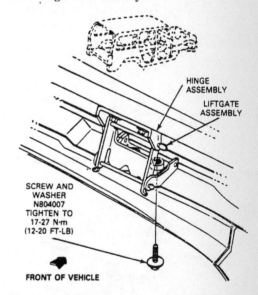

Liftgate and hinge assembly — Explorer

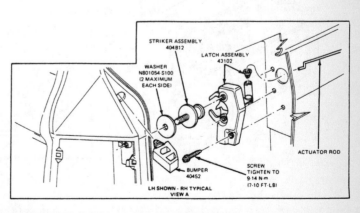

Liftgate striker and latch assembly — Bronco II

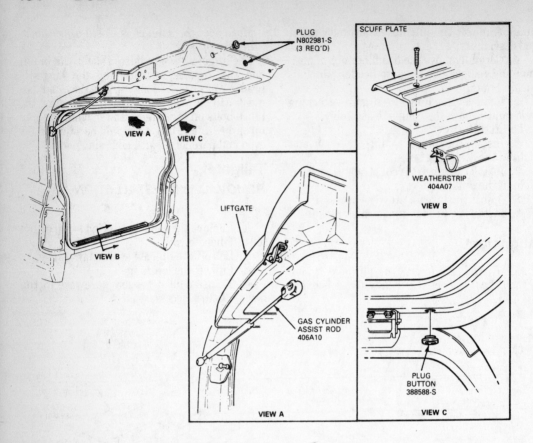

PLUG
N802981-S
(3 REQ'D)

SCUFF PLATE

LIFTGATE

GAS CYLINDER
ASSIST ROD
406A10

WEATHERSTRIP
404A07

VIEW B

PLUG
BUTTON
388588-S

VIEW A

VIEW C

VIEW A

VIEW C

VIEW B

Liftgate gas cylinder assist rods

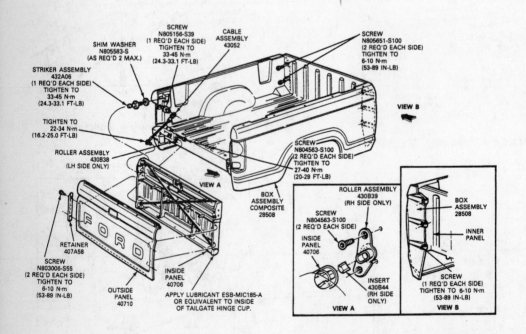

SHIM WASHER
N805583-S
(AS REQ'D 2 MAX.)

SCREW
N805156-S39
(1 REQ'D EACH SIDE)
TIGHTEN TO
33-45 N·m
(24.3-33.1 FT-LB)

CABLE
ASSEMBLY
43052

SCREW
N805651-S100
(2 REQ'D EACH SIDE)
TIGHTEN TO
6-10 N·m
(53-89 IN-LB)

STRIKER ASSEMBLY
432A06
(1 REQ'D EACH SIDE)
TIGHTEN TO
33-45 N·m
(24.3-33.1 FT-LB)

TIGHTEN TO
22-34 N·m
(16.2-25.0 FT-LB)

ROLLER ASSEMBLY
430B38
(LH SIDE ONLY)

VIEW A

VIEW B

SCREW
N804563-S100
(2 REQ'D EACH SIDE)
TIGHTEN TO
27-40 N·m
(20-29 FT-LB)

BOX
ASSEMBLY
COMPOSITE
28508

RETAINER
407A58

SCREW
N803006-S55
(2 REQ'D EACH SIDE)
TIGHTEN TO
6-10 N·m
(53-89 IN-LB)

OUTSIDE
PANEL
40710

INSIDE
PANEL
40706

APPLY LUBRICANT ESB-MIC185-A
OR EQUIVALENT TO INSIDE
OF TAILGATE HINGE CUP.

ROLLER ASSEMBLY
430B39
(RH SIDE ONLY)

SCREW
N804563-S100
(2 REQ'D EACH SIDE)

INSIDE
PANEL
40706

INSERT
430B44
(RH SIDE
ONLY)

VIEW A

BOX
ASSEMBLY
28508

INNER
PANEL

SCREW
(1 REQ'D EACH SIDE)
TIGHTEN TO 6-10 N·m
(53-89 IN-LB)

VIEW B

Tailgate and related hardware — Ranger with High Strength Composite Pickup Box

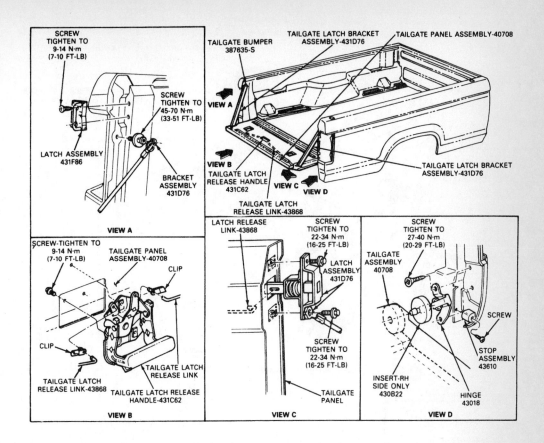

Tailgate and related hardware — Ranger

5. Installation is the reverse of removal.

Front and Rear Bumpers

REMOVAL AND INSTALLATION

1. Support the bumper. Disconnect electrical pigtails, if applicable.

2. Remove the nuts and bolts attaching the bumper brackets to the frame. Once the bumper is removed from the truck, remove the brackets from the bumper.

3. Remove the valance panel and rubstrip from the bumper as required.

4. Installation is the reverse of removal. Use a leveling tool to ensure a level installation before tightening the bolts.

5. Support the bumper and torque the bracket-to-frame bolts to specifications.

Outside Mirrors

REMOVAL AND INSTALLATION

1. On Explorer, the door panel must first be removed to gain access to the mounting nuts. Disconnect the harness connector if equipped with power mirrors.

2. Remove the mounting screws or nuts and lift off the mirror. Remove and discard the gasket.

3. When installing, make sure the gasket is properly positioned before tightening the screws.

4. If equipped with power mirror, plug in the electrical connector and test the operation of the power mirror before installing the door panel.

Antenna

REPLACEMENT

1. If the antenna cable plugs directly into the radio, pull it straight out of the set. Otherwise, disconnect the antenna lead-in cable from the cable assembly in-line connector above the glove box.

2. Working under the instrument panel, disengage the cable from its retainers.

NOTE: *On some models, it may be necessary to remove the instrument panel pad to get at the cable.*

3. Outside, unsnap the cap from the antenna base.

4. Remove the 3 screws and lift off the antenna, pulling the cable with it, carefully.

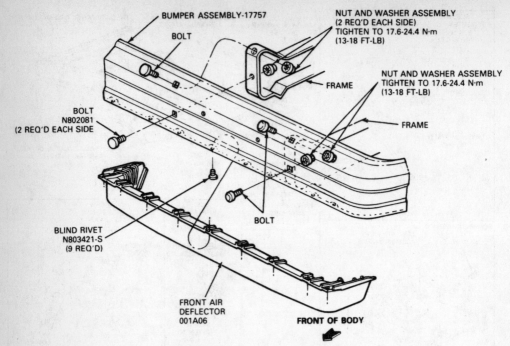

BUMPER ASSEMBLY-17757

BOLT

NUT AND WASHER ASSEMBLY
(2 REQ'D EACH SIDE)
TIGHTEN TO 17.6-24.4 N·m
(13-18 FT-LB)

FRAME

NUT AND WASHER ASSEMBLY
TIGHTEN TO 17.6-24.4 N·m
(13-18 FT-LB)

FRAME

BOLT
N802081
(2 REQ'D EACH SIDE)

BOLT

BLIND RIVET
N803421-S
(9 REQ'D)

FRONT AIR
DEFLECTOR
001A06

FRONT OF BODY

Front bumper assembly — Bronco II

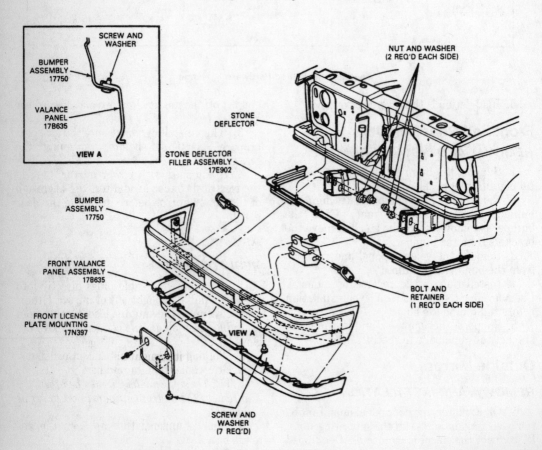

SCREW AND
WASHER

BUMPER
ASSEMBLY
17750

VALANCE
PANEL
17B635

VIEW A

NUT AND WASHER
(2 REQ'D EACH SIDE)

STONE
DEFLECTOR

STONE DEFLECTOR
FILLER ASSEMBLY
17E902

BUMPER
ASSEMBLY
17750

FRONT VALANCE
PANEL ASSEMBLY
17B635

FRONT LICENSE
PLATE MOUNTING
17N397

BOLT AND
RETAINER
(1 REQ'D EACH SIDE)

VIEW A

SCREW AND
WASHER
(7 REQ'D)

Front bumper assembly — Ranger and Explorer

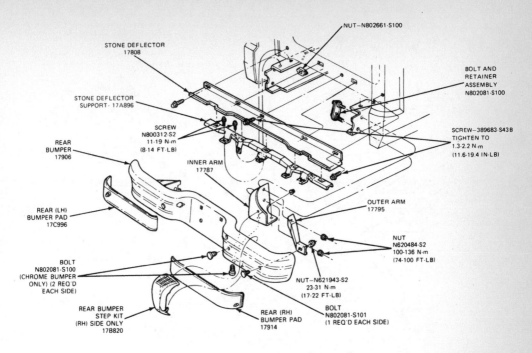

Rear bumper assembly — Bronco II

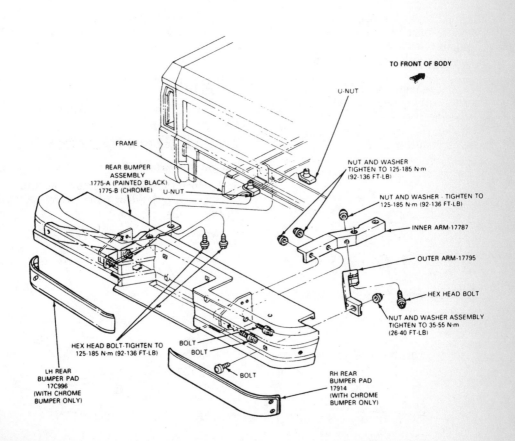

Rear bumper assembly — Ranger

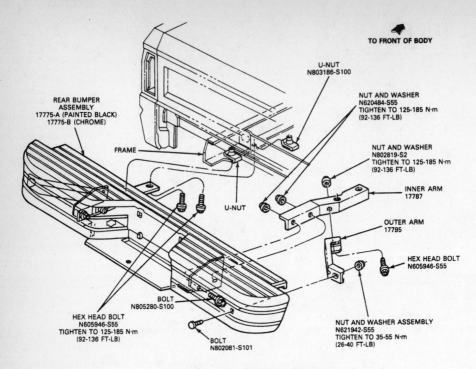

Rear bumper assembly — Explorer

5. Remove and discard the gasket.

To install:

6. Place the gasket in position on the cowl panel.

7. Insert the antenna cable through the hole and seat the antenna base on the cowl. Secure with the 3 screws.

8. Position the cap over the antenna base and snap it into place.

9. Route the cable in exactly the same position as before removal behind the instrument panel.

10. Connect the cable to the radio or in-line connector.

INTERIOR

Door Panels

REMOVAL AND INSTALLATION

Ranger and Bronco II

1. Open the window. Remove the armrest.

2. Remove the door handle screw and pull off the handle.

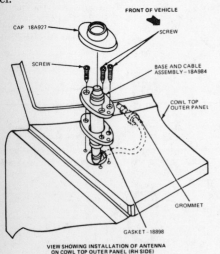

Antenna mounting on the cowl

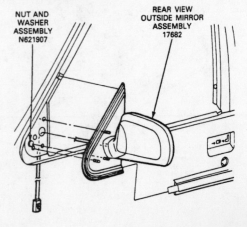

Outside mirror mounting — Explorer

3. If equipped with manual windows, remove the window regulator handle screw and pull off the handle. If equipped with power windows, remove the power window switch housing.

4. If equipped with manual door locks, remove the door lock control. If equipped with power door locks, remove the power door lock switch housing.

5. If equipped with electric outside rear view mirrors, remove the power mirror switch housing.

6. Using a flat wood spatula, insert it carefully behind the panel and slide it along to find the push-pins. When you encounter a pin, pry the pin outward. Do this until all the pins are out. NEVER PULL ON THE PANEL TO REMOVE THE PINS!

7. Installation is the reverse of removal.

Explorer

1. Open the window. Remove the 2 screws retaining the trim panel located above the door handle.

2. Remove the rim cup behind the door handle using a small prying tool. Retention nibs will flex for ease of removal.

3. If equipped with power accessories, use the notch at the lower end of the plate and pry the plate off. Remove the plate from the trim panel and pull the wiring harness from behind the panel. Disconnect the harness from the switches.

4. Using a flat wood spatula, insert it carefully behind the panel and slide it along to find the push-pins. When you encounter a pin, pry the pin outward. Do this until all the pins are out. NEVER PULL ON THE PANEL TO REMOVE THE PINS!

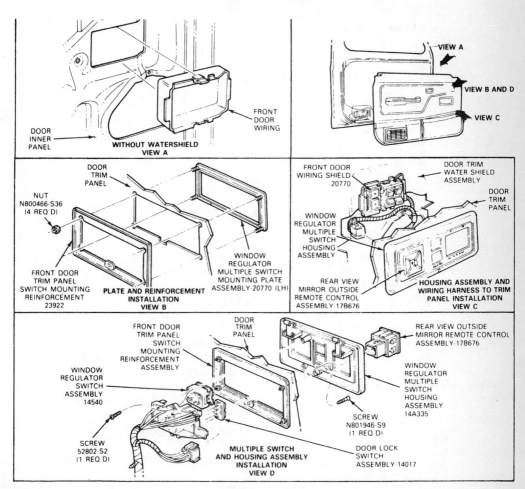

Door trim panel — Ranger and Bronco II

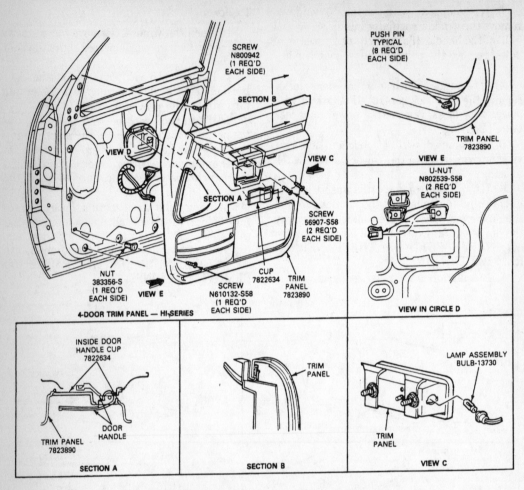

Front door trim panel — Explorer; Hi line shown

5. Lift slightly to disengage the panel from the flange at the top of the door.

6. Disconnect the door courtesy lamp and remove the panel completely. Replace any damaged or bent attaching clips.

7. Installation is the reverse of removal.

Door Locks

REMOVAL AND INSTALLATION

Door Latch

1. Remove the door trim panel and watershield.

2. Disconnect the rods from the handle and lock cylinder, and from the remote control assembly.

3. Remove the latch assembly attaching screws and remove the latch from the door.

4. Installation is the reverse of removal.

Door Lock Cylinder

1. Open the window.

2. Remove the trim panel and watershield.

3. Disconnect the actuating rod from the lock control link clip.

4. Slide the retainer away from the lock cylinder.

5. Remove the cylinder from the door.

6. Use a new gasket when installing to ensure a watertight fit.

7. Lubricate the cylinder with suitable oil recommended for this application.

Door Glass and Regulator

REMOVAL AND INSTALLATION

Glass

1. Remove the door trim panel and speaker if applicable.

2. Remove the screw from the division bar.

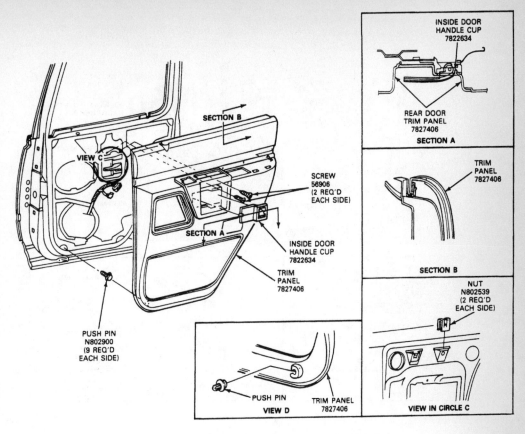

Rear door trim panel — Explorer; Hi line shown

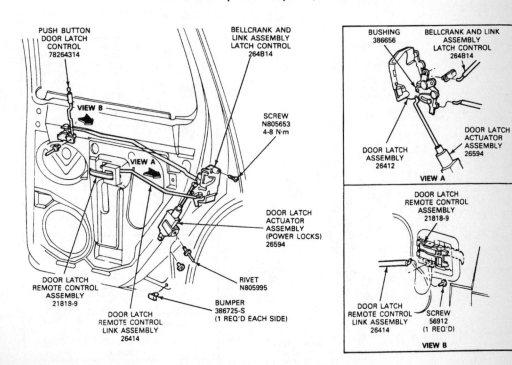

Rear door latch assembly — Explorer

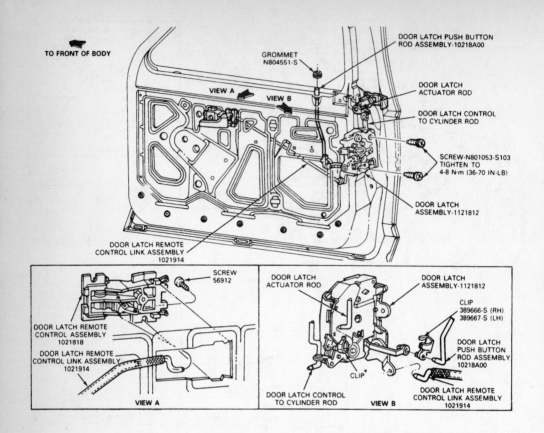

TO FRONT OF BODY

DOOR LATCH PUSH BUTTON
ROD ASSEMBLY-10218A00

GROMMET
N804551-S

VIEW A   VIEW B

DOOR LATCH
ACTUATOR ROD

DOOR LATCH CONTROL
TO CYLINDER ROD

SCREW-N801053-S103
TIGHTEN TO
4-8 N·m (36-70 IN-LB)

DOOR LATCH
ASSEMBLY-1121812

DOOR LATCH REMOTE
CONTROL LINK ASSEMBLY
1021914

SCREW
56912

DOOR LATCH
ACTUATOR ROD

DOOR LATCH
ASSEMBLY-1121812

CLIP
389666-S (RH)
389667-S (LH)

DOOR LATCH REMOTE
CONTROL ASSEMBLY
1021818

DOOR LATCH REMOTE
CONTROL LINK ASSEMBLY
1021914

DOOR LATCH
PUSH BUTTON
ROD ASSEMBLY
10218A00

CLIP

DOOR LATCH CONTROL
TO CYLINDER ROD

DOOR LATCH REMOTE
CONTROL LINK ASSEMBLY
1021914

VIEW A   VIEW B

Door latch assembly — Ranger and Bronco II

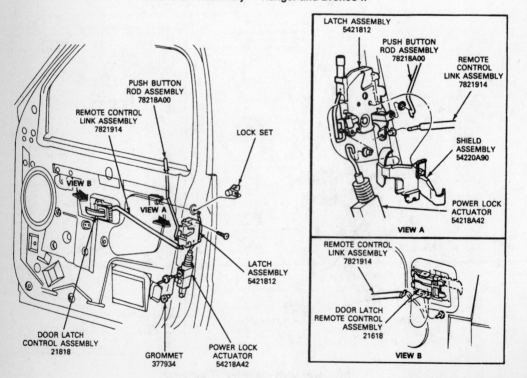

LATCH ASSEMBLY
5421812

PUSH BUTTON
ROD ASSEMBLY
78218A00

REMOTE
CONTROL
LINK ASSEMBLY
7821914

PUSH BUTTON
ROD ASSEMBLY
78218A00

REMOTE CONTROL
LINK ASSEMBLY
7821914

LOCK SET

SHIELD
ASSEMBLY
54220A90

POWER LOCK
ACTUATOR
54218A42

VIEW B

VIEW A

LATCH
ASSEMBLY
5421812

VIEW A

REMOTE CONTROL
LINK ASSEMBLY
7821914

DOOR LATCH
CONTROL ASSEMBLY
21818

GROMMET
377934

POWER LOCK
ACTUATOR
54218A42

DOOR LATCH
REMOTE CONTROL
ASSEMBLY
21618

VIEW B

Front door latch assembly — Explorer

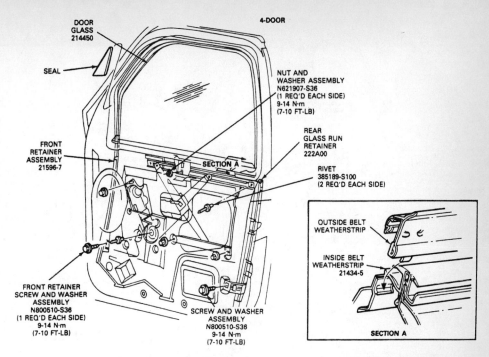

Rear door glass and regulator assembly — Explorer

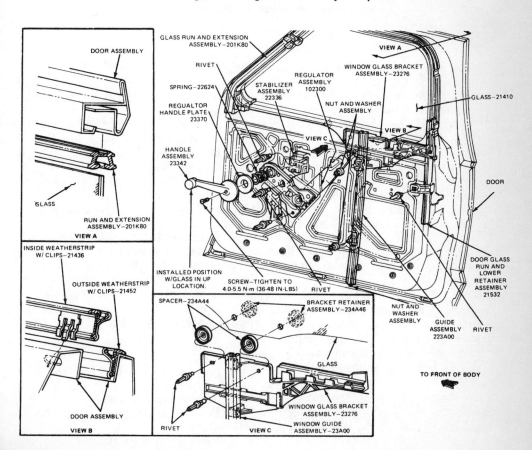

Door glass and regulator assembly — Ranger and Bronco II

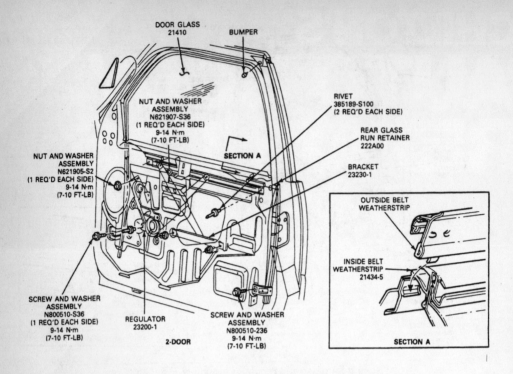

Front door glass and regulator assembly — Explorer

Remove the inside belt weatherstrip(s) if equipped.

3. Remove the 2 vent window attaching screws from the front edge of the door.

4. Lower the glass and pull the glass out of the run retainer near the vent window division bar, just enough to allow the removal of the vent window, if equipped.

5. Push the front edge of the glass downward and remove the rear glass run retainer from the door.

6. If equipped with retaining rivets, remove them carefully. Otherwise, remove the glass from the channel using Glass and Channel Removal Tool 2900, made by the Sommer and Mala Glass Machine Co. of Chicago, ILL., or its equivalent. Remove the glass through the belt opening if possible.

To install:

7. Install the glass spacer and retainer into the retention holes.

8. Install the glass into the door, position on the bracket and align the retaining holes.

9. Carefully install the retaining rivets or equivalent.

10. Raise the glass to the full closed position.

11. Install the rear glass run retainer and glass run. Install the inside belt weatherstrip(s).

12. Check for smooth operation before installing the trim panel.

Regulator

EXCEPT FRONT DOOR — EXPLORER

1. Remove the door trim panel. If equipped with power windows, disconnect the wire from the regulator

2. Support the glass in the full UP position or remove completely.

3. Remove the window guide and glass bracket if equipped.

4. Remove the center pins from the regulator attaching rivets.

5. Drill out the regulator attaching rivets using a $1/4$ in. (6mm) drill bit.

6. Disengage the regulator arm from the glass bracket and remove the regulator.

7. Installation is the reverse of removal. $1/4$ in.-20 $\times$ $1/2$ in. bolts and nuts may be used in place of the rivets to attach the regulator.

FRONT DOOR — EXPLORER

1. Remove the door trim panel and watershield.

2. Remove the inside door belt weatherstrip and glass stabilizer.

3. Remove the door glass.

4. Remove the 2 nuts attaching the equalizer bracket.

5. Remove the rivets attaching the regulator base plate to the door.

6. Remove the regulator and glass bracket

CHILTON'S
AUTO BODY REPAIR TIPS

**Tools and Materials • Step-by-Step Illustrated Procedures
How To Repair Dents, Scratches and Rust Holes
Spray Painting and Refinishing Tips**

With a little practice, basic body repair procedures can be mastered by any do-it-yourself mechanic. The step-by-step repairs shown here can be applied to almost any type of auto body repair.

TOOLS & MATERIALS

You may already have basic tools, such as hammers and electric drills. Other tools unique to body repair — body hammers, grinding attachments, sanding blocks, dent puller, half-round plastic file and plastic spreaders — are relatively inexpensive and can be obtained wherever auto parts or auto body repair parts are sold. Portable air compressors and paint spray guns can be purchased or rented.

Auto Body Repair Kits

The best and most often used products are available to the do-it-yourselfer in kit form, from major manufacturers of auto body repair products. The same manufacturers also merchandise the individual products for use by pros.

Kits are available to make a wide variety of repairs, including holes, dents and scratches and fiberglass, and offer the advantage of buying the materials you'll need for the job. There is little waste or chance of materials going bad from not being used. Many kits may also contain basic body-working tools such as body files, sanding blocks and spreaders. Check the contents of the kit before buying your tools.

BODY REPAIR TIPS

Safety

Many of the products associated with auto body repair and refinishing contain toxic chemicals. Read all labels before opening containers and store them in a safe place and manner.

• Wear eye protection (safety goggles) when using power tools or when performing any operation that involves the removal of any type of material.

• Wear lung protection (disposable mask or respirator) when grinding, sanding or painting.

Sanding

1 Sand off paint before using a dent puller. When using a non-adhesive sanding disc, cover the back of the disc with an overlapping layer or two of masking tape and trim the edges. The disc will last considerably longer.

2 Use the circular motion of the sanding disc to grind *into* the edge of the repair. Grinding or sanding away from the jagged edge will only tear the sandpaper.

3 Use the palm of your hand flat on the panel to detect high and low spots. Do not use your fingertips. Slide your hand slowly back and forth.

WORKING WITH BODY FILLER

Mixing The Filler

Cleanliness and proper mixing and application are extremely important. Use a clean piece of plastic or glass or a disposable artist's palette to mix body filler.

1 Allow plenty of time and follow directions. No useful purpose will be served by adding more hardener to make it cure (set-up) faster. Less hardener means more curing time, but the mixture dries harder; more hardener means less curing time but a softer mixture.

2 Both the hardener and the filler should be thoroughly kneaded or stirred before mixing. Hardener should be a solid paste and dispense like thin toothpaste. Body filler should be smooth, and free of lumps or thick spots.

Getting the proper amount of hardener in the filler is the trickiest part of preparing the filler. Use the same amount of hardener in cold or warm weather. For contour filler (thick coats), a bead of hardener twice the diameter of the filler is about right. There's about a 15% margin on either side, but, if in doubt use less hardener.

3 Mix the body filler and hardener by wiping across the mixing surface, picking the mixture up and wiping it again. Colder weather requires longer mixing times. Do not mix in a circular motion; this will trap air bubbles which will become holes in the cured filler.

Applying The Filler

1 For best results, filler should not be applied over 1/4" thick.

Apply the filler in several coats. Build it up to above the level of the repair surface so that it can be sanded or grated down.

The first coat of filler must be pressed on with a firm wiping motion.

Apply the filler in one direction only. Working the filler back and forth will either pull it off the metal or trap air bubbles.

REPAIRING DENTS

Before you start, take a few minutes to study the damaged area. Try to visualize the shape of the panel before it was damaged. If the damage is on the left fender, look at the right fender and use it as a guide. If there is access to the panel from behind, you can reshape it with a body hammer. If not, you'll have to use a dent puller. Go slowly and work the metal a little at a time. Get the panel as straight as possible before applying filler.

1 This dent is typical of one that can be pulled out or hammered out from behind. Remove the headlight cover, headlight assembly and turn signal housing.

2 Drill a series of holes ½ the size of the end of the dent puller along the stress line. Make some trial pulls and assess the results. If necessary, drill more holes and try again. Do not hurry.

3 If possible, use a body hammer and block to shape the metal back to its original contours. Get the metal back as close to its original shape as possible. Don't depend on body filler to fill dents.

4 Using an 80-grit grinding disc on an electric drill, grind the paint from the surrounding area down to bare metal. Use a new grinding pad to prevent heat buildup that will warp metal.

5 The area should look like this when you're finished grinding. Knock the drill holes in and tape over small openings to keep plastic filler out.

6 Mix the body filler (see Body Repair Tips). Spread the body filler evenly over the entire area (see Body Repair Tips). Be sure to cover the area completely.

7 Let the body filler dry until the surface can just be scratched with your fingernail. Knock the high spots from the body filler with a body file ("Cheese-grater"). Check frequently with the palm of your hand for high and low spots.

8 Check to be sure that trim pieces that will be installed later will fit exactly. Sand the area with 40-grit paper.

9 If you wind up with low spots, you may have to apply another layer of filler.

10 Knock the high spots off with 40-grit paper. When you are satisfied with the contours of the repair, apply a thin coat of filler to cover pin holes and scratches.

11 Block sand the area with 40-grit paper to a smooth finish. Pay particular attention to body lines and ridges that must be well-defined.

12 Sand the area with 400 paper and then finish with a scuff pad. The finished repair is ready for priming and painting (see Painting Tips).

Materials and photos courtesy of Ritt Jones Auto Body, Prospect Park, PA.

REPAIRING RUST HOLES

There are many ways to repair rust holes. The fiberglass cloth kit shown here is one of the most cost efficient for the owner because it provides a strong repair that resists cracking and moisture and is relatively easy to use. It can be used on large and small holes (with or without backing) and can be applied over contoured areas. Remember, however, that short of replacing an entire panel, no repair is a guarantee that the rust will not return.

1 Remove any trim that will be in the way. Clean away all loose debris. Cut away all the rusted metal. But be sure to leave enough metal to retain the contour or body shape.

2 Grind away all traces of rust with a 24-grit grinding disc. Be sure to grind back 3-4 inches from the edge of the hole down to bare metal and be sure all traces of paint, primer and rust are removed.

3 Block sand the area with 80 or 100 grit sandpaper to get a clear, shiny surface and feathered paint edge. Tap the edges of the hole inward with a ball peen hammer.

4 If you are going to use release film, cut a piece about 2-3″ larger than the area you have sanded. Place the film over the repair and mark the sanded area on the film. Avoid any unnecessary wrinkling of the film.

5 Cut 2 pieces of fiberglass matte to match the shape of the repair. One piece should be about 1″ smaller than the sanded area and the second piece should be 1″ smaller than the first. Mix enough filler and hardener to saturate the fiberglass material (see Body Repair Tips).

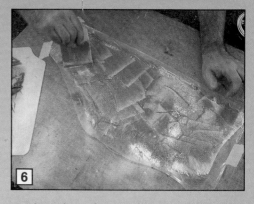

6 Lay the release sheet on a flat surface and spread an even layer of filler, large enough to cover the repair. Lay the smaller piece of fiberglass cloth in the center of the sheet and spread another layer of filler over the fiberglass cloth. Repeat the operation for the larger piece of cloth.

7 Place the repair material over the repair area, with the release film facing outward. Use a spreader and work from the center outward to smooth the material, following the body contours. Be sure to remove all air bubbles.

8 Wait until the repair has dried tack-free and peel off the release sheet. The ideal working temperature is 60°-90° F. Cooler or warmer temperatures or high humidity may require additional curing time. Wait longer, if in doubt.

9 Sand and feather-edge the entire area. The initial sanding can be done with a sanding disc on an electric drill if care is used. Finish the sanding with a block sander. Low spots can be filled with body filler; this may require several applications.

10 When the filler can just be scratched with a fingernail, knock the high spots down with a body file and smooth the entire area with 80-grit. Feather the filled areas into the surrounding areas.

11 When the area is sanded smooth, mix some topcoat and hardener and apply it directly with a spreader. This will give a smooth finish and prevent the glass matte from showing through the paint.

12 Block sand the topcoat smooth with finishing sandpaper (200 grit), and 400 grit. The repair is ready for masking, priming and painting (see Painting Tips).

Materials and photos courtesy Marson Corporation, Chelsea, Massachusetts

PAINTING TIPS

Preparation

1 SANDING — Use a 400 or 600 grit wet or dry sandpaper. Wet-sand the area with a 1/4 sheet of sandpaper soaked in clean water. Keep the paper wet while sanding. Sand the area until the repaired area tapers into the original finish.

2 CLEANING — Wash the area to be painted thoroughly with water and a clean rag. Rinse it thoroughly and wipe the surface dry until you're sure it's completely free of dirt, dust, fingerprints, wax, detergent or other foreign matter.

3 MASKING — Protect any areas you don't want to overspray by covering them with masking tape and newspaper. Be careful not get fingerprints on the area to be painted.

4 PRIMING — All exposed metal should be primed before painting. Primer protects the metal and provides an excellent surface for paint adhesion. When the primer is dry, wet-sand the area again with 600 grit wet-sandpaper. Clean the area again after sanding.

Painting Techniques

P aint applied from either a spray gun or a spray can (for small areas) will provide good results. Experiment on an old piece of metal to get the right combination before you begin painting.

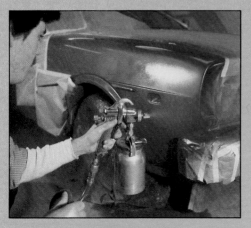

SPRAYING VISCOSITY (SPRAY GUN ONLY) — Paint should be thinned to spraying viscosity according to the directions on the can. Use only the recommended thinner or reducer and the same amount of reduction regardless of temperature.

AIR PRESSURE (SPRAY GUN ONLY) — This is extremely important. Be sure you are using the proper recommended pressure.

TEMPERATURE — The surface to be painted should be approximately the same temperature as the surrounding air. Applying warm paint to a cold surface, or vice versa, will completely upset the paint characteristics.

THICKNESS — Spray with smooth strokes. In general, the thicker the coat of paint, the longer the drying time. Apply several thin coats about 30 seconds apart. The paint should remain wet long enough to flow out and no longer; heavier coats will only produce sags or wrinkles. Spray a light (fog) coat, followed by heavier color coats.

DISTANCE — The ideal spraying distance is 8"-12" from the gun or can to the surface. Shorter distances will produce ripples, while greater distances will result in orange peel, dry film and poor color match and loss of material due to overspray.

OVERLAPPING — The gun or can should be kept at right angles to the surface at all times. Work to a wet edge at an even speed, using a 50% overlap and direct the center of the spray at the lower or nearest edge of the previous stroke.

RUBBING OUT (BLENDING) FRESH PAINT — Let the paint dry thoroughly. Runs or imperfections can be sanded out, primed and repainted.

Don't be in too big a hurry to remove the masking. This only produces paint ridges. When the finish has dried for at least a week, apply a small amount of fine grade rubbing compound with a clean, wet cloth. Use lots of water and blend the new paint with the surrounding area.

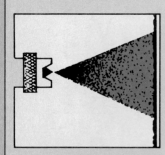

WRONG

Thin coat. Stroke too fast, not enough overlap, gun too far away.

CORRECT

Medium coat. Proper distance, good stroke, proper overlap.

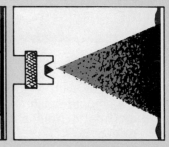

WRONG

Heavy coat. Stroke too slow, too much overlap, gun too close.

as an assembly from the door and transfer to a workbench.

7. Carefully bend the tab flat in order to remove the air slides from the glass bracket C-channel.

8. Install new regulator arm plastic guides into the C-channel and bend the tab back 90°. If the tab is broken or cracked, replace the glass bracket assembly. Make sure the rubber bumper is installed properly on the new glass bracket, if applicable.

CAUTION: *If the regulator counterbalance spring is to be removed, make sure the regulator arms are in a fixed position prior to removal. This will prevent possible injury when the C-spring unwinds.*

To install:

9. Assemble the glass bracket and regulator assembly.

10. Install the assembly in the door. Set the regulator base plate to the door using the base plate locator tab as a guide.

11. Attach the regulator to the door using new rivets. $1/4$ in.-20 × $1/2$ in. bolts and nuts may be used in place of the rivets to attach the regulator.

12. Install the equalizer bracket, door belt weatherstrip and glass stabilizer.

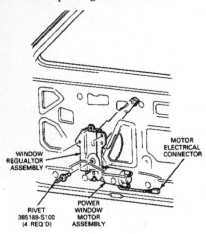

Power window motor and regulator assembly — Ranger and Bronco II

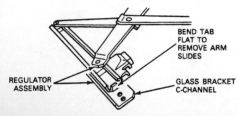

Regulator assembly — Explorer front door

13. Install the glass and check for smooth operation before installing the door trim panel.

Electric Window Motor

REMOVAL AND INSTALLATION

Ranger and Bronco II

1. Disconnect the negative battery cable.

2. Open the window. Remove the trim panel and watershield and support the window.

3. Disconnect the power window motor connector.

4. There may be a drill dimple in the door panel, opposite the concealed motor retaining bolt. Drill out the dimple to gain access to the bolt. Be careful to avoid damage to the wires. Remove the motor mounting bolts and remove the motor and regulator assembly.

5. Separate the motor and drive from the regulator on a workbench.

6. Installation is the reverse of removal.

7. Check for smooth operation before installing the trim panel.

Explorer

1. Raise the window fully if possible. If not, you will have to support the window during this procedure. Disconnect the battery ground.

2. Remove the door trim panel.

3. Disconnect the window motor wiring harness.

4. There may be a drill dimple in the door panel, opposite the concealed motor retaining bolt. Drill out the dimple to gain access to the bolt. Be careful to avoid damage to the wires.

5. Remove the motor mounting bolts (front door) or rivets(rear door).

6. Push the motor towards the outside of the door to disengage it from the gears. You'll have to support the window glass once the motor is disengaged.

7. Remove the motor from the door.

8. Installation is the reverse of removal. To avoid rusting in the drilled areas, prime and paint the exposed metal, or, cover the holes with waterproof body tape. Make sure that the motor works properly before installing the trim panel.

Windshield Glass and Bronco II Side Body Windows

This job requires a high level of skill, a number of special tools, and must be performed to Federal Motor Vehicle Safety Standards. It is highly recommended that you have a professional shop replace your windshield or window.

Stationary Glass

REMOVAL AND INSTALLATION

Fixed Side Window

RANGER SUPER CAB AND EXPLORER

1. Remove the interior trim around the window.

2. Remove the nuts from inside window assembly and remove the molding.

3. Remove the glass by pushing on it with enough force to separate the butyl seal.

4. Clean all traces of the original seal from the window opening and repair the sheet metal as required.

   To install:

5. If the replacement window is not complete with sealer tape, then apply a continuous strip of $\frac{5}{16} \times \frac{5}{16}$ in. (8mm × 8mm) Foam Core Butyl Tape, or equivalent, to the back of the window. The ends must meet at the bottom and overlap 1–2 in. (25–50mm).

6. Press the window in place with just enough force to seat the window firmly into the sealing material.

7. Install the retaining nuts.

8. Leak test the installation. If it is satisfactory, install the interior trim.

Stationary or Sliding Back Window

RANGER

1. From inside the cab, pull down the weatherstrip and push the back window and weatherstrip out of the window opening from inside the cab.

2. If reusing the window, remove the weatherstrip from the window.

3. If equipped with a sliding window, the window may be removed separately if necessary:

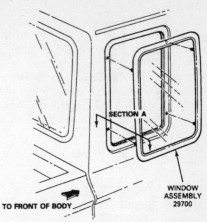

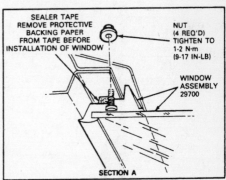

Fixed side window assembly — Ranger Super Cab

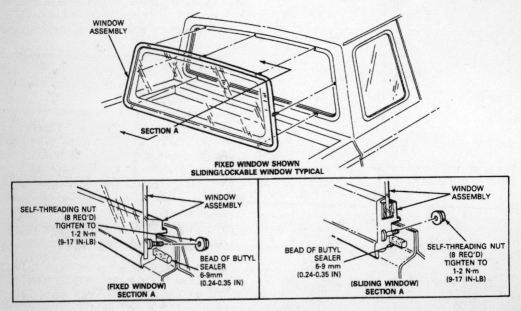

Back window assembly — Ranger Super Cab

a. Open the window and remove the screw retaining each division bar. Also, remove the anchor plate from the track.

b. Spread the window frame and work the movable glass out of its track. Then remove it from its frame.

c. Remove the division bar if necessary, and separate the rear window from the frame.

4. Thoroughly clean the opening in the back of the truck.

To install:

5. Assemble the sliding window to the back window if necessary. Lubricate all seals to ease assembly.

6. Install the outside molding if equipped. Position the weatherstrip to the back window glass.

7. Install a draw cord all around the weatherstrip in the flange crevice, allowing the cord to overlap at the bottom center of the glass. Coat the weatherstrip mounting surface with an appropriate Rubber Lubricant.

8. Position the glass and weatherstrip to the window opening. With the aid of an assistant, apply hand pressure from outside the cab and pull (from inside) the weatherstrip lip over the window opening flange with the draw cord.

9. Pull the weatherstrip over the lower flange, pulling one end of the cord at a time. Then pull the weatherstrip over the side flanges and upper flange.

10. Clean the glass and area around the window to remove all excess sealer.

11. Leak test the installation.

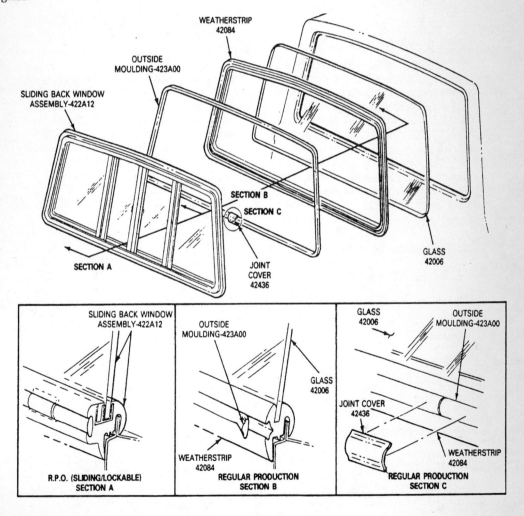

Back window assembly — Ranger

RANGER SUPER CAB

1. Remove the interior trim around the back window.

2. Remove the 8 self-threading nuts from inside the window.

3. Remove the glass by pushing on it with enough force to separate the butyl seal.

4. Clean all traces of the original seal from the window opening and repair the sheet metal as required.

To install:

5. Apply new Liquid Butyl around the perimeter of the body recess.

6. Press the window in place with just enough force to seat the window firmly into the sealing material.

7. Install the self-threading nuts.

8. Leak test the installation. If it is satisfactory, install the interior trim.

Inside Rear View Mirror

The mirror is held in place with a single setscrew. Loosen the screw and lift the mirror off. Don't forget to unplug the electrical connector if the truck has an electric Day/Night mirror.

Repair kits for damaged mirrors are available and most auto parts stores. The most important part of the repair is the beginning. Mark the outside of the windshield to locate the pad, then scrape the old adhesive off with a razor blade. Clean the remaining adhesive off with chlorine-based window cleaner (not petroleum-based solvent) as thoroughly as possible.

Follow the manufacturers instructions exactly to complete the repair..

Seats

REMOVAL AND INSTALLATION

Bench Seat

1. On the right side, remove the seat track insulator.

2. Remove 4 seat track-to-floor retaining screws (2 each side) and lift the seat and track assembly from vehicle.

3. To remove the tracks from the seat, place the seat upside-down on a clean bench.

4. Disconnect the track latch tie rod assembly from latch lever and hook in the center of the cushion assembly.

5. Remove 4 track-to-seat cushion retaining screws (2 each side) and remove the tracks from the cushion assembly.

To install:

6. Position the track to the cushion assembly. Install the 4 track-to-seat retaining screws and tighten.

7. Connect the track latch tie rod assembly to the latch lever and hook in center of cushion.

8. Position the seat and track assembly in the vehicle.

9. Install the 4 seat track-to-floor retaining screws and tighten to specification.

10. On the right side, install the seat track insulator.

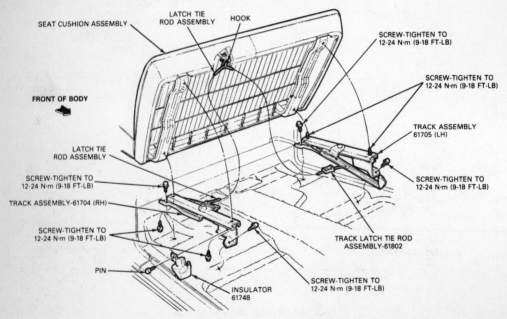

Bench seat and track — Ranger

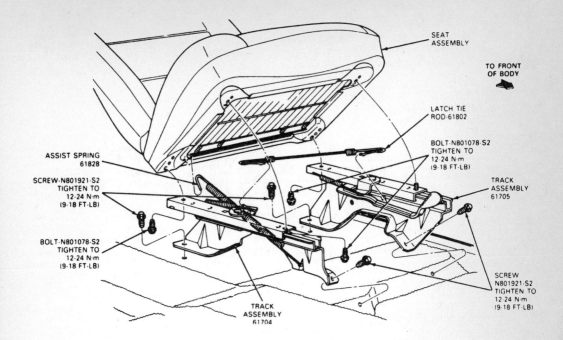

Bucket seat and track — Bronco II

Bucket and 60/40 Seats

1. Remove the seat track insulator (Ranger passenger seat only).

2. Remove the 4 seat track-to-floorpan screws (2 each side) and lift the seat and track assembly from the vehicle.

3. To remove the seat tracks from the seat cushion, position the seat upside down on a clean bench.

4. Disconnect the latch tie rod assembly and assist spring from the tracks.

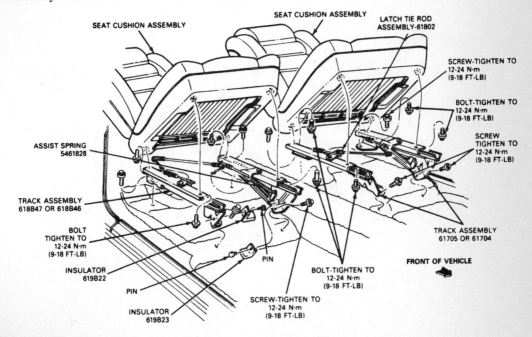

Bucket seats and tracks — Ranger

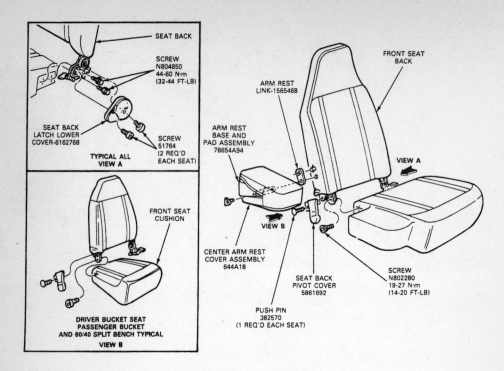

60/40 split seat — Explorer

5. Remove 4 track-to-seat cushion screws (2 each side) from the track assemblies. Remove the tracks from seat cushion.

To install:

6. Position the tracks to the seat cushion. Install the 4 track-to-seat cushion screws (2 each side) and tighten.

7. Connect the latch tie rod assembly and assist spring to the tracks.

8. Position the seat and track assembly in the vehicle.

9. Install 4 track-to-floorpan screws and tighten to specification.

10. Install the seat track insulators (Ranger passenger seat only).

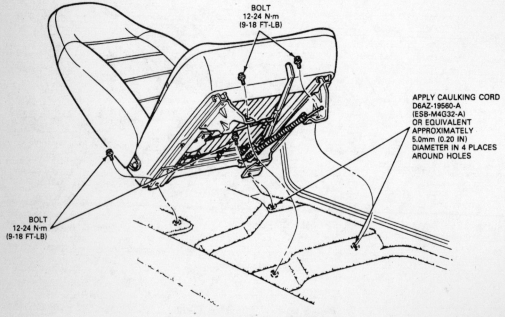

Bucket seat and track — Explorer

1":254mm
TAX
10.16mm
Liter
Parts
Overhaul

General Conversion Table

Multiply By	To Convert	To	
		LENGTH	
2.54	Inches	Centimeters	.3937
25.4	Inches	Millimeters	.03937
30.48	Feet	Centimeters	.0328
.304	Feet	Meters	3.28
.914	Yards	Meters	1.094
1.609	Miles	Kilometers	.621
		VOLUME	
.473	Pints	Liters	2.11
.946	Quarts	Liters	1.06
3.785	Gallons	Liters	.264
.164	Cubic inches	Liters	61.02
16.39	Cubic inches	Cubic cms.	.061
28.32	Cubic feet	Liters	.0353
		MASS (Weight)	
28.35	Ounces	Grams	.035
.4536	Pounds	Kilograms	2.20
—	To obtain	From	Multiply by

Multiply By	To Convert	To	
		AREA	
6.45	Square inches	Square cms.	.155
.836	Square yds.	Square meters	1.196
		FORCE	
4.448	Pounds	Newtons	.225
.138	Ft. lbs.	Kilogram/meters	7.23
1.356	Ft. lbs.	Newton-meters	.737
.113	In. lbs.	Newton-meters	8.844
		PRESSURE	
.068	Psi	Atmospheres	14.7
6.89	Psi	Kilopascals	.145
		OTHER	
1.104	Horsepower (DIN)	Horsepower (SAE)	.9861
.746	Horsepower (SAE)	Kilowatts (KW)	1.34
1.609	Mph	Km/h	.621
.425	Mpg	Km/L	2.35
—	To obtain	From	Multiply by

Tap Drill Sizes

National Coarse or U.S.S.

Screw & Tap Size	Threads Per Inch	Use Drill Number
No. 5	40	39
No. 6	32	36
No. 8	32	29
No. 10	24	25
No. 12	24	17
1/4	20	8
5/16	18	F
3/8	16	5/16
7/16	14	U
1/2	13	27/64
9/16	12	31/64
5/8	11	17/32
3/4	10	21/32
7/8	9	49/64

National Coarse or U.S.S.

Screw & Tap Size	Threads Per Inch	Use Drill Number
1	8	7/8
1 1/8	7	63/64
1 1/4	7	1 7/64
1 1/2	6	1 11/32

National Fine or S.A.E.

Screw & Tap Size	Threads Per Inch	Use Drill Number
No. 5	44	37
No. 6	40	33
No. 8	36	29
No. 10	32	21

National Fine or S.A.E.

Screw & Tap Size	Threads Per Inch	Use Drill Number
No. 12	28	15
1/4	28	3
6/16	24	1
3/8	28	Q
7/16	20	W
1/2	20	29/64
9/16	18	33/64
5/8	18	37/64
3/4	16	11/16
7/8	14	13/16
1 1/8	12	1 3/64
1 1/4	12	1 11/64
1 1/2	12	1 27/64

Drill Sizes In Decimal Equivalents

Inch	Decimal	Wire	mm
1/64	.0156		.39
	.0157		.4
	.0160	78	
	.0165		.42
	.0173		.44
	.0177		.45
	.0180	77	
	.0181		.46
	.0189		.48
	.0197		.5
	.0200	76	
	.0210	75	
	.0217		.55
	.0225	74	
	.0236		.6
	.0240	73	
	.0250	72	
	.0256		.65
	.0260	71	
	.0276		.7
	.0280	70	
	.0292	69	
	.0295		.75
	.0310	68	
1/32	.0312		.79
	.0315		.8
	.0320	67	
	.0330	66	
	.0335		.85
	.0350	65	
	.0354		.9
	.0360	64	
	.0370	63	
	.0374		.95
	.0380	62	
	.0390	61	
	.0394		1.0
	.0400	60	
	.0410	59	
	.0413		1.05
	.0420	58	
	.0430	57	
	.0433		1.1
	.0453		1.15
	.0465	56	
3/64	.0469		1.19
	.0472		1.2
	.0492		1.25
	.0512		1.3
	.0520	55	
	.0531		1.35
	.0550	54	
	.0551		1.4
	.0571		1.45
	.0591		1.5
	.0595	53	
	.0610		1.55
1/16	.0625		1.59
	.0630		1.6
	.0635	52	
	.0650		1.65
	.0669		1.7
	.0670	51	
	.0689		1.75
	.0700	50	
	.0709		1.8
	.0728		1.85

Inch	Decimal	Wire	mm
	.0730	49	
	.0748		1.9
	.0760	48	
	.0768		1.95
5/64	.0781		1.98
	.0785	47	
	.0787		2.0
	.0807		2.05
	.0810	46	
	.0820	45	
	.0827		2.1
	.0846		2.15
	.0860	44	
	.0866		2.2
	.0886		2.25
	.0890	43	
	.0906		2.3
	.0925		2.35
	.0935	42	
3/32	.0938		2.38
	.0945		2.4
	.0960	41	
	.0965		2.45
	.0980	40	
	.0981		2.5
	.0995	39	
	.1015	38	
	.1024		2.6
	.1040	37	
	.1063		2.7
	.1065	36	
	.1083		2.75
7/64	.1094		2.77
	.1100	35	
	.1102		2.8
	.1110	34	
	.1130	33	
	.1142		2.9
	.1160	32	
	.1181		3.0
	.1200	31	
	.1220		3.1
1/8	.1250		3.17
	.1260		3.2
	.1280		3.25
	.1285	30	
	.1299		3.3
	.1339		3.4
	.1360	29	
	.1378		3.5
	.1405	28	
9/64	.1406		3.57
	.1417		3.6
	.1440	27	
	.1457		3.7
	.1470	26	
	.1476		3.75
	.1495	25	
	.1496		3.8
	.1520	24	
	.1535		3.9
	.1540	23	
5/32	.1562		3.96
	.1570	22	
	.1575		4.0
	.1590	21	
	.1610	20	

Inch	Decimal	Wire & Letter	mm
	.1614		4.1
	.1654		4.2
	.1660	19	
	.1673		4.25
	.1693		4.3
	.1695	18	
11/64	.1719		4.36
	.1730	17	
	.1732		4.4
	.1770	16	
	.1772		4.5
	.1800	15	
	.1811		4.6
	.1820	14	
	.1850	13	
	.1850		4.7
	.1870		4.75
3/16	.1875		4.76
	.1890	12	
	.1890		4.8
	.1910	11	
	.1929		4.9
	.1935	10	
	.1960	9	
	.1969		5.0
	.1990	8	
	.2008		5.1
	.2010	7	
13/64	.2031		5.16
	.2040	6	
	.2047		5.2
	.2055	5	
	.2067		5.25
	.2087		5.3
	.2090	4	
	.2126		5.4
	.2130	3	
	.2165		5.5
7/32	.2188		5.55
	.2205		5.6
	.2210	2	
	.2244		5.7
	.2264		5.75
	.2280	1	
	.2283		5.8
	.2323		5.9
	.2340	A	
15/64	.2344		5.95
	.2362		6.0
	.2380	B	
	.2402		6.1
	.2420	C	
	.2441		6.2
	.2460	D	
	.2461		6.25
	.2480		6.3
1/4	.2500	E	6.35
	.2520		6.
	.2559		6.5
	.2570	F	
	.2598		6.6
	.2610	G	
	.2638		6.7
17/64	.2656		6.74
	.2657		6.75
	.2660	H	
	.2677		6.8

Inch	Decimal	Letter	mm
	.2717		6.9
	.2720	I	
	.2756		7.0
	.2770	J	
	.2795		7.1
	.2810	K	
9/32	.2812		7.14
	.2835		7.2
	.2854		7.25
	.2874		7.3
	.2900	L	
	.2913		7.4
	.2950	M	
	.2953		7.5
19/64	.2969		7.54
	.2992		7.6
	.3020	N	
	.3031		7.7
	.3051		7.75
	.3071		7.8
	.3110		7.9
	.3125		7.93
5/16	.3150		8.0
	.3160	O	
	.3189		8.1
	.3228		8.2
	.3230	P	
	.3248		8.25
	.3268		8.3
21/64	.3281		8.33
	.3307		8.4
	.3320	Q	
	.3346		8.5
	.3386		8.6
	.3390	R	
	.3425		8.7
11/32	.3438		8.73
	.3445		8.75
	.3465		8.8
	.3480	S	
	.3504		8.9
	.3543		9.0
	.3580	T	
	.3583		9.1
23/64	.3594		9.12
	.3622		9.2
	.3642		9.25
	.3661		9.3
	.3680	U	
	.3701		9.4
	.3740		9.5
3/8	.3750		9.52
	.3770	V	
	.3780		9.6
	.3819		9.7
	.3839		9.75
	.3858		9.8
	.3860	W	
	.3898		9.9
25/64	.3906		9.92
	.3937		10.0
	.3970	X	
	.4040	Y	
13/32	.4062		10.31
	.4130	Z	
	.4134		10.5
27/64	.4219		10.71

Inch	Decimal	mm
	.4331	11.0
7/16	.4375	11.11
	.4528	11.5
29/64	.4531	11.51
15/32	.4688	11.90
	.4724	12.0
31/64	.4844	12.30
	.4921	12.5
1/2	.5000	12.70
	.5118	13.0
	.5156	13.09
33/64	.5156	13.09
17/32	.5312	13.49
	.5315	13.5
35/64	.5469	13.89
	.5512	14.0
9/16	.5625	14.28
	.5709	14.5
37/64	.5781	14.68
	.5906	15.0
19/32	.5938	15.08
39/64	.6094	15.47
	.6102	15.5
5/8	.6250	15.87
	.6299	16.0
41/64	.6406	16.27
	.6496	16.5
21/32	.6562	16.66
	.6693	17.0
43/64	.6719	17.06
11/16	.6875	17.46
	.6890	17.5
45/64	.7031	17.85
	.7087	18.0
23/32	.7188	18.25
	.7283	18.5
47/64	.7344	18.65
	.7480	19.0
3/4	.7500	19.05
49/64	.7656	19.44
	.7677	19.5
25/32	.7812	19.84
	.7874	20.0
51/64	.7969	20.24
	.8071	20.5
13/16	.8125	20.63
	.8268	21.0
53/64	.8281	21.03
27/32	.8438	21.43
	.8465	21.5
55/64	.8594	21.82
	.8661	22.0
7/8	.8750	22.22
	.8858	22.5
57/64	.8906	22.62
	.9055	23.0
29/32	.9062	23.01
59/64	.9219	23.41
	.9252	23.5
15/16	.9375	23.81
	.9449	24.0
61/64	.9531	24.2
	.9646	24.5
31/32	.9688	24.6
	.9843	25.0
63/64	.9844	25.0
1	1.0000	25.4

AIR/FUEL RATIO: The ratio of air to gasoline by weight in the fuel mixture drawn into the engine.

AIR INJECTION: One method of reducing harmful exhaust emissions by injecting air into each of the exhaust ports of an engine. The fresh air entering the hot exhaust manifold causes any remaining fuel to be burned before it can exit the tailpipe.

ALTERNATOR: A device used for converting mechanical energy into electrical energy.

AMMETER: An instrument, calibrated in amperes, used to measure the flow of an electrical current in a circuit. Ammeters are always connected in series with the circuit being tested.

AMPERE: The rate of flow of electrical current present when one volt of electrical pressure is applied against one ohm of electrical resistance.

ANALOG COMPUTER: Any microprocessor that uses similar (analogous) electrical signals to make its calculations.

ARMATURE: A laminated, soft iron core wrapped by a wire that converts electrical energy to mechanical energy as in a motor or relay. When rotated in a magnetic field, it changes mechanical energy into electrical energy as in a generator.

ATMOSPHERIC PRESSURE: The pressure on the Earth's surface caused by the weight of the air in the atmosphere. At sea level, this pressure is 14.7 psi at 32°F (101 kPa at 0°C).

ATOMIZATION: The breaking down of a liquid into a fine mist that can be suspended in air.

AXIAL PLAY: Movement parallel to a shaft or bearing bore.

BACKFIRE: The sudden combustion of gases in the intake or exhaust system that results in a loud explosion.

BACKLASH: The clearance or play between two parts, such as meshed gears.

BACKPRESSURE: Restrictions in the exhaust system that slow the exit of exhaust gases from the combustion chamber.

BAKELITE: A heat resistant, plastic insulator material commonly used in printed circuit boards and transistorized components.

BALL BEARING: A bearing made up of hardened inner and outer races between which hardened steel balls roll.

BALLAST RESISTOR: A resistor in the primary ignition circuit that lowers voltage after the engine is started to reduce wear on ignition components.

BEARING: A friction reducing, supportive device usually located between a stationary part and a moving part.

BIMETAL TEMPERATURE SENSOR: Any sensor or switch made of two dissimilar types of metal that bend when heated or cooled due to the different expansion rates of the alloys. These types of sensors usually function as an on/off switch.

BLOWBY: Combustion gases, composed of water vapor and unburned fuel, that leak past the piston rings into the crankcase during normal engine operation. These gases are removed by the PCV system to prevent the buildup of harmful acids in the crankcase.

BRAKE PAD: A brake shoe and lining assembly used with disc brakes.

BRAKE SHOE: The backing for the brake lining. The term is, however, usually applied to the assembly of the brake backing and lining.

BUSHING: A liner, usually removable, for a bearing; an anti-friction liner used in place of a bearing.

BYPASS: System used to bypass ballast resistor during engine cranking to increase voltage supplied to the coil.

CALIPER: A hydraulically activated device in a disc brake system, which is mounted straddling the brake rotor (disc). The caliper contains at least one piston and two brake pads. Hydraulic pressure on the piston(s) forces the pads against the rotor.

CAMSHAFT: A shaft in the engine on which are the lobes (cams) which operate the valves. The camshaft is driven by the crankshaft, via a belt, chain or gears, at one half the crankshaft speed.

CAPACITOR: A device which stores an electrical charge.

CARBON MONOXIDE (CO): A colorless, odorless gas given off as a normal byproduct of combustion. It is poisonous and extremely dangerous in confined areas, building up slowly to toxic levels without warning if adequate ventilation is not available.

CARBURETOR: A device, usually mounted on the intake manifold of an engine, which mixes the air and fuel in the proper proportion to allow even combustion.

CATALYTIC CONVERTER: A device installed in the exhaust system, like a muffler, that converts harmful byproducts of combustion into carbon dioxide and water vapor by means of a heat-producing chemical reaction.

CENTRIFUGAL ADVANCE: A mechanical method of advancing the spark timing by using fly weights in the distributor that react to centrifugal force generated by the distributor shaft rotation.

CHECK VALVE: Any one-way valve installed to permit the flow of air, fuel or vacuum in one direction only.

CHOKE: A device, usually a movable valve, placed in the intake path of a carburetor to restrict the flow of air.

CIRCUIT: Any unbroken path through which an electrical current can flow. Also used to describe fuel flow in some instances.

CIRCUIT BREAKER: A switch which protects an electrical circuit from overload by opening the circuit when the current flow exceeds a predetermined level. Some circuit breakers must be reset manually, while most reset automatically

COIL (IGNITION): A transformer in the ignition circuit which steps up the voltage provided to the spark plugs.

COMBINATION MANIFOLD: An assembly which includes both the intake and exhaust manifolds in one casting.

COMBINATION VALVE: A device used in some fuel systems that routes fuel vapors to a charcoal storage canister instead of venting

them into the atmosphere. The valve relieves fuel tank pressure and allows fresh air into the tank as the fuel level drops to prevent a vapor lock situation.

COMPRESSION RATIO: The comparison of the total volume of the cylinder and combustion chamber with the piston at BDC and the piston at TDC.

CONDENSER: 1. An electrical device which acts to store an electrical charge, preventing voltage surges.
2. A radiator-like device in the air conditioning system in which refrigerant gas condenses into a liquid, giving off heat.

CONDUCTOR: Any material through which an electrical current can be transmitted easily.

CONTINUITY: Continuous or complete circuit. Can be checked with an ohmmeter.

COUNTERSHAFT: An intermediate shaft which is rotated by a mainshaft and transmits, in turn, that rotation to a working part.

CRANKCASE: The lower part of an engine in which the crankshaft and related parts operate.

CRANKSHAFT: The main driving shaft of an engine which receives reciprocating motion from the pistons and converts it to rotary motion.

CYLINDER: In an engine, the round hole in the engine block in which the piston(s) ride.

CYLINDER BLOCK: The main structural member of an engine in which is found the cylinders, crankshaft and other principal parts.

CYLINDER HEAD: The detachable portion of the engine, fastened, usually, to the top of the cylinder block, containing all or most of the combustion chambers. On overhead valve engines, it contains the valves and their operating parts. On overhead cam engines, it contains the camshaft as well.

DEAD CENTER: The extreme top or bottom of the piston stroke.

DETONATION: An unwanted explosion of the air/fuel mixture in the combustion chamber caused by excess heat and compression, advanced timing, or an overly lean mixture. Also referred to as ''ping''.

DIAPHRAGM: A thin, flexible wall separating two cavities, such as in a vacuum advance unit.

DIESELING: A condition in which hot spots in the combustion chamber cause the engine to run on after the key is turned off.

DIFFERENTIAL: A geared assembly which allows the transmission of motion between drive axles, giving one axle the ability to turn faster than the other.

DIODE: An electrical device that will allow current to flow in one direction only.

DISC BRAKE: A hydraulic braking assembly consisting of a brake disc, or rotor, mounted on an axle, and a caliper assembly containing, usually two brake pads which are activated by hydraulic pressure. The pads are forced against the sides of the disc, creating friction which slows the vehicle.

DISTRIBUTOR: A mechanically driven device on an engine which is responsible for electrically firing the spark plug at a predetermined point of the piston stroke.

DOWEL PIN: A pin, inserted in mating holes in two different parts allowing those parts to maintain a fixed relationship.

DRUM BRAKE: A braking system which consists of two brake shoes and one or two wheel cylinders, mounted on a fixed backing plate, and a brake drum, mounted on an axle, which revolves around the assembly. Hydraulic action applied to the wheel cylinders forces the shoes outward against the drum, creating friction, slowing the vehicle.

DWELL: The rate, measured in degrees of shaft rotation, at which an electrical circuit cycles on and off.

ELECTRONIC CONTROL UNIT (ECU): Ignition module, amplifier or igniter. See Module for definition.

ELECTRONIC IGNITION: A system in which the timing and firing of the spark plugs is controlled by an electronic control unit, usually called a module. These systems have no points or condenser.

ENDPLAY: The measured amount of axial movement in a shaft.

ENGINE: A device that converts heat into mechanical energy.

EXHAUST MANIFOLD: A set of cast passages or pipes which conduct exhaust gases from the engine.

FEELER GAUGE: A blade, usually metal, of precisely predetermined thickness, used to measure the clearance between two parts. These blades usually are available in sets of assorted thicknesses.

F-HEAD: An engine configuration in which the intake valves are in the cylinder head, while the camshaft and exhaust valves are located in the cylinder block. The camshaft operates the intake valves via lifters and pushrods, while it operates the exhaust valves directly.

FIRING ORDER: The order in which combustion occurs in the cylinders of an engine. Also the order in which spark is distributed to the plugs by the distributor.

FLATHEAD: An engine configuration in which the camshaft and all the valves are located in the cylinder block.

FLOODING: The presence of too much fuel in the intake manifold and combustion chamber which prevents the air/fuel mixture from firing, thereby causing a no-start situation.

FLYWHEEL: A disc shaped part bolted to the rear end of the crankshaft. Around the outer perimeter is affixed the ring gear. The starter drive engages the ring gear, turning the flywheel, which rotates the crankshaft, imparting the initial starting motion to the engine.

FOOT POUND (ft.lb. or sometimes, ft. lbs.): The amount of energy or work needed to raise an item weighing one pound, a distance of one foot.

FUSE: A protective device in a circuit which prevents circuit overload by breaking the circuit when a specific amperage is present. The device is constructed around a strip or wire of a lower amperage rating than the circuit it is designed to protect. When an amperage higher than that stamped on the fuse is present in the circuit, the strip or wire melts, opening the circuit.

GEAR RATIO: The ratio between the number of teeth on meshing gears.

GENERATOR: A device which converts mechanical energy into electrical energy.

HEAT RANGE: The measure of a spark plug's ability to dissipate heat from its firing end. The higher the heat range, the hotter the plug fires. **HUB:** The center part of a wheel or gear.

HYDROCARBON (HC): Any chemical compound made up of hydrogen and carbon. A major pollutant formed by the engine as a byproduct of combustion.

HYDROMETER: An instrument used to measure the specific gravity of a solution.

INCH POUND (in.lb. or sometimes, in. lbs.): One twelfth of a foot pound.

INDUCTION: A means of transferring electrical energy in the form of a magnetic field. Principle used in the ignition coil to increase voltage.

INJECTION PUMP: A device, usually mechanically operated, which meters and delivers fuel under pressure to the fuel injector.

INJECTOR: A device which receives metered fuel under relatively low pressure and is activated to inject the fuel into the engine under relatively high pressure at a predetermined time.

INPUT SHAFT: The shaft to which torque is applied, usually carrying the driving gear or gears.

INTAKE MANIFOLD: A casting of passages or pipes used to conduct air or a fuel/air mixture to the cylinders.

JOURNAL: The bearing surface within which a shaft operates.

KEY: A small block usually fitted in a notch between a shaft and a hub to prevent slippage of the two parts.

MANIFOLD: A casting of passages or set of pipes which connect the cylinders to an inlet or outlet source.

MANIFOLD VACUUM: Low pressure in an engine intake manifold formed just below the throttle plates. Manifold vacuum is highest at idle and drops under acceleration.

MASTER CYLINDER: The primary fluid pressurizing device in a hydraulic system. In automotive use, it is found in brake and hydraulic clutch systems and is pedal activated, either directly or, in a power brake system, through the power booster.

MODULE: Electronic control unit, amplifier or igniter of solid state or integrated design which controls the current flow in the ignition primary circuit based on input from the pickup coil. When the module opens the primary circuit, the high secondary voltage is induced in the coil.

NEEDLE BEARING: A bearing which consists of a number (usually a large number) of long, thin rollers.

OHM:(Ω) The unit used to measure the resistance of conductor to electrical flow. One ohm is the amount of resistance that limits current flow to one ampere in a circuit with one volt of pressure.

OHMMETER: An instrument used for measuring the resistance, in ohms, in an electrical circuit.

OUTPUT SHAFT: The shaft which transmits torque from a device, such as a transmission.

OVERDRIVE: A gear assembly which produces more shaft revolutions than that transmitted to it.

OVERHEAD CAMSHAFT (OHC): An engine configuration in which the camshaft is mounted on top of the cylinder head and operates the valves either directly or by means of rocker arms.

OVERHEAD VALVE (OHV): An engine configuration in which all of the valves are located in the cylinder head and the camshaft is located in the cylinder block. The camshaft operates the valves via lifters and pushrods.

OXIDES OF NITROGEN (NOx): Chemical compounds of nitrogen produced as a byproduct of combustion. They combine with hydrocarbons to produce smog.

OXYGEN SENSOR: Used with the feedback system to sense the presence of oxygen in the exhaust gas and signal the computer which can reference the voltage signal to an air/fuel ratio.

PINION: The smaller of two meshing gears.

PISTON RING: An open ended ring which fits into a groove on the outer diameter of the piston. Its chief function is to form a seal between the piston and cylinder wall. Most automotive pistons have three rings: two for compression sealing; one for oil sealing.

PRELOAD: A predetermined load placed on a bearing during assembly or by adjustment.

PRIMARY CIRCUIT: Is the low voltage side of the ignition system which consists of the ignition switch, ballast resistor or resistance wire, bypass, coil, electronic control unit and pick-up coil as well as the connecting wires and harnesses.

PRESS FIT: The mating of two parts under pressure, due to the inner diameter of one being smaller than the outer diameter of the other, or vice versa; an interference fit.

RACE: The surface on the inner or outer ring of a bearing on which the balls, needles or rollers move.

REGULATOR: A device which maintains the amperage and/or voltage levels of a circuit at predetermined values.

RELAY: A switch which automatically opens and/or closes a circuit.

RESISTANCE: The opposition to the flow of current through a circuit or electrical device, and is measured in ohms. Resistance is equal to the voltage divided by the amperage.

RESISTOR: A device, usually made of wire, which offers a preset amount of resistance in an electrical circuit.

RING GEAR: The name given to a ring-shaped gear attached to a differential case, or affixed to a flywheel or as part a planetary gear set.

ROLLER BEARING: A bearing made up of hardened inner and outer races between which hardened steel rollers move.

ROTOR: 1. The disc-shaped part of a disc brake assembly, upon which the brake pads bear; also called, brake disc.
2. The device mounted atop the distributor shaft, which passes current to the distributor cap tower contacts.

SECONDARY CIRCUIT: The high voltage side of the ignition system, usually above 20,000 volts. The secondary includes the ignition coil, coil wire, distributor cap and rotor, spark plug wires and spark plugs.

SENDING UNIT: A mechanical, electrical, hydraulic or electromagnetic device which transmits information to a gauge.

SENSOR: Any device designed to measure engine operating conditions or ambient pressures and temperatures. Usually electronic in nature and designed to send a voltage signal to an on-board computer, some sensors may operate as a simple on/off switch or they may provide a variable voltage signal (like a potentiometer) as conditions or measured parameters change.

SHIM: Spacers of precise, predetermined thickness used between parts to establish a proper working relationship.

SLAVE CYLINDER: In automotive use, a device in the hydraulic clutch system which is activated by hydraulic force, disengaging the clutch.

SOLENOID: A coil used to produce a magnetic field, the effect of which is to produce work.

SPARK PLUG: A device screwed into the combustion chamber of a spark ignition engine. The basic construction is a conductive core inside of a ceramic insulator, mounted in an outer conductive base. An electrical charge from the spark plug wire travels along the conductive core and jumps a preset air gap to a grounding point or points at the end of the conductive base. The resultant spark ignites the fuel/air mixture in the combustion chamber.

SPLINES: Ridges machined or cast onto the outer diameter of a shaft or inner diameter of a bore to enable parts to mate without rotation.

TACHOMETER: A device used to measure the rotary speed of an engine, shaft, gear, etc., usually in rotations per minute.

THERMOSTAT: A valve, located in the cooling system of an engine, which is closed when cold and opens gradually in response to engine heating, controlling the temperature of the coolant and rate of coolant flow.

TOP DEAD CENTER (TDC): The point at which the piston reaches the top of its travel on the compression stroke.

TORQUE: The twisting force applied to an object.

TORQUE CONVERTER: A turbine used to transmit power from a driving member to a driven member via hydraulic action, providing changes in drive ratio and torque. In automotive use, it links the driveplate at the rear of the engine to the automatic transmission.

TRANSDUCER: A device used to change a force into an electrical signal.

TRANSISTOR: A semi-conductor component which can be actuated by a small voltage to perform an electrical switching function.

TUNE-UP: A regular maintenance function, usually associated with the replacement and adjustment of parts and components in the electrical and fuel systems of a vehicle for the purpose of attaining optimum performance.

TURBOCHARGER: An exhaust driven pump which compresses intake air and forces it into the combustion chambers at higher than atmospheric pressures. The increased air pressure allows more fuel to be burned and results in increased horsepower being produced.

VACUUM ADVANCE: A device which advances the ignition timing in response to increased engine vacuum.

VACUUM GAUGE: An instrument used to measure the presence of vacuum in a chamber.

VALVE: A device which control the pressure, direction of flow or rate of flow of a liquid or gas.

VALVE CLEARANCE: The measured gap between the end of the valve stem and the rocker arm, cam lobe or follower that activates the valve.

VISCOSITY: The rating of a liquid's internal resistance to flow.

VOLTMETER: An instrument used for measuring electrical force in units called volts. Voltmeters are always connected parallel with the circuit being tested.

WHEEL CYLINDER: Found in the automotive drum brake assembly, it is a device, actuated by hydraulic pressure, which, through internal pistons, pushes the brake shoes outward against the drums.

A: Ampere

AC: Alternating current

A/C: Air conditioning

A–h: Amper hour

AT: Automatic transmission

ATDC: After top dead center

μA: Microampere

bbl: Barrel

BDC: Bottom dead center

bhp: Brake horsepower

BTDC: Before top dead center

BTU: British thermal unit

C: Celsius (Centigrade)

CCA: Cold cranking amps

cd: Candela

cm^2: Square centimeter

cm^3, cc: Cubic centimeter

CO: Carbon monoxide

CO_2: Carbon dioxide

cu.in., in^3: Cubic inch

CV: Constant velocity

Cyl.: Cylinder

DC: Direct current

ECM: Electronic control module

EFE: Early fuel evaporation

EFI: Electronic fuel injection

EGR: Exhaust gas recirculation

Exh.: Exhaust

F: Farenheit

F: Farad

pF: Picofarad

μF: Microfarad

FI: Fuel injection

ft.lb., ft. lb., ft. lbs.: foot pound(s)

gal: Gallon

g: Gram

HC: Hydrocarbon

HEI: High energy ignition

HO: High output

hp: Horsepower

Hyd: Hydraulic

Hz: Hertz

ID: Inside diameter

in.lb; in. lbs.; in. lbs.: inch pound(s)

Int: Intake

K: Kelvin

kg: Kilogram

kHz: Kilohertz

km: Kilometer

km/h: Kilometers per hour

kΩ: Kilohm

kPa: Kilopascal

kV: Kilovolt

kW: Kilowatt

l: Liter

l/s: Liters per second

m: Meter

mA: Milliampere

mg: Milligram

mHz: Megahertz

mm: Millimeter

mm^2: Square millimeter

m^3: Cubic meter

$M\Omega$: Megohm

m/s: Meters per second

MT: Manual transmission

mV: Millivolt

μm: Micrometer

N: Newton

N–m: Newton meter

NOx: Nitrous oxide

OD: Outside diameter

OHC: Over head camshaft

OHV: Over head valve

Ω: Ohm

PCV: Positive crankcase ventilation

psi: Pounds per square inch

pts: Pints

qts: Quarts

rpm: Rotations per minute

rps: Rotations per second

R–12: refrigerant gas (Freon)

SAE: Society of Automotive Engineers

SO_2: Sulfur dioxide

T: Ton

t: Megagram

TBI: Throttle Body Injection

TPS: Throttle Position Sensor

V: 1. Volt; 2. Venturi

μV: Microvolt

W: Watt

∞: Infinity

<: Less than

>: Greater than

Part No.	Model	Repair Manual Title	Part No.	Model	Repair Manual Title
6980	Accord	Honda 1973-88	6739	Cherokee 1974-83	Jeep Wagoneer, Commando, Cherokee, Truck 1957-86
7747	Aerostar	Ford Aerostar 1986-90			
7165	Alliance	Renault 1975-85	7939	Cherokee 1984-89	Jeep Wagoneer, Comanche, Cherokee 1984-89
7199	AMX	AMC 1975-86			
7163	Aries	Chrysler Front Wheel Drive 1981-88	6840	Chevelle	Chevrolet Mid-Size 1964-88
7041	Arrow	Champ/Arrow/Sapporo 1978-83	6836	Chevette	Chevette/T-1000 1976-88
7032	Arrow Pick-Ups	D-50/Arrow Pick-Up 1979-81	6841	Chevy II	Chevy II/Nova 1962-79
6637	Aspen	Aspen/Volare 1976-80	7309	Ciera	Celebrity, Century, Ciera, 6000 1982-88
6935	Astre	GM Subcompact 1971-80			
7750	Astro	Chevrolet Astro/GMC Safari 1985-90	7059	Cimarron	Cavalier, Skyhawk, Cimarron, 2000 1982-88
6934	A100, 200, 300	Dodge/Plymouth Vans 1967-88			
5807	Barracuda	Barracuda/Challenger 1965-72	7049	Citation	GM X-Body 1980-85
6844	Bavaria	BMW 1970-88	6980	Civic	Honda 1973-88
5796	Beetle	Volkswagen 1949-71	6817	CJ-2A, 3A, 3B, 5, 6, 7	Jeep 1945-87
6837	Beetle	Volkswagen 1970-81			
7135	Bel Air	Chevrolet 1968-88	8034	CJ-5, 6, 7	Jeep 1971-90
5821	Belvedere	Roadrunner/Satellite/Belvedere/GTX 1968-73	6842	Colony Park	Ford/Mercury/Lincoln 1968-88
			7037	Colt	Colt/Challenger/Vista/Conquest 1971-88
7849	Beretta	Chevrolet Corsica and Beretta 1988			
7317	Berlinetta	Camaro 1982-88	6634	Comet	Maverick/Comet 1971-77
7135	Biscayne	Chevrolet 1968-88	7939	Comanche	Jeep Wagoneer, Comanche, Cherokee 1984-89
6931	Blazer	Blazer/Jimmy 1969-82			
7383	Blazer	Chevy S-10 Blazer/GMC S-15 Jimmy 1982-87	6739	Commando	Jeep Wagoneer, Commando, Cherokee, Truck 1957-86
7027	Bobcat	Pinto/Bobcat 1971-80	6842	Commuter	Ford/Mercury/Lincoln 1968-88
7308	Bonneville	Buick/Olds/Pontiac 1975-87	7199	Concord	AMC 1975-86
6982	BRAT	Subaru 1970-88	7037	Conquest	Colt/Challenger/Vista/Conquest 1971-88
7042	Brava	Fiat 1969-81			
7140	Bronco	Ford Bronco 1966-86	6696	Continental 1982-85	Ford/Mercury/Lincoln Mid-Size 1971-85
7829	Bronco	Ford Pick-Ups and Bronco 1987-88			
7408	Bronco II	Ford Ranger/Bronco II 1983-88	7814	Continental 1982-87	Thunderbird, Cougar, Continental 1980-87
7135	Brookwood	Chevrolet 1968-88			
6326	Brougham 1975-75	Valiant/Duster 1968-76	7830	Continental 1988-89	Taurus/Sable/Continental 1986-89
6934	B100, 150, 200, 250, 300, 350	Dodge/Plymouth Vans 1967-88	7583	Cordia	Mitsubishi 1983-89
			5795	Corolla 1968-70	Toyota 1966-70
7197	B210	Datsun 1200/210/Nissan Sentra 1973-88	7036	Corolla	Toyota Corolla/Carina/Tercel/Starlet 1970-87
7659	B1600, 1800, 2000, 2200, 2600	Mazda Trucks 1971-89	5795	Corona	Toyota 1966-70
			7004	Corona	Toyota Corona/Crown/Cressida/Mk.II/Van 1970-87
6840	Caballero	Chevrolet Mid-Size 1964-88			
7657	Calais	Calais, Grand Am, Skylark, Somerset 1985-86	6962	Corrado	VW Front Wheel Drive 1974-90
			7849	Corsica	Chevrolet Corsica and Beretta 1988
6735	Camaro	Camaro 1967-81	6576	Corvette	Corvette 1953-62
7317	Camaro	Camaro 1982-88	6843	Corvette	Corvette 1963-86
7740	Camry	Toyota Camry 1983-88	6542	Cougar	Mustang/Cougar 1965-73
6695	Capri, Capri II	Capri 1970-77	6696	Cougar	Ford/Mercury/Lincoln Mid-Size 1971-85
6963	Capri	Mustang/Capri/Merkur 1979-88			
7135	Caprice	Chevrolet 1968-88	7814	Cougar	Thunderbird, Cougar, Continental 1980-87
7482	Caravan	Dodge Caravan/Plymouth Voyager 1984-89			
			6842	Country Sedan	Ford/Mercury/Lincoln 1968-88
7163	Caravelle	Chrysler Front Wheel Drive 1981-88	6842	Country Squire	Ford/Mercury/Lincoln 1968-88
7036	Carina	Toyota Corolla/Carina/Tercel/Starlet 1970-87	6983	Courier	Ford Courier 1972-82
			7004	Cressida	Toyota Corona/Crown/Cressida/Mk.II/Van 1970-87
7308	Catalina	Buick/Olds/Pontiac 1975-90			
7059	Cavalier	Cavalier, Skyhawk, Cimarron, 2000 1982-88	5795	Crown	Toyota 1966-70
			7004	Crown	Toyota Corona/Crown/Cressida/Mk.II/Van 1970-87
7309	Celebrity	Celebrity, Century, Ciera, 6000 1982-88			
			6842	Crown Victoria	Ford/Mercury/Lincoln 1968-88
7043	Celica	Toyota Celica/Supra 1971-87	6980	CRX	Honda 1973-88
8058	Celica	Toyota Celica/Supra 1986-90	6842	Custom	Ford/Mercury/Lincoln 1968-88
7309	Century FWD	Celebrity, Century, Ciera, 6000 1982-88	6326	Custom	Valiant/Duster 1968-76
			6842	Custom 500	Ford/Mercury/Lincoln 1968-88
7307	Century RWD	Century/Regal 1975-87	7950	Cutlass FWD	Lumina/Grand Prix/Cutlass/Regal 1988-90
5807	Challenger 1965-72	Barracuda/Challenger 1965-72			
7037	Challenger 1977-83	Colt/Challenger/Vista/Conquest 1971-88	6933	Cutlass RWD	Cutlass 1970-87
			7309	Cutlass Ciera	Celebrity, Century, Ciera, 6000 1982-88
7041	Champ	Champ/Arrow/Sapporo 1978-83			
6486	Charger	Dodge Charger 1967-70	6936	C-10, 20, 30	Chevrolet/GMC Pick-Ups & Suburban 1970-87
6845	Charger 2.2	Omni/Horizon/Rampage 1978-88			

Chilton's Repair Manuals are available at your local retailer or by mailing a check or money order for **$15.95** per book plus **$3.50** for 1st book and **$.50** for each additional book to cover postage and handling to:

Chilton Book Company
Dept. DM
Radnor, PA 19089

NOTE: When ordering be sure to include your name & address, book part No. & title.

CHILTON'S REPAIR MANUAL MODEL INDEX
Car and truck model names are listed in alphabetical and numerical order

Part No.	Model	Repair Manual Title
8055	C-15, 25, 35	Chevrolet/GMC Pick-Ups & Suburban 1988-90
6324	Dart	Dart/Demon 1968-76
6962	Dasher	VW Front Wheel Drive 1974-90
5790	Datsun Pickups	Datsun 1961-72
6816	Datsun Pickups	Datsun Pick-Ups and Pathfinder 1970-89
7163	Daytona	Chrysler Front Wheel Drive 1981-88
6486	Daytona Charger	Dodge Charger 1967-70
6324	Demon	Dart/Demon 1968-76
7462	deVille	Cadillac 1967-89
7587	deVille	GM C-Body 1985
6817	DJ-3B	Jeep 1945-87
7040	DL	Volvo 1970-88
6326	Duster	Valiant/Duster 1968-76
7032	D-50	D-50/Arrow Pick-Ups 1979-81
7459	D100, 150, 200, 250, 300, 350	Dodge/Plymouth Trucks 1967-88
7199	Eagle	AMC 1975-86
7163	E-Class	Chrysler Front Wheel Drive 1981-88
6840	El Camino	Chevrolet Mid-Size 1964-88
7462	Eldorado	Cadillac 1967-89
7308	Electra	Buick/Olds/Pontiac 1975-90
7587	Electra	GM C-Body 1985
6696	Elite	Ford/Mercury/Lincoln Mid-Size 1971-85
7165	Encore	Renault 1975-85
7055	Escort	Ford/Mercury Front Wheel Drive 1981-87
7059	Eurosport	Cavalier, Skyhawk, Cimarron, 2000 1982-88
7760	Excel	Hyundai 1986-90
7163	Executive Sedan	Chrysler Front Wheel Drive 1981-88
7055	EXP	Ford/Mercury Front Wheel Drive 1981-87
6849	E-100, 150, 200, 250, 300, 350	Ford Vans 1961-88
6320	Fairlane	Fairlane/Torino 1962-75
6965	Fairmont	Fairmont/Zephyr 1978-83
5796	Fastback	Volkswagen 1949-71
6837	Fastback	Volkswagen 1970-81
6739	FC-150, 170	Jeep Wagoneer, Commando, Cherokee, Truck 1957-86
6982	FF-1	Subaru 1970-88
7571	Fiero	Pontiac Fiero 1984-88
6846	Fiesta	Fiesta 1978-80
5996	Firebird	Firebird 1967-81
7345	Firebird	Firebird 1982-90
7059	Firenza	Cavalier, Skyhawk, Cimarron, 2000 1982-88
7462	Fleetwood	Cadillac 1967-89
7587	Fleetwood	GM C-Body 1985
7829	F-Super Duty	Ford Pick-Ups and Bronco 1987-88
7165	Fuego	Renault 1975-85
6552	Fury	Plymouth 1968-76
7196	F-10	Datsun/Nissan F-10, 310, Stanza, Pulsar 1976-88
6933	F-85	Cutlass 1970-87
6913	F-100, 150, 200, 250, 300, 350	Ford Pick-Ups 1965-86
7829	F-150, 250, 350	Ford Pick-Ups and Bronco 1987-88
7583	Galant	Mitsubishi 1983-89
6842	Galaxie	Ford/Mercury/Lincoln 1968-88
7040	GL	Volvo 1970-88
6739	Gladiator	Jeep Wagoneer, Commando, Cherokee, Truck 1962-86
6981	GLC	Mazda 1978-89
7040	GLE	Volvo 1970-88
7040	GLT	Volvo 1970-88
7593	Golf	VW Front Wheel Drive 1974-90
7165	Gordini	Renault 1975-85
6937	Granada	Granada/Monarch 1975-82
6552	Gran Coupe	Plymouth 1968-76
6552	Gran Fury	Plymouth 1968-76
6842	Gran Marquis	Ford/Mercury/Lincoln 1968-88
6552	Gran Sedan	Plymouth 1968-76
6696	Gran Torino 1972-76	Ford/Mercury/Lincoln Mid-Size 1971-85
7346	Grand Am	Pontiac Mid-Size 1974-83
7657	Grand Am	Calais, Grand Am, Skylark, Somerset 1985-86
7346	Grand LeMans	Pontiac Mid-Size 1974-83
7346	Grand Prix	Pontiac Mid-Size 1974-83
7950	Grand Prix FWD	Lumina/Grand Prix/Cutlass/Regal 1988-90
7308	Grand Safari	Buick/Olds/Pontiac 1975-87
7308	Grand Ville	Buick/Olds/Pontiac 1975-87
6739	Grand Wagoneer	Jeep Wagoneer, Commando, Cherokee, Truck 1957-86
7199	Gremlin	AMC 1975-86
6575	GT	Opel 1971-75
7593	GTI	VW Front Wheel Drive 1974-90
5905	GTO 1968-73	Tempest/GTO/LeMans 1968-73
7346	GTO 1974	Pontiac Mid-Size 1974-83
5821	GTX	Roadrunner/Satellite/Belvedere/GTX 1968-73
5910	GT6	Triumph 1969-73
6542	G.T.350, 500	Mustang/Cougar 1965-73
6930	G-10, 20, 30	Chevy/GMC Vans 1967-86
6930	G-1500, 2500, 3500	Chevy/GMC Vans 1967-86
8040	G-10, 20, 30	Chevy/GMC Vans 1987-90
8040	G-1500, 2500, 3500	Chevy/GMC Vans 1987-90
5795	Hi-Lux	Toyota 1966-70
6845	Horizon	Omni/Horizon/Rampage 1978-88
7199	Hornet	AMC 1975-86
7135	Impala	Chevrolet 1968-88
7317	IROC-Z	Camaro 1982-88
6739	Jeepster	Jeep Wagoneer, Commando, Cherokee, Truck 1957-86
7593	Jetta	VW Front Wheel Drive 1974-90
6931	Jimmy	Blazer/Jimmy 1969-82
7383	Jimmy	Chevy S-10 Blazer/GMC S-15 Jimmy 1982-87
6739	J-10, 20	Jeep Wagoneer, Commando, Cherokee, Truck 1957-86
6739	J-100, 200, 300	Jeep Wagoneer, Commando, Cherokee, Truck 1957-86
6575	Kadett	Opel 1971-75
7199	Kammback	AMC 1975-86
5796	Karmann Ghia	Volkswagen 1949-71
6837	Karmann Ghia	Volkswagen 1970-81
7135	Kingswood	Chevrolet 1968-88
6931	K-5	Blazer/Jimmy 1969-82
6936	K-10, 20, 30	Chevy/GMC Pick-Ups & Suburban 1970-87
6936	K-1500, 2500, 3500	Chevy/GMC Pick-Ups & Suburban 1970-87
8055	K-10, 20, 30	Chevy/GMC Pick-Ups & Suburban 1988-90
8055	K-1500, 2500, 3500	Chevy/GMC Pick-Ups & Suburban 1988-90
6840	Laguna	Chevrolet Mid-Size 1964-88
7041	Lancer	Champ/Arrow/Sapporo 1977-83
5795	Land Cruiser	Toyota 1966-70
7035	Land Cruiser	Toyota Trucks 1970-88
7163	Laser	Chrysler Front Wheel Drive 1981-88
7163	LeBaron	Chrysler Front Wheel Drive 1981-88
7165	LeCar	Renault 1975-85

Chilton's Repair Manuals are available at your local retailer or by mailing a check or money order for **$15.95** per book plus **$3.50** for 1st book and **$.50** for each additional book to cover postage and handling to:

Chilton Book Company
Dept. DM
Radnor, PA 19089

NOTE: When ordering be sure to include your name & address, book part No. & title.

CHILTON'S REPAIR MANUAL MODEL INDEX
Car and truck model names are listed in alphabetical and numerical order

Part No.	Model	Repair Manual Title	Part No.	Model	Repair Manual Title
5905	LeMans	Tempest/GTO/LeMans 1968-73	5790	Patrol	Datsun 1961-72
7346	LeMans	Pontiac Mid-Size 1974-83	6934	PB100, 150, 200, 250, 300, 350	Dodge/Plymouth Vans 1967-88
7308	LeSabre	Buick/Olds/Pontiac 1975-87			
6842	Lincoln	Ford/Mercury/Lincoln 1968-88	5982	Peugeot	Peugeot 1970-74
7055	LN-7	Ford/Mercury Front Wheel Drive 1981-87	7049	Phoenix	GM X-Body 1980-85
6842	LTD	Ford/Mercury/Lincoln 1968-88	7027	Pinto	Pinto/Bobcat 1971-80
6696	LTD II	Ford/Mercury/Lincoln Mid-Size 1971-85	6554	Polara	Dodge 1968-77
			7583	Precis	Mitsubishi 1983-89
7950	Lumina	Lumina/Grand Prix/Cutlass/Regal 1988-90	6980	Prelude	Honda 1973-88
6815	LUV	Chevrolet LUV 1972-81	7658	Prizm	Chevrolet Nova/GEO Prizm 1985-89
6575	Luxus	Opel 1971-75	8012	Probe	Ford Probe 1989
7055	Lynx	Ford/Mercury Front Wheel Drive 1981-87	7660	Pulsar	Datsun/Nissan F-10, 310, Stanza, Pulsar 1976-88
6844	L6	BMW 1970-88	6529	PV-444	Volvo 1956-69
6344	L7	BMW 1970-88	6529	PV-544	Volvo 1956-69
6542	Mach I	Mustang/Cougar 1965-73	6529	P-1800	Volvo 1956-69
6812	Mach I Ghia	Mustang II 1974-78	7593	Quantum	VW Front Wheel Drive 1974-87
6840	Malibu	Chevrolet Mid-Size 1964-88	7593	Rabbit	VW Front Wheel Drive 1974-87
6575	Manta	Opel 1971-75	7593	Rabbit Pickup	VW Front Wheel Drive 1974-87
6696	Mark IV, V, VI, VII	Ford/Mercury/Lincoln Mid-Size 1971-85	6575	Rallye	Opel 1971-75
			7459	Ramcharger	Dodge/Plymouth Trucks 1967-88
7814	Mark VII	Thunderbird, Cougar, Continental 1980-87	6845	Rampage	Omni/Horizon/Rampage 1978-88
			6320	Ranchero	Fairlane/Torino 1962-70
6842	Marquis	Ford/Mercury/Lincoln 1968-88	6696	Ranchero	Ford/Mercury/Lincoln Mid-Size 1971-85
6696	Marquis	Ford/Mercury/Lincoln Mid-Size 1971-85			
			6842	Ranch Wagon	Ford/Mercury/Lincoln 1968-88
7199	Matador	AMC 1975-86	7338	Ranger Pickup	Ford Ranger/Bronco II 1983-88
6634	Maverick	Maverick/Comet 1970-77	7307	Regal RWD	Century/Regal 1975-87
6817	Maverick	Jeep 1945-87	7950	Regal FWD 1988-90	Lumina/Grand Prix/Cutlass/Regal 1988-90
7170	Maxima	Nissan 200SX, 240SX, 510, 610, 710, 810, Maxima 1973-88			
			7163	Reliant	Chrysler Front Wheel Drive 1981-88
6842	Mercury	Ford/Mercury/Lincoln 1968-88	5821	Roadrunner	Roadrunner/Satellite/Belvedere/GTX 1968-73
6963	Merkur	Mustang/Capri/Merkur 1979-88			
6780	MGB, MGB-GT, MGC-GT	MG 1961-81	7659	Rotary Pick-Up	Mazda Trucks 1971-89
			6981	RX-7	Mazda 1978-89
6780	Midget	MG 1961-81	7165	R-12, 15, 17, 18, 18i	Renault 1975-85
7583	Mighty Max	Mitsubishi 1983-89	7830	Sable	Taurus/Sable/Continental 1986-89
7583	Mirage	Mitsubishi 1983-89	7750	Safari	Chevrolet Astro/GMC Safari 1985-90
5795	Mk.II 1969-70	Toyota 1966-70			
7004	Mk.II 1970-76	Toyota Corona/Crown/Cressida/Mk.II/Van 1970-87	7041	Sapporo	Champ/Arrow/Sapporo 1978-83
			5821	Satellite	Roadrunner/Satellite/Belvedere/GTX 1968-73
6554	Monaco	Dodge 1968-77			
6937	Monarch	Granada/Monarch 1975-82	6326	Scamp	Valiant/Duster 1968-76
6840	Monte Carlo	Chevrolet Mid-Size 1964-88	6845	Scamp	Omni/Horizon/Rampage 1978-88
6696	Montego	Ford/Mercury/Lincoln Mid-Size 1971-85	6962	Scirocco	VW Front Wheel Drive 1974-90
			6936	Scottsdale	Chevrolet/GMC Pick-Ups & Suburban 1970-87
6842	Monterey	Ford/Mercury/Lincoln 1968-88			
7583	Montero	Mitsubishi 1983-89	8055	Scottsdale	Chevrolet/GMC Pick-Ups & Suburban 1988-90
6935	Monza 1975-80	GM Subcompact 1971-80			
6981	MPV	Mazda 1978-89	5912	Scout	International Scout 1967-73
6542	Mustang	Mustang/Cougar 1965-73	8034	Scrambler	Jeep 1971-90
6963	Mustang	Mustang/Capri/Merkur 1979-88	7197	Sentra	Datsun 1200, 210, Nissan Sentra 1973-88
6812	Mustang II	Mustang II 1974-78			
6981	MX6	Mazda 1978-89	7462	Seville	Cadillac 1967-89
6844	M3, M6	BMW 1970-88	7163	Shadow	Chrysler Front Wheel Drive 1981-88
7163	New Yorker	Chrysler Front Wheel Drive 1981-88	6936	Siera	Chevrolet/GMC Pick-Ups & Suburban 1970-87
6841	Nova	Chevy II/Nova 1962-79			
7658	Nova	Chevrolet Nova/GEO Prizm 1985-89	8055	Siera	Chevrolet/GMC Pick-Ups & Suburban 1988-90
7049	Omega	GM X-Body 1980-85			
6845	Omni	Omni/Horizon/Rampage 1978-88	7583	Sigma	Mitsubishi 1983-89
6575	Opel	Opel 1971-75	6326	Signet	Valiant/Duster 1968-76
7199	Pacer	AMC 1975-86	6936	Silverado	Chevrolet/GMC Pick-Ups & Suburban 1970-87
7587	Park Avenue	GM C-Body 1985			
6842	Park Lane	Ford/Mercury/Lincoln 1968-88	8055	Silverado	Chevrolet/GMC Pick-Ups & Suburban 1988-90
6962	Passat	VW Front Wheel Drive 1974-90			
6816	Pathfinder	Datsun/Nissan Pick-Ups and Pathfinder 1970-89	6935	Skyhawk	GM Subcompact 1971-80
			7059	Skyhawk	Cavalier, Skyhawk, Cimarron, 2000 1982-88
			7049	Skylark	GM X-Body 1980-85

Chilton's Repair Manuals are available at your local retailer or by mailing a check or money order for **$15.95** per book plus **$3.50** for 1st book and **$.50** for each additional book to cover postage and handling to:

Chilton Book Company
Dept. DM
Radnor, PA 19089

NOTE: When ordering be sure to include your name & address, book part No. & title.

CHILTON'S REPAIR MANUAL MODEL INDEX
Car and truck model names are listed in alphabetical and numerical order

Part No.	Model	Repair Manual Title	Part No.	Model	Repair Manual Title
7675	Skylark	Calais, Grand Am, Skylark, Somerset 1985-86	7040	Turbo	Volvo 1970-88
			5796	Type 1 Sedan 1949-71	Volkswagen 1949-71
7657	Somerset	Calais, Grand Am, Skylark, Somerset 1985-86	6837	Type 1 Sedan 1970-80	Volkswagen 1970-81
7042	Spider 2000	Fiat 1969-81	5796	Type 1 Karmann Ghia 1960-71	Volkswagen 1949-71
7199	Spirit	AMC 1975-86			
6552	Sport Fury	Plymouth 1968-76	6837	Type 1 Karmann Ghia 1970-74	Volkswagen 1970-81
7165	Sport Wagon	Renault 1975-85			
5796	Squareback	Volkswagen 1949-71	5796	Type 1 Convertible 1964-71	Volkswagen 1949-71
6837	Squareback	Volkswagen 1970-81			
7196	Stanza	Datsun/Nissan F-10, 310, Stanza, Pulsar 1976-88	6837	Type 1 Convertible 1970-80	Volkswagen 1970-81
6935	Starfire	GM Subcompact 1971-80	5796	Type 1 Super Beetle 1971	Volkswagen 1949-71
7583	Starion	Mitsubishi 1983-89			
7036	Starlet	Toyota Corolla/Carina/Tercel/Starlet 1970-87	6837	Type 1 Super Beetle 1971-75	Volkswagen 1970-81
7059	STE	Cavalier, Skyhawk, Cimarron, 2000 1982-88	5796	Type 2 Bus 1953-71	Volkswagen 1949-71
			6837	Type 2 Bus 1970-80	Volkswagen 1970-81
5795	Stout	Toyota 1966-70	5796	Type 2 Kombi 1954-71	Volkswagen 1949-71
7042	Strada	Fiat 1969-81			
6552	Suburban	Plymouth 1968-76	6837	Type 2 Kombi 1970-73	Volkswagen 1970-81
6936	Suburban	Chevy/GMC Pick-Ups & Suburban 1970-87			
			6837	Type 2 Vanagon 1981	Volkswagen 1970-81
8055	Suburban	Chevy/GMC Pick-Ups & Suburban 1988-90	5796	Type 3 Fastback & Squareback 1961-71	Volkswagen 1949-71
6935	Sunbird	GM Subcompact 1971-80			
7059	Sunbird	Cavalier, Skyhawk, Cimarron, 2000 1982-88	7081	Type 3 Fastback & Squareback 1970-73	Volkswagen 1970-70
7163	Sundance	Chrysler Front Wheel Drive 1981-88	5796	Type 4 411 1971	Volkswagen 1949-71
7043	Supra	Toyota Celica/Supra 1971-87	6837	Type 4 411 1971-72	Volkswagen 1970-81
8058	Supra	Toyota Celica/Supra 1986-90	5796	Type 4 412 1971	Volkswagen 1949-71
6837	Super Beetle	Volkswagen 1970-81	6845	Turismo	Omni/Horizon/Rampage 1978-88
7199	SX-4	AMC 1975-86	5905	T-37	Tempest/GTO/LeMans 1968-73
7383	S-10 Blazer	Chevy S-10 Blazer/GMC S-15 Jimmy 1982-87	6836	T-1000	Chevette/T-1000 1976-88
			6935	Vega	GM Subcompact 1971-80
7310	S-10 Pick-Up	Chevy S-10/GMC S-15 Pick-Ups 1982-87	7346	Ventura	Pontiac Mid-Size 1974-83
			6696	Versailles	Ford/Mercury/Lincoln Mid-Size 1971-85
7383	S-15 Jimmy	Chevy S-10 Blazer/GMC S-15 Jimmy 1982-87			
			6552	VIP	Plymouth 1968-76
7310	S-15 Pick-Up	Chevy S-10/GMC S-15 Pick-Ups 1982-87	7037	Vista	Colt/Challenger/Vista/Conquest 1971-88
7830	Taurus	Taurus/Sable/Continental 1986-89	6933	Vista Cruiser	Cutlass 1970-87
6845	TC-3	Omni/Horizon/Rampage 1978-88	6637	Volare	Aspen/Volare 1976-80
5905	Tempest	Tempest/GTO/LeMans 1968-73	7482	Voyager	Dodge Caravan/Plymouth Voyager 1984-88
7055	Tempo	Ford/Mercury Front Wheel Drive 1981-87			
7036	Tercel	Toyota Corolla/Carina/Tercel/Starlet 1970-87	6326	V-100	Valiant/Duster 1968-76
			6739	Wagoneer 1962-83	Jeep Wagoneer, Commando, Cherokee, Truck 1957-86
7081	Thing	Volkswagen 1970-81			
6696	Thunderbird	Ford/Mercury/Lincoln Mid-Size 1971-85	7939	Wagoneer 1984-89	Jeep Wagoneer, Comanche, Cherokee 1984-89
7814	Thunderbird	Thunderbird, Cougar, Continental 1980-87	8034	Wrangler	Jeep 1971-90
7055	Topaz	Ford/Mercury Front Wheel Drive 1981-87	7459	W100, 150, 200, 250, 300, 350	Dodge/Plymouth Trucks 1967-88
6320	Torino	Fairlane/Torino 1962-75	7459	WM300	Dodge/Plymouth Trucks 1967-88
6696	Torino	Ford/Mercury/Lincoln Mid-Size 1971-85	6842	XL	Ford/Mercury/Lincoln 1968-88
			6963	XR4Ti	Mustang/Capri/Merkur 1979-88
7163	Town & Country	Chrysler Front Wheel Drive 1981-88	6696	XR-7	Ford/Mercury/Lincoln Mid-Size 1971-85
6842	Town Car	Ford/Mercury/Lincoln 1968-88			
7135	Townsman	Chevrolet 1968-88	6982	XT Coupe	Subaru 1970-88
5795	Toyota Pickups	Toyota 1966-70	7042	X1/9	Fiat 1969-81
7035	Toyota Pickups	Toyota Trucks 1970-88	6965	Zephyr	Fairmont/Zephyr 1978-83
7004	Toyota Van	Toyota Corona/Crown/Cressida/Mk.II/Van 1970-87	7059	Z-24	Cavalier, Skyhawk, Cimarron, 2000 1982-88
7459	Trail Duster	Dodge/Plymouth Trucks 1967-88	6735	Z-28	Camaro 1967-81
7046	Trans Am	Firebird 1967-81	7318	Z-28	Camaro 1982-88
7345	Trans Am	Firebird 1982-90	6845	024	Omni/Horizon/Rampage 1978-88
7583	Tredia	Mitsubishi 1983-89	6844	3.0S, 3.0Si, 3.0CS	BMW 1970-88
			6817	4-63	Jeep 1981-87

Chilton's Repair Manuals are available at your local retailer or by mailing a check or money order for **$15.95** per book plus **$3.50** for 1st book and **$.50** for each additional book to cover postage and handling to:

Chilton Book Company
Dept. DM
Radnor, PA 19089

NOTE: When ordering be sure to include your name & address, book part No. & title.

CHILTON'S REPAIR MANUAL MODEL INDEX
Car and truck model names are listed in alphabetical and numerical order

Part No.	Model	Repair Manual Title	Part No.	Model	Repair Manual Title
6817	4 × 4-63	Jeep 1981-87	6932	300ZX	Datsun Z & ZX 1970-87
6817	4-73	Jeep 1981-87	5982	304	Peugeot 1970-74
6817	4 × 4-73	Jeep 1981-87	5790	310	Datsun 1961-72
6817	4-75	Jeep 1981-87	7196	310	Datsun/Nissan F-10, 310, Stanza,
7035	4Runner	Toyota Trucks 1970-88			Pulsar 1977-88
6982	4wd Wagon	Subaru 1970-88	5790	311	Datsun 1961-72
6982	4wd Coupe	Subaru 1970-88	6844	318i, 320i	BMW 1970-88
6933	4-4-2 1970-80	Cutlass 1970-87	6981	323	Mazda 1978-89
6817	6-63	Jeep 1981-87	6844	325E, 325ES, 325i,	BMW 1970-88
6809	6.9	Mercedes-Benz 1974-84		325iS, 325iX	
7308	88	Buick/Olds/Pontiac 1975-90	6809	380SEC, 380SEL,	Mercedes-Benz 1974-84
7308	98	Buick/Olds/Pontiac 1975-90		380SL, 380SLC	
7587	98 Regency	GM C-Body 1985	5907	350SL	Mercedes-Benz 1968-73
5902	100LS, 100GL	Audi 1970-73	7163	400	Chrysler Front Wheel Drive 1981-88
6529	122, 122S	Volvo 1956-69	5790	410	Datsun 1961-72
7042	124	Fiat 1969-81	5790	411	Datsun 1961-72
7042	128	Fiat 1969-81	7081	411, 412	Volkswagen 1970-81
7042	131	Fiat 1969-81	6809	450SE, 450SEL, 450	Mercedes-Benz 1974-84
6529	142	Volvo 1956-69		SEL 6.9	
7040	142	Volvo 1970-88	6809	450SL, 450SLC	Mercedes-Benz 1974-84
6529	144	Volvo 1956-69	5907	450SLC	Mercedes-Benz 1968-73
7040	144	Volvo 1970-88	6809	500SEC, 500SEL	Mercedes-Benz 1974-84
6529	145	Volvo 1956-69	5982	504	Peugeot 1970-74
7040	145	Volvo 1970-88	5790	510	Datsun 1961-72
6529	164	Volvo 1956-69	7170	510	Nissan 200SX, 240SX, 510, 610,
7040	164	Volvo 1970-88			710, 810, Maxima 1973-88
6065	190C	Mercedes-Benz 1959-70	6816	520	Datsun/Nissan Pick-Ups and Path-
6809	190D	Mercedes-Benz 1974-84			finder 1970-89
6065	190DC	Mercedes-Benz 1959-70	6844	524TD	BMW 1970-88
6809	190E	Mercedes-Benz 1974-84	6844	525i	BMW 1970-88
6065	200, 200D	Mercedes-Benz 1959-70	6844	528e	BMW 1970-88
7170	200SX	Nissan 200SX, 240SX, 510, 610,	6844	528i	BMW 1970-88
		710, 810, Maxima 1973-88	6844	530i	BMW 1970-88
7197	210	Datsun 1200, 210, Nissan Sentra	6844	533i	BMW 1970-88
		1971-88	6844	535i, 535iS	BMW 1970-88
6065	220B, 220D, 220Sb,	Mercedes-Benz 1959-70	6980	600	Honda 1973-88
	220SEb		7163	600	Chrysler Front Wheel Drive 1981-88
5907	220/8 1968-73	Mercedes-Benz 1968-73	7170	610	Nissan 200SX, 240SX, 510, 610,
6809	230 1974-78	Mercedes-Benz 1974-84			710, 810, Maxima 1973-88
6065	230S, 230SL	Mercedes-Benz 1959-70	6816	620	Datsun/Nissan Pick-Ups and Path-
5907	230/8	Mercedes-Benz 1968-73			finder 1970-89
6809	240D	Mercedes-Benz 1974-84	6981	626	Mazda 1978-89
7170	240SX	Nissan 200SX, 240SX, 510, 610,	6844	630 CSi	BMW 1970-88
		710, 810, Maxima 1973-88	6844	633 CSi	BMW 1970-88
6932	240Z	Datsun Z & ZX 1970-87	6844	635CSi	BMW 1970-88
7040	242, 244, 245	Volvo 1970-88	7170	710	Nissan 200SX, 240SX, 510, 610,
5907	250C	Mercedes-Benz 1968-73			710, 810, Maxima 1973-88
6065	250S, 250SE,	Mercedes-Benz 1959-70	6816	720	Datsun/Nissan Pick-Ups and Path-
	250SL				finder 1970-89
5907	250/8	Mercedes-Benz 1968-73	6844	733i	BMW 1970-88
6932	260Z	Datsun Z & ZX 1970-87	6844	735i	BMW 1970-88
7040	262, 264, 265	Volvo 1970-88	7040	760, 760GLE	Volvo 1970-88
5907	280	Mercedes-Benz 1968-73	7040	780	Volvo 1970-88
6809	280	Mercedes-Benz 1974-84	6981	808	Mazda 1978-89
5907	280C	Mercedes-Benz 1968-73	7170	810	Nissan 200SX, 240SX, 510, 610,
6809	280C, 280CE, 280E	Mercedes-Benz 1974-84			710, 810, Maxima 1973-88
6065	280S, 280SE	Mercedes-Benz 1959-70	7042	850	Fiat 1969-81
5907	280SE, 280S/8,	Mercedes-Benz 1968-73	7572	900, 900 Turbo	SAAB 900 1976-85
	280SE/8		7048	924	Porsche 924/928 1976-81
6809	280SEL, 280SEL/8,	Mercedes-Benz 1974-84	7048	928	Porsche 924/928 1976-81
	280SL		6981	929	Mazda 1978-89
6932	280Z, 280ZX	Datsun Z & ZX 1970-87	6836	1000	Chevette/1000 1976-88
6065	300CD, 300D,	Mercedes-Benz 1959-70	6780	1100	MG 1961-81
	300SD, 300SE		5790	1200	Datsun 1961-72
5907	300SEL 3.5,	Mercedes-Benz 1968-73	7197	1200	Datsun 1200, 210, Nissan Sentra
	300SEL 4.5				1973-88
5907	300SEL 6.3,	Mercedes-Benz 1968-73	6982	1400GL, 1400DL,	Subaru 1970-88
	300SEL/8			1400GF	
6809	300TD	Mercedes-Benz 1974-84	5790	1500	Datsun 1961-72

Chilton's Repair Manuals are available at your local retailer or by mailing a check or money order for **$15.95** per book plus **$3.50** for 1st book and **$.50** for each additional book to cover postage and handling to:

Chilton Book Company
Dept. DM
Radnor, PA 19089

NOTE: When ordering be sure to include your name & address, book part No. & title.

CHILTON'S REPAIR MANUAL MODEL INDEX
Car and truck model names are listed in alphabetical and numerical order

Part No.	Model	Repair Manual Title	Part No.	Model	Repair Manual Title
6844	1500	DMW 1970-88	6844	2000	BMW 1970-88
6936	1500	Chevy/GMC Pick-Ups & Suburban 1970-87	6844	2002, 2002Ti, 2002Tii	BMW 1970-88
8055	1500	Chevy/GMC Pick-Ups & Suburban 1988-90	6936	2500	Chevy/GMC Pick-Ups & Suburban 1970-87
6844	1600	BMW 1970-88	8055	2500	Chevy/GMC Pick-Ups & Suburban 1988-90
5790	1600	Datsun 1961-72	6844	2500	BMW 1970-88
6982	1600DL, 1600GL, 1600GLF	Subaru 1970-88	6844	2800	BMW 1970-88
6844	1600-2	BMW 1970-88	6936	3500	Chevy/GMC Pick-Ups & Suburban 1970-87
6844	1800	BMW 1970-88	8055	3500	Chevy/GMC Pick-Ups & Suburban 1988-90
6982	1800DL, 1800GL, 1800GLF	Subaru 1970-88	7028	4000	Audi 4000/5000 1978-81
6529	1800, 1800S	Volvo 1956-69	7028	5000	Audi 4000/5000 1978-81
7040	1800E, 1800ES	Volvo 1970-88	7309	6000	Celebrity, Century, Ciera, 6000 1982-88
5790	2000	Datsun 1961-72			
7059	2000	Cavalier, Skyhawk, Cimarron, 2000 1982-88			